Learn to Navigate

Learn to Navigate
by the Tutorial System Developed at Harvard

by Charles A. Whitney and Frances W. Wright

Cornell Maritime Press
Centreville, Maryland

Library of Congress Cataloging-in-Publication Data

Whitney, Charles Allen.
    Learn to navigate by the tutorial system developed at Harvard / by
Charles A. Whitney and Frances W. Wright. — 1st ed.
        p.   cm.
    Includes index.
    ISBN 0-87033-426-3 (paper)
    1. Navigation. I. Wright, Frances Woodworth. II. Title.
VK555.W339 1992
    623.89—dc20   92-10108
                                                       CIP

Manufactured in the United States of America
First edition

Contents

Preface

In 1942, during the early days of the United States' direct involvement in World War II, the Harvard College Observatory offered to provide intensive training in navigation for several branches of the armed forces. Bart Bok, professor of astronomy, gave the lectures and Frances Wright ran laboratory sections in which the students applied the ideas developed in lecture. Several letters attested to the lives saved by the techniques the servicemen had learned from Bok and Wright, whose book *Basic Marine Navigation,* was published in 1944 (second edition, 1952).

After the war Wright continued to offer the course to Harvard students and, through the Hayden Planetarium of the Boston Museum of Science, to the public, while earning her Ph. D. in astronomy and carrying on a research career. During this time, she published three books, *Celestial Navigation* (1969), *Particularized Navigation* (1973, describing emergency techniques in a compact form), and *Coastwise Navigation* (1980, describing piloting techniques).

In 1988, after more than forty-five years of teaching, Dr. Wright relinquished the helm of the course to me, and I held it for two years, until my retirement from Harvard. This coincided with the sale of the last copies of Wright's books, so we decided to attempt an updated amalgamation of her books. This is the result, and it is a testimonial to Frances Wright's long dedication to her students in the art and science of navigation.

But it is is not simply a compendium of what has come before. While attempting to retain the flavor of the earlier books—with their emphasis on *practice* and on *constant vigilance*—we have have added a number of exercises and diagrams to help students learn the fundamental concepts; as well, we have revised the sight-reduction forms and added a number of useful shortcuts for performing various navigational operations. The Introduction describes our philosophy of learning and specifies the unique features of our book.

I wish to express our gratitude to those who have helped us over the years. For the most part, they must go unnamed, but I would like to thank Philip Sadler for his many ingenious contributions to the exercises, and to mention Harvard students Brett Humphreys and Robert Campbell, who served as course assistants and helped with the exercises. John M. Hodgson helped redesign the forms for sight reduction. Professors Irwin Shapiro and George Field gave support and encouragement, material and otherwise, over the years.

The sky charts in this book were created on an Apple Macintosh with the program called Voyager, the Interactive Desktop Planetarium, which is available from Carina Software, 830 Williams Street, San Leandro, California 94577; telephone 415-352-7328. This program can also be used to generate star altitudes for comparison with your sextant sights.

During the final stages of preparing this book, I was fortunate to have the assistance of Nancy Lee Snyder, who read the copy and verified the calculations.

I am sad to report that Frances Wright died while this book was in preparation. Without her inspiration this project never would have been started. Proceeds from the sale of this book will go to the Frances W. Wright Navigation Fund at Harvard University.

To past and future navigators

I. Coastwise Navigation

Introduction

This book is written for the mariner who wants to learn the concepts of piloting and navigation and do more than merely follow a closely prescribed set of rules. The reader is expected to be an active participant, and many exercises have been designed to help along the way.

This is not the *only* book you will need when you go to sea, so we provide references to other books that are more specialized or more compendious. But we have tried to deal with all the topics usually considered essential for coastal and blue-water boating.

OUR APPROACH

Henry David Thoreau was a Harvard student during the nineteenth century. In his chapter titled "Economy" in *Walden,* he wrote, "To my astonishment I was informed on leaving college that I had studied navigation!—why, if I had taken one turn down the harbor I should have known more about it." We cannot offer a boat ride in Boston Harbor, but our book is a response to Thoreau's plea for a *practical* approach. Its methods were initiated by Frances Wright and Professor Bart Bok at Harvard during the Second World War, and they were developed and refined during four decades of teaching by Dr. Wright and her assistants, and then by Professor Whitney, Philip Sadler, and many course assistants.

Three of our methods are common to many books: (1) hands-on involvement, (2) practical applications and the use of concise forms, and (3) emphasis on the need for constant vigilance. This book provides problems and answers for each chapter, and it includes practical lists of resources for the navigator who is preparing to set out. A set of reduction forms is provided at the rear of the book. These forms will help you with all the common types of sextant sight reduction. They are intended to be self-guided, and they may be photocopied and put into a ring binder for use at sea.

What makes our book different from most others is its focus on the three further methods: (4) *confrontation with misconceptions,* (5) the use of *definitions based on procedures,* and (6) the use of *imaginary scenarios* or "thought experiments." We feel these methods are keys to learning, and we owe thanks to our colleague, Philip Sadler, and his cohorts in the education department of the Harvard-Smithsonian Center for Astrophysics for helping us understand their value.

What do they mean? How do they affect this book?

Confrontation with misconceptions

Our minds are not empty buildings into which we merely bring furniture and tools. We all have ideas about almost any topic, whether we have studied it or not, so the process of learning is somewhat like constructing a new wing on an existing building. If a new idea is presented to us, we will add it to the existing superstructure—which often consists of naive ideas that we have invented for ourselves—and the result is often a bizarre floor plan. The old house will remain, and the naive ideas will still be available to mislead us into dead ends or through doorways that have no balconies.

So, it is not enough merely to give you the correct explanation, expecting you to grasp its full implications and throw out the naive ideas. Learning can only occur when you are able to confront your preconceptions and see that they do not work. You must, in many cases, be convinced of the need to restructure the old house. This confrontation can be achieved by having you make a prediction based on your preconceptions. If the prediction fails and you can admit that something is wrong with the old idea, you are then ready to work toward a new conception.

Many sections of this book have questions to help you explore your preconceptions. These are the "pretests" and they will enable you to confront your ideas. Write your predictions in a notebook before looking at the answers found in the Appendix. Exercises are included to help make some of the ideas more obvious. Posttests (with answers in the Appendix) have been supplied to give you a chance to try out the new ideas.

Procedural definitions

By themselves, concepts and data are meaningless. Only when they are seen as part of a procedure are they useful to the navigator, just as a window frame is not much use until it is set into the framework of a house. The confident navigator is one who has a grasp of the procedures by which the navigational concepts are defined.

For example, when we introduce the concept of angular size we outline a series of steps starting with simple distance measurements and gradually coming to the idea of *apparent angular size*. Each section of the book starts with a statement of the concept to be treated and then focuses on a step-by-step procedure that will lead you to the concept.

Using imaginary scenarios

Our approach in this book is to help you visualize each concept by way of a *scenario,* which is our word for an imaginary experiment. Scenarios don't have to be real to be useful, as they can simplify and clarify our thinking. For example, in coping with time zones we imagine a flight around the world in a super-fast jet plane. We imagine starting at a point just west of the international dateline, wherever that may be— for the moment, we don't need to know. We take off at dawn and fly westward at 24,000 miles per hour,

away from the sun. In our mind's eye the sun sinks below the eastern horizon again. This tells us that the local time has become earlier, so we must set our clock earlier. By imagining that we fly all the way around the globe in one hour, we can decide what to do when we cross the date line again. (We will complete this discussion in Chapter 13.)

The type of understanding that comes from imaginary scenarios is much more powerful than memorized rules. It will prepare you to handle situations that are not in any textbook. Scenarios not only *connect facts* and help you remember them, they can also *generate new insights.* One aspect of learning to navigate—or of learning any technical skill—is to build up a repertory of scenarios that can be used to solve new types of problems as they arise.

SPECIAL FEATURES

We have added three features to assist the navigator, whether beginner or expert:

1. A discussion of the Polynesian and other natural methods of determining positions and directions by noting the positions of the stars, as well as simple methods for determining latitude and longitude with an almanac and accurate timings of sunrise and sunset;

2. A set of self-guided concise forms for carrying out the reduction of a variety of sextant sights;

3. A mini-almanac giving the sun's declination and time of local noon for 1992-2001, and numerous other tables and lists.

Remember to pay constant vigilance, not only to the sea and your vessel, but to your misconceptions as well.

Happy and safe voyaging!

CHAPTER ONE

Estimating Distances and Angles

Navigation, a word derived from the Latin *navis,* "ship," and *agere,* "to drive," originally denoted the art of ship driving, including steering and setting the sails . . .

The New Encyclopædia Britannica

It really gnaws at your stomach not to know where you are.

Circumnavigator Tania Aebi, quoted by Greg Walsh, Ocean Navigator

INTRODUCTION

Navigation has been described as the art and science of "determining position, course, and distance travelled." More briefly, it is finding yourself in space, and it involves the determination of distances and directions. This must be done with measurement, not guesswork. But measurement of what? That will depend on the weather and where you are.

If you are sailing within sight of a shoreline, you will probably measure the directions of prominent features with your compass or radar and then use your navigational chart to find your position from these data. This is the science of *piloting,* treated in the first part of this book.

If you are out of sight of land, you will have to use celestial objects: the sun, moon, planets, and stars. With your sextant you measure the angular height of a few of these objects above the horizon, and from those angles you derive a position. This is *celestial navigation,* treated in the second part of this book.

If the sky is cloudy and you are far from land (or worse, if you are in a fog) you will have to depend on guesswork, called *deduced reckoning.* Starting from where you know you were at some definite time, you estimate how fast you have gone and in what direction. You draw this line on the chart from the starting point, and the end of the line is your best guess. The name of the process has been shortened to "ded reckoning," and it is usually spelled "dead reckoning" for some reason—probably a landlubber's joke.

BRIEF HISTORY OF NAVIGATIONAL TECHNIQUES

The techniques of coastal piloting are treated first in this book because they are easier to visualize; they deal with flat maps and plane geometry. Historically, they are the older, and many students find they are easier to visualize than the techniques of celestial navigation, which depend on the fact that the earth is nearly a sphere.

The first navigators have long been lost in the mists of time, but they almost certainly were hunters and nomads who moved from place to place on land. They worked with familiar landmarks by day, and at night they probably estimated directions by the stars. Distances would have been estimated from the time it took to make a trip—a method we often use today when we measure a trip by airplane or automobile. Under most conditions, the passage of time is a more immediate impression than the passage of distance. Today, in fact, we take for granted the easy measurement of time—a glance at a wristwatch takes only an instant.

The earliest navigators on water had no way of measuring time accurately, so they developed piloting techniques that did not depend on time. They adopted the methods of the nomads and kept close to shore, where they could depend on visible landmarks. Today, we call this "coastwise piloting." It is based on simple geometry and it assumes that the earth is flat.

But people sailed beyond sight of land long before compasses or other devices had been invented. (Noah used a dove to locate the direction of dry land.)

North American Indians may have arrived by sea. The Phoenicians, inhabitants of the Mediterranean shores, and the Polynesians made long voyages between landfalls. (The biographer of Jonah put him far from shore when he was thrown overboard.) One of the earliest recorded voyages took place in the fourth century B.C., by Pytheas of Massalia, a Greek who sailed to England and beyond. We know little about his techniques and, unfortunately, the later techniques of the Norsemen have also been mostly lost from recorded history.

Without the concept of a spherical earth, navigation by the stars would have been limited to a form of dead reckoning in which the navigator adopts a course and keeps going in the same direction until land is sighted. Stars near the horizon can give reliable indications of direction, no matter what shape you may believe the earth to have, and this fact was at the heart of the Polynesian methods. The Magi of the New Testament evidently navigated by the stars, but we do not know whether they believed in a spherical earth. In any case, the distinction would have been irrelevant for their short trip. One thing is certain: They could not have believed that a natural star would stand all night over the town of Bethlehem; they had spent many nights out in the open and had watched the stars move westward, following the setting sun. In Judges 5:20, for example, we find a clear allusion to such motion: "From heaven fought the stars, from their courses they fought against Sisera."

The Magi might have followed the direction of a twilight comet, star, or planet—or a conjunction of such objects. The inspiration for the story of the Christmas star is a much-discussed topic, yet it seems unlikely that we will ever find a simple natural explanation.

It may be true that the Babylonians of the first millennium B.C. believed the earth to be circular, that is, round but flat; however, it is a myth that Christopher Columbus was one of the first to believe that the earth was spherical. Many of the ancient Greeks believed it, and they surely were not the only ones—nor the first.

When the great navigators began to sail across oceans and around the world at the end of the fifteenth century, they carried magnetic compasses and they used Polaris by night. They knew that the North Star (Polaris) could be used to infer directions from any place in the northern hemisphere.

They also knew that the height of Polaris above the horizon told the distance to the earth's equator. (A nocturnal, a device for measuring the orientation of the sky in its daily motion around the pole, was used to correct the measured altitude for the fact that Polaris is a little more than 1° from the true pole.) By keeping Polaris to starboard, they could sail westward and at the same time keep a constant distance from the equator.

Moderately accurate measurement (say, to 1°) of the height of Polaris was achieved with a variety of simple, ingenious devices, such as astrolabes and cross-staffs. Accurate time was not needed for the interpretation of such measurements—nor could it be found at sea. (The interval between sunrise and sunset was divided into twelve hours whose length depended on the time of year. Hours were marked with a variety of "clocks" such as sand-filled hourglasses and carefully marked candles.) Precise measurement of the height of Polaris came with the invention of a device that used glass mirrors (a "sextant") in 1730. This gave a factor 100 improvement in the accuracy of angular measurement and permitted determining north-south location with an error of one nautical mile or less.

But the earth spins, and the determination of east-west location with comparable accuracy required being able to determine the time with an error of a few seconds or less. This accuracy was finally achieved during the eighteenth century by elaborate clocks with ingenious temperature-compensation mechanisms. Gradually these "chronometers" became smaller and more rugged, as well as more accurate and reliable. Navigation to within a few miles became commonplace during the nineteenth century. Electronic time and position determination were developed by the middle of the twentieth century, and it is now possible to find oneself electronically using shore-based radio transmitters (Loran, for example) to within a few tens of meters with equipment costing a thousand dollars. Loran is limited to the northern hemisphere, but global satellite-location systems are commercially available and becoming more widespread.

Given these electronic aids, why must sailors study piloting and celestial navigation? In order to get to port when the electronics fail. Remember the Peter Principle: If anything can fail, it will. But, unless you drop it, your sextant will always work for you—if you know how to use it.

THE MOON ILLUSION AND ANGULAR MEASUREMENT

Today, accurate measurement is at the heart of navigation, and we will start with the measurement of angles and the estimation of distances. But first, let us explore a vagary of visual perception that is the bane of navigators—our inability to reliably estimate distances and angles with the naked eye.

How many times has a sailor stood on the deck of a boat near shore and misjudged the length of the swim to the beach? And who has not noticed the enormous, but illusory, size of the full moon as it rises over a distant horizon? As different as they may seem to be, these illusions are both related to our difficulty in estimating angular sizes. For reasons that are not well understood, our eye and brain are not very good at this task, as you can easily prove to yourself, as follows.

PRETEST*

1.1 Which of the following objects, if held at arm's length, would come closest to exactly covering the face of the moon?

small pea _____ quarter _____
four-inch saucer _____ volley ball _____

Next time you see the moon, try the comparison for yourself. Most people are surprised by the result.

If you have trouble finding the moon, try this one. The angles are nearly the same. Find a dish that is six inches across. Place it twenty-five feet away and imagine that it is the face of the moon. Now answer the same question:

1.2 Which of the following objects, if held at arm's length, would come closest to exactly covering the face of the dish?

small pea _____ quarter _____
four-inch saucer _____ volley ball _____

You will find that the small pea does the trick nicely. Now let's try to express this quantitatively. First we need a few definitions.

Distance-to-size ratio

In Figure 1.1, D is an object's distance from an observer at O, and S is its diameter or greatest linear dimension as seen by the observer. The distance-to-

---

*Answers to pretest and posttest questions are given in appendix 7.

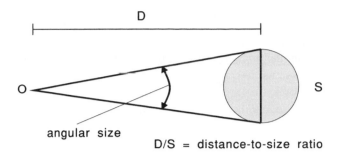

Figure 1.1a. An observer at O on the left looks at a ball whose diameter is S and distance is D. Two strings (indicated by heavy lines) are stretched between the observer and the sides of the ball. The angle between the strings is the angular size as seen from point O. For different people looking at the same ball, the distance-to-size ratio increases with distance while the angular size decreases.

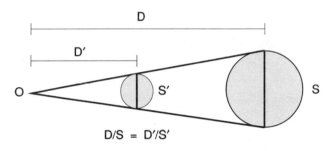

Figure 1.1b. All objects that fit between the same strings will have the same angular size as seen from O. They have the same distance-to-size ratios, D/S. A 6-inch dish at a distance of 25 feet has a distance-to-size ratio D/S = 50.

size ratio is the ratio of the distance to the actual size: D/S. *It increases with distance,* and it cannot reliably be estimated by eye; it must be measured. In the case of the dish, S = 0.5 feet and D = 25 feet, so D/S = 50. The distance-to-size ratio is fifty to one.

Angular size

This is the angle across an object as seen from a defined observer's location. Intuitively, it is obvious that angular size *decreases with distance.* This chapter explores the relation between angular size and distance-to-size ratio.

Apparent size and the moon illusion

Apparent size is the psychological impression of the angular size as judged by the eye and brain. It is strongly influenced by visual background and surroundings. The moon illusion is an example.

PRETEST

1.3 Is the distance-to-size ratio of the moon larger or smaller when it is on the horizon compared to when it is high in the sky?

larger _____ smaller _____ same _____

1.4 Is the angular size of the moon larger or smaller when it is on the horizon?

larger _____ smaller _____ same _____

1.5 Is the apparent size of the moon larger or smaller when it is on the horizon?

larger _____ smaller _____ same _____

For most people, the moon looks much larger when it is near the horizon, but in truth it is not. The moon is actually a little bit smaller when seen on the horizon, despite the strong visual impression to the contrary. This is known as the "moon illusion." To convince yourself that the large size of the moon is an illusion, look at the rising moon through a small gap between your fingers. It will appear to collapse, almost like a deflated balloon, to its "normal" size. This behavior implies that apparent size does not obey the ordinary laws of geometry. It is strongly influenced by the poorly understood processes of visual perception.

Prediction—Figure 1.2 shows an experimental set-up related to the moon illusion. It consists of two identical dishes propped on chairs. If you make an eye estimate of the angular sizes, $A1$ and $A2$, of two 12-inch dishes seen at distances of 5 feet and 10 feet, which relationship do you expect to find?

A1/A2 = 10/5 ____ A1/A2 = 5/10 ____ other: A1/A2 = ____

Procedure—Now carry out an experiment like that in Figure 1.2 to test your prediction:

a. Place two identical dishes in two chairs, C1 and C2, about 10 feet apart. Then stand in front of the nearer chair so the two chairs are in line, and estimate the ratio of the angular sizes of the two dishes from where you are standing: Eye estimate of ratio of apparent sizes: A1/A2 = _____ .

b. Now measure your distances from the two chairs, D1 and D2, and compute the ratio: Measured ratio of distances: D2/D1 = _____ .

According to geometry, these ratios ought to be the same. However, most people find a ratio of apparent sizes, A1/A2, that is much closer to 1 than it ought to be. In other words the more distant dish appears much larger than would be predicted by geometry. This discrepancy, which arises in the brain, is probably at the root of the moon illusion.

USING THE DISTANCE-TO-SIZE RATIO

Suppose a boat is coming up behind you and you want to estimate its distance. The distance-to-size ratio of the boat can be useful because you can measure it without knowing the boat's distance. You can measure the distance-to-size ratio of its mast (as described below) and if you know how tall the

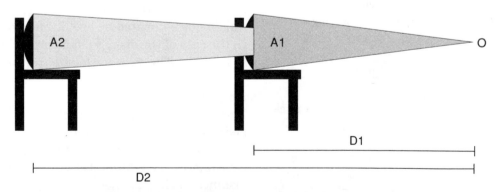

Figure 1.2. This diagram shows an experiment that may convince you of the need for objective measurement rather than relying on eye estimates when you are determining distances and sizes from a boat. Two identical dishes are propped on chairs, C1 and C2. The viewer stands so one is twice the distance of the other, D2 = 2 × D1. The angular size of the closer dish is twice that of the more distant dish—but that is not the way you will see it. The two dishes will probably appear to be about the same size. Most people find it very difficult to estimate the geometric sizes of the dishes from their perceived sizes.

mast is, you can easily calculate the boat's distance. As an example, if the mast is 60 feet tall, and you measure its distance-to-size ratio to be D/S = 100, you know the boat is $60 \times 100 = 6,000$ feet, or about one nautical mile, away. (A nautical mile is 6,080 feet, slightly longer than a statute mile of 5,280 feet.) If the boat is overtaking you at two knots, it will catch up with you in half an hour. Or suppose you identify a 100-foot lighthouse on your chart and you measure its distance-to-size ratio as D/S = 150. You can calculate its distance as 15,000 feet, or about 2.5 nautical miles.

PRETEST

1.6 As an observer moves toward a lighthouse, its distance-to-size ratio increases. T _____ F _____

1.7 Boat masts that are 50 feet tall will show distance-to-size ratios that are in proportion to the boats' distances from the observer. T _____ F _____

Concepts

a. Larger objects at the same distance have smaller distance-to-size ratios.

b. Boat masts of the same height will show angular sizes that are inversely related to the boats' distances.

Procedure

a. Find a coin and a dish and measure their diameters as accurately as you can with a ruler. Write the results here, noting the units (inches or millimeters). Measured size (diameter) of coin: Sc = _____ . Measured size (diameter) of dish: Sd = _____ .

b. Prop the dish upright on a chair at a distance of about 10 feet (120 inches). Measure the distance and enter it here: Distance of dish: Dd = _____ .

PRETEST

1.8 How far from your eye will you will have to hold the coin in order for it to exactly cover the face of the dish, as in Figure 1.5? You may use any information available to calculate your prediction. Predicted distance of coin: Dc = _____ .

Procedure

c. Now test your prediction. Hold the coin between your eye and the dish and adjust the position of your hand until the coin exactly covers the dish. (You may have to adjust the distance of the dish if your arm is not long enough. If you do, enter the new value for Dd and make a new prediction for the coin's distance.)

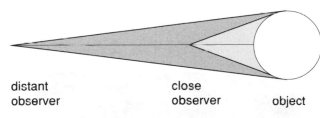

distant observer   close observer   object

Figure 1.3. When an observer is closer to an object it covers a larger angle.

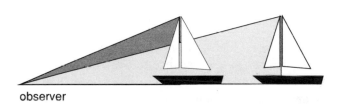

observer

Figure 1.4. Boats of the same height have angular sizes that decrease in proportion to distance from the observer.

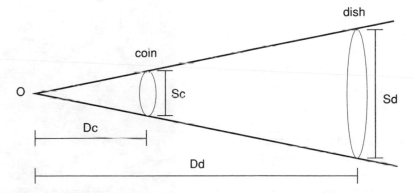

Figure 1.5. Coin covers face of dish. Diagram shows definitions of distances and sizes.

d. Measure the distance between your eye and the coin, and also try to estimate the uncertainty of your measurement, in inches: Measured distance of coin: Dc = _____ ± _____ (estimated error).

Did your prediction agree with the measurement, to within the estimated error?

Prediction—You now have four measured quantities—Sc, Sd, Dd, and Dc—corresponding to a coin covering the face of a dish in Figure 1.5. Check the relationship you expect to find when you have computed the distance-to-size ratios of the coin and dish, Dc/Sc and Dd/Sd.

Coin   Dish
Dc/Sc greater than Dd/Sd _____
Dc/Sc equal to Dd/Sd _____
Dc/Sc less than Dd/Sd _____

Test of prediction—Now test your prediction by computing the actual ratios from the data. Check the correct relationship:

Coin   Dish
Dc/Sc greater than Dd/Sd _____
Dc/Sc equal to Dd/Sd _____
Dc/Sc less than Dd/Sd _____

Was your prediction correct?

Conclusion—This scenario ought to verify that objects with the same distance-to-size ratio will have the same angular size. That is, the nearer one will cover the farther one. If you failed to confirm the concept, try to figure out where you might have gone wrong. Repeat the work until you have confirmed the concept.

Figure 1.6 shows diagrams of the sun and the moon on the same scale. If you measure their apparent diameters with a ruler you will find that they are nearly the same. Astronomers have found that the distance-to-size ratios are 100 for these objects, so: distance/diameter = 100.

POSTTEST
1.9 a) The moon is known to be 240,000 miles away. Use this expression to determine its diameter.
Moon's diameter = _____ miles
b) If the sun's diameter is 800,000 miles, what is its approximate distance from earth?
Sun's distance = _____ miles

1.10 Figure 1.7 is a photograph of two boats of the same true size. Measure their apparent sizes in the photograph and determine their relative distances. Distance of further boat/Distance of closer boat = _____

DEVICES FOR MEASURING DISTANCE-TO-SIZE RATIOS

Distance-to-size ratios can be measured in a variety of ways, using rulers and protractors. Your hand also makes a useful device, once you have measured it and practiced a bit.

The handiest of all

PRETEST
1.11 What is the distance-to-size ratio of the width of your little finger at arm's length? _____

Procedure

a. Measure the width of your little finger: width = _____ . Now measure its distance from your eye when your arm is comfortably extended: Arm length = _____ . Compute the distance-to-size ratio: Distance-to-size ratio = Arm length/finger width = _____ .

Many people find that the ratio is 50:1 if they hold it at the right distance. One way to find the right distance is to make a 6-inch mark on a piece of paper and then stand 25 feet away. Learn to hold your finger so it just covers the 6-inch mark at 25 feet.

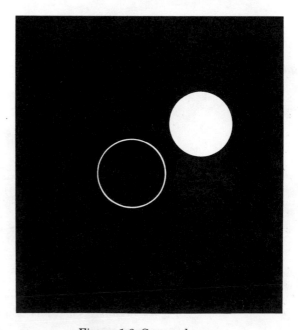

Figure 1.6. Sun and moon.

b. Here is another way to determine the distance-to-size ratio of your little finger when held at arm's length. It is similar to the experiment you performed earlier with the dish. First, with a ruler measure the size of a convenient small object, such as a dish or a book: Size of object (covered by finger) = _____ .

Now stand the object on its edge so you see it face-on and back away from it, holding your little finger at arm's length, until your finger just covers the object. Then measure your distance from the object: Distance to object (covered by finger) = _____ . Distance/size of finger = _____ .

Example—If the object is ½ foot across, and you have to stand 25 feet away in order to exactly cover it with your finger, the distance/size ratio = 25/0.5 = 50:1.

Cross-staff

Before the days of sextants, navigators used a variety of machines for measuring distance-to-size ratios. One such device was the cross-staff, shown in Figure 1.8. A yardstick and a ruler make good components for such a device.

Binoculars

A cross-staff is not the ideal instrument for measuring the angular sizes of distant objects, such as lighthouses and boats at sea. A far handier and

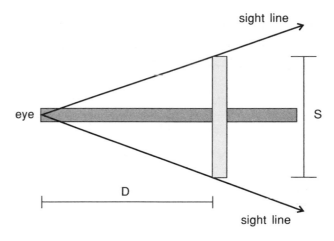

Figure 1.8. Cross-staff for measuring distance-to-size ratio. Sighting from the eye end, the user slides the cross-piece back and forth until its ends match the top and bottom of the object being measured. The ratio of the lengths D and S then give the distance-to-size ratio of the object.

more accurate device is a pair of binoculars with an eyepiece scale.

Figure 1.9 shows a schematic view through a pair of binoculars equipped with an eyepiece scale for estimating the distance of an object seen from your boat. The scale is specially constructed so that an object covering a single division has a distance-to-size ratio of 1,000. If the object covers two divisions, its distance-to-size ratio is 1,000/2 = 500.

Figure 1.7. Photograph of two boats of nearly the same true size. Measurement of their apparent sizes will give their relative distances from the camera. (Photo courtesy Peter Duff)

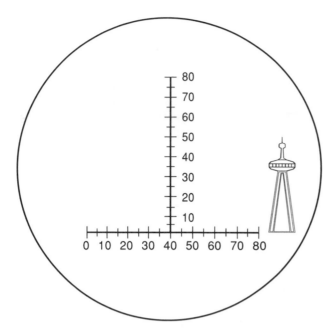

Figure 1.9. Schematic view through binoculars with scale for estimating distance of objects of known size. The object on the right has a height of 55 scale units, so its distance-to-size ratio is 1,000/55. Multiplying by the object's known true height in feet gives the distance in feet, as described in the text.

Here is how you can make use of such a device. Start by finding the true height of the object, perhaps from a chart. (Do this first, because there's little point in measuring an object whose height you can't find on a chart or in a book.) Suppose it is 100 feet. Point the binoculars so the bottom of the scale is at the foot of the object and read the scale at the point corresponding to the top of the object. Suppose, as in the diagram, you read five scale divisions. (This means that the object has a distance-to-size ratio of 1,000/5.) Compute the distance from the relation.

Distance = 1,000/(scale reading) × size

In our example,

Distance = 1,000/5 × 100 = 20,000 feet

Convert this to nautical miles.

Distance = 20,000/6,080 = 3.3 NM

1.12 Verify for yourself that a 75-foot tower that matches 35 scale units is at a distance of 0.35 NM. What would its distance be if it measured 17 scale units? _____

MEASURING BY DEGREES

Not every boat has a pair of binoculars with an eyepiece scale. But if you have a sextant handy, you can achieve the same goal, because it will have a scale marked in degrees and a drum for reading to the nearest minute of arc (60′ = 1°). This section explores the relation between distance-to-size ratios and angular sizes in degrees. Practicing this piloting technique with a sextant will help you become familiar with the use of the sextant and prepare you for celestial navigation.

PRETEST
1.13 Suppose an object has a distance-to-size ratio of 100:1. What would be its angular size in degrees?

_____

1.14 What is the angular size in degrees of a 100-foot mast at a distance of 1 nautical mile? _____

Two Definitions
• An angle is a measure of the difference in direction between two intersecting straight lines.

• One degree (1°) is 1/360 of a circle. That is, a degree is a unit of angle such that 360° make one complete circle.

Concept
• Objects that cover an angle of 1° have a distance-to-size ratio of about 57:1 (or 60:1 if you need not be too fussy). This is a very useful fact when you are piloting along a coast.

Suppose you see an object whose size, S, you know. For example, a lighthouse on a chart might have S = 50 feet. You measure the angular size of the object with a sextant and find it covers an angle of 1°. At once, you know it is at a distance of 60S = 3,000 feet, or about half a nautical mile. (We will abbreviate this as NM from now on.) This is the kind of knowledge that can keep you from going on the rocks.

The remainder of this section will show you how to prove this and to derive it for yourself in case you forget the exact ratio.

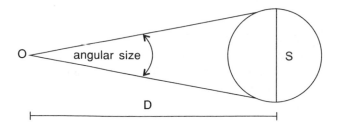

Figure 1.10. What is the quantitative relationship between angular size, A, and the distance-to-size ratio, D/S?

Your first step is to determine a numerical relationship between angular size in degrees, A, and the distance-to-size ratio, D/S (see Figure 1.10).

Procedure

a. Instead of working with 1°, which is a bit narrow for easy work, let us start with an angle of 45° and find its corresponding distance-to-size ratio. Draw a circle of radius D, and at its center, draw an angle of 45° (see Figure 1.11, and don't confuse D with diameter— it is the radius). The arc of the circle represents an object whose size is S and whose distance is D.

b. How do you find S/D? One way is to use a ruler. On the circle, measure S and D and evaluate the ratio: S/D = _____ .

c. Now do this for circles of a few other sizes and prove to yourself that *the ratio does not depend on the size of the circle;* it only depends on the angle at the center.

d. The 45° angle cuts off exactly ⅛ of the full circumference of a circle (Figure 1.11). So

$$S(45°) = \text{Circumference}/8$$

Instead of using a ruler on the circle you have drawn, which is a bit tricky, you can determine the circumference another way. You can, so to speak, straighten out the circumference by rolling a dish along a table in a straight line without letting it slip. The distance it moves in one complete revolution is the circumference. Do this for a number of dishes of different sizes and verify the relationship.

$$\text{Circumference} = 2\pi \text{ radius}$$

where $\pi = 3.1416$ (π is the Greek letter pi. If you take $\pi = 22/7$ you will come pretty close.)
So

$$S(45°) = 2\pi \text{ radius}/8$$

or

$$S(45°)/\text{radius} = 2\pi/8 = 0.7854$$

This says that the arc corresponding to 45° is 0.7854 times the radius of the circle. What about the arc corresponding to 1°? The length of the arc is proportional to the angle at the center, $S/S' = A/A'$.
Write this as

$$S(1°)/S(45°) = 1/45$$

or

$$S(1°) = S(45°)/45$$

So from the expression for S(45°) above, we find

$$S(1°)/\text{radius} = 0.7854/45 = 1/57.3$$

And for any other angle

$$S(A°)/\text{radius} = A/57.3$$

Turning this upside down, and replacing the radius by the distance, D, we find the relationship we were looking for.

$$D/S = 57.3/A$$

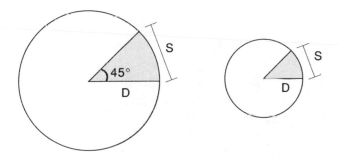

Figure 1.11. A 45° angle cuts off 1/8 of a circle: S = circumference/8. This is true for a circle of any size. The ratio D/S depends only on the angle as seen from the center.

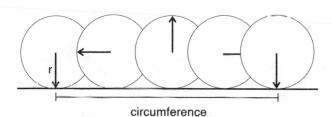

circumference

Figure 1.12. A circle moves a distance equal to its circumference when it rolls once without slipping. Circumference = 2π radius.

This tells us that the distance-to-size ratio is 57.3 divided by the angular size *measured in degrees*. As an example, an object subtending an angle of 6′ (= 0.1°) will have a distance-to-size ratio of D/S = 57.3/A = 57.3/0.1 = 573. If the object is 10 feet tall, it must be at a distance of $10 \times 573 = 5,730$ feet, or about 0.94 NM.

Here is a table illustrating the relationship.

Table 1.1. Angular size and distance-to-size ratio

Angular Size (°) A	Distance-to-size ratio D/S
0.01	5730
0.03	1910
0.1	573
0.3	191
1	57
3	19
10	5.7
30	1.9

Figure 1.13. Diagram of the phases of the moon and Venus on October 26, 1984, when the moon passed close to Venus. They are separated by about 0.6 degrees or 36 minutes of arc.

POSTTEST

1.15 Figure 1.13 shows a photograph on which the moon and Venus can be seen. Measure the diameters of both images with a fine ruler. Then using what you know about the moon, compute the distance-to-size ratio of Venus. _____

What is the angular diameter of Venus in degrees as seen from the earth? _____

If you assume Venus has approximately the same diameter as the earth (8,000 miles) what is the distance to Venus? _____

1.16 Figure 1.14 shows a photograph of an airplane passing in front of the moon. Determine the distance of the airplane from the camera, using what you know about the moon plus the fact that the airplane is about 230 feet long.

Figure 1.14. Airplane passing in front of the moon. (Photo courtesy Bryon Hogan, Clifton, NJ)

CHAPTER TWO

Putting Yourself on the Map

The men went on their way to map out the land after Joshua had given them these instructions: "Go all over the land and map it out, and come back to me. And then here in Shiloh I will consult the LORD for you by drawing lots." So the men went all over the land and set down in writing how they divided it into seven parts, making a list of the towns. Then they went back to Joshua in the camp at Shiloh. Joshua drew lots to consult the LORD for them, and assigned each of the remaining tribes of Israel a certain part of the land.

Book of Joshua, 18:8-10

INTRODUCTION

This chapter describes how to make a map without measuring angles and how to make a simple chart with contour lines. Actually doing the work will provide a pleasant and profitable day's activity, and will take the mystery out of charts and perhaps prepare you for unusual or emergency situations. Later in the chapter, we will describe the latitude and longitude system of coordinates on the surface of the earth.

MAKING YOUR OWN PLANE-TABLE CHART

For our purposes, a map (or chart) is a scaled-down representation of a vertical view of a region of the earth. It is flat and usually printed on a sheet of paper. Maps of small regions can be quite accurate, but maps of large regions are the result of compromises and always contain distortions. The distortions could be eliminated if we were willing to carry globes for the purpose of navigation. But to be useful, the globe would have to be nearly as large as a ship. Maps and charts are the fruit of trying to put small portions of a globe onto a convenient sheet of paper.

Each point on the earth is represented by a corresponding point on the map, and each point must be in exactly the right position. Making a map can be a tedious and demanding job (lots of arithmetic)—but not necessarily. You are about to be introduced to a painless way to make a map. You may never need to use this method again, but it will demonstrate what mapping is all about.

Overview of procedure

A plane-table chart treats a small region of the earth as though it were a flat sheet. A number of *stations* are selected and landmarks are sighted from each station. Each landmark is located geometrically, by triangulation. Lines are drawn on the chart from the stations in the direction of the landmarks, and the intersections of lines from different stations define the locations of the landmarks. The scale of the map is determined by the ratio of distances measured between the stations on the earth and on the map.

Equipment required

- Clean white paper mounted on stiff board

- Triangular ruler for sighting and drawing

- Masking tape

- Pencil (#3)

- Large eraser (nobody is perfect)

- Pen for final drawing

- Tape measure or other method of measuring true distance between at least one pair of stations

- Portable *plane table* for holding the paper horizontal. (This is what gives the method its name.) You may use any small table and a piece of foam board (available from art-supply or stationery stores) to support the drawing paper.

Step-by-step procedure for mapping a room
The following procedure ought to be practiced first in a room, and it can then be adapted to mapping a body of water. The word "station" will refer to an actual location on the ground or water; "point" will refer to its representation on the chart.

- **Step 1**—Select three stations that are well separated and placed so that all the interesting locations of the room can be seen from at least two stations. (If you are doing this on the water, you may use moorings and a station on the shore.)

- **Step 2**—Set the plane table and paper over Station 1 and make sure it is horizontal. Orient the paper to conform to the long dimension of the room. Mark a point on the paper to represent Station 1. This will be called Point 1.

- **Step 3**—Using a triangular ruler or other straight sighting device, draw pencil lines from Point 1 toward Stations 2 and 3. Label the lines so you will know where they pointed after you move the plane table. (You do not know where the other points are yet, only their directions from Point 1.) It is crucial that the orientation of the paper remain the same during the rest of the mapping, so check it from time to time by resighting one of the stations and turn the map if necessary. (This is the most difficult part of making a plane-table map, especially on water, where the boat will tend to turn.)

- **Step 4**—In a similar fashion, draw lines toward the corners of the room and any other key points you wish to locate. Label each of them for identification later.

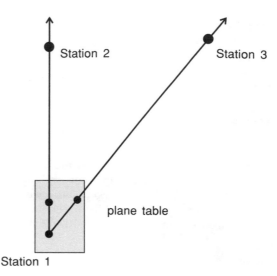

Figure 2.2. Vertical view looking down on plane table located over Station 1. Sight lines have been drawn to two other stations in Steps 1–4.

- **Step 5**—Move the plane table to Station 2. Do a back sight on Station 1 and rotate the map until the line from Point 1 to Point 2 is aligned toward Station 1. This will ensure that the paper is oriented in the same direction as before.

- **Step 6**—With a tape measure, determine the horizontal distance between Station 1 and Station 2.

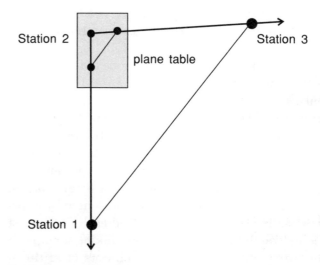

Figure 2.3. Back sighting from Station 2 to Station 1 in Step 5, for aligning the plane table in preparation for triangulating to other objects. Station 3, for example, is located by the intersection of the sight lines from the two stations.

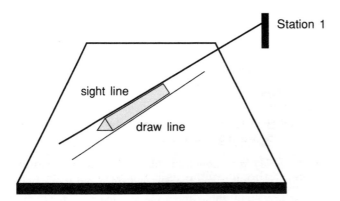

Figure 2.1. Sighting along the top edge of a triangular rule to find the direction of an object on the chart in Step 3.

- **Step 7**—Select a map scale so the line from Point 1 to Point 2 will be a convenient length on the paper. Using this scale, convert the measured distance to a chart-distance. (For example, suppose the measured distance is 50 feet and you wish this to be about 4 inches on the chart. As 50 feet = 600 inches, adopting a scale of 1: 150 will give 4 inches. Write the scale in the corner of the map.) Measure from Point 1 and mark the location of Point 2.

- **Step 8**—From Point 2, draw lines in the directions of the key points of the room. This time, instead of labeling each line, you may draw a small circle around the intersection of the two related lines, indicating the position of each key point.

- **Step 9**—Complete the map by drawing the outlines of the room; locate the key objects and label them.

Testing your map

Verify the scale of the map as follows. Measure the distance between the two stations as they appear on the map, in inches or centimeters. Then measure the distance between the actual locations of the stations in the room, and convert the result to the same units, inches or centimeters. Suppose you found that the stations were separated by 10 cm on the paper and 200 cm in the room. Take the ratio and set up the proportion 10:200 = 1:20. The scale ratio of your map is 1:20. This means that all distances on the map are just $\frac{1}{20}$ of their length in the real world.

Using your chart and its scale, determine a few other distances in the room, such as its length and width and the distance between Stations 2 and 3. After you have done this, measure the actual distances with a tape measure and compare the two sets of measures. The ratios of the true and the mapped distances ought to be equal to the scale ratio you just determined.

GUNKHOLE CHARTING

Using the plane table gives a useful introduction to mapping, but it has a limitation. You must have solid land underfoot to orient the table at each station and carry out the triangulation on the paper. In a boat, this is out of the question, so we need another technique for making nautical charts. Specifically, we need a method of determining relative directions that is not dependent on our being able

to fix the direction of the paper. The magnetic compass is the answer.

In the July 1988 issue of *Cruising World,* Alison Ball described a method of charting a small bay from a dinghy, with a hand bearing compass, paper, pencil, and protractor. (She also describes an alternative method using a sextant in place of the hand bearing compass.)

The method can be thought of as an extension of the plane-table method we just described. Ball's method uses one shore station (selected so the shoreline of the bay is visible) and one boat station (somewhere near the middle and marked by a buoy, either permanent or temporary). Instead of using a plane table and orienting by back sights on other stations, you first select a shore station, and then row out to the boat station with your hand bearing compass and a notepad. Tie up and then measure the compass bearings to all key points along the shore and make a carefully labelled list of the measurements—and don't forget to measure the direction to the shore station. (The fact that the compass doesn't point toward true north need not bother you. You don't need true directions at this point; compass bearings will suffice, as the chart can be oriented later if you wish.)

Move to the shore station and measure the new compass bearings to all the key points on your list. Also measure the direction to the boat station. Then go back to your drawing board.

Take out a big sheet of blank paper and start by plotting the position of the boat station. It will be near the center of the small bay (gunkhole), so put it near the center of the paper. Select a direction for compass north and draw a line in the north-south direction passing through the boat station. Use this line with the protractor to draw a line in the direction of the shore station. At a convenient distance along this line make a mark representing the shore station, and draw a north-south line through it. Now plot the directions to each of the landmarks from both stations using your protractor. Locate the key points at the intersections of the lines from different stations, as you did when making the plane-table chart. Label the landmarks and sketch the shape of the shoreline as a dot-to-dot among the plotted points.

Your next step is to determine the scale ratio of the chart. Think about this problem for a moment. How could you do it without measuring the distance from the shore station to the boat station? (That would be difficult, unless you have radar!)

All you have to do is measure the straight-line distance between any two of the landmarks. Presumably, now that you know you are going to have to do this, you can choose them so this measurement will be easy. Then measure the distance on the map and take the ratio. The scale ratio is given by the ratio of distances between any two objects in the real world and on the map.

The next part of Ball's method is to draw a contour map of the bottom of the gunkhole. To do this, you must first determine the depth of the water at several dozen points—the more the better, of course. Locate a few prominent points on the chart and draw lines between them with a ruler. Measure their compass directions to help you find your way. (Or better yet, establish some *range lines* with trees and stakes on the shore. See Chapter 3 for a discussion of range lines.) Then go out in the dinghy and row along these lines, stopping every 5 or 10 feet to measure the depth. You can measure the depths using a marked string with a small, but heavy, weight on the end. Depths to the nearest foot are probably accurate enough in most situations. Write the measurements directly on the chart at the proper locations. Then, back at the drawing board, draw

smooth curves to connect points of equal depth. (See Ball's article for further hints.)

THE HORIZON AND CARDINAL DIRECTIONS

PRETEST
2.1 Altitude is measured upward from the horizon.
   T _____ F _____
2.2 Polaris is at the zenith no matter where you are on earth. T _____ F _____
2.3 Azimuth is the angle measured from the horizon up to an object. T _____ F _____
2.4 The cardinal directions are up, down, right, left.
   T _____ F _____

Zenith and horizon

Tip your head back and look straight up or, better yet, lie on your back in the open air and look straight ahead. You will be looking at the zenith, which is the center of the overhead sky. It is straight up. You have a private zenith which is different from anyone else's. One way to find it is to hang a small weight on a string. The string will point straight up and down. It points to the zenith. The direction of the zenith is along the line from the center of the earth through your body up toward the sky.

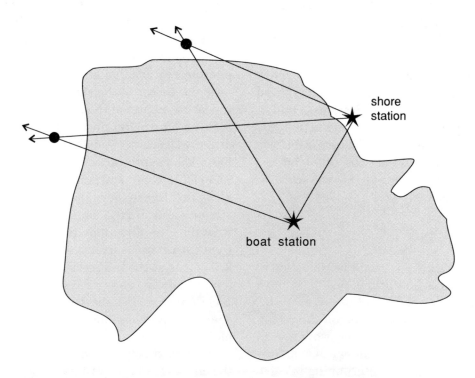

Figure 2.4. Triangulation lines to two of the landmarks as seen from the two stations.

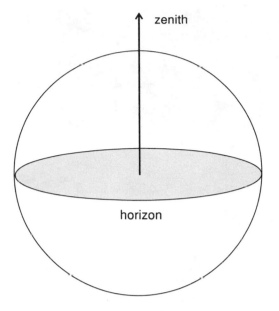

Figure 2.5. The zenith is directly overhead. It is along the line of a plumb bob and it lies perpendicular to a perfectly calm surface of water. The horizon divides the sphere symmetrically into two equal parts.

When you are at sea, the horizon is the line that divides the sky from the water (Figure 2.5). It defines the horizontal direction.

Altitude and zenith distance

The altitude of a star is the angle between the horizon and the star, measured upward toward the zenith (Figure 2.6). To find the altitude of the sun, for example, measure the angle from the horizon toward the zenith.

Now imagine a circle around the sky parallel to the horizon, as in Figure 2.6. All objects on the circle, which is parallel to the horizon and passes through the sun, at that moment have the same altitude as the sun. The angle measured from the zenith is the zenith distance and it obeys the following relation.

$$\text{Zenith distance} = 90° - \text{altitude}$$

Celestial pole and meridian

The axis of the earth's daily rotation can be imagined as a straight line through the center of the earth which pierces the sky at the celestial poles. The stars appear to rotate about the poles, as shown by the time exposure of the northern sky in Figure 2.7. Polaris (the North Star) is the bright star near the center of the circular arcs produced by the other stars. It is not overhead, unless you are at the north pole of the earth. Ordinarily, Polaris is partway down toward the horizon.

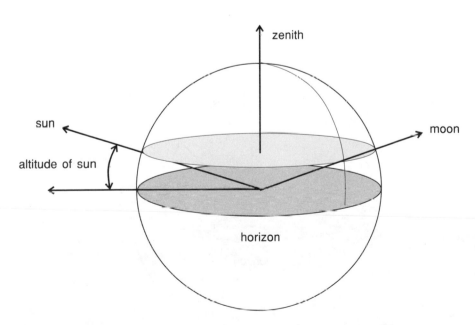

Figure 2.6. The altitude of the sun is the angle from the horizon toward the zenith. If the moon happens to have the same altitude as the sun at that moment it will lie on the same circle parallel to the horizon.

Imagine that you are standing at the center of an immense hemispherical tent and you can see Polaris through the tent. If an arc is drawn along the surface from the zenith down through the celestial pole to the horizon, it will pass close to Polaris and it will touch the ground at the north point of the horizon (Figure 2.8).

The cardinal directions

These mark four key places on the horizon (N, E, S, W). If you are in the northern hemisphere, north is directly below the north celestial pole. (From the southern hemisphere, the NCP is invisible, so you determine south by dropping a line from the south celestial pole.) East is halfway from north to south, measured clockwise around the horizon. West is opposite east.

The north-south line is the meridian passing through the celestial poles and the navigator's zenith. So every navigator has a north-south line. The first step in determining the direction of your north-south line is to find the celestial pole.

Azimuth

In addition to altitude, we need another angle if we are to specify completely the direction of an object on the sky—unless it happens to lie in one of the cardinal directions. There are many possible choices, but the most common angle is the azimuth, measured along the horizon from the north through east (Figure 2.9).

Figure 2.7. Time exposure of the region of the north celestial pole (NCP) showing the apparent counterclockwise motion of the stars about the axis of rotation. The bright star near the center is Polaris. At the south pole, the stars will appear to rotate clockwise in a similar pattern.

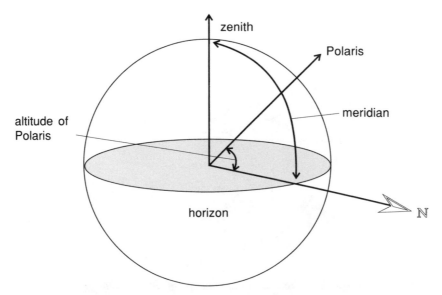

Figure 2.8. Diagram showing the meridian passing from the zenith through Polaris and the north celestial pole. The altitude of Polaris will depend on your latitude.

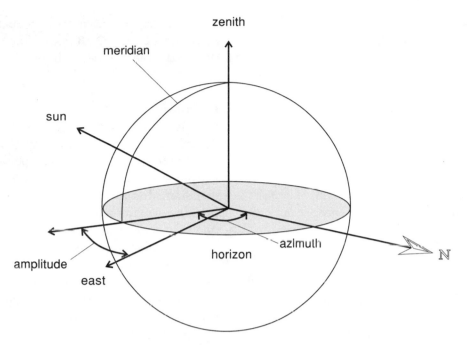

Figure 2.9. The azimuth of an object is a measure of its direction on the horizon. It is given by the angle from north through east to the line that passes down from the zenith through the object. East is 90°, south is 180°, and west is 270°. The amplitude of an object is measured from the east or the west direction, whichever is closer. In this example the amplitude of the sun is measured from the east.

Amplitude

This is similar to azimuth, but it is measured along the horizon from the east-west line (Figure 2.9). It is useful for discussing the direction of the sun at sunrise and sunset. At the spring and fall equinoxes, for example, the sun rises due east, and its amplitude is 0°. Chapter 17 describes the use of the solar amplitude at sunrise and sunset for compass testing.

POSTTEST

2.5 What are the azimuths of the cardinal points?

   N ____ E ____ S ____ W ____

2.6 What are the amplitudes of the cardinal points?

   N ____ E ____ S ____ W ____

2.7 What are the amplitudes of points whose azimuths are the following?

   130° ____ 020° ____ 290° ____ 195° ____

2.8 What is the altitude of the zenith? ____

LATITUDE AND LONGITUDE

PRETEST

2.9 Latitude lines are closer together near the poles.

   T ____ F ____

2.10 Latitude increases from 0° to 360° around the equator. T ____ F ____

2.11 Longitude lines all go through the north and south poles. T ____ F ____

The earth spins daily about an axis that defines the north and south poles (Figure 2.10). This spinning motion defines two poles and an equator that can be used for setting up a coordinate system.

Longitude

Imagine a plane fixed in the earth that includes the earth's axis of rotation (Figure 2.11). This plane will intersect the earth's surface in a line that is approximately a circle. Such a line is a line of longitude or a meridian.

All points on a meridian have the same numerical value of longitude. Greenwich, England (the site of an observatory near London), has the privileged 0° of longitude because London was once the hub of the world's shipping. To find the longitude of another city, say New York, we imagine a second plane containing the earth's axis and oriented so it passes through New York (Figure 2.12). The angle by which

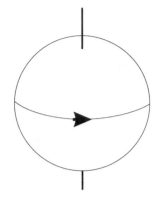

Figure 2.10. The earth spins eastward once per day, and this motion provides a natural basis for the measurement of longitude and latitude.

the plane is rotated clockwise to carry it through New York is the west longitude of New York. Longitude is measured westward to 180°W for the western hemisphere and eastward to 180°E for the eastern hemisphere. Therefore it is necessary to label longitudes E or W depending on the direction in which they are measured.

The poles are the pivots for longitude measurement, and Figure 2.13 shows the view down onto the north pole where the lines of longitude meet at a point.

Latitude

Latitude is an angular measure of position on a meridian. Taken together, latitude and longitude completely specify the location of a point on the surface. (Airplane pilots and submariners need a third dimension: distance above or below the surface.) Imagine a plane perpendicular to the axis of rotation that divides the earth into equal northern and southern hemispheres (Figure 2.14). The circle where this plane intersects the surface is the equator. Its latitude is 0°. As shown in Figure 2.15, latitude is the angle between the equator and a line from the center of the earth to the point of interest. The north pole is at 90°N and the south pole is at 90°S. Figure 2.16 shows the plane parallel to the equator that goes through all points with the latitude of Miami.

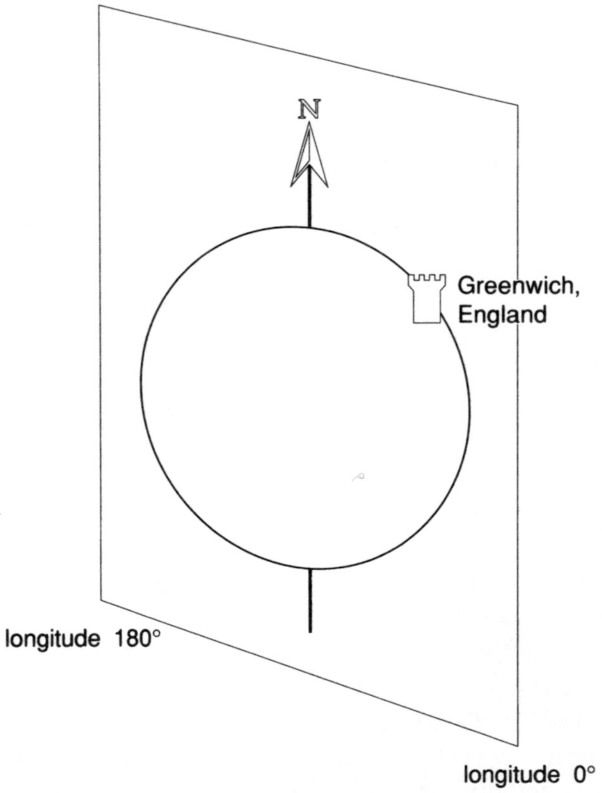

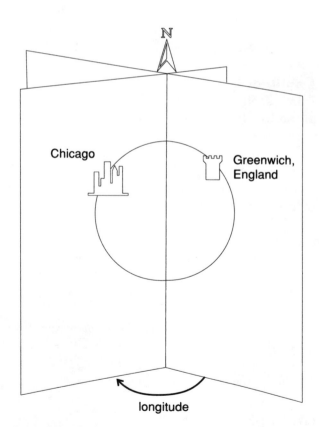

Figure 2.11. Lines of longitude (meridians) are defined by the intersection of the earth's surface with a plane that includes the axis of rotation. Greenwich is the starting point for longitude.

Figure 2.12. Longitude is the angle by which a plane through the earth's axis must be rotated to carry it from Greenwich to the point of interest. In this illustration it is measured westward and labelled W.

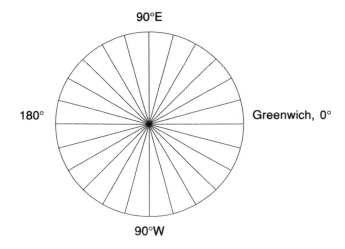

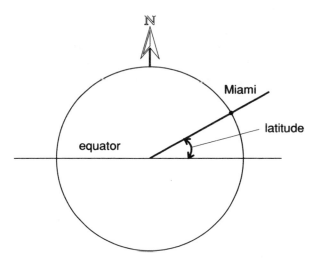

Figure 2.13. Longitude lines in 15° intervals looking down on the north pole. West longitude is measured clockwise from the meridian of Greenwich, England.

Figure 2.15. Cross section of the earth, showing the complete meridian through Miami. Latitude is measured from the equator. It is labelled N or S depending on the hemisphere.

Rather than make a separate construction for each location on a globe, it is handier to set up a grid of latitude and longitude lines that completely cover the earth, as in Figure 2.17. With this, the location of a point may be estimated by noting its position relative to the lines of labeled latitude and longitude.

Distance scales and nautical miles

Nautical miles are defined so that 60 NM = 1° of latitude. And because 1° = 60 minutes of arc, we have

1 NM = 1 minute of arc of latitude = 6,080 feet

Remember, this is measured *from the equator along the meridians.* What happens if we measure min-

utes of arc along a latitude circle instead of along the meridians? Trouble. Figure 2.18 shows that the meridians get closer together in nautical miles as we approach the poles. A nautical mile measured along the equator will cover 1 minute of arc of longitude, but if we go away from the equator it will cover a greater range of longitude. The relationship is shown in Figure 2.19.

Some important differences between the properties of latitude and longitude lines are summarized in Table 2.1.

For example, a distance of 1° of longitude in the east-west direction along a latitude circle will stretch across 52 NM at a latitude of 30°N or S. At a higher latitude of 70°, the distance of 1° in longitude is only 20 NM.

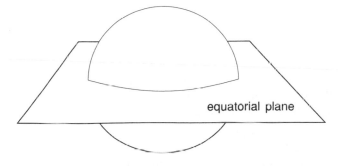

Figure 2.14. The equatorial plane of the earth provides a natural starting point for measuring latitude, which is the angle from the equator along a meridian.

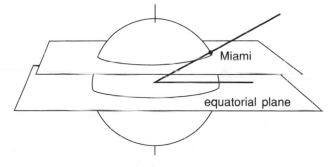

Figure 2.16. A plane through Miami parallel to the equator goes through points of the same latitude. The latitude of Miami is the angle between the straight lines from the center of the earth.

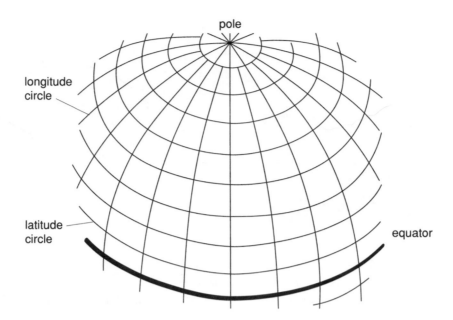

Figure 2.17. The longitude and latitude lines provide a grid covering the globe.

Table 2.1. Properties of latitude and longitude lines

Latitude
Measured along a meridian: 0°–90°N, 0°–90°S
Equal latitudes are marked by small circles parallel to equator.
Small circles are always equal distances apart.

Longitude
. . . along equator: 0–180°W, 0–180°E
. . . by great circles through poles

Great circles converge at poles.

POSTTEST

2.12 Make a short list of cities with similar latitudes.

2.13 Make a short list of cities with similar longitudes.

2.14 Measure the distances between longitude lines (meridians) at several latitudes and compare the variation with what you find in Figure 2.19.

2.15 Suppose you wish to fly by a great circle route from City A to City B as shown in Figure 2.20 below. Use the compass diagrams to indicate your initial direction along this route. (Mark your guess in pencil; then find a globe and stretch a string between the cities to find a more reliable value.)

2.16 Suppose two cities are at longitude 75°W. If one of them is at latitude 43°45′N and the other is at 42°00′N, how many miles apart are they, as measured along the longitude circle?

2.17 Suppose two cities are at latitude 48°N. If one of them is at longitude 84°45′ W and the other is at 82°00′W, how many miles apart are they as measured along the latitude circle?

2.18 If the latter distance were measured along a great circle, would it be shorter or longer than the distance measured along the latitude circle?

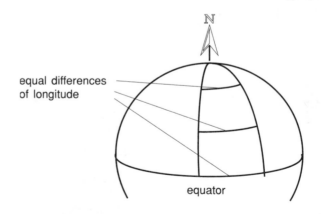

Figure 2.18. Meridians are parallel to each other at the equator, but they converge toward each other as the pole is approached. This means that a certain angle of longitude will cover a smaller span of nautical miles along a latitude circle as we approach the poles.

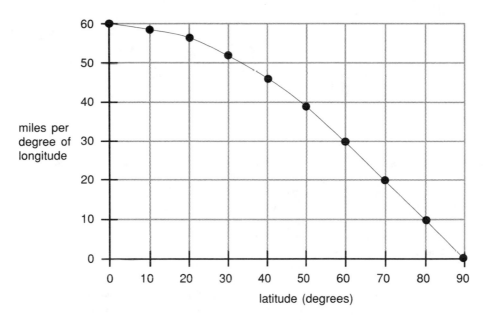

Figure 2.19. The number of nautical miles spanned by 1° of longitude decreases as we get farther from the equator. For latitude the relationship is constant: 1° of latitude = 60 NM.

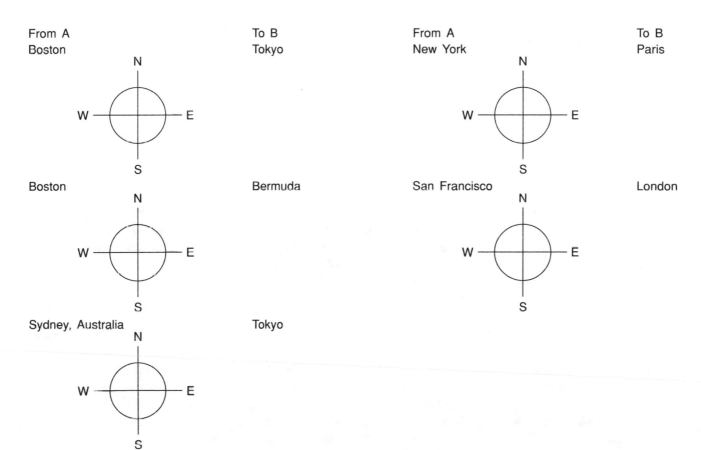

Figure 2.20.

CHAPTER THREE

Using Nautical Charts

Had you followed Captain Ahab down into his cabin . . . you would have seen him go to a locker in the transom, and bringing out a large wrinkled roll of yellowish sea charts, spread them before him on his screwed down table. Then seating himself before it, you would have seen him intently study the various lines and shadings which there met his eye; and with slow but steady pencil trace additional courses over spaces that before were blank. At intervals, he would refer to piles of old log-books beside him, wherein were set down the seasons and places in which, on various former voyages of various ships, sperm whales had been captured or seen . . .

But it was not this night in particular that, in the solitude of his cabin, Ahab thus pondered over his charts. Almost every night they were brought out; almost every night some pencil marks were effaced, and others were substituted. For with the charts of all four oceans before him, Ahab was threading a maze of currents and eddies, with a view to the more certain accomplishment of the monomaniac thought of his soul.

Melville, Moby Dick

The pilot chart, that precious and indispensable compendium for the navigator, which I carried on every voyage, gives for September-December a probable mean of twenty-seven days per month of winds force 8 (37-44 knots). And it was precisely in those months that I was to attempt the crossing of the whole breadth of the Indian Ocean.

Vito Dumas, Alone through the Roaring Forties

INTRODUCTION

At sea, the most dangerous regions are usually in sight of land, near shallow water or strong currents. Piloting, or coastwise navigation, is the art and science of guiding your boat and keeping track of your position on a chart when in sight of land. At all times, you must know your location on a chart—whether you are in fog, rain, or sunshine.

The surest way to keep track of your position on a chart is to update it frequently and at every change of course. If you do this, you will be able to find yourself within seconds when you need to. This is far easier than starting from scratch and trying to figure out where you are with no clues but a thin shoreline and a few buoys around you.

As an example of the need to keep track of your position and to verify your hunches rather than trusting them, I remember one misty morning off Casco Bay when we had sailed with friends overnight from Marblehead, Mass. In fog, we had not been able to update our track and when the fog lifted, we thought we recognized a particular buoy. We did not bother to go off course for a closer look,

and during the next half hour we gradually realized that other buoys were not where they belonged. So we started from scratch to figure out where we were. Try as we might, we couldn't find a convincing place on the chart. Finally, in desperation, I simply closed my eyes and pinned my finger on the chart. Amazingly enough, we were then able to locate ourselves. This is not guaranteed as a method of navigation.

THE CHART IS YOUR MOST VALUABLE TOOL

After the boat, charts are the sailor's most precious possession. When you learn to read a chart, it may warn you of reefs and submerged wrecks and show the way to safe harbors. If you can locate yourself on a chart and identify surrounding landmarks, there is no need to use your compass to find north. Some say it is better to lose your sextant or your compass than your charts.

Charts will not speak for themselves. Plotting (with a pencil) is one safety procedure you should always practice. Stories of misadventure through neglect abound. According to a description on the back of the U. S. Navy Hydrographic Office *Pilot Chart 1400* for August 1963, a large ore carrier was passing through Serpent's Mouth, south of Trinidad. Onboard they had the most advanced equipment—radar, course recorder, fathometer with recorder—but the ship went aground. No one had plotted the course on a chart, where the shallows of Icacos Point were clearly marked. *The truth is, it could happen to you!*

FEATURES AND PROPERTIES OF A CHART

PRETEST

3.1 What is a compass rose?

3.2 On a chart with a scale of 1:10,000, how long is 10 nautical miles?

3.3 What does the contour interval of a chart tell you?

For our purposes, a *chart* is a map representing the view looking down on a restricted region of the earth. It is called a "chart" rather than a "map" when the region that it depicts is largely covered with water, or when it is used for air navigation.

If the chart covers a small area, say several hundred miles or less, it can be a faithful geometric replica of the region. Charts of larger areas necessarily have various types of distortion to be discussed later in this chapter.

Refer to Nautical Training Chart 116-SC Tr for what follows.

Scale

A scale of 1:100 means that any length on the chart represents 100 times that length on the actual earth. For example, 1 inch on such a chart would depict 100 inches on earth. A 3-foot chart with a scale of 1:100 could only show a region the size of a

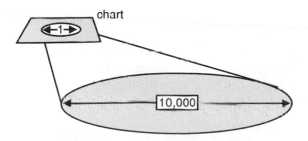

Figure 3.1. If the chart scale is 1:10,000, each centimeter on the chart is 10,000 centimeters (100 meters) on the earth's surface.

football field, so most navigational charts have scales from 1:10,000 to 1:200,000.

It is helpful to think of the scale of 1:10,000 as the ratio 1/10,000. (See Figure 3.1). *The scale is the ratio of the object's size on a chart to its true size.* Charts on which objects are relatively large are large-scale charts; charts making objects look smaller are small-scale charts. The smaller the scale, the larger the area will be, but the fewer the details that can be shown.

Orientation

On a proper chart, the direction of north is always indicated by an arrow. This arrow is often found in a *compass rose,* which is a circular scale usually several inches in diameter, on which the compass directions are indicated by their degrees from north. Most roses have two such scales. The outer scale starts from *true north;* the inner scale starts from *magnetic north* at the region of the chart and on the date indicated. The difference between true and magnetic north is called *magnetic variation.*

Find the compass rose on the left-hand side of Chart 116-SC Tr. Notice the longitude lines are aligned with true north and the latitude lines are perpendicular to them. Also, magnetic and true north in 1970 differed by 13°30′W and the difference was increasing by 2′ per year. (More on this in Chapter 5, where we discuss the compass.)

Depths and Contours

Elevations and depths cannot be shown directly on navigational charts, because the view is straight down, so they are often shown quantitatively with numbers or contour lines. The reference level for water depth is usually *mean low water* (so the actual depth will usually be somewhat greater) and the units are specified on each chart with a statement such as "Soundings in feet at mean low water." Land heights are usually measured in feet from *mean high water* (so the actual height above sea level will usually be somewhat greater).

Each contour line shows points along it of equal height or depth. Another way to think of a contour line is that it would be a shoreline if the water were at exactly that height. The vertical distance between adjacent contour lines is the *contour interval.* The contours are close together where the slope is steep. Contours are labelled with their depth or height, and they are often confined to the region near the shore.

Colors

The types of surfaces in various region are often distinguished by color on the chart. On Chart 116-SC Tr, the shallowest water is shown in light blue.

Legend

This is the portion of a chart where most of the symbols are collected and described. The scale is usually stated in the legend, as well as the date of the chart. Find the legend on Chart 116-SC Tr.

TYPES OF NAVIGATIONAL CHARTS

Harbor charts (1:10,000 to 1:50,000)

These are the largest-scale charts usually available and they are used for entering and leaving harbors, where the greatest detail is needed. Chart 116-SC Tr is an example of this type.

Coastal charts (1:50,000 to 1:150,000)

These are for navigation near the shore, for entering bays and harbors of considerable width, and for sailing among reefs. There are also several Intracoastal Waterway charts covering partially protected waterways from New Jersey to Mexico, with scale usually 1:40,000. Because these and the harbor charts cover a small portion of the earth, it is possible to use a single scale for the entire chart.

General charts (1:150,000 to 1:600,000)

These are for coastwise navigation outside reefs and shoals.

Pilot charts/sailing charts (1:600,000 or smaller)

These cover an entire ocean, and are useful for planning ocean crossings. An example is the *Pilot Chart of the North Atlantic Ocean* (1:15,700,000), which is published in quarterly sets showing averaged ocean currents, water and air temperatures, iceberg limits, and percentage of wind speed from various directions. Data on pilot charts are historical and they are helpful in planning but should not be taken as predictions.

Chart kits (various scales)

Government charts are sold individually (see Appendix 4). With an index chart you can select a convenient set of charts for any particular voyage. Alternatively, you may purchase regional sets of charts that have been reprinted privately from the government charts. These sets contain a variety of scales and come on heavy paper in a spiral binder for easy manipulation on a boat. Because government prices have become so high, these private kits are, for the most part, a bargain. And where they are reproduced directly from the government charts, they ought to be reliable. On the other hand, an article in *Practical Sailor* (16:1; Jan. 1, 1990) mentions several errors that have been found on such charts—such as a reversed compass rose.

Electronic charts

With the advent of shipboard computers and electronic charts, the problems of cost, reliability, and rapid updating ought to be alleviated. See Chapter 22 for more details.

UPDATING CHARTS

Charts become outdated as buoys and lights are added, removed, or shifted, and shoals and bars are moved by the currents. Even the most recent printing of a chart will almost certainly need updating in a half-dozen details. You ought to apply these with ink. The U.S. government publishes weekly *Notices to Mariners* in which the corrections may be found arranged by geographical location. Alternatively, it is possible to get lists by chart number (which is considerably more convenient) through the *Automated Notices to Mariners*. These lists may be obtained with a computer and a modem directly from the government, to be printed with your own printer and then applied to the charts by hand. (See Chapter 22 for details.) Having the corrections summarized by chart number will save you from the need to leaf through seemingly endless *Notices to Mariners*. Alternatively, printed copies of the lists may be purchased by chart number from private suppliers at about $5 per chart.

MAPPING THE GLOBE ONTO A CHART

PRETEST

3.4 What is a rhumb line? Why is it useful?

3.5 Which type of chart is best for finding rhumb lines?

3.6 What is a great circle?

The spherical earth poses a problem to mappers: how to represent the spherical surface on a flat map? Representing a large portion of the earth on a single, flat chart is a difficult job. Not because the earth is rough—on a global scale, the surface of the earth is extremely smooth, even in the mountain ranges, and especially on the ocean surface. To get an idea of just how smooth it is, imagine a bowling ball that has been dipped into water and pulled out again. If the ball represents the earth, the mountains of the earth would all be inside the layer of water clinging to the ball.

Accurate charting is difficult because the earth is not flat; it is nearly spherical. In our daily life, we tend to forget this, because we see only a small portion of the sphere, and it looks relatively flat. But the curvature is important if the chart is to extend more than a few hundred miles. If you have ever tried to wrap an apple or peach in tissue paper, you will know why this curvature makes mapping difficult. The paper wrinkles as soon as it is forced to the curvature of the fruit. Only if you use small pieces, no larger than a postage stamp, can you make the paper lie on the surface without wrinkling. And when you peel an orange, the skin cannot be made to lie flat on the table unless you cut it into very small pieces.

Hundreds of compromises and partial solutions to this problem have been proposed, each with its peculiar advantages and shortcomings. We will mention only three types, and it is a safe bet that these three will cover essentially all of your needs. Each chart should have its type clearly stated in the legend.

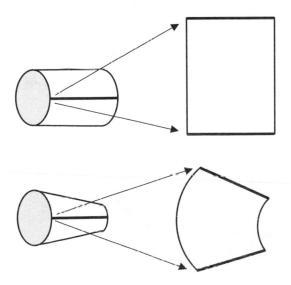

Figure 3.2. Cylindrical and conical surfaces may be rolled out flat after they have been cut. Heavy line is the cut.

The first two types are *central projections;* that is, they may be generated by imagining a tiny (but very bright) light bulb at the center of the earth sending out rays that trace the outlines of the continents onto a *projection surface* that intercepts the rays. The shape and location of the surface will determine the nature of the projection. Usually the projection surface is flat or conical, as these are shapes that can be opened out flat with a single cut (Figure 3.2).

In describing the relative advantage of various types of charts, we will relate them to the two types of ocean tracks that are often used for planning a voyage. These are *great circles* and *rhumb lines.* See Chapter 18 for more on great circles, but all you need to know at the moment is that *the great circle is the shortest track between two points.* As you progress along a great-circle voyage, the true heading of the ship will gradually change. You might start a great-circle passage across the Pacific Ocean sailing northeast; in midocean you would be sailing eastward, and at the time of your landfall you would be sailing southeast.

The great-circle route requires adjusting the helm every hundred miles or so. By contrast, *a rhumb line is the track of constant true heading between two points.* (There is a discussion of true heading in Chapter 4.) It is simpler to steer along a rhumb line than a great circle: you simply hold the same course the entire way. But the rhumb line is a longer course. Figure 3.3 shows a comparison of a track across the Atlantic Ocean on the gnomonic projection (upper) and the Mercator map (lower).

Gnomonic projection

This is the simplest map to describe, although its name is the trickiest to pronounce. (Hint: the g is silent and the word rhymes with *tonic.*) In this case, the mapping surface is a plane that just touches (is tangent to) the sphere. Lines are drawn from the center of the globe through each point on the surface and they are extended to the tangent plane. All points that are connected by a great circle on the globe will lie along *a straight line* on the gnomonic projection. And conversely, all straight lines on the gnomonic projection represent *great circles* on the globe.

The gnomonic chart is handy for planning trips longer than a few thousand miles, such as ocean crossings. And, because radio signals travel nearly along great circles (under ideal conditions), the gnomonic map is handy for radio direction finding over long distances. Ham radio operators often have a gnomonic chart of the world on the wall of their radio shack. The chart is centered on their location and gives the directions to operators on other continents. This is useful for orienting directional radio antennas.

Advantage of gnomonic projection: Great circles are straight lines.

Disadvantages: Scale changes drastically from center outward. True directions are difficult to read if you are not at the center of the chart. Shapes become distorted away from the equator.

Uses: Trips longer than a thousand miles; plotting bearings in radio direction finding.

Lambert projection

Picture a cone which intersects the earth along two circles of latitude not more than about 10° to 15° apart. Project the outlines of the continents onto this cone and then cut the cone in a straight line from its vertex to its base. It can then be laid out flat on a table. The circles of latitude (which are technically *small circles* and are often called *parallels*) will project into circles that are nearly concentric and equidistant. The longitude lines are straight lines that converge at the north (or south) pole.

Advantages of Lambert projection: Scale changes slowly with latitude, so this is useful for large areas and is popular in air navigation. Longitude lines are straight lines. Great circles are nearly straight lines. Shapes of regions are pretty well preserved. Can be constructed for any latitude.

Disadvantages: Routes of constant heading are curved on this projection, just as they are on the gnomonic. Mileage scales in latitude and longitude are slightly different so shapes of regions are slightly distorted.

Uses: General-purpose map, good for coastwise or oceanic sailing.

Mercator mapping

This kind of map or chart is created by a mathematical formula, not a projection, although it is

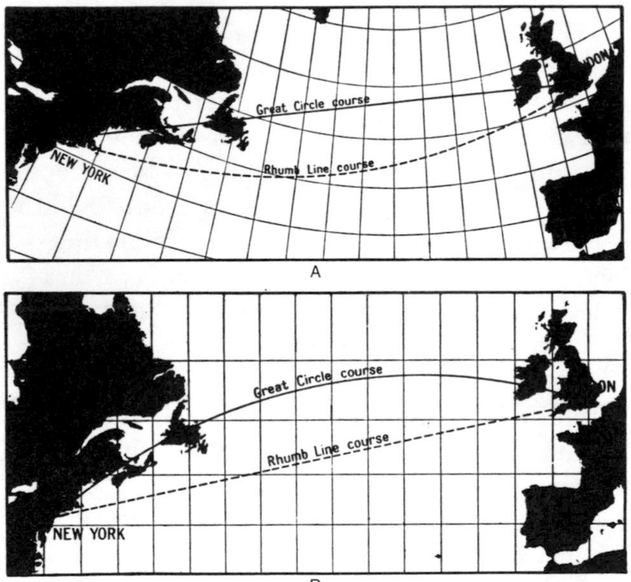

Figure 3.3. Comparison of great-circle and rhumb-line courses on two map projections. Top, Gnomonic projection: The great-circle route from New York to London is a straight line on a gnomonic projection. It starts on a northeast heading and becomes due east off the coast of Ireland, before turning to southeast. The rhumb-line course holds a constant heading, but it is a curve on this type of map. Bottom, Mercator map: The rhumb-line course is a straight line on the Mercator map because it has a constant heading. The great-circle route is curved on this type of map.

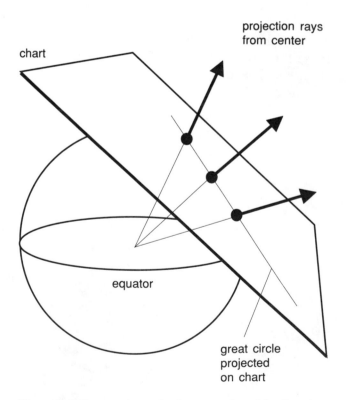

Figure 3.4. Gnomonic projection is produced by drawing rays from the center of the earth onto a tangent plane. This example shows three points lying on a great circle; they project onto a straight line.

often (somewhat inaccurately) described as a central projection onto a cylinder that is tangent to the sphere. Thinking of it that way will not put you on the shoals. Near the equator, the Mercator and the Lambert maps are nearly identical, but the usual Mercator map cannot be used in polar regions. Chart 116-SC Tr is an example of a Mercator map.

Advantages of Mercator mapping: Rhumb lines are straight. Mileage scales in latitude and longitude are the same, so angles are precisely preserved. However, the scale changes as either pole is approached.

Disadvantages: Scale changes away from the equator, becoming very small as the pole is approached. Great circles are curved.

Uses: Sight reduction and a variety of problems where short distances are involved and equal latitude and longitude scales are essential, such as dead reckoning (Chapter 6). Can be used for radio direction finding (Chapter 7) if the transmitting station is not more than 100 miles away.

Making a Mercator chart—Chapter 23 describes how to construct your own Mercator chart starting with a blank sheet of paper. Many navigators prefer to have a good supply of the handy universal plotting sheets (UPS) on hand. Their use is described in Chapter 7.

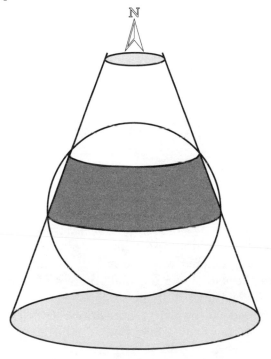

Figure 3.5. Lambert projection for a limited region of latitude is obtained by projecting from the center of the Earth onto a cone that cuts the surface near the region of interest.

Transferring a track from a gnomonic to a Mercator chart—Once a great-circle track has been laid out on a gnomonic chart, it is easy to transfer it to another type of chart. Merely read off the latitude and longitude at equally spaced points and plot them one by one on the new chart. Then connect them with short straight lines. Look carefully at Figure 3.3, where both types of charts are shown, and you will see how it is done.

GENERAL COMMENTS ON READING A COASTAL CHART

The goal in reading a chart of a strange territory is to transform it into a visual image as seen from your location in the boat. For example, you may want to spot a particular buoy that can be seen on the chart. Three things make the reading of a chart rather tricky and they will require conscious effort and practice on your part. We will discuss each of them briefly, and recommend study of an article by Ralph Naranjo in the June 1988 issue of *Sail* magazine, entitled "Read a Chart in Three Dimensions."

Point of view

The chart gives you a view looking down, which would be fine if you were in an airplane. From a boat, you look at the world edgewise, so to speak. Reading a chart requires the ability to imagine how the downward view would translate to this edgewise view.

Foreground-background confusion

Our eye/brain provides depth perception and a three-dimensional picture when we look at objects that are not more than a few hundred feet away. We unconsciously use a variety of clues to estimate depth (such as size, darkness and atmospheric haze, hiding of background objects, texture, etc.), but these don't work at great distances. We have difficulty determining what is closer and what is farther so we must look carefully and consciously for these types of clues.

Curvature of earth's surface

Because the earth is approximately a sphere with a radius of 4,000 miles, the surface of a calm ocean may rise as much as 6 feet between you and a low-lying beach 5 miles away. This means that if you are 6 feet above the water, you are cut off from a 6-foot-high band of shoreline. So don't look for

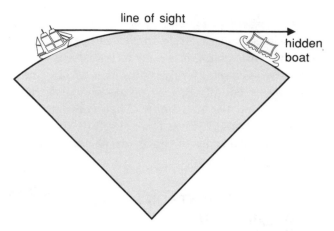

Figure 3.6. Curvature of the earth's surface causes low objects to be hidden when viewed from a great distance.

buoys that are more than a few miles away. (These matters will be discussed more fully in Chapter 8.)

As Naranjo points out, "Don't fall into the habit of ignoring your chart once you recognize the surroundings. This is the best time to learn to use the chart effectively by comparing real-world inputs with charted data."

SYMBOLS

There are many dozens of symbols used on navigational charts. Most of these can be found on the back of Chart 1210 Tr, an inexpensive training chart available at most nautical supply stores. Also, the U.S. Government Defense Mapping Agency publishes a pamphlet (Chart No. 1) with a complete listing. This chart should be a standard part of your navigation kit, kept at a handy spot near the chart table. Many a disaster has occurred through misidentification of a buoy or misinterpretation of a chart symbol. Get to know them.

The symbols are divided into categories as follows:

- coastline features
- natural land features
- survey control points whose locations are accurately known
- lights
- buoys
- radio and radar stations
- dangers

- various limits
- soundings
- depth contours
- quality of the bottom
- tide and current indicators

The light symbols are crucial for coastwise navigation at night. They tell the pattern and color of flashing, as well as the expected range of visibility, and they will be discussed in Chapter 8. Whistles, bells, and horns are crucial in foggy weather. Become familiar with these types before you need them.

PLOTTING ON CHART 116-SC Tr

To prepare for plotting, you will need to assemble the following equipment:

Equipment needed for plotting a course

- dividers
- drawing compass
- protractor
- parallel rulers or sliding ruler equipped with roller to keep it parallel to itself as it moves (12″ size is convenient)
- several sharp pencils (#3) and a small sharpener
- eraser
- 4-function calculator
- drawing board or table
- transparent triangle (optional)

Many navigators use a plotter-protractor with a rectangular grid and two circular scales. This can be readily aligned with the meridians and can replace the use of the parallel rulers and compass rose for plotting headings.

Spread out the chart on the drawing table so the side showing Long Island Sound is facing up. The lines marked 41°18′, 41°20′, etc., are parallels of latitude and they are separated by 2′ or 2 NM (NM = nautical mile = 6,080 feet = 1.15 statute miles). The lines perpendicular to them, marked 71°52′, 71°54′, etc., are lines of longitude or meridians.

This is a Mercator chart so the mileage scale at any point is the same in the north-south direction as it is in the east-west direction. But, by measuring with your dividers you can see that 1' of latitude is longer than 1' of longitude in miles. This occurs because the meridians all converge toward the poles. Use the latitude scale (north-south lines) for nautical miles. One nautical mile = 1' of latitude. *Never use the longitude scale for measuring distances on a chart.*

You are now ready to try a practice cruise on your chart. You will sail out of New London harbor southward and then westward, beyond and south of Bartlett Reef Light. Then you will turn east, toward a point about 0.4 miles south of Groton Long Pt. (All miles in this book are nautical miles.) The log in Table 3.1 will describe your cruise.

First plot the point of departure (PoD) found at the top of the log. The latitude of this point is easy, as it is right on a latitude line. The next step is to plot the longitude line of the PoD, and this is not so easy as the longitude is 72°05′05″. You can find this longitude line by offsetting from the nearest printed meridian, which is at 72°06′W. You want to go 55 (60″ – 5″) east from that meridian, so take the dividers and spread their points to correspond to 55″ by using the latitude scale (north-south) near Bartlett Reef. Carefully holding your dividers so this distance is not lost, place one tip on the 72°06′W longitude line at its intersection with the 41°18′N latitude line; mark the point where the other tip falls when it is directly east, on the same latitude. This is your PoD. Label it with the time of departure and draw a small circle around it. Write PoD after the time, and you are now ready to plot the cruise.

True courses with the compass rose and parallel rulers

You now transfer directions from the compass rose using the parallel rulers. The course legs listed in Table 3-1 are relative to *true* north, so you should use the outer scale (true directions) of the compass rose. The less you move the parallel rulers, the less will be the danger of their slipping, and the work will be easier if you start by holding the two rulers together and aligning the left ruler to the 168° mark. Then bear down on the left ruler and move the right ruler toward the PoD, to the east, as far as you can go comfortably. Now hold the right ruler down firmly and move the left to join the right again. One further move of the right will cause it to pass through the PoD, where you want to be careful to make it go exactly through this point.

With a pencil, draw a course line through your PoD in the direction of 168° and write 168T above the line (T stands for *true,* as measured from true north) and write S10 kn below the line (for *speed 10 knots*).

Measuring distances

Your next task is to lay off the length of leg 1. The distance covered is 1.46 miles according to the log, and we will estimate to the nearest 0.01 mile using the distance scale at the top of the chart. Note that the left end of the scale is marked in tenths of miles reading from right to left. Place one point of the dividers on the "1" NM mark. To measure an additional 0.46 miles, the other end of the dividers should be placed 0.6 of the way from the 0.4 to the 0.5 mark measuring from right to left, as indicated in the diagram below. Being careful to avoid changing the separation of the dividers, you can now transfer this distance to the plotted leg and indicate the end of the leg with a pencil mark.

The time required for the leg can be found by simple arithmetic with a small calculator from the formula:

$$\text{Time (hours)} = \text{distance (NM)}/\text{speed (knots)}$$

We may also write this as:

Table 3.1 Cruise of *Vega*

Point of departure (PoD): Lat. 41°18′N, Long. 72°05′05″W
LOG

Leg	True Heading	Speed (kn)	Dist. (NM)	Time (EST) Start leg	End of leg Lat.	End of leg Long.
1	168°	10	1.46	0736	41°16.6N	72°04.7W
2	256°	10	4.00	0745	41°15.6N	72°09.8W
3	091°	10	4.00	0809		
4	050°	10	3.73		41°18.0N	72°00.7W

Distance (NM) = time (hours) × speed (knots)
Speed (knots) = distance (NM)/time (hours)

Using a hand calculator, even for these simple calculations, is a good idea, as it will avoid errors. Also note, speed is measured in *knots* (NM/hour). Don't get caught referring to "knots per hour."

In our example, Time = 1.46/10 = 0.146 (hours) = 60 × 0.146 (minutes) = 9 (minutes).

Courses are usually plotted to the nearest minute.

POSTTEST

3.7 Plot the cruise of the *Vega* (Table 3.1) on the chart and verify the times and latitude and longitude at the end of each leg with your dividers. Fill out the missing entries in the log.

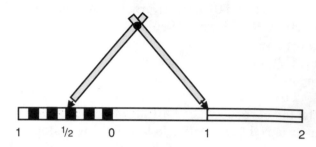

Figure 3.8. *Using the distance scale to measure 1.46 miles with a pair of dividers. One nautical mile = 1' of latitude. Do not use the longitude scale for measuring distances on a chart.*

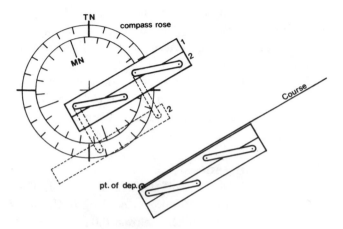

Figure 3.7. *Plotting a course with parallel rulers.*

CHAPTER FOUR

Measuring True and Relative Directions

The land ahead was undoubtedly the north coast of Spain, somewhere, we thought, in the neighborhood of Coruna. With the aid of binoculars, the hand-bearing compass, and the appropriate "Pilot", we speedily identified the Tower of Hercules, a square dark tower at the western entrance of Coruna bay. Proctor, who two months before had been there in my old acquaintance *Iyruna* on her way home from Oporto, recognised it, and the adjacent features seemed to fit. After one wrong assumption it is remarkable how easily the neighbouring marks on a coast line can be made to conform and how long it is before discrepancies become so glaring that the original assumption has to be abandoned. Prominent buildings noted in the "Pilot" are cheerfully allowed to have been knocked down or put up since the invaluable guide was written, woods to have been planted or felled; and awkward hills which refuse to fit into the picture are either ignored or assumed to have been swallowed by an earthquake. Until at last common sense prevails and one is obliged sadly to admit that nothing fits and that one is looking at an entirely different piece of coast. We were all adrift. We were off Cape Ortegal . . .

That we were out in our reckoning and had made a bad landfall was attributed to our being set by the tide. The navigator can always attribute his errors—unless, of course, they are fatal—to abnormal tidal sets or the perverse behavior of currents, whereas the man who leads his party into the wrong valley or on to the wrong ridge has no such scapegoat and is written down an ass

H. W. Tilman, Adventures under Sail

INTRODUCTION

After you have found yourself on a chart, how can you use the chart to measure directions to visible objects? That is the primary subject of this chapter. You will also learn how to triangulate a fix and how to estimate the accuracy of the location provided by the fix.

A few definitions

Before getting started, we need to define a few new terms.

- *True heading*—Standing on the deck of your boat, you are at the center of an imaginary circle of 360° around the horizon. The direction of the axis of the earth's rotation, marked quite closely by Polaris, is *true north*. (In case you are wondering about *untrue* north, we come to that in the next chapter.) If your vessel is pointing true north, its true heading is 000T, if toward the true east, your heading is 090T, and so forth. The reference direction from which the angle is measure (true north) is indicated by the letter T following the numbers. Directions should always be quoted in groups of three integers and a letter: 185T, 003T, etc.

- *Bearing*—Angles measured from north along the horizon to the right are *azimuths*, but we will reserve that term for star directions. When referring to boats we will use the term *heading* to indicate the direction a boat is pointing. *Bearing* is the direction to an object sighted from the boat. Both are measured from north.

Figure 4.1 illustrates these definitions. In this case, the boat is on a heading of 270T. In the northeasterly direction there is a TV tower whose bearing is about 040T. Polaris marks true north in this diagram.

PRETEST

4.1 What are the true headings corresponding to the intercardinal directions?

NE _____ SE _____ SW _____ NW _____

To review, the direction of an object measured from true north as seen from your boat is its true bearing. It ranges from 000 to 359. An island with a true bearing of 090 is due east. (Note: The true bearing of an object is not related to the heading of the boat.)

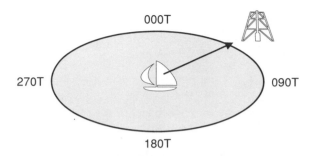

Figure 4.1. The horizon circle with azimuths of the four cardinal directions indicated. The boat is on a heading of 270T and the tower has a bearing of about 040T.

The scenario

We introduce the subject of measuring directions by means of a short fiction that begins high on a windy hill on St. Thomas in the American Virgin Islands. We choose that spot for its excellent view and the solid ground underfoot. The current chapter picks up plane-table mapping where we left it in Chapter 2 and extends those techniques to the nautical charts of Chapter 3.

All measurements in this chapter will be from true north, so you may put away your magnetic compass until the next chapter.

Figure 4.2 is a portion of NOAA Chart No. 25641 showing the region around the island of St. Thomas. This is a Mercator chart on which the soundings are in fathoms (1 fathom = 6 feet) from *mean low water,* while heights are in feet above *mean high water.* (This convention implies that the actual values of *depth* and *height* will typically be *greater* than the chart values.) The outer circle of the compass rose shows true north and gives angular bearings relative to true north.

Look carefully near the "T" in "Thomas" on the island. There you will find a TV tower whose height is given as 1,712 ft. This is the height of the top of the tower above mean high water.

Imagine you are at the foot of the tower looking out over the water toward the north. It is a bright, sunny day and the trade wind is gently blowing from the east. You see a sailboat that appears to be in trouble, and you decide to try to measure the bearing of the boat, just in case you need to report it to the Coast Guard. You spread the chart out before you and try to orient yourself by identifying

some of the islands. You manage to find Little Tobago Island, toward the northeast, and then you decide to identify some of the other islands by measuring their bearings. As luck would have it, you brought a piece of angle-measuring equipment, your trusty *pelorus.*

USING A PELORUS

A pelorus is a device for measuring bearings (Figure 4.3). It is, in effect, a gunsight that swings about the horizon and is mounted on swivels (gimbals) to remain vertical.

A plastic pelorus costs less than $50 and is a good investment for the coastal navigator. It can be bolted near the helm when needed and can be dismounted and stored when not needed. Let us imagine that yours is new, so it has not yet been mounted on your boat. Instead, you have temporarily mounted it on a board.

A simple pelorus has a frame that is fixed to the mounting; in addition, there are two moving parts. One is the *sighting vane;* the other is an *index scale* that may be rotated with respect to the index marks. The fixed mounting is bolted to the boat in a place of good visibility and is marked with two short *index lines* that are to be aligned with the keel of the boat. (For the moment, you can forget the boat and its keel; they are far below you in the harbor.) Figure 4.4 is a schematic diagram looking down onto a pelorus.

First scenario: Identifying the islands when north is known

Set your pelorus on a level piece of ground and make sure the 000 on the index scale is set opposite the index mark, as shown in Figure 4.4. Then rotate the board and the pelorus with it until the index marks are oriented north and south. (We assume you observed the North Star last evening from this site.)

Now, when you point the sighting vane at an island, the pelorus reading (where the sighting vane crosses the index scale) will give the true bearing of the island. Figure 4.4 shows the situation when you point it at Little Tobago Island, which has a bearing of about 051T from the TV tower.

Next, you swing the sighting vane toward the boat in trouble and the two islands that you want to identify, and measure their true bearings. The results are:

Figure 4.2. Chart showing a portion of the American Virgin Islands.

Description	Bearing
Island 1, small rock to the NW	298T
Island 2, farther island to the SW	226T
Boat in trouble	016T

You decide to identify the islands first, to make sure you are doing things correctly before calling the Coast Guard. You spread out your chart (Figure 4.2) and find the compass rose. On it, you set your parallel rulers to the first bearing (298T) and transfer the line to your location at the TV tower. If you draw a line in the direction 298T through the TV tower and extend it far enough, it will intersect Cricket Rock. That is Island 1. Doing the same for the second bearing, you find that a line from the TV tower in the direction 226T intersects Saba Island. That is Island 2.

The appearance on the chart seems to agree with your visual impression, so you have some confidence in what you are doing. Next you draw a line on the chart from the TV tower toward the boat, with a bearing 016T, and prepare to pack up.

Second scenario: Finding north by sighting a known object

Suppose you had not observed the North Star, so you did not know how to align the index marks of your pelorus to the north-south line. You can get true bearings by using some additional information.

You know where Little Tobago Island is, because you are able to identify it without making any measurements. You can measure its true bearing on the chart, and once you have done that, you can align the index marks and find true bearings of other objects. Here's how.

On your chart, draw a line from the TV tower toward Little Tobago Island. This represents your line of sight to the island. Get out your parallel rulers and transfer this sight line to the outer compass rose. You find a bearing of 051T. When the index mark of your pelorus has been aligned correctly with the north-south direction, you should find this reading when you swing the sighting vane to Little Tobago Island.

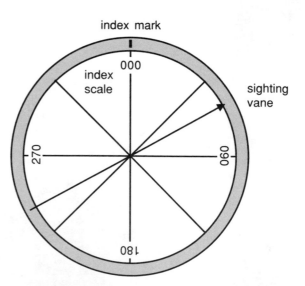

Figure 4.3. Pelorus for determining relative directions from onboard a vessel. (Photo courtesy Davis Instruments, Hayward, CA)

Figure 4.4. Diagram of pelorus. The outer circ (shaded) is fixed to the mounting. The inner circle can be rotated and it carries the index scale, which is used to read the angle of the sighting vane. As shown, the index scale 000 is set to the index mark, so the scale gives the angle of the sighting vane from the index mark. In this case the reading is about 51°.

You achieve this by the following steps:

1. Set the index scale 000 to the index mark, as shown in Figure 4.4.

2. Set the sighting vane to 051 on the index scale.

3. Without touching the pelorus, rotate the board and the pelorus until you see Little Tobago Island in the sighting vane.

True north is now in the direction of the index mark. If you turn the sighting vane to 000, it will be pointing to true north. You are now ready to measure the true bearings of other objects, by swinging the sighting vane and reading the scale.

POSITION OF AN OBJECT BY TRIANGULATION

In making the plane-table map in Chapter 2, you triangulated locations by establishing sight lines from two or more separate stations. With the help of a collaborator, you can do the same with pelorus measures on St. Thomas to establish the position of the boat in trouble. On your chart you have already drawn one sight line to the boat from the TV tower. One more is needed, and it must be obtained from another location.

Intersecting sight lines

Suppose this boat had also been sighted by the crew of a boat that was one nautical mile north of Rough Point, and they determine its true bearing at the same time to be 059.

If this information is telephoned to the Coast Guard they can draw the two sight lines on the chart from the known locations of the sighters, and they will get a fix on the position of the boat. The result is shown schematically in Figure 4.5.

The next question is, how precise is the fix? That is, how close to this position should they expect to find the boat?

Estimating the uncertainty of a fix

The two sight lines intersect at a point if they are not parallel. That much we know from Euclid. If the sight lines were precise, the fix would be, too. But the Coast Guard knows that would be too good to be true. The directions of the sight lines are uncertain by a few degrees. This means that if the measures were repeated a large number of times their inter-

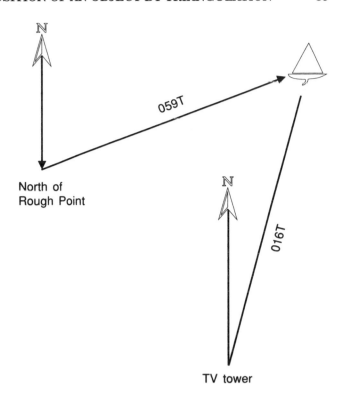

Figure 4.5. Triangulation using true bearings toward a boat in trouble from two known points on the chart.

sections would have produced a scatter-shot diagram, as in Figure 4.6. The size of the pattern would give an idea of the area that ought to be covered in a preliminary search (assuming the boat did not drift). How big would the pattern be?

To predict the size of the pattern that would be created by the measurements, the Coast Guard (or whoever is doing the error estimate) adopts a reasonable guess for the uncertainty of each measure (let us say ±2°) and then draws lines that far on each side of the sight lines, as in Figure 4.7. The intersections of these lines define the four corners of a trapezoid. The size of this trapezoid is the estimated uncertainty of the fix.

If the errors from one station were known to be larger than the errors from the other (either because it is farther away or because the angles were not measured as well) the trapezoid will be elongated.

This narrative illustrates the importance of estimating the uncertainty of your measurement when the results are crucial.

Suppose a third group had measured the direction of the boat in trouble and the Coast Guard found that the lines did not all intersect at the same

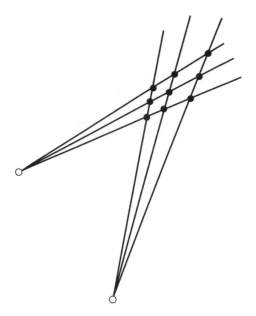

Figure 4.6. If the sight lines were repeated many times, they would produce a small scatter-shot diagram, due to the errors of individual measurements. The width of the fan of possible sight lines from each observer is a measure of the uncertainty of measurement. This is usually several degrees.

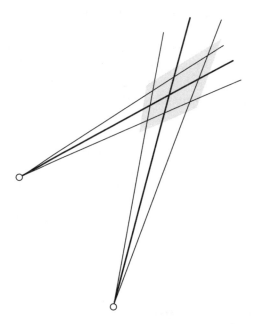

Figure 4.7. Rather than plotting a bundle of sight lines (which may not be practical), you may estimate the uncertainty of a fix as follows. Using a guess of the errors of measurement, each actual sight line (heavy) is bracketed with thinner lines that enclose the expected region (shaded) of uncertainty of the fix.

point. A typical intersection might resemble the small triangle in Figure 4.8.

Question: Does the size of the triangle indicate the uncertainty of the fix? The answer to this question is emphatically *no.* Although the best guess for the location of the fix will be at the center of the triangle, there is little to be learned from the size of the triangle. You must not use the size as an estimate of the error. You must instead draw the small fan about each sight line, as indicated in Figure 4.9.

To see why the size of the intersection triangle can be misleading, let us assume that each sight line has the same angular uncertainty and try to visualize how the triangle was built up. If we represent the actual position of the fix by the lighthouse in Figure 4.9a, the first measured sight line will be somewhere in the fan-shaped region.

Similarly the second sight line will fall at a random direction inside the fan-shaped region of uncertainty for the second station, as in Figure 4.9b. It will intersect the first sight line in a point.

The first two sight lines will always define a single point. When the third sight line is drawn, it might fall close to that point or far from it, depending on the random error of that particular measurement (Figure 4.9c). This means that the size of the triangle depends entirely on the behavior of that final sight line. The triangle could be quite small, even if the error were large, as in Figure 4.9c. All we can say is that the fix probably does not have an uncertainty *smaller* than is implied by the size of the triangle, and it may be considerably *larger.*

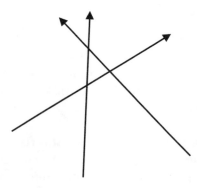

Figure 4.8. Three sight lines intersect to form a small triangle. Some navigators are tempted to use the size of this triangle to estimate the uncertainty of the fix. This is bad practice.

The only reliable way to estimate errors is to repeat the measurement several times to obtain an estimate for the angular uncertainty (in degrees) from the scatter of the results. For example, if you find 51, 53, 55, 51, you would take $53° \pm 2$ as an estimate of the uncertainty.

MOUNTING A PELORUS ON YOUR BOAT

Having come down from the windy hill, you decide it is time to mount the pelorus on your boat. Pick a spot close to the helm, where the sighting vanes can sweep most of the horizon. You must align the index marks of the pelorus parallel to the keel.

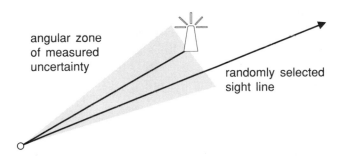

Figure 4.9a. The first sight line has a random position inside the fan-shaped zone of uncertainty of the measurement.

Challenge: Before looking ahead, try to imagine a way of drawing a line down the middle of the deck of your sailboat. Your equipment can be a piece of chalk and a string or a tape measure.

A good way to do this is to make a chalked *lubber's line* where you wish to mount the pelorus. The lubber's line is an imaginary line that defines the direction the boat is pointing—its *heading*. The lubber's line is parallel to the keel of the boat, as indicated in Figure 4.10. The central lubber's line lies directly above the keel, but others may be offset to one side or the other, as long as they remain parallel to the central lubber's line. These lubber's lines define convenient references for measuring directions *relative to the heading of your boat,* rather than referring to true north.

Your goal is to find a straight line parallel to the keel, lying halfway between the sides of the boat, and there are many ways to do this. Guessing the location of the lubber's line can be deceptive on a curvaceous boat, so take the time to make a few measurements. One way is to measure across the boat with a tape measure. Another is to use a string to find the full width and then fold it in half to find the midline.

On some vessels, you may require a more elaborate method, illustrated in Figure 4.11. Imagine a

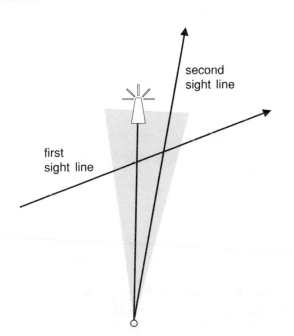

Figure 4.9b. The second sight line will fall inside the fan-shaped region of uncertainty and it will intersect the first in a single point. In this case the intersection is not exactly at the object.

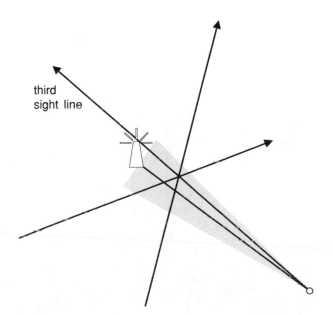

Figure 4.9c. When the third sight line is drawn, it might accidentally pass right through the intersection of the first two, giving the erroneous impression of high accuracy. The intersection does not fall at the object.

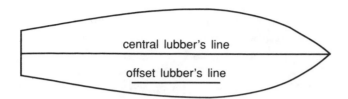

Figure 4.10. View looking down on boat, showing two lubber's lines, which are parallel to the keel. A lubber's line defines the direction the boat is pointing.

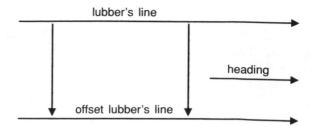

Figure 4.12. Offset lubber's lines may be constructed by measuring equal perpendicular distances to one side of the central lubber's line. This new lubber's line also defines the heading of the boat.

circle concentric with the bow. It will intersect the sides at equal distances from the bow. Find these points with a string, stretched first to one side and marked with a knot, then stretched to the other side. Then shorten the string and draw portions of a circle from one side. Take this string to the other side and draw another circle with the same radius. These two circles intersect at two points that define a lubber's line. Mark them with chalk or small

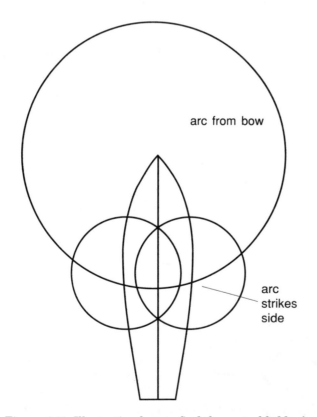

Figure 4.11. Illustrating how to find the central lubber's line of a boat using strings, as described in the text. Secondary lubber's lines parallel to the first may be found by measuring equal offsets.

pieces of tape. (If the circles drawn from the sides have unequal radii, the lubber's line will be offset, but it will be parallel to the keel.)

Once you have marked a lubber's line, you may construct other lubber's lines at other positions by using a string to measure offsets toward one side or another, as illustrated in Figure 4.12.

RELATIVE AND TRUE BEARINGS

Imagine yourself standing on the deck of a small cutter approaching a tropical island (or a Norwegian fjord, if you prefer!). You are facing *forward*, toward the *bow*. To your right is the *starboard beam*, to your left the *port beam*. Behind you is the *stern*. The island is *dead ahead*, and if you see another boat to starboard or port you would properly say it is *abeam to starboard*, or *abeam to port*, while a boat that is directly behind you would be *dead astern*. Further refinements are shown in Figure 4.13.

Relative bearings are measured from dead ahead toward the right, or clockwise looking down on the boat. An object abeam to starboard would have a relative heading of 090. An object broad on the port bow has a bearing of about 315 degrees, but rather than stating that it has a relative bearing of "315 degrees" it is more common to give it a bearing of "45 degrees off the port bow."

Relative bearings with the pelorus
When the index scale is set to 000, the pelorus reading indicates relative bearings, that is, angles measured from the boat's heading. In this case, to get a relative bearing you simply swing the sighting vane and line it up; then read the index scale. The settings in Figure 4.14 indicate a relative bearing of 225.

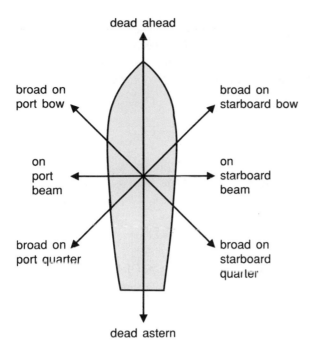

dead ahead

broad on port bow

broad on starboard bow

on port beam

on starboard beam

broad on port quarter

broad on starboard quarter

dead astern

Figure 4.13. Diagram illustrating verbal descriptions of relative bearings.

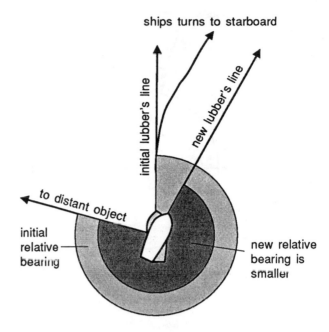

ships turns to starboard

initial lubber's line

new lubber's line

to distant object

initial relative bearing

new relative bearing is smaller

Figure 4.15. When the ship turns to starboard, the relative bearings of all stationary objects decrease.

When the vessel turns, the relative bearings of all stationary objects change. The effect of a rotation to the starboard is indicated in Figure 4.15.

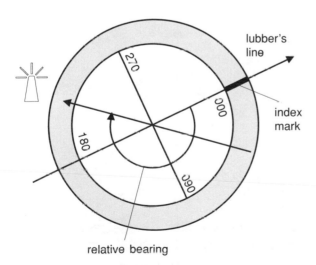

lubber's line

270

000

180

090

index mark

relative bearing

Figure 4.14. When the scale reading 000 is set to the index mark, the sighting vane indicates relative bearings. The relative bearing is measured clockwise from the ship's heading, indicated by the lubber's line. In this case the relative bearing of the lighthouse is about 225.

POSTTEST

4.2 If the vessel turns to port, the relative bearing of the lighthouse in Figure 4.14 will increase _____ decrease _____ .

4.3 When the vessel turns to starboard, the relative bearings of objects on the port and starboard sides of the lubber's line behave as follows.
both decrease _____ both increase __
one increases while the other decreases _____

4.4 When the vessel is on a northerly heading, 000T, relative and true bearings of objects seen in the sighting vane are equal. T _____ F _____

True bearings with a pelorus

Now we introduce another aspect of using a pelorus: setting the index scale so the pelorus gives true bearings directly.

Suppose you are sailing due north through Middle Passage, on the chart in Figure 4.2. Thatch Cay is on your port beam and Little Tobago Island is 10° off the port bow, or at a true bearing of 350T. You instruct the helm to head for Little Tobago Island and you ask the navigator to let you know when the southern tip of Hans Lollik Island has a bearing 270T. The navigator knows her stuff, so she goes to the pelorus and rotates the index card until the scale reads the heading of the vessel (350T)

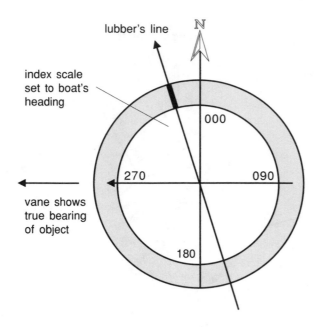

Figure 4.16. The boat is heading toward 350T and the island is at a true heading of 270T. When the index scale is set to the ship's true heading, the vane will show the true heading of an object.

against the index mark. Then she swings the sighting vane to 270 on the index scale. She knows that when the tip of the island appears in the sighting vane, it will have a true bearing of 270T.

Here is the rule: *The sighting vane reads true bearings when the index scale is set to the true heading of the vessel.* This is illustrated in Figure 4.16. The relationships can also be expressed in the following equation.

Vane reading = relative bearing + index reading

When the index reading is set to the boat's heading, the vane reads the true bearing, so the equation becomes:

True bearing = relative bearing + boat's heading

In this case, the numbers in the equation are: 270 = 280 + 350. Adding 350 is the same as subtracting 10, so this might also be written 270 = 280 − 10.

POSTTEST

4.5 For each of the diagrams in Figure 4.17, fill out the values of the following:

	Left	Right
Ship's true heading	___	___
True bearing of lighthouse	___	___
Relative bearing of lighthouse	___	___

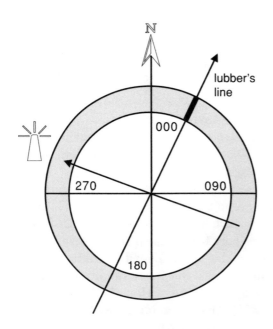

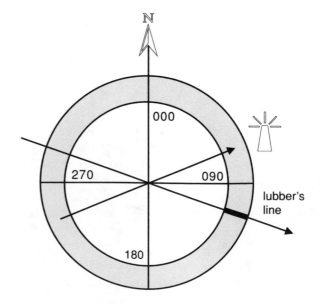

Figure 4.17.

CHAPTER FIVE

Care and Reading of Magnetic Compasses

On the 13th of September [1492], in the evening, being about 200 leagues from the island of Ferro, Columbus for the first time noticed the variation of the [compass] needle; a phenomenon which had never before been remarked. He perceived about nightfall that the needle, instead of pointing to the north star, varied about half a point, or between five and six degrees, to the northwest, and still more on the following morning. Struck with this circumstance, he observed it attentively for three days, and found that the variation increased as he advanced. He at first made no mention of this phenomenon, knowing how ready his people were to take alarm, but it soon attracted the attention of his pilots, and filled them with consternation. It seemed as if the very laws of nature were changing as they advanced, and that they were entering another world, subject to unknown influences. They apprehended that the compass was about to lose its mysterious virtues, and without this guide, what was to become of them in a vast and trackless ocean?

Columbus tasked his science and ingenuity for reasons with which to allay their terror. He told them that the direction of the needle was not to the polar star, but to some fixed and invisible point. The variation therefore was not caused by any fallacy in the compass . . .

Washington Irving, The Life and Voyages of Christopher Columbus

Compass: Navigational instrument that records a variety of directional errors and indicates the presence of machinery and magnets on board ship by spinning wildly.

Henry Beard and Roy McKie, Sailing, A Sailor's Dictionary

INTRODUCTION

The realization that the magnetic compass is guided by the earth's global magnetic field is probably one of the greatest discoveries since fire. It is usually attributed to William Gilbert in the sixteenth century, although such devices were almost certainly used before his time.

The magnetic compass provides a portable direction finder that operates independently of the weather and can be used night and day. It is still a prime instrument on small vessels. Larger vessels use magnetic compasses as backup, but they usually rely on gyroscopic compasses—which have nothing to do with magnetism, are expensive, and can break.

The magnetic compass needle is delicately balanced and it is influenced not only by the earth's magnetic field, but also by the magnetic fields of the vessel and the electrical equipment carried onboard. And, as Columbus discovered, even on a wooden ship the compass does not always point toward true north—in fact, it seldom does. The magnetic compass has its own poles.

This chapter describes how to use the compass and cope with some of its vagaries.

Experiments on compass behavior

Compasses and magnetic materials have many interesting quirks. The following exercise will help you become acquainted with some of them. Try to predict answers to each question and then carry out the experiments.

Obtain a small pocket compass and and several magnets and some pins or nails and try to find answers to the following questions.

- *Part 1*—Can you shield a magnetic field with your hand? What objects in your pocket affect the compass? What objects are attracted to the compass? Which part of a radio affects the compass? Does it make any difference whether it is turned on or off? How do two compasses affect each other? How does the effect alter with the separation of the compasses? When you rub a pin with the north end of the magnet, where is the north end of the magnetized pin? If you heat the pin, does its magnetism increase or decrease?

- *Part 2*—Magnetize a nail by rubbing it on a magnet. Determine which end attracts the north end of the compass and mark it with a small piece of tape. Place a compass on a table and let it come to rest, pointing north and south. Place the nail on the table next to the compass on the east side and notice its effect on the compass. Place the nail at the other three cardinal points of the compass and note the effects. Make a series of diagrams like Figure 5.1.

PRETEST

5.1. What is compass variation? Does it depend on the heading of the boat?

5.2. What is compass deviation? Does it depend on the heading of the boat?

5.3. A nearby radio can deflect a compass.
T ____ F ____

5.4. Compass compensation makes a compass point toward true north. T ____ F ____

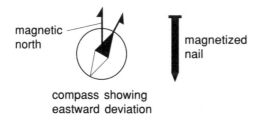

Figure 5.1a. The nail represents the magnetized boat, and its influence on the compass (deviation) depends on its orientation with respect to the earth's magnetic meridians. In this situation the deviation is eastward. Compare with Figure 5.1b.

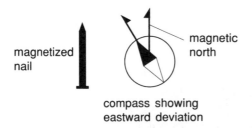

Figure 5.1b. Now the magnetized nail has turned 180° and has been moved to the other side, as though the boat had reversed its heading. The nail now influences the needle in the opposite direction, causing westward deviation. These figures illustrate how the compass deviation will change when the heading of the vessel changes.

MAGNETIC DIRECTIONS

Figure 5.2 illustrates two types of compasses: a pocket compass with a *needle* that swings above a directional scale, and a ship's compass in which a *compass card* replaces the needle and rotates against an index mark. The point of the needle and the north arrow on the compass card align themselves along the direction of the magnetic field in the immediate vicinity of the compass.

For the moment, we will consider only the magnetic field of the earth, which is created by mysterious electrical currents deep inside the planet. This field may be represented by lines that converge toward the north and south magnetic poles. Through any point there is only one magnetic line, and the direction of that line defines the magnetic north-south line at that point (see Figure 5.3).

Directions measured from magnetic north are called *magnetic directions*. (This is the first type of *non-true* directions you will encounter in this chapter.) The lines are slightly deflected here and there; and the poles are nearly 1,000 miles from the geographic poles and are constantly on the move.

Figure 5.2. Marine compass. A horizontal card rotating on a pin acts as the compass needle. It aligns with the local magnetic field, and the orientation of the lubber's line of the vessel is indicated by the white index mark above the card. (Photo courtesy E. S. Ritchie & Sons, Inc., Pembroke, MA)

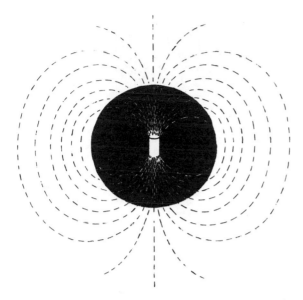

Figure 5.3. Schematic diagram with arrows indicating the directions of the north celestial pole and the north magnetic pole of the earth. Two loops of the magnetic field are also indicated. Because the loops are magnetic, they do not point to the celestial pole. As a result, magnetic compasses do not point to the celestial pole.

Magnetic variations

The angular difference between the directions of true north and magnetic north at each point on the earth is called the *magnetic variation* at that point (Figure 5.4). If the magnetic meridian points to the west of true north, the variation is westward and is labeled W. Otherwise it is eastward and is labeled E. Away from the polar regions, the values of variation typically range from 15W to 15E. Changes inside the earth cause the magnetic poles to shift gradually and rotate the magnetic lines slightly. As a consequence, the value of the variation at any point changes by as much as several minutes of arc each year. The changes stay nearly the same from one year to the next, and they are usually stated on each compass rose. In principle, you can use that figure, multiplied by the appropriate number of years since the date of the chart, to update the compass rose for several decades—although you probably won't let your charts get that old.

Figure 5.5 is a Mercator map from *Bowditch* showing the magnetic variation all over the globe, and Figure 5.6 shows a portion of a pilot chart giving a more detailed picture of the contour lines. (These contours of equal variation are, of course, not the same as the magnetic lines.)

POSTTEST

5.5 Examine the pattern of magnetic lines in Figure 5.3, and try to compare it with Figure 5.5. See if you can predict the places on the earth where the variation would be very small. Can you see why the largest values of variation are found near the magnetic poles?

5.6 Using Figure 5.5, what is the approximate magnetic variation (E or W) at the following places on earth:
Cape Horn_____ Chicago _____ Paris _____
Tokyo _____ Melbourne _____

Magnetic bearings

These are measured in degrees from the direction of magnetic north as determined by the earth's field at your location. They are indicated with the letter M. Magnetic north is 000M, and an object that is seen 45 to the right of the magnetic north is said to have a bearing 045M.

But the earth's field is very elusive; it is easily distorted by stray magnetic fields that deflect the compass. So, in order to measure magnetic bearings, we send you back to the hill on St. Thomas with a compass and pelorus. You won't have to worry about a boat's magnetic field, and if you stand far enough from the TV tower and all the other transmitting equipment, you can assume that the earth's field is not disturbed. This implies that magnetic north has exactly the amount of variation shown on the chart in Figure 4.2, about 012W.

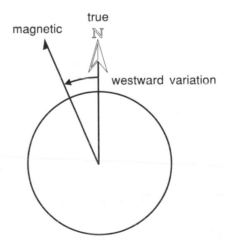

Figure 5.4. True and magnetic norths, looking down on compass rose. The variation is the angle from the true north to the magnetic north. In this figure, the magnetic north is to the west, so this is called westward variation.

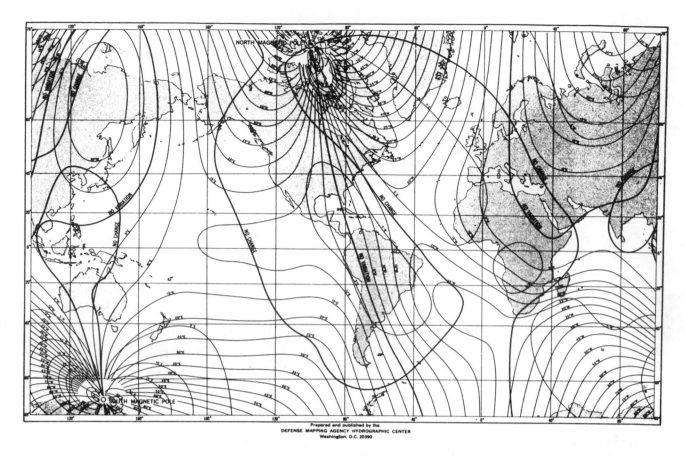

Figure 5.5. Map showing magnetic variation on the surface of the earth. The north and south magnetic poles are also indicated. The contours are lines of equal variation. Along the line of no variation, the magnetic lines are oriented north and south. Note that a line of no variation lies directly south of the north magnetic pole and directly north of the south magnetic pole. (Map reprinted from Bowditch)

Put your compass on the ground with the index mark aligned with the true north-south line determined by Polaris. You will notice that the needle does not point directly north. It will probably point about 12° west of true north. If you rotate the compass and the index mark until the mark is aligned with the compass needle, it will look something like Figure 5.7a. The right side of the figure shows the compass needle, pointing toward the magnetic north, indicated by the half-arrow. True north is indicated by the full arrow.

By sighting over the compass, you will find that the true and magnetic headings of Little Tobago Island are 051T and 063M. These are also the values you would obtain directly from the chart using par-allel rulers and the two compass roses. The rule relating magnetic and true bearings is the following.

True bearing + variation (W) = magnetic bearing
(add west)

That is, in order to find the magnetic bearing from the true bearing, you would *add westward variation* to the true bearing.

To clarify this rule, assume for the moment that you travel to another island, where the variation is 015E (Figure 5.7b). To find the magnetic bearing in this case, you would *subtract eastward variation* from the true bearing. This convention gives the rule:

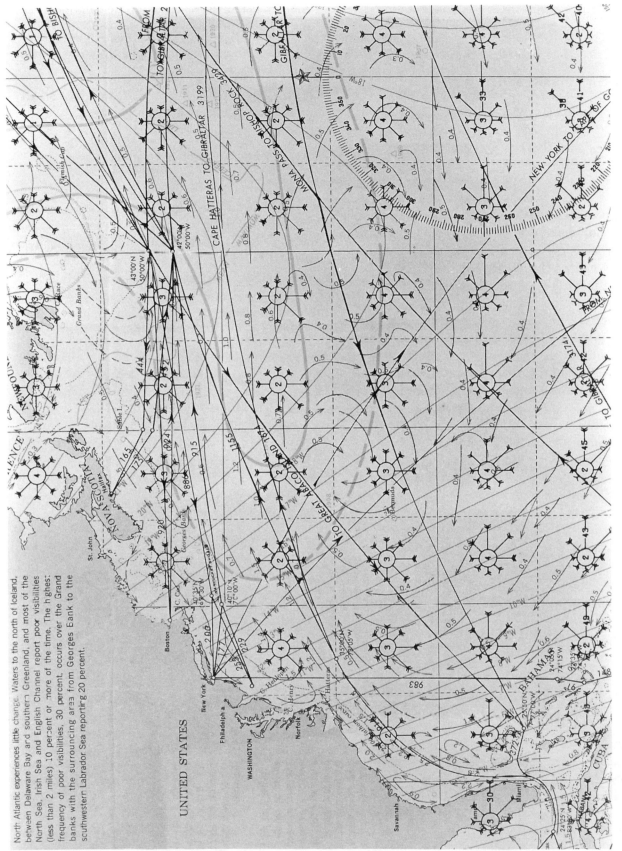

Figure 5.6. Pilot chart showing a great deal of information about a particular region of the ocean during a two-month interval. The curved lines sweeping down and diverging to the right and left are contours of constant magnetic variation. This chart also shows currents and winds. Each chart has a complete explanation printed on its face.

True bearing – variation (E) = magnetic bearing
(subtract east)

POSTTEST

5.7. Suppose you are on an island where the variation is 13E and you measure the true bearings of two rocks as listed below. What will be their magnetic bearings?

	True Bearing	Magnetic Bearing
Rock 1	100T	
Rock 2	238T	

Magnetic bearings with a pelorus—Now, back to St. Thomas. Your next task is to use your pelorus to measure the magnetic bearings of a few other islands as seen from the TV tower.

Set the pelorus near the compass. It is mostly plastic and it will not influence the compass noticeably. Do not worry about the orientation of the index mark; it will be aligned with the lubber's line of your boat, but for the moment it is irrelevant.

You need to find the correct orientation of the index card so that it will indicate magnetic bearings of objects seen in the sighting vane. Here are the steps:

- **Step 1**—Find the magnetic bearing of a known object. To do this, draw a line on the chart from your location near the TV tower to Little Tobago Island. Using the inner compass rose and your parallel rulers, measure the bearing of this line. You should find 063M.

- **Step 2**—Rotate the sighting vane over the index card until it reads the magnetic bearing 063.

- **Step 3**—With a piece of tape, fix the vane to the index card.

- **Step 4**—Rotate the index card and vane together until the vane points at Little Tobago Island.

- **Step 5**—Remove the tape from the vane and use it to fix the card to the pelorus mounting.

The pelorus is now ready for use. Swing the vane to Cricket Rock. You will find a scale reading of 310°, and this is the magnetic bearing 310M. Similarly, for Saba Island you will find a magnetic bearing of 238M. The data along with true bearings and the magnetic variation are listed in Table 5.1.

Table 5.1. Bearings of islands from TV tower on St. Thomas

Identification	True Bearing	Variation	Magnetic Bearing
Little Tobago Is.	051T	12W	063M
Cricket Rock	226T	12W	310M
Saba Island	226T	12W	238M

If your measurements match these, they confirm the formula given above:

True bearing + variation (W) = magnetic bearing
(add west)

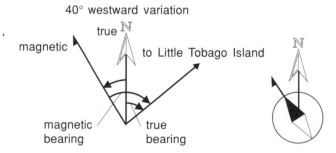

Figure 5.7a. The effect of westward variation. From the TV tower on St. Thomas (Figure 4.2), the true and magnetic bearings of Little Tobago are 051T and 063M. The variation is 012W, counterclockwise, so the magnetic bearing is 12° greater than the true bearing. The compass needle is shown on the right and a diagram of the angles is shown on the left.

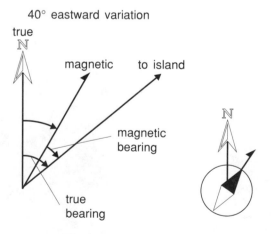

Figure 5.7b. Effect of eastward variation. If you are at a spot where the variation is eastward, the true bearings will be larger than the magnetic bearings.

COMPASS DIRECTIONS

Now you return to your boat, which is at a mooring in St. Thomas harbor. You must depend on the compass to determine magnetic north, but (as we keep saying) the metal and electrical parts of your boat will distort the magnetic field around the compass. This distortion is called the *compass deviation*. It is the discrepancy between magnetic north and the pointing of the compass. The deviation and variation are illustrated in Figure 5.8.

Note the distinction: *Variation* is produced by irregularities in the interior of the earth and refers to the direction of the earth's field. It is a quantity that has been mapped carefully and indicates the direction that a perfect compass would point if there were no magnetic disturbance in its neighborhood. On the other hand, *deviation* is produced by the boat's interaction with the earth's magnetism. The compass needle feels both the earth's field and the boat's field. Thus, the sum of the variation and the deviation gives the total discrepancy between the compass needle and true north.

As another illustration of the meaning of deviation, think of the magnetic disturbance produced by the TV tower on top of St. Thomas. This disturbance changes the direction of the magnetic meridians nearby, so a compass carried to various parts of the hill would point in slightly different directions. Variation indicates the direction of the needle in the absence of the TV tower. Deviation indicates the additional disturbance produced by the tower. Variation plus deviation indicates the net difference between compass north and true north.

Compass bearings

There are two kinds of compass directions: Compass *bearing* refers to the direction of a sighted object, while compass *heading* refers to the direction of the lubber's line—it is the bearing of an object that is dead ahead. To indicate a compass direction, the suffix C is often added to distinguish it from a true (T) or magnetic (M) direction. Alternatively, some navigators use *psc,* which is an abbreviation of *per steering compass,* indicating that it was read with the ship's steering compass.

The compass bearing is measured clockwise from compass north, and it is related to the magnetic bearing by the formula:

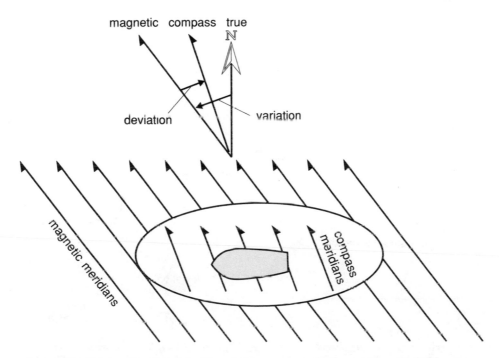

Figure 5.8. Schematized view looking down on a vessel whose magnetic field causes a local deviation in the direction of the magnetic meridians. On this vessel and in this heading the compass will point to the right of the magnetic north.

Magnetic bearing + deviation = compass bearing
(add west)

If the deviation is westward, it is added to the magnetic bearing to find compass bearing; if east, it is subtracted.

By this time, the list of relationships may have gotten a bit intimidating, but if you look back at this chapter, you will notice that the following sequence is always obeyed:

True + Variation →
Magnetic + Deviation → Compass
Add West

The last two words carry the instruction to add variation and deviation if they are westward, otherwise subtract. Here's how to remember the sequence. The following sentence has initial letters in the same order: *Timid Virgins Make Dull Company At Weddings*. As long as you remember this, you will not have difficulty coping with these compass relations.

As an example, if the TV tower produced a compass deviation of 3° eastward, all of the compass bearings would be 3° less than the magnetic bearings. Table 5.2 repeats the data of Tables 5.1 and includes the effect of such an eastward compass deviation. The rule is written beneath.

Table 5.2. Bearings illustrating the rule TVMDCAW

Identification	True Bearing	Var.	Magnetic Bearing	Dev.	Compass Bearing
Little Tobago Is.	051T	12W	063M	3E	060psc
Cricket Rock	298T	12W	310M	3E	307psc
Saba Island	226T	12W	238M	3E	235psc
	True +	Var →	Magnetic +	Dev →	Compass

POSTTEST

5.8. Fill in the blank spaces in the following table by using the relationships just described.

Identification	True	Var.	Magnetic	Dev.	Compass
Island 1	055T		063M		065psc
Island 2	090T	10E		12W	
Island 3		12W		8E	090psc

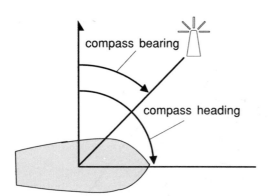

Figure 5.9. Compass bearing *refers to the direction of a sighted object as determined by the compass, while compass* heading *is the bearing of an object that is dead ahead.*

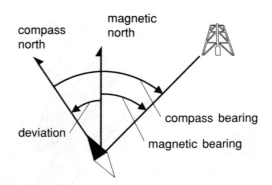

Figure 5.10. In this diagram, the compass points west of magnetic north, and it is said to have westward deviation. The compass bearing is the sum of the westward deviation and the magnetic bearing.

Compass deviation

Deviation is the rotation required to bring the compass needle to magnetic north. The amount of deviation depends on the heading of the boat, so the *compass bearing of a distant object will vary with the heading of the ship*. Therefore you must, in principle, always note the heading of the ship when you read the compass. You will need to set up a detailed table or graph of the deviations of your steering compass for piloting and passage making. Much of the deviation can be removed by "compensating the compass," as the next section describes.

Quick survey by sighting over the compass needle— Suppose you are at anchor one morning and the wind is shifting, so the boat swings in a complete circle. As the boat turns, the compass feels a slightly altered magnetic field and the deviation of the needle changes in response.

The direction of compass north depends on the heading of the boat, and on some boats the effect is large enough to be measured by sighting over the compass. This should be good to a few degrees with a little practice. As a practical matter, errors of 1° or 2° are usually ignored in small boat piloting, so this method is adequate for many piloting needs. It is easy to do, and when the boat is underway the helmsperson should be doing it as a matter of habit from time to time.

Here is a way to see how compass north depends on the heading of your boat if you are lying at anchor and a breeze is blowing so your boat swings on its anchor. (Or, lacking a breeze, you can send somebody to pull the boat's stern with the dinghy.) Find a fixed object (preferably on the shore) that is lined up with your compass needle and is so far away that the swinging of the boat on its anchor does not affect the object's direction from your boat. A mile or two is sufficient. Then watch the behavior of your compass as the boat swings around its anchor. You will find that the needle wanders to the right and left of the object as the heading of the boat changes. This corresponds to various amounts of eastward and westward deviation as the heading of the boat changes.

On some boats the change of deviation is so small that you must use a pelorus and sighting vane to detect it. Or perhaps you want to use the pelorus to get a more complete tabulation of your own compass behavior, to verify the compensation

and make up a detailed steering card to put near the helm. This subject is treated next.

Determining compass deviations with a pelorus— When more precision is needed, you may put the pelorus to work. Using the pelorus will usually require two people, one to operate the pelorus and the other to handle the helm. And you may want a third person in a dinghy to help turn the boat if you do this at a mooring. With practice, a team should be able to achieve an accuracy of 2° or 3°. Doing each measurement three or four times and averaging the results will reduce the inevitable measuring errors and will eliminate large accidental errors. Calm water and careful steering are essential for this procedure to work well. You start, as follows, by finding the magnetic bearing of a known object.

- *Step 1*—Using piloting techniques, locate the ship on a chart. Suppose you are near the radio tower at the head of St. Thomas harbor.

- *Step 2*—Find the true bearing of a distant object from the chart. From a mooring at the head of St. Thomas harbor, Buck Island will serve the purpose. According to the chart Buck Island has a true bearing of 140T from your mooring.

- *Step 3*—Convert from true to magnetic direction by adding the local variation. The variation can be found in the compass roses on the chart. Ordinarily you can round the variation to the nearest degree, as that is the usual limit in reading your ship's compass.

The magnetic bearing of the distant object is found from "Timid Virgins Make . . . At Weddings," which recalls the rule:

True + variation = magnetic (add west)

The variation is 12W, and the true bearing is 140T, so the magnetic bearing of Buck Island is 140 + 12 = 152M. Enter this in column 2 of Table 5.3.

- *Step 4*—Point the ship on each of the cardinal compass headings (N, E, S, W psc) and in each heading find the compass bearing of Buck Island, using one of the methods described below. Enter the values in column 4. A typical set of bearings that would be found for Buck Island is shown in Table 5.3. The compass directions are labelled psc, which stands for per steering compass.

- **Step 5**—Compute the deviation (column 3) at each of the compass headings from the key ". . . Make Dull Company," which translates as:

$$\text{Magnetic + deviation = compass}$$

or

$$\text{Deviation = compass − magnetic}$$
(Deviation is E if negative and W if positive.)

These values in column 3 indicate the amount of deviation on each heading.

Table 5.3. Deviations on compass headings (example)

(1) Ship's Comp. hdg. (psc)	(2) Magnetic Bearing	(3) Deviation (psc)	(4) Compass Bearing
000	152M	16E	136
015	152M	23E	129
030	152M	26E	126
045	152M	27E	125
060	152M	23E	129
075	152M	15E	137
090	152M	6E	146
105	152M	3W	155
120	152M	11W	163
135	152M	17W	169
150	152M	19W	171
165	152M	17W	169
180	152M	14W	166
195	152M	10W	162
210	152M	6W	158
225	152M	5W	157
240	152M	5W	157
255	152M	6W	158
270	152M	8W	160
285	152M	9W	161
300	152M	9W	161
315	152M	5W	157
330	152M	000	152
345	152M	8E	144
360	152M	16E	136

Notice first that the magnetic bearing of the island does not change as the boat turns. On the other hand, the compass bearing increases and then decreases by 40° as the boat swings. This is deviation and is due to the changing influence of the boat on the compass needle. Table 5.3 tells the deviation of the compass for different headings of the boat.

Instead of listing the deviations in a table, the data can be plotted against ship's compass heading, as in Figure 5.11.

Having shown the results of measuring the compass deviation, let us now describe how you might find them. There are two popular methods, and you can use the one that seems easier.

First method: Mark by pelorus—This is the basic procedure often used with the shipboard compass, and it is diagrammed in Figure 5.12.

- **Step 1**—Set the 000 of the index card of the pelorus to coincide with the lubber's line and clamp it. Now the scale readings of the pelorus give relative bearings.

- **Step 2**—The helmsperson then sets the ship on a compass heading that can be held for 5 minutes or so.

- **Step 3**—The second person ("pelorus-person") points the pelorus vane toward a distant fixed object.

- **Step 4**—Sighting through the pelorus without turning it, the pelorus-person instructs the helmsperson to turn the ship slowly to port or starboard until the object is exactly in the sighting vane. When this occurs, the pelorus-person calls, "Mark" and the helmsperson reads the compass heading of the ship, CHS.

The compass bearing of the object, CBO, is then found from the relationship shown in Figure 5.13:

$$\text{Compass bearing of the object =}$$
$$\text{compass heading of ship + pelorus reading}$$

or in shorthand,

$$\text{CBO = CHS + PR}$$

Second method: Mark by compass—A commonly used variant of this procedure is the following, which is illustrated in Figure 5.14.

- **Step 1**—Same as Step 1 of first method: Set the index of the pelorus to 000 and clamp it, so its scale readings correspond to relative bearings.

- **Step 2**—The helmsperson steers the ship and calls "Mark" when the compass heading of the ship is in a cardinal direction (N, E, S, W).

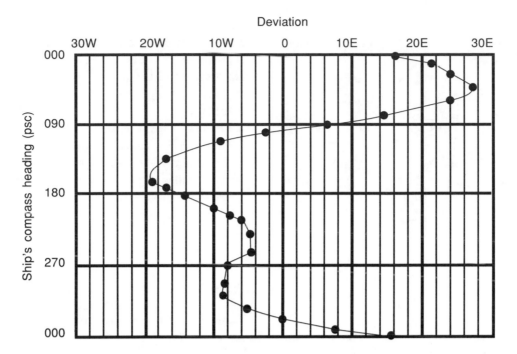

Figure 5.11. Sample graph of compass deviation for various headings of the vessel, based on the compass data of Table 5.3. For example, when the ship is heading on a 270 psc course, the helmsperson knows the compass needle deviates 8° westward from magnetic north. Each vessel will have a different graph.

- **Step 3**—At that instant, the pelorus handler aligns the sighting vane with the object and reads the pelorus scale. The compass bearing of the object may be computed from the formula used with the first method.

Try both methods and choose the one you prefer, then practice until you are confident and get a sense of the accuracy attainable.

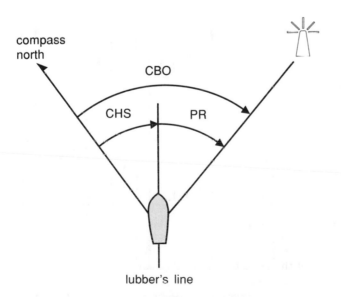

Figure 5.12. View looking down on vessel, its compass, and pelorus while obtaining a compass bearing by first method.

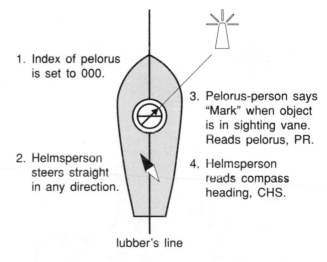

Fig. 5.13. The compass bearing of an object (CBO) is the sum of the compass heading of the ship (CHS) and the pelorus reading (PR) if the pelorus index is aligned with the lubber's line. The CBO is then derived from CBO = CHS + PR.

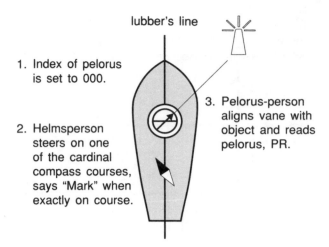

1. Index of pelorus is set to 000.

2. Helmsperson steers on one of the cardinal compass courses, says "Mark" when exactly on course.

3. Pelorus-person aligns vane with object and reads pelorus, PR.

Figure 5.14. View looking down on vessel, its compass, and pelorus while obtaining a compass bearing by second method.

Three types of compass deviation—There are three distinct types of compass deviation you might find while studying your compass. They each have a different behavior as the vessel swings through different headings. It pays to learn to recognize them, because they each have a different cure. (The next two sections may seem rather complicated on first reading. They will make more sense after you have started working with an actual compass.)

Constant deviation—This is a mechanical deviation caused by improper installation of the compass. Suppose the index mark (000) on the compass is not aligned with the lubber's line, but actually points 10° to the east (clockwise) of the lubber's line (Figure 5.15). Then all compass readings will be 10° too small. For example, when the compass heading of the ship is actually 90°, the compass will give it as 80°. If the helmsperson steers an average

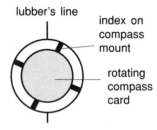

Figure 5.15. Constant deviation is indicated when the compass index is rotated from the lubber's line. In this case, the compass index is 10° east of the lubber's line, or clockwise. All compass readings will be 10° too small, regardless of the heading of the boat. This corresponds to an eastward deviation.

course of 90° per compass, the track will be toward 100°. On a day's trip of 150 miles, this error will correspond to a departure of about 26 miles to the clockwise (right) side of the intended course.

POSTTEST

5.9 If, after one day on this heading, the vessel is put onto a reciprocal course and steered toward 270°, will the vessel return to the starting point or will it be 52 miles off to the side? (Assume no currents and no leeway, so the boat actually moves in the direction it is heading.)

The compass card in this situation looks like Table 5.4, and a graph of these data is shown in Figure 5.16.

Table 5.4. Compass card for constant deviation

Ship's Heading (psc)	Deviation
000	10E
090	10E
180	10E
270	10E

Compensation for constant deviation consists in remounting the compass or rotating its mounting so it is accurately aligned with the lubber's line.

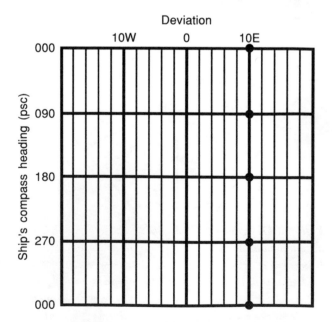

Figure 5.16. Deviation curve for constant deviation of 10E, when the compass index is rotated 10° clockwise from the lubber's line.

Semicircular deviation—Every boat carries a permanent magnetic field of its own, due to magnetized materials (such as radio speakers) or electrical equipment (such as lights). It is called "permanent" because it is not affected by the magnetic field of the earth; it keeps a fixed orientation *relative to the boat* wherever the boat may find itself. Although the magnetic field is fixed, its effect on the compass is not. The effect will depend on the heading of the boat. There are two directions in which this deviation vanishes, hence the name "semicircular."

The earth's magnetism, as well as the boat's, may be pictured as arrows (Figure 5.17). The earth's arrow points along the magnetic meridian, which defines magnetic north. The permanent portion of the boat's magnetism is an arrow that keeps a fixed direction relative to the boat. In this example, it is pointed forward along the lubber's line.

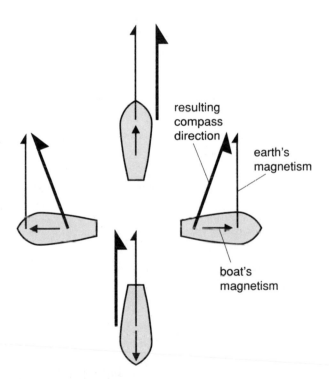

Figure 5.17. Schematic diagram showing how the boat's magnetism adds to the earth's magnetism when the boat is pointed in the cardinal directions. The heavy arrow in each diagram is the direction the compass needle will point, and it is found by attaching the earth's arrow to the tip of the boat's arrow. In this example, the boat's magnetism is assumed to point forward along the lubber's line at all times. When the boat is heading magnetic north or south, there is no deviation.

Each arrow represents the direction a compass would point if that were the only magnetism acting on it. When two magnetisms act simultaneously, we may find their net effect by attaching one arrow to the tip of the other and finding the resulting arrow. So, to find the direction the compass will point, we attach the earth's arrow to the end of the boat's arrow in each orientation. Notice the differences in the way the arrows combine. When the boat is heading east, the compass is deflected to the right (eastward deviation). When the boat is heading north, the arrows are all in the same direction, so there is no deviation, etc. This accounts for the semicircular nature of the deviation produced by the boat's permanent magnetism.

Finally, we notice that the deviation is greatest on the east/west headings because we have assumed the boat's magnetism to be aligned with the lubber's line. This is, in fact, fairly typical of real boats.

Table 5.5 shows a typical summary of this type of deviation. Such a table is called a *compass card*. The data are plotted in Figure 5.18.

Table 5.5. Compass card for semicircular deviation

Ship's Heading (psc)	Deviation
000	0
090	10E
180	0
270	10W

POSTTEST

5.10 Construct curves for a boat in which the permanent magnetism is (a) toward the stern, (b) toward the starboard beam.

Quadrantal deviation—Some pieces of metal become temporarily magnetized when placed near another magnet. This *induced* magnetism can affect a nearby compass and produce what is called *quadrantal deviation*—so named because it vanishes in four directions. These four directions are typically the four cardinal directions (N, E, S, W), so quadrantal deviation is usually noticed only along the intercardinal directions (NE, SE, SW, NW). Figure 5.19 shows the resulting behavior of quadrantal deviation in a typical metal-hulled boat. Table 5.6 and Figure 5.20 show the deviation curve.

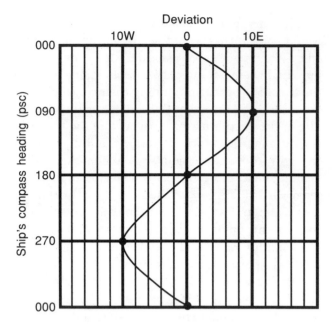

Figure 5.18. Deviations from Table 5.5, for semicircular deviation caused by permanent magnetism aligned forward along the lubber's line. In this case, the deviation vanishes when the ship is heading north or south (psc).

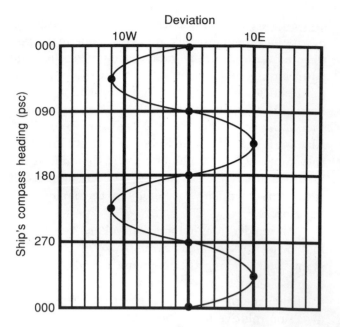

Figure 5.20. Graph of compass card (Table 5.6) for quadrantal deviation. The deviation vanishes on the four cardinal headings, so it would not be noticed unless you made a detailed study. It is usually not serious on wooden boats.

The extra complexity of quadrantal deviation arises because (unlike permanent magnetism) *induced magnetism is aligned with the earth's magnetism,* so it does not have a constant direction with respect to the lubber's line.

Table 5.6. Compass card for quadrantal deviation

Ship's Heading (psc)	Deviation
000	0
045	10E
090	0
135	10W
180	0
225	10E
270	0
315	10W

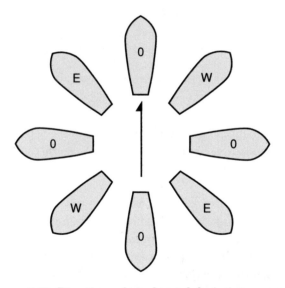

Figure 5.19. Directions of quadrantal deviation on a typical metal-hulled boat. Magnetic north is upward and each deviation is indicated on the hull heading along one of the 12 major compass points. Notice there are four directions of zero deviation. Also, the deviations are the same on reciprocal headings. These are the identifying characteristics of quadrantal deviation produced by induced magnetism in a boat.

Combining the deviations—We have discussed the three types of deviation as though each could appear without the others. We did this to clarify the behavior of each type, but a real compass will show all three at once—although probably not as severely as in the examples.

The next step is to show how they would combine into a more realistic composite curve. With fair accuracy, we can do this by simply adding together the types of deviations for each compass heading. For example, at a compass heading of 090 psc, we had:

Type	Amount
Constant	10E
Semicircular	10E
Quadrantal	0
Total	20E

(In carrying out the arithmetic when both E and W deviations occur, you should treat E as *negative* and W as *positive*.)

Combining the measures at every heading, we find data in Table 5.7 and the curve in Figure 5.21.

Table 5.7. Compass card for composite deviation

Ship's Heading (psc)	Total Deviation
000	10E
0405	20E
090	20E
135	0
180	10E
225	20E
270	0
315	0

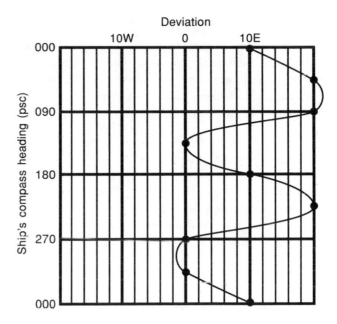

Figure 5.21. Compass deviation curve for combined effect of the constant, semicircular, and quadrantal deviations discussed in this section, based on Table 5.7.

This curve has some of the quirkiness of a real curve, and its shift to the right is a clear indication of a constant deviation. The sum of the deviations on all headings ought to equal zero if there is no constant deviation.

Now you are ready to start trying to reduce the deviations so the compass will point closer to magnetic north. This is called "compensating the compass."

Compensating your compass—A good job of compensation can reduce the deviation to one or two degrees, and this amount can be ignored for most purposes. Then you can read your compass as though it pointed toward magnetic north. (Remember, nothing you can do will make it reliably point toward true north—until you learn to make elephants fly!)

This section describes two methods of compensation. The first method will give you a complete picture of the behavior of your compass, but it will require 2 or 3 hours. The second method is far

quicker, but it will not reveal all the deviations. It should be used from time to time *after* you have become familiar with the behavior of your compass. It is useful for verifying the compensation of the semicircular deviation. For a slightly different description and further details and examples, see the excellent pamphlet "How to Adjust Your Own Compass," by K. W. David, revised by Wm. E. Elmhart (1982), and published by Bee Marine Service, Inc., 234 S.W. 30th Street, Ft. Lauderdale, FL 33315.

First method: constant and semicircular deviations—The actual compensation to reduce the compass deviation is done by adjusting small magnets mounted inside the compass, using a nonmagnetic screwdriver. (Occasionally it may be necessary to use small, externally mounted deck magnets to supplement the built-in magnets. Their use is described in the pamphlet, "How to Adjust Your Own Compass.")

The compensation process should be done while steering the vessel on magnetic headings, rather than compass headings, as this is more effective in eliminating the variation. (All ship headings are psc, per steering compass, in what follows.)

- **Step 1**—Neutralize the adjusting magnets in the compass by setting their screw slots vertical or horizontal, depending on the model of the compass. Use a nonmagnetic screwdriver made of brass. (The rod in a toilet mechanism can be hammered and filed into an excellent screwdriver.)

- **Step 2**—Steer the ship on a magnetic east heading by clamping the index of the pelorus to 90° on the lubber's line and setting the sighting vane reading to the magnetic bearing of the object (141° in the example). Then instruct the helm to turn port or starboard until the object is sighted through the pelorus. At that moment, the ship is headed toward magnetic east.

- **Step 3**—Remove the full compass deviation on this heading by rotating the fore-and-aft adjusting shaft until the compass indicates an east heading, 090.

- **Step 4**—Steer the ship on a westerly heading, as follows. Clamp the pelorus scale so 270 is on the index at the lubber's line, and set the sighting vane to the magnetic bearing of the distant object. Swing the ship until the distant object is sighted through the pelorus. At this moment the ship is on a magnetic west heading, 270M.

- **Step 5**—Remove half of the remaining deviation by rotating the same (fore-and-aft) adjusting shaft. For example, if the compass reads 290, rotate the shaft until it reads 280.

- **Step 6**—Clamp the pelorus index to 000 and steer the ship on a north magnetic heading by again sighting on the distant object with the vane set to the magnetic bearing.

- **Step 7**—Remove the full deviation on this heading using the thwartship (from side to side) adjusting shaft.

- **Step 8**—Finally, clamp the pelorus index at 180° and set the ship on a south magnetic heading by sighting on the distant object.

- **Step 9**—Remove half the remaining deviation by turning the thwartship adjusting shaft.

- **Step 10**—Now check your success—measure the deviation on the four cardinal magnetic headings using one of the methods described earlier in this chapter. If they are not 0°, add the west deviations together and then subtract each of the east deviations. If the sum is not 0° you probably have a constant deviation whose amount is one-quarter of the sum you just

found. For example in Table 5.7, the sum of deviations is 80°E. Dividing by 8 gives 10E for the constant deviation. This is compensated by rotating the compass index by 10° clockwise (i.e., toward the east).

At this point, you can look for quadrantal deviation by steering on the intercardinal directions (NE, SE, SW, NW) and seeing whether the deviations are all 0°. If not, make note of them on a small card and keep the card near the compass. You probably will not be able to compensate them unless you are on a large boat (see below).

Second method: semicircular deviation on reciprocal headings—There is a simpler process that can be done in the open ocean without charts or known magnetic directions. This method requires a moderately low sun and it is the one most often described in magazine articles (see, for example, "Checking Your Compass at Sea," by Phillip Mason, *Sail,* September 1987, p. 19). It does not give a complete compensation of the compass, and it should not be used until you have eliminated the constant deviation as described above and have assured yourself that the quadrantal deviation is unimportant. This method assumes that the compass only has semicircular deviation.

- **Step 1**—Head the boat eastward on a compass heading 090 psc.

- **Step 2**—Determine the relative bearing of the sun with a pelorus. (To do this, clamp the index card in line with the lubber's line, sight the sun with the sighting vane, and read the relative bearing from the scale.)

- **Step 3**—Swing the vessel to a reciprocal course so the relative bearing of the sun is increased by 180°, as determined by the pelorus.

- **Step 4**—Read the new compass heading. It would be 180° + 90° = 270° in the absence of semicircular deviation. In this case, be grateful and skip to Step 6. Suppose, however, the compass reads 290°. This means that the combined deviations on east and west headings is 20°.

- **Step 5**—Remove half the discrepancy by turning the fore-and-aft screw that adjusts the compensating magnets in the compass. In this case, turn the screw so the compass heading becomes 270° + 20°/2 = 280°.

- **Step 6**—Steer north by compass so the compass heading is 000 and determine the relative bearing of the sun again.

- **Step 7**—Swing to a reciprocal heading and if the compass heading is not 180° remove half the discrepancy with the thwartship (from side to side) adjusting screw.

Quadrantal deviation—Compensation for quadrantal deviation is accomplished by placing spheres of iron on either side of the compass and adjusting their separation. They are called "quadrantal spheres" and their induced magnetism is intended to annul the induced magnetism of the iron in the boat. They are only installed on large boats with metal hulls. Most small-boat skippers find their quadrantal deviation is small enough (a few degrees) so that it can be tabulated on a *compass deviation card* and referred to when high accuracy is needed.

Two words of caution—In principle, your job is finished, but if the initial deviations were greater than 10°, the process you have just gone through may not have been adequate to eliminate them the first time. You should check the deviations and repeat the compensation process if necessary. There is little point in trying to reduce the deviations below, say 5°.

Although there is no reason to think the semi-circular deviation will change significantly once it has been measured, the vigilant skipper will verify the compass on reciprocal headings after each week of sailing to avoid unpleasant surprises.

SPECIAL TOPICS

The lore of compasses sometimes seems endless, and here are a few more pointers concerning their use.

Making a steering card and Napier curve

Table 5.3 and Figure 5.11 show the deviations of your fictional compass for every 15° of ship's compass heading. The data were obtained before the compass was compensated, and by this time your compass deviations may look quite a bit smaller.

The purpose of the steering card and Napier curve is to display the deviations in a form that is convenient for steering, and we will use the original data in Table 5.3 as an illustration. Ordinarily, you would construct these steering aids from the final deviations after the compensation has been completed.

Steering will usually be done with the steering compass, as you have no direct way of observing true or magnetic north from the helm. When laying out a course on a chart, you will use the inner compass rose and read magnetic directions. These must then be converted to compass headings for the helmsperson. (We will assume the course and the heading are the same direction for the purpose of this discussion.)

There are two approaches you might take to the problem of finding the compass heading: (1) a table of the deviations found on a compass card, or (2) a table or graph showing directly the relation between magnetic and compass headings. The first method requires little explanation. It consists of finding the variation for each magnetic heading and applying it to find the compass heading. We shall not discuss it further in this chapter. The second method permits a direct conversion from one type of heading to the other without adding or subtracting.

If you plan to use the second method, which is generally preferred because of its simplicity, you should first add a column to Table 5.3 giving the ship's magnetic headings. The completed table would look like Table 5.8, below.

Suppose you wish to steer 145M. Scan the right-hand column to the two values on either side of that value, namely 131 and 148. The value you want can be found by interpolation in the left-hand column. A first glance tells you it is approximately 160psc. You may find it more reliably by linear interpolation, as follows:

- **Step 1**—First find the fractional distance from the lower value in the right hand column:

$$(145 - 131)/(148 - 131) = 14/17$$

- **Step 2**—Multiply this by the total interval in the left-hand column:

$$14/17 \times (165 - 150) = 12$$

- **Step 3**—Add to the lower value in the left-hand column:
$$150 + 12 = 162$$

This is the compass course.

Table 5.8. Sample of steering card to be mounted near helm

Ship's Comp. hdg. (psc)	Deviation	Ship's Mag. hdg. (M)
000	16E	016
015	23E	038
030	26E	056
045	27E	072
060	23E	083
075	15E	090
090	6E	096
105	3W	102
120	11W	109
135	17W	118
150	19W	131
165	17W	148
180	14W	166
195	10W	185
210	6W	204
225	5W	220
240	5W	235
255	6W	249
270	8W	262
285	9W	276
300	9W	291
315	5W	310
330	000	330
345	8E	353
360	16E	016

This steering card can be used to convert either way—from magnetic to compass or from compass to magnetic. It is easy to set up, but it requires a little arithmetic each time it is used.

The Napier curve eliminates the need for arithmetic. You do some graphing to set it up, and then you read it with a ruler. The goal is to set up a graph that will be accurate and can be used to make the conversion in either direction. The Napier diagram ingeniously achieves both goals, although the graph may look a little different from anything you have seen before. Figure 5.22 is an example of a portion of a Napier diagram, and a blank form (form F12) is given in Appendix 2.

The coordinate lines in a Napier diagram are diagonals rather than vertical or horizontal as they are in most graphs. One set (magnetic headings in solid lines) slopes 30° upward to the right; the compass headings are dotted and they slope 30° downward to the right. Each line represents a constant value of the corresponding type of heading. Along the solid lines, magnetic heading is constant. Numerical values for each line are shown along the scale in the middle of the diagram.

The plotted points are taken from Table 5.8, reading from the top. Point A corresponds to ship's compass heading 000 psc and magnetic heading 016M. The remaining points are included in the posttest.

POSTTEST
5.11 Fill in the gaps in the following table, finding headings and then the deviation using Figure 5.22.

Point	Magnetic (M)	Deviation	Compass (psc)
A	016	16E	000
B	038	23E	015
C			
D			
E			
F			

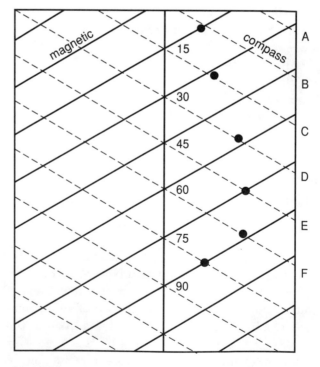

Figure 5.22. Portion of a Napier diagram for converting between compass and magnetic headings. Lines of equal magnetic heading (solid) and equal compass heading (dashed) intersect at specific values of deviation. The plotted points indicate the deviations in Table 5.8.

How to find a reciprocal heading using the sun

The low sun provides a useful target to steer by when you are seeking a reciprocal course. Two points should be noted: one concerns the motion of the sun and the other is an alternative to the use of a pelorus.

Sun's change of bearing—In average conditions, the sun's true bearing (azimuth) increases by 1° every 5 minutes when it is moderately high in the sky. This means you must work fast if you wish to use it as a fixed mark. If the sun is higher than 70° its bearing can change much more rapidly, so the method should not be used around midday in the tropics. On the other hand, within an hour or two of sunset or sunrise, the motion in azimuth is very slow in the tropics, so the method is quite good at those times.

Sun compass as an alternative to a pelorus—If a gimballed pelorus is not at hand, you can substitute a sun compass if the boat is not heeling (tilting). The sun compass is a long straight nail stuck vertically into a small flat board. (Take great care to make the nail exactly perpendicular to the board.) A straight index line is drawn across the board through the foot of the nail.

Here is how you use it. In Step 2 above, instead of finding the the sun's relative bearing, place the sun compass on a level spot and rotate it until the shadow of the nail falls on one half of the index line. When you swing the ship in Step 3, you will see the shadow gradually move around the board. You will know you are on a reciprocal course when the shadow falls on the other half of the index line. That's all there is to it. It's much simpler than a pelorus, but you must be sure the nail is exactly vertical or the method will not work.

Finding magnetic headings at sea

If you have been away from land for more than a week and have not had a chance to verify your compass against a known magnetic heading, now is the time to use the North Star or the sun.

With the North Star—The North Star is within a degree of the pole, so you may assume it to show true north for most compass work. But you will need *magnetic* north, so pull out your pilot chart and find the magnetic variation in your location. This will be the magnetic bearing of the North Star.

(For example, if the variation is 5°W, the magnetic bearing of the North Star will be 5°. Remember TVMDCAW, which means we add west variation to find magnetic bearing from true bearing.) If you then find that its compass bearing is the same as this magnetic bearing, then you have no deviation on that heading. This would be reassuring, but it is more likely that you will find a small deviation. (For example, if you find a compass bearing of 7°, you have a deviation of 2°W on that heading of the ship.) The deviation will depend on the heading of your ship, and there is not much you can do with a single measurement unless you happen to be sailing on that heading. But if you want more information you can head the boat in the cardinal directions and determine the compass bearing of the North Star on each heading. In other words, you can use the North Star as the object of known magnetic bearing and go through the full compensation process.

With the sun—The same can be achieved with the sun, but it takes a little more work because the sun moves across the sky each day. So you start by computing the sun's azimuth for 10-minute intervals over a period of an hour or so. (This process is described in chapter 17.) Adding the local magnetic variation to each computed azimuth will give you a list of magnetic bearings for 10-minute intervals. You can use these for a spot check of your compass, as with the North Star. Or if you have reason to suspect your compass, you can use this list of known magnetic bearings and carry out the compensation described earlier in this chapter.

The use of hand-held compasses

If the permanently mounted ship's compass is the archangel of the pilot's equipment, the pilot may also call upon two lesser angels: the *hand bearing compass* and the *binocular compass*. Either of these devices may be carried to a convenient viewing spot; both permit the rapid determination of compass bearing with an apparent precision somewhat greater than can be attained by sighting over the top of the ship's compass.

Hand bearing compass—This device is little more than a good pocket compass mounted with a handle and a viewing vane that works as a gun sight. Holding it at arm's length and sighting an object will give you the compass bearing of that object in a matter of seconds. For good accuracy, it should be arranged so that you can see the object and read the compass simultaneously. Better models come with a small light for reading the compass, and this is essential for night piloting. These devices need not be very expensive and every boat should be equipped with one.

Binocular compass—This type of device permits the pilot to identify the marking on a buoy, determine compass heading, and estimate distance at the same time. It is only found in the best marine binoculars so it is considerably more expensive than a simple hand bearing compass. (They cost in the neighborhood of $500, but those who own them claim they are worth every dollar of the price.)

Deviant deviations—If it were not for one shortcoming, these auxiliary compasses could replace the ship's compass for most purposes. But, because they are portable, these compasses cannot be compensated. They do not come equipped with compensating magnets, and if they did the magnets would be useless. Compensation of a compass is only possible when the compass is mounted in a fixed position on the boat. So you always face the problem of compass deviation when you use an auxiliary compass, and this can easily throw you off by 10° or more.

The best strategy is to get to know your equipment and become familiar with the pattern of deviations produced by the boat. You will probably discover that the pattern is rather complicated, because it will be affected, not only by the heading of the boat, but by your location on the boat as well. Perhaps the best procedure is to select one or two "pilot stations" for using the auxiliary compasses.

During a quiet day in a harbor, where you are surrounded by landmarks, enlist a friend to help you determine the deviation of your auxiliary compass. Do it from one of your pilot stations by sighting on a dozen objects distributed about the compass rose. Note the heading of your boat and compare the compass bearings you find with the magnetic bearings given by your ship's compass and pelorus or derived from a chart. If you are lucky, the deviation will be the same for all objects as long as the boat's heading is fixed. Turn the boat to various headings and again compare the compass bearings of all objects with the known magnetic bearings. (You may have to remeasure the magnetic headings if the boat has moved more than one boat-length from the original position when you changed heading.)

If the deviations at each pilot station depend only on the boat's heading, so much the better. You will be able to use a single compass deviation card for each pilot station, listing the deviation you find at each heading. You may, on the other hand, find a more complicated behavior and be forced to content yourself with a rough knowledge of the maximum deviation to be expected on each heading. This maximum (which may be 5° or 10°, or as much as 30° in severe cases) will serve as a limit on the accuracy you can expect from the auxiliary compass.

The best strategy will depend on your boat, the compass, and your personal inclination.

CHAPTER SIX

Dead Reckoning

Take off from a known position on a course for something that makes a noise. A bell, gong, or whistle is ideal. Lacking that, the bold shore of an island will do very well. You will surely hear the surf and see the loom of the shore before you are in trouble. Make some allowances for tide, a bit less than you think.

Roger F. Duncan and John P. Ware, A Cruising Guide to the New England Coast

Dead Reckoning: Traditional form of rough-estimate navigation used for hundreds of years by sailors, almost all of whom are dead. As it is practiced today, the technique involves the use of three special "chart darts" which are "entered" in the appropriate region of the chart from 8 feet away. The resulting holes are joined by pencil lines to form a triangle whose central point is taken to be the boat's position.

Henry Beard and Roy McKie, Sailing, A Sailor's Dictionary

INTRODUCTION

Dead reckoning is what you do when you are not determining bearings from land objects or determining celestial fixes. According to *Bowditch,* dead reckoning (DR) is "the determination of position by advancing a known position for courses and distances . . . It is reckoning relative to something stationary or 'dead' in the water, and hence applies to courses and speeds *through the water.*"

Let us take apart this definition and expand it slightly. It has four elements:

1. *Determination of position*—The central purpose of DR is the determination of position, and it is the only method that can provide a position at *any* time, whether in fog or under a clear sky, night or day. It is an approximate method, based on measurement, but often requiring estimation and the application of judgment. Every navigator, whether on a small cruiser or an ocean liner ought to have a notebook and chart containing enough information to determine a DR position at any moment.

2. *Advancing a known position*—The DR plot starts from a previously measured position, and it carries this position forward in time to the present and into the near future. This is called advancing the position, and it is based solely on measurement or estimation of the progress of the vessel through the water.

3. *Courses*—The direction of the vessel's progress is specified by its heading (course) as determined by

ship's compass or other orienteering methods, such as the known directions of celestial bodies.

4. *Distances*—The amount of progress is specified by the distance travelled, and this is calculated from speed through the water and lapsed time or is measured by a ship's log—a device that senses the motion of the boat through the water.

The accuracy of a DR position depends on the accuracy of the measurements and of the estimates that went into it. The vigilant navigator constantly verifies the equipment used for this purpose and keeps it in top shape.

The DR plot serves many purposes. When carried forward a day or so, it is the basis for predicting the times of sunrise and sunset or local noon, and it can be the basis for predicting landfalls or the sighting of navigation lights. In the fog, it will tell you when to expect the sound of the gong.

Horizontal motion of the water (currents) and the leeway of a sailboat (see "Determining Leeway" later in this chapter) will tend to introduce geographical errors into the DR position, so whenever possible the pilot makes additional measurements (bearings, transits, celestial sights, etc.) that serve to correct the DR plot. *Bowditch* suggests that DR "might be considered *basic* navigation, with all other methods only appendages to provide means for correcting the dead reckoning." If so, this chapter is the basic chapter of this book, and all others are appendages.

MAKING A DR PLOT

Before starting on a day sail you should verify that your piloting kit includes the following items.

- Binoculars

- Hand bearing compass

- Watch that can be read to the nearest second, or a stopwatch plus ship's chronometer

- Charts

- Drawing equipment: pencils, triangles, parallel rulers

- Notebook to act as navigator's logbook

Scenario for a day's sail

It is a bright morning in July 1990, and you are anchored in Dutch Island Harbor in the West Passage to Narragansett Bay, Rhode Island. (Find this on the chart in Figure 6.1). You chose the harbor after reading the description in the *Cruising Guide to the New England Coast*, by Duncan and Ware:

> Dutch Island Harbor. Among many Rhode Island yachtsmen this is the most popular harbor on the Bay, not for its facilities, for there are almost none, but partly because of the lack of them. It is unspoiled, uncrowded even when a yacht-club fleet makes it a rendezvous; the swimming is fine; and except in blows from the north it is fairly well protected.

Today a fair wind blows from the west, and you plan to sail due south between Whale Rock and the bell near Beavertail Point, past the Brenton Reef Horn to the bell on buoy "H," and due east until noon; then you'll do a turnabout and return along the same track. (Before drawing the track on the chart, scan the proposed route and look for danger spots and objects that might make useful marks along the way. Adjust the track to avoid dangers.)

Taking departure

The captain has decided to leave the anchorage under sail, so when the galley is cleared and the gear has all been stowed you raise the jib and hoist the anchor. You will sail out to the gong just south of Dutch Island and raise the mainsail on the way. The gong will be your point of departure (PoD).

Mark it on the chart with a small circle, and draw a line due south (180T) indicating your intended track over the bottom.

You need a compass heading for the helm. The magnetic variation, according to the compass rose on the chart, is 15°15′ in 1990, so your magnetic heading will be 180 + 015 = 195M. (Ignore fractions of a degree because the helm cannot be held that closely.) You need the deviation, and from your compass table, you find 2°W on this heading. So the compass course is 197C. You call out this course to the helmsperson, who repeats it to make sure it was understood.

From the appearance of the water flowing past the gong at your PoD, you guess that the current is running out at about 1 knot. You write this in the log and note time and write it as well (0930 EDT). The current will increase your speed over the bottom.

(In making your DR estimates of arrival at points along the way, you do not include this estimate of current. Rather you improve your knowledge of the current by noting whether, and by how much, you arrive early or late at the way points. DR estimates are best made with respect to motion through the water, not the ground. This is less confusing in the long run and facilitates keeping track of what you have done.)

POSTTEST

6.1 According to the compass rose in Figure 6.1, what was the compass variation in 1985? If the annual increase of the variation is 3′ per year, what will be the variation in 1996?

6.2 What would the compass course be in 1996 on a course 090T if the deviation were 5°E?

Symbols for plotting the course—Write the compass course along the track and in your log. Ask the helmsperson for the ship's speed (4 knots) and write it beneath the track. (Methods for getting the speed are discussed below.) Your line on the chart looks like Figure 6.2a.

Estimating time

Next you need to estimate the time of arrival at the first way point, the bell off Beavertail Point. On the track near the bell, draw a half circle, as in Figure 6.2b and then measure the distance along the track from the PoD to the mark (3.2 NM). The time interval to sail that distance is calculated as follows.

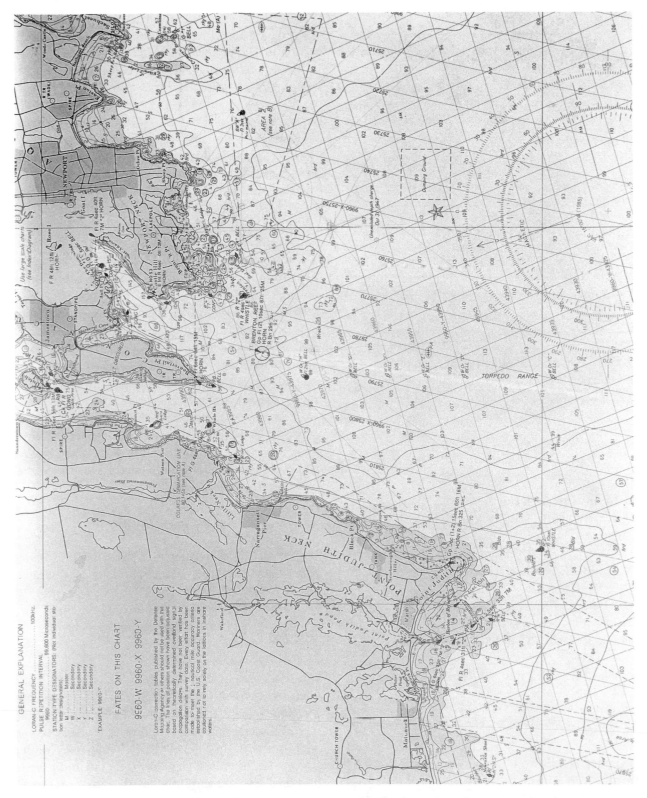

Figure 6.1 Chart of entrance to Narragansett Bay, Rhode Island.

Elapsed time (hours) = distance (NM)/speed (knots)

$$= 3.2/4 = 0.80 \text{ hours}$$

$$= 48 \text{ minutes}$$

Your estimated time at the bell is 0930 + 0048 = 1018 EDT. Near the half-circle, you write this DR time estimate. Now you can estimate times anywhere along the track, if needed.

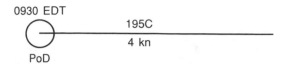

Figure 6.2a. Symbols on DR track indicating point of departure, time, course, and speed. The circle indicates a fix. The course is written above the track and the speed is written below.

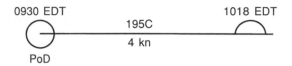

Figure 6.2b. DR track after the time of arrival near the bell has been estimated. The semicircle indicates a point on the DR track near the bell.

POSTTEST

6.3 Using the equation for elapsed time, supply the missing entries in the following table:

Elapsed time (h)	Distance (NM)	Speed (kn)
1.25	6.0	
	15	6
2.5		8

Sample navigator's log

By this time, your notebook will look something like this:

Date: July 15, 1990; Vessel Lynx
Wind: West, Force 3
PoD: Gong s. of Dutch Is. 0930 EDT
Current: 1 kn. ebb. = following
DR course: 180T + 15 = 195M + 2 = 197C/speed = 4 kn
ETA at Beavertail Point: 3.2 NM/4 = 0.8 = 48 min.
    0930
    0048
    1018

If the fog should roll in, you would want an estimate of when to start listening for the bell off Beavertail Point, and you don't want to be late starting, so you might recompute the time, increasing your speed by the observed current. This would give for the new interval: t = 3.2/5 = 0.64 hours = 36 minutes. So the revised time is 1006, and you would start at least five minutes before that.

Once you have passed the bell, you will write the actual time at the way point, and you might use it to revise your estimate of the current.

Next you must make a DR estimate of arrival at the next way point, but the current will probably change when you pass Beavertail Point, so the revised information will not be of much use. (That is the trouble with observing the current—the relevant water is always behind your vessel, and there is little reason to suppose the water ahead is moving the same way as the water behind.)

And so it goes. One leg follows another, and at all times you have enough information to pinpoint your location on the chart at a moment's notice.

Methods for determining vessel's speed with a stopwatch

With experience, you will be able to judge the speed of your vessel from the appearance of the wake and the sound of the water flowing past the hull. But in order to gain this ability (assuming you lack a knot-meter) you need a quantitative method for determining speed through the water.

The essential equipment is a stop watch and a tape measure. With the stop watch you will measure intervals of 1 to 10 seconds accurately. With the tape measure, you will set up a distance scale based on the following definition:

1 knot = 6,080 feet per hour

If we round the distance to 6,000 feet, we find an easy rule which is accurate enough for dead reckoning:

1 knot = 100 feet per $\frac{1}{60}$ hour or 1 minute
    = 10 feet per $\frac{1}{600}$ hour or 6 seconds
    = 5 feet per 3 seconds

The knot board and string—This method harks back to the original definition of the "knot" as a measure of ship's speed. Cut a small square board (about 6 inches on a side) and weight one edge with some short bolts so the board floats more or less upright in the water. Drill a small hole in the center and feed a string through it with a knot on the end so the string won't pull through. The string should be about 100 feet long and it should be wrapped around a free-running spool. At about 15 feet from the board make the first knot and tie a small piece of wool to it to mark it. Then carefully measure off an interval of 61 inches. Tie a knot and measure off another interval of the same length. Tie another knot and repeat until you have about 15 knots equally spaced.

To use the knot board, sit next to the railing of your boat when it is underway and drop the board into the water. Let the string run out and start your stopwatch when the first knot goes through your fingers. When exactly 3 seconds have passed, grab the string tightly and count the number of knots that have passed after the first one. That will be your speed in knots.

Speed in knots = knots counted in 3 seconds

Alternatively you can use a small bucket with a line through the handle and bits of tape wrapped around the line every 61 inches. Then drop the bucket overboard so it fills with water and pulls out the line. (The line must be strong enough to permit retrieving the bucket!) Whatever you use, it is im-portant that the line be stationary in the water while it runs freely through your fingers.

POSTTEST

6.4 Suppose you wish to develop a knotted string for timing a 5-second interval. How far apart should the knots be?

Chips and nomogram—Here is another way to use the same relationship. Find a convenient place along the rail of your boat that is an exact number of feet from the stern and mark it with a piece of tape. Suppose the distance is exactly 20 feet. Drop a small floating chip over the rail—on the lee side so it doesn't have far to fall before it hits the water. With your stop watch, time the interval required for the chip to come opposite the stern. Suppose it requires 3 seconds. Lay one edge of a ruler at the 20-foot mark on the right-hand scale of the nomo-gram in Figure 6.3. Rotate the ruler until the edge

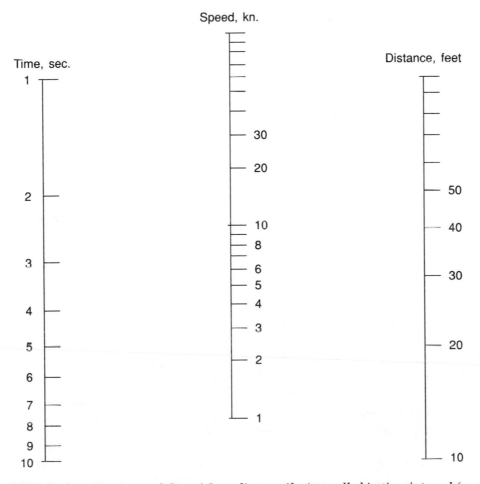

Figure 6.3. Nomogram for determining speed (knots) from distance (feet) travelled in time interval (seconds). To deter-mine speed, lay a ruler across the time interval and the number of feet travelled. The ruler will intersect the speed scale at the appropriate value.

is at the 3-second mark on the left-hand scale. Then you can read the speed in knots on the middle scale. (The result is 3.9 knots. This table and nomogram are computed using the correct length of the nautical mile, so they are slightly different from the approximate rule for the string.)

You can compute the speed from this equation:

$$\text{Speed (kn)} = 0.592 \times \text{distance (feet)} /$$
$$\text{time interval (sec)} = 0.592 \times 20 / 3 = 3.9 \text{ knots}$$

or you may get an approximate value from a glance at Table 6.1.

POSTTEST

6.5. With the nomogram fill in the missing entries.

Elapsed time (sec.)	Distance (feet)	Speed (kn.)
2	20	
	35	6
4		25

Table 6.1. Conversion from feet/second to knots

f/s	kn.	f/s	kn.	f/s	kn.
1.7	1	10.1	6	18.6	11
2.5	1.5	11.0	6.5	19.4	11.5
3.4	2	11.8	7	20.3	12
4.2	2.5	12.7	7.5	21.1	12.5
5.1	3	13.5	8	22.0	13
5.9	3.5	14.4	8.5	22.8	13.5
6.8	4	15.2	9	23.7	14
7.6	4.5	16,0	9.5	24.5	14.5
8.4	5	16.9	10	25.3	15
9.3	5.5	17.7	10.5		

Determining leeway

As illustrated in Figure 6.4 sailboats tend to slip sideways downwind, so their actual track through the water is not always aligned with the lubber's line of the boat. This is called the *leeway,* and you will notice that the leeway is in the same direction (to the right in this example) whether you are looking forward or aft.

The leeway depends on the boat and on the speed and direction of the wind relative to the boat's heading. With experience, the helmsperson will come to know the behavior of the boat and will be able to estimate the leeway well enough to compensate at the helm. This is, in fact, the usual practice: to compensate for leeway by steering the boat

so the track through the water will have the desired compass heading.

But until the helmsperson knows how to predict the leeway, it must be measured for each set of conditions. The quickest way is to look over the stern, as illustrated in Figure 6.5. The difference between the direction of the lubber's line extended over the water and the center line of the wake is the amount of the leeway. In this example it is to the right. This means that, when the helmsperson looks forward, the boat's track through the water will be to the right of the lubber's line.

When the centerline of the wake is difficult to judge, you may throw a small buoyant object, such as a wad of paper, overboard. (Be sure it's degradable and will rot in the sea.) Then the leeway can be estimated by eye or measured with a pelorus when the object is about 100 feet astern.

POSTTEST

6.6 Compute the compass headings to steer for the following data.

Desired Magnetic Course	Deviation	Leeway	Compass Heading to Steer
090	4E	12° clockwise	
180	10W	5° counterclockwise	
350	15E	7° clockwise	

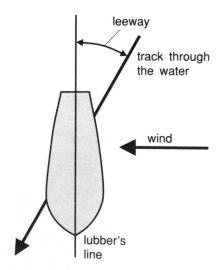

Figure 6.4. Leeway is the angle between the lubber's line and the boat's track through the water. It is always downwind. In this case it is to the right. To determine its amount, look over the stern and imagine the lubber's line extended over the water, as in Figure 6.5.

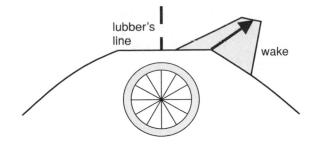

Figure 6.5. *Sternward view of the center of the boat's wake and the extended lubber's line. The angle between them as seen from straight overhead is the leeway of the boat, and it will depend on the relative speed and direction of the wind.*

Using a speed-distance scale

Many navigational charts show a scale for evaluating the relation among elapsed time, distance, and speed. It is used with a pair of dividers, and once you have caught on, you will find it to be a quick way to avoid the arithmetic—and at the same time avoid making simple arithmetic errors. Figure 6.6 is a scale, and the caption of Figure 6.7 tells how to use it.

POSTTEST

6.7 Use the scale in Figure 6.6 to verify your answers to Posttest 6.3.

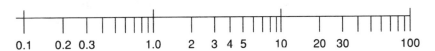

Figure 6.6. *Speed-distance scale for solving the relation t = d/s with a pair of dividers. In this scale, time is in hours, distance in nautical miles, and speed in knots.*

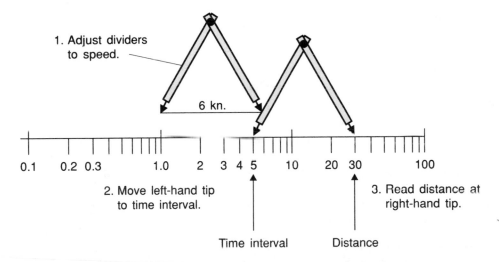

Figure 6.7. *There are three steps to using the speed-distance scale to find distance travelled in a given time and at a given speed. First put the left-hand tip of a pair of dividers at the 1.0 mark and spread them until the right-hand tip lies opposite the speed. Then move the dividers, without changing their spread, until the left-hand tip is on the correct time interval mark. Read the distance at the right-hand tip. You may also solve the related problems of finding the time required to go a certain distance at a given speed and then finding the speed required to go a given distance in a certain time. You can discover the techniques for these problems by playing awhile and then trying Posttest 6.7.*

SUMMARY OF GUIDELINES FOR DEAD RECKONING

We begin with an object lesson in the fallibility of dead reckoning by pure estimation.

"It was a dark and stormy night." My wife and I had gone to bed at our summer home on an inland lake. A thunderstorm raged outside and a few members of our family had stayed up to play cards. Shortly after turning off our light, we heard a strange crash outside. We assumed a tree had fallen in the wind, but a minute later our daughter came into the house and shouted that she had heard someone calling for help out on the lake. I put on shoes without socks and slipped a rain jacket over my pyjamas and called to my son and daughter to meet me at the dock. Through the rain, we could see flashlights a hundred yards down the shore, and in a flash of lightning we saw a terrible sight—a large white boat was perched on the shore among the bushes and a person sat in the stern waving a light.

After a quarter hour of bouncing among the rocks with our small boat, we managed to haul two dazed passengers into our boat, and then we brought them back to our house, where we telephoned the volunteer rescue team. (One of the passengers had broken three ribs and had cut a vein in his neck; the other, a young boy, had broken an arm and cut his forehead. A third youngster had managed to climb out of the boat and had disappeared into the woods by the time we arrived. He had headed for home, hoping to get to a telephone.)

As we waited for the ambulance, the boat driver told us with a sheepish grin that he had done what he always did when coming home in the dark at night. "I drove between the islands and waited until I got to the red light. Then I counted to 60 and turned hard left. I thought I was going into the bay. But I hit the shore this side of the bay. I just don't know how that could have happened. I guess I was going 35 miles an hour."

This person went aground with a crash and ended up in the trees when he tried to estimate time by counting to himself, rather than using a watch. His internal clock was running faster than he thought, and he had no independent method of verifying his position when he turned the boat. A lantern on the dock would probably have been visible, and his inability to see it might have served to warn him of problems. (Hindsight is infallible.)

Do's and don'ts for DR

In an article titled "Plotting to Find Your Position," in the May 1987 issue of *Sail* magazine, Fred Edwards discussed the prudent practice of DR when cruising, and to his list of guidelines we can add a few based on the experience just cited.

1. Make a DR plot on your chart whenever you leave a known position. Mark the time, and lay out the new course being steered. (Many sailors prefer to use directions relative to true north rather than compass headings for the DR course.) Write the course just above the track and write the estimated speed through the water just below the track. (See earlier discussion of estimating ship's speed.) Some small boats drag a "log" which has a small propeller whose turns are recorded on a dial that indicates distance in

1. Error of estimated speed

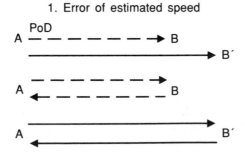

Figure 6.8. Top, *A boat takes departure at PoD and sails to B according to the DR track and estimated speed. If the true speed is greater, the actual leg will end at B'.* Bottom, *In a round trip, the second leg is also longer than the DR estimate, so the vessel comes back to the starting point despite the error. The error on the outgoing leg was compensated by the error on the return leg.*

2. Steering error

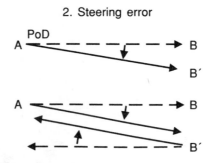

Figure 6.9. Top, *A boat steers to starboard due to a compass error and arrives at point B' rather than the DR position, B.* Bottom, *In a round trip with a constant steering error to starboard, the boat will arrive back at the starting point despite the error. The return leg compensated for the outgoing leg.*

nautical miles. If you do estimate the speed of the current, make a separate notation and use speed through the water for estimating distance. This way, you will have a better control over your estimates of current, which can be deceptive.

2. Plot a new leg on your DR track every time the boat changes course or speed. Indicate the new course and speed on the track, and verify that the implied change of course is consistent with the change of the boat's heading.

3. Indicate a new DR position (with a semicircle) every hour on the hour and label it with the time. You will find it much easier and more reliable to average over intervals of one hour than several hours.

4. Even if you do not plot a detailed DR track during a long cruise in open water, *always log enough information to permit you or someone else to construct a DR track and determine your position at any time.*

5. Never rely on estimates of time or distance. These are notoriously unreliable at sea. Measure time with a watch. When you compute DR distances, use your best estimate of speed and multiply by elapsed time. Speed estimates are more reliable than time or distance estimates.

6. Always assume you are wrong until you have proven yourself right. If at all possible, *use more than one piece of information when making a crucial decision or change of course, and look for inconsistencies* among your clues. We all have a tendency to assume we know what is going on, even when we are on the wrong track. For example, we tend to assume that the number on the buoy is what we expect it to be.

7. Trust your instruments and check your calculations. But to be trustworthy, your instruments must be kept in order.

Effects of errors in DR plotting
In discussing the possible errors of DR plotting, we shall assume that you use a reliable watch and have kept accurate track of the time. There are four basic types of error that may creep into your DR plot, and we treat them separately, although they may come in bunches. The interesting thing about these errors is that their effects depend on whether or not you intend your DR track to bring you back to your destination. Their effect on a one-way passage is quite different from their effect on a round trip, as illustrated in the upper and lower portions of Figures 6.8 through 6.11.

Note that, if the boat reverses its heading when returning to the PoD, the error on the return leg can, under some circumstances, compensate the error on the outgoing leg. Also, although the steering error and the effect of leeway may be similar on a one-way trip, their effects on a round trip are quite different.

ACTIVITY
Construct diagrams showing the effect of these errors in a triangular course of three equal legs that is intended to return to the starting point.

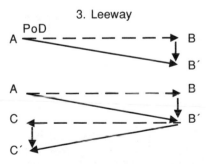

Figure 6.10. Top, *A boat drifts downwind due to leeway; in this case, the error is to starboard as indicated by the arrow B-B' connecting the ends of the DR track and the true track.* Bottom, *On the return leg, the boat again drifts downwind. Assuming the wind has not changed, this error will be added to the error of the outgoing leg and the boat will arrive at C' instead of C.*

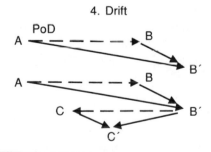

Figure 6.11. Top, *In the presence of drift due to tides or ocean currents, the boat deviates from the DR track in much the same way as for leeway. (See Chapter 10 for a discussion of tidal currents.) However, the drift is not necessarily downwind, so it can affect the speed as well as the course.* Bottom, *On the return leg, if the current is the same, the effect will be added to the effect of the outward leg. More commonly, the tide will have changed and there will be no relationship between the errors on the two legs.*

CHAPTER SEVEN

Direction Finding by Radio

Besides not being able to get a sun sight my navigation was complicated by not being able to pick up any of the radio beacons listed in the latest Admiralty manual. At last, by searching the frequency band, I located Cape Otway on 314 kcs [kHz] instead of the 289 given in the manual—the latest available when I left. I also managed to find Cape Wickham's frequency, and I got a rough fix from the two. My run to noon of December 3 [1966] was only 53-½ miles.

Sir Francis Chichester, Gypsy Moth Circles the World

INTRODUCTION

Radio direction finding (RDF) permits taking bearings from a vessel near a coastline in foggy weather. In principle, the technique is simple, and gives the compass bearing of the great circle toward a radio beacon whose coordinates are known. The compass bearing is converted to true bearing and a line of position is drawn from the beacon. In practice, the use of RDF can be tricky, if the wrong beacon is identified, or if the weakness or bending of the signal prevents a good fix.

EQUIPMENT REQUIRED

AM Radios

RDF receivers come in a variety of shapes and qualities. You can usually have some success with a simple AM (standard broadcast) receiver because most built-in antennas are directional. That is, they are more sensitive in the direction faced by the flat side of the radio than along the radio. Hold the radio vertical and rotate it about a vertical axis. When the signal fades, the long side of the radio is pointing toward or away from the beacon. When the signal is strongest, the flat side of the radio is facing toward or away from the station (Figure 7.1).

Remember, if you try to obtain an RDF bearing using an AM radio with a speaker, the magnet in the speaker may cause a compass deviation, so *do not use a magnetic compass within several feet of a radio.*

RDFs

RDFs are available with a swivel mounting calibrated in degrees. This may be aligned with the lubber's line so the relative bearings may be read directly. They are then converted to magnetic bearings by adding the magnetic heading of the vessel.

There are also hand-held RDFs with a compass mounted on them; they are relatively inexpensive ($100 or so) and are convenient to stow in a crowded vessel. To avoid magnetic disturbances, they are equipped with small earphones rather than a speaker.

PLOTTING

When you use RDF for piloting, you will tune into several radio beacons and determine their bearings. Then you plot the coordinates of the beacons

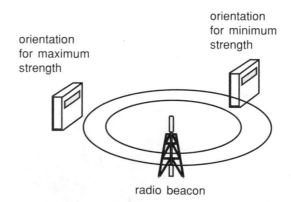

Figure 7.1. Schematic view looking down on radio waves coming from a beacon. If a portable AM radio is used to derive a radio bearing, the signal will be at maximum strength when the radio is perpendicular to the line of sight toward the beacon. Sometimes is it easier to detect the direction of the null that occurs when the radio is oriented for minimum strength.

and the lines of position corresponding to your measurements. The plotting can be done on a government chart or on a Mercator chart that you have made for the purpose.

Correction

There is a slight error incurred in using a Mercator chart at latitudes greater than about 10° north or south because radio waves travel along great circles, which are slightly curved on a Mercator chart. In view of the uncertainties of radio propagation, this error will not be a concern unless the radio station is more than 200 miles away. When it is, you should use a gnomonic chart where great circles are exactly straight, or a Lambert chart where they are approximately straight. Lacking these, you may use a table of corrections. Figure 7.2 illustrates the correction, and Table 7.1. gives some representative values. The correction vanishes at the equator, where the lines of longitude are parallel to each other. It also vanishes when the beacon is on the same line of longitude as the receiver.

In all other cases, the correction is such as would be produced by *moving the beacon toward the equator*. To see how this works, let us take an ex-

treme example. Suppose the vessel is at a latitude of 40°N by dead reckoning, and the navigator has identified a beacon that is at the same latitude. The rhumb line along the circle of latitude would point due east, but the great circle to the station would be slightly north of east. That is the direction observed by the RDF, so it must be corrected slightly south to the rhumb line. To put in some numbers, the bearing of a station which is 8° of longitude away from the vessel is observed to be 087T. The correction will turn the line 3° southward to 090T, as indicated in the figure.

Table 7.1. Correction (in degrees) to great-circle bearings for Mercator plotting*

Latitude (°N or °S)	Difference of Longitude (°E or °W)						
	4	8	12	16	20	24	28
4	0	0	0	1	1	1	1
8	0	1	1	1	1	2	2
12	0	1	1	2	2	2	3
16	1	1	2	2	3	3	4
20	1	1	2	3	3	4	5
24	1	2	2	3	4	5	6
28	1	2	3	4	5	6	7
32	1	2	3	4	5	6	7
36	1	2	4	5	6	7	8
40	1	3	4	5	6	8	9
44	1	3	4	6	7	8	10
48	1	3	4	6	7	9	10
52	2	3	5	6	8	9	11
56	2	3	5	7	8	10	12
60	2	3	5	7	9	10	12

Corrections from this table should be applied in the direction that takes the radio bearing *south* if you are in the northern hemisphere and *north* if you are in the southern hemisphere—in other words, it always moves the beacon toward the hemisphere that lies across the equator.

Examples—

1. You are at latitude 32N and you observe a radio beacon that is about 12° of longitude east of your estimated position. You detect it in the direction 055T and want to draw a line of position from the charted position of the beacon toward your boat. First you add 180° to find the reciprocal bearing, 180 + 055 = 235.

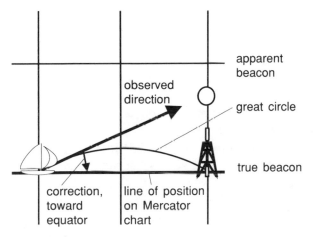

Figure 7.2. The measured bearing of a radio beacon lying due east would be along the great circle. Due to the distortion of a Mercator chart, this will appear to lie away from the equator compared to the rhumb line on the Mercator map. Therefore before plotting on the Mercator chart, a correction from Table 7.1 must be made to the observed bearing to bring it to the equator. (This is in addition to the correction for magnetic variation.) When the beacon is closer than 5° of longitude or radio bearings are plotted on a Lambert chart, this distortion is usually small enough to be ignored.

*See explanation of how to apply these corrections in the text below.

If you are working on a Lambert chart, you locate the beacon and draw a line toward 235T. This will be your line of position for that observation.

If you are working on a Mercator or universal plotting sheet (UPS, described later in this chapter), you first look in Table 7.1 for a correction. Scan across to 12° longitude difference (this is the same whether the beacon is west or east of you) and then scan down to your latitude, 32° (whether N or S). You find a correction of 3°. The bearing is in the NE direction, so if the beacon were moved toward the equator, its bearing would be increased. So you must *add* 003 to the observed bearing 055T. You find 058T as the corrected bearing, then add 180 to find the reciprocal direction and draw a line of position from the beacon.

2. Suppose you are in the southern hemisphere at 40S and you observe a beacon whose longitude is 8° west of your dead reckoning (DR) position. The bearing of the beacon is 270T, due west, and you wish to plot this on a UPS, so you find the tabulated correction, 3°. To decide whether to add or subtract the correction, you figure that if the beacon is to be moved toward the equator its bearing will move toward the right and increase. So you add and find 273T. If the beacon had been observed in the east, at 087T, the bearing would be moved toward the left and decrease. In that case you would subtract the correction, finding 084T.

INFORMATION AVAILABLE ON RDF BEACONS

Lists of radio beacons (many of which are primarily intended for aeronautical navigation) near the coastal waters of the world are found in several publications that differ in their coverage.

POSTTEST

7.1 Fill in the corrected bearings for the following situations:

- ***Radio Navigational Aids, Pub. 117,*** Defense Mapping Agency, Hydrographic/Topographic Center, Washington, D.C. 20315-0030. Updates to the tabulated information are listed weekly in the *Notice to Mariners,* also published by the Defense Mapping Agency.

- ***Admiralty List of Radio Signals,*** published in many volumes by the Hydrographer of the Navy, Taunton, Somerset, England.

- ***Reed's Nautical Almanac and Coast Pilot,*** published annually by Thomas Reed Publications, Ltd., 80 Coombe Road, New Malden, Surrey KT3 4QS, England, and distributed in the United States by Better Boating Association, Inc., Box 407, Needham, MA 02192. (This almanac also has a wealth of other information, including tide tables and data for sextant sights on the sun, moon, planets, and stars.)

The ranges of most radio beacons are limited to less than 100 miles and many of them are only 10 miles or so. Hence they are useful only close to shore. Marine radio beacon signals are in the frequency range 285-325 kHz (kiloHerz) which is the low-frequency end of the AM band used for commercial broadcast. (Aeronautical signals are in the slightly wider band from 200 to 415 kHz.) You will occasionally pick up a commercial station with your RDF equipment. The announcer will identify the call letters and, if you are lucky, give the name of the city at the time of a station break. This may be sufficient for you to obtain a line of position, but remember, the radio station is not necessarily at the center of the town.

As an example, Figure 7.3 is excerpted from *Reed's Almanac* and shows beacons along the Atlantic coast from New York to Cape Breton Island. Table 7.2 gives the data for the corresponding beacons identified by station number.

| DR Pos. | | Beacon | Diff. of | Tabulated | Observed | Corrected |
Lat.	Long.	Long.	Long.	Correction	Bearing	Bearing
40S	80W	88W	8	3	270T	273T
40S	80W	72W	8	3	087T	084T
16N	60E	72E			040T	
16S	60E	72E			040T	
45N	120W	140W			220T	
45S	120W	140W			310T	

Table 7.2. Data on radio beacons between New York and Cape Breton Island*

*Reed's Station No.	Type	Station Name and Grouping	Morse Ident.	Freq. kHz.	Mode	Sequence	Range or Power (kW)	Position Lat. N. ° '	Long. W. ° '
1	RC	St Paul Is (North Point Lt)	P ·--·	286	A2A	1	70m	47 13.6	60 08.4
3	RC	Scatarie Is NE Lt	Y -·--	286	A2A	3	100m	46 02.1	59 40.6
4	RC	Cranberry Is Lt	G --·	286	A2A	4	100m	45 19.5	60 55.7
11	RC	Sambro Is Lt	Q --·-	296	A2A	3	125m	44 26.2	63 33.9
16	Aero RC	Sable Is	SA ··· ·-	374	A2A		200m	43 56.0	60 01.7
19	RC	Outer Island Lt	IN ·· -·	272	A2A		25m	43 27.4	65 44.7
20	Aero RC	Yarmouth	QI --·- ··	206	A2A		50m	43 47.6	66 07.6
26	RC	St John	J ·---	397	A2A		45m	45 13.8	65 57.7
30	RC	Partridge Is	U ··-	308	A2A	2	50m	45 14.2	66 03.3
34	RC	Seal Is Lt	H ····	308	A2A	6	75m	45 23.7	66 00.9
40	RC Marker	The Cuckolds Lt	CU -·-· ··-	320	A2A		10m	43 46.8	69 39.0
44	RC	Matinicus Rock Lt	MR -- ·-·	314	A2A		20m	43 47.0	68 51.4
45	RC	Gt Duck Is Lt	GD --· -··	286	A2A	5	50m	44 08.5	68 15.3
46	RC	Manana Is Sig Sta	MI -- ··	286	A2A	0	100m	43 45.8	69 19.6
55	RC	Highland Lt Cape Cod	HI ···· ··	286	A2A	1	100m	42 02.4	70 03.7
79	RC	Montauk Point Lt	MP -- ·--·	286	A2A	3	125m	41 04.0	71 51.8
88	RC	Ambrose Lt	T -	286	A2A	4	125m	40 27.6	73 49.8
56	RC	Nantucket Shoals Lanby	NS -· ···	299	A2A		50m	40 30.0	69 26.0
57	RC	Chatham Lt	CH -·-· ····	311	A2A		20m	41 40.3	69 57.0
47	RC	Halfway Rock Lt	HR ···· ·-·	291	A2A		10m	43 39.3	70 02.3
48	RC	Portland Lt By 'P'	PH ·--· ····	301	A2A		30m	43 31.6	70 05.5
49	RC	Eastern Pt Lt	EP · ·--·	325	A2A		10m	42 34.8	70 39.9
50	RC	New Castle Lt Portsmouth Hr	NCE -· -·-· ·	322	A2A		10m	43 04.3	70 42.6
51	RC Marker	Scituate Harbor	SH ··· ····	295	A2A		10m	42 12.0	70 43.2
53	Aero RC	Lynnfield	LQ ·-·· --·-	382	NON A2A		100m	42 27.1	70 57.8
54	RC	Boston Lt By 'B'	BH -··· ····	304	A2A		30m	42 22.7	70 47.0
58	RC	Buzzards Bay Lt	BB -··· -···	314	A2A		20m	41 23.8	71 02.1
59	RC	Point Judith Lt	PJ ·--· ·---	325	A2A		10m	41 21.7	71 28.9
65	RC	Cape Cod Canal	CC -·-· -·-·	318	A2A		20m	41 46.3	70 30.1
66	RC	Cleveland Ledge Lt	CL -·-· ·-··	308	A2A		10m	41 37.8	70 41.7
67	RC	Nobska Point Lt	NP -· ·--·	291	A2A		20m	41 30.9	70 39.4
68	RC	New Bedford East Barrier Lt	NB -· -···	322	A2A		10m	41 37.5	70 54.4
71	RC Marker	Brant Pt Lt	BP -··· ·--·	325	A2A		10m	41 17.4	70 05.5
72	RC	Brenton Reef Lt	BR -··· ·-·	295	A2A		10m	41 25.6	71 23.3
73	Aero RC	Nantucket Is	TUK - ··- -·-	194			2.0kW	41 16.1	70 10.8
78	RC Marker	Saybrook Lt	SB ··· -···	320	A2A		10m	41 15.8	72 20.6
80	RC	Little Gull Is Lt	J ·---	306	A2A	2	20m	41 12.4	72 06.5
81	RC	Clinton Hr	CL -·-· ·-··	306	A2A	1, 4	20m	41 16.0	72 31.2
82	RC	Horton Pt. Lt.	HP ···· ·--·	306	A2A	3, 6	20m	41 05.1	72 26.8
83	RC	Watch Hill Lt.	WH ·-- ····	306	A2A	5	10m	41 18.3	71 51.6
84	RC	Block Is SE Lt	BI -··· ··	301	A2A		20m	41 09.2	71 33.1
86	RC	Fire Is	RT ·-· -	291	A2A		15m	40 38.3	73 18.9
85	RC	Old Field Point Lt.	OP --- ·--·	316	A2A	2, 5	20m	40 58.6	73 07.1
87	RC	Execution Rocks Lt	XR -··- ·-·	316	A2A	1, 4	20m	40 52.7	73 44.3
89	RC	Stratford Pt. Lt.	SP ··· ·--·	316	A2A	3, 6	20m	41 09.1	73 06.2
93	RC Marker	Shinnecock Lt	SN ··· -·	311	A2A		20m	40 50.5	72 28.8
97	RC Marker	Jones Inlet	JI ·--- ··	319	A2A		10m	40 34.8	73 34.4
98	RC	East Rockaway Inlet	ER · ·-·	302	A2A		10m	40 35.2	73 45.2
99	Aero RC	New York (John F. Kennedy)	JF ·--- ··-·	373	NON		25m	40 35.2	73 48.0
105	RC Marker	Manasquan Inlet	MI -- ··	308	A2A		20m	40 06.0	74 02.0
106	RC Marker	Barnegat Inlet	BI -··· ··	322	A2A		20m	39 45.5	74 06.5
107	RC Marker	Atlantic City Absecon Inlet ...	AC ·- -·-·	316	A2A		15m	39 22.0	74 24.6
108	RC Marker	Cape May	CM -·-· --	325	A2A		10m	38 56.6	74 52.4
110	RC Marker	Indian River Inlet	IR ·· ·-·	308	A2A		10m	38 36.6	75 04.1
111	RC Marker	Ocean City Lt	OC --- -·-·	293	A2A		10m	38 19.5	75 05.3
112	RC Marker	Wachapreague Inlet	WI ·-- ··	324	A2A		10m	37 34.4	75 37.1
115	RC	Delaware Lt Ho By 'D'	N -·	319	A2A		10m	38 27.3	74 41.8
116	RC	Five Fathom Lt Ho By 'F'	F ··-·	312	A2A		10m	38 47.3	74 34.6
118	RC	Cape Henlopen	HL ···· ·-··	298	A2A	3	125m	38 46.6	75 05.3
119	RC	Cape Henry Lt	CB -·-· -···	298	A2A	4	150m	36 55.6	76 00.4
131	RC	Oregon Inlet Lt	PI ·--· ··	298	A2A	5	125m	35 46.1	75 31.5
132	RC	Fort Macon	CL -·-· ·-··	298	A2A	6	150m	34 41.9	76 41.0
133	RC	Oak Island Lt	OA --- ·-	298	A2A	2	70m	33 53.6	78 02.1
146	RC	Charleston Lt	S ···	298	A2A	3	125m	32 45.5	79 50.6

* These numbers correspond with the numbers on the Radio Beacon Charts.
Service: All radiobeacons transmit continuously unless stated.

USING A RADIO DIRECTION FINDER AND MORSE CODE

Think of the radio signals as coming to you the way water comes from a hose. When an ordinary radio is held facing toward or away from the stream, it catches the most water, and the antenna catches the maximum amount of radio energy. With this orientation, the signal is strongest. By noting the direction the radio is facing, you can determine the orientation of the line of position.

Tune the dial and swing the radio slowly right and left until you find the direction of greatest signal strength. Special-purpose RDFs have highly di-

*(Courtesy *Reed's Almanac*, 1990)

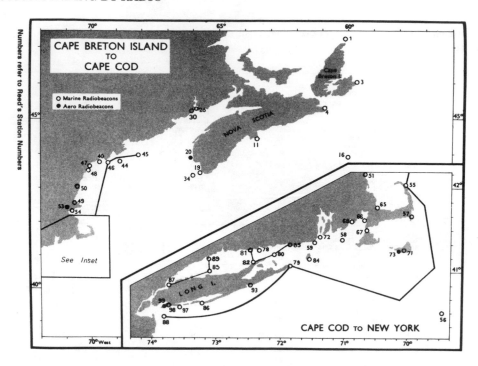

Figure 7.3. Map of radio beacons between New York and Cape Breton Island. (Courtesy Reed's Almanac, 1990)

rective antennas and an arrow pointing along the line of position. (Alternatively, you can look for a *minimum* in the signal, and then your antenna is aligned broadside to the beacon.)

Determining the observed bearing

Unfortunately you cannot tell whether the radio is facing *toward* or *away from* the station, because the antenna cannot tell the difference; the signal is just as strong with either orientation. But you will usually have a fair idea of the general direction of the radio beacon from your dead reckoning position and you will be able to resolve this ambiguity.

With luck, you may be able to obtain compass bearings to two beacons and determine a fix from the intersection of the two lines of position.

The measurements of direction are always uncertain to at least several degrees and often as much as 10° or 20°, and this must be taken into account when you interpret the information. So when you measure the bearing, also note how many degrees on each side of this direction would also be possible bearings. Then when you plot the line you will draw lines lying that far on each side to enclose

the best guess. The fix will actually be an area on the chart, rather than a point.

Identification by Morse code

The identification of the radio beacon is achieved by noticing the Morse code signal, which is usually a series of two or three letters, such as BH (– · · · · · · ·) or LQ (· – · · – – · –). The complete Morse code is shown below. It is not necessary to memorize it entirely, but a few hours spent listening to it will make the recognition of signals much easier and will repay the navigator. The Amateur Radio Relay League (Newington, CT) broadcasts announcements and text from *QST* magazine on its station W1AW in lower-side-band (LSB, a mode of shortwave broadcast that permits using a narrower frequency band, leaving more room for other stations). The following schedule (EST) is typical, but is subject to change:

1. Monday, Wednesday, and Friday at 9 AM and 7 PM

2. Tuesday, Thursday, Saturday, and Sunday at 4 and 10 PM

The approximate broadcast frequencies are 3580, 7048, and 14700 kHz, and the code is transmitted at speeds of 5 to 35 words per minute. If you tape-record the transmissions directly off the air, you will be able to play them back repeatedly.

Morse Code

a	· —	j	· — — —	s	· · ·	1	· — — — —
b	— · · ·	k	— · —	t	—	2	· · — — —
c	— · — ·	l	· — · ·	u	· · —	3	· · · — —
d	— · ·	m	— —	v	· · · —	4	· · · · —
e	·	n	— ·	w	· — —	5	· · · · ·
f	· · — ·	o	— — —	x	— · · —	6	— · · · ·
g	— — ·	p	· — — ·	y	— · — —	7	— — · · ·
h	· · · ·	q	— — · —	z	— — · ·	8	— — — · ·
i	· ·	r	· — ·			9	— — — — ·
						0	— — — — —

Period (.)	· — · — · —	Error	· · · · · · · ·
Comma (,)	— — · · — —	Wait	· — · · ·
Question (?)	· · — — · ·	End	· — · — ·
Dash (—)	— · · · · —	Go ahead	— · —
		Replying	· — ·

The identification of a beacon requires knowing its radio frequency and setting your RDF accordingly. For this reason, it is important that the dial be set properly and that you verify its proper functioning before you actually need it. Digital dials permit precise setting and for this reason they are much easier to use.

PLOTTING THE LINES OF POSITION

The principle is exactly the same as for daytime sightings of, say, a lighthouse or a buoy. You may proceed in either of two ways.

First method

If you have a Lambert chart showing the coastal region and the beacons, you may identify the radio beacon on the chart. Then convert the compass bearing you have obtained to true bearing (or magnetic) and use the compass rose on the chart to draw a line with that orientation from the beacon. (The great circles may be plotted directly onto the Lambert chart without too much error.) Remember the line goes *in both directions* from the beacon. Ordinarily one of them will go inland and can be rejected—if you are afloat.

Always try to estimate the uncertainty of the fix by drawing lines on each side of the lines of position, as in Figure 7.4 below. (See Chapter 4 for an earlier discussion of estimating uncertainties.)

Second method

Lacking such a chart, or if you are too far from shore to be on the appropriate chart, you may construct your own Mercator chart (according to the directions in Chapter 20) or use a UPS (described below). In either case, you begin by selecting the central latitude and longitude and the scale of nautical miles so that the beacons and your vessel will all appear on the same chart. Locate the beacons by latitude and longitude, and then draw the lines of position. Determine the best fix and read off your latitude and longitude. (Remember to correct the observed bearings, if necessary, according to Table 7.1)

SETTING UP A UNIVERSAL PLOTTING SHEET

You may construct a Mercator chart centered on Boston using a universal plotting sheet (DMA Stock No. VPOS 001; see Appendix 2, form F11) as follows, referring to Figure 7.5.

* **Step 1**—Label the central latitude line (horizontal) 43°N, and label the other latitude lines in 1° increments.

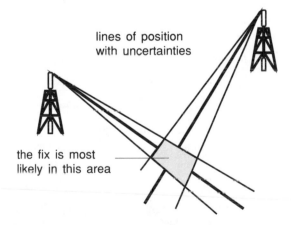

Figure 7.4. After determining the bearing of the strongest signal, the navigator estimates the likely error on either side by swinging the radio back and forth. In this case, an uncertainty of ±5° was estimated, and this is typical of RDF bearings. All bearings are converted to true bearings for plotting and the error lines are drawn to indicate the likely area of the fix.

- **Step 2**—Label the central longitude line (vertical) with the longitude of Boston, 71°W.

- **Step 3**—Your next task is to construct the remaining longitude lines. Their separation depends on latitude. To find the separation for your central latitude, make four marks on the compass rose in the center of the sheet. Here is how to find where to draw these marks. Think of the compass rose as a side view of the earth, on which the poles are up and down and the equator is horizontal. Measure up and down from the equator to the central latitude (±43°) and put a little mark in each quadrant. This will give you two marks on each side of the central longitude.

- **Step 4**—Draw vertical longitude lines through the pairs of marked points, one on each side of the central meridian. (Notice these lines will be closer together if you use a higher central latitude. This corresponds to the convergence of the longitude lines on the globe of the earth.) Label the line on the right 70°W and the one on the left 72°W. (A common mistake is to reverse the order of the longitudes in the western hemisphere. Remember numbers increase to the left.)

- **Step 5**—If needed, you may add further lines of longitude by measuring equal horizontal intervals and drawing lines parallel to the central longitude.

POSTTEST

7.2. Refer to the chart in Figure 6.1. You are sailing at night off the coast of Rhode Island and you take bearings on two radio beacons:

Frequency	Code	True bearing
295 kHz	– · · · – ·	020T
325 kHz	· – – · – – –	270T

What are your latitude and longitude?

7.3. Find three or four radio beacons that you expect to be able to hear from your home port. Write the

relevant information in the spaces below. Then set up a UPS and plot the locations of the broadcasting beacons. Attempt to measure their directions and estimate the uncertainty of these measures. Enter these data in the table and plot the lines of position. Determine a fix and draw a circle indicating the estimated uncertainty.

Signal (code)	Freq.	Range	Lat.	Long.	Observed bearing M or T	Uncertainty (Degrees)
1.						
2.						
3.						
4.						

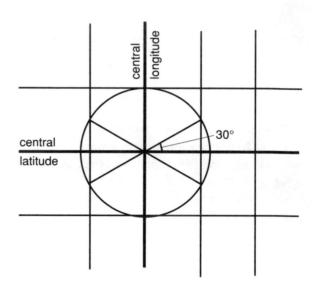

Figure 7.5. Appearance of universal plotting sheet set up for 30° latitude after the adjacent longitude lines have been drawn. Another longitude line has been added at an equal distance to the east. Because this is a Mercator map, the distance scales in miles are the same in the latitude and longitude directions.

CHAPTER EIGHT

Piloting Techniques

Excitement grew as I approached it [the Cape of Good Hope]. The swell was getting up; as it came from astern it helped the wind to carry me on. The cape was now abeam, but I had to continue steering South for half a mile in order to clear two rocks that mount guard seaward. I took a bearing and when I was sure of being clear of danger I tacked due East.

Vito Dumas, Alone through the Roaring Forties

INTRODUCTION

Piloting is the art of guiding a vessel safely through coastal waters. It uses a wide variety of techniques, and when you have learned the basics, you will be able to invent methods of your own. If you practice your piloting techniques during times of favorable wind and weather, you will find your efforts repaid tenfold when wind and weather are foul. You will know how to cope with fogs, and at night you will be able to proceed without endangering your vessel.

A summary list of techniques is given at the end of this chapter. They may be divided into two categories: *Primary techniques* give a position by pure geometry. These positions are called *fixes,* and they are the most reliable. When the situation prevents using a primary technique, you can often call upon a *secondary technique* and locate the vessel by invoking an assumption about its speed and direction of motion. Such positions are called *running fixes.*

PRETEST

8.1 What is a bearing line? a range line?

8.2 What is an advantage of obtaining a fix from two range lines?

8.3 With compass observations, how can you tell that you are on a collision course with another vessel?

A few definitions

- *Position*—Geographical position is defined by a point on a chart and is specified by *latitude* and *longitude.* Of course, without the *time,* such a position is not of much use.

- *Line of position (LOP)*—This is the key to piloting. It is a line on a chart locating the vessel at a specified time. The vessel can be anywhere on the line, so a single line of position does not completely determine position. Various methods for determining lines of position will be described below under *bearing line, range line,* and *circle of position.*

- *Fix*—A purely geometric determination of the location of the vessel at a known time, usually by the intersection of at least two simultaneous lines of position. No assumptions about the motion of the vessel are needed. Various methods of determining fixes will be described below.

- *Running fix*—If the lines of position were determined at different times and one of them is advanced to the time of the other, they provide a *running fix.* This is probably the most frequently used technique in coastal piloting.

- *Estimated position (EP)*—A determination of location at a known time using one or more assumptions about the motion of the vessel, such as its speed and direction or the distance it has moved in the interval between two sightings. This is usually more reliable than a dead reckoning (DR) position, which often involves more assumptions. This distinction between EP and DR position is somewhat moot. Don't worry about it.

- *Bearing line*—If a known object is observed from a boat, the bearing line is the locus of points on the chart consistent with the observed bearing. (If the bearing was obtained with a compass, it should be converted to magnetic or true before being plotted.) A bearing line and the corresponding time at which the bearing was observed constitute a line of position.

For example, on the chart in Figure 8.1 a line has been drawn with a bearing of 120T from the flagpole on Newport Neck. A pilot anywhere on that line will see the pole on a reciprocal bearing, namely at 120T ± 180 = 300T. A person on land on the other (northern) half of the line will see the pole with a bearing of 120T (see Figure 8.2).

To construct a line of position from an observed bearing, compute the reciprocal bearing (by adding or subtracting 180) and draw the bearing line from the observed object. Bearing lines are always drawn from the known object.

POSTTEST

8.4 A pilot near Brenton Reef Horn observes the flagpole on Newport Neck (Figure 8.1). What will be the observed true bearing?

- **Range line**—Suppose you are sailing near Brenton Reef (Figure 8.1) and notice that two charted objects,

such as the cupola on Brenton Point and the flagpole on Newport Neck, are directly in line with each other. This fact can give you a quick line of position.

When two objects are directly in line with one another, they are said to be in *range*. All points from which the objects will be in line with each other are on the *range line*. Geometrically, the range line is the line containing the two objects, and it extends as far as the eye can see in both directions. It is usually possible to determine which object is in front, and thus to determine which half of the range line is relevant to the vessel's location (see Figure 8.3). The range line can be constructed by drawing a straight line through the two objects, and it does not require knowing their bearings. *A range line and the corresponding time constitute a line of position.*

Range lines can be useful for checking compass deviation. The vessel is put onto the range line and the measured compass bearing of the objects is compared with the magnetic bearing of the range line as read from the compass rose on the chart.

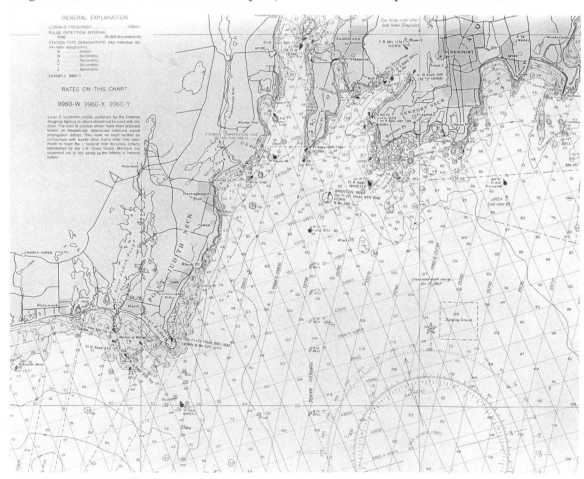

Figure 8.1. Portion of chart of Narragansett Bay, Rhode Island.

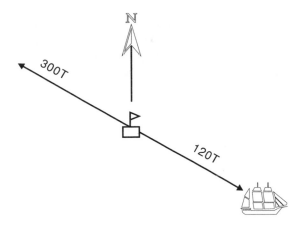

Figure 8.2. Points seen from the flagpole having a bearing of 120° are on a bearing line of 120°. From a boat on this bearing line, the flagpole has the reciprocal bearing, 300T.

POSTTEST

8.5 What are the bearing and reciprocal bearing of the range line between the two towers on Beavertail Point as seen from the south, near Brenton Reef?

PRIMARY TECHNIQUES TO DETERMINE FIX

Any position determined from the intersection of two or more simultaneous lines of position is a fix. (Because a fix does not require assumptions about the motion of the vessel, it is usually more reliable than the running fixes described later.)

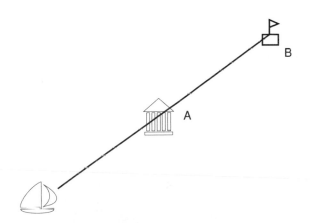

Figure 8.3. This range line, determined by objects at A (cupola) and B (flagpole), is the set of locations from which the two objects will appear in line with each other. On a chart, the range line is determined by drawing a straight line through the two objects. No measurements of bearing are needed. If A is known to be in front of B, you know which half of the line is relevant.

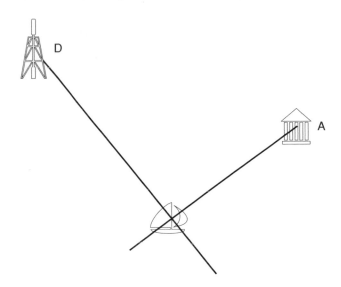

Figure 8.4. Intersection of two bearing lines from A and D determine the vessel's location. The orientation of the bearing lines must be determined as true or magnetic bearings. Hence the compass deviation must be known.

Crossed bearings (compass deviation must be known)

Two simultaneous bearing lines intersect at the vessel's location, as indicated in Figure 8.4.

POSTTEST

8.6 You are south of Sheep Point and you observe two bearings: Brenton Point cupola (288T), Cormorant Rock (043T). What letter is written on the buoy nearest you?

Intersection of two ranges

Two simultaneous range lines intersect at the vessel's location, as indicated in Figure 8.5. This is a powerful method, as it is independent of compass deviation, and it does not depend on the measurement of bearings. Unfortunately, this type of fix is relatively rare due to the scarcity of good range lines and the need to be on two of them at the same instant.

POSTTEST

8.7 You are near Brenton Reef and you observe two ranges: (1) the two towers on Beavertail Point and (2) the cupola on Brenton Point and the flagpole on Newport Neck. What is the charted depth of water at your position? (Depths are in feet below mean low water on this chart.)

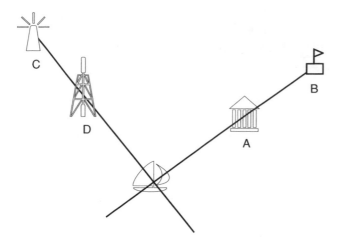

Figure 8.5. The intersection of two simultaneous range lines may be found on the chart when the four objects have been identified. This determines a primary fix without requiring the measurement of bearings.

Intersection of range and bearing (deviation must be known)

A mixture of the two preceding methods is often a good tactic, and there are two ways to do it. One way uses a compass and requires you to know its deviation; the other uses the true bearing of the range and the relative bearing of another object, so no compass is needed.

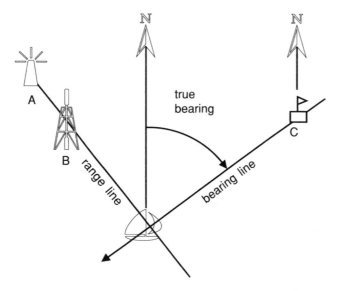

Figure 8.6. Typical mixture of primary methods in determining a fix. Here the compass bearing of C is determined at the instant the vessel crosses the range line A–B and is then reduced to a true bearing using the known variation and deviation. The bearing line is drawn from the object back toward the vessel, and its intersection with the range line is your fix.

Range line and compass bearing of third object—On crossing a range line (A–B in Figure 8.6), measure the bearing of a third object, C. To use the range line, merely draw it directly on the chart. To use the observation of the third object, first reduce the compass bearing to a magnetic or true bearing, and then draw a bearing line from the object. The intersection with the range line is your fix.

Range line and relative bearing—At the moment you cross a range line, you measure the relative bearing from the range line to a third object (Figure 8.7). Draw the range line on the chart, and with a protractor measure from the range line an angle equal to the relative bearing. Draw a line with this bearing. With parallel rulers shift this line so it passes through object C. The intersection of this bearing line with the range line is your fix.

POSTTEST

8.8 You find the flagpole on Newport Neck to have a bearing of 042T. At the same time you see that the two towers on Beavertail Point form a range line. What is the letter on the buoy nearest your vessel?

Bearing and distance by radar

Most of the primary techniques rely only on angles and they require observations of at least two objects. With radar, however, it is possible to determine the relative bearing and the distance of a

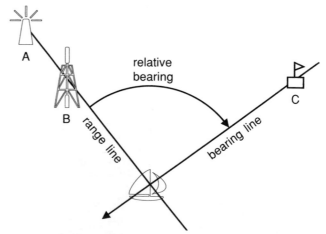

Figure 8.7. Here the relative bearing of C from the range line A–B is determined at the instant the vessel crosses the range line. This permits drawing a line with the correct bearing on the chart; when this line is drawn from the object back toward the vessel with parallel rulers, its intersection with the range line is your fix.

single object, and this is sufficient to provide a fix. The distance gives a circle of position, and the relative bearing, when converted to true or magnetic by knowing the heading of the vessel, gives a bearing line as indicated in Figure 8.8.

Two circles of position by horizontal angles

This can be done with radar or a sextant. The sextant method requires accurate measurement of the apparent angles between two pairs of objects on the horizon, and it is described in the next chapter.

Obtain more data than you need for a fix

Do not suppose that because you have been very careful your results must be very accurate. Even experienced pilots make mistakes, and they try to protect themselves by obtaining more than the necessary minimum of data to determine a fix. For example, they may determine the intersections of three rather than two lines of position.

If you use three or more position lines and they happen to intersect in a single point, do not be misled by what appears to be an accurate intersection. The uncertainty of your fix is determined by measurement error, not by the size of the resulting triangle (see Chapter 2).

The extra line of position can signal an alarm in case of large mistakes or misidentifications of ob-

jects. In Figure 8.9, the bearing line is mistakenly drawn from D′ instead of D, resulting in a gross error that would not have been detected without bearings from both E and A.

If you seem to have a large discrepancy, do not ignore it. Take more bearings, because you have made a mistake somewhere along the line.

SECONDARY TECHNIQUES— RUNNING FIXES

When conditions prevent applying a primary fix to obtain a good solid position, it is time to apply a secondary method and derive an estimated position.

These methods are based on an estimate of the vessel's *course and distance travelled* during a short interval. The course is determined by watching the compass. The distance is derived from the time interval and the estimated speed, as determined by your knowledge of the boat or from reading the ship's log (speedometer or distance meter). The secondary methods use the assumption that short time intervals imply small errors of estimated distance. This assumption permits treating observations made at different times *as though they were simultaneous*. This is a very powerful trick. The basic idea is to *advance* an LOP obtained at an earlier time so that it can be used with a later observation.

Figure 8.8. Radar determination of range plus true bearing of a known object yield a fix. The range gives a circle of position, and the bearing gives a line of position. They intersect at the vessel's position. (You must know the vessel's true heading to convert from the radar bearing to true bearing.)

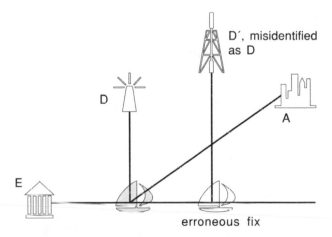

Figure 8.9. Incorrect identifications can be detected by using more than the minimum number of lines of position. Errors may reveal themselves by giving highly discordant results. In this case the erroneous LOP from D′ would not have been detected if only the line from A had been available. There is usually no way to tell which is the bad line, so the next step is to obtain more bearings on different objects.

The following methods are merely a sample of the variety of techniques that can be used if you can make a good estimate of the distance and the direction travelled between the times of making two measurements.

Advancing a line of position

First method: Two observations of a single object—It is a spring afternoon and you are sailing due eastward (090T) near Brenton Reef. You go belowdecks to make a sandwich and when you come back up, you see that the boat is about to sail into a fogbank. In minutes, the world is cut off from view. Added to this, the tide is about to start coming in and it will set you toward the shore, so you must try to keep a close watch on your position.

The depth sounder is reassuring. It shows 95 feet of water below your hull, so the bottom is about 92 feet below the keel and 100 feet below the surface. You get out the chart (Figure 8.1) and see that the Brenton Reef beacon has a radio transmitter on 295 kHz broadcasting Morse code — · · · — ·.

POSTTEST
8.9 What letters does this code signify?

With your RDF (discussed in Chapter 7) you obtain a compass bearing of 030 psc at 1600 hours. Looking at the steering card in Table 5.8 you find that the compass deviation while heading due east is 6E. From the compass rose, you compute that the variation is 15°15′W in 1990. Adding these together, you obtain a total correction of V+D = 9°15′W and you subtract this from the compass bearing to find a true bearing of 021T .

> Did you follow that? Remember TVMDC(AW) and see if you can figure it out. If not, you ought to go back and review Chapter 5.

So the bearing line from Brenton Reef beacon has a true bearing of 180 + 21T = 201T, and you draw this first line of position from the beacon. You label it 1600.

There is another radio beacon on the chart, but you can't seem to get a fix on it so you decide to wait a while and take another observation of the Brenton Reef beacon. To prepare for this, you watch the ship's log and see that you are making a steady 6

knots. As you sail, the beacon is on the port side, and its bearing gradually decreases.

After 40 minutes, its bearing has decreased by 60°, so when you repeat the RDF observation you find 330 psc or 321T. You plot the second bearing line in a reciprocal direction, 180 + 321T = 141T, and label it 1640. Now you have two lines of position, as in Figure 8.10. Also, you know your vessel's motion during that interval is represented by an arrow pointing east and 4 nautical miles long. You can slide this arrow around the chart, always keeping it pointing in the same direction, until you find where it fits between the two LOPs. When you fit it in there, you will know how far from the beacon you are, because the difference between the directions of the LOPs can only be matched by one position of the arrow. The tip of the arrow is your location at 1640. It is a running fix.

This description was designed to show how the method of running fixes works, but it is not the easiest way to carry it out. In practice most pilots do something that is closer to Figure 8.11. Redraw Figure 8.10 with the two LOPs. First, look at the left-hand side of Figure 8.11. If you suppose you

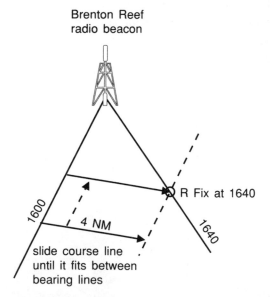

Brenton Reef
radio beacon

R Fix at 1640

1600

4 NM

1640

slide course line
until it fits between
bearing lines

Figure 8.10. You are sailing eastward and take two radio bearings of the Brenton Reef radio beacon at a 40-minute interval. These give the two LOPs corresponding to different times. You estimate you travelled 4 NM during that interval, so you construct an arrow and slide it until it just fits between the LOPs. The tip of the arrow is your running fix for 1640. See Figure 8.11 for an easier method of construction.

were at point A at 1600, then you must have been at point A' at 1640. But that point lies beyond the second LOP. On the other hand, if you assume your 1600 position was at B, your 1640 position would be B', which lies inside the second LOP. To find the correct assumption, merely draw a line between A' and B', as in the right-hand side of the figure. This line will intersect the second LOP at your 1640 position. It is called the "1600 LOP advanced to 1640."

Here is a summary of the method for the running fix with a single object illustrated in Figure 8.11.

1. Plot the LOP for 1600.

2. Estimate as accurately as possible the distance and direction travelled to the time of the second LOP (4 NM on course 090T).

3. Plot the second LOP (for 1640).

4. Advance the first LOP to the time of the second. Do this by selecting any two points on the first LOP; draw arrows from these points indicating the distance travelled in the interval; draw a line between the tips of the two arrows. This is the advanced LOP.

The intersection of this advanced LOP with the second LOP is your running fix at 1640.

Second method: Bearings of two objects—If you lost contact with the radio beacon after the first LOP, you might still be able to use that LOP if you sighted another object at a later time and advanced the first LOP to the time of the second. Nothing about the method requires that the two object be the same, as long as you can identify them on the chart.

Figure 8.12 shows an example. After making the second observation of the Brenton Reef radio beacon at 1640, you sailed an hour at 6 knots on a slightly altered course 080T (allowing for the set of the tide). You were then able to glimpse the flagpole on Newport Neck and obtain a bearing of 000T at 1740. Plotting both LOPs and then advancing the first by the distance travelled you were able to obtain a running fix. The depth sounder verified your expected water depth at that point.

Uncertainty of the fix—The resulting fix has an uncertainty that depends on your ability to estimate the distance travelled between the two observa-

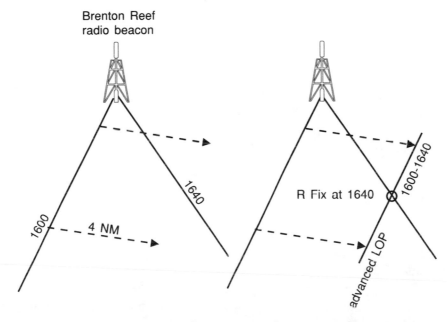

Figure 8.11. Running fix by two bearings of the Brenton Reef radio beacon. The left part of the figure shows the two lines of position observed 40 minutes apart, at 1600 and 1640. From two points on the first line of position (LOP), construct arrows showing the distance and direction travelled in the 40-minute interval. Draw the advanced LOP as a dashed line through the tips of the arrows, as shown in the right-hand diagram. Label it with the two times and find your running fix at 1640 as the intersection with the second LOP.

tions. This uncertainty will slide the advanced LOP forward and back slightly and shift the intersection of the two LOPs. This is illustrated in Figure 8.13, where the uncertainty in the estimated distance is indicated by the small error circle and the resulting uncertainty in the fix is indicated by the heavy line.

The size of the error of the final fix depends on the direction of the second bearing line relative to the first. If the two are nearly perpendicular to each other, the uncertainty of the fix will be about the same size as the error circle. If the second bearing line is nearly parallel to the first, the running fix is weak, because the uncertainty will be very large in a direction perpendicular to the course. So it pays to think of the geometry of the intersection when selecting objects for a fix.

Try to select objects so the two lines of position are nearly perpendicular to each other. This simple rule will lead to the best results when dealing with bearing lines or range lines. If you follow this rule, you may take comfort in knowing you will obtain the best accuracy that the conditions permit.

INTRODUCTION TO TRIANGLES

If you are sailing on a straight line along a coast and can identify a charted object broad on the bow (see Figure 4.13 if you have forgotten the meaning of this phrase), you can quite easily obtain a running fix if you estimate distance travelled. As a preparation for understanding the methods—and so you can invent other methods for yourself—it is helpful to study a bit about triangles and the angles that compose them.

Some properties of triangles

Figure 8.14 shows the *interior angle* and *turning angle* at the vertex, C. The turning angle is the amount you must turn at a vertex if you wish to walk along the next side of the triangle.

PRETEST
8.10 What are your predictions for the three questions below?

What is the sum of A + A'?
90° ____ 180° ____ 270° ____ 360° ____ Other ____
What is the sum of A + B + C?
90° ____ 180° ____ 270° ____ 360° ____ Other ____
What is the sum of A' + B' + C'?
90° ____ 180° ____ 270° ____ 360° ____ Other ____

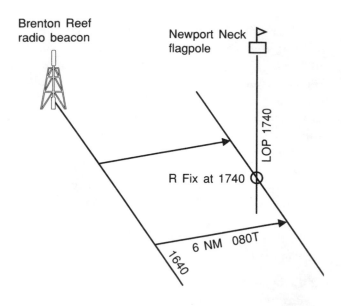

Figure 8.12. For a running fix, the two lines of position need not be measured to the same object.

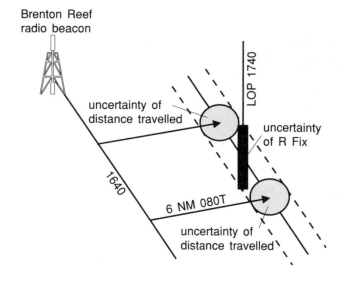

Figure 8.13. After an hour's travel, the best estimate of the distance travelled is indicated by the line and the uncertainty is represented by the small circle. The advanced line of position must pass through a point inside this circle, but you do not know which point. You assume it passes through the center and attach an uncertainty equal to the size of the circle. This is reflected as an uncertainty in the fix indicated by the heavy short line. The amount of uncertainty will depend on the angles with which the LOPs intersect.

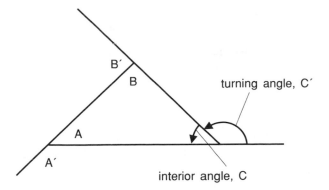

Figure 8.14. Interior angles, A, B, and C, and the corresponding turning angles, A', B', C'.

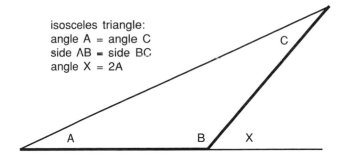

isosceles triangle:
angle A = angle C
side AB = side BC
angle X = 2A

Figure 8.15. In this isosceles triangle, the angles at A and C are equal, and the sides AB and BC are equal. As described in the text, this can be constructed by drawing AB, constructing angle A (22° in this figure) and then constructing angle X so that is it twice as great as A.

Measure the first sum with a protractor. Then find the second and third sum by tracing the figure and cutting out the triangle with a pair of scissors. Then cut apart the vertices so you can lay the angles together at a common vertex. What do they form? (Before you cut, plan ahead so you don't lose the turning angles.)

Property 1—At each vertex, the sum of the interior angle and the turning angle makes a straight line. At vertex C, for example, the sum of the turning angle, C', and the interior angle, C, obeys: C + C' = 180°—as they make a straight line.

Property 2— The sum of the three turning angles in any plane triangle is 360°. That is, A' + B' + C' = 360. Proof: Imagine walking along the sides of the triangle in Figure 8.14. At each vertex, the exterior angle is the amount you must turn to walk along the next side. By the time you have walked past the three angles, you will have turned through a full circle or 360°.

Property 3—The sum of the three interior angles in any plane triangle is 180°; thus, A + B + C = 180. Proof: From Property 2: A' + B' + C' = 360. From Property 1: A' = 180 – A, B' = 180 – B, C' = 180 – C. Substituting these into the first expression gives: 180 – A + 180 – B + 180 – C = 360. With a little rearranging, 540 – 360 = 180 = A + B + C. QED.

Constructing an isosceles triangle

An isosceles triangle is one in which two or more sides are equal. Figure 8.15 shows an isosceles triangle in which angles A and C are equal. The sides opposite these angles are shown in heavier lines; they are of equal length.

The following method of constructing this figure is the basis for the piloting method known as "doubling the angle off the bow."

- *Step 1*—Draw the side AB, making it 3 inches long.

- *Step 2*—Lay off an angle A, say 22°, as in the figure. Draw a line in the direction of the second side AC. You don't know how long that side is yet.

- *Step 3*—At B, measure an angle that is twice as great as A, 45°, and draw the side BC to intersect the third side.

This will give an isosceles triangle, and side BC will also be 3 inches.

EXERCISES

8.11 Use a protractor to verify these rules about the sums of the exterior and interior angles in the triangles shown below. Determine the average accuracy of your measurements.

8.12 Carry out the construction of Figure 8.15 and verify that the heavy sides are equal.

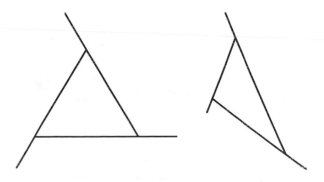

Figure 8.16.

TECHNIQUES DEPENDENT ON TRIANGLES

Distance off by doubling the angle off the bow

Now you are ready to put your knowledge of triangles to use. Referring to Figure 8.17, suppose you are sailing along a coast, and you see a tower that is 45° off the port bow at 1415 according to your watch. Then 30 minutes later, at 1445, you notice the tower is 90° off the bow.

You construct in your mind a right triangle and notice that the two shorter sides are the same length. So the distance run is the same as your distance from the object at 1445. If your speed was 8 knots, your run in 30 minutes was 4 NM, and this is your distance from the tower at 1445. Now you can draw a circle centered on the tower with a radius of 4 NM. This is a circle of position.

If you are sailing a straight track, the distance run while the angle off the bow doubles is equal to the distance from the object to the vessel at the end of the run. This same relationship holds any time you double the angle on the bow.

Figure 8.18 shows another example. This time the angles are 30° and 60°. Any such pair will work (such as 16° and 32°; 23° and 46°). It gives you the distance from an object, even if you don't know what the true or magnetic bearing is. All you need to do is sail a straight line and measure the relative bearings at two times, and this will give you a circle of position.

You can also do it for objects that have already been passed, as the actual direction of motion of the ship does not affect the figure.

And there is a bonus if you measure the magnetic heading of the boat as it sails along the straight line. Add the boat's heading to the relative bearing of the object. This will give you the magnetic bearing of the object and you will then be able to plot a line of position. Here's the formula; it works for true or magnetic values.

Bearing of LOP = heading of boat +
relative bearing of object

Plot the LOP from the object, then measure off a distance equal to your run, and you have a secondary fix. Figure 8.19 is an example.

This method is so easy you should use it frequently as a check on your dead reckoning.

POSTTEST

8.13 You are sailing on a course 060T and observe Brenton Reef Horn at a relative bearing of 30° off the port bow (Figure 8.1). After sailing 1.5 NM you find that the relative bearing has changed to 60° off the port bow. Draw a circle of position from the horn and plot the line of position to find your running fix. What should the approximate depth of the water be at your location?

Distance abeam by two angles and run

Here is a variation on the previous theme. It uses Table 8.1, which gives pairs of angles. The result is distance abeam—in a direction at right angles to the lubber's line (Figure 4.13)—rather than distance off.

While sailing on a straight course, you notice a fixed object at a relative bearing, 30°. You note the time to the nearest second and estimate the speed of your vessel. Then you wait until the bearing has increased to 54°. Again noting the time, you estimate the distance run during that interval, using the table T1 in Appendix 3. Suppose you find that you have run 2 NM between the two sightings. The two angles in this example (30° and 54°) were chosen from Table 8.1, so the distance abeam equals the distance run. This means that the object will be 2 NM from the vessel when the object comes abeam (Figure 8.20). Or, to put it another way, if you ex-

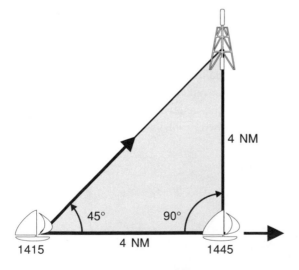

Figure 8.17. At 1415 the tower was 45° off the bow. After you have sailed 4 NM you find that it is 90° off the bow. By the geometry of isosceles triangles, you know you are 4 NM from the tower at the time of the second observation.

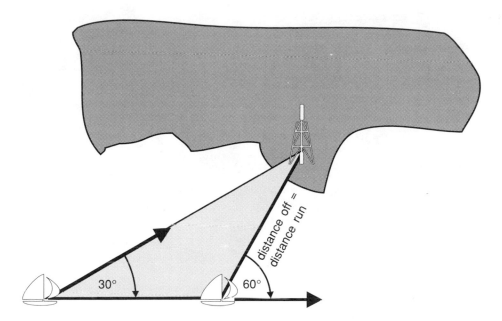

Figure 8.18. Another example of doubling the angle off the bow. In this case the first angle was 30° and the second was 60°. Again, the length of the run in the interval is equal to the distance from the object at the end of the run. This relationship holds for any such pair of angles. Notice the actual direction of motion of the vessel has no effect on the geometry, so this method can be applied to objects that have already been passed (see Figure 8.19).

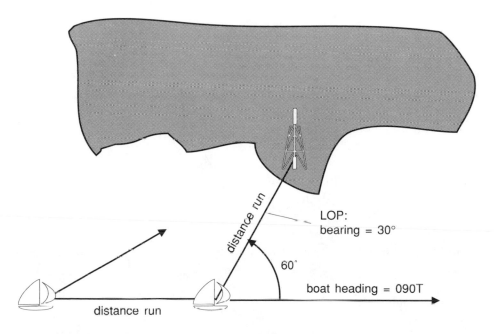

Figure 8.19. Obtaining an LOP and a secondary fix after doubling the angle on the bow (see Figure 8.18). The bearing of the LOP from the tower is determined by adding the heading of the boat to the relative bearing of the tower. The known distance off (Figure 8.18) establishes the secondary fix.

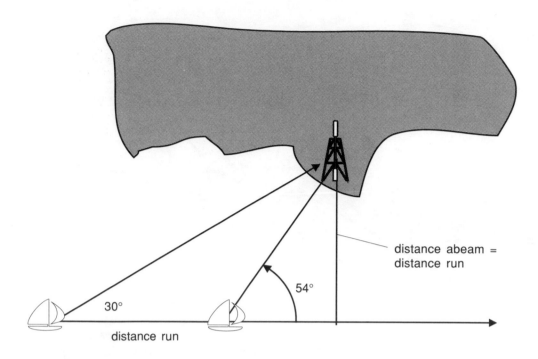

Figure 8.20. Determining distance abeam by two angles and distance run. The navigator sees an object at 30° off the port bow and notes the time. At a later time, the object is seen at 54° off the port bow. The distance run between the two sightings is the distance to the object when the object comes directly abeam. Table 8.1 and Figure 8.21 give other pairs of angles for which this equality holds. If the true bearing of the object is known, the LOP may be drawn and a running fix will be obtained.

tend your course line to the point where the object is directly abeam, it will pass exactly 2 NM from the object.

Figure 8.21 is a graph of Table 8.1; it can be used for odd angles that are not included in the table.

The distance abeam can be used to find a secondary fix if the magnetic (or true) heading of the ship is known so the true bearing of the object may be calculated. To find the magnetic (or true) orientation of the object simply add the relative bearing to the heading of the boat.

$$\text{Bearing of LOP} = \text{heading of boat} + \text{relative bearing}$$

Draw a line with this orientation from the charted object and mark off the distance, D. That is your running fix.

Table 8.1. Pairs of angles (B1, B2) off the bow giving distance abeam equal to run

B1	B2	B1	B2
20	30	50	99
22	34	52	102
24	39	54	105
26	44	56	108
28	49	58	111
30	54	60	113
32	59	62	115
34	64	64	117
36	69	66	119
38	74	68	121
40	79	70	122
42	84	72	124
44	88	74	125
46	92	76	127
48	96	80	129

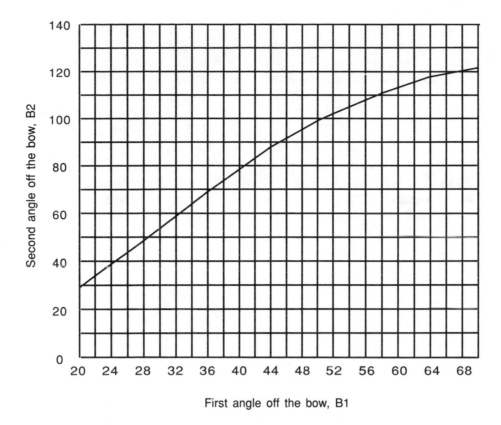

Figure 8.21. Graph of the angles listed in Table 8.1 for determining distance abeam from two relative bearings, B1 and B2, and distance run.

USING DEPTH CONTOURS

Line of Position

Depth sounders are not only useful in avoiding dangerously shallow water. They can also provide you a good line of position. Read the depth sounder, then pull out your charts showing the depth contours where you are sailing. You are directly above the contour (or one of the contours) labelled with the depth you just measured. Suppose you are south of Newport Neck (Figure 8.1) due east of the tank on Judith Neck and sailing 090T in about 100–110 feet of water. You notice the water begin to get shallower, and when the depth decreases to 90 feet, you can make a good estimate of your position on the chart.

The contour on a chart for a particular depth is probably long and devious, but with a single bearing on a charted object you can often get a reliable fix. An example is shown schematically in Figure 8.22, where water depth is used with a range line to determine an approximate fix. (The fix is approximate because the water-depth measurement may

be affected by tide, list of the boat, or irregularity of the bottom.)

In some cases, the contours make closed loops and the solution is ambiguous. There will be more than one location that will lie on the LOP at the indicated depth. In this case, you may have to abandon the method and use the depth contours

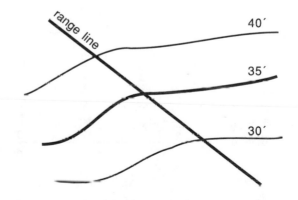

Figure 8.22. Using depth contour for a line of position. If your depth sounder says you are in 35 feet of water, you may locate yourself on the chart contour by crossing it with a second line of position, such as a range line.

merely to test a fix determined by other methods. If the depth is not what the chart suggests it ought to be, look for the cause of the discrepancy. You can assume the chart is correct and you have goofed somewhere along the line.

Running fix

Your depth-sounder may come in handy when you are in the fog and can't obtain a second line of position; a variety of tricks have been described by Tom Vesey (*Cruising World,* October 1989, p. 33). In a letter to the editor (*Cruising World,* February 1990, p. 9), Robert Wendt describes a method for obtaining a running fix from a series of depth measurements

and a process called bottom-contour matching. It is illustrated in Figure 8.23 and works as follows.

Set your vessel on a fixed heading and move with a constant and known (or estimated) speed through the water. With a stopwatch, you can note the depth of the water every minute and write it in a small table. Do this until the depth has changed significantly; then stop the boat to give yourself time for some chartwork. First, compute how far the boat has moved from the first depth point at the time of each successive depth sounding. (Look back at Chapter 4 if you need reminding how to do this.)

Now make a graph showing the depth along your track. To do this, take a separate piece of pa-

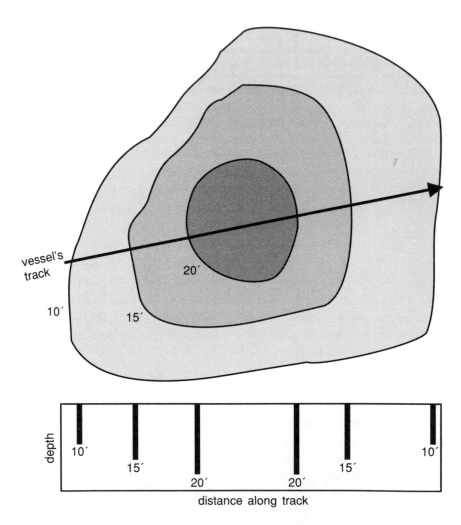

Figure 8.23. *You may obtain a running fix by using the profile of depth obtained from your sounder. As described in the text, make a profile of the bottom while the vessel moves along a known direction. Mark the contours on a ruler made from a separate piece of paper (below) and orient it in the direction of the vessel's track. Then slide it around the chart until the depths coincide with those on the chart.*

per and draw a straight line representing your track over the bottom. Using the distance scale of your chart, mark off the locations of your depth-soundings as accurately as you can, and then draw a series of perpendicular lines whose lengths represent the depths of the water at each point. For these depths, you will use a much larger scale, say 10 feet to the inch. Draw a smooth curve through the ends of the depth lines to make the depth profile you want to compare with the chart.

As you can see, unknown currents will falsify the method, as will a perfectly flat bottom beneath you. But with a little luck you will find some useful variation of depth. To make the comparison between your measures and the depths on the chart you first look for the depths that are plotted as contours on your chart. Suppose the contour interval is 15 feet. Then mark the track of the vessel at each place where the depth profile crossed one of the contour depths: 15, 30, etc. (If there are no depth contours, you will have to use the numbers themselves.) Take a pair of scissors and cut along the track, making a little ruler with the contour crossings marked. Then orient this ruler on the chart in the chosen heading of your vessel's track and slide it around until you find a place where the marks can be made to coincide with the contours. In principle, this will be the true location of your vessel, but success depends on accurate measurements and an uneven bottom. Try it sometime before you are caught in a fog. This will help improve your technique, and you may be encouraged to try it when you really need it.

DANGER BEARING

Several types of critical situations can arise when piloting near a shore or among boats. The boat can enter on a collision course with another boat, or it can be set by a current so that it runs onto shoals despite the fact that it appears to be heading into safe water. A few simple tricks will help you spot such situations before they become disastrous.

These techniques require measuring the direction of the danger at several times, and *it is far safer to use magnetic (or compass) bearings than relative bearings.* The reason is very simple. The true heading of the boat can change from one moment to the next—especially in moderate and heavy seas—and this will affect the relative bearing of the danger and possibly lead to confusion.

Constant bearing means collision

The navigator and helmsperson should always be on the lookout for an object whose bearing does not change. If the object is a stationary one, it is in the boat's path. If the object is a moving boat, then it is on a collision course. On the other hand, bearings that change with time indicate that the two objects will probably pass safely. The different situations are illustrated in Figures 8.24 through 8.27. Study them carefully and exercise *constant vigilance!*

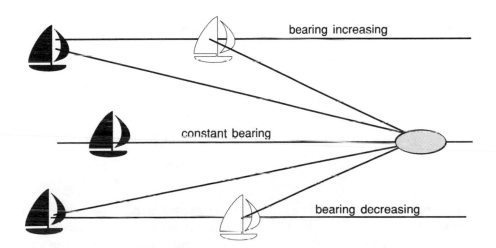

Figure 8.24. When approaching a stationary object such as a shoal, if that object holds a constant bearing from your ship, you are going to hit it. On the other hand, if the bearing increases, you will leave the obstacle to starboard; if the bearing decreases, you will leave it to port.

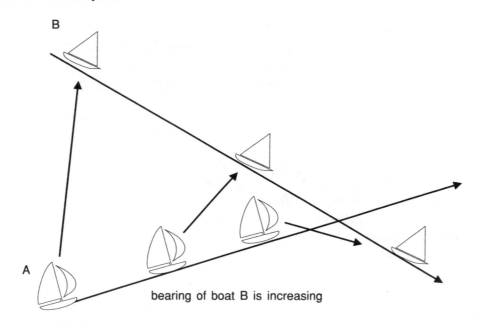

Figure 8.25. In this example, boat B is moving down toward the right. As seen from boat A, the bearing of boat B increases steadily, and the helmsperson knows that boat B will pass safely in front of the bow. Compare with Figures 6.21 and 6.22.

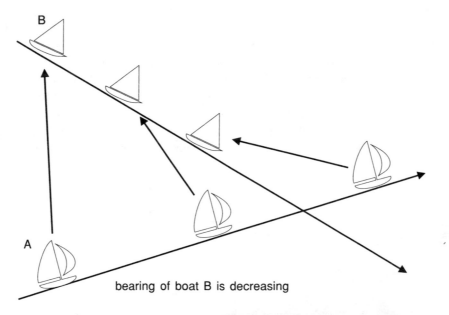

Figure 8.26. The bearing of boat B steadily decreases and boat A passes safely ahead of it. Compare with Figure 8.27.

Establishing and using a danger bearing
Suppose you are sailing near an invisible shoal in a tidal current. You see an island off the port, but are not sure where the current is taking you. You need a simple and sure method of avoiding the shoal. Or you are sailing near an unlit island at night. Ahead you see a charted light, but the island lurks invis-

ibly somewhere off to port. How can you be sure you have not been set dangerously close to the island?

Danger bearings provide an answer in both situations. The first step is to get out your chart and mark your estimated position. It need not be precise, just an indication of your position, taking into account the magnetic bearing of the visible mark—

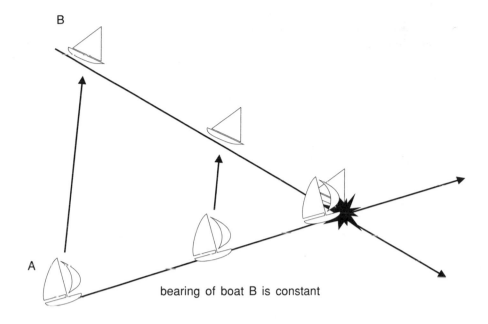

bearing of boat B is constant

Figure 8.27. "Constant bearing means collision." If the helmsperson sees a moving boat whose bearing does not change, a collision is in the making.

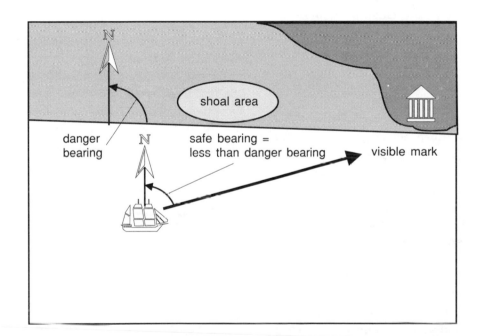

Figure 8.28. The danger line from a visible mark to the dangerous object is the boundary between safe and dangerous waters. In this case, the navigator must be sure the bearing of the mark remains less than the danger bearing. In this way, dangers may be avoided without the need for fixes.

the light or the island. Suppose it is a light and you have identified it on your chart using the characteristics described in the next section of this chapter. Put one edge of your ruler over the mark and swing the ruler until the edge comes between you and the danger, as in Figure 8.28. This is the *danger line,* and its orientation is the *danger bearing.* Measure the bearing with the compass rose and mark it on the danger line, remembering to indicate *true* or *magnetic.*

This danger bearing will warn you of the danger. No matter what your heading or the nature of the current, if you monitor the magnetic (or true) bearing of the visible mark you can be sure you are in safe water as long as the measured bearing remains less than the danger bearing. (Depending on the location of the boat, the safe bearing may in some cases be *greater* than the danger bearing. You can tell whether it should be greater or less than the danger bearing from the relative locations of the visible mark, the danger, and your estimated position.)

The technique of danger bearings avoids the need for fixes. All that's needed is a glance at the compass to determine the bearing of the visible mark.

PILOTING AT NIGHT

The nature of the task

The principles of night piloting are no different from those of day piloting, but the practice can be quite different. Most of the clues that pilots use during the day are lost or altered at night. Land masses are vaguely outlined and barely visible against a pale sky; all buoy lights look more or less white and are mixed with lights from shore; the waves all but vanish in the gloom.

Experience is the best teacher. Awareness of buoys, lights, and depth contours are the best guides unless your boat is equipped with radar. At night, the prudent pilot's time is largely spent updating a dead reckoning position, attempting to identify lights, and verifying the water depth. Few tasks are more difficult than attempting to locate oneself at night when the DR position has not been updated adequately. We have already discussed DR plotting, so the focus of this section will be on the identification of lights.

Color of the light is seldom a help, as the long-range lights are usually white, and colors fade in faint light. Red sensitivity is relatively enhanced at night, but faint green lights are particularly difficult to see. White lights at a great distance tend to look yellow or orange, while red is often confused with white.

In a brightly lit cabin, the sensitivity of your eyes is greatly reduced; you will need to spend at least 10-15 minutes on a dark deck before their sensitivity is reasonably recovered. Wearing dark red glasses while in the cabin and using red flashlights while on deck will help a great deal. Covering the cabin lights with red cellophane will preserve night vision.

Bright lights at great distances are often confused with faint lights close at hand. (As an extreme example, think how much brighter the moon looks to us than the light of a distant street lamp!) Do not attempt to judge distance by brightness alone.

Approaching a light

The pilot's world is circumscribed by the horizon, imposed by the fact that the earth is spherical. Objects of different height are treated differently by the horizon. Tall objects may be seen at greater distances; pilots on a high bridge can see farther than those near the water. If you ignore atmospheric bending of light (which you may do if you do not fly upward a mile or two in an airplane), the idea of the distance to the horizon is not difficult to visualize.

Geographical range—This is the distance that a straight line goes from the navigator's eye to become tangent to the surface. Every navigator has a horizon whose distance depends on height of eye above the surface of the water. (Let us ignore waves for a moment.)

Figure 8.29 shows a ray from a lighthouse to a navigator's eye at the moment when the lighthouse

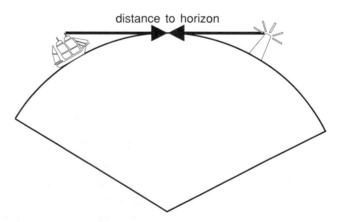

Figure 8.29. Arrows indicate distances to horizon for sailor standing in small boat and for light house. The higher the object, the greater the distance to the horizon. The sum of the two distances is the geographical range of the light for this sailor.

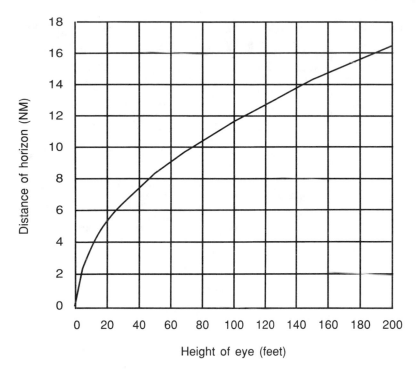

Figure 8.30. The distance to the horizon increases with the square root of height of eye.

is exactly on the navigator's horizon. The ray goes from the lighthouse to the navigator by just grazing the surface of the ocean, so the distance to the lighthouse is the sum of the distances to the sailor's horizon and the lighthouse's horizon. This depends on the height of both objects and it is called the *geographical range* of the lighthouse for this navigator.

Table 8.2 and Figure 8.29 give distance to horizon for various heights. As the reader may verify, the distance in nautical miles may be estimated from the height in feet by use of the following formula:

Distance to horizon (NM) =
1.17 × square root of height (feet)

As an example of this formula, suppose you are 16 feet above the water. The distance to the horizon is 4.7 NM according to the table, while the formula gives 1.17 × 4 = 4.68 NM That's good agreement.

The implication of this rule is important. The distance to the horizon does not increase proportionally to the navigator's height, but as its square root. So, to double the distance of the horizon, the navigator must ascend to 4 times the original height.

Table 8.2. Distance to horizon (adapted from *Bowditch*, Table 8)

Height Feet	Distance NM	Height Meters
1	1.2	0.30
2	1.7	0.61
4	2.3	1.22
8	3.3	2.44
12	4.1	3.66
16	4.7	4.88
24	5.7	7.32
32	6.6	9.75
40	7.4	12.2
50	8.3	15.2
60	9.1	18.3
70	9.8	21.3
80	10.5	24.4
90	11.1	27.4
100	11.7	30.5
150	14.3	45.7
200	16.5	61.0

This table may be used to determine the geographical range of a lighthouse. Suppose the lighthouse is 70 feet high (measured from the water

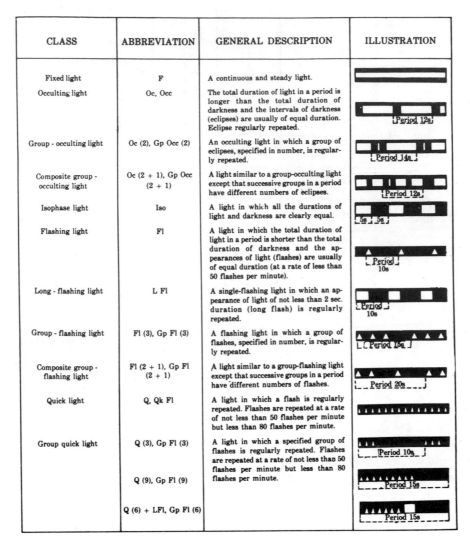

CLASS	ABBREVIATION	GENERAL DESCRIPTION	ILLUSTRATION
Fixed light	F	A continuous and steady light.	
Occulting light	Oc, Occ	The total duration of light in a period is longer than the total duration of darkness and the intervals of darkness (eclipses) are usually of equal duration. Eclipse regularly repeated.	Period 12s
Group - occulting light	Oc (2), Gp Occ (2)	An occulting light in which a group of eclipses, specified in number, is regularly repeated.	Period 14s
Composite group - occulting light	Oc (2 + 1), Gp Occ (2 + 1)	A light similar to a group-occulting light except that successive groups in a period have different numbers of eclipses.	Period 12s
Isophase light	Iso	A light in which all the durations of light and darkness are clearly equal.	5s 5s
Flashing light	Fl	A light in which the total duration of light in a period is shorter than the total duration of darkness and the appearances of light (flashes) are usually of equal duration (at a rate of less than 50 flashes per minute).	Period 10s
Long - flashing light	L Fl	A single-flashing light in which an appearance of light of not less than 2 sec. duration (long flash) is regularly repeated.	Period 10s
Group - flashing light	Fl (3), Gp Fl (3)	A flashing light in which a group of flashes, specified in number, is regularly repeated.	Period 15s
Composite group - flashing light	Fl (2 + 1), Gp Fl (2 + 1)	A light similar to a group-flashing light except that successive groups in a period have different numbers of flashes.	Period 20s
Quick light	Q, Qk Fl	A light in which a flash is regularly repeated. Flashes are repeated at a rate of not less than 50 flashes per minute but less than 80 flashes per minute.	
Group quick light	Q (3), Gp Fl (3)	A light in which a specified group of flashes is regularly repeated. Flashes are repeated at a rate of not less than 50 flashes per minute but less than 80 flashes per minute.	Period 10s
	Q (9), Gp Fl (9)		Period 15s
	Q (6) + LFl, Gp Fl (6)		Period 15s

Figure 8.31a. Light phase characteristic. (Reprinted from Bowditch*)*

level at the moment), and you are 16 feet above the water. You look up the corresponding distances to the horizon and add them, according to the following expression:

Geographical range = distance to horizon of navigator + distance to horizon of object

In this example, you find geographical range = 9.8 + 4.7 = 14.5 NM If the navigator is only 8 feet off the water, the geographical range is reduced to 9.8 + 3.3 = 13.1 NM. This relatively minor reduction is a result of the much greater height of the lighthouse.

Loom of a light—On a dark, fogless night, when a light is beyond its geographical range, the navigator may glean a clue to its location by the faint glow it produces in the atmosphere. This is the loom of the light and it consists of light that has been scattered helter-skelter by the atmospheric molecules. The loom is brightest in the direction of the light, and with a little care, the navigator may take a bearing on it. Of course, this assumes you are able to identify the light without seeing it. Coastal towns may be located by their loom before they are in a direct line of vision.

Fix by bobbing a light on the horizon—In an article on nighttime navigation in *Ocean Navigator* (Jan./Feb. 1989, p. 64), Gregg Walsh describes a useful technique for estimating the distance of a light that is close to its geographical range. As soon as the light becomes visible over the horizon (or shortly before it is due to vanish over the horizon), the navigator bobs up and down a distance of 3 or 4

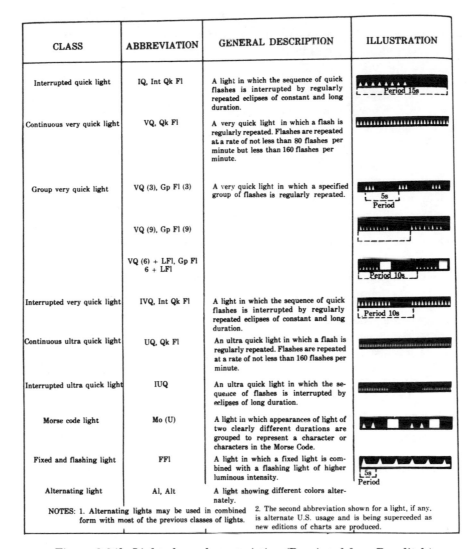

CLASS	ABBREVIATION	GENERAL DESCRIPTION	ILLUSTRATION
Interrupted quick light	IQ, Int Qk Fl	A light in which the sequence of quick flashes is interrupted by regularly repeated eclipses of constant and long duration.	
Continuous very quick light	VQ, Qk Fl	A very quick light in which a flash is regularly repeated. Flashes are repeated at a rate of not less than 80 flashes per minute but less than 160 flashes per minute.	
Group very quick light	VQ (3), Gp Fl (3)	A very quick light in which a specified group of flashes is regularly repeated.	
	VQ (9), Gp Fl (9)		
	VQ (6) + LFl, Gp Fl 6 + LFl		
Interrupted very quick light	IVQ, Int Qk Fl	A light in which the sequence of quick flashes is interrupted by regularly repeated eclipses of constant and long duration.	
Continuous ultra quick light	UQ, Qk Fl	An ultra quick light in which a flash is regularly repeated. Flashes are repeated at a rate of not less than 160 flashes per minute.	
Interrupted ultra quick light	IUQ	An ultra quick light in which the sequence of flashes is interrupted by eclipses of long duration.	
Morse code light	Mo (U)	A light in which appearances of light of two clearly different durations are grouped to represent a character or characters in the Morse Code.	
Fixed and flashing light	FFl	A light in which a fixed light is combined with a flashing light of higher luminous intensity.	
Alternating light	Al, Alt	A light showing different colors alternately.	

NOTES: 1. Alternating lights may be used in combined form with most of the previous classes of lights. 2. The second abbreviation shown for a light, if any, is alternate U.S. usage and is being superceded as new editions of charts are produced.

Figure 8.31b. Light phase characteristics. (Reprinted from Bowditch)

feet. If the light appears and disappears, then its distance is somewhere between the geographical ranges corresponding to the two heights. This distance can be used for a fix if you measure the magnetic bearing of the light, draw the corresponding line of position on a chart, and mark off the distance to the light.

For example, suppose a lighthouse is 70 feet above sea level, as in the previous example. If you can make the light disappear and reappear by bobbing up and down between heights of 8 and 12 feet, then the distance of the light is between 9.8 + 3.3 = 13.1 NM and 9.8 + 4.1 = 13.9 NM. This is an excellent determination, and the navigator should constantly be watching for the chance to use it.

One good way to prepare your chart for night piloting is to draw a circle around important lights

with a radius equal to the visual range of the light for a height that is typical of your boat. This will help you know which lights to be looking for, and it will alert you to the possibility of bobbing a helpful light. The next section tells how to determine the visual range.

Recognizing navigational lights

The characteristics of each light are listed on the chart where it appears, and they are given in full detail in its *Light List* entry. In addition to its identification number, the characteristics of a light fall into two categories:

Phase characteristics—These define the pattern of flashing that will be seen by the navigator at night. (Most lights are turned off during daylight.) An example is Fl(2) 10s, which states there are two flashes in a period of 10 seconds. Figures 8.31a and 8.31b provide a summary, and details can be found in *Bowditch,* Chapters IV and V.

General characteristics—These are the color, height, and range at which a light can normally be seen under good conditions. For each light, there are four types of range that are defined by *Bowditch:*

1. The *nominal range* is the maximum distance at which the light can be seen in clear weather (with at least 10 NM visibility) assuming a sufficient height of eye.

2. The *luminous range* is the maximum distance the light can be seen under existing visibility conditions. It takes no account of the height of light or of navigator nor of background lights that might interfere.

3. The *geographical range* is the distance to the horizon from the light at its height above mean high water. This is the maximum distance you could see the light if you were swimming.

4. The *visual range* of a light is the maximum distance you will see the light under existing conditions from your height of eye.

A typical set of characteristics might look as follows:

Property	Example	Meaning
Color	R	red
Height	16m	16 meters, above mean high water unless otherwise stated on chart
Nominal range	16M	16 nautical miles

Determining the visual range of a light from your boat on a particular night

- *Step 1*—Estimate the luminous range from the nominal range and the quality of the visibility. (The visibility must be estimated from the appearance of the horizon during the day or from the appearance of the stars.) The luminous range will approach the nominal range under excellent conditions, but typically it will be 20 to 40 percent smaller if the visibility is good but not excellent.

- *Step 2*—Compute the geographical range for your boat by finding the distance to your horizon in Table 8.2 and adding it to the stated geographical range of the light.

- *Step 3*—Compare the luminous and the geographical ranges and take the *smaller.* This is the visual range of the light. It is the radius to use if you draw circles of visual range about the lights you will be passing at night.

CHAPTER NINE

The Sextant in Piloting

It became pretty obvious that my [plastic sextant] was defective. It was kind of like a warped record. Maybe it had been left in the sun one day. At that point I closed it up in its case and tossed it into the bottom of a locker and never touched it again . . . From that point on I became a perfect celestial navigator with total confidence . . . The amazing thing was that I could have been so dense over the first three thousand miles about not trying a different sextant.

Tania Aebi, quoted by Greg Walsh, in Ocean Navigator

INTRODUCTION

Now we get down to accurate measurement of angles with a modern sextant. This will be a key step in celestial navigation, but for the moment, we will concentrate on using the sextant to determine distances for coastwise navigation. This can provide valuable practice for sun shots, and it will eliminate a certain amount of fumbling in the dark when you come to twilight celestial navigation using star shots. A further advantage of starting to use the sextant in daytime piloting is that the requirement for precision is much more relaxed than it will be when you come to celestial navigation. In most coastal piloting techniques, it is sufficient to obtain 1° of precision, while you will try to do fifty times better when you take a shot at the sky.

The first sextants were constructed in 1730 by the Englishman John Hadley and by the American Thomas Godfrey. Until that time, navigators had measured the angular heights of stars with cross-staffs and astrolabes, and for a number of reasons—among them the need to look in two directions at once—they rarely did better than a degree or so. The sextant avoids the need to look at two places at once by the use of mirrors and partially silvered glass. These days, they cost anywhere from $50 in plastic to $1,000 or more in metal. For a long voyage, it is wise to carry more than one, and a plastic sextant makes an economical backup, although the plastic may tend to warp or break more easily than metal.

Figure 9.1 is a diagram of a typical sextant. It is meant to be held firmly with the right hand, while the left hand is used to adjust the scale and turn the micrometer drum. (Left-handed sextants are available.)

POSTTEST
9.1 How many mirrors are there in a typical sextant?
9.2 What was the sextant's advantage over older methods such as the cross-staff?

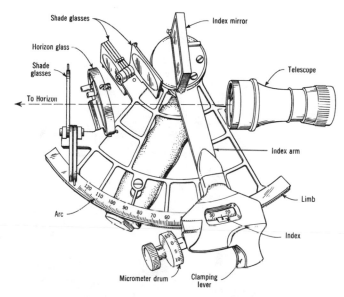

Figure 9.1. Diagram of a typical sextant, showing two mirrors. The upper mirror can be pivoted with the arm that hangs down. The lower mirror is half-silvered, so the horizon and a star may be seen at the same time.

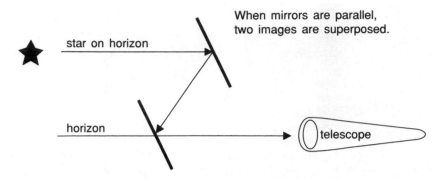

Figure 9.2a. Schematic diagram of sextant. Light from a star reflects off the pivoted mirror and then off the partially silvered fixed mirror into a telescope. Light from the horizon passes through the fixed mirror and enters the telescope, where it is compared with the star. When the mirrors are parallel, the light they send to the telescope comes from a single direction.

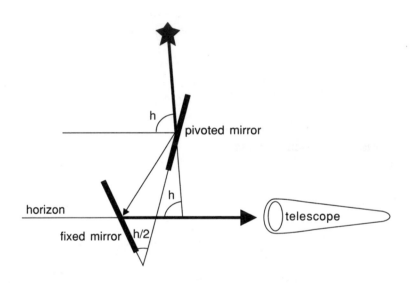

Figure 9.2b. The angle, h, of the star above the horizon is measured by pivoting the mirror until the star and the horizon are superposed. For each 1° above the horizon, the mirror is tilted ½°. Thus, the angle between the two mirrors is exactly one-half the angle between the light rays from the star and the horizon.

USING A SEXTANT

PRETEST

9.3 What is the meaning of index error?

9.4 How do you determine the size of index error?

9.5 How accurately should you try to read angles with a sextant?

Reading the angle

Figure 9.3 shows the window where the measured angle is read. The position of the arrow gives you a reading in degrees. Each division is one degree and you can interpolate to the nearest quarter of a degree, which is adequate for some piloting purposes. However, for celestial navigation and for determin-

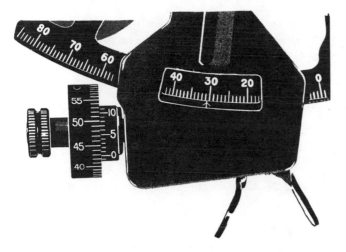

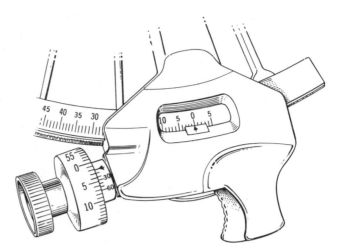

Figure 9.3. The sextant reading is 30°42.7'. (Courtesy Frederick L. Devereux, Jr., Practical Navigation for the Yachtsman, *New York: Norton, 1972)*

ing distances by angular size, you will need to read the sextant angle to the nearest minute of arc. The minutes are found on the micrometer drum to the left. In this case the reading is 30° 42.7'. (You can use the small vernier scale just to the right of the drum if you need to read to 0.1' of arc.)

Finding the index error

Whenever you use a sextant, your first act should be to determine the index error of the sextant. When you become familiar with the process, it will only take a few seconds and it may save you from a large error. Here are the steps.

- *Step 1*—Move the arm so the reading of the sextant is approximately 0°.

- *Step 2*—Hold the sextant in your right hand *vertically,* with the plane of the arc at a right angle to the plane of the horizon.

- *Step 3*—With the sextant vertical, look in the eyepiece at the distant horizon (or the roof of a building at least a quarter-mile away), and see two horizons in the field of the eyepiece—one in the clear glass portion, the other in the silvered half, of the horizon glass. (Some sextants do not split the horizon glass into two portions this way, but have the entire glass partially silvered. In this case you will see the two horizons superposed rather than side by side.)

- *Step 4*—Focus the eyepiece for clear images.

- *Step 5*—By turning the micrometer drum with your left hand, make the two horizons come directly in line

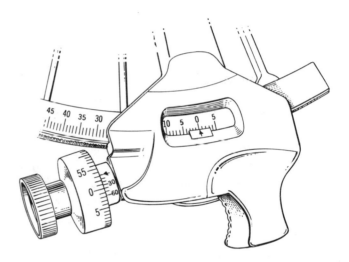

Figure 9.4. Reading the index error (IE) of two sextants. Top, The index error is about 2' on the arc. Bottom, The index error is a bit more than 3' off the arc and is determined by subtracting the drum reading from 60'.

with each other, so they form a single continuous line (or are exactly superposed).

- *Step 6*—Take the reading, which should be less than a degree for most sextants. Note that it may be *on the arc* (with the arrow on the positive side of 0°) or *off the arc* (with the arrow on the negative side of 0°). Always write "off" or "on" next to the number you have found, so you don't need to rely on your memory (Figure 9.4).

Applying the correction for index error

When the index error is *on the arc,* this means the 0° mark should be inside the scale. That is, the numbers you will read when you measure an angle will be a little too large. You should subtract the index error.

Rather than trying to figure out which way it goes each time, you may use a simple rule to remember whether to add or subtract the index error.

Rule for Index Error
If it's on (the arc) *it's off*—to be subtracted from your sextant reading. *If it's off* (the arc) *it's on*—to be added to your sextant reading.

For example: You read a sextant altitude (h_s) of 34°50′ and your index error (IE) is 2′ off the arc. The error is added, so the corrected reading is 34°52′.

POSTTEST
9.6 The sextant reads 49°03′ and the index error is 10′ on the arc. What is the corrected reading?

Sextant adjustment
Most instruments are subject to a small index error, and it does no harm, as long as you remember to correct for it. But if you find an index error greater than half a degree, your sextant probably needs adjusting. This is something you can learn to do for yourself, with a cautious approach, a small screwdriver, and guidance from an expert or a good book. There's little virtue in struggling to obtain a *zero* index error, because you'll still have to check it each time to make sure it is still zero. All that really matters is that the index error doesn't change in the midst of your observations.

Sextant backlash
If the micrometer for measuring minutes of arc is worn, you will find the drum moves a little without moving the two images in the telescope. It will feel loose. This is called "backlash." The way to avoid being bothered by it is to get into the habit of turning the drum *in the same direction* (clockwise or counterclockwise, whichever is handier for you) when you make the final reading. This way, its effect will be as harmless as an index error, and you will remove it automatically when you correct for index error.

Exercises with the sextant

Determining mast height—Find a boat tied to a dock and determine the height of its mast by mea-

suring its angular height with a sextant. (Preferably this will be a mast whose height you already know or can find by asking. A flagpole will also suffice, or a building.)

- *Step 1*—Mark a convenient place on the dock where you have a good view of the base and top of the mast and, if possible, the distant horizon beyond the boat (Figure 9.5).

- *Step 2*—Measure the distance from this spot to the mast.

- *Step 3*—Put a tape on the mast that is at the same height above water as your eye when you stand on the dock. (One way to do this is to have someone move a finger up and down the mast until it is exactly in line with the distant ocean horizon. Put a piece of tape there.)

- *Step 4*—Measure the angular height of the top of the mast above the tape.

- *Step 5*—With a protractor, ruler, and pencil, make an accurate drawing of the triangle defined by the tape, the top of the mast, and the location of your sextant using these measurements. Then measure the height on the diagram and convert it to true height using the scale of the diagram. Alternatively, you can use the tangent function on your calculator.

Measuring angles between stars—While you are getting used to the sextant by using it in the daytime, you might also want to start some night work. The trick is to know how well you are doing, and Commander Bauer comes to the rescue here. In his book, he has given a "Table of Interstellar Angles for Practice Sighting and Sextant Testing." A portion of this table is copied in Table 9.1. It gives angles between Vega and three stars in the same region of the sky.

Table 9.1. Angles between Vega and three stars

Arcturus	Deneb	Alkaid
59°06.5′	23°50.9′	51°01.0′

The first part of your task is to find these stars. Then check the index error and leave the sextant set for a very small angle. Point it toward Vega and tilt it toward the second star. Then slide the index arm out slowly until the second star comes into view. (Start with Deneb, as it is closest to Vega and

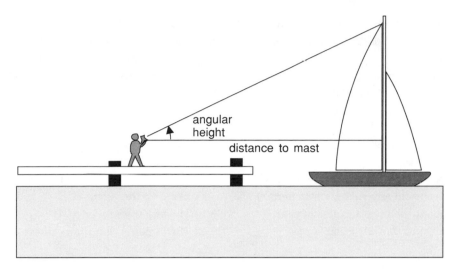

Figure 9.5. Setup for measuring the height of a mast near a dock. Determine the angle from the top of the mast to a point that is level with your sextant. Measure your distance from the mast and, using a convenient scale, plot the triangle with a protractor and ruler. You may then measure the height on the drawing.

will be easiest to find.) Make the same measures several times to get an idea of your personal accuracy.

Refraction will alter the measures a fraction of a degree, but if both stars are at the same altitude or are higher than 50° the effect will be negligible.

ESTIMATING DISTANCE BY ANGULAR SIZE

Now we get to the piloting. You can use your sextant to estimate distance to an object. You measure the angular size of the object and convert this to a distance-to-size ratio, then multiply by the known size to find the distance.

Angular size → distance-to-size ratio

× known size = distance

Here are the details:

- *Step 1*—From a chart or book find the true height of a visible object .

- *Step 2*—Measure the angular height of the object (remembering to apply the index correction).

- *Step 3a*—Using the angular height, find the distance-to-size ratio from the table in Chapter 1, and multiply by the known true height to find distance, or

- *Step 3b*—Alternatively, you may use Table 41 in *Bowditch*, which has columns for objects of different true heights, a portion of which is shown below. This will save you the need to multiply. The alert reader will notice a number of proportionalities among the entries in Table 9.2. For example, if the height of the object is 25 feet, its vertical angle is halved from 0°30′ to 0°15′ when its distance is doubled.

Table 9.2. Extract of Table 41, *Bowditch*: Distance in miles by vertical angle measured between bottom and top of object

	Height of object in feet							
	10	15	20	25	50	75	100	150
Angle								
0°15′	0.38	0.57	0.75	0.94	1.89	2.83	3.77	–
0°30′	0.19	0.28	0.38	0.47	0.94	1.41	1.89	2.83
0°45′	0.13	0.19	0.25	0.31	0.63	0.94	1.26	1.89
1°00′	–	0.14	0.19	0.24	0.47	0.71	0.94	1.41
2°00′	–	–	–	0.12	0.24	0.35	0.47	0.71

POSTTEST

Take a 6-inch dish and stand it on its edge. Then measure a distance of 25 feet. With your sextant determine the angular diameter of the object.

9.7 What angle should you expect?

9.8 What is the distance-to-size ratio of the dish?

9.9 Suppose you were to measure the angular size of a 12-inch dish and you found 0.25°. What is the distance?

9.10 With a sextant, measure the angular size of the moon as accurately as you can and determine its distance-to-size ratio. What value did you get? By doing this four or five times and comparing the results, you will be able to estimate the uncertainty of your measurements.

9.11 Measure the moon several times during the day and see whether you find any variation. In light of what you know about the uncertainties of your measures, do you think this variation is real?

FIX BY TWO HORIZONTAL ANGLES

Here is a very powerful way of fixing the location of your boat without depending on your compass. It may seem complicated at first, but it will become quite easy with a bit of practice.

Brief overview of the method

Identify three charted objects from your boat; hold your sextant horizontal and measure the angle between the left pair; then do the same for the right pair. On your chart, you will construct one circle of position from each of these angles. These two circles will intersect at two points (if you have done it correctly) and your location is one of the intersections.

The heart of the method is the construction of each circle of position, and before giving the rules, which you may follow slavishly if you wish, we will try to explain what lies behind them. If you understand this, you will be able to reinvent the method when you need it.

A Property of Angles in Circles—The property we will describe is at the heart of this piloting technique. In Figures 9.6a and b below, let O be the center of a circle; A, B, and C are three points on its perimeter.

PRETEST

By eye, compare the angles AOB (where the vertex is at the center) and ACB (where the vertex is at point C on the circle). What do you predict as the answer to these questions?

9.12 The larger angle is: AOB ____ ACB ____

9.13 The larger is how many times the other?

½ ____ 2 ____ 4 ____

Test your prediction by measuring the angles with a protractor.

∠AOB = ____° ∠ACB = ____° Ratio AOB/ACB = ____

9.14 If point C moves to the bottom of the circle as in Figure 9.6b, how will the angle ACB change?

increase ____ decrease ____

stay nearly the same ____

Pick a point near the bottom of the circle as a new C and check your prediction by measuring the new angle. The new one is:

bigger ____ same ____ smaller ____

Here is the rule governing the behavior of the angles inside the circle:

The angle AOB, as measured from the center, is twice the angle ACB as measured from any point on the circle.

Figure 9.7 shows an application of this rule. Use it a guide for this exercise.

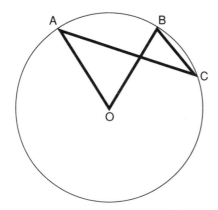

Figure 9.6a. Points A, B, and C are on the circle whose center is at O. What is the relation between the two angles AOB and ACB?

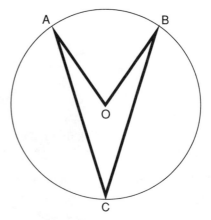

Figure 9.6b. What happens to the size of angle ACB when the point C moves to the far side of the circle? See pretest 9.12 through 9.14.

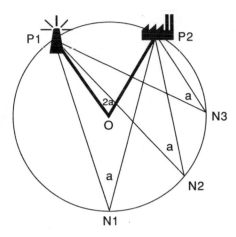

Figure 9.7. Three navigators at N1, N2, and N3 on a circle will measure the same value, a, for the horizontal angles between the points P1 and P2. This is the basis for the circle of position using a horizontal angle, as described in the text.

POSTTEST

9.15 Suppose three navigators (N1, N2, N3) are on a circle whose center is at O. If they each measure the horizontal angles, a, made by points P1 and P2 as seen from their locations, how will the values of the angles compare?

If you are not sure of the answer, do the exercise as follows: Draw two vertical marks to represent P1 and P2 about 2 feet apart on a blackboard (or use two poles stuck in the ground). Then get out your sextant and set it to read 10°; hold it horizontal and move to a point where the lines are superposed, indicating that they are 10° apart. Make a mark on the floor and, without changing the sextant setting, move to another spot where they are superposed again. In other words, play the roles of the three navigators. You should find that your positions lie on a circle. From the center of the circle, the two marks should be 20° apart.

This rule works both ways: Every navigator who finds the angle to be equal to a will be on the same circle; all navigators on the same circle passing through P1 and P2 will measure the same angle between them.

Figure 9.8a. First step: Draw a straight line between the first pair of charted points.

Thus, the circle whose center is at O will be a circle of position for any navigator who finds the value, a, for that horizontal angle.

Here is the way to use this rule if you wish to determine a fix by measuring the horizontal angle between two pairs of points.

Constructing the circle of position

Here are the steps to follow:

- **Step 1**—Find the first pair of points, P1 and P2, on the chart and draw a straight line between them, as in Figure 9.8a.

- **Step 2**—Suppose the horizontal angle is a. Draw two lines making an angle 90° − a with the line between the two points as shown in Figure 9.8b. Their intersection is the center of your first circle of position. (This construction makes the angle at O equal to a, as you can see if you remember that the sum of the interior angles in any triangle is 180°.)

- **Step 3**—With O as the center and the distance O-P1 as the radius, draw the first circle of position with a compass, giving a diagram like Figure 9.8c.

- **Step 4**—Repeat this process with the second pair of points, finding the second circle of position. You are at the intersection.

POSTTEST

9.16 On the chart in Figure 8.1, construct two circles of position from the following horizontal angles.

Between	Angle
Brenton Reef Horn and Flagpole on Newport Neck:	59°
Flagpole on Newport Neck and buoy BW "A" fl 3sec:	54°

What is your approximate position?

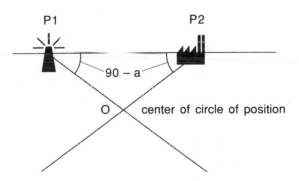

Figure 9.8b. Second step: Find the intersection of lines making an angle 90 − a with the line connecting the charted points whose horizontal angle is a.

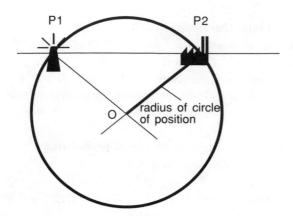

Figure 9.8c. Third step: Draw the first circle of position by starting with the pin of your compass at O and the pencil at P1 or P2.

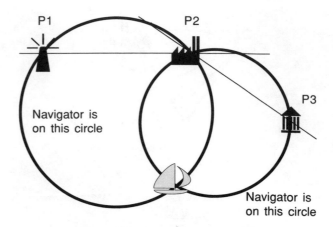

Figure 9.8d. Fourth step: Repeat the process for the second horizontal angle between another pair of points. One of the points may be the same as P2.

CHAPTER TEN

Tides and Currents

"The steamer went that way, and will come back that way. We must go inside over the sands. Am I dreaming, though? Can you possibly find the way?"

"I shouldn't wonder. But I don't believe you see the hitch. It's the *time* and the falling tide. High water was about 8.15; it's now 10.15, and all those sands are drying off. We must cross the See-Gat and strike that boomed channel, the Memmert Balje; strike it, freeze on it—can't cut off an inch—and pass that 'watershed' you see there before it's too late. It's an infernally bad one, I can see. Not even a dinghy will cross it for an hour each side of low water."

Erskine Childers, Riddle of the Sands

INTRODUCTION

The soundings given on charts for coastwise navigation tell the *depth* of the water at the time of *mean low water* (if not stated otherwise under the chart's title). If you add this to the *height* of the *tide* (height of the water above mean low water), you will know how deep the water is at each point on the chart. Compare this to the *draft* of your own vessel (depth to which the vessel reaches below the water surface) and you will know where you can go without danger of grounding—assuming that the tide is behaving normally. Figure 10.1 depicts a ship that draws 22 feet of water. The tide at this moment is 3 feet above the *datum*. (The datum is the reference level from which the tides are measured: usually the mean level at the time of low tide.) An obstruction on the bottom is charted at a depth of 21 feet below the datum. This makes the water depth 24 feet over the obstruction, giving the ship 2 feet of clearance. So the ship looks slightly worried.

PRETEST

10.1 Why are there two tides per day?

10.2 Why is the moon's tide so much larger than the sun's?

10.3 Are there places where only one tide occurs per day?

10.4 Why isn't there a tide in the middle of the ocean?

10.5 Why do the tides come at such different times in nearby ports?

The rise and fall of the surface water is the result of *tidal currents* that carry water hither and yon. Currents can be dangerous, if they carry your boat horizontally toward shallow water, and they can be helpful, when they speed you on your way. Knowledge of currents is vital. Among coastal waters, a tidal current—which can easily attain 2 knots—can deflect your course-made-good far astray from the apparent heading of the boat. It can also drift you ahead or behind the speed you may estimate by looking at the wake of your boat. Figure 10.2 shows a current flowing past a cluster of pilings, and Figure 10.3 shows that the velocity over the bottom is the sum of the ship's velocity through the water plus the velocity of the current.

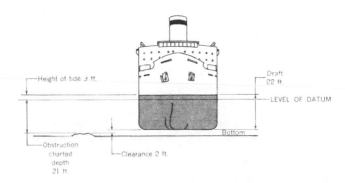

Figure 10.1. Tides and the ship (Bowditch). The droll face on this ship suggests a sense of humor in government publications. See text for an explanation of the level of datum.

Figure 10.2. Tidal currents can be visible when an object stands still in the water, as in the case of these pilings which are driven into the bottom. The ripple pattern can be used to estimate the speed of the current.

Figure 10.4 shows the pattern of tides in Long Island Sound, and it is clear that "constant vigilance" is the watchword when you are in such playgrounds of the tides.

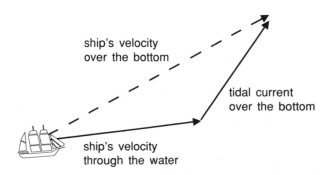

Figure 10.3. Vector diagram showing how the tidal current is added to the ship's velocity through the water to produce the net velocity over the bottom (dashed line).

TIDES

If the tides are a coastal pilot's nightmare, they can be a mathematician's dream. Behavior that appears capricious and erratic as esoteric jazz to some can seem a wonderfully syncopated song to another.

Isaac Newton taught us how to start understanding the tides, but the theory is still not fully developed. Fortunately for the pilot, the full theory is not needed. Just as a baseball player can learn to hit a pitched ball without understanding what Newton had to say about gravity and trajectories, mathematicians and pilots can predict tides by watching closely and practicing.

The present theory of tides can give a satisfactory answer to many of the fundamental questions:

- Why are there usually two tides per day? Because the tidal force of the moon pulls the sea *away* from the moon on the far side of the earth and *toward* the moon on the near side.

- Why is the moon's tide twice as great as the sun's? Because the sun, which has 27 million times as much mass as the moon, is 400 times as far from earth. This greater distance weakens the tidal force by a factor 1/64 million.

- Are there places with only one tide per day? Yes, for example, in the South China Sea and regions of the Pacific Ocean when the moon is farthest south in its orbit.

- Why isn't there a tide in the middle of the ocean? There is a tide, but it is too small to be noticed in the deep water.

- Why can the high tide be a half-hour later just a short way down the coast? The water takes time to flow from one place to another.

But these are not the crucial questions to a pilot. They do not keep the vessel out of danger. The crucial questions are such as these:

- When will low tide occur today?

- How high will the tide get tomorrow?

- Which way is the current flowing at this moment?

Exact answers to these questions are, in a practical sense, beyond today's theories. Although a supercomputer and a dedicated scientist might be

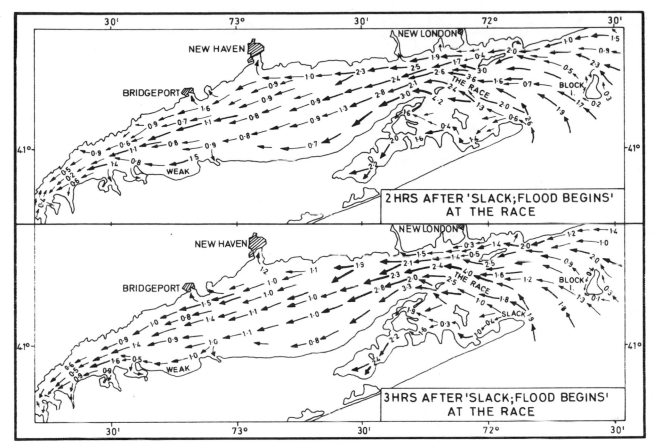

Velocities are for the time of Spring currents and consequently are the strongest normally encountered.

Figure 10.4. Chart of tidal currents at one moment of the day in Long Island Sound.

able to find answers by using the basic laws of Newton, the answer would hardly be worth the effort, because there is a simpler way: watch the tide for a month—or, better yet, for a year. The patterns that emerge at a single spot will be seen to repeat quite well from one month to the next and very well from year to year. They do, however, vary from week to week and they are wonderfully varied from one port to another.

If the wind is not too spectacular and the barometer is fairly steady, observations of previous tides can be used to predict future tides, to within a foot or so. And when the data are plotted over a period of 18 years, they can be matched with mathematical patterns that can be used for making precise predictions. A careful look at some of the typical patterns will make it easier for you to use the tide and current tables.

Figures 10.5a, b, and c show three types of daily patterns; the distinction is produced by differences in the moon's influence.

Tide patterns

Half-daily tides—Also called *semidiurnal,* these tides are the most common in the temperate zones, outside the tropics; they show two highs and two lows per day (Figure 10.5a).

Daily tides—Also called *diurnal,* these tides show a single high and low per day. They are most common in the tropics, especially the South Pacific Ocean, and the Gulf of Mexico (Figure 10.5b).

Mixed tides—Many regions show two highs of different extent and lows of different depth in the course of a single day. Where mixed tides occur, the

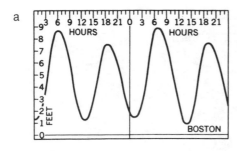

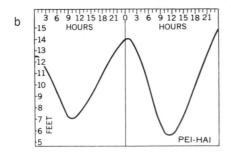

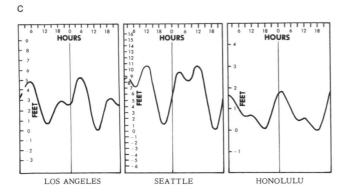

LOS ANGELES   SEATTLE   HONOLULU

Figure 10.5 a, b, c. Various mixtures of half-daily and daily tides. The nature of the mixture varies, not only with location, but also during the month.

pattern is apt to change radically from one part of the month to another due to changes in the geographical location of the moon and the moon's relation to the sun (Figure 10.5c).

Cycles of the tides

Figure 10.6 shows the tidal plots for the month of September in a particular year at six locations scattered over the world. Look carefully at the monthly patterns and see how many characteristics you can discover. Some of them are globally typical of tides, while others are a result of the particular location, so these curves illustrate variety rather than provide a basis for generalizing.

Here are a few of the more obvious characteristics; note that the particular dates on which they occur will change from month to month.

- In most places, the character of the tide changes significantly during the month in its amplitude and mixture of daily and half-daily components.

- The least-changeable pattern occurred in New York, where the maximum swing of the tide occurred that month on the 8th and the 23rd, when the sun and moon were working together. These are the spring tides. The lower tides occurring halfway between are the neap tides. A similar behavior was seen at other stations, except Pei-hai in the Gulf of Tonkin.

- Around the 23rd of the month that year, the moon was at perigee (closest to earth) and the tide was greatest at all places shown, except Pei-hai.

- In Los Angeles and Honolulu, the tide becomes daily when the moon is farthest south, which occurred around the 16th of that month.

- In Seattle and Pei-hai there was a mixed tide around the time of the spring tides.

Newton's theory of the tides points to the predominance of nine different cycles in the motions of the sun and moon. They modulate the tides, and their rhythms and beats lead to the complexity of the tidal curves shown in Figure 10.6. These cycles are listed in Table 10.1 and described in the notes.

Lunitidal interval—Although the time of high tide varies through the month and from port to port, there is one interval that can be most helpful in making a rough prediction. This is the *lunitidal interval,* or the time interval from the time the moon crosses the local meridian (north-south line) to the observed time of high tide. The crossing of the meridian is called a *transit*. The time of lunar transit is the key to the time of high tide because the moon is usually more important than the Sun in producing the tide. Once you have measured it for a particular port, you can assume it will change very little during the weeks to come.

If the lunitidal interval of a port is 4 hours, then adding this to the time of the moon's transit will give the time of high tide. For example, if the transit occurs at 1100 hours, the high tide is expected at

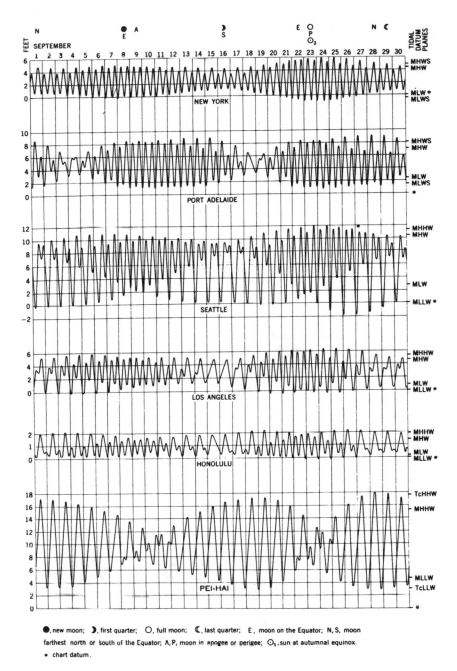

Figure 10.6. Representative tide curves during one month. The positions of the moon during the month are indicated by small characters at the top. (Bowditch)

1500. The time of transit can be found from the *Nautical Almanac* (as described later) or can be estimated from a newspaper by taking the midpoint between times of moonrise and moonset. (For example, if moonrise is at 0500 and moonset is at 1700, then the transit will occur at 1100.)

The time of lunar transit can be estimated from Table 10.2, if you know the phase of the moon on that date. For example, when the moon is at third quarter, it will pass the meridian at sunrise and sunset. If the lunitidal interval is 1 hour, you should expect high tide to occur 1 hour after sunrise or sunset.

Table 10.1. Tidal cycles

Six Cycles of the Moon

Type	Effect	Period
Geographical longitude[1]	Half-daily tide	12h 13m
Geographical latitude[2]	Strength of daily tide	27.32 days
Distance from Earth[3]	Strength of all tides	27.55 days
Lunar Phase[4]	Neap and spring tides	29.53 days
Position of moon's node[5]	Strength of daily tide	18.61 years
Position of moon's perigee[6]	Strength of spring tide	8.85 years

Three Cycles of the Sun

Type	Effect	Period
Geographical longitude[7]	Half-daily tide	12h
Distance from earth[8]	Strength of solar tide	1 year
Geographical latitude[9]	Strength of daily tide	1 year

Notes:

1. Due to the eastward rotation of the earth and the moon's eastward orbital motion, the moon appears to move westward around the earth once in 24 hours 25 minutes.

2. The moon's path is tilted by about 5° from the plane of the earth's orbit, and this, added to the tilt of the earth's axis, carries the moon north and south in the course of a month. The latitude of the moon repeats in a cycle known as the *tropical* month, of 27.32 days.

3. The moon's orbit is slightly out of round, and its distance from the earth varies by about 5 percent during a month. The point of closest approach is called the *perigee,* and the interval between perigee passages is the *anomalistic* month of 27.55 days.

4. Lunar phase is the relation of the moon's position to the position of the sun, and the time between new moons in the *synodic* month of 29.53 days.

5. The intersection of the moon's path with the earth's orbit is the *node,* and it rotates once in 18.61 years.

6. The point of closest approach to the earth is the perigee and it rotates about the orbit in 8.85 years. When perigee occurs at spring tides, they will be particularly high.

7. The sun appears to move around the earth once in 24 hours. This is the solar day to which most clocks are attuned.

8. The earth is slightly farther from the sun in summer than in winter, and this causes a slight decrease in the solar tide each summer.

9. The sun's apparent annual path around the earth is tilted by 23° from the equator of the earth, and this causes the sun to move north and south, producing the seasons and altering the role of the sun.

Table 10.2. Times at which the moon is due south or north

Lunar Phase	Times of day	
	Above horizon	*Below horizon*
New	Noon	Midnight
First quarter	Sunset	Sunrise
Full	Midnight	Noon
Third quarter	Sunrise	Sunset

POSTTEST

10.6 The moon is at first quarter and the lunitidal interval is 2 hours. What are the expected times of low tide?

10.7 Use a coastal newspaper's tide reports to determine the lunitidal interval for that port.

Phases of the moon—To take advantage of the lunitidal interval in predicting the tides for your port, it helps to learn how to predict the time of the moon's crossing of your meridian from the moon's *phase* in its monthly cycle. The phase can be described in *quarters* of the month (new, first quarter, full, third quarter, new, etc.). To make matters a bit confusing, the term *quarter* refers to a fraction of the month, not the face of the moon. So the moon at first quarter is actually half-full.

The lunar phase can also be described in terms of its age: the number of days since new moon. Both can be found in the *Nautical Almanac* on the daily pages, as shown in Table 10.3. (See Chapter 14 and the Appendix for a fuller introduction to the *Almanac.*)

Table 10.3. Excerpt from daily pages showing ages and phase of the moon

	SUN			MOON			
Day	Eqn. of Time		Mer. Pass.	Mer. Pass.		Age	Phase
	00 h	12 h		Upper	Lower		
	m s	m s	h m	h m	h m	d	
29	01 09	01 00	12 01	18 54	06 29	09	
30	00 51	00 42	12 01	19 46	07 20	10	◖
31	00 32	00 23	12 00	20 37	08 12	11	

Lacking an almanac you can estimate the phase by looking at the moon's face and noting its shape and relationship to the position of the sun. As an example, if the moon is full, it will be highest in the sky at midnight. Now suppose your lunitidal interval is 1 hour. The high tides would occur one hour after the time the moon is due south—1:00 AM and 1:00 PM. The low tides would occur about 6 hours later.

POSTTEST

10.8 You are to arrange the photos of the moon shown in Figure 10.7 into a sequence of ages, beginning with picture A. To help you do this, you may want to make a photocopy of the page or a tracing of the outlines of the moon's shapes. Then cut this copy into separate images and arrange them on a flat surface.
   a) Write your list of letters describing the sequence: _____
   b) What approximate age corresponds to each of these images?
   A _____   D _____   G _____
   B _____   E _____   H _____
   C _____   F _____
   c) If the moon appeared as in picture B, what time would it be at its highest point in the sky?

10.9 Assume your lunitidal interval is 1h 30m and answer the following:
   a) When does the third-quarter moon rise?

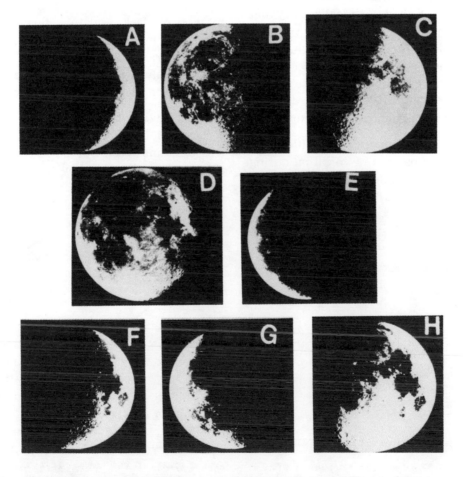

Figure 10.7. Images of the moon arranged in random order. Your task is to arrange them in the sequence that corresponds to the phases during a month, starting from the new moon. (Adapted from photo courtesy Wellesley College.)

b) When would the high tide occur at third-quarter moon?

c) When does the first-quarter moon set?

d) When does the high tide occur at first-quarter moon?

Tidal currents

Tides rise and fall because the water moves horizontally in tidal currents. These currents alternately pile up the water (*flood tide*) and cause it to withdraw (*ebb tide*). The time relationship between the currents and the height of the tide varies from place to place. For example, if a bay has a wide entrance and does not extend far inland, the time of fastest flood will occur halfway between low and high tide. Slack water will occur at high and low water. On the other hand, at a narrow entrance to a large bay, the current will rush through the entrance most rapidly when the difference in height between the bay and the ocean is greatest. This will usually occur at the times of high and low water outside the bay. Figure 10.8 shows an idealized bay that is exposed to tidal rise and fall of the ocean level outside a narrow inlet. When the ocean is high and the difference between the levels of the ocean and the bay is greatest, the current will flow into the bay at its greatest speed. The time of greatest depth in the bay will come later, as indicated in Figure 10.9.

Reversing currents—Tidal currents also differ from place to place in their pattern of variation during the tidal cycle. Some are called *reversing currents* because they slosh back and forth, alternating between two opposite directions. For example, it might flow northwest during flood stage, pass through an

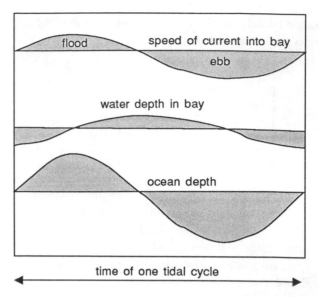

Figure 10.9. Reversing current at the mouth of a bay (top). *The tide runs out most rapidly when the water in the bay is highest. The water depths in the ocean* (middle) *and in the bay* (bottom) *are also shown.*

interval of slack, and then flow southeast during ebb stage. Figure 10.9 shows the velocity diagram for a reversing current at the mouth of the bay. Positive values correspond to one direction, negative to the opposite. (Flood is inward; ebb is outward.)

Rotating currents—*Rotating currents* are more common and they are characterized by a more or less constant speed but a rotating direction. Like the hand of a clock, they constantly turn in the same direction, and in their purest form, there is no slack water. Figure 10.10 shows the pattern of a

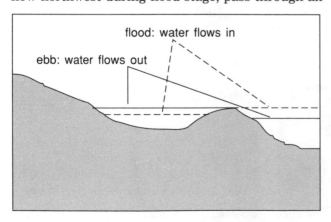

Figure 10.8. Schematic profile of water depths in a bay that is exposed to an ocean (on right) *whose level rises and falls with the tide. Water alternately flows into and out of the bay through an inlet* (not shown).

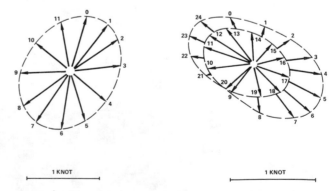

Figure 10.10. Current roses depict the hourly patterns of the current. Arrows are plotted at an hourly interval with respect to high and low water to show the direction of the current, and the length of the arrow shows the speed of the current at that time. (Oceanography and Seamanship, William G. van Dorn, *Dodd, Mead & Co. New York, adapted from* Bowditch)

rotary current in the form of a *current rose.* An arrow is plotted at an hourly interval with respect to high and low water to show the direction of the current, and the length of the arrow shows the speed of the current at that time.

Set, drift, and strength—The direction toward which a current is flowing is called its *set.* So an eastward current would have a set of 090T. (This is the opposite of the convention used in labelling winds. An east wind blows *from* the east.) The speed of a current is called its *drift,* and it is measured in knots. (One knot is one nautical mile per hour.) The *strength* of a current usually refers to the maximum speed between times of slack water. It varies over the month in much the same way that the height of the tide varies at that location. It is greatest at the time of spring tides and least at neap tides.

Tide tables

Just before the end of the nineteenth century (according to G. R. Newell in *SOS North Pacific*) Captain Lewis, skipper of the steamboat *Victorian,* used his tide tables to extricate his ship when it became impaled on a jagged rock off the mountainous coast of northern British Columbia. Much against the young captain's better judgment, he had followed an older captain close to the shore in order to fill the steamer's tanks with water from the waterfalls. The older captain had been successful in obtaining water and getting away, but as the tide ebbed, Capt. Lewis found himself in a predicament. A sharp rock, in the shape of a miniature pinnacle, pierced his hull, and the ship settled down until the rock protruded 5 feet above the lower deck. (At low tide in that region, the water can fall

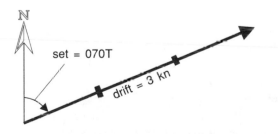

Figure 10.11. Tidal current vector is described by its drift (speed) and set (direction of flow). An easterly tide is moving toward the east. This is different from the convention used for winds. In this case the set is about 075T and the drift is 3 kn.

by 20 feet or more.) While Capt. Lewis was waiting for help to come, he used some timbers to build a cofferdam around the rock inside the ship. He had his tide tables with him, and he saw from them that an unusually high tide was due. As the tide rose, it lifted the ship off the rock and the *Victorian* floated into safer waters.

Tables are published annually to permit you to calculate the times of high and low tide at hundreds of coastal stations, as well as interpolating for the depth of water at any arbitrary time. To reduce the length of such tables, daily details are given for a small number of reference stations, and *differences* are given for the other locations, as we now describe.

Table 10.4 shows a list of stations and gives reference numbers for finding the data in the *Tide Tables,* a government publication from which this is excerpted.

Times of high and low tide—Let us assume you are interested in tides at Stonington, CT, on Fisher's Island Sound (see Chart 116-SC Tr), and the date is October 27, 1977. If you pick up the *Tide Tables (1977), East Coast of North and South America,* you will be able to do the following steps (using tables for other years will lead to minor differences):

- *Step 1*—In the index, Table 10.4, search for Stonington, CT, or Fisher's Island Sound. Both names appear in the index, with the key number 1187 following.

- *Step 2*—Find the key number in the left margin of Table 10.5, which gives the latitude and longitude of Stonington, CT, to help you find it on a chart. It also gives the time and height differences from the appropriate reference station. The name of the reference station is found in bold face in the column of differences; in this case you find the phrase "on NEW LONDON, p. 44."

- *Step 3*—Copy out the crucial numbers in a form such as the following:

Stonington
–0h 33m HWDT (High Water Difference in Time)
–0h 41m LWDT (Low Water Difference in Time)
+0.1 feet HWDH (High Water Difference in Height)
 0.0 feet LWDH (Low Water Difference in Height)

The final three figures in the row for Stonington show the general situation. The mean range is 2.7

Table 10.4. Index to reference stations (from
Tide Tables)

	NO.			NO.
STONE HARBOR, N. J.	1741		THREEMILE HARBOR ENTRANCE, N. Y.	1399
STONE ISLAND, MAINE	657		THROGS NECK, N. Y.	1263
STONINGTON, CONN.	1187		THUNDERBOLT, GA.	2727
STONINGTON, MAINE	743		TICORALAK ISLAND, LABRADOR	167
STONO RIVER, S. C.	2617-2621		TIDNISH HEAD, NEW BRUNSWICK	415
STONY BROOK, N. Y.	1355		TIERRA DEL FUEGO	3841-3847
STRAIT OF BELLE ISLE	181-185		TIGNISH, PRINCE EDWARD ISLAND	417
STRATFORD, CONN.	1231		TIMBALIER ISLAND, LA.	3247
STRATFORD SHOAL, N. Y.	1357		TIVERTON, NOVA SCOTIA	555
STRAWBERRY HILL, MASS.	985		TIVERTON, R. I.	1149
STUPART BAY	137		TIVOLI, N.Y.	1555
STURGEON ISLAND, MAINE	835		TODD CREEK, GA.	2809
STURGEON POINT, VA.	2403		TODDVILLE, S. C.	2537
SUCCONNESSET POINT, MASS.	1037		TOLCHESTER BEACH, MD.	2079
SUFFOLK, VA.	2373		TOM NEVERS HEAD, MASS.	1041
SULLIVAN, MAINE	705		TOMS RIVER (town), N. J.	1661
SULLIVANS ISLAND, S. C.	2569		TOOGOODOO CREEK, S. C.	2629
SUMMERHOUSE POINT, S. C.	2661		TORRESDALE, PA.	1885
SUMMERSIDE HARBOUR, PRINCE EDWARD I-	437		TOTTENVILLE, N. Y.	1599
SUMMIT BRIDGE, DEL.	1837		TOWN POINT, VA.	2369
SUNBURY, GA.	2749		TOWN POINT NECK, MD.	2087
SUNNYBANK, VA.	2259		TOWNSEND INLET, N. J.	1735
SUNNY ISLES, BISCAYNE CREEK, FLA.	2917		TRACADIE, NEW BRUNSWICK	403
SURINAM	3593-3597		TRAFTON ISLAND, MAINE	673
SURINAME RIVIER ENTRANCE * (164)	3595		TRAVIS POINT, VA.	2171
SUSQUEHANNA RIVER, MD.	2095, 2097		TRED AVON RIVER, MD.	2037, 2039
SUWANNEE RIVER, FLA.	3121		TRENTON, N. J.	1895
SWAIN CHANNEL, N. J.	1751		TREPASSEY HARBOUR, NEWFOUNDLAND	223
SWAN CREEK, MD.	2077		TRINIDAD	3577-3587
SWAN ISLANDS, WEST INDIES	3326		TRINITY BAY, TEX.	3283
SWEET HALL LANDING, VA.	2337		TROIS RIVIERES, QUEBEC	371
SWIM POINT, NOVA SCOTIA	547		TROPICAL HOMESITES LANDING, FLA.	3062
			TROUP CREEK, GA.	2785

feet, the spring tide range is 3.2 feet, and the mean tide level is 1.3 feet. The units are at the top of the page.

- **Step 4**—For computing tide at a specific time, you will need the data for New London on p. 44 of the *Tide Tables* in *Times and Heights of High and Low Waters*. New London is one of 48 reference stations for which data are given for every day of the current year. (Times and heights at other stations, such as Stonington, CT, are found by adding these figures to the differences found in Step 3.)

Scan down the table until you find the correct date. Typically there will be four rows for each date, corresponding to the two high tides and two low tides. HT stands for the height of the water at the time given, and it is generally understood (and confirmed in a footnote on that page) that all heights are reckoned from datum of soundings of the locality. This is *mean low water* in the majority of cases. Copy out the data as shown in the first two columns below.

The second and fourth entries indicate highest water, so the times of high tide are 09 10 and 21 38.

Mark them H and mark the lows with L, as in the third column.

on New London—27 Oct.

TIME	HT.		Stonington			
h m	ft.		Differences		Tides	
03 09	0.2	L	−0 41	0.0	02 28	0.1
09 10	3.1	H	−0 33	+0.1	08 37	3.2
15 46	−0.1	L	−0 41	0.0	15 05	−0.1
21 38	2.4	H	−0 33	+0.1	21 05	2.5

- **Step 5**—Recopy the Stonington differences into the next two columns and add the figures algebraically (i.e., subtract negative numbers) to the reference data to obtain the tides shown in boldface in the final two columns. They will apply if all conditions are normal, but see next section.

Further stations referred to New London may be added to the right in case you need them.

Finding tide depth at a particular time—Suppose you want to take advantage of the height of tide at a special time, 07h 40m, at the same place. Table

Table 10.5. Tidal differences and other constants
(from *Tide Tables*)

No.	PLACE	POSITION		DIFFERENCES				RANGES		Mean Tide Level
				Time		Height				
		Lat.	Long.	High water	Low water	High water	Low water	Mean	Spring	
		° ′ N.	° ′ W.	h. m.	h. m.	feet	feet	feet	feet	feet
	RHODE ISLAND and MASSACHUSETTS									
	Narragansett Bay — Continued			on NEWPORT, p.40						
	Time meridian, 75°W.									
1159	Fall River, Massachusetts-----------	41 44	71 08	+0 31	+0 34	+0.9	0.0	4.4	5.5	2.2
1161	Taunton, Taunton River, Mass--------	41 53	71 06	+1 09	+2 26	-0.7	0.0	2.8	3.5	1.4
1163	Bristol------------------------------	41 40	71 16	+0 10	0 00	+0.6	0.0	4.1	5.1	2.0
1165	Warren------------------------------	41 44	71 17	+0 21	+0 04	+1.1	0.0	4.6	5.7	2.3
1167	Nayatt Point------------------------	41 43	71 20	+0 12	+0 03	+1.1	0.0	4.6	5.7	2.3
1169	Providence--------------------------	41 48	71 24	+0 14	+0 05	+1.1	0.0	4.6	5.7	2.3
1171	Pawtucket, Seekonk River------------	41 52	71 23	+0 21	+0 14	+1.1	0.0	4.6	5.8	2.3
1173	East Greenwich---------------------	41 40	71 27	+0 16	+0 08	+0.5	0.0	4.0	5.0	2.0
1175	Wickford-----------------------------	41 34	71 27	+0 12	+0 07	+0.3	0.0	3.8	4.7	1.9
1177	Narragansett Pier-------------------	41 25	71 27	-0 08	+0 16	-0.3	0.0	3.2	4.0	1.6
	RHODE ISLAND, Outer Coast									
1179	Point Judith Harbor of Refuge-------	41 22	71 29	-0 07	+0 22	-0.4	0.0	3.1	3.9	1.5
1181	Block Island (Great Salt Pond)------	41 11	71 35	+0 05	+0 12	-0.9	0.0	2.6	3.2	1.3
1183	Block Island (Old Harbor)-----------	41 10	71 33	-0 14	+0 17	-0.6	0.0	2.9	3.6	1.4
1185	Watch Hill Point--------------------	41 18	71 52	+0 44	+1 21	-0.9	0.0	2.6	3.2	1.3
				on NEW LONDON, p.44						
1186	Westerly, Pawcatuck River-----------	41 23	71 50	-0 27	+0 02	+0.1	0.0	2.7	3.2	1.3
	CONNECTICUT, Long Island Sound									
1187	Stonington, Fishers Island Sound----	41 20	71 54	-0 33	-0 41	+0.1	0.0	2.7	3.2	1.3
1189	Noank, Mystic River entrance--------	41 19	71 59	-0 23	-0 08	-0.3	0.0	2.3	2.7	1.2
1191	West Harbor, Fishers Island, N. Y---	41 16	72 00	-0 01	-0 06	-0.1	0.0	2.5	3.0	1.2
1192	Silver Eel Pond, Fishers I., N. Y---	41 15	72 02	-0 17	-0 04	-0.3	0.0	2.3	2.7	1.1
	Thames River									
1193	NEW LONDON, State Pier-----------	41 22	72 06	Daily predictions				2.6	3.1	1.3
1195	Smith Cove entrance-------------	41 24	72 06	-0 01	+0 10	-0.1	0.0	2.5	3.0	1.2
1197	Norwich-------------------------	41 31	72 05	+0 09	+0 20	+0.4	0.0	3.0	3.6	1.5
1199	Millstone Point---------------------	41 18	72 10	+0 08	+0 01	+0.1	0.0	2.7	3.2	1.3
	Connecticut River									
1200	Saybrook Jetty---------------------	41 16	72 21	+1 10	+0 45	+0.9	0.0	3.5	4.2	1.7
1201	Saybrook Point---------------------	41 17	72 21	+1 10	+0 53	+0.6	0.0	3.2	3.8	1.6
1202	Lyme, highway bridge-------------	41 19	72 21	+1 24	+1 10	+0.5	0.0	3.1	3.7	1.5
1203	Essex-------------------------------	41 21	72 23	+1 38	+1 38	+0.4	0.0	3.0	3.6	1.5
1204	Hadlyme†----------------------------	41 25	72 26	+2 18	+2 23	+0.1	0.0	2.7	3.2	1.3
1205	East Haddam------------------------	41 27	72 28	+2 41	+2 53	+0.3	0.0	2.9	3.5	1.4
1206	Haddam†----------------------------	41 29	72 30	+2 47	+3 08	-0.1	0.0	2.5	3.0	1.2
1207	Higganum Creek--------------------	41 30	72 33	+2 54	+3 25	0.0	0.0	2.6	3.1	1.3
1209	Portland†---------------------------	41 34	72 38	+3 50	+4 28	-0.4	0.0	2.2	2.6	1.1
1211	Rocky Hill†-------------------------	41 39	72 38	+4 43	+5 44	-0.6	0.0	2.0	2.4	1.0
1213	Hartford†---------------------------	41 46	72 40	+5 39	+6 52	-0.7	0.0	1.9	2.3	1.0
				on BRIDGEPORT, p.48						
1214	Westbrook, Duck Island Roads--------	41 16	72 28	-0 23	-0 34	-2.6	0.0	4.1	4.7	2.0
1215	Duck Island-------------------------	41 15	72 29	-0 25	-0 37	-2.2	0.0	4.5	5.2	2.2
1217	Madison-----------------------------	41 16	72 36	-0 20	-0 32	-1.8	0.0	4.9	5.6	2.4
1219	Falkner Island---------------------	41 13	72 39	-0 13	-0 27	-1.3	0.0	5.4	6.2	2.7
1220	Sachem Head------------------------	41 15	72 42	-0 10	-0 17	-1.3	0.0	5.4	6.2	2.7
1221	Money Island-----------------------	41 15	72 45	-0 11	-0 25	-1.1	0.0	5.6	6.4	2.8
1223	Branford Harbor--------------------	41 16	72 49	-0 07	-0 20	-0.8	0.0	5.9	6.8	2.9
1225	New Haven Harbor entrance----------	41 14	72 55	-0 08	-0 16	-0.5	0.0	6.2	7.1	3.1
1227	New Haven (city dock)--------------	41 18	72 55	+0 02	-0 03	-0.7	0.0	6.0	6.9	3.0
1229	Milford Harbor---------------------	41 13	73 03	-0 07	-0 12	-0.1	0.0	6.6	7.6	3.3
1231	Stratford, Housatonic River--------	41 11	73 07	+0 27	+0 59	-1.2	0.0	5.5	6.3	2.7
1233	Shelton, Housatonic River----------	41 19	73 05	+1 36	+2 42	-1.7	0.0	5.0	5.8	2.5

†Tidal information applies only during low river stages.

10.7 (*Tide Tables*, Table 3) permits this calculation from data you obtained in Step 4 above. It may seem tricky the first time, but you'll soon get used to it.

- ***Step 1***—Is the tide rising or falling? Your desired time, 0740 hours, falls between the first low and high, so the water is rising. Find the *duration of rise* from the difference: 0837 − 0228 = 0609 hours.

Table 10.6. Times and heights of high and low water (from *Tide Tables*)

OCTOBER

DAY	TIME h.m.	HT. ft.	DAY	TIME h.m.	HT. ft.
1 SA	0548	0.3	16 SU	0534	0.0
	1141	2.8		1129	3.4
	1828	0.2		1823	-0.3
2 SU	0011	2.3	17 M	0008	2.6
	0637	0.5		0632	0.1
	1226	2.7		1226	3.3
	1919	0.3		1922	-0.2
3 M	0101	2.2	18 TU	0111	2.5
	0731	0.6		0733	0.2
	1316	2.6		1330	3.1
	2012	0.4		2022	-0.1
4 TU	0156	2.1	19 W	0217	2.5
	0825	0.7		0840	0.3
	1410	2.5		1439	2.9
	2108	0.5		2124	0.0
5 W	0257	2.1	20 TH	0327	2.5
	0923	0.7		0948	0.3
	1509	2.4		1551	2.7
	2201	0.5		2224	0.0
6 TH	0354	2.1	21 F	0434	2.6
	1020	0.7		1052	0.2
	1606	2.4		1657	2.7
	2252	0.4		2321	0.1
7 F	0448	2.3	22 SA	0533	2.7
	1111	0.6		1151	0.1
	1700	2.5		1759	2.6
	2338	0.3			
8 SA	0535	2.4	23 SU	0012	0.0
	1201	0.4		0625	2.8
	1749	2.6		1245	0.0
				1852	2.6
9 SU	0022	0.2	24 M	0100	0.0
	0616	2.6		0712	3.0
	1246	0.2		1334	-0.1
	1834	2.7		1939	2.6
10 M	0106	0.1	25 TU	0144	0.0
	0657	2.9		0753	3.0
	1331	0.0		1421	-0.1
	1916	2.8		2020	2.5
11 TU	0145	0.0	26 W	0227	0.0
	0739	3.1		0832	3.1
	1415	-0.2		1503	-0.2
	2001	2.9		2058	2.5
12 W	0227	-0.1	27 TH	0309	0.1
	0820	3.3		0910	3.1
	1500	-0.3		1546	-0.1
	2045	2.9		2138	2.4
13 TH	0309	-0.2	28 F	0349	0.2
	0902	3.5		0948	3.0
	1546	-0.4		1628	-0.1
	2132	2.9		2216	2.4
14 F	0353	-0.2	29 SA	0433	0.3
	0948	3.6		1025	2.9
	1635	-0.5		1712	0.0
	2219	2.9		2256	2.3
15 SA	0440	-0.1	30 SU	0517	0.4
	1037	3.5		1104	2.8
	1727	-0.4		1758	0.1
	2312	2.8		2339	2.2
			31 M	0605	0.5
				1146	2.7
				1845	0.2

NOVEMBER

DAY	TIME h.m.	HT. ft.	DAY	TIME h.m.	HT. ft.
1 TU	0029	2.2	16 W	0055	2.6
	0656	0.6		0717	0.1
	1232	2.5		1314	2.9
	1935	0.3		1959	-0.2
2 W	0117	2.1	17 TH	0201	2.5
	0749	0.7		0823	0.1
	1322	2.4		1421	2.7
	2028	0.3		2100	-0.1
3 TH	0217	2.1	18 F	0309	2.5
	0847	0.7		0929	0.1
	1418	2.3		1532	2.5
	2120	0.4		2158	0.0
4 F	0313	2.2	19 SA	0414	2.6
	0944	0.7		1034	0.1
	1517	2.3		1638	2.4
	2210	0.3		2253	0.0
5 SA	0405	2.3	20 SU	0514	2.7
	1038	0.5		1133	0.0
	1615	2.3		1740	2.3
	2257	0.2		2346	0.0
6 SU	0455	2.5	21 M	0604	2.8
	1129	0.3		1228	0.0
	1709	2.4		1833	2.2
	2343	-0.1			
7 M	0540	2.7	22 TU	0033	0.0
	1218	0.1		0651	2.9
	1759	2.5		1315	-0.1
				1918	2.2
8 TU	0027	0.0	23 W	0118	0.0
	0622	3.0		0731	2.9
	1305	-0.1		1400	-0.2
	1847	2.6		2000	2.2
9 W	0110	-0.1	24 TH	0200	0.1
	0707	3.3		0809	2.9
	1351	-0.4		1442	-0.2
	1936	2.7		2037	2.2
10 TH	0155	-0.2	25 F	0242	0.1
	0752	3.5		0845	2.8
	1438	-0.5		1523	-0.2
	2023	2.8		2114	2.2
11 F	0241	-0.3	26 SA	0324	0.1
	0838	3.6		0921	2.9
	1526	-0.7		1603	-0.2
	2112	2.8		2151	2.2
12 SA	0329	-0.3	27 SU	0405	0.2
	0927	3.7		0957	2.8
	1616	-0.7		1645	-0.1
	2203	2.8		2232	2.2
13 SU	0419	-0.3	28 M	0449	0.3
	1018	3.6		1035	2.7
	1709	-0.6		1728	-0.1
	2256	2.7		2312	2.2
14 M	0515	-0.2	29 TU	0534	0.4
	1112	3.4		1115	2.6
	1803	-0.5		1813	0.0
	2354	2.6		2357	2.1
15 TU	0613	-0.1	30 W	0624	0.5
	1211	3.2		1156	2.5
	1900	-0.4		1901	0.1

DECEMBER

DAY	TIME h.m.	HT. ft.	DAY	TIME h.m.	HT. ft.
1 TH	0045	2.1	16 F	0139	2.5
	0717	0.5		0802	-0.1
	1240	2.4		1357	2.4
	1949	0.1		2030	-0.3
2 F	0135	2.1	17 SA	0241	2.5
	0811	0.5		0907	0.0
	1332	2.2		1503	2.2
	2039	0.2		2126	-0.1
3 SA	0227	2.2	18 SU	0343	2.5
	0907	0.5		1010	0.0
	1431	2.2		1611	2.0
	2128	0.2		2221	-0.1
4 SU	0320	2.3	19 M	0445	2.6
	1005	0.4		1111	0.0
	1529	2.1		1711	1.9
	2216	0.1		2316	0.0
5 M	0412	2.5	20 TU	0539	2.6
	1058	0.2		1204	-0.1
	1629	2.1		1807	1.9
	2303	0.0			
6 TU	0503	2.7	21 W	0005	0.0
	1150	-0.1		0625	2.6
	1725	2.2		1252	-0.1
	2353	-0.1		1854	1.9
7 W	0550	3.0	22 TH	0051	0.0
	1239	-0.3		0707	2.7
	1818	2.3		1336	-0.2
				1936	1.9
8 TH	0039	-0.2	23 F	0135	0.0
	0639	3.2		0745	2.7
	1328	-0.5		1419	-0.2
	1912	2.4		2014	2.0
9 F	0129	-0.3	24 SA	0217	0.0
	0730	3.4		0821	2.7
	1417	-0.7		1459	-0.3
	2003	2.5		2051	2.0
10 SA	0218	-0.4	25 SU	0300	0.0
	0819	3.5		0856	2.7
	1507	-0.8		1539	-0.3
	2054	2.6		2129	2.1
11 SU	0309	-0.5	26 M	0342	0.0
	0910	3.5		0932	2.7
	1557	-0.9		1619	-0.3
	2147	2.7		2207	2.1
12 M	0403	-0.5	27 TU	0424	0.1
	1002	3.5		1010	2.6
	1649	-0.8		1701	-0.3
	2241	2.7		2246	2.1
13 TU	0459	-0.4	28 W	0509	0.1
	1057	3.3		1046	2.5
	1741	-0.7		1743	-0.2
	2337	2.6		2327	2.1
14 W	0557	-0.2	29 TH	0555	0.2
	1153	3.0		1126	2.4
	1837	-0.6		1826	-0.2
15 TH	0036	2.6	30 F	0011	2.2
	0658	-0.2		0643	0.2
	1253	2.7		1209	2.3
	1933	-0.4		1909	-0.1
			31 SA	0053	2.2
				0737	0.3
				1256	2.2
				1956	0.0

TIME MERIDIAN 75° W. 0000 IS MIDNIGHT. 1200 IS NOON.
HEIGHTS ARE RECKONED FROM THE DATUM OF SOUNDINGS ON CHARTS OF THE LOCALITY WHICH IS MEAN LOW WATER.

- *Step 2*—What is the *time interval from the nearest high water or low water?* The nearest time to 0740 is the high water at 0837, and the interval is 57m.

- *Step 3*—What is the range of that tide? You find 3.2 − 0.1 = 3.1 feet.

- *Step 4*—Now enter the table at the value nearest the appropriate *duration of rise or fall* (6h00m) and go across to the value nearest the *time from nearest high water or low water* (1h). Put one finger on that entry and scan down the column with your other finger until you come to the value nearest the appropriate *range of tide* (3.0 ft.). The corresponding entry is 0.2 feet.

- *Step 5*—This entry is to be applied to the height at the nearest high or low water, and it is to be subtracted or added depending on the case. Our special time was an hour before high water, so we subtract 0.2 from the high tide, finding 3.2 − 0.2 = 3.0 feet.

Table 10.7. Height of tide at any time—for interpolation (from *Tide Tables*)

Time from the nearest high water or low water

Duration of rise or fall, see footnote

h. m.	h. m.	h. m.	h. m.	h. m.	h. m.	h. m.	h. m.	h. m.	h. m.	h. m.	h. m.	h. m.	h. m.	h. m.	h. m.
4 00	0 08	0 16	0 24	0 32	0 40	0 48	0 56	1 04	1 12	1 20	1 28	1 36	1 44	1 52	2 00
4 20	0 09	0 17	0 26	0 35	0 43	0 52	1 01	1 09	1 18	1 27	1 35	1 44	1 53	2 01	2 10
4 40	0 09	0 19	0 28	0 37	0 47	0 56	1 05	1 15	1 24	1 33	1 43	1 52	2 01	2 11	2 20
5 00	0 10	0 20	0 30	0 40	0 50	1 00	1 10	1 20	1 30	1 40	1 50	2 00	2 10	2 20	2 30
5 20	0 11	0 21	0 32	0 43	0 53	1 04	1 15	1 25	1 36	1 47	1 57	2 08	2 19	2 29	2 40
5 40	0 11	0 23	0 34	0 45	0 57	1 08	1 19	1 31	1 42	1 53	2 05	2 16	2 27	2 39	2 50
6 00	0 12	0 24	0 36	0 48	1 00	1 12	1 24	1 36	1 48	2 00	2 12	2 24	2 36	2 48	3 00
6 20	0 13	0 25	0 38	0 51	1 03	1 16	1 29	1 41	1 54	2 07	2 19	2 32	2 45	2 57	3 10
6 40	0 13	0 27	0 40	0 53	1 07	1 20	1 33	1 47	2 00	2 13	2 27	2 40	2 53	3 07	3 20
7 00	0 14	0 28	0 42	0 56	1 10	1 24	1 38	1 52	2 06	2 20	2 34	2 48	3 02	3 16	3 30
7 20	0 15	0 29	0 44	0 59	1 13	1 28	1 43	1 57	2 12	2 27	2 41	2 56	3 11	3 25	3 40
7 40	0 15	0 31	0 46	1 01	1 17	1 32	1 47	2 03	2 18	2 33	2 49	3 04	3 19	3 35	3 50
8 00	0 16	0 32	0 48	1 04	1 20	1 36	1 52	2 08	2 24	2 40	2 56	3 12	3 28	3 44	4 00
8 20	0 17	0 33	0 50	1 07	1 23	1 40	1 57	2 13	2 30	2 47	3 03	3 20	3 37	3 53	4 10
8 40	0 17	0 35	0 52	1 09	1 27	1 44	2 01	2 19	2 36	2 53	3 11	3 28	3 45	4 03	4 20
9 00	0 18	0 36	0 54	1 12	1 30	1 48	2 06	2 24	2 42	3 00	3 18	3 36	3 54	4 12	4 30
9 20	0 19	0 37	0 56	1 15	1 33	1 52	2 11	2 29	2 48	3 07	3 25	3 44	4 03	4 21	4 40
9 40	0 19	0 39	0 58	1 17	1 37	1 56	2 15	2 35	2 54	3 13	3 33	3 52	4 11	4 31	4 50
10 00	0 20	0 40	1 00	1 20	1 40	2 00	2 20	2 40	3 00	3 20	3 40	4 00	4 20	4 40	5 00
10 20	0 21	0 41	1 02	1 23	1 43	2 04	2 25	2 45	3 06	3 27	3 47	4 08	4 29	4 49	5 10
10 40	0 21	0 43	1 04	1 25	1 47	2 08	2 29	2 51	3 12	3 33	3 55	4 16	4 37	4 59	5 20

Correction to height

Range of tide, see footnote

Ft.	Ft.	Ft.	Ft.	Ft.	Ft.	Ft.	Ft.	Ft.	Ft.	Ft.	Ft.	Ft.	Ft.	Ft.	Ft.
0.5	0.0	0.0	0.0	0.0	0.0	0.0	0.1	0.1	0.1	0.1	0.1	0.2	0.2	0.2	0.2
1.0	0.0	0.0	0.0	0.0	0.1	0.1	0.1	0.2	0.2	0.2	0.3	0.3	0.4	0.4	0.5
1.5	0.0	0.0	0.0	0.1	0.1	0.1	0.2	0.2	0.3	0.4	0.4	0.5	0.6	0.7	0.8
2.0	0.0	0.0	0.0	0.1	0.1	0.2	0.3	0.3	0.4	0.5	0.6	0.7	0.8	0.9	1.0
2.5	0.0	0.0	0.1	0.1	0.2	0.2	0.3	0.4	0.5	0.6	0.7	0.9	1.0	1.1	1.2
3.0	0.0	0.0	0.1	0.1	0.2	0.3	0.4	0.5	0.6	0.8	0.9	1.0	1.2	1.3	1.5
3.5	0.0	0.0	0.1	0.2	0.2	0.3	0.4	0.6	0.7	0.9	1.0	1.2	1.4	1.6	1.8
4.0	0.0	0.0	0.1	0.2	0.3	0.4	0.5	0.7	0.8	1.0	1.2	1.4	1.6	1.8	2.0
4.5	0.0	0.0	0.1	0.2	0.3	0.4	0.6	0.7	0.9	1.1	1.3	1.6	1.8	2.0	2.2
5.0	0.0	0.1	0.1	0.2	0.3	0.5	0.6	0.8	1.0	1.2	1.5	1.7	2.0	2.2	2.5
5.5	0.0	0.1	0.1	0.2	0.4	0.5	0.7	0.9	1.1	1.4	1.6	1.9	2.2	2.5	2.8
6.0	0.0	0.1	0.1	0.3	0.4	0.6	0.8	1.0	1.2	1.5	1.8	2.1	2.4	2.7	3.0
6.5	0.0	0.1	0.2	0.3	0.4	0.6	0.8	1.1	1.3	1.6	1.9	2.2	2.6	2.9	3.2
7.0	0.0	0.1	0.2	0.3	0.5	0.7	0.9	1.2	1.4	1.8	2.1	2.4	2.8	3.1	3.5
7.5	0.0	0.1	0.2	0.3	0.5	0.7	1.0	1.2	1.5	1.9	2.2	2.6	3.0	3.4	3.8
8.0	0.0	0.1	0.2	0.3	0.5	0.8	1.0	1.3	1.6	2.0	2.4	2.8	3.2	3.6	4.0
8.5	0.0	0.1	0.2	0.4	0.6	0.8	1.1	1.4	1.8	2.1	2.5	2.9	3.4	3.8	4.2
9.0	0.0	0.1	0.2	0.4	0.6	0.9	1.2	1.5	1.9	2.2	2.7	3.1	3.6	4.0	4.5
9.5	0.0	0.1	0.2	0.4	0.6	0.9	1.2	1.6	2.0	2.4	2.8	3.3	3.8	4.3	4.8
10.0	0.0	0.1	0.2	0.4	0.7	1.0	1.3	1.7	2.1	2.5	3.0	3.5	4.0	4.5	5.0
10.5	0.0	0.1	0.3	0.5	0.7	1.0	1.3	1.7	2.2	2.6	3.1	3.6	4.2	4.7	5.2
11.0	0.0	0.1	0.3	0.5	0.7	1.1	1.4	1.8	2.3	2.8	3.3	3.8	4.4	4.9	5.5
11.5	0.0	0.1	0.3	0.5	0.8	1.1	1.5	1.9	2.4	2.9	3.4	4.0	4.6	5.1	5.8
12.0	0.0	0.1	0.3	0.5	0.8	1.1	1.5	2.0	2.5	3.0	3.6	4.1	4.8	5.4	6.0
12.5	0.0	0.1	0.3	0.5	0.8	1.2	1.6	2.1	2.6	3.1	3.7	4.3	5.0	5.6	6.2
13.0	0.0	0.1	0.3	0.6	0.9	1.2	1.7	2.2	2.7	3.2	3.9	4.5	5.1	5.8	6.5
13.5	0.0	0.1	0.3	0.6	0.9	1.3	1.7	2.2	2.8	3.4	4.0	4.7	5.3	6.0	6.8
14.0	0.0	0.2	0.3	0.6	0.9	1.3	1.8	2.3	2.9	3.5	4.2	4.8	5.5	6.3	7.0
14.5	0.0	0.2	0.4	0.6	1.0	1.4	1.9	2.4	3.0	3.6	4.3	5.0	5.7	6.5	7.2
15.0	0.0	0.2	0.4	0.6	1.0	1.4	1.9	2.5	3.1	3.8	4.4	5.2	5.9	6.7	7.5
15.5	0.0	0.2	0.4	0.7	1.0	1.5	2.0	2.6	3.2	3.9	4.6	5.4	6.1	6.9	7.8
16.0	0.0	0.2	0.4	0.7	1.1	1.5	2.1	2.6	3.3	4.0	4.7	5.5	6.3	7.2	8.0
16.5	0.0	0.2	0.4	0.7	1.1	1.6	2.1	2.7	3.4	4.1	4.9	5.7	6.5	7.4	8.2
17.0	0.0	0.2	0.4	0.7	1.1	1.6	2.2	2.8	3.5	4.2	5.0	5.9	6.7	7.6	8.5
17.5	0.0	0.2	0.4	0.8	1.2	1.7	2.2	2.9	3.6	4.4	5.2	6.0	6.9	7.8	8.8
18.0	0.0	0.2	0.4	0.8	1.2	1.7	2.3	3.0	3.7	4.5	5.3	6.2	7.1	8.1	9.0
18.5	0.1	0.2	0.5	0.8	1.2	1.8	2.4	3.1	3.8	4.6	5.5	6.4	7.3	8.3	9.2
19.0	0.1	0.2	0.5	0.8	1.3	1.8	2.4	3.1	3.9	4.8	5.6	6.6	7.5	8.5	9.5
19.5	0.1	0.2	0.5	0.8	1.3	1.9	2.5	3.2	4.0	4.9	5.8	6.7	7.7	8.7	9.8
20.0	0.1	0.2	0.5	0.9	1.3	1.9	2.6	3.3	4.1	5.0	5.9	6.9	7.9	9.0	10.0

Obtain from the predictions the high water and low water, one of which is before and the other after the time for which the height is required. The difference between the times of occurrence of these tides is the duration of rise or fall, and the difference between their heights is the range of tide for the above table. Find the difference between the nearest high or low water and the time for which the height is required.

Enter the table with the duration of rise or fall, printed in heavy-faced type, which most nearly agrees with the actual value, and on that horizontal line find the time from the nearest high or low water which agrees most nearly with the corresponding actual difference. The correction sought is in the column directly below, on the line with the range of tide.

When the nearest tide is high water, subtract the correction.

When the nearest tide is low water, add the correction.

After a few trials, you will find that you can often do the interpolation in your head. Or you might prefer to sketch a complete tide curve, as described in the next section.

Sketching the tide curve with the "One-quarter, One-tenth" rule—You can quite easily draw a curve showing the hour-by-hour variation of tide through the day, as in Figure 10.12, using the one-quarter, one-tenth rule and the data collected for Stonington. You need, in addition, a sheet of graph paper to help in the plotting. Choose a scale such that 24 hours will fit across the paper and the vertical range of the tide on the paper corresponds to about the same horizontal distance as 12 hours.

- *Step 1*—Plot the four high and low tide points for Stonington. For example, for the first point find 2h 28m on the horizontal scale and go above this point to a height of 0.1 feet. Draw a small circle around the point, and then do the same for the other three points.

- *Step 2*—Draw straight sloping lines between all adjacent pairs of points. Each line will be between a low and a high or vice versa. Find the midpoint of each line and draw a small circle around it. You can do this quickly by making the divisions first by eye and then adjusting them with dividers.

- *Step 3*—Find the midpoints of each of the halves. Draw vertical lines at each of the two outside quarter points in each segment.

- *Step 4*—The one-quarter, one-tenth rule tells you to take 1/10 of the range. The range in this case for the Stonington curve was 3.1 feet between the first low-high pair. One-tenth is 0.3 (no need to carry more accuracy than tenths of a foot). On the vertical line through the first quarter point lay off this distance *downward* and draw a small circle around the point; on the next vertical line lay off the same distance *upward* and draw a small circle. Now determine the range for the succeeding high-low pair. (In this case there is no significant difference from the previous range.) Take 1/10 of it and lay it off on the vertical lines through the two quarter-points between the first high and the second low. The rule is *up around highs* and *down around lows*. Repeat for the next low-high and high-low. Draw circles around each of the points found this way.

- *Step 5*—Now draw freehand a smooth curve through the circled points, trying to avoid kinks. This is the tide curve for the day.

From such a tide curve you can read the tide at any arbitrary moment during the day.

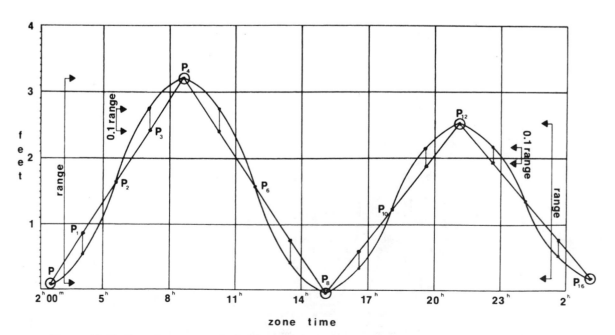

Figure 10.12. Drawing a smoothed tide curve for a day using the one-quarter, one-tenth rule.

CURRENTS

Current tables and charts

Currents vary with the same period as the tides, but there is no simple rule to describe the relationship between, say, flooding current and high tide. The diagram in Figure 10.9 showed an idealized example, but these relationships are subject to local quirks and you must seek them by becoming familiar with the waters about you or find them by scanning the published tables and charts.

Tidal current tables—There are three tables in one volume:

1. The first (Table 10.8) gives *time differences* and *velocity ratios*. You will use time differences between events at the reference station and at the desired place—as you did with the tides.

2. The second (Table 10.9) gives the *set* (direction) and *drift* (speed) of the current for each day of the year at reference stations.

3. The third (not shown) gives corrections from the set and drift of the reference station to those of the desired place.

Let us study the currents at Stonington, Fisher's Island Sound, on October 27, 1977, where we previously studied the tides, and let us assume you want the full details for the day.

- *Step 1*—Pick up the *Tidal Current Tables, Atlantic Coast of North America.* This time you will not find Stonington in the index, but you will see Fisher's Island Sound, with numbers 1605-1650.

- *Step 2*—Find the index numbers 1605-1650. You will still not find Stonington, but by hunting around a bit you will find that the latitude and longitude of No. 1605, *Edwards Pt.—Sandy Pt. (between),* correspond to station No. 1187, Stonington, as listed in the *Tide Tables* (see Table 10.5 above). So you will use No. 1605.

- *Step 3*—Scan the data and see whether there are any peculiar characteristics. In this case, there are. You will see references to footnote 1 in the columns subheaded *Maximum current* and *Maximum ebb.* This note (See Table 10.8) tells you that there are two ebb tides separated by a minimum, and it gives the three corresponding velocity ratios and time differences, as well as a time difference for maximum flood.

  Rather than copy the data at this point, look up at the TIME DIFFERENCES column; you will see *on THE RACE,* which is the name of the reference station.

- *Step 4*—Set up a form like the following and copy out the data for The Race on October 27 into the first two columns. (We have numbered the columns for clarity.) Leave extra rows after each ebb for the double ebb you found in the footnote for No. 1605. When you have finished this step, the form will look like this:

Current Data, Oct. 27, 1977

The Race   Desired Place: Stonington

(1)	(2)	(3)	(4)	(5)	(6)	(7)
Time	*Max currents*	*Time*	*Time*	*Velocity*	*Drift*	*Set*
H M	*and slacks*	*diff.*		*ratio*		
0225	3.5E					
—						
—						
0536	Slack					
0822	3.2F					
1123	Slack					
1448	3.9E					
—						
—						
1808	Slack					
2050	3.0F					
2351	Slack					

Current Data, Oct. 27, 1977

The Race   *Desired Place: Stonington (No. 1605)*

(1)	(2)	(3)	(4)	(5)	(6)	(7)
Time	*Max currents*	*Time*	*Time*	*Velocity*	*Drift*	*Set*
H M	*and slacks*	*diff.*		*ratio*		
02 25	3.5E	−03 40(1E)	22 45	0.3	1.0	035
—		−01 30(Min)	00 55	0.1	0.4	
—		−00 05(2E)	02 20	0.2	0.7	
05 36	Slack	−02 30	03 06	—	Slack, flood beg.	
08 22	3.2F	−03 15	05 07	0.4	1.3	235
11 23	Slack	−02 30	08 53	—	Slack, ebb beg.	
14 48	3.9E	−03 40(1E)	11 08	0.3	1.2	035
—		−01 30(Min)	13 18	0.1	0.4	
—		−00 05(2E)	14 43	0.2	0.8	
18 08	Slack	−02 30	15 38	—	Slack, flood beg.	
20 50	3.0F	−03 15	15 35	0.4	1.2	235
23 51	Slack	−02 30	21 21	—	Slack, ebb beg.	

Note: Columns (1) and (2) are taken from Table 10.9 (*Tidal Current Tables,* Table 1) for reference station, The Race. Columns (3) and (5) are taken from Table 10.8 for place No. 1605. Columns (4) and (6) are computed from the other columns.

- *Step 5*—Now turn back to No. 1605 in Table 2, Current Differences and Other Constants (illustrated in Table 10.8), and copy out the data in the appropriate places, as above.

  Insert the time differences into column (3) and use them to compute the times in column (4).

  Insert the velocity ratios in column (5) and use them to compute the drift in column (6), rounded to the nearest 0.1 knot.

  Insert the set for the floods and ebbs in column (7). When you are done, the table will appear as above.

Tidal current charts—In addition to current tables, there are many *Tidal Current Charts* published for various sounds and harbors, such as *Block Island and Eastern Long Island Sound, Narragansett Bay to Nantucket Sound, Puget Sound,* and *San Francisco Bay.* (See Figure 10.4 for an example.) They depict, by means of arrows and numbers, the direction and speed (which together define the velocity) of the tidal current for each hour of a typical tidal cycle. The charts may be used for any year, but of course they are only approximate. They show graphically the tidal currents in waterways as a whole and also permit finding for any time the velocities at specific points in the region depicted. Most of them require the annual *Tidal Current Tables,* while the New York and Narragansett Bay tidal current charts are to be used with the annual *Tide Tables.* In addition, there are sets of 12 monthly current diagrams for various large harbors. Directions for use of the charts and diagrams are given in each publication.

Current problems

There are three current problems you will need to cope with at one time or another.

Finding track and speed over the bottom—A vessel's speed and the direction of its track over the bottom will be altered by a current. This first type of current problem arises when you know the tidal current and you know your true heading (for example, from a compass reading) and speed through the water (from a ship's log), and you wish to predict the effect of the current, that is, find your actual course and speed over the bottom.

- *Step 1*—Referring to Figure 10.13a, mark a point to represent your starting point (the ship).

- *Step 2*—Then lay off a line with the heading of your vessel (true or magnetic, as long as you are consistent) and mark the distance you will travel through the water in 1 hour, or any convenient length of time.

- *Step 3*—From the tip of that arrow, draw a line in the direction (set) of the current.

Table 10.8. Current differences and other constants (from *Tidal Current Tables*)

No.	PLACE	POSITION		TIME DIFFERENCES		VELOCITY RATIOS		MAXIMUM CURRENTS			
								Flood		Ebb	
		Lat.	Long.	Slack water	Maximum current	Maximum flood	Maximum ebb	Direction (true)	Average velocity	Direction (true)	Average velocity
		° ′	° ′	h. m.	h. m.			deg.	knots	deg.	knots
	GARDINERS BAY, etc.—Continued *Time meridian, 75°W.*	N.	W.	on THE RACE, p.34							
1587	Jennings Point, 0.2 mile NNW. of	41 04	72 22	+0 25	+0 05	0.6	0.4	290	1.6	055	1.5
1590	Cedar Point, 0.2 mile west of	41 02	72 16	0 00	-0 30	0.6	0.5	195	1.8	005	1.6
1592	North Haven Peninsula, north of	41 02	72 19	+0 15	-0 30	0.8	0.6	230	2.4	035	2.1
1593	Paradise Point, 0.4 mile east of	41 03	72 23	+0 25	+0 05	0.5	0.4	145	1.5	345	1.5
1595	Little Peconic Bay entrance	41 02	70 33	+0 35	+0 10	0.6	0.4	240	1.6	015	1.5
1600	Robins Island, 0.5 mile south of	40 57	72 27	+0 35	+0 10	0.6	0.2	245	1.7	065	0.6
	FISHERS ISLAND SOUND										
1605	Edwards Pt.-Sandy Pt. (between)	41 20	71 54	-2 30	(1)	0.4	(1)	035	1.1	235	----
1610	Napatree Point, 0.7 mile SW. of	41 18	71 54	-0 55	-1 10	0.6	0.6	285	1.7	115	2.2
1620	Little Narragansett Bay entrance	41 20	71 53	-2 00	-2 15	0.4	0.3	090	1.3	270	1.3
1625	Avondale, Pawcatuck River	41 20	71 51	-2 05	(2)	0.2	(2)	060	0.6	255	----
1630	Ram Island Reef, south of	41 18	71 58	-0 45	-0 50	0.4	0.4	255	1.3	090	1.6
1635	Noank	41 19	71 59	(3)	(3)	0.2	(3)	340	0.5	----	----
1640	Mystic, Highway Bridge, Mystic River	41 21	71 58	-2 05	(4)	0.2	(4)	040	0.5	230	----
1645	Clay Point, 1.3 miles NNE. of	41 18	71 58	-0 40	-1 00	0.5	0.5	265	1.4	035	1.9
1650	North Hill Pt., 1.1 miles NNW. of	41 18	72 02	(5)	(5)	0.5	0.4	260	1.5	080	1.2
	LONG ISLAND SOUND										
	The Race										
1655	Race Point, 0.4 mile SW. of	41 15	72 03	-0 35	-0 40	0.9	1.0	290	2.6	135	3.5
1660	THE RACE, near Valiant Rock	41 14	72 04	Daily predictions				295	2.9	100	3.5
1665	0.5 mile NE. of Little Gull Island	41 13	72 06	-0 20	-0 20	1.0	0.7	000	3.3	105	3.1
1670	Little Gull I., 1.1 mi. ENE. of	41 13	72 05	-0 05	-0 30	1.4	1.3	300	4.0	130	4.7
1675	Great Gull Island, 0.7 mile WSW. of	41 12	72 08	-0 40	(6)	0.9	0.9	300	2.6	135	3.2
1680	Plum Gut	41 10	72 13	-1 10	-1 50	1.2	1.2	325	3.5	125	4.3
1685	Eastern Point, 1.5 miles south of	41 18	72 05	-1 30	-1 50	0.1	0.1	250	0.4	055	0.4
1690	New London Harbor entrance	41 19	72 05	-1 45	-1 35	0.1	0.1	350	0.1	210	0.2
	Thames River										
1695	Winthrop Point	41 22	72 06	-1 05	(7)	0.1	(7)	010	0.4	185	----
1700	Off Smith Cove	41 24	72 05	-1 25	(8)	0.2	(8)	020	0.7	200	----
1705	Off Stoddard Hill	41 28	72 04	-1 00	(9)	0.2	(9)	330	0.7	165	----
1710	Lower Coal Dock	41 31	72 05	*Current too weak and variable to be predicted.*							

[1] A double ebb occurs at this station (see note *). Time differences: first ebb, -3^h 40^m; minimum ebb, -1^h 30^m; second ebb, -0^h 05^m; maximum flood, -3^h 15^m. Velocity ratio for first ebb is 0.3; minimum ebb, 0.1; second ebb, 0.2.

[2] A double ebb occurs at this station (see note *). Time differences: first ebb, -3^h 40^m; minimum ebb, -1^h 10^m; second ebb, +0^h 05^m; maximum flood, -2^h 40^m. Velocity ratio for first ebb is 0.2; second ebb, 0.1. Minimum ebb is extremely weak, possibly flooding for a short period.

[3] Flood begins, -1^h 35^m; ebb begins, -4^h 10^m. A double ebb occurs at this station (see note *). Time differences: first ebb, -4^h 30^m; minimum ebb, -1^h 25^m; second ebb, +0^h 20^m; maximum flood, -3^h 15^m. Velocity ratio for first ebb is 0.1; second ebb, 0.1. Minimum ebb is extremely weak, possibly flooding for a short period.

[4] A double ebb occurs at this station (see note *). Time differences: first ebb, -3^h 40^m; minimum ebb, -1^h 40^m; second ebb, -0^h 20^m; maximum flood, -2^h 50^m. Velocity ratio for first ebb is 0.1; second ebb, 0.1. Minimum ebb is weak.

[5] Flood begins, -1^h 05^m; maximum flood, -0^h 25^m; ebb begins, -0^h 20^m; maximum ebb, -1^h 35^m.

[6] Maximum flood, -0^h 35^m; maximum ebb, -1^h 40^m.

[7] A double ebb occurs at this station (see note *). Time differences: first ebb, -2^h 35^m; minimum ebb, -1^h 10^m; second ebb, +0^h 05^m; maximum flood, -2^h 00^m. Velocity ratio for first ebb is 0.1; second ebb, 0.1. Minimum ebb is weak.

[8] A double ebb occurs at this station (see note *). Time differences: first ebb, -1^h 55^m; minimum ebb, -1^h 30^m; second ebb, +0^h 15^m; maximum flood, -2^h 20^m. Velocity ratio for first ebb is 0.2; minimum ebb, 0.1; second ebb, 0.2.

[9] A double ebb occurs at this station (see note *). Time differences: first ebb, -2^h 30^m; minimum ebb, -1^h 10^m; second ebb, +0^h 25^m; maximum flood, -2^h 25^m. Velocity ratio for first ebb is 0.1; second ebb, 0.2. Minimum ebb is weak.

* A double ebb occurs at this station. A similar slackening occurs during the ebb period as is described for the flood period in "footnote *, page 140". Differences and ratios given for first, minimum, and second ebbs should be applied to the time and velocity of maximum ebb at the reference station. Other values should be applied to the corresponding phases at the reference station.

Table 10.9. The Race, Long Island Sound, 1977
(from *Tidal Current Tables*)

SEPTEMBER

DAY	SLACK WATER TIME H.M.	MAXIMUM CURRENT TIME H.M.	VEL. KNOTS	DAY	SLACK WATER TIME H.M.	MAXIMUM CURRENT TIME H.M.	VEL. KNOTS
1 TH	0122	0445	3.6E	16 F	0052	0408	3.8E
	0754	1038	3.2F		0713	1010	3.7F
	1344	1710	3.6E		1313	1635	4.1E
	2026	2301	2.8F		1948	2238	3.5F
2 F	0206	0528	3.2E	17 SA	0141	0459	3.7E
	0838	1120	2.8F		0801	1058	3.6F
	1428	1757	3.3E		1403	1727	4.0E
	2116	2347	2.5F		2042	2331	3.4F
3 SA	0253	0619	2.8E	18 SU	0235	0552	3.5E
	0926	1205	2.5F		0856	1153	3.4F
	1514	1847	3.0E		1458	1828	3.8E
	2209				2142		
4 SU	0343	0038	2.2F	19 M	0334	0027	3.1F
	1018	0710	2.5E		0959	0657	3.3E
	1604	1254	2.2F		1600	1252	3.2F
	2305	1942	2.7E		2249	1932	3.7E
5 M	0437	0132	1.9F	20 TU	0438	0130	3.0F
	1116	0806	2.3E		1108	0804	3.2E
	1659	1349	2.0F		1705	1355	3.1F
		2037	2.6E		2357	2038	3.7E
6 TU	0004	0229	1.9F	21 W	0545	0237	2.9F
	0535	0903	2.2E		1220	0911	3.3E
	1215	1449	2.0F		1813	1506	3.1F
	1755	2133	2.7E			2143	3.7E
7 W	0100	0332	1.9F	22 TH	0103	0349	3.0F
	0634	1000	2.3E		0651	1012	3.5E
	1313	1549	2.0F		1327	1617	3.2F
	1851	2226	2.8E		1918	2244	3.9E
8 TH	0152	0428	2.1F	23 F	0203	0457	3.3F
	0728	1053	2.5E		0753	1112	3.8E
	1405	1644	2.2F		1428	1722	3.4F
	1944	2315	3.0E		2019	2339	4.1E
9 F	0239	0518	2.3F	24 SA	0258	0554	3.5F
	0818	1142	2.8E		0850	1207	4.1E
	1452	1731	2.5F		1524	1820	3.6F
	2033				2114		
10 SA	0321	0002	3.2E	25 SU	0349	0032	4.2E
	0902	0601	2.6F		0941	0645	3.6F
	1535	1224	3.1E		1615	1258	4.2E
	2118	1814	2.8F		2205	1911	3.6F
11 SU	0400	0045	3.5E	26 M	0436	0120	4.2E
	0943	0640	2.9F		1027	0730	3.7F
	1615	1309	3.4E		1702	1345	4.3E
	2201	1856	3.1F		2250	1954	3.6F
12 M	0437	0127	3.7E	27 TU	0520	0207	4.1E
	1023	0718	3.2F		1110	0812	3.6F
	1654	1347	3.7E		1747	1430	4.2E
	2243	1937	3.3F		2333	2035	3.5F
13 TU	0512	0208	3.8E	28 W	0601	0250	3.9E
	1103	0759	3.5F		1150	0848	3.5F
	1734	1428	3.9E		1830	1512	4.0E
	2324	2019	3.5F			2113	3.2F
14 W	0549	0246	3.9E	29 TH	0014	0333	3.6E
	1144	0840	3.7F		0642	0926	3.2F
	1815	1507	4.1E		1230	1553	3.8E
		2102	3.6F		1912	2149	3.0F
15 TH	0007	0327	3.9E	30 F	0054	0416	3.3E
	0629	0923	3.7F		0721	1002	3.0F
	1227	1550	4.1E		1309	1636	3.5E
	1900	2149	3.6F		1954	2229	2.7F

OCTOBER

DAY	SLACK WATER TIME H.M.	MAXIMUM CURRENT TIME H.M.	VEL. KNOTS	DAY	SLACK WATER TIME H.M.	MAXIMUM CURRENT TIME H.M.	VEL. KNOTS
1 SA	0135	0459	2.9E	16 SU	0126	0442	3.9E
	0802	1045	2.7F		0744	1039	3.8F
	1349	1722	3.2E		1345	1712	4.3E
	2039	2311	2.4F		2026	2311	3.6F
2 SU	0218	0543	2.6E	17 M	0221	0540	3.7E
	0846	1126	2.4F		0843	1134	3.6F
	1432	1808	2.9E		1442	1812	4.1E
	2127	2358	2.2F		2127		
3 M	0305	0634	2.3E	18 TU	0321	0012	3.4F
	0936	1215	2.1F		0949	0644	3.5E
	1520	1900	2.6E		1544	1234	3.3F
	2219				2232	1916	3.8E
4 TU	0047	0047	2.0F	19 W	0425	0115	3.2F
	0357	0729	2.2E		1059	0749	3.4E
	1033	1308	1.9F		1650	1343	3.1F
	1613	1955	2.5E		2339	2021	3.7E
	2316						
5 W	0454	0142	1.9F	20 TH	0531	0224	3.1F
	1134	0826	2.2E		1210	0855	3.5E
	1710	1404	1.9F		1758	1457	3.0F
		2052	2.5E			2124	3.7E
6 TH	0012	0241	1.9F	21 F	0043	0339	3.1F
	0551	0923	2.3E		0636	0956	3.6E
	1233	1505	2.0F		1316	1611	3.1F
	1808	2147	2.6E		1904	2226	3.7E
7 F	0105	0339	2.1F	22 SA	0143	0444	3.3F
	0646	1015	2.6E		0737	1055	3.8E
	1328	1601	2.2F		1416	1714	3.2F
	1904	2238	2.9E		2004	2319	3.8E
8 SA	0154	0431	2.4F	23 SU	0238	0539	3.4F
	0736	1103	2.9E		0831	1148	4.0E
	1417	1652	2.5F		1510	1809	3.3F
	1957	2326	3.1E		2059		
9 SU	0238	0515	2.7F	24 M	0328	0010	3.8E
	0822	1151	3.3E		0920	0629	3.5F
	1501	1739	2.8F		1600	1238	4.1E
	2045				2148	1858	3.4F
10 M	0318	0011	3.4E	25 TU	0414	0059	3.8E
	0907	0601	3.1F		1004	0710	3.4F
	1544	1233	3.7E		1645	1323	4.1E
	2131	1824	3.2F		2232	1940	3.3F
11 TU	0358	0056	3.7E	26 W	0456	0142	3.7E
	0949	0643	3.5F		1045	0749	3.3F
	1626	1316	4.0E		1728	1406	4.1E
	2215	1909	3.5F		2312	2017	3.2F
12 W	0438	0136	3.9E	27 TH	0536	0225	3.5E
	1032	0728	3.8F		1123	0822	3.2F
	1708	1357	4.3E		1808	1448	3.9E
	2300	1956	3.8F		2351	2050	3.0F
13 TH	0519	0219	4.0E	28 F	0614	0307	3.3E
	1117	0812	4.0F		1159	0857	3.0F
	1753	1440	4.5E		1847	1528	3.7E
	2346	2039	3.9F			2125	2.8F
14 F	0603	0303	4.1E	29 SA	0029	0347	3.0E
	1203	0859	4.0F		0652	0931	2.8F
	1840	1528	4.6E		1236	1608	3.4E
		2128	3.9F		1926	2201	2.6F
15 SA	0034	0351	4.0E	30 SU	0108	0429	2.8E
	0651	0948	4.0F		0730	1010	2.6F
	1252	1617	4.5E		1314	1651	3.1E
	1931	2219	3.8F		2006	2242	2.5F
				31 M	0149	0511	2.5E
					0812	1053	2.3F
					1355	1733	2.9E
					2048	2323	2.3F

TIME MERIDIAN 75° W.   0000 IS MIDNIGHT.   1200 IS NOON.

- **Step 4**—Compute how far the current will carry you and make the second arrow of the appropriate length.

- **Step 5**—Now refer to Figure 10.13b. Draw the arrow from the starting point to the tip of the second arrow.

The direction of this arrow will be your course made good over the bottom, and its length will be the distance you will travel in 1 hour, or whatever interval you used. This distance will give you the speed over the bottom. With it, you may estimate how long it will take you to go any distance along that line—as long as the same current applies.

POSTTEST

10.10 You are heading due north at 6 knots through the water. The current is due east at 2 knots. What will be your course and speed over the bottom?

Finding set and drift of current—This problem arises when you want to verify that the current is behaving the way you expected. You must first determine your actual track over the bottom by using piloting methods, such as discussed in Chapter 8. Once that has been accomplished, refer to Figure 10.13b.

- **Step 1**—Draw an arrow from your starting point representing the track and speed made good over the bottom.

- **Step 2**—Then from the same starting point draw another arrow for your course and speed *through the water*. The direction of this arrow is determined by your compass reading, and its length is determined by your speed and the time interval.

- **Step 3**—Finally, draw an arrow from the tip of the second to the tip of the first. The direction and length of this arrow will give you the set and drift of the current.

Remember, this tells you what the current *was*, not necessarily what it *will be*. It is useful for comparison with what you may have predicted from the tide and current tables, but be cautious when you make further predictions.

POSTTEST

10.11 Your piloting tells you that your track over the bottom was due west 6 NM during the last 45 minutes. Your vessel's heading was southwest and your speed through the water was 8 knots. What were the set and drift of the current?

Finding desired true heading and speed through the water—This is the basis of the conventional rendezvous problem for powered vessels. You know the set and drift of the current, and you know the direction and speed you want to travel in order to arrive at a desired point at the appointed time. The question is, which way should you head and how fast should you go to overcome the effects of set and current?

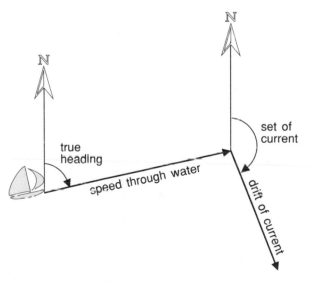

Figure 10.13a. Knowing your heading and speed, and knowing the set and drift of the current, find your track over the bottom.

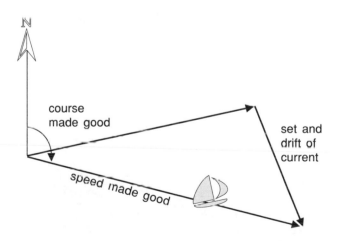

Figure 10.13b. Draw the third arrow, representing your track over the bottom and showing the net result of your boat's motion through the water and the motion of the water over the bottom

- **Step 1**—On the chart, measure the true heading and the distance to the destination.

- **Step 2**—Find the desired speed over the bottom by dividing the distance by the time available until the rendezvous. This heading and speed will give you the desired track.

- **Step 3**—Referring to Figure 10.14a, draw the desired track from your starting point and make its length equal to the distance travelled in one hour at the desired speed. Label its end with the letter B.

- **Step 4**—Next, draw an arrow whose heading is the set of the current and whose length is the drift of the current, or the distance it would carry you in one hour. Label its end with the letter A.

- **Step 5**—Now refer to Figure 10.14b, and draw the arrow from A to B. This will be your desired heading and its length will be your speed through the water— that is, the distance you would travel in one hour. If your vessel can attain the desired speed, go for it. Otherwise you may have to turn the problem around and find the desired track when the speed is set by the vessel's limitation.

POSTTEST

10.12 You wish to rendezvous at a point due west 8 NM in 1h 15m. The tide is due north at 1.5 knots. What

should be your heading and speed through the water?

Finding desired true heading and resulting speed over the bottom—This is probably the most important problem to be encountered by the sailor who cannot set the vessel's speed at an arbitrary value, but must sail at a convenient speed that will be dictated by the wind and the vessel. It will also apply in a powered boat if the engine is not sufficient to push the boat at the desired speed.

- **Step 1**—Referring to Figure 10.15a, draw an arrow from the starting point in the direction of the current and with a length equal to the distance the current would move in one hour. Label its end with the letter A.

- **Step 2**—Then draw a line from the starting point in the direction of the destination. This is the direction of the track.

- **Step 3**—Next, decide on a convenient speed for the vessel and draw a circle centered on A with a radius equal to the distance the boat would move in one hour. Label the intersection of this circle with the track as point B.

- **Step 4**—Now refer to Figure 10.15b and draw the arrow from point A to point B. This is the desired heading of the vessel, that is, the direction in which to steer.

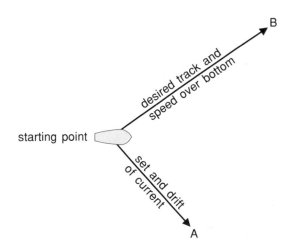

Figure 10.14a. First two steps in finding true heading and speed through the water. You must know desired track and speed to rendezvous point and know drift and set of current to find desired heading and speed through the water. This is particularly useful for a powered vessel, whose speed may be set by the throttle.

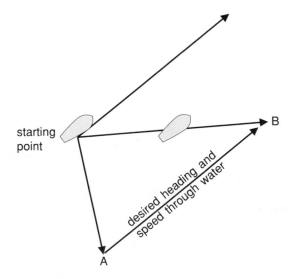

Figure 10.14b. The final step is to draw an arrow from A to B. This is the desired heading and speed through the water. If your vessel cannot make that speed through the water, you may wish to try a different method.

As is clear from Figure 10.15a, the length of this arrow is the same as the radius of the circle, which was the distance the boat would move in one hour at the convenient speed through the water. Thus steering at this heading and with this speed will take the vessel along the desired track. The vessel's actual speed made good over the bottom is determined by the length of the arrow from the starting point to point B.

POSTTEST

10.13 You wish to rendezvous at a point due north 6 NM; the current is toward the southeast at 2 knots. Your boat will sail at a speed of 6 knots through the water on any heading. What should be your course, and what will be the time of arrival?

ABNORMAL TIDES AND WAVES

Tides

The regular pattern of rise and fall is occasionally disturbed by unusual conditions of weather or sea, or by the effect of an earthquake. The chances are in favor of your sailing for years without encountering abnormal tides or waves, but they make good subjects for stories on long watches.

Storm surges—Hurricanes can produce abnormally high tides if they coincide with the normal high, and under certain conditions they can create abrupt rises or surges in sea level. *Bowditch* states that it has been estimated that three-fourths of the deaths on land attributed to hurricanes are caused by such storm tides.

River bores—Some rivers, the Amazon in Brazil and the Petitcodiac in the Bay of Fundy among them, are famous for the appearance of a *tidal bore* that heralds each high tide. They are somewhat akin to the sonic boom that accompanies the passage of a supersonic airplane. Tidal bores occur when the change of water level is too great to be accommodated by a gradual rise, and the result is a foaming, steplike wave that moves rapidly up the river. Typically a few feet high, they can achieve 25 feet in the Amazon. Van Dorn (1974) states that "dangerous bores are well noted in the sailing directions, and are devoutly to be eschewed by small vessels."

Influence of atmospheric pressure—These tides are not wind-driven, and they are quite mild, but interesting nevertheless. On a day of low atmospheric pressure, the ocean surface will act as though it is being drawn upward, and the resulting tides may rise a foot higher than normal. And, conversely, lower tides can occur on days of high atmospheric pressure. In some regions of the earth this effect will be larger than the normal tide. It is discussed in Section 3115 of *Bowditch*.

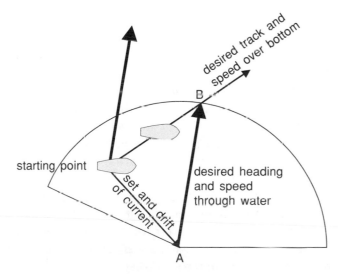

Figure 10.15b. Second part of solution: The direction of the line from A to B is the desired heading through the water. Its length is the convenient speed adopted by the pilot. The speed that will be made good over the bottom is determined by measuring the length of the track from the starting point to point B.

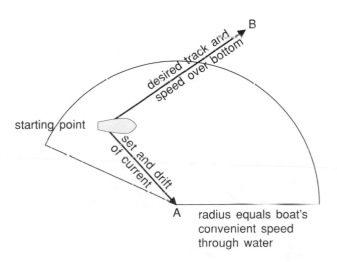

Figure 10.15a. First steps in solving the problem: knowing drift and set of current and knowing the boat's speed through the water, as well as the direction of the desired track, to find the course to steer.

Waves

Earthquake tsunamis and "tidal waves"—Tsunami is the name for the earthquake-generated monsters that are popularly called tidal waves, but have nothing to do with the tides. Tsunamis are a series of waves that travel rapidly from the epicenter and pile up against a shore. In deep water, they are probably no more than two or three feet high, but they can be 100 miles long and in shallow water they can build to 50 feet or more and can inflict widespread damage. Let us quote from *Bowditch,* p. 831:

> On April 1, 1946, seismic sea waves originating at an epicenter near the Aleutians spread over the entire Pacific. Scotch Cap Light on Unimak Island, 57 feet above sea level, was completely destroyed. Travelling at an average speed of 490 miles per hour, the waves reached the Hawaiian Islands in 4 hours and 34 minutes, where they arrived as waves 50 feet above the high water level, and flooded a strip of coast more than 1,000 feet wide at some places. They left a death toll of 173, and property damage of $25 million. Less destructive waves reached the shores of North and South America, and Australia, 6,700 miles from the epicenter.

But here is the good news. "After this disaster, a tsunami warning system was set up in the Pacific, even though destructive waves are relatively rare (averaging about one in 20 years in the Hawaiian Islands.)"

Van Dorn's 1974 data suggest they occur about ten times a century somewhere in the Pacific, but the other good news is that they are even rarer in oceans where earthquakes are less frequent. Warnings are broadcast on commercial and marine radio, and can give the alert navigator several hours to prepare. If you are at an isolated atoll, you may not get the radio warning, but the other side of that coin is that tsunamis are usually less severe near smaller islands—if you are in deep water. Like the surf, tsunamis build to destructive height in the shallows.

If you have reason to think that a tsunami may be heading your way, make for deep water, trying to get a mile or two beyond the 10-fathom line. There you will probably be safe. Van Dorn (1974, Chapter 18) discusses other alternatives.

Rogue waves—Occasionally an extraordinarily high wave will appear as if from nowhere. Joshua Slocum in Chapter 7 of his *Sailing Alone around the World* tells of one such wave. So huge was the apparition that Slocum could see it coming at him.

> One day, well off the Patagonian coast, while the sloop was reaching under short sail, a tremendous wave, the culmination, it seemed, of many waves, rolled down upon her in a storm, roaring as it came. I had only a moment to get all sail down and myself up on the peak halliards, out of danger, when I saw the mighty crest towering over my vessel. The mountain of water submerged my vessel. She shook in every timber and reeled under the weight of the sea, but rose quickly out of it, and rode grandly over the rollers that followed. It may have been a minute that from my hold in the rigging I could see no part of the *Spray*'s hull. Perhaps it was even less than that, but it seemed a long while, for under great excitement one lives fast . . .

Sir Ernest Shackleton described a similar monster in the chapter titled "The Boat Journey" in his book, *South.* He and five other men were sailing the *James Caird,* a 20-foot ship's whaler, toward South Georgia in the hope of finding a ship to rescue his polar expedition party that had been stranded on Elephant Island off the coast of Antarctica. One night, the sky

> . . . was overcast and occasional snow-squalls added to the discomfort produced by a tremendous cross-sea—the worst, I thought, that we had experienced. At midnight [May 5-6, 1916], I was at the tiller and suddenly noticed a line of clear sky between the south and south-west. I called to the other men that the sky was clearing, and then a moment later I realized that what I had seen was not a rift in the clouds but the white crest of an enormous wave. During twenty-six years' experience of the ocean in all its moods I had not encountered a wave so gigantic. It was a mighty upheaval of the ocean, a thing quite apart from the big white-capped seas that had been our tireless enemies for days. I shouted, "For God's sake, hold on! It's got us." Then came a moment of suspense that seemed drawn into hours. White surged the foam of the breaking sea around

us. We felt our boat lifted and flung forward like a cork in breaking surf. We were in a seething chaos of tortured water; but somehow the boat lived through it, half full of water, sagging to the dead weight and shuddering under the blow.

Very little scientific or quantitative literature exists on these rogue waves. They are evidently unpredictable, although they appear to be more common in regions of rough ocean where waves of many different lengths and directions are superposed on each other—"cross-sea" in Shackleton's words. In such regions, the waves will usually tend to interfere and cancel each other, producing a mixed and unpleasant sea, but on rare occasions they culminate—to use Slocum's apt expression—in a destructive wave that stampedes like a foaming herd of buffalo.

How far can they travel? How high can they get? How fast do they move? Are they statistically predictable, like tornadoes in the Plains states? These questions are largely unanswered, but van Dorn (1974) discusses the statistics of wave heights in a wind-driven sea and suggests that some rogues are simply the extreme samples from a statistical distribution. He says "the chance [of encountering a rogue] is best following a succession of abnormally high waves." He provides graphs for predicting the likelihood of waves of various heights in well-developed seas under various conditions. But, of course, these are merely averages. Who can say what the next wave will bring?

CHAPTER ELEVEN

A Cruise on Long Island Sound

INTRODUCTION

This chapter provides a chance for you to apply some of the techniques discussed in earlier chapters. We will leave it up to you to procure a copy of training chart 116-SC Tr for plotting the cruise. Figure 11.1 is the Napier diagram for your compass. Chapter references and answers to questions are given in Appendix 7.

GETTING READY

An essential and enjoyable part of most coastwise navigation is plotting your cruise in advance. The weather the next day promises to be fine; the wind will blow from the north at 10 knots. You are in the harbor of Stonington, CT, on a 32-foot cruiser with a few friends, and you decide to sail around part of Long Island Sound. The boat makes about 4 knots through the water with a fair breeze. It has a radio direction finder, a marine compass, and a pelorus, and you have a pair of binoculars equipped with a compass.

Scan the chart and find the compass rose that is nearest Stonington.

QUESTION

11.1 What is the magnetic variation for 1990? _____

You have checked the tide tables and have found that the high tide comes at about 0600 AM, so it will be ebbing during the morning. In this region, that means that the current will be from west to east, and you can expect currents up to 1 or 2 knots.

You decided to sail out of the harbor to the Middle Ground Horn and then turn west, sailing past Eel Grass Ground and North Dumpling. From there you will turn southeast across The Race toward Little Gull Island. From there you will sail north to Bartlett Reef, and then you will turn eastward and sail directly back to Stonington.

With a pencil and a straightedge, plot a series of straight legs from your point of departure to your destination. Then look for dangers along each leg, and look for waymarks that will help you know how far you have come. Mark each leg with its true direction. Measure an approximate distance and estimate the time it will take. Add up the times, and estimate your arrival time. Of course, the wind and water will appear to have minds of their own, and you will probably deviate from your plan as you go, but this preliminary planning is never a waste of time. In case of unexpected circumstances, it will be a help in setting a new course. (Who knows, this imaginary trip may be the only time you will get to your planned destination that day!)

QUESTION

11.2 What are the approximate distance (NM) and time required for this tour, if you assume a nominal speed of 4 kn? _____

This planning stage is also the time to look for special features on the chart that may be of help in piloting, such as airports, cupolas, water tanks, radio towers, and radio beacons. Make sure you are familiar with the symbols on the chart.

Assemble your drawing tools and charts, and sharpen your pencils. Time for bed.

TAKING DEPARTURE

You get up at dawn and sail out of Stonington Harbor due south, passing between a green and a red flashing light toward the Middle Ground light. You will be making a dead reckoning (DR) plot and correcting it throughout the day, and unless you start accurately, you may become lost or confused, so the point of departure (POD) must be established carefully.

When you come near the red nun buoy marked "2," you decide to head the boat on course heading 270T (in order to avoid Latimer Reef), and then take some relative bearings to fix your location as the POD.

QUESTIONS

11.3 What should be your magnetic heading? _____

11.4 Using the Napier diagram in Figure 11.1, what is your compass heading? _____

With your boat on a heading 270T, you measure the following relative bearings with a pelorus:

Watch Hill Hotel cupola	179T
Fishers Island cupola	314T
Middle Ground Light	109T

QUESTION

11.5 Using this information find your location on the chart and determine the latitude and longitude.
Lat. _____ Long. _____

UNDERWAY

You sail on the new course until Latimer Reef bell passes to port and is seen at a relative bearing of 270 and a distance of about ¼ NM. Then you turn 20° to port, heading on a course of 250T.

QUESTION

11.6 What are your new headings?
magnetic _____ compass _____

On this course, you estimate your speed as 4 knots through the water, and you pass Eel Grass abeam to starboard at 0900 EDT.

QUESTIONS

11.7 When do you expect to arrive at Ram Island Gong? _____ EDT

11.8 When do you expect to arrive at North Dumpling Light? _____ EDT

You find North Dumpling directly abeam to port at 1012 EDT. This is a little later than you antici-

pated, so you use this information to estimate the effect of the tidal current.

QUESTIONS

11.9 What were your distance and average speed over the bottom from Eel Grass to North Dumpling?
_____

11.10 What can you say about the tidal current? _____

You pass North Dumpling Horn on your port side, and before turning south toward Little Gull Island, you decide to take another fix. One line of position at 1020 EDT is determined by the fact that you are on a range line with Seaflower Reef and Vixen Ledge. Scanning the water with your compass-binoculars, you determine that the magnetic heading of Horseshoe Reef is 014M. (You have previously found a place on the boat where the compass deviation is small enough to be ignored, so you may assume that the binoculars give magnetic bearings.)

QUESTION

11.11 What is the true heading of Horseshoe Reef at that moment? _____

Mark your location on the chart, and measure the true course to Little Gull Island.

QUESTIONS

11.12 What are the true course and distance to Little Gull Island? _____

11.13 After you have passed the flashing red light R "2" near Fishers Island, what is the shallowest water you should expect on the depth-sounder until you are within a mile of Little Gull Island? _____

You turn to that course at 1022 EDT and paying careful attention to the wake of your boat, you assure yourself there is very little leeway. But, after 41 minutes, you see that Race Rock is 45° off the port bow. Four minutes later (1107 EDT) you find that Race Rock is abeam to port, and the water is only about 50 feet deep. Something is not right. You decide to heave-to for a few minutes, heading the boat into the wind and bringing it to a standstill while you figure out what is going on.

QUESTION

11.14 Using these data, determine your distance-off from Race Rock and find an approximate fix.

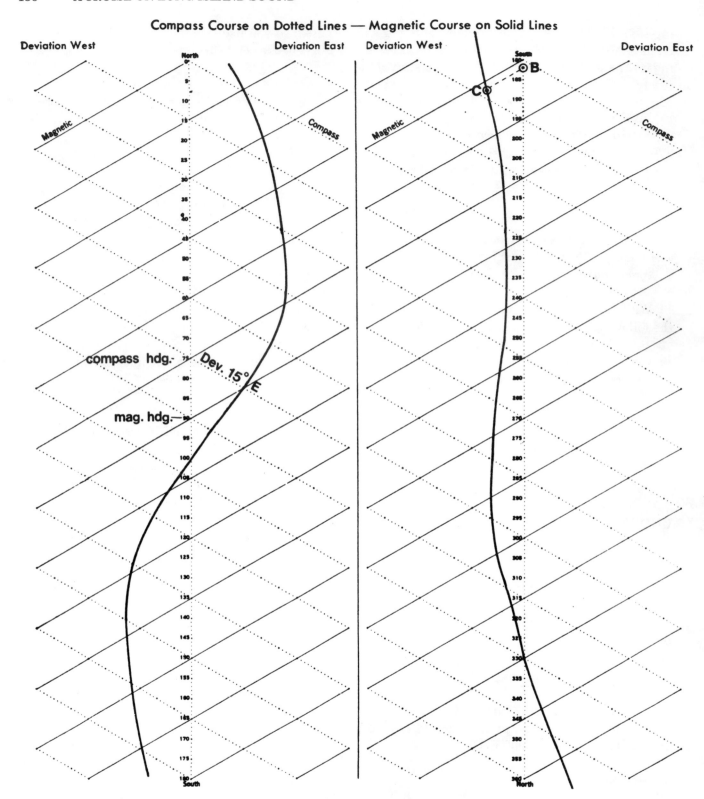

Figure 11.1.

It seems clear that the tide has set you to port, so you decide to solve for the speed of the current by comparing your true location with what you DR had predicted.

QUESTION
11.15 What are the set and drift of the tide? _____

Now you need to set the new course to account for this tide, assuming that its effect will stay the same all the way to Little Gull Island. You decide to follow a track at 225T over the bottom.

QUESTION
11.16 What should be your new true course, and what speed do you expect to make over the bottom if you make 4 kn through the water? _____

Having stopped for 3 minutes to figure out the tide, you set sail, and at about 1152 EDT you pass over a deep channel (250 feet) and into shallower water. Little Gull Island is dead ahead, and you decide to head toward Bartlett Reef. The tide has gone slack, so you may ignore it for the next leg of the trip.

QUESTION
11.17 What is the true course toward Bartlett Reef?

_____

At 1155 EDT you head on the new course sailing at about 3.5 kn through the water. You measure the distance to R "44" and Bartlett Reef and estimate your arrivals.

QUESTIONS
11.18 When do you expect to see R"44" abeam to port?

_____

11.19 When do you expect to arrive near Bartlett Reef?

_____

In order to avoid going aground on the reefs just to the east of Bartlett Reef you measure a "danger bearing" using the tank near Seaside Point. If the true bearing of the tank becomes greater than this danger bearing, you know you are getting too close to the reef.

QUESTION
11.20 What is the true danger bearing, and what are the magnetic and compass values of the danger bearing? _____

At 1255 EDT you get a fix from magnetic bearings of Bartlett Reef and the tank near Seaside Point:

| Bartlett Reef | 294M |
| Tank near Seaside Point | 001M |

QUESTION
11.21 What are the true bearings to these marks? _____

Mark your position and time on the chart.
At this time you decide to head back toward Stonington Harbor. Your first goal will be Seaflower Reef.

QUESTIONS
11.22 What is your course and distance to Seaflower Reef? _____
11.23 At what time will you arrive, assuming no tide?

_____

11.24 If you arrive 15 minutes earlier than expected, what can you say about the effect of the tidal current? _____
11.25 Assuming the same current will hold all the way back, when should you expect to arrive at the Eel Grass Ground? _____
11.26 Did you manage to convince yourself that you knew what you were doing the whole time?

II. Celestial Navigation

CHAPTER TWELVE

Watching the Sky

"See, Buddy? Dat de north star . . . Dat is one thing you can count on. Everything else in dis goddom world changin so fast dat a mon cannot keep up no more, but de north star is always dere, boy, de cold eye of it, watching de seasons come and go . . .

"It were watchin on de night dat you were borned, and it be watchin when dat night comes dat you die."

Peter Mathiessen, Far Tortuga

INTRODUCTION

This chapter describes what the navigator should watch for in the sky, in order to anticipate the data that can be found in the *Nautical Almanac.* Some aspects of the sky alter from one night to the next; others change more slowly. And—just as important for the navigator—some aspects of the sky depend very little on the observer's location, while others depend on latitude.

MAKING A JOURNAL OF THE SKY

One way to learn the sky is to read it. Whenever you have a chance, stop, orient yourself, check the time, and look up. Even on a cloudy day, there is something useful to be learned. (You can, for example, become familiar with the approach of evening darkness.)

Make written notes of what you see, including the date, the time to the nearest minute, the condition of the sky (overcast, partly cloudy, or clear), and your location. If it is daylight and not overcast, locate the sun; try to estimate its altitude and azimuth. You will quickly learn where to look, depending on the time of day. Stand a few minutes and see whether you can detect its westward motion. Notice how low the sun is even around noon in the winter months.

Look for the moon. Chances are, you will be able to find it if you look very carefully, because the moon is visible at some time during the night or day for about twenty-six out of the twenty-nine days that lie between one new moon and the next. What is

the shape of the crescent? Which way is it oriented? Is the moon waxing or waning? (See if you can develop simple rules for predicting the answers to such questions by noting the relationship between the appearance of the moon and the relative position of the sun.) If you study the comic strips, you will quickly find that the artists often exercise their imagination and draw the moon in ways that are impossible: a full moon rising at midnight, for example; or a crescent that is backward.

At night, orient yourself by finding the celestial pole in your hemisphere (described below). Watch for a while and see if you can detect the motion of the stars. This will usually take a half-hour or so, but it can be done more quickly if you line up a star or the moon with a tree or a building. Make a note of where you stand and make a sketch of the stars you observe. Then return a few nights later and see whether the stars are in the same place at the same time by your watch.

Here are some other activities that will be useful to the navigator: Find several star patterns that can be used to locate Polaris; see whether you can tell time by the orientations of the constellations or their settings and risings, and try to determine how much time on your watch (which is sun time) is required for the star clock to move ahead one day.

PRETEST

12.1 How long does it take the sun to set?

12.2 In exactly 24 hours, does the moon return to the same place in the sky?

12.3 In exactly 24 hours, do the stars return to the same place in the sky?

FINDING THE CELESTIAL POLES

North celestial pole

Figure 2.10 shows a long-exposure photograph of the region of the north celestial pole (NCP) and the direction of motion in that photograph is indicated in Figure 12.1. The bright star near the center of Figure 12.1 is the North Star, Polaris. Find it by locating the Big Dipper (in Ursa Major, the Great Bear) and extending a line from the pointer stars (Figure 12.2). If the Big Dipper is not visible, you may be able to find the W of Cassiopeia. (It will look like an M in some orientations.) Follow the direction indicated by the arrow formed by the central three stars, as in Figure 12.3.

Polaris is about 1° from the actual celestial pole. (In the year 2102 it will be only 0.5° from the pole.) So it traces a small circle about the pole, and its geographic point is at latitude 89° on the earth's surface. Hence it swings 1° east and west of the pole each day. Figure 12.4 shows how to locate the pole more accurately, using Ruchbah, a star in Cassiopeia. Extend a line from Ruchbah through Polaris and then 1° beyond. That will put you quite close to the pole.

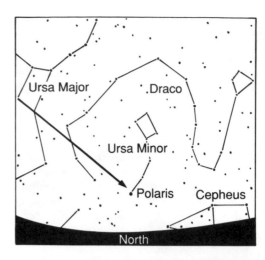

Figure 12.2. Locating the North Star (Polaris) by extending the line between the two stars at the end of the bowl of the Big Dipper (Ursa Major).

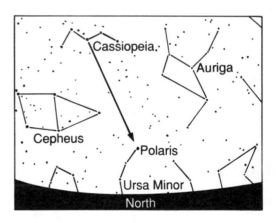

Figure 12.3. When the Big Dipper is not visible, the W of Cassiopeia points to Polaris.

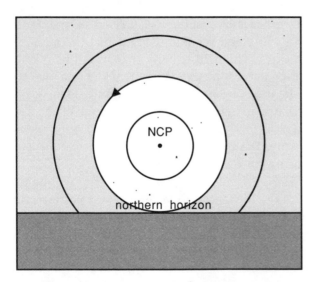

Figure 12.1. Looking north toward the north celestial pole (NCP). During a day, the stars in the northern sky trace counterclockwise circles about the NCP, which is about 1° from Polaris. At a latitude of 20°N, the stars within 20° of the north celestial pole never set (light region in this diagram). They are called circumpolar stars.

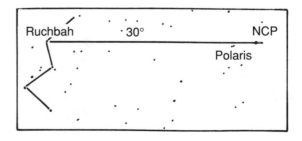

Figure 12.4. To locate the pole, extend a line from Ruchbah in Cassiopeia through Polaris (30°) and extend it 1° beyond. That point will be within 0.1° of the pole.

If you need even greater accuracy, you may turn to Chapter 16 and use the Polaris Tables in the *Nautical Almanac*.

South celestial pole

This pole is not marked by a star, but it can be located approximately by following the axis of the Southern Cross (Crux), as indicated in Figure 12.5, to the region between Octans and Chameleon. Stars in the southern sky move in a clockwise direction about the south celestial pole.

FINDING THE ZENITH

If you can find the celestial pole and can estimate accurately the location of the zenith, the north-south line is the circle passing through them (Figure 12.6). The zenith is directly overhead. It is at the intersection of all the lines coming straight up from the horizon, but determining the precise direction of the zenith is very difficult. It requires considerable practice because there is a tendency to put it in front of you, as indicated in Figure 12.7.

When you have picked out a star that you think is at the zenith, turn 180° and see whether is still appears at the zenith. If it does not, pick another spot halfway between the old and the new apparent zenith. Then turn again; keep trying until you are satisfied.

East and west

These directions are just as useful as north and south, and sometimes they are easier to determine.

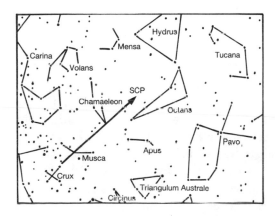

Figure 12.5. There is no star at the south celestial pole (SCP), but the pole can be located by extending the axis of the Southern Cross (Crux).

To find them, you can make use of the fact that the celestial equator crosses the horizon at the east and west points, no matter where on earth you are—as long as you are not at one of the poles, where east and west are undefined (see Figures 12.8 through 12.11). One marker for the celestial equator is the belt of Orion.

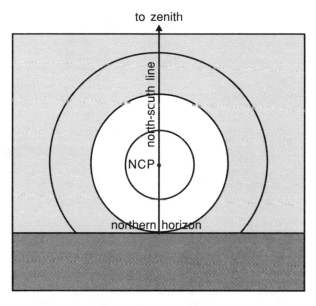

Figure 12.6. The north-south line rises perpendicular to the northern horizon and passes through the north celestial pole and the zenith.

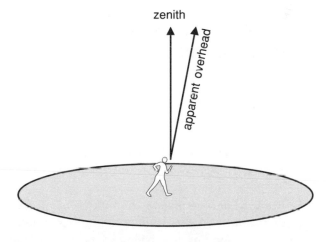

Figure 12.7. Illustration of a tendency to put the zenith in front of you. In this example, you are facing east, and you tend to see the zenith east of its true position, as indicated by the arrow. You must test your estimate by turning 180°.

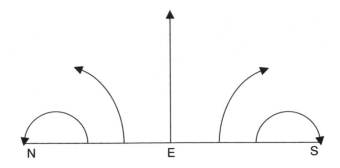

Figure 12.8. Tracks of the stars moving upward across the eastern half of the horizon as seen from the equator, where the stars rise vertically.

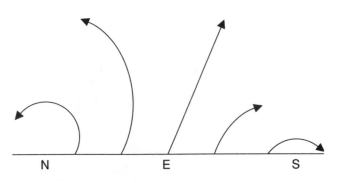

Figure 12.9. Eastern half of the horizon as seen from a moderate northern latitude, where the stars rise obliquely. At the horizon, the amount of tilt from the vertical is equal to the latitude. The north celestial pole is above the horizon but the south celestial pole is not.

WATCHING THE THE SKY FROM DIFFERENT LATITUDES

PRETEST

12.4 The sun moves overhead every noon. T _____ F _____

12.5 The sun always sets straight down toward the horizon. T _____ F _____

12.6 The sun never rises for a person standing at the north pole. T _____ F _____

In order to get a sense of the motion of the sky and how it might be useful to navigators, it is helpful to imagine moving to various parts of the globe and looking upward. Let us start on the equator at the time of the spring equinox.

From the equator

Suppose we sail from the tropics toward the equator in mid-March. Each evening the sun descends

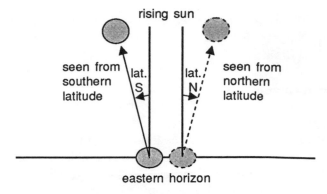

Figure 12.10. The apparent paths of the rising sun relative to the horizon in the eastern sky. When seen from the northern hemisphere, the sun's upward path tilts toward the south, which is to the right when facing east. The amount of tilt from the vertical equals the navigator's latitude.

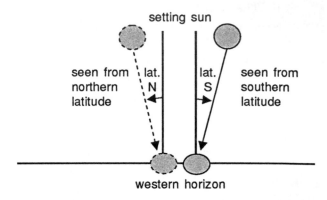

Figure 12.11. The apparent paths of the setting sun relative to the horizon in the western sky. When seen from the northern hemisphere, the sun's downward path tilts down toward the north, which is to the right when facing west. The amount of tilt from the vertical equals the navigator's latitude.

vertically toward the horizon and, almost before we are aware, the twilight has vanished and the stars have come out. Orion sinks toward the western horizon and we see most of the familiar northern winter constellations, but we look in vain for Polaris. It has vanished into the thick air near the northern horizon. During the night, all stars rise straight up from the horizon (Figure 12.12) in the eastern half of the sky and trace a semicircle that carries them across the meridian and straight down toward the western half of the horizon. Stars that rise in the southeast will set in the southwest. Stars that rise in the northeast will set in the northwest. They are above the horizon for twelve hours.

Morning twilight is abrupt and "the sun comes up like thunder" in the east because it moves straight up, regardless of the time of year.

If we return three months later, we will find much the same behavior, except the constellations will have shifted westward and the sun will rise in the northeast instead of due east. It remains above the horizon twelve hours each day, year around.

From an intermediate latitude

Let us turn north and sail toward Bermuda. When we reach a latitude of about 5°N, Polaris emerges from the northern horizon. The stars and sun no longer rise straight up. Their paths slant toward the south (to the right looking east) more and more as we sail north (Figures 12.10-12.11).

From the north pole

Now let us wait until mid-December and fly to the north pole. The sun is invisible and the sky is totally dark, except for the stars that wheel around the sky. Polaris traces a small circle (1° radius) about the north celestial pole. The stars and planets all move parallel to the horizon, neither setting nor rising. Each one traces a complete circle about the zenith in twenty-four hours, as though attached to the pole by the ribbon of a celestial May pole (Figure 12.12). The belt of Orion is dimly visible on the horizon, wheeling about the sky once a day.

There is no east or west; all directions are south. If we walk in a straight line for 120 nautical miles, we notice that the circular paths of the stars have tilted slightly (by 2°). Behind us (north), a few stars dip below the horizon for part of their path. Ahead (south), we see an occasional star gleam above the horizon for an hour or so before dipping down and vanishing again.

From the south pole

If we could fly at once (it is still mid-December) from the north pole toward the south pole, we might catch the sun rising above the southern horizon as we pass the arctic circle. By the time we have reached the antarctic circle, the sun remains in the sky twenty-four hours a day. Landing at the pole, we see that the sun traces a circle about the zenith, but it is going clockwise, contrary to the motions we saw at the north pole (Figure 12.13).

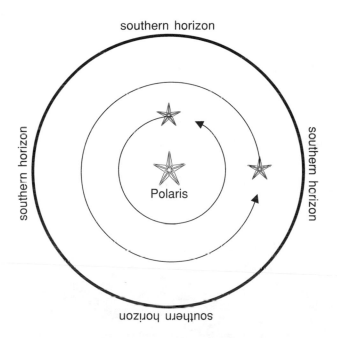

Figure 12.12. Looking toward the zenith while standing at the north pole, the stars daily trace a circle counterclockwise about the north celestial pole, which is approximately marked by Polaris. All directions are south.

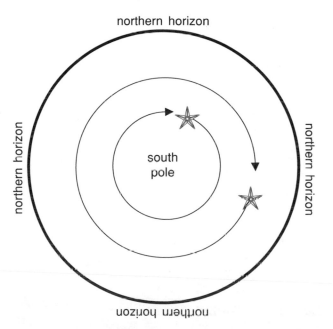

Figure 12.13. Looking toward the zenith while standing at the south pole, the stars daily trace a circle clockwise about the south celestial pole. All directions are north.

CHAPTER THIRTEEN

Sun Time

Time, except dawn and nightfall, meant nothing to daily life in that immensity of sea, yet I had to take meticulous care to know the time accurately to within a second for navigation. The dateline has given mariners a headache since it was first invented. After crossing the dateline, the only way that I could avoid making mistakes over the time was to head every page of the log with my local date and day of the week, as well as the difference between my local time and Greenwich time.

Sir Francis Chichester, Gypsy Moth Circles the World

INTRODUCTION

The sun is the key figure is most celestial navigation, and your clock will help you predict the position of the sun and deduce your location from observations of the sun's position.

Your "ship's watch" may be a modern digital watch or an old-fashioned chronometer. Whichever it may be, it is set to Greenwich mean time (GMT); this in turn is derived from the motion of the sun.

This chapter assumes you know your dead reckoning position and describes methods for predicting the behavior of the sun from an approximate location. You will learn how to determine the time and to use some of the tables for the sun in the *Nautical Almanac.*

PRETEST

13.1 The sun is always directly south when your watch says 1200 standard time. T _____ F _____

13.2 Sunrise comes earlier in the west. T _____ F _____

13.3 When you cross the international date line going east, you should add a day to the date.
T _____ F _____

13.4 A sundial tells standard time. T _____ F _____

Building a sundial

A sundial is a clock with just one moving part: the sun. It is easy to build a sundial, and if you are careful you will be able to tell sun time to within a few minutes. The sundial also makes a good instrument for discovering some things about the oddity of sun time and its daughter, Greenwich mean time.

You can build one on the ground or on a board. If you opt for the ground, find a flat piece of terrain

and drive a tall stick into the ground so it is good and sturdy. The stick will serve as the gnomon and cast a shadow on the ground. As the sun moves westward around the gnonom, the shadow moves eastward. To mark the passage of the hours you can put a small stick in the ground at the tip of the shadow exactly at the start of each hour of daylight.

Alternatively, you can use a large board (about two feet on a side), and a thin dowel about one foot long will serve as the gnomon. Drill a hole near the center for the dowel so that it will stand exactly perpendicular to the board, and mount a small magnetic compass as shown in Figure 13.1. Draw a north-south line through the centers of the dowel and the compass.

You can set the board on a windowsill and line it up with true north whenever you want to know the

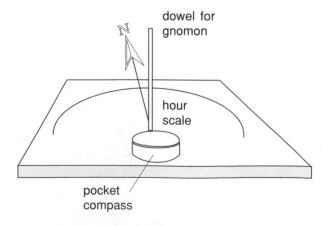

Figure 13.1. Design for simple sundial with compass and north-south line for finding the time of noon. Remember to correct for compass variation. The north-south line should point to true north.

sun time. If you do the alignment with the compass, you must find the effect of magnetic variation and compass deviation. You can find the variation from a nautical chart of your region, or, if you live in the northern hemisphere, you can check the pointing of the compass against the North Star some night. Or, if you have a south-facing window, you can go out and stand so the North Star is directly over the window. Then mark the spot where you are standing (perhaps next to a tree), go up to the window, and use the mark to indicate true south. This will give you a reference for lining up the sundial. In the southern hemisphere, you can use your compass.

To mark the hours, all you need to do is set your watch accurately and when each hour arrives, put a small nail into the board at the center of the gnomon shadow, or at its tip. To make it easier to read, the nails should be arranged along a curve (it is actually an ellipse) as far from the gnomon as possible. Once the hours have been marked, you can estimate fractions of an hour by eye, using divisions of one-quarter hour, or fifteen minutes.

LOCAL APPARENT NOON (LAN)

One of the easiest ways to determine your latitude at sea is to measure the altitude of the sun with a sextant when it is exactly on the north-south line (Figure 13.2). At that moment the sun is on the meridian and the sun time is "local apparent noon." We will call it LAN for short, and your task is to determine when LAN occurs.

The first step is to level the board and turn it so the north-south line is lined up with true north.

Once you have done this, you simply wait until the gnomon shadow falls on the north-south line.

POSTTEST

13.5 If you forgot to take into account a 15°W compass variation when you lined your sundial up with the compass, how would this affect the measured time of your LAN? Would it be early or late, and by how much?

Look at the name of LAN carefully. It is called "local" because the time depends on your location; it is called "apparent" because it is determined by the apparent (visible) sun. We now take each of these terms in turn.

Local vs. zone time

Suppose the date is April 13 and you have measured the time of LAN in a city at a longitude of 71°W (the latitude makes no difference). You will find that the sun crosses the meridian at 1144 EST (eastern standard time).

Later that day, you drive west to longitude 78°W. If you set up your sundial the next day and measure the time of LAN you will find it to occur about 28 minutes later, at 1212 EST. The extra 28 minutes was required for the sun to move westward by the additional 7° of longitude. Thus, the time of LAN is affected by your longitude, as illustrated in Figure 13.3.

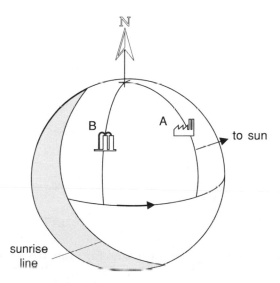

Figure 13.3. Diagram of the earth showing the time of local apparent noon (LAN) at city A. The direction of the earth's rotation is indicated at the equator. City B is west of A and it has just emerged from the sunrise line, so its LAN will be later.

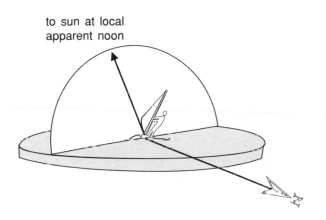

Figure 13.2. At the time of local apparent noon (LAN), the sun is on the north-south line and is highest in the sky. This is a handy situation for accurate latitude determination, and you should know how to predict it.

It would be very awkward if everyone agreed to set their clocks so the sun would be on the meridian when they read 1200 hours. Every city would have a different time, and radio stations in different locations would be giving station breaks at different times.

Time zones were invented to take care of this problem. The equator is divided into 24 zones of 15° width. Each zone corresponds to one hour and within each zone, all clocks are set to zone time (ZT), which is the sun time at the center of the zone. Figure 13.4 shows the layout of actual time zones; they are bent here and there for convenience and for political reasons. There are 360° along the equator, and if there are to be 24 zones, each will have 15°. The first one is centered on Greenwich, England, and reaches from longitude 7°30′E to 7°30′W. The zones are centered at longitudes 0°, ±15°, ±30°, ±45°, ±60°, ±75°, ±90°, etc.

Like GMT, zone time (ZT) is matched to the mean daily motion of the sun. But ZT differs by a whole number of hours from GMT. It is the time to which most watches are set. On land it is called "standard time."

The zone description (ZD) is the number of hours to be added to zone time to find the GMT:

$$GMT = ZT + ZD$$
(1 hour per 15°; – if east, + if west longitude)

If you are in an eastern longitude, compute your ZD by finding the multiple of 15° nearest to your longitude and taking that multiplier as the ZD. For example at 56°E the nearest multiple is 60° and the multiplier is 4, and the ZD is –4h.

If you are in a western longitude, take that multiplier with a positive sign as the ZD. For example at 56°W, the multiplier is 4 and the ZD is 4h.

Longitude 180° is the theoretical position of the international date line (IDL). The ZD for the time zone centered on the IDL is ±12h, depending on your location in the zone. It is given by ZD = +12h if you are west of the IDL and ZD = –12h if you are east. Thus, the ZD changes by 24h when you cross

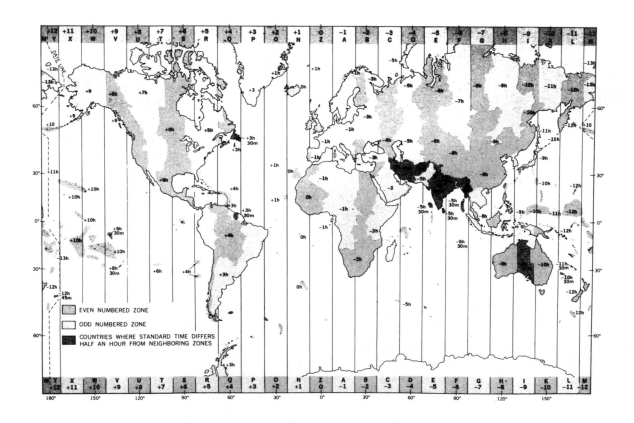

Figure 13.4. Time zones of the world. Each zone is nominally 15° wide in longitude, and their centers are at longitudes 0°, ±15°, ±30°, ±45° . . . The standard time in each zone is found by adding the zone description to the UTC, which is nearly the same as GMT.

the IDL. The date advances when you move westward and it falls back a day when you move eastward across the date line.

Here's how to remember how to treat the date line. Imagine you are flying westward along the equator at about 1,000 statute miles per hour and the sun is over head. You will have perpetual noon, but after you have gone once around the world, it must be a day later. So, advance your calendar a day when crossing the date line moving westward.

POSTTEST

13.6 What are the zone descriptions for the following longitudes?

14W ____

125E ____

125W ____

181E ____

13.7 You are flying eastward at 2,000 mph (statute miles) along the equator in a plane that is refueled in the air. How often do you you have to adjust your watch to account for the new zone times, and in which direction?

13.8 When you fly across the date line eastward which way do you change the calendar?

Apparent vs. mean sun time

Suppose you are in a city that lies at the center of your time zone. In the contiguous United States, this would be longitude 75°W (eastern), 90°W (central), 105°W (mountain) or 120°W (Pacific). It is April 13, and you have an excellent watch that you set to 1200 hours when the sun crosses the meridian (LAN). You then observe the times of LAN through the year, checking your watch as you go. You soon find that your watch runs regularly, but the sun does not. Figure 13.5 shows the difference in minutes throughout the year. This pattern is repeated from one year to the next.

By May 16, the sun is running early by 3 minutes: LAN occurs at 1157. On June 12 it is correct again, but by July 22 it is 6 minutes late: LAN occurs at 1206. Again reversing its trend, the sun catches up with your watch and by September 1 LAN occurs exactly at 1200. By November 3, the sun is 16 minutes early: LAN occurs at 1144; on December 21 it is on time again. From January to mid-April, the sun is late, and by May 16 it has caught up again.

On the average through the year, the sun agrees with your watch because your watch is built to keep

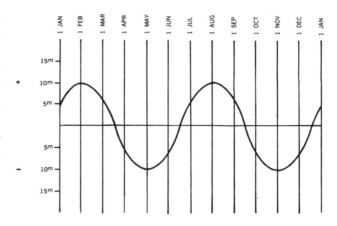

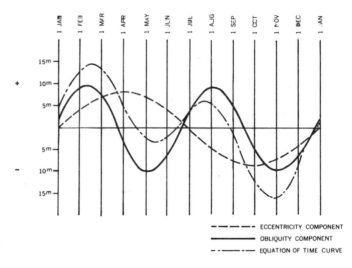

- - - - - - ECCENTRICITY COMPONENT

————————— OBLIQUITY COMPONENT

- · — · — EQUATION OF TIME CURVE

Figure 13.5. Yearly pattern in the time of local apparent noon (LAN) at the center of each time zone. The sun crosses the meridian at 1200 standard time on April 13, June 12, September 1, and December 21. At other times it is early or late by as much as 16 minutes. This curve is called the equation of time.

mean sun time. But on any particular date, the sun will be ahead or behind your watch because the earth's orbit is not quite round and because the orbit is tilted with respect to the earth's equator. The difference is called the equation of time.

Another way to display the equation of time is shown in Figure 13.6, which displays the position of the sun relative to the meridian at 1200 hours throughout the year.

Your watch keeps mean sun time and it runs at a constant rate. Before going any further, you must know how to set your watch accurately. Telephone service is usually a reliable way to find zone time, but the safest method is to use the signals that are

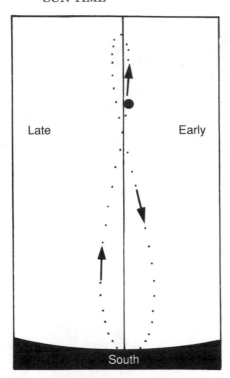

Late

Early

South

Figure 13.6. The large dot shows the position of the sun at 1200 standard time on March 24 as seen looking south from latitude 68°N, at the arctic circle. The vertical line represents the meridian. The dots show successive positions of the sun at 1200 each week of the year. The arrows indicate the direction of motion from one noon to the next. When the sun is east, its meridian passage occurs after 1200 and the equation of time is positive. The north-south motion corresponds to the seasons, and the east-west motion is the equation of time. Note the sun is below the horizon at noon for a few days near the winter solstice, when there is no daylight.

broadcast continuously on shortwave radio. The next section describes them.

POSTTEST

13.9 How many times a year does the sun cross the meridian exactly at 1200?

13.10 If the sun is late on a particular day , is it east or west of the meridian at 1200?

GREENWICH MEAN TIME

PRETEST

13.11 How long does it take a radio signal to travel all the way around the world? Same as sound _____ Approximately one day _____ one hour _____ one minute _____ one second _____ $\frac{1}{10}$ second _____

The worldwide reference for time is Greenwich mean time (GMT). This is the time that is determined by the rotation of the earth and it is used in the nautical almanacs. It is very close to *universal time coordinated* (UTC), which is broadcast on shortwave. For most purposes of navigation, you may assume UTC and GMT are the same, as they almost never differ by more than 1 second.

Shortwave time signals

With an ordinary shortwave (high frequency or HF) receiver, you can tune into a time service anywhere in the world. The *Admiralty List of Radio Signals* has a complete list, but for the U.S. coastal waters, the following will suffice.

WWV and WWVH: 2.5, 5.0, 10.0, 15.0, 20 MHz—The U.S. National Bureau of Standards broadcasts continuously from Fort Collins, CO, and Kauai, HI. The call letters of these stations are WWV and WWVH. Voice announcements give the hours and minutes of UTC just before the start of each minute. The start of the beep indicates the start of the minute.

These signals also carry the DUT1 code, as described in *Bowditch* for corrections to the nearest 0.1 second of UT1 (see below for definitions).

The quality of the received signal will vary from frequency to frequency and with time of day, so you should hunt for the one giving the best signal. The best signals are usually found at 10.0 MHz or 15.0 MHz.

The following information is carried by WWV at a certain number of minutes after each hour.

Table 13.1. WWV voice announcements each hour

Minutes after the hour	*Topic*
8, 9, 10	Storm announcements provide the latitude and longitude of low-pressure regions, tropical storms, hurricanes, and regions of thunderstorm activity
14	Preliminary NASTAR GPS announcement (see Chapter 22)
15	Report on status of GPS
16	Status of Omega navigation system (see Chapter 22)
18	Solar flux and geomagnetic activity report and prediction

CHU: 3.33, 7.335, and 14.670 MHz—Station CHU, Canada, broadcasts UTC with voice announcements alternating in French and English each minute. This is an excellent signal for the East Coast of the United States.

Telephone time signals

If you don't have access to a shortwave receiver, you may check the time by telephone from the government agencies:

NBS: Fort Collins, CO, 303-499-7111

NBS: Kauai, HI 808-335-4363

Naval Observatory: Washington, DC,
900-410-8463

Local phone companies also provide automatic voice announcement of time signals, and they appear to be good to the nearest second, but they should be verified by comparison with the government signals.

Setting your ship's watch

The ship's watch is a good clock or watch that has been dedicated to its task and is kept at the navigation station, out of harm's way. The time shown by ship's watch is called watch time (WT). The ship's watch will not keep perfect time, so you should also keep a graph showing its watch error (WE), and verify the time every few days, or when feasible. (Rather then resetting the watch when it runs ahead or behind, it is better practice to simply keep a record of its behavior. That way you will be able to predict its error if you lose contact with radio signals. Details are given in the next section.)

In this day of inexpensive electronic watches, the prudent navigator will have three or four watches that can serve as ship's watch, and each will have its own graph of watch error. Each should be given a name or letter designation and the navigator should be sure to note which one is used for each log entry or sextant sight.

The ship's watch may be set to zone time and updated periodically, or it may be kept on GMT. This is a matter of personal preference, but keeping it on GMT will eliminate a lot of uncertainty when you reduce a sighting. (With more than one watch on hand, you can set some on GMT and others on zone time.)

TIMELY DETAILS

This section collects some definitions concerning time and gives some details that are useful to the navigator.

Greenwich mean time (GMT)

This is the time used in calculating the *Nautical Almanac*. It is matched to the average (mean) daily motion of the sun and it is needed for the reduction of celestial sights. One day of GMT is the mean (average) time interval between noon one day and noon the next day. GMT is also known as UT1 (universal time).

Watch time (WT)

The time shown on your watch. It will vary from the "correct" time and you must keep track of the watch error (WE), which is defined by the time shown on the watch minus the true time:

$$WE \text{ (fast)} = WT - GMT$$

Figure 13.7 shows a plot of a typical watch error, determined by comparing a watch with a radio or telephone signal each week and noting whether the watch is fast or slow.

If your watch error does not follow a straight line to within ±1 second, get another watch—better yet, get three and be safe.

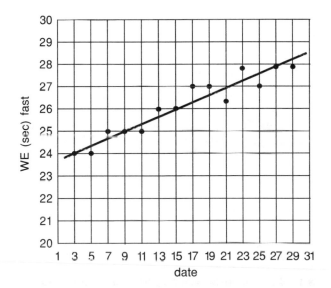

Figure 13.7. Watch error (WE) is determined by comparing a good watch with a radio signal every few days. It is the time shown on the watch minus the true time, so it is positive when the watch is fast, as in this diagram. The key factor in judging the quality of the watch is the straightness of the line through the measured differences. Deviations from a straight line should not exceed ±1 second. You may read off the WE at any date and predict it in advance.

If your watch is fast, you subtract the WE from your watch time to find GMT, and do the opposite if it is slow:

$$GMT = WT - WE \text{ (fast)}$$
$$GMT = WT + WE \text{ (slow)}$$

POSTTEST

13.12 Your watch says 12 03 05 when the radio says it is 12 00 00 GMT. What is your watch error?

13.13 Assuming the same WE, what is the GMT when your watch says 05 57 55?

Local mean time (LMT)

Zone time is a round number of hours from GMT, and it is the LMT at the center of the zone. If you are not exactly at the theoretical center of your time zone (0°, ± 15°, ± 30°, ± 45°. . .), your mean noon will occur a few minutes earlier or later than it does at the central longitude—later if you are west and earlier if east.

To predict accurately the times of sunrise, noon, or sunset, you will have to adjust your zone time to the LMT that corresponds to your longitude, because these are the times used in the *Almanac*. The correction is to make time earlier by 1 hour for each 15°W of longitude, or 4 minutes earlier for each 1°W of longitude.

$$LMT = ZT - [\text{longitude (°W)} - \text{center of time zone}] \times 4 \text{ minutes}$$

For example, if your longitude is 71°W, your equation is:

$$LMT = ZT - [71 - 75] \times 4 = ZT + 16 \text{ minutes}$$

so it is 16 minutes later than eastern standard time.

POSTTEST

13.14 Your longitude is 104°E. What is your LMT at GMT = 1300?

13.15 If your watch is set to ZT and is 5 seconds fast, what will it read at GMT = 15 01 15?

Universal time coordinated (UTC)

This is the time that is broadcast over shortwave by various time-keeping agencies, and it is used in setting standard time. UTC is a smooth-running time determined by atomic clocks. It is adjusted in whole seconds from time to time to keep it within 1 second of GMT, which is the astronomical time that is affected by the slightly erratic rotation of the earth.

The UTC radio signal (which moves quickly enough to go around the earth seven times in 1 second) typically takes a few hundredths of a second to come to your radio, so you are always a little behind, but the effect on celestial sights is trivial. Thus, the celestial navigator can assume that the UTC as given by the radio and GMT used in the *Almanac* are nearly the same. The fine points discussed in the next definition, UT1, are not usually needed for sight reduction.

Universal time (UT1)

This is another name for GMT. It is always within 1 second of the atomic time given by UTC, and it may be obtained from UTC by decoding the radio signal, which gives DUT1 = UT1 - UTC, as described in *Bowditch*. It is only needed for specialized navigation and surveys in which the slight irregularities of the earth's rotation cannot be ignored. (Unfortunately, the almanacs sometimes refer to UT1 as UT).

WHEN WILL THE SUN CROSS THE MERIDIAN?

Now let us put all of this to practice and show how you would prepare for a noon sight by predicting the time of passage of the sun across the local meridian at your dead reckoning position. We will simplify matters slightly by assuming that your boat is dead in the water, either becalmed or at anchor.

- *Step 1*—As described earlier, the sun runs about a quarter-hour ahead or behind its average position at various times in the course of the year. The difference is called the equation of time, and the daily pages of the *Nautical Almanac* give values of the equation of time for every 12 hours of GMT (Figure 13.8).

  As an example, suppose you are at longitude 70°30'W and the date is July 15, 1990. On this day, the column headed Mer. Pass. gives 1206 LMT.

  For more precision: A more accurate estimate can be found from the values given for the equation of time by noting that your ZD is –5h, so local noon will occur at about 1200 + 500 = 1700 GMT. Looking at the second column, for 15 July 12h GMT we see the equation of time given as 5m 55s, and looking ahead to the value for 0000 GMT the next day (5m 58s), we

| Day | SUN | | | MOON | | | Phase |
| | Eqn. of Time | | Mer. Pass. | Mer. Pass. | | Age | |
	00 h	12 h		Upper	Lower		
	m s	m s	h m	h m	h m	d	
15	05 52	05 55	12 06	05 33	17 58	23	
16	05 58	06 01	12 06	06 25	18 52	24	
17	06 03	06 06	12 06	07 21	19 50	25	

Figure 13.8. Portion of the daily pages giving the equation of time and the time of meridian passage of the sun for July 15-17, 1990.

interpolate to 5m 56s, giving a meridian passage at 12 05 56 LMT.

- **Step 2**—Ordinarily your watch is set to zone time, not LMT, so you must correct for your longitude, 70°30′W. You are 4°30′ east of the central meridian of the zone. Use the table called "Conversion from Arc to Time" in the first yellow page of the *Nautical Almanac*. Your work will look as follows:

Meridian passage		12 05 56 LMT
Longitude	4° E:	−16 00
correction	30′ E:	−02 00
Total correction		−18 00 (earlier because you are east)
Corrected time on meridian		11 47 56

POSTTEST

13.16 Find the GMT and LMT of local apparent noon for July 17, 1990, at a longitude 14°E.

HOW ACCURATELY DO YOU NEED TO KNOW THE TIME?

In the quotation at the head of this chapter Chichester says he needed to time his sights to within one second. You can calculate the requirements from the known speed of the earth's rotation.

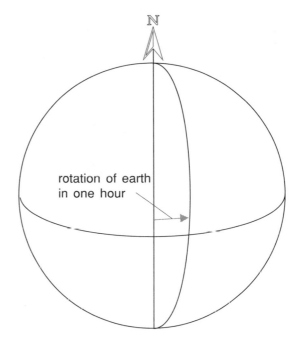

Figure 13.9. The rotational speed of the earth's surface is about 0.25 nautical miles per second at the equator, so you must known the Greenwich time to within a few seconds for celestial navigation.

PRETEST

13.17 How many nautical miles per hour is an object on the equator carried by the rotation of the earth?

13.18 How long does it take for the surface of the earth to move 1 NM at the equator?

First you need the circumference of the earth in nautical miles. The circumference of the equator is 360° × 60 NM per degree = 21,600 NM. The earth rotates once in 24 × 60 × 60 = 86,400 seconds. Hence the surface of the earth moves 0.25 NM/second at the equator. Suppose you want to determine your longitude to ±1 NM. You would need to know the time to ±4 seconds. So, it's a good practice to do everything to the nearest second. That explains Chichester's remark.

CHAPTER FOURTEEN

Tracking the Sun

On the day that the LORD gave the men of Israel victory over the Amorites, Joshua spoke to the LORD. In the presence of the Israelites he said,

"Sun, stand still over Gibeon;
Moon, stop over Aijalon Valley."

The sun stood still and the moon did not move until the nation had conquered its enemies. This is written in the Book of Jashar. The sun stood still in the middle of the sky and did not go down for a whole day. Never before, and never since, has there been a day like it . . .

Book of Joshua, 10:12-14

INTRODUCTION

Keeping track of the motion of the sun is a fascinating and valuable exercise for the navigator, not only for timekeeping, but also for determining your latitude and longitude and for orienting your compass. This chapter introduces the daily and yearly ambulations of the sun and sets up a coordinate system for measurement and calculation.

PRETEST

14.1. The sun is overhead at noon every day at the equator. T _____ F _____

14.2. The sun is farthest north on the first day of northern spring each year. T _____ F _____

PLOTTING THE DAILY MOTION OF THE SUN

To collect data for study in this chapter, you should start the following activity and prepare a graph of the track of the sun across the sky, as illustrated in Figure 14.1 (for the northern hemisphere) or 14.2 (for the southern hemisphere). If possible, make the observations in a single day, or within a week at most.

ACTIVITY

Equip yourself with a notebook, a watch, a compass, a protractor, and a piece of string with a small weight on the end. Measure the azimuth and the altitude every half hour or so and record the time and the data in the notebook.

POSTTEST

14.3 After noon has passed, how long does it take the sun to descend halfway to the horizon according to your graph?

TRACKING THE YEARLY MOTION OF THE SUN

The daily pattern of the sun's track across the sky changes from one season to the next—in fact, from one day to the next. The *Nautical Almanac* keeps track of the changes for you, using a coordinate system that is described later in this chapter. In order to describe what is contained in the *Almanac,* let us take another imaginary and leisurely trip from one pole to another.

We start at the south pole as the new year rolls in.

At the south pole

By the middle of January we notice that the sun's circle about the zenith has begun to expand slowly. The sun, which was 23° from the horizon when we arrived in mid-December, is spiralling toward the horizon. Its downward motion gradually accelerates, and by the middle of March it drops nearly 1° while moving 360° around the horizon each day.

In the beginning of the third week of March, a day after the equinox, the sun touches the horizon and 12 hours later its disc sinks from sight. (Refraction delays the sunset.) For the next two weeks, we can watch the fading glow of twilight move leftward around the horizon, completing the circuit every 24

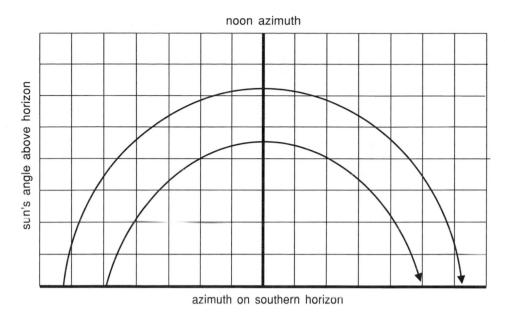

Figure 14.1 Daily motion of the sun as seen looking south from two latitudes in the northern hemisphere. The sun moves upward from the east, reaches its greatest height at local apparent noon, and then descends toward the west. The height of the sun is affected by latitude, so a measurement of this height permits determining your latitude.

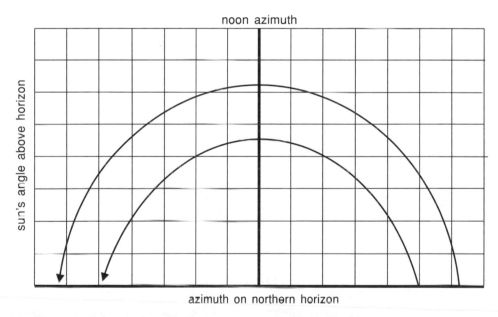

Figure 14.2 Daily motion of the sun as seen looking north from two latitudes in the southern hemisphere. The sun moves upward from the east, reaches its greatest height at local apparent noon, and then descends toward the west.

hours. Stars begin to emerge and gradually the sky becomes dark. For another 4 months we will not see a glimmer of twilight if we stay at the pole. But we move on.

At the equator

We fly to the equator in early April, just after the equinox, and we find the sun rising slightly north of due east and setting slightly north of due west.

During the three following months, the sun swings northward, gradually slowing its progress northward until it halts 23° north of east on June 21. This is the solstice, when the sun reaches its northernmost limit and begins to swing south. By mid-July, it has a moved a few degrees south and by the end of September it has reached the equator, rising due east. On December 21, the time of the solstice, we see it rising 23° south of due east.

Days are 12 hours long at the equator, regardless of the time of year, and the sun rises high in the sky at noon. (If you measure precisely the interval between sunset and sunrise at the equator, you will find it slightly more than 12 hours because the earth's atmosphere tends to lift the image of the sun. This effect makes the sun appear 1 minute early and vanish about 1 minute late.)

If we were to judge by the sun alone, we would hardly notice the seasons at the equator, although the shifting constellations mark the passing of the year, as discussed in Chapter 15.

POSTTEST

14.4 If you are standing at the equator, the sun rises and sets perpendicular to the horizon every day of the year. T _____ F _____

14.5 The sun is never overhead to a navigator at 30° from the equator. T _____ F _____

14.6 Seen from the north pole, the sun is about 23° above the horizon on June 21. T _____ F _____

FINDING TIMES OF TWILIGHT, SUNRISE, AND SUNSET

The daily pages give the LMT of risings and settings as seen from sea level in a clear sky. The times listed in the *Almanac* include the effect of refraction. The seasonal variations of sunset and sunrise are quite obvious to people who live in the middle and high latitudes, but they are barely noticeable at the equator (Figure 14.3, 14.4).

Suppose you are in the North Atlantic, and you wish to plan for star sights the next day. These sights are made with a sextant when the horizon is faintly illuminated by twilight. (A bright moon can also show you the horizon, but be careful to avoid its sparkling reflection on the water, which will produce a spurious horizon. Moon sights are difficult for this reason.) A few definitions are needed.

- **Sunrise and sunset**—The moments when the upper limb (edge of the sun's disc) is on the horizon. (The sun is assumed to be lifted by a standard 16′, which makes it appear about 1 minute early and vanish 1 minute late at the equator. The effect on time is greater at other latitudes.)

- **Civil twilight**—The sun's center is 6° below the horizon. At this time, the brighter stars are visible and the horizon is bright enough to be seen in the sextant.

- **Nautical twilight**—The sun's center is 12° below the horizon. By this time the horizon is dark and sextant sights are difficult.

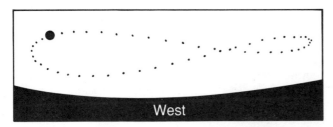

Figure 14.3. Weekly snapshots of the sun at 1730 zone time as seen from the equator. As we are looking west, the sun sets directly downward in this picture. The circle shows the sun on January 19, a month after its southernmost excursion. The north and south swings of about 46° correspond to the seasons. At all times of the year, the sun sets at approximately 1800 at the equator.

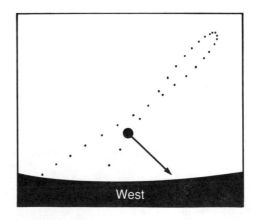

Figure 14.4. Weekly snapshots of the sun at 1730 zone time as seen from latitude 45°N. The circle shows the sun on September 13 as it is moving south. The arrow indicates the motion of the setting sun that day. The sun is below the horizon at this time of evening between October 11 and March 1.

Table 14.1. Risings and settings for May 8, 1990

Latitude	Twilight		Sunrise	Twilight		Sunset
	Civil	Nautical		Civil	Nautical	
52N	02 44	03 38	04 18	19 36	20 16	21 11
50N	02 58	03 47	04 25	19 29	20 07	20 57
51N	02 51	03 42	04 22	19 33	20 11	21 04
3W(+)	12	12	12	12	12	12
63W	03 03	03 54	04 34	19 45	20 23	21 16

Thus, you should plan to make star and planet sights between civil twilight and nautical twilight. Most navigators find morning sights to be easier because their eyes are dark-adapted and they have had plenty of time to locate the navigation stars before the sights must be made.

As an example, suppose the date is May 8, 1990, and you are at longitude 63W and latitude 51N. Refer to Figure 14.16 for the extract from the daily pages for this date. Read out the times for the two latitudes surrounding your estimated position that day and set up a table as above to interpolate to your latitude. The final lines show the correction to your longitude, which is 3° west of the central meridian of your zone.

POSTTEST

14.7 When will the sunrise occur at latitude 63N and longitude 10E?

FIX BY THE TIMES OF SUNSET AND SUNRISE

The times of sunrise and sunset (and hence also the length of daylight) depend on time of year, latitude, and longitude. The cause is illustrated in Figure 14.5.

Longitude

If you know the date, you can find the time of local noon by averaging the times of sunrise and sunset. If your watch is set to GMT, you may look up the Greenwich hour angle (GHA) of the sun for that time. This will be your longitude. It is a fairly good method, but it assumes a clear horizon so you can time the events accurately, and this is not easy to come by.

Latitude

At certain times of the year (away from the equinoxes) latitude may be estimated by measuring the interval between sunrise and sunset and finding the corresponding value in the twilight tables of the

Almanac. For example, suppose the date is November 28 (the year is not important) and you measure the length of daylight to be 10h 35m using your watch. To compare this with the *Almanac* values, prepare a table of intervals like Table 14.2, using the daily pages in Figure 14.6 for the appropriate range of latitudes. Then scan the table looking for the entries that bracket your measured interval. In this case they are at latitudes 20N (11h 02m) and 30N (10h 24m). Interpolating to the measured value gives

$$\text{Latitude} = 30\text{N} - (11/38)10 = 27\text{N}$$

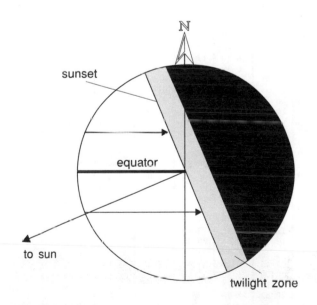

Figure 14.5. Diagram of the twilight zone (light gray) on the earth's surface during northern autumn showing the earth as seen from space. The heavy horizontal line is the equator. The southern latitude line is more than half covered by daylight, and the fractional daylight depends on latitude. The south pole has no sunset. Arrows indicate the direction of the earth's daily rotation.

Lat.	Twilight Naut.	Twilight Civil	Sunrise	Moonrise 27	Moonrise 28	Moonrise 29	Moonrise 30
° h m	h m	h m	h m	h m	h m	h m	h m
N 72	07 42	09 35	■	12 41	12 08	11 19	▭
N 70	07 27	09 00	■	12 46	12 22	11 50	10 30
68	07 14	08 35	10 17	12 50	12 34	12 14	11 39
66	07 04	08 15	09 35	12 53	12 43	12 32	12 16
64	06 55	07 59	09 07	12 56	12 51	12 47	12 42
62	06 47	07 46	08 45	12 58	12 58	12 59	13 03
60	06 41	07 35	08 28	13 01	13 04	13 10	13 20
N 58	06 34	07 25	08 14	13 03	13 10	13 20	13 34
56	06 29	07 16	08 01	13 04	13 15	13 28	13 47
54	06 24	07 09	07 50	13 06	13 19	13 35	13 57
52	06 19	07 02	07 41	13 07	13 23	13 42	14 07
50	06 15	06 55	07 32	13 09	13 27	13 48	14 16
45	06 05	06 41	07 14	13 12	13 34	14 01	14 34
N 40	05 56	06 29	06 59	13 14	13 41	14 12	14 49
35	05 48	06 19	06 47	13 16	13 47	14 21	15 02
30	05 40	06 10	06 36	13 18	13 52	14 29	15 13
20	05 26	05 53	06 17	13 22	14 01	14 44	15 33
N 10	05 11	05 37	06 00	13 24	14 08	14 56	15 50
0	04 56	05 22	05 44	13 27	14 16	15 08	16 06
S 10	04 39	05 06	05 28	13 30	14 23	15 20	16 22
20	04 19	04 47	05 11	13 33	14 31	15 33	16 40
30	03 53	04 25	04 52	13 37	14 41	15 48	17 00
35	03 36	04 11	04 40	13 39	14 46	15 57	17 12
40	03 15	03 55	04 27	13 41	14 52	16 07	17 25
45	02 49	03 35	04 11	13 44	14 59	16 19	17 42
S 50	02 11	03 09	03 51	13 47	15 08	16 33	18 02
52	01 51	02 56	03 42	13 49	15 12	16 40	18 11
54	01 23	02 42	03 31	13 51	15 16	16 47	18 22
56	00 39	02 24	03 19	13 53	15 21	16 56	18 35
58	////	02 02	03 05	13 55	15 27	17 05	18 49
S 60	////	01 33	02 49	13 57	15 33	17 17	19 06

Lat.	Sunset	Twilight Civil	Twilight Naut.	Moonset 27	Moonset 28	Moonset 29	Moonset 30
° h m	h m	h m	h m	h m	h m	h m	h m
N 72	■	14 00	15 53	01 13	03 26	06 02	▭
N 70	■	14 35	16 08	01 12	03 15	05 33	08 51
68	13 18	15 01	16 21	01 11	03 06	05 12	07 44
66	14 00	15 20	16 31	01 10	02 58	04 55	07 08
64	14 28	15 36	16 40	01 10	02 52	04 42	06 43
62	14 50	15 49	16 48	01 09	02 46	04 31	06 23
60	15 07	16 00	16 55	01 09	02 42	04 21	06 07
N 58	15 22	16 10	17 01	01 08	02 38	04 13	05 53
56	15 34	16 19	17 06	01 08	02 34	04 05	05 42
54	15 45	16 27	17 12	01 07	02 31	03 59	05 32
52	15 55	16 34	17 16	01 07	02 28	03 53	05 23
50	16 03	16 40	17 21	01 07	02 25	03 48	05 15
45	16 21	16 54	17 31	01 06	02 19	03 36	04 58
N 40	16 36	17 06	17 40	01 06	02 15	03 27	04 44
35	16 49	17 17	17 48	01 05	02 10	03 19	04 32
30	17 00	17 26	17 55	01 05	02 07	03 12	04 22
20	17 19	17 43	18 10	01 04	02 01	03 00	04 04
N 10	17 36	17 58	18 24	01 04	01 55	02 50	03 49
0	17 52	18 14	18 40	01 03	01 50	02 40	03 35
S 10	18 07	18 30	18 57	01 02	01 45	02 30	03 21
20	18 25	18 49	19 17	01 02	01 39	02 20	03 06
30	18 44	19 11	19 44	01 01	01 33	02 08	02 49
35	18 56	19 25	20 01	01 01	01 30	02 02	02 39
40	19 10	19 41	20 21	01 00	01 26	01 54	02 28
45	19 26	20 01	20 48	01 00	01 21	01 45	02 14
S 50	19 46	20 27	21 26	00 59	01 15	01 35	01 58
52	19 55	20 40	21 47	00 58	01 13	01 30	01 51
54	20 06	20 55	22 15	00 58	01 10	01 24	01 43
56	20 18	21 13	23 02	00 58	01 07	01 18	01 33
58	20 32	21 36	////	00 57	01 04	01 12	01 23
S 60	20 49	22 06	////	00 57	01 00	01 04	01 11

Day	SUN Eqn. of Time 00ʰ	SUN Eqn. of Time 12ʰ	SUN Mer. Pass.	MOON Mer. Pass. Upper	MOON Mer. Pass. Lower	Age	Phase
	m s	m s	h m	h m	h m	d	
27	12 35	12 25	11 48	19 39	07 15	10	
28	12 16	12 06	11 48	20 28	08 03	11	◖
29	11 55	11 45	11 48	21 22	08 54	12	

Table 14.2. Duration of daylight on November 28

Latitude	Sunrise	Sunset	Duration
64	09 07	14 28	5 21
60	08 28	15 07	6 39
50	07 32	16 03	8 31
40	06 59	16 36	9 37
30	06 36	17 00	10 24
20	06 17	17 19	11 02
10N	06 00	17 36	11 36
0	05 44	17 52	12 08
10S	05 28	18 07	12 39
20	05 11	18 25	13 14
30	04 52	18 44	13 52
40	04 27	19 10	14 43
50	03 51	19 46	15 55
60	02 49	20 49	18 00

These data are plotted in Figure 14.7.

Example—Suppose you wish to compute the times of sunrise and sunset at latitude 40°N, longitude 71°W on November 28, 1990. Using the data in Figure 14.6, find the LMT in the second column:

	LMT	Corr.	ZT	ZD	GMT
Sunrise	0659	−16	0643	0500	1143
Sunset	1636	−16	1620	0500	2120

The *Almanac* entries are the values of zone time as observed from the central longitude of the zone, 75°W. Correction to your longitude is $(71 - 75) \times 4 = 16$ minutes earlier, and this is entered in the third column, to give the ZT in the fourth column. The zone description is 0500, giving GMT in the last column.

POSTTEST

14.8 Carry out the same calculations for November 29, 1990, at latitude 37°30′N and longitude 77°W.

CREAMER'S METHOD FOR ROUNDING CAPE HORN

Marvin Creamer sailed around the world in the 1980s without instruments of any kind. This was a tour de force of ingenuity—and a wonderful exam-

Figure 14.6. Excerpt from daily pages showing times of sunset and sunrise for November 27-30. Table 14.2 is derived from these data, which apply to all three days on the daily page.

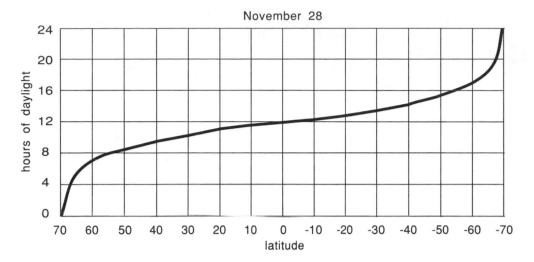

November 28

Figure 14.7. Hours of daylight at various latitudes on a day in northern autumn when the declination of the sun is 21S. Midnight sun then occurs at latitudes south of 69S and there is no daylight north of 69N.

ple of doing things the hard way. (The feat was described by Greg Walsh in *Ocean Navigator* No. 28, Sept./Oct. 1989, p. 23.)

To understand the method, look at the daily pages for November 27 in whatever almanac you have at hand. You will notice that there are no times given for nautical twilight on that date for latitudes south of 58S. This means that the sky never becomes completely dark if you are sufficiently far south on that day. The reason for this is illustrated in Figure 14.8, which shows a profile of the earth looking toward the twilight region, with the sun to the left. The navigator is on the right side at midnight. The declination of the sun that day is about 21S so the sun would graze the southern horizon at a latitude of 90S − 21 = 69S. Ten degrees north of that point, the sun would sink 10° below the horizon and the sky would become dark. So we would expect dark skies at all latitudes north of 59S during that night. If the sky becomes totally dark at midnight (or sooner) you would know you were north of 59S. That is the essence of Creamer's method. The artistry comes in knowing how to distinguish a dark sky from deep twilight, and Creamer cultivated his ability to do this through extensive practice.

His actual rounding of the cape took place near the time of the solstice, December 21, when the sun's declination is 23S. This is 2° farther south than the example we just computed, so the critical latitude was 57S. As shown in Figure 14.9, this

is just the latitude of the tip of South America. Creamer approached from the west and sailed east-southeast until he was able to detect a faint glow in the southern sky at midnight. This told him he was sufficiently south, so he turned due east and successfully rounded the cape!

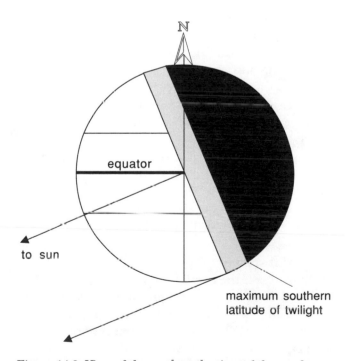

Figure 14.8. View of the earth at the time of the southern solstice, when the south pole and all latitudes south of 67S enjoy a midnight sun.

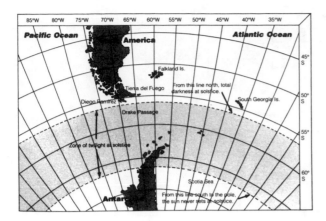

Figure 14.9. Marvin Creamer's strategy for rounding Cape Horn without instruments relied on the fact that total darkness only occurred at latitudes north of 57°S at the solstice. He sailed south until he left the zone of total darkness and then he knew he was safely south of the cape (from Ocean Navigator *No. 28, Sept./Oct. 1989, p. 27).*

Figure 14.10. Diagram of the earth, showing how a line from the center of the earth toward the sun will intersect the surface of the earth at the sun's geographic point. The geographic point moves westward along the surface as the earth turns eastward.

CELESTIAL COORDINATES

To construct a set of coordinates for specifying the locations of the celestial bodies, we start from the surface of the earth and the familiar system of longitude and latitude.

Geographic point

If we could draw a line from the center of the earth toward the sun at a particular moment, it would intersect the earth's surface at the sun's geographic point (Figure 14.10). Standing at the sun's geographic point, we would see the sun directly overhead.

The westward longitude of the geographic point increases as the world turns on its axis, by 15° per hour. The latitude of the geographic point changes much more slowly, so the geographic point sweeps out a line that is nearly a circle of latitude.

Celestial sphere

We now fly off the earth and watch the earth being reduced to a dot. We imagine it surrounded by a large transparent sphere on which are painted the constellations. This is the "celestial sphere" (Figure 14.11). Navigators have established a coordinate system on this imaginary sphere for finding the geographical positions of celestial bodies at any instant.

In order to set up the coordinate system, we project the earth's latitude and longitude grid outward onto the celestial sphere. This produces the celestial coordinates called declination (latitude) and Greenwich hour angle (longitude W). The Greenwich hour angle (GHA) will range from 0° to 360° and it is measured westward. The relationships are shown in Figure 14.12 and are summarized in Table 14.3.

At any instant, the sun can be located by specifying its geographical point. To determine each geographical point, we could travel around the world looking for the place where that star is overhead. The longitude (W) would be the Greenwich hour angle and the latitude would be the declination of the sun at that moment.

Table 14.3. Corresponding coordinates

Geographic point on earth	Object on celestial sphere	Measure
Longitude (W)	Greenwich hour angle	0–360°
Latitude (N, S)	Declination (N, S)	0–90°

Due to the rotation of the earth, the geographic point speeds westward. This rotation does not move the equator, so declinations are not affected. But the Greenwich hour angle increases about 15° every hour, and a table of Greenwich hour angles

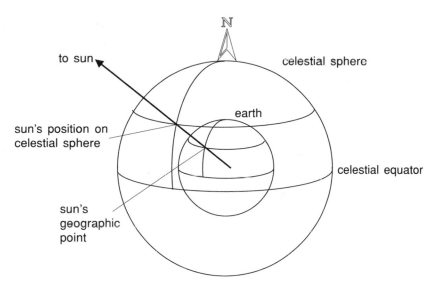

Figure 14.11. Diagram of the earth surrounded by the celestial sphere on which the celestial coordinates are measured.

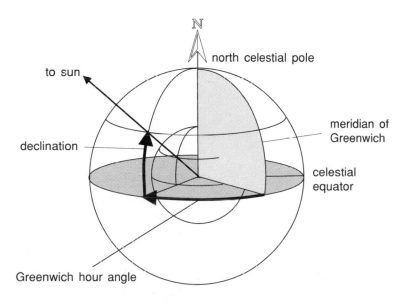

Figure 14.12. Diagram of the celestial sphere showing the Greenwich hour angle (GHA) and declination of the geographic point.

for all 57 of the navigation stars would be very awkward.

Astronomers have met this problem by adopting a point on the celestial sphere that rotates with the stars and serves as the starting point for celestial coordinates. The point, called the *first point of Aries,* is on the celestial equator at the spot where the meridian of Greenwich crosses the equator at midnight on the first day of spring. (In ancient times, this point was in the constellation Aries, hence the name.)

Celestial longitude measured westward from the first point of Aries is called *sidereal hour angle* (SHA). The key relation is:

$$GHA (sun) = SHA (sun) + GHA \, Aries$$

Expressed in words:

> Geographic longitude = celestial longitude +
> geographic longitude of first point of Aries

This is illustrated in Figure 14.13.

For example, suppose the sun's SHA is 35° and the GHA Aries is 134°. The GHA of the sun would be 169°. This would put the geographic point of the sun at longitude 169W.

One more definition will be useful. The *local hour angle* (LHA) of an object is the difference of longitude between the navigator and the object's geographic point (Figure 14.14):

$$LHA \text{ (object)} = GHA \text{ (object)} - \text{longitude}$$

The LHA of the sun is 0° at the instant of local noon, because at that time the sun is at the navigator's longitude. Suppose the GHA of the sun is 100° at a particular moment. For a navigator at 130°W, the LHA of the sun is 30° westward, and for a navigator at 70°W, the LHA of the sun is –30°, or 30° eastward.

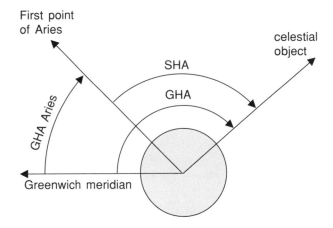

Figure 14.13. Looking down on the north pole of the earth. The Greenwich hour angle of the celestial object (GHA) is longitude measured westward from Greenwich, while the sidereal hour angle (SHA) is measured from the first point of Aries, the origin of the celestial coordinates that rotate with the sky. The GHA Aries increases 15° per hour, but the SHA of each celestial object is approximately constant. These are the quantities found in the Almanac, *and from them the geographic longitude of the object may be found, as is described in the text.*

POSTTEST

14.9 Compute the GHA, longitude of the geographic point, and LHA for each of the following pairs of SHA and GHA Aries if the navigator is at longitude 100°W.

Aries		Sun		
GHA	SHA	GHA	Longitude	LHA
23	133	____	____	____
189	28	____	____	____
290	187	____	____	____
300	160	____	____	____

Comparing the behavior of GHA and SHA

To see the meaning of GHA Aries and its usefulness, imagine yourself on a rotating merry-go-round using a walkie-talkie to help someone find you. You might proceed in several ways. For example, you might say, "I am due north of the center of the merry-go-round right now, and we are spinning once a minute counterclockwise." On the other hand, you might say, "Look for the big white horse. I am on the second horse behind it." The latter method is closer to what the astronomer does when he or she specifies the position of the sun or a star on a rotating sky relative to the first point of Aries, which plays the role of the white horse.

The difference between the behaviors of the GHA and SHA of the sun can be seen in Figure 14.15 which shows *Almanac* data for three days in May 1990. (The data are taken from Figure 14.16.)

Because the declinations of the sun, moon, and planets change fairly rapidly, the *Almanac* gives the GHA and declination of these objects for every hour of the year. On the other hand, the navigation stars are almost motionless on the celestial sphere, so they are listed by SHA and declination every three days.

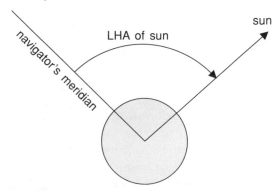

Figure 14.14. The local hour angle (LHA) of a celestial object is the difference of longitude between the geographic point of the object and the navigator.

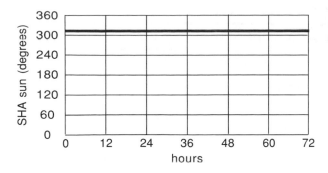

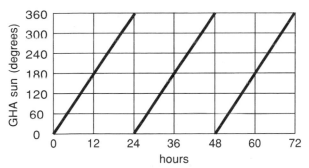

Figure 14.15. Plots of the SHA (top) and GHA (bottom) of the sun over a period of three days. The GHA increases 360° per day, as the geographic point of the sun moves around the earth once a day. The SHA decreases very slowly (1° per day) as the sun moves around the celestial sphere on its yearly track.

USING THE *ALMANAC* TO FIND THE GEOGRAPHIC POINT OF THE SUN

A key step in locating yourself with the celestial bodies is to find the geographic point of the bodies by using the *Almanac*. Then you measure your location with respect to those geographic points, and that's all there is to celestial navigation—except filling out the forms.

As an example of finding the geographic point, suppose we are in England and we wish to find the geographic point of the sun at 0821 AM standard time on May, 8, 1990. The *Almanac* page for that day is shown in Figure 14.16.

There are four steps to be followed, and carrying them out will help prepare you for sight reduction in later chapters:

- *Step 1*—Find the Greenwich mean time (GMT) of the observation, as this is the time used in the *Almanac*. The conversion to GMT is trivial, because standard time in England is the same as GMT. (For our purpose it is also equivalent to UTC, universal time coordinated, as discussed in Chapter 13.)

- *Step 2*—Now turn to the daily pages and look for the date May 8, 1990. The corresponding portion of the *Almanac* is shown in Figure 14.16. We scan down to the nearest hour (08) *and scan across to the correct column*. (Failure to use the correct column is a common source of error in using the almanac.) Read out the values bracketing our desired time:

Time (GMT)		GHA Sun	Declination
May 9, 1990	08 00 00	300° 53.7′	N17° 19.1′
	09 00 00	315° 53.8′	N17° 19.8′
	Differences	15° 00.1′	0° 00′

At the bottom of the column find *d 0.7*. This is the change of declination of the sun in 1 hour for most of this page. Note that the declination is *increasing*. The GHA sun increased by about 15°, as we should expect (15° = 360°/24).

- *Step 3*—We first interpolate the GHA sun to the exact time 08 21 05 GMT. This can be done with a hand calculator, but it is quicker and safer to use the table called "Increments and Corrections" in the yellow pages at the back of the *Almanac* (Figure 14.17).

  We find the page with 21^m at the top and then scan down to 05 seconds in the column for the "Sun and Planets." There we read 5° 16.3′, which we add:

GHA sun	08 00 00	300° 53.7′
Increment for 21m 05s		5° 16.3′
GHA sun	08 21 05	306° 10.0′

Double-check your use of the table. The most common mistake is to confuse the minutes and seconds headings.

- *Step 4*—Finally, we must interpolate the declination, which increased 0.7′ during the hour. With a calculator we find that in 21m it will increase 0.7 × 21/60 = 0.3′. Alternatively (and preferably) we may use the same "Increments and Corrections" table that we just used for the GHA sun. On the page marked 21^m (ignoring the seconds, because the change of declination is so slight) we scan down the column marked *v or d corrn* to the proper entry, 0.7 in the left-hand column. Next to it we see 0.3, which is the value to be added to the declination for the start of the hour:

Declination of sun	08 00 00	N17° 19.1′
Increment for 21m		0.3′
Declination of sun	08 21 05	N17° 19.4′

Thus, the geographic point of the sun is at longitude 306° 10.0′ W and latitude N17° 19.4′.

POSTTEST

14.10 Find the geographic point of the sun for 1305 GMT on May 9, 1990.

1990 MAY 7, 8, 9 (MON., TUES., WED.)

UT (GMT)	ARIES G.H.A.	VENUS −4.1 G.H.A.	Dec.	MARS +0.7 G.H.A.	Dec.	JUPITER −2.0 G.H.A.	Dec.	SATURN +0.5 G.H.A.	Dec.
7 00	224 34.7	221 04.1	S 0 05.2	240 32.3	S 8 34.3	125 52.9	N23 19.9	287 18.9	S20 54.7
01	239 37.2	236 03.9	04.2	255 33.0	33.6	140 54.9	19.9	302 21.3	54.7
02	254 39.6	251 03.8	03.1	270 33.7	32.9	155 56.8	19.9	317 23.8	54.7
03	269 42.1	266 03.6	·· 02.1	285 34.4	·· 32.2	170 58.8	·· 19.9	332 26.3	·· 54.7
04	284 44.6	281 03.4	01.1	300 35.1	31.5	186 00.8	19.8	347 28.8	54.7
05	299 47.0	296 03.3	S 0 00.1	315 35.8	30.8	201 02.8	19.8	2 31.2	54.7
06	314 49.5	311 03.1	N 0 00.9	330 36.6	S 8 30.1	216 04.8	N23 19.8	17 33.7	S20 54.7
07	329 52.0	326 02.9	01.9	345 37.3	29.5	231 06.7	19.8	32 36.2	54.7
08	344 54.4	341 02.8	02.9	0 38.0	28.8	246 08.7	19.7	47 38.7	54.7
M 09	359 56.9	356 02.6	·· 03.9	15 38.7	·· 28.1	261 10.7	·· 19.7	62 41.1	·· 54.7
O 10	14 59.3	11 02.5	05.0	30 39.4	27.4	276 12.7	19.7	77 43.6	54.7
N 11	30 01.8	26 02.3	06.0	45 40.1	26.7	291 14.7	19.7	92 46.1	54.7
D 12	45 04.3	41 02.1	N 0 07.0	60 40.8	S 8 26.0	306 16.6	N23 19.7	107 48.6	S20 54.7
A 13	60 06.7	56 02.0	08.0	75 41.6	25.3	321 18.6	19.6	122 51.0	54.7
Y 14	75 09.2	71 01.8	09.0	90 42.3	24.6	336 20.6	19.6	137 53.5	54.7
15	90 11.7	86 01.6	·· 10.0	105 43.0	·· 24.0	351 22.6	·· 19.6	152 56.0	·· 54.7
16	105 14.1	101 01.5	11.1	120 43.7	23.3	6 24.6	19.6	167 58.5	54.8
17	120 16.6	116 01.3	12.1	135 44.4	22.6	21 26.5	19.5	183 00.9	54.8
18	135 19.1	131 01.1	N 0 13.1	150 45.1	S 8 21.9	36 28.5	N23 19.5	198 03.4	S20 54.8
19	150 21.5	146 01.0	14.1	165 45.8	21.2	51 30.5	19.5	213 05.9	54.8
20	165 24.0	161 00.8	15.1	180 46.6	20.5	66 32.5	19.5	228 08.4	54.8
21	180 26.5	176 00.6	·· 16.1	195 47.3	·· 19.8	81 34.5	·· 19.4	243 10.8	·· 54.8
22	195 28.9	191 00.5	17.2	210 48.0	19.1	96 36.4	19.4	258 13.3	54.8
23	210 31.4	206 00.3	18.2	225 48.7	18.4	111 38.4	19.4	273 15.8	54.8
8 00	225 33.8	221 00.2	N 0 19.2	240 49.4	S 8 17.8	126 40.4	N23 19.4	288 18.3	S20 54.8
01	240 36.3	236 00.0	20.2	255 50.1	17.1	141 42.4	19.3	303 20.7	54.8
02	255 38.8	250 59.8	21.2	270 50.9	16.4	156 44.3	19.3	318 23.2	54.8
03	270 41.2	265 59.7	·· 22.2	285 51.6	·· 15.7	171 46.3	·· 19.3	333 25.7	·· 54.8
04	285 43.7	280 59.5	23.3	300 52.3	15.0	186 48.3	19.3	348 28.2	54.8
05	300 46.2	295 59.3	24.3	315 53.0	14.3	201 50.3	19.2	3 30.6	54.8
06	315 48.6	310 59.2	N 0 25.3	330 53.7	S 8 13.6	216 52.2	N23 19.2	18 33.1	S20 54.8
07	330 51.1	325 59.0	26.3	345 54.4	12.9	231 54.2	19.2	33 35.6	54.8
T 08	345 53.6	340 58.8	27.3	0 55.2	12.2	246 56.2	19.2	48 38.1	54.8
U 09	0 56.0	355 58.7	·· 28.3	15 55.9	·· 11.6	261 58.2	·· 19.1	63 40.6	·· 54.8
E 10	15 58.5	10 58.5	29.4	30 56.6	10.9	277 00.1	19.1	78 43.0	54.8
S 11	31 01.0	25 58.3	30.4	45 57.3	10.2	292 02.1	19.1	93 45.5	54.8
D 12	46 03.4	40 58.2	N 0 31.4	60 58.0	S 8 09.5	307 04.1	N23 19.1	108 48.0	S20 54.9
A 13	61 05.9	55 58.0	32.4	75 58.7	08.8	322 06.1	19.0	123 50.5	54.9
Y 14	76 08.3	70 57.8	33.4	90 59.5	08.1	337 08.0	19.0	138 52.9	54.9
15	91 10.8	85 57.7	·· 34.5	106 00.2	·· 07.4	352 10.0	·· 19.0	153 55.4	·· 54.9
16	106 13.3	100 57.5	35.5	121 00.9	06.7	7 12.0	19.0	168 57.9	54.9
17	121 15.7	115 57.3	36.5	136 01.6	06.0	22 14.0	19.0	184 00.4	54.9
18	136 18.2	130 57.2	N 0 37.5	151 02.3	S 8 05.3	37 15.9	N23 18.9	199 02.9	S20 54.9
19	151 20.7	145 57.0	38.5	166 03.1	04.6	52 17.9	18.9	214 05.3	54.9
20	166 23.1	160 56.8	39.6	181 03.8	04.0	67 19.9	18.9	229 07.8	54.9
21	181 25.6	175 56.7	·· 40.6	196 04.5	·· 03.3	82 21.9	·· 18.9	244 10.3	·· 54.9
22	196 28.1	190 56.5	41.6	211 05.2	02.6	97 23.8	18.8	259 12.8	54.9
23	211 30.5	205 56.3	42.6	226 05.9	01.9	112 25.8	18.8	274 15.3	54.9
9 00	226 33.0	220 56.1	N 0 43.6	241 06.6	S 8 01.2	127 27.8	N23 18.8	289 17.7	S20 54.9
01	241 35.4	235 56.0	44.7	256 07.4	8 00.5	142 29.8	18.8	304 20.2	54.9
02	256 37.9	250 55.8	45.7	271 08.1	7 59.8	157 31.7	18.7	319 22.7	54.9
03	271 40.4	265 55.6	·· 46.7	286 08.8	·· 59.1	172 33.7	·· 18.7	334 25.2	·· 54.9
04	286 42.8	280 55.5	47.7	301 09.5	58.4	187 35.7	18.7	349 27.7	54.9
05	301 45.3	295 55.3	48.8	316 10.2	57.7	202 37.6	18.7	4 30.2	54.9
06	316 47.8	310 55.1	N 0 49.8	331 11.0	S 7 57.0	217 39.6	N23 18.6	19 32.6	S20 55.0
W 07	331 50.2	325 55.0	50.8	346 11.7	56.4	232 41.6	18.6	34 35.1	55.0
E 08	346 52.7	340 54.8	51.8	1 12.4	55.7	247 43.6	18.6	49 37.6	55.0
D 09	1 55.2	355 54.6	·· 52.8	16 13.1	·· 55.0	262 45.5	·· 18.6	64 40.1	·· 55.0
N 10	16 57.6	10 54.5	53.9	31 13.8	54.3	277 47.5	18.5	79 42.6	55.0
E 11	32 00.1	25 54.3	54.9	46 14.6	53.6	292 49.5	18.5	94 45.0	55.0
S 12	47 02.6	40 54.1	N 0 55.9	61 15.3	S 7 52.9	307 51.5	N23 18.5	109 47.5	S20 55.0
D 13	62 05.0	55 53.9	56.9	76 16.0	52.2	322 53.4	18.5	124 50.0	55.0
A 14	77 07.5	70 53.8	58.0	91 16.7	51.5	337 55.4	18.4	139 52.5	55.0
Y 15	92 09.9	85 53.6	0 59.0	106 17.4	·· 50.8	352 57.4	·· 18.4	154 55.0	·· 55.0
16	107 12.4	100 53.4	1 00.0	121 18.2	50.1	7 59.3	18.4	169 57.5	55.0
17	122 14.9	115 53.3	01.0	136 18.9	49.4	23 01.3	18.3	184 59.9	55.0
18	137 17.3	130 53.1	N 1 02.1	151 19.6	S 7 48.7	38 03.3	N23 18.3	200 02.4	S20 55.0
19	152 19.8	145 52.9	03.1	166 20.3	48.0	53 05.2	18.3	215 04.9	55.0
20	167 22.3	160 52.7	04.1	181 21.0	47.3	68 07.2	18.3	230 07.4	55.0
21	182 24.7	175 52.6	·· 05.1	196 21.8	·· 46.7	83 09.2	·· 18.2	245 09.9	·· 55.0
22	197 27.2	190 52.4	06.2	211 22.5	46.0	98 11.2	18.2	260 12.4	55.1
23	212 29.7	205 52.2	07.2	226 23.2	45.3	113 13.1	18.2	275 14.9	55.1
Mer. Pass. 8 56.3		v −0.2	d 1.0	v 0.7	d 0.7	v 2.0	d 0.0	v 2.5	d 0.0

STARS

Name	S.H.A.	Dec.
Acamar	315 31.8	S40 20.5
Achernar	335 39.9	S57 17.0
Acrux	173 28.6	S63 03.1
Adhara	255 26.4	S28 57.6
Aldebaran	291 09.6	N16 29.5
Alioth	166 35.1	N56 00.7
Alkaid	153 11.9	N49 21.6
Al Na'ir	28 05.4	S47 00.3
Alnilam	276 04.2	S 1 12.4
Alphard	218 13.1	S 8 37.1
Alphecca	126 25.3	N26 44.6
Alpheratz	358 01.8	N29 02.1
Altair	62 25.0	N 8 50.4
Ankaa	353 32.9	S42 21.3
Antares	112 47.2	S26 24.8
Arcturus	146 11.2	N19 13.8
Atria	108 04.3	S69 00.7
Avior	234 25.4	S59 29.0
Bellatrix	278 50.9	N 6 20.5
Betelgeuse	271 20.3	N 7 24.4
Canopus	264 04.2	S52 41.6
Capella	281 00.6	N45 59.5
Deneb	49 43.3	N45 14.4
Denebola	182 51.1	N14 37.5
Diphda	349 13.5	S18 02.3
Dubhe	194 12.2	N61 48.4
Elnath	278 34.9	N28 36.1
Eltanin	90 53.8	N51 29.1
Enif	34 04.2	N 9 49.7
Fomalhaut	15 43.1	S29 40.3
Gacrux	172 20.1	S57 03.9
Gienah	176 10.0	S17 29.5
Hadar	149 12.2	S60 19.9
Hamal	328 20.8	N23 25.0
Kaus Aust.	84 06.5	S34 23.4
Kochab	137 17.7	N74 11.6
Markab	13 55.8	N15 09.1
Menkar	314 33.5	N 4 03.2
Menkent	148 27.8	S36 19.6
Miaplacidus	221 43.7	S69 41.0
Mirfak	309 05.9	N49 49.7
Nunki	76 19.6	S26 18.6
Peacock	53 46.2	S56 45.8
Pollux	243 49.0	N28 03.1
Procyon	245 18.0	N 5 15.0
Rasalhague	96 22.3	N12 33.8
Regulus	208 01.8	N12 00.8
Rigel	281 29.0	S 8 12.7
Rigil Kent.	140 15.0	S60 47.9
Sabik	102 32.2	S15 43.0
Schedar	350 01.1	N56 28.9
Shaula	96 45.1	S37 05.9
Sirius	258 49.2	S16 42.2
Spica	158 49.3	S11 06.9
Suhail	223 05.4	S43 23.9
Vega	80 50.4	N38 46.1
Zuben'ubi	137 24.3	S16 00.3

	S.H.A.	Mer. Pass.
Venus	355 26.3	9 16
Mars	15 15.6	7 56
Jupiter	261 06.5	15 31
Saturn	62 44.4	4 46

Figure 14.16. Portion of daily pages of the Nautical Almanac *for the sun, Wednesday, May 9, 1990.*

1990 MAY 7, 8, 9 (MON., TUES., WED.)

SUN and MOON

UT (GMT)	SUN G.H.A.	SUN Dec.	MOON G.H.A.	MOON v	MOON Dec.	MOON d	MOON H.P.
7 (MONDAY)							
00	180 51.6	N16 40.9	32 11.4	15.9	S10 11.0	12.7	54.4
01	195 51.6	41.6	46 46.3	15.9	10 23.7	12.6	54.4
02	210 51.7	42.3	61 21.2	15.8	10 36.3	12.6	54.3
03	225 51.7 ..	43.0	75 56.0	15.8	10 48.9	12.6	54.3
04	240 51.8	43.7	90 30.8	15.8	11 01.5	12.6	54.3
05	255 51.8	44.4	105 05.6	15.8	11 14.1	12.4	54.3
06	270 51.9 N16	45.1	119 40.4	15.7	S11 26.5	12.5	54.3
07	285 51.9	45.8	134 15.1	15.7	11 39.0	12.4	54.3
08	300 51.9	46.5	148 49.8	15.7	11 51.4	12.3	54.3
09	315 52.0 ..	47.2	163 24.5	15.6	12 03.7	12.3	54.3
10	330 52.0	47.9	177 59.1	15.6	12 16.0	12.2	54.3
11	345 52.1	48.6	192 33.7	15.5	12 28.2	12.2	54.2
12	0 52.1 N16	49.3	207 08.2	15.6	S12 40.4	12.1	54.2
13	15 52.2	50.0	221 42.8	15.4	12 52.5	12.1	54.2
14	30 52.2	50.6	236 17.2	15.5	13 04.6	12.0	54.2
15	45 52.2 ..	51.3	250 51.7	15.4	13 16.6	12.0	54.2
16	60 52.3	52.0	265 26.1	15.4	13 28.6	11.9	54.2
17	75 52.3	52.7	280 00.5	15.3	13 40.5	11.9	54.2
18	90 52.4 N16	53.4	294 34.8	15.3	S13 52.4	11.8	54.2
19	105 52.4	54.1	309 09.1	15.2	14 04.2	11.7	54.2
20	120 52.4	54.8	323 43.3	15.2	14 15.9	11.7	54.2
21	135 52.5 ..	55.5	338 17.5	15.2	14 27.6	11.6	54.2
22	150 52.5	56.1	352 51.7	15.1	14 39.2	11.6	54.1
23	165 52.6	56.8	7 25.8	15.0	14 50.8	11.5	54.1
8 (TUESDAY)							
00	180 52.6 N16	57.5	21 59.8	15.1	S15 02.3	11.4	54.1
01	195 52.6	58.2	36 33.9	14.9	15 13.7	11.4	54.1
02	210 52.7	58.9	51 07.8	15.0	15 25.1	11.3	54.1
03	225 52.7 16	59.6	65 41.8	14.9	15 36.4	11.3	54.1
04	240 52.8 17	00.2	80 15.7	14.8	15 47.7	11.1	54.1
05	255 52.8	00.9	94 49.5	14.8	15 58.8	11.2	54.1
06	270 52.8 N17	01.6	109 23.3	14.7	S16 10.0	11.0	54.1
07	285 52.9	02.3	123 57.0	14.7	16 21.0	11.0	54.1
08	300 52.9	03.0	138 30.7	14.7	16 32.0	10.9	54.1
09	315 52.9 ..	03.6	153 04.4	14.6	16 42.9	10.9	54.1
10	330 53.0	04.3	167 38.0	14.5	16 53.8	10.7	54.1
11	345 53.0	05.0	182 11.5	14.5	17 04.5	10.7	54.1
12	0 53.0 N17	05.7	196 45.0	14.5	S17 15.2	10.7	54.1
13	15 53.1	06.4	211 18.5	14.4	17 25.9	10.5	54.0
14	30 53.1	07.0	225 51.9	14.3	17 36.4	10.5	54.0
15	45 53.2 ..	07.7	240 25.2	14.3	17 46.9	10.4	54.0
16	60 53.2	08.4	254 58.5	14.2	17 57.3	10.4	54.0
17	75 53.2	09.1	269 31.7	14.2	18 07.7	10.3	54.0
18	90 53.3 N17	09.7	284 04.9	14.1	S18 18.0	10.1	54.0
19	105 53.3	10.4	298 38.0	14.1	18 28.1	10.2	54.0
20	120 53.3	11.1	313 11.1	14.0	18 38.3	10.0	54.0
21	135 53.4 ..	11.8	327 44.1	14.0	18 48.3	10.0	54.0
22	150 53.4	12.4	342 17.1	13.9	18 58.3	9.8	54.0
23	165 53.4	13.1	356 50.0	13.9	19 08.1	9.8	54.0
9 (WEDNESDAY)							
00	180 53.5 N17	13.8	11 22.9	13.7	S19 17.9	9.7	54.0
01	195 53.5	14.5	25 55.6	13.8	19 27.6	9.7	54.0
02	210 53.5	15.1	40 28.4	13.7	19 37.3	9.5	54.0
03	225 53.6 ..	15.8	55 01.1	13.6	19 46.8	9.5	54.0
04	240 53.6	16.5	69 33.7	13.6	19 56.3	9.4	54.0
05	255 53.6	17.1	84 06.3	13.5	20 05.7	9.3	54.0
06	270 53.7 N17	17.8	98 38.8	13.5	S20 15.0	9.2	54.0
07	285 53.7	18.5	113 11.3	13.4	20 24.2	9.1	54.0
08	300 53.7	19.1	127 43.7	13.3	20 33.3	9.0	54.0
09	315 53.8 ..	19.8	142 16.0	13.3	20 42.3	9.0	54.0
10	330 53.8	20.5	156 48.3	13.2	20 51.3	8.8	54.0
11	345 53.8	21.1	171 20.5	13.2	21 00.1	8.8	54.0
12	0 53.8 N17	21.8	185 52.7	13.1	S21 08.9	8.7	54.0
13	15 53.9	22.5	200 24.8	13.1	21 17.6	8.6	54.0
14	30 53.9	23.1	214 56.9	13.0	21 26.2	8.5	54.0
15	45 53.9 ..	23.8	229 28.9	12.9	21 34.7	8.4	54.0
16	60 54.0	24.5	244 00.8	12.9	21 43.1	8.3	54.0
17	75 54.0	25.1	258 32.7	12.8	21 51.4	8.2	54.0
18	90 54.0 N17	25.8	273 04.5	12.8	S21 59.6	8.1	54.0
19	105 54.0	26.5	287 36.3	12.7	22 07.7	8.0	54.0
20	120 54.1	27.1	302 08.0	12.6	22 15.7	7.9	54.0
21	135 54.1 ..	27.8	316 39.6	12.6	22 23.6	7.9	54.0
22	150 54.1	28.4	331 11.2	12.5	22 31.5	7.7	54.0
23	165 54.2	29.1	345 42.7	12.5	22 39.2	7.6	54.0
	S.D. 15.9	d 0.7	S.D. 14.8	14.7			14.7

Twilight, Sunrise and Moonrise

Lat.	Naut.	Civil	Sunrise	Moonrise 7	8	9	10
N 72	////	////	00 32	19 52	■	■	■
N 70	////	////	01 48	19 21	21 57	■	■
68	////	////	02 25	18 58	21 01	■	■
66	////	01 06	02 51	18 40	20 28	22 36	■
64	////	01 52	03 11	18 26	20 04	21 49	23 52
62	////	02 21	03 27	18 14	19 45	21 19	22 55
60	00 59	02 43	03 40	18 04	19 29	20 56	22 22
N 58	01 40	03 00	03 52	17 55	19 16	20 38	21 57
56	02 07	03 15	04 02	17 48	19 05	20 23	21 38
54	02 28	03 27	04 10	17 41	18 55	20 10	21 22
52	02 44	03 38	04 18	17 35	18 47	19 59	21 08
50	02 58	03 47	04 25	17 29	18 39	19 48	20 56
45	03 25	04 07	04 40	17 18	18 22	19 27	20 31
N 40	03 46	04 22	04 52	17 08	18 09	19 10	20 11
35	04 02	04 35	05 03	17 00	17 58	18 56	19 54
30	04 15	04 46	05 12	16 52	17 48	18 44	19 40
20	04 36	05 04	05 27	16 40	17 31	18 23	19 16
N 10	04 53	05 18	05 41	16 29	17 16	18 05	18 55
0	05 06	05 31	05 53	16 19	17 02	17 48	18 35
S 10	05 18	05 43	06 05	16 09	16 49	17 31	18 16
20	05 29	05 55	06 18	15 59	16 34	17 13	17 56
30	05 39	06 08	06 33	15 47	16 18	16 53	17 32
35	05 45	06 15	06 42	15 40	16 08	16 41	17 18
40	05 50	06 23	06 51	15 32	15 57	16 27	17 02
45	05 56	06 31	07 03	15 23	15 45	16 11	16 43
S 50	06 03	06 41	07 16	15 12	15 29	15 51	16 19
52	06 05	06 46	07 23	15 07	15 22	15 42	16 08
54	06 08	06 51	07 30	15 01	15 14	15 31	15 55
56	06 11	06 56	07 38	14 55	15 06	15 20	15 40
58	06 15	07 03	07 47	14 49	14 56	15 06	15 22
S 60	06 18	07 09	07 57	14 41	14 44	14 50	15 01

Sunset, Twilight and Moonset

Lat.	Sunset	Civil	Naut.	Moonset 7	8	9	10
N 72	▢	▢	▢	01 33	00 45	■	■
N 70	22 11	////	////	01 50	01 18	00 12	■
68	21 32	////	////	02 03	01 42	01 10	■
66	21 05	22 56	////	02 14	02 01	01 44	01 11
64	20 44	22 05	////	02 23	02 17	02 09	01 59
62	20 28	21 35	////	02 31	02 30	02 29	02 29
60	20 14	21 13	23 02	02 38	02 41	02 45	02 52
N 58	20 03	20 55	22 17	02 44	02 50	02 58	03 11
56	19 53	20 40	21 49	02 50	02 59	03 10	03 27
54	19 44	20 27	21 28	02 55	03 06	03 21	03 40
52	19 36	20 16	21 11	02 59	03 13	03 30	03 52
50	19 29	20 07	20 57	03 03	03 19	03 38	04 03
45	19 14	19 47	20 29	03 12	03 32	03 56	04 25
N 40	19 01	19 31	20 08	03 19	03 43	04 11	04 43
35	18 51	19 18	19 52	03 26	03 53	04 23	04 58
30	18 42	19 07	19 38	03 31	04 01	04 34	05 11
20	18 26	18 49	19 17	03 41	04 15	04 52	05 33
N 10	18 12	18 35	19 00	03 49	04 28	05 09	05 52
0	18 00	18 22	18 47	03 57	04 40	05 24	06 10
S 10	17 48	18 09	18 35	04 06	04 52	05 39	06 29
20	17 34	17 57	18 24	04 14	05 04	05 56	06 48
30	17 19	17 45	18 13	04 24	05 19	06 15	07 11
35	17 11	17 37	18 08	04 30	05 28	06 26	07 24
40	17 01	17 30	18 02	04 37	05 37	06 40	07 40
45	16 50	17 21	17 56	04 44	05 49	06 54	07 58
S 50	16 36	17 11	17 50	04 53	06 03	07 12	08 21
52	16 30	17 06	17 47	04 58	06 09	07 21	08 32
54	16 22	17 01	17 44	05 03	06 17	07 31	08 45
56	16 15	16 56	17 41	05 08	06 25	07 42	08 59
58	16 06	16 50	17 37	05 14	06 34	07 55	09 16
S 60	15 55	16 43	17 34	05 20	06 45	08 11	09 37

SUN and MOON

Day	SUN Eqn. of Time 00h	12h	Mer. Pass.	MOON Mer. Pass. Upper	Lower	Age	Phase
7	03 26	03 28	11 57	22 29	10 08	12	
8	03 30	03 32	11 56	23 13	10 51	13	
9	03 34	03 35	11 56	23 59	11 36	14	○

Figure 14.16. (cont.)

20ᵐ   INCREMENTS AND CORRECTIONS   21ᵐ

20	SUN PLANETS	ARIES	MOON	v or Corrⁿ / d		v or Corrⁿ / d		v or Corrⁿ / d	
s	° ′	° ′	° ′	′	′	′	′	′	′
00	5 00·0	5 00·8	4 46·3	0·0	0·0	6·0	2·1	12·0	4·1
01	5 00·3	5 01·1	4 46·6	0·1	0·0	6·1	2·1	12·1	4·1
02	5 00·5	5 01·3	4 46·8	0·2	0·1	6·2	2·1	12·2	4·2
03	5 00·8	5 01·6	4 47·0	0·3	0·1	6·3	2·2	12·3	4·2
04	5 01·0	5 01·8	4 47·3	0·4	0·1	6·4	2·2	12·4	4·2
05	5 01·3	5 02·1	4 47·5	0·5	0·2	6·5	2·2	12·5	4·3
06	5 01·5	5 02·3	4 47·8	0·6	0·2	6·6	2·3	12·6	4·3
07	5 01·8	5 02·6	4 48·0	0·7	0·2	6·7	2·3	12·7	4·3
08	5 02·0	5 02·8	4 48·2	0·8	0·3	6·8	2·3	12·8	4·4
09	5 02·3	5 03·1	4 48·5	0·9	0·3	6·9	2·4	12·9	4·4
10	5 02·5	5 03·3	4 48·7	1·0	0·3	7·0	2·4	13·0	4·4
11	5 02·8	5 03·6	4 49·0	1·1	0·4	7·1	2·4	13·1	4·5
12	5 03·0	5 03·8	4 49·2	1·2	0·4	7·2	2·5	13·2	4·5
13	5 03·3	5 04·1	4 49·4	1·3	0·4	7·3	2·5	13·3	4·5
14	5 03·5	5 04·3	4 49·7	1·4	0·5	7·4	2·5	13·4	4·6
15	5 03·8	5 04·6	4 49·9	1·5	0·5	7·5	2·6	13·5	4·6
16	5 04·0	5 04·8	4 50·2	1·6	0·5	7·6	2·6	13·6	4·6
17	5 04·3	5 05·1	4 50·4	1·7	0·6	7·7	2·6	13·7	4·7
18	5 04·5	5 05·3	4 50·6	1·8	0·6	7·8	2·7	13·8	4·7
19	5 04·8	5 05·6	4 50·9	1·9	0·6	7·9	2·7	13·9	4·7
20	5 05·0	5 05·8	4 51·1	2·0	0·7	8·0	2·7	14·0	4·8
21	5 05·3	5 06·1	4 51·3	2·1	0·7	8·1	2·8	14·1	4·8
22	5 05·5	5 06·3	4 51·6	2·2	0·8	8·2	2·8	14·2	4·9
23	5 05·8	5 06·6	4 51·8	2·3	0·8	8·3	2·8	14·3	4·9
24	5 06·0	5 06·8	4 52·1	2·4	0·8	8·4	2·9	14·4	4·9
25	5 06·3	5 07·1	4 52·3	2·5	0·9	8·5	2·9	14·5	5·0
26	5 06·5	5 07·3	4 52·5	2·6	0·9	8·6	2·9	14·6	5·0
27	5 06·8	5 07·6	4 52·8	2·7	0·9	8·7	3·0	14·7	5·0
28	5 07·0	5 07·8	4 53·0	2·8	1·0	8·8	3·0	14·8	5·1
29	5 07·3	5 08·1	4 53·3	2·9	1·0	8·9	3·0	14·9	5·1
30	5 07·5	5 08·3	4 53·5	3·0	1·0	9·0	3·1	15·0	5·1
31	5 07·8	5 08·6	4 53·7	3·1	1·1	9·1	3·1	15·1	5·2
32	5 08·0	5 08·8	4 54·0	3·2	1·1	9·2	3·1	15·2	5·2
33	5 08·3	5 09·1	4 54·2	3·3	1·1	9·3	3·2	15·3	5·2
34	5 08·5	5 09·3	4 54·4	3·4	1·2	9·4	3·2	15·4	5·3
35	5 08·8	5 09·6	4 54·7	3·5	1·2	9·5	3·2	15·5	5·3
36	5 09·0	5 09·8	4 54·9	3·6	1·2	9·6	3·3	15·6	5·3
37	5 09·3	5 10·1	4 55·2	3·7	1·3	9·7	3·3	15·7	5·4
38	5 09·5	5 10·3	4 55·4	3·8	1·3	9·8	3·3	15·8	5·4
39	5 09·8	5 10·6	4 55·6	3·9	1·3	9·9	3·4	15·9	5·4
40	5 10·0	5 10·8	4 55·9	4·0	1·4	10·0	3·4	16·0	5·5
41	5 10·3	5 11·1	4 56·1	4·1	1·4	10·1	3·5	16·1	5·5
42	5 10·5	5 11·4	4 56·4	4·2	1·4	10·2	3·5	16·2	5·5
43	5 10·8	5 11·6	4 56·6	4·3	1·5	10·3	3·5	16·3	5·6
44	5 11·0	5 11·9	4 56·8	4·4	1·5	10·4	3·6	16·4	5·6
45	5 11·3	5 12·1	4 57·1	4·5	1·5	10·5	3·6	16·5	5·6
46	5 11·5	5 12·4	4 57·3	4·6	1·6	10·6	3·6	16·6	5·7
47	5 11·8	5 12·6	4 57·5	4·7	1·6	10·7	3·7	16·7	5·7
48	5 12·0	5 12·9	4 57·8	4·8	1·6	10·8	3·7	16·8	5·7
49	5 12·3	5 13·1	4 58·0	4·9	1·7	10·9	3·7	16·9	5·8
50	5 12·5	5 13·4	4 58·3	5·0	1·7	11·0	3·8	17·0	5·8
51	5 12·8	5 13·6	4 58·5	5·1	1·7	11·1	3·8	17·1	5·8
52	5 13·0	5 13·9	4 58·7	5·2	1·8	11·2	3·8	17·2	5·9
53	5 13·3	5 14·1	4 59·0	5·3	1·8	11·3	3·9	17·3	5·9
54	5 13·5	5 14·4	4 59·2	5·4	1·8	11·4	3·9	17·4	5·9
55	5 13·8	5 14·6	4 59·5	5·5	1·9	11·5	3·9	17·5	6·0
56	5 14·0	5 14·9	4 59·7	5·6	1·9	11·6	4·0	17·6	6·0
57	5 14·3	5 15·1	4 59·9	5·7	1·9	11·7	4·0	17·7	6·0
58	5 14·5	5 15·4	5 00·2	5·8	2·0	11·8	4·0	17·8	6·1
59	5 14·8	5 15·6	5 00·4	5·9	2·0	11·9	4·1	17·9	6·1
60	5 15·0	5 15·9	5 00·7	6·0	2·1	12·0	4·1	18·0	6·2

21	SUN PLANETS	ARIES	MOON	v or Corrⁿ / d		v or Corrⁿ / d		v or Corrⁿ / d	
s	° ′	° ′	° ′	′	′	′	′	′	′
00	5 15·0	5 15·9	5 00·7	0·0	0·0	6·0	2·2	12·0	4·3
01	5 15·3	5 16·1	5 00·9	0·1	0·0	6·1	2·2	12·1	4·3
02	5 15·5	5 16·4	5 01·1	0·2	0·1	6·2	2·2	12·2	4·4
03	5 15·8	5 16·6	5 01·4	0·3	0·1	6·3	2·3	12·3	4·4
04	5 16·0	5 16·9	5 01·6	0·4	0·1	6·4	2·3	12·4	4·4
05	5 16·3	5 17·1	5 01·8	0·5	0·2	6·5	2·3	12·5	4·5
06	5 16·5	5 17·4	5 02·1	0·6	0·2	6·6	2·4	12·6	4·5
07	5 16·8	5 17·6	5 02·3	0·7	0·3	6·7	2·4	12·7	4·6
08	5 17·0	5 17·9	5 02·6	0·8	0·3	6·8	2·4	12·8	4·6
09	5 17·3	5 18·1	5 02·8	0·9	0·3	6·9	2·5	12·9	4·6
10	5 17·5	5 18·4	5 03·0	1·0	0·4	7·0	2·5	13·0	4·7
11	5 17·8	5 18·6	5 03·3	1·1	0·4	7·1	2·5	13·1	4·7
12	5 18·0	5 18·9	5 03·5	1·2	0·4	7·2	2·6	13·2	4·7
13	5 18·3	5 19·1	5 03·8	1·3	0·5	7·3	2·6	13·3	4·8
14	5 18·5	5 19·4	5 04·0	1·4	0·5	7·4	2·7	13·4	4·8
15	5 18·8	5 19·6	5 04·2	1·5	0·5	7·5	2·7	13·5	4·8
16	5 19·0	5 19·9	5 04·5	1·6	0·6	7·6	2·7	13·6	4·9
17	5 19·3	5 20·1	5 04·7	1·7	0·6	7·7	2·8	13·7	4·9
18	5 19·5	5 20·4	5 04·9	1·8	0·6	7·8	2·8	13·8	4·9
19	5 19·8	5 20·6	5 05·2	1·9	0·7	7·9	2·8	13·9	5·0
20	5 20·0	5 20·9	5 05·4	2·0	0·7	8·0	2·9	14·0	5·0
21	5 20·3	5 21·1	5 05·7	2·1	0·8	8·1	2·9	14·1	5·1
22	5 20·5	5 21·4	5 05·9	2·2	0·8	8·2	2·9	14·2	5·1
23	5 20·8	5 21·6	5 06·1	2·3	0·8	8·3	3·0	14·3	5·1
24	5 21·0	5 21·9	5 06·4	2·4	0·9	8·4	3·0	14·4	5·2
25	5 21·3	5 22·1	5 06·6	2·5	0·9	8·5	3·0	14·5	5·2
26	5 21·5	5 22·4	5 06·9	2·6	0·9	8·6	3·1	14·6	5·2
27	5 21·8	5 22·6	5 07·1	2·7	1·0	8·7	3·1	14·7	5·3
28	5 22·0	5 22·9	5 07·3	2·8	1·0	8·8	3·2	14·8	5·3
29	5 22·3	5 23·1	5 07·6	2·9	1·0	8·9	3·2	14·9	5·3
30	5 22·5	5 23·4	5 07·8	3·0	1·1	9·0	3·2	15·0	5·4
31	5 22·8	5 23·6	5 08·0	3·1	1·1	9·1	3·3	15·1	5·4
32	5 23·0	5 23·9	5 08·3	3·2	1·1	9·2	3·3	15·2	5·4
33	5 23·3	5 24·1	5 08·5	3·3	1·2	9·3	3·3	15·3	5·5
34	5 23·5	5 24·4	5 08·8	3·4	1·2	9·4	3·4	15·4	5·5
35	5 23·8	5 24·6	5 09·0	3·5	1·3	9·5	3·4	15·5	5·6
36	5 24·0	5 24·9	5 09·2	3·6	1·3	9·6	3·4	15·6	5·6
37	5 24·3	5 25·1	5 09·5	3·7	1·3	9·7	3·5	15·7	5·6
38	5 24·5	5 25·4	5 09·7	3·8	1·4	9·8	3·5	15·8	5·7
39	5 24·8	5 25·6	5 10·0	3·9	1·4	9·9	3·5	15·9	5·7
40	5 25·0	5 25·9	5 10·2	4·0	1·4	10·0	3·6	16·0	5·7
41	5 25·3	5 26·1	5 10·4	4·1	1·5	10·1	3·6	16·1	5·8
42	5 25·5	5 26·4	5 10·7	4·2	1·5	10·2	3·7	16·2	5·8
43	5 25·8	5 26·6	5 10·9	4·3	1·5	10·3	3·7	16·3	5·8
44	5 26·0	5 26·9	5 11·1	4·4	1·6	10·4	3·7	16·4	5·9
45	5 26·3	5 27·1	5 11·4	4·5	1·6	10·5	3·8	16·5	5·9
46	5 26·5	5 27·4	5 11·6	4·6	1·6	10·6	3·8	16·6	5·9
47	5 26·8	5 27·6	5 11·9	4·7	1·7	10·7	3·8	16·7	6·0
48	5 27·0	5 27·9	5 12·1	4·8	1·7	10·8	3·9	16·8	6·0
49	5 27·3	5 28·1	5 12·3	4·9	1·8	10·9	3·9	16·9	6·1
50	5 27·5	5 28·4	5 12·6	5·0	1·8	11·0	3·9	17·0	6·1
51	5 27·8	5 28·6	5 12·8	5·1	1·8	11·1	4·0	17·1	6·1
52	5 28·0	5 28·9	5 13·1	5·2	1·9	11·2	4·0	17·2	6·2
53	5 28·3	5 29·1	5 13·3	5·3	1·9	11·3	4·0	17·3	6·2
54	5 28·5	5 29·4	5 13·5	5·4	1·9	11·4	4·1	17·4	6·2
55	5 28·8	5 29·7	5 13·8	5·5	2·0	11·5	4·1	17·5	6·3
56	5 29·0	5 29·9	5 14·0	5·6	2·0	11·6	4·2	17·6	6·3
57	5 29·3	5 30·2	5 14·3	5·7	2·0	11·7	4·2	17·7	6·3
58	5 29·5	5 30·4	5 14·5	5·8	2·1	11·8	4·2	17·8	6·4
59	5 29·8	5 30·7	5 14·7	5·9	2·1	11·9	4·3	17·9	6·4
60	5 30·0	5 30·9	5 15·0	6·0	2·2	12·0	4·3	18·0	6·5

Figure 14.17. Portion of "Increments and Corrections" table in yellow pages of Almanac.

CHAPTER FIFTEEN

Latitude and Longitude from the Sun

The *Mayflower* made a slow and rough voyage because she left at the wrong time of year. If the Pilgrims' plans had been carried out promptly, she would have started in May and enjoyed fair winds. But in September the season of westerly gales had begun, and she encountered plenty.

. . . Master Jones . . . had some inaccurate charts of the Atlantic, and knew the straight course for Cape Cod; but for more than half the voyage the west wind prevented his steering the straight course. Every noon he checked his latitude by observing the sun with a crude instrument called a cross-staff, and applying the figures from an almanac. But he had no means of measuring longitude or how far west he had sailed, except by tracing on the chart his compass course and estimated distance.

. . . The *Mayflower* took sixty-five days to sail from Plymouth, England, to Cape Cod, and one day more to her first American harbor. That was exactly twice what Columbus took on his first voyage. The *Mayflower* might have made a shorter and easier passage by the southern route, but she would have run the risk of being captured by the Spaniards or wrecked off Cape Hatteras.

Samuel Eliot Morison, The Story of the "Old Colony" of New Plymouth 1620-1692

As the harbor pilots guided the *Flying Fish* into the Norwegian port, officers and crew alike scratched their heads at the mystery. How had they managed to miss Gibraltar by 2000 miles . . . to make landfall at the edge of the Arctic Circle? Three officers had taken regular sightings, and all their calculations agreed that they were on track to Gibraltar. What could possibly have gone wrong?

Finally the mystery was solved—traced to a single arithmetic error. In calculating their position, all three officers had *subtracted* the sun's increasing declination after March 20 instead of adding it—and had dutifully altered their course ever northward to keep to what they thought was the latitude . . . of the route to Gibraltar!

John Townley, Ocean Navigator

INTRODUCTION

The discussions of the sky and the sun have so far assumed you wanted to follow the sun's behavior from a known position. This chapter will permit using the sun to determine your latitude and longitude. All you need to know is the date.

Latitude is determined by measuring the height of the celestial pole, and this can be done in many ways, by measuring Polaris or by measuring the height of the sun or a star when it is on the meridian. This chapter concentrates on the sun because it is the easiest celestial object to observe and is a good place to start.

Greenwich is the starting point of longitude, and you cannot determine your longitude from the sun without knowing the time in Greenwich. The westward track of the sun is like the motion of an hour hand that completes one rotation per day. The longitude of Greenwich is the starting mark.

RULE FOR LATITUDE BY NOON SIGHT

A noon sight of the sun is probably the easiest and most commonly used method of latitude determination, and there are at least three reasons for this popularity. First, the mathematics are minimal and there are no double-entry tables to be used. In fact, the only table you need is the declination of the sun. Second, a sextant sight of the sun is much easier to obtain than a sight of a star. (The star is faint and the horizon may be hard to find in the twilight.) Third, many navigators like to make a habit of determining noon positions. The day begins at noon, so to speak, and the noon updating becomes part of the daily ritual. The updating is achieved by combining the noon latitude with a

DR estimate of longitude or with a running fix from an early morning sun sight, as described in Chapter 20.

The rule

Apparent noon is the instant when the sun is on the navigator's meridian and is highest in the sky. If you measure the sun's altitude with a sextant at that instant, you can find its zenith distance (Figure 12.1) from the formula:

$$\text{Zenith distance} = 90° - \text{altitude}$$

and then can find your latitude from:

Latitude = sun's declination ± sun's zenith distance
(subtract when sun is north of zenith)

For example, if the sun is straight overhead the zenith distance is 0° and your latitude is the same as its declination. When the sun is not overhead, you must note whether it is north or south of your zenith to decide whether to add or subtract the zenith distance. The rule can be inferred from Figures 15.1a or 15.1b, and when you are in doubt you can draw a diagram like one of these. Southern latitudes and declinations are treated as negative angles.

As another example, suppose the sun is in the south at a zenith distance of 60° when at a declination of 30S. In this case, the navigator's latitude is −30° + 60° = 30°N.

POSTTEST

15.1 Fill in the blanks and compute the navigator's latitude from the following data on the sun:

Sun's declination	Sun N or S of zenith	Sun's height	Zenith distance	Latitude
24N	S	80°	____	____
10N	N	40°	____	____
30S	N	30°	____	____
10S	S	60°	____	____

GETTING THE NOON SIGHT

First you must predict the time of local noon from your DR longitude and the *Almanac*. One method (using the equation of time) was described in Chapter 13, and another method is described below and

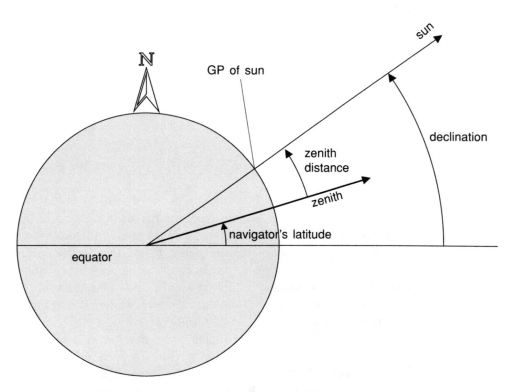

Figure 15.1a. When the sun is on your meridian, its distance from the zenith gives your distance from its geographical position (GP). In this case the sun is north of the navigator's zenith, and the relationship is latitude = declination − zenith distance.

is used in the reduction form. Next you determine the index correction of your sextant (see Chapter 9). Then you measure the sun's altitude above the horizon at the time of predicted noon. This can be done with a protractor, as in the activity described at the start of this chapter, or with a sextant. If you use a protractor, your accuracy will be limited to a few degrees, equivalent to several hundred miles on the earth's surface. With a sextant you can find yourself to within a few miles.

It is crucial that the sextant, or other measuring device, be straight up and down when making the measurement so the angle is taken along the true vertical (Figure 15.2).

Reduction tables and tables giving positions of celestial bodies are based on the *centers* of the bodies. The navigator cannot use the center of the sun in taking a sun sight, because it is too difficult to estimate its location precisely. Instead, the upper or lower limb is used (Figures 15.2, 15.3).

Ordinarily you will observe the lower limb of the sun, unless it is covered by clouds, and you should make three or four measures in the space of a minute or so and average them. The average time is needed to the nearest minute, but it is good practice

to get in the habit of working to the nearest second of time. A correction to the center of the sun is then applied, as described below.

CORRECTIONS TO THE SEXTANT ALTITUDE OF THE SUN

Three corrections must be made to the sextant sight, h_S. Ideally, the first two should be made before the third, as shown in Figure 15.4.

1. *Index correction (IC)*—All sextant sights begin with a determination of the index error and end with a verification that it has not changed during the measurement. The method is described in Chapter 9. Let us suppose you find an error of IC = 2′ off the arc. This implies that you must add 2′ to h_S. (Remember, if it's *on, it's off;* if it's *off, it's on.*)

2. *Dip of the horizon*—The measured value, h_S, must be corrected for the height of your eye above the water. This height causes a dip of the horizon (Figure 15.5), and the corrections are found on the inside front cover of the *Nautical Almanac,* which is excerpted in Table 15.1 and is reproduced in the Appendix.

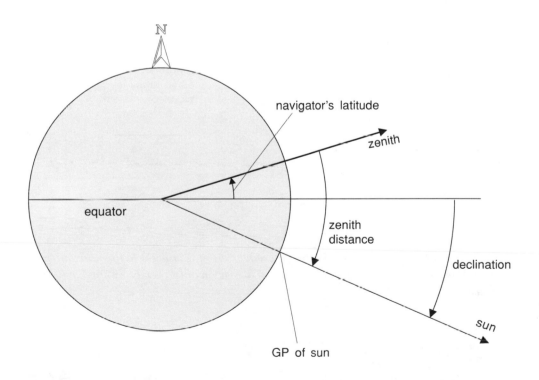

Figure 15.1b. In this case, the sun is south of the navigator's zenith, and the relationship determined by inspecting the diagram is latitude – declination + zenith distance.

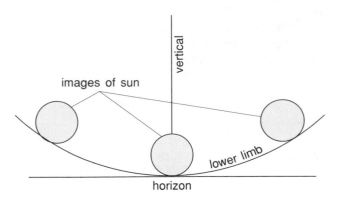

Figure 15.2. Making a sextant sight of the sun by rock-ing the sextant to find the true vertical.

Table 15.1. Dip correction to sextant height

Height of eye (feet)	8	16	32	64
Dip of horizon (arc minutes)	−2.8	−3.9	−5.5	−7.8

For example, if h_s = 60°30′ and your eye is 16 feet above the water, you must subtract 4′ from the reading to find 60° 26′.

3. *"3rd correction" for refraction and semidiameter—* When light rays from a celestial body enter the earth's atmosphere, they are bent slightly downward, as illustrated in Figure 15.6. This has the effect of

making the object look a little too high. The effect vanishes overhead and it is greatest at the horizon, where it becomes about one-half degree. This is ap-proximately equal to the diameter of the sun and has the effect of lifting the entire sun above the horizon before sunrise and after sunset.

When the sun's lower limb is observed, 16′ must be added to hs to get the height of the sun's center; when the lower limb is observed, 16′ must be sub-tracted (see Figure 15.3). The amount of this correc-tion varies slightly in the course of the year, due to the earth's varying distance from the sun, which makes the sun appear larger in winter than sum-mer. (The amount of change is only 1 percent, and this is too small to be noticed without careful mea-surement.)

To save time, the *Almanac* combines this semi-diameter correction with the refraction correction for the sun. The result is called the "3rd correction" because it comes after index correction and dip cor-rection. These corrections are inside the front cover, and they are given for both limbs and for the two halves of the year when the earth is closer to and farther from the sun.

The following table gives sample corrections de-rived from the *Almanac*.

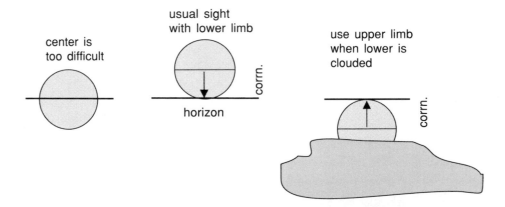

Figure 15.3. Usually, the lower limb of the sun or moon is brought to the horizon, but when it is clouded, the upper limb is used. A correction must then be applied to bring the center to the horizon.

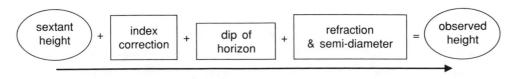

Figure 15.4. Three corrections to the sextant height, h_s, lead to the observed height H_o.

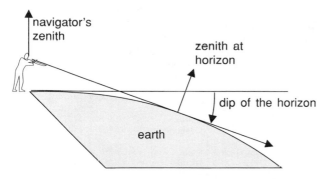

Figure 15.5. Dip of the horizon. The navigator's eye is above the curved surface, so the horizon (arrow to right) appears more than 90° from the zenith. Sextant height must be decreased slightly to correct for the dip, and the amount of correction depends on the height of the navigator's eye above the surface. The correction is found inside the front cover of the Almanac.

Table 15.2. Sample altitude corrections to h_s for the sun

Date: May 5; IE = 2′ off the arc; height of eye = 16 feet; h_s = 60°30′ (lower limb)

h_s	60°30′
IC	+ 2′
Dip	− 4′
3rd corr.	+ 15′
H_o	60° 43′

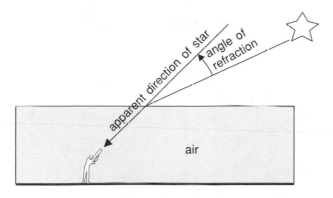

Figure 15.6. The effect of refraction by earth's atmosphere is to make objects appear slightly higher. The correction to be applied is found inside the front cover of the Almanac. *For the sun, the correction is combined with a correction for the apparent radius (semidiameter) of the sun.*

POSTTEST

15.2 Using the following data, compute the observed height H_o.

Date: Nov 10; IE = 3′ on the arc; height of eye = 8 feet; h_s = 49°20′ (upper limb)

h_s	
IC	
Dip	
3rd corr.	
H_o	_____

USING THE FORM F2

After making all these altitude corrections, you calculate the zenith distance, find the noon declination of the sun from the *Almanac,* and solve for latitude. The details of all these steps (including the altitude corrections) are shown on the sample form F2. If you follow it step by step, you will find your latitude.

Date: February 25, 1990
Time: 1105 ZT
DR position: long. 61°20′W; lat. 23°30′N
Index error: 1′ on the arc
Watch error: 5 sec. slow

You wish to make a sighting of the sun at noon to determine your latitude. (You can't determine both latitude and longitude from a single sun sight, because you will assume your longitude in calculating the time of noon.)

The first task is to predict the time of local noon for your DR longitude using the successive parts of form F2. This calculation involves finding the local hour angle of the sun and computing how long it will take to reach your meridian.

Read the description for each part and then look at the form and the *Almanac* data in Figures 15.7-15.9 to identify the numbers that have been entered. You may refer back to Chapter 14 for hints on the use of the *Almanac* yellow pages.

- *Part 1*—Enter the current watch time (WT) and compute the GMT corresponding to when you were at the DR position.

- *Part 2*—Enter the GHA sun from the daily pages (Figure 15.7) for the current hours GMT (15) and then find the correction for 5 minutes from the yellow pages (Figure 15.8). This gives the GHA sun and,

1990 FEBRUARY 24, 25, 26 (SAT., SUN., MON.)

UT (GMT) d h	ARIES G.H.A.	VENUS −4.6 G.H.A.	Dec.	MARS +1.3 G.H.A.	Dec.	JUPITER −2.4 G.H.A.	Dec.	SATURN +0.6 G.H.A.	Dec.	STARS Name	S.H.A.	Dec.
24 00	153 36.7	217 25.0	S15 29.2	223 30.6	S22 51.2	62 43.8	N23 26.9	220 15.7	S21 28.1	Acamar	315 31.6	S40 20.8
01	168 39.2	232 26.1	29.3	238 31.1	51.0	77 46.2	26.9	235 17.9	28.1	Achernar	335 39.8	S57 17.3
02	183 41.6	247 27.2	29.4	253 31.6	50.8	92 48.7	26.9	250 20.1	28.1	Acrux	173 28.7	S63 02.7
03	198 44.1	262 28.3 ..	29.4	268 32.1 ..	50.6	107 51.2 ..	26.9	265 22.3 ..	28.0	Adhara	255 26.0	S28 57.6
04	213 46.6	277 29.4	29.5	283 32.6	50.3	122 53.7	26.9	280 24.5	28.0	Aldebaran	291 09.4	N16 29.5
05	228 49.0	292 30.5	29.6	298 33.1	50.1	137 56.1	26.9	295 26.7	28.0			
S 06	243 51.5	307 31.5	S15 29.6	313 33.5	S22 49.9	152 58.6	N23 27.0	310 28.9	S21 27.9	Alioth	166 35.2	N56 00.4
A 07	258 54.0	322 32.6	29.7	328 34.0	49.7	168 01.1	27.0	325 31.1	27.9	Alkaid	153 12.1	N49 21.3
T 08	273 56.4	337 33.7	29.8	343 34.5	49.5	183 03.5	27.0	340 33.3	27.8	Al Na'ir	28 05.9	S47 00.6
U 09	288 58.9	352 34.7 ..	29.8	358 35.0 ..	49.2	198 06.0 ..	27.0	355 35.5 ..	27.8	Alnilam	276 04.0	S 1 12.5
R 10	304 01.3	7 35.8	29.9	13 35.5	49.0	213 08.5	27.0	10 37.7	27.8	Alphard	218 13.0	S 8 37.1
D 11	319 03.8	22 36.9	30.0	28 36.0 .	48.8	228 10.9	27.0	25 39.9	27.7			
A 12	334 06.3	37 37.9	S15 30.0	43 36.5	S22 48.6	243 13.4	N23 27.0	40 42.1	S21 27.7	Alphecca	126 25.7	N26 44.4
Y 13	349 08.7	52 39.0	30.1	58 37.0	48.4	258 15.9	27.0	55 44.4	27.7	Alpheratz	358 02.0	N29 02.2
14	4 11.2	67 40.0	30.2	73 37.5	48.1	273 18.3	27.0	70 46.6	27.6	Altair	62 25.5	N 8 50.3
15	19 13.7	82 41.1 ..	30.2	88 37.9 ..	47.9	288 20.8 ..	27.0	85 48.8 ..	27.6	Ankaa	353 33.1	S42 21.7
16	34 16.1	97 42.1	30.3	103 38.4	47.7	303 23.3	27.0	100 51.0	27.6	Antares	112 47.8	S26 24.8
17	49 18.6	112 43.2	30.4	118 38.9	47.5	318 25.7	27.0	115 53.2	27.5			
18	64 21.1	127 44.2	S15 30.4	133 39.4	S22 47.2	333 28.2	N23 27.0	130 55.4	S21 27.5	Arcturus	146 11.4	N19 13.7
19	79 23.5	142 45.3	30.5	148 39.9	47.0	348 30.7	27.0	145 57.6	27.5	Atria	108 05.5	S69 00.5
20	94 26.0	157 46.3	30.5	163 40.4	46.8	3 33.1	27.0	160 59.8	27.4	Avior	234 24.8	S59 28.8
21	109 28.4	172 47.3 ..	30.6	178 40.9 ..	46.6	18 35.6 ..	27.0	176 02.0 ..	27.4	Bellatrix	278 50.7	N 6 20.5
22	124 30.9	187 48.4	30.6	193 41.4	46.3	33 38.1	27.0	191 04.2	27.4	Betelgeuse	271 20.1	N 7 24.4
23	139 33.4	202 49.4	30.7	208 41.9	46.1	48 40.5	27.0	206 06.5	27.3			
25 00	154 35.8	217 50.4	S15 30.8	223 42.4	S22 45.9	63 43.0	N23 27.0	221 08.7	S21 27.3	Canopus	264 03.6	S52 41.6
01	169 38.3	232 51.5	30.8	238 42.8	45.7	78 45.4	27.1	236 10.9	27.2	Capella	281 00.2	N45 59.6
02	184 40.8	247 52.5	30.9	253 43.3	45.4	93 47.9	27.1	251 13.1	27.2	Deneb	49 43.9	N45 14.5
03	199 43.2	262 53.5 ..	30.9	268 43.8 ..	45.2	108 50.4 ..	27.1	266 15.3 ..	27.2	Denebola	182 51.1	N14 37.4
04	214 45.7	277 54.5	31.0	283 44.3	45.0	123 52.8	27.1	281 17.5	27.1	Diphda	349 13.6	S18 02.5
05	229 48.2	292 55.5	31.1	298 44.8	44.7	138 55.3	27.1	296 19.7	27.1			
S 06	244 50.6	307 56.5	S15 31.1	313 45.3	S22 44.5	153 57.7	N23 27.1	311 21.9	S21 27.1	Dubhe	194 12.0	N61 48.1
U 07	259 53.1	322 57.5	31.2	328 45.8	44.3	169 00.2	27.1	326 24.1	27.0	Elnath	278 34.6	N28 36.2
N 08	274 55.6	337 58.6	31.2	343 46.3	44.1	184 02.7	27.1	341 26.3	27.0	Eltanin	90 54.5	N51 29.0
D 09	289 58.0	352 59.6 ..	31.3	358 46.8 ..	43.8	199 05.1 ..	27.1	356 28.6 ..	27.0	Enif	34 04.6	N 9 49.6
A 10	305 00.5	8 00.6	31.3	13 47.3	43.6	214 07.6	27.1	11 30.8	26.9	Fomalhaut	15 43.5	S29 40.6
Y 11	320 02.9	23 01.6	31.4	28 47.7	43.4	229 10.0	27.1	26 33.0	26.9			
12	335 05.4	38 02.6	S15 31.4	43 48.2	S22 43.1	244 12.5	N23 27.1	41 35.2	S21 26.9	Gacrux	172 20.2	S57 03.5
13	350 07.9	53 03.6	31.5	58 48.7	42.9	259 15.0	27.1	56 37.4	26.8	Gienah	176 10.1	S17 29.4
14	5 10.3	68 04.5	31.5	73 49.2	42.7	274 17.4	27.1	71 39.6	26.8	Hadar	149 12.7	S60 19.5
15	20 12.8	83 05.5 ..	31.6	88 49.7 ..	42.4	289 19.9 ..	27.1	86 41.8 ..	26.7	Hamal	328 20.8	N23 25.1
16	35 15.3	98 06.5	31.6	103 50.2	42.2	304 22.3	27.1	101 44.0	26.7	Kaus Aust.	84 07.1	S34 23.5
17	50 17.7	113 07.5	31.7	118 50.7	42.0	319 24.8	27.1	116 46.2	26.7			
18	65 20.2	128 08.5	S15 31.7	133 51.2	S22 41.7	334 27.2	N23 27.1	131 48.5	S21 26.6	Kochab	137 18.4	N74 11.3
19	80 22.7	143 09.5	31.8	148 51.7	41.5	349 29.7	27.1	146 50.7	26.6	Markab	13 56.1	N15 09.1
20	95 25.1	158 10.4	31.8	163 52.2	41.3	4 32.1	27.1	161 52.9	26.6	Menkar	314 33.4	N 4 03.1
21	110 27.6	173 11.4 ..	31.9	178 52.7 ..	41.0	19 34.6 ..	27.2	176 55.1 ..	26.5	Menkent	148 28.1	S36 19.4
22	125 30.1	188 12.4	31.9	193 53.1	40.8	34 37.1	27.2	191 57.3	26.5	Miaplacidus	221 42.8	S69 40.7
23	140 32.5	203 13.4	32.0	208 53.6	40.6	49 39.5	27.2	206 59.5	26.5			
26 00	155 35.0	218 14.3	S15 32.0	223 54.1	S22 40.3	64 42.0	N23 27.2	222 01.7	S21 26.4	Mirfak	309 05.7	N49 49.9
01	170 37.4	233 15.3	32.1	238 54.6	40.1	79 44.4	27.2	237 03.9	26.4	Nunki	76 20.1	S26 18.7
02	185 39.9	248 16.3	32.1	253 55.1	39.8	94 46.9	27.2	252 06.2	26.4	Peacock	53 47.0	S56 46.0
03	200 42.4	263 17.2 ..	32.2	268 55.6 ..	39.6	109 49.3 ..	27.2	267 08.4 ..	26.3	Pollux	243 48.7	N28 03.1
04	215 44.8	278 18.2	32.2	283 56.1	39.4	124 51.8	27.2	282 10.6	26.3	Procyon	245 17.7	N 5 15.0
05	230 47.3	293 19.1	32.2	298 56.6	39.1	139 54.2	27.2	297 12.8	26.3			
06	245 49.8	308 20.1	S15 32.3	313 57.1	S22 38.9	154 56.7	N23 27.2	312 15.0	S21 26.2	Rasalhague	96 22.8	N12 33.7
07	260 52.2	323 21.0	32.3	328 57.6	38.7	169 59.1	27.2	327 17.2	26.2	Regulus	208 01.7	N12 00.8
08	275 54.7	338 22.0	32.4	343 58.1	38.4	185 01.6	27.2	342 19.4	26.1	Rigel	281 28.8	S 8 12.8
M 09	290 57.2	353 22.9 ..	32.4	358 58.6 ..	38.2	200 04.0 ..	27.2	357 21.6 ..	26.1	Rigil Kent.	140 15.6	S60 47.6
O 10	305 59.6	8 23.9	32.4	13 59.0	37.9	215 06.5	27.2	12 23.9	26.1	Sabik	102 32.7	S15 43.0
N 11	321 02.1	23 24.8	32.5	28 59.5	37.7	230 08.9	27.2	27 26.1	26.0			
D 12	336 04.5	38 25.7	S15 32.5	44 00.0	S22 37.5	245 11.4	N23 27.2	42 28.3	S21 26.0	Schedar	350 01.3	N56 29.2
A 13	351 07.0	53 26.7	32.6	59 00.5	37.2	260 13.8	27.2	57 30.5	26.0	Shaula	96 45.8	S37 05.9
Y 14	6 09.5	68 27.6	32.6	74 01.0	37.0	275 16.3	27.2	72 32.7	25.9	Sirius	258 48.9	S16 42.2
15	21 11.9	83 28.5 ..	32.6	89 01.5 ..	36.7	290 18.7 ..	27.2	87 34.9 ..	25.9	Spica	158 49.5	S11 06.8
16	36 14.4	98 29.5	32.7	104 02.0	36.5	305 21.2	27.3	102 37.1	25.9	Suhail	223 05.0	S43 23.7
17	51 16.9	113 30.4	32.7	119 02.5	36.2	320 23.6	27.3	117 39.4	25.8			
18	66 19.3	128 31.3	S15 32.8	134 03.0	S22 36.0	335 26.1	N23 27.3	132 41.6	S21 25.8	Vega	80 51.0	N38 46.1
19	81 21.8	143 32.2	32.8	149 03.5	35.8	350 28.5	27.3	147 43.8	25.8	Zuben'ubi	137 24.7	S16 00.3
20	96 24.3	158 33.2	32.8	164 04.0	35.5	5 31.0	27.3	162 46.0	25.7		S.H.A.	Mer. Pass.
21	111 26.7	173 34.1 ..	32.9	179 04.5 ..	35.3	20 33.4 ..	27.3	177 48.2 ..	25.7	Venus	63 14.6	9 28
22	126 29.2	188 35.0	32.9	194 05.0	35.0	35 35.8	27.3	192 50.4	25.7	Mars	69 06.5	9 05
23	141 31.7	203 35.9	32.9	209 05.5	34.8	50 38.3	27.3	207 52.6	25.6	Jupiter	269 07.1	19 42
Mer. Pass. 13 39.4		v 1.0	d 0.1	v 0.5	d 0.2	v 2.5	d 0.0	v 2.2	d 0.0	Saturn	66 32.8	9 14

Figure 15.7. Daily page for February 25, 1990.

1990 FEBRUARY 24, 25, 26 (SAT., SUN., MON.)

UT (GMT) d h	SUN G.H.A.	SUN Dec.	MOON G.H.A.	v	MOON Dec.	d	H.P.
24 00	176 40.1	S 9 38.3	193 46.2	10.7	S15 32.0	13.4	58.2
01	191 40.2	37.4	208 15.9	10.7	15 18.6	13.6	58.2
02	206 40.3	36.4	222 45.6	10.8	15 05.0	13.6	58.2
03	221 40.4	.. 35.5	237 15.4	10.8	14 51.4	13.7	58.3
04	236 40.5	34.6	251 45.2	10.8	14 37.7	13.8	58.3
05	251 40.6	33.7	266 15.0	10.8	14 23.9	13.9	58.3
06	266 40.7	S 9 32.7	280 44.8	10.9	S14 10.0	14.0	58.4
07	281 40.7	31.8	295 14.7	10.9	13 56.0	14.1	58.4
S 08	296 40.8	30.9	309 44.6	10.9	13 41.9	14.1	58.4
A 09	311 40.9	.. 30.0	324 14.5	11.0	13 27.8	14.3	58.4
T 10	326 41.0	29.1	338 44.5	11.0	13 13.5	14.3	58.5
U 11	341 41.1	28.1	353 14.5	11.0	12 59.2	14.4	58.5
R 12	356 41.2	S 9 27.2	7 44.5	11.1	S12 44.8	14.5	58.5
D 13	11 41.3	26.3	22 14.6	11.1	12 30.3	14.5	58.6
A 14	26 41.4	25.4	36 44.7	11.1	12 15.8	14.7	58.6
Y 15	41 41.5	.. 24.4	51 14.8	11.1	12 01.1	14.7	58.6
16	56 41.6	23.5	65 44.9	11.2	11 46.4	14.8	58.6
17	71 41.7	22.6	80 15.1	11.2	11 31.6	14.8	58.7
18	86 41.8	S 9 21.7	94 45.3	11.2	S11 16.8	15.0	58.7
19	101 41.8	20.7	109 15.5	11.2	11 01.8	15.0	58.7
20	116 41.9	19.8	123 45.7	11.3	10 46.8	15.1	58.8
21	131 42.0	.. 18.9	138 16.0	11.2	10 31.7	15.1	58.8
22	146 42.1	18.0	152 46.2	11.3	10 16.6	15.2	58.8
23	161 42.2	17.0	167 16.5	11.4	10 01.4	15.3	58.8
25 00	176 42.3	S 9 16.1	181 46.9	11.3	S 9 46.1	15.3	58.9
01	191 42.4	15.2	196 17.2	11.4	9 30.8	15.4	58.9
02	206 42.5	14.2	210 47.6	11.4	9 15.4	15.5	58.9
03	221 42.6	.. 13.3	225 18.0	11.4	8 59.9	15.5	58.9
04	236 42.7	12.4	239 48.4	11.4	8 44.4	15.6	59.0
05	251 42.8	11.5	254 18.8	11.4	8 28.8	15.7	59.0
06	266 42.9	S 9 10.5	268 49.2	11.5	S 8 13.1	15.8	59.0
07	281 43.0	09.6	283 19.7	11.4	7 57.5	15.8	59.0
S 08	296 43.1	08.7	297 50.1	11.5	7 41.7	15.8	59.1
U 09	311 43.2	.. 07.7	312 20.6	11.5	7 25.9	15.8	59.1
N 10	326 43.3	06.8	326 51.1	11.5	7 10.1	15.9	59.1
D 11	341 43.4	05.9	341 21.6	11.5	6 54.2	16.0	59.1
A 12	356 43.5	S 9 05.0	355 52.1	11.5	S 6 38.2	16.0	59.2
Y 13	11 43.6	04.0	10 22.6	11.6	6 22.2	16.0	59.2
14	26 43.7	03.1	24 53.2	11.5	6 06.2	16.1	59.2
15	41 43.8	.. 02.2	39 23.7	11.6	5 50.1	16.1	59.2
16	56 43.9	01.2	53 54.3	11.5	5 34.0	16.2	59.2
17	71 44.0	9 00.3	68 24.8	11.6	5 17.8	16.2	59.3
18	86 44.1	S 8 59.4	82 55.4	11.5	S 5 01.6	16.2	59.3
19	101 44.2	58.4	97 25.9	11.6	4 45.4	16.3	59.3
20	116 44.3	57.5	111 56.5	11.6	4 29.1	16.3	59.3
21	131 44.4	.. 56.6	126 27.1	11.5	4 12.8	16.4	59.4
22	146 44.5	55.6	140 57.6	11.6	3 56.4	16.3	59.4
23	161 44.6	54.7	155 28.2	11.6	3 40.1	16.4	59.4
26 00	176 44.7	S 8 53.8	169 58.8	11.5	S 3 23.7	16.5	59.4
01	191 44.8	52.8	184 29.3	11.6	3 07.2	16.4	59.4
02	206 44.9	51.9	198 59.9	11.5	2 50.8	16.5	59.4
03	221 45.0	.. 51.0	213 30.4	11.6	2 34.3	16.5	59.5
04	236 45.1	50.0	228 01.0	11.5	2 17.8	16.5	59.5
05	251 45.2	49.1	242 31.5	11.6	2 01.3	16.6	59.5
06	266 45.3	S 8 48.2	257 02.1	11.5	S 1 44.7	16.5	59.5
07	281 45.4	47.2	271 32.6	11.5	1 28.2	16.6	59.5
08	296 45.5	46.3	286 03.1	11.5	1 11.6	16.6	59.6
M 09	311 45.6	.. 45.4	300 33.6	11.5	0 55.0	16.6	59.6
O 10	326 45.7	44.4	315 04.1	11.5	0 38.4	16.6	59.6
N 11	341 45.8	43.5	329 34.6	11.5	0 21.8	16.7	59.6
D 12	356 45.9	S 8 42.6	344 05.1	11.4	S 0 05.1	16.6	59.6
A 13	11 46.0	41.6	358 35.5	11.5	N 0 11.5	16.6	59.6
Y 14	26 46.1	40.7	13 06.0	11.4	0 28.1	16.7	59.6
15	41 46.2	.. 39.8	27 36.4	11.4	0 44.8	16.6	59.7
16	56 46.3	38.8	42 06.8	11.4	1 01.4	16.7	59.7
17	71 46.4	37.9	56 37.2	11.4	1 18.1	16.6	59.7
18	86 46.5	S 8 37.0	71 07.6	11.3	N 1 34.7	16.7	59.7
19	101 46.6	36.0	85 37.9	11.3	1 51.4	16.6	59.7
20	116 46.7	35.1	100 08.2	11.3	2 08.0	16.7	59.7
21	131 46.8	.. 34.1	114 38.5	11.3	2 24.7	16.6	59.7
22	146 46.9	33.2	129 08.8	11.2	2 41.3	16.6	59.8
23	161 47.1	32.3	143 39.1	11.2	2 57.9	16.7	59.8
	S.D. 16.2	d 0.9	S.D. 15.9		16.1		16.2

Lat.	Twilight Naut.	Twilight Civil	Sunrise	Moonrise 24	Moonrise 25	Moonrise 26	Moonrise 27
N 72	05 31	06 49	08 00	08 37	07 49	07 14	06 39
N 70	05 34	06 44	07 47	08 11	07 38	07 12	06 46
68	05 36	06 40	07 37	07 52	07 29	07 10	06 51
66	05 38	06 37	07 29	07 36	07 21	07 08	06 56
64	05 39	06 34	07 22	07 23	07 15	07 07	07 00
62	05 40	06 31	07 16	07 12	07 09	07 06	07 03
60	05 41	06 29	07 11	07 02	07 04	07 05	07 07
N 58	05 41	06 27	07 06	06 54	07 00	07 04	07 09
56	05 42	06 25	07 02	06 46	06 56	07 04	07 12
54	05 42	06 23	06 59	06 40	06 52	07 03	07 14
52	05 42	06 21	06 55	06 34	06 49	07 02	07 16
50	05 42	06 19	06 52	06 28	06 46	07 02	07 18
45	05 42	06 16	06 45	06 17	06 39	07 01	07 22
N 40	05 41	06 13	06 40	06 07	06 34	07 00	07 25
35	05 40	06 09	06 35	05 58	06 29	06 59	07 28
30	05 39	06 06	06 31	05 51	06 25	06 58	07 31
20	05 35	06 01	06 23	05 38	06 18	06 57	07 35
N 10	05 30	05 55	06 16	05 27	06 12	06 55	07 40
0	05 25	05 49	06 10	05 16	06 06	06 54	07 43
S 10	05 17	05 42	06 03	05 05	05 59	06 53	07 47
20	05 07	05 34	05 56	04 54	05 53	06 52	07 52
30	04 54	05 23	05 48	04 41	05 46	06 51	07 57
35	04 46	05 17	05 43	04 33	05 41	06 50	07 59
40	04 36	05 10	05 38	04 24	05 37	06 49	08 03
45	04 24	05 01	05 31	04 14	05 31	06 48	08 06
S 50	04 08	04 49	05 23	04 02	05 24	06 47	08 11
52	04 00	04 44	05 20	03 56	05 21	06 47	08 13
54	03 51	04 38	05 16	03 49	05 17	06 46	08 16
56	03 41	04 31	05 11	03 42	05 14	06 45	08 18
58	03 29	04 24	05 07	03 34	05 09	06 45	08 21
S 60	03 15	04 15	05 01	03 24	05 04	06 44	08 24

Lat.	Sunset	Twilight Civil	Twilight Naut.	Moonset 24	Moonset 25	Moonset 26	Moonset 27
N 72	16 29	17 40	18 58	14 47	17 20	19 42	22 10
N 70	16 41	17 44	18 55	15 11	17 28	19 39	21 55
68	16 50	17 48	18 52	15 28	17 34	19 37	21 43
66	16 58	17 51	18 51	15 42	17 40	19 35	21 34
64	17 05	17 54	18 49	15 54	17 44	19 34	21 25
62	17 11	17 57	18 48	16 04	17 48	19 32	21 19
60	17 16	17 59	18 47	16 12	17 51	19 31	21 13
N 58	17 21	18 01	18 46	16 19	17 54	19 30	21 07
56	17 25	18 03	18 46	16 25	17 57	19 29	21 03
54	17 29	18 04	18 45	16 31	17 59	19 28	20 59
52	17 32	18 06	18 45	16 36	18 02	19 28	20 55
50	17 35	18 08	18 45	16 41	18 03	19 27	20 51
45	17 41	18 11	18 45	16 51	18 08	19 25	20 44
N 40	17 47	18 14	18 46	16 59	18 11	19 24	20 38
35	17 52	18 17	18 47	17 06	18 14	19 23	20 33
30	17 56	18 20	18 48	17 12	18 17	19 22	20 28
20	18 03	18 26	18 51	17 22	18 21	19 20	20 20
N 10	18 10	18 31	18 55	17 31	18 25	19 19	20 14
0	18 16	18 37	19 02	17 40	18 29	19 17	20 07
S 10	18 23	18 44	19 09	17 48	18 32	19 16	20 01
20	18 30	18 52	19 18	17 57	18 36	19 14	19 54
30	18 38	19 02	19 31	18 07	18 40	19 13	19 46
35	18 43	19 09	19 41	18 13	18 43	19 12	19 42
40	18 48	19 16	19 49	18 19	18 45	19 11	19 37
45	18 54	19 25	20 01	18 27	18 48	19 09	19 31
S 50	19 02	19 36	20 17	18 35	18 52	19 08	19 24
52	19 05	19 41	20 25	18 40	18 54	19 07	19 21
54	19 09	19 47	20 33	18 44	18 55	19 06	19 17
56	19 13	19 53	20 43	18 49	18 57	19 05	19 14
58	19 18	20 01	20 55	18 54	19 00	19 04	19 09
S 60	19 24	20 09	21 09	19 01	19 02	19 03	19 05

Day	SUN Eqn. of Time 00h	SUN Eqn. of Time 12h	SUN Mer. Pass.	MOON Mer. Pass. Upper	MOON Mer. Pass. Lower	Age	Phase
24	13 20	13 15	12 13	11 28	23 53	29	●
25	13 11	13 06	12 13	12 17	24 41	00	
26	13 02	12 57	12 13	13 06	00 41	01	

Figure 15.7. (cont.)

4ᵐ INCREMENTS AND CORRECTIONS 5ᵐ

4ᵐ	SUN PLANETS	ARIES	MOON	v or Corrn d	v or Corrn d	v or Corrn d
s	° ′	° ′	° ′	′ ′	′ ′	′ ′
00	1 00·0	1 00·2	0 57·3	0·0 0·0	6·0 0·5	12·0 0·9
01	1 00·3	1 00·4	0 57·5	0·1 0·0	6·1 0·5	12·1 0·9
02	1 00·5	1 00·7	0 57·7	0·2 0·0	6·2 0·5	12·2 0·9
03	1 00·8	1 00·9	0 58·0	0·3 0·0	6·3 0·5	12·3 0·9
04	1 01·0	1 01·2	0 58·2	0·4 0·0	6·4 0·5	12·4 0·9
05	1 01·3	1 01·4	0 58·5	0·5 0·0	6·5 0·5	12·5 0·9
06	1 01·5	1 01·7	0 58·7	0·6 0·0	6·6 0·5	12·6 0·9
07	1 01·8	1 01·9	0 58·9	0·7 0·1	6·7 0·5	12·7 1·0
08	1 02·0	1 02·2	0 59·2	0·8 0·1	6·8 0·5	12·8 1·0
09	1 02·3	1 02·4	0 59·4	0·9 0·1	6·9 0·5	12·9 1·0
10	1 02·5	1 02·7	0 59·7	1·0 0·1	7·0 0·5	13·0 1·0
11	1 02·8	1 02·9	0 59·9	1·1 0·1	7·1 0·5	13·1 1·0
12	1 03·0	1 03·2	1 00·1	1·2 0·1	7·2 0·5	13·2 1·0
13	1 03·3	1 03·4	1 00·4	1·3 0·1	7·3 0·5	13·3 1·0
14	1 03·5	1 03·7	1 00·6	1·4 0·1	7·4 0·6	13·4 1·0
15	1 03·8	1 03·9	1 00·8	1·5 0·1	7·5 0·6	13·5 1·0
16	1 04·0	1 04·2	1 01·1	1·6 0·1	7·6 0·6	13·6 1·0
17	1 04·3	1 04·4	1 01·3	1·7 0·1	7·7 0·6	13·7 1·0
18	1 04·5	1 04·7	1 01·6	1·8 0·1	7·8 0·6	13·8 1·0
19	1 04·8	1 04·9	1 01·8	1·9 0·1	7·9 0·6	13·9 1·0
20	1 05·0	1 05·2	1 02·0	2·0 0·2	8·0 0·6	14·0 1·1
21	1 05·3	1 05·4	1 02·3	2·1 0·2	8·1 0·6	14·1 1·1
22	1 05·5	1 05·7	1 02·5	2·2 0·2	8·2 0·6	14·2 1·1
23	1 05·8	1 05·9	1 02·8	2·3 0·2	8·3 0·6	14·3 1·1
24	1 06·0	1 06·2	1 03·0	2·4 0·2	8·4 0·6	14·4 1·1
25	1 06·3	1 06·4	1 03·2	2·5 0·2	8·5 0·6	14·5 1·1
26	1 06·5	1 06·7	1 03·5	2·6 0·2	8·6 0·6	14·6 1·1
27	1 06·8	1 06·9	1 03·7	2·7 0·2	8·7 0·7	14·7 1·1
28	1 07·0	1 07·2	1 03·9	2·8 0·2	8·8 0·7	14·8 1·1
29	1 07·3	1 07·4	1 04·2	2·9 0·2	8·9 0·7	14·9 1·1
30	1 07·5	1 07·7	1 04·4	3·0 0·2	9·0 0·7	15·0 1·1
31	1 07·8	1 07·9	1 04·7	3·1 0·2	9·1 0·7	15·1 1·1
32	1 08·0	1 08·2	1 04·9	3·2 0·2	9·2 0·7	15·2 1·1
33	1 08·3	1 08·4	1 05·1	3·3 0·2	9·3 0·7	15·3 1·1
34	1 08·5	1 08·7	1 05·4	3·4 0·3	9·4 0·7	15·4 1·2
35	1 08·8	1 08·9	1 05·6	3·5 0·3	9·5 0·7	15·5 1·2
36	1 09·0	1 09·2	1 05·9	3·6 0·3	9·6 0·7	15·6 1·2
37	1 09·3	1 09·4	1 06·1	3·7 0·3	9·7 0·7	15·7 1·2
38	1 09·5	1 09·7	1 06·3	3·8 0·3	9·8 0·7	15·8 1·2
39	1 09·8	1 09·9	1 06·6	3·9 0·3	9·9 0·7	15·9 1·2
40	1 10·0	1 10·2	1 06·8	4·0 0·3	10·0 0·8	16·0 1·2
41	1 10·3	1 10·4	1 07·0	4·1 0·3	10·1 0·8	16·1 1·2
42	1 10·5	1 10·7	1 07·3	4·2 0·3	10·2 0·8	16·2 1·2
43	1 10·8	1 10·9	1 07·5	4·3 0·3	10·3 0·8	16·3 1·2
44	1 11·0	1 11·2	1 07·8	4·4 0·3	10·4 0·8	16·4 1·2
45	1 11·3	1 11·4	1 08·0	4·5 0·3	10·5 0·8	16·5 1·2
46	1 11·5	1 11·7	1 08·2	4·6 0·3	10·6 0·8	16·6 1·2
47	1 11·8	1 11·9	1 08·5	4·7 0·4	10·7 0·8	16·7 1·3
48	1 12·0	1 12·2	1 08·7	4·8 0·4	10·8 0·8	16·8 1·3
49	1 12·3	1 12·4	1 09·0	4·9 0·4	10·9 0·8	16·9 1·3
50	1 12·5	1 12·7	1 09·2	5·0 0·4	11·0 0·8	17·0 1·3
51	1 12·8	1 12·9	1 09·4	5·1 0·4	11·1 0·8	17·1 1·3
52	1 13·0	1 13·2	1 09·7	5·2 0·4	11·2 0·8	17·2 1·3
53	1 13·3	1 13·5	1 09·9	5·3 0·4	11·3 0·8	17·3 1·3
54	1 13·5	1 13·7	1 10·2	5·4 0·4	11·4 0·9	17·4 1·3
55	1 13·8	1 14·0	1 10·4	5·5 0·4	11·5 0·9	17·5 1·3
56	1 14·0	1 14·2	1 10·6	5·6 0·4	11·6 0·9	17·6 1·3
57	1 14·3	1 14·5	1 10·9	5·7 0·4	11·7 0·9	17·7 1·3
58	1 14·5	1 14·7	1 11·1	5·8 0·4	11·8 0·9	17·8 1·3
59	1 14·8	1 15·0	1 11·3	5·9 0·4	11·9 0·9	17·9 1·3
60	1 15·0	1 15·2	1 11·6	6·0 0·5	12·0 0·9	18·0 1·4

5ᵐ	SUN PLANETS	ARIES	MOON	v or Corrn d	v or Corrn d	v or Corrn d
s	° ′	° ′	° ′	′ ′	′ ′	′ ′
00	1 15·0	1 15·2	1 11·6	0·0 0·0	6·0 0·6	12·0 1·1
01	1 15·3	1 15·5	1 11·8	0·1 0·0	6·1 0·6	12·1 1·1
02	1 15·5	1 15·7	1 12·1	0·2 0·0	6·2 0·6	12·2 1·1
03	1 15·8	1 16·0	1 12·3	0·3 0·0	6·3 0·6	12·3 1·1
04	1 16·0	1 16·2	1 12·5	0·4 0·0	6·4 0·6	12·4 1·1
05	1 16·3	1 16·5	1 12·8	0·5 0·0	6·5 0·6	12·5 1·1
06	1 16·5	1 16·7	1 13·0	0·6 0·1	6·6 0·6	12·6 1·2
07	1 16·8	1 17·0	1 13·3	0·7 0·1	6·7 0·6	12·7 1·2
08	1 17·0	1 17·2	1 13·5	0·8 0·1	6·8 0·6	12·8 1·2
09	1 17·3	1 17·5	1 13·7	0·9 0·1	6·9 0·6	12·9 1·2
10	1 17·5	1 17·7	1 14·0	1·0 0·1	7·0 0·6	13·0 1·2
11	1 17·8	1 18·0	1 14·2	1·1 0·1	7·1 0·7	13·1 1·2
12	1 18·0	1 18·2	1 14·4	1·2 0·1	7·2 0·7	13·2 1·2
13	1 18·3	1 18·5	1 14·7	1·3 0·1	7·3 0·7	13·3 1·2
14	1 18·5	1 18·7	1 14·9	1·4 0·1	7·4 0·7	13·4 1·2
15	1 18·8	1 19·0	1 15·2	1·5 0·1	7·5 0·7	13·5 1·2
16	1 19·0	1 19·2	1 15·4	1·6 0·1	7·6 0·7	13·6 1·2
17	1 19·3	1 19·5	1 15·6	1·7 0·2	7·7 0·7	13·7 1·3
18	1 19·5	1 19·7	1 15·9	1·8 0·2	7·8 0·7	13·8 1·3
19	1 19·8	1 20·0	1 16·1	1·9 0·2	7·9 0·7	13·9 1·3
20	1 20·0	1 20·2	1 16·4	2·0 0·2	8·0 0·7	14·0 1·3
21	1 20·3	1 20·5	1 16·6	2·1 0·2	8·1 0·7	14·1 1·3
22	1 20·5	1 20·7	1 16·8	2·2 0·2	8·2 0·8	14·2 1·3
23	1 20·8	1 21·0	1 17·1	2·3 0·2	8·3 0·8	14·3 1·3
24	1 21·0	1 21·2	1 17·3	2·4 0·2	8·4 0·8	14·4 1·3
25	1 21·3	1 21·5	1 17·5	2·5 0·2	8·5 0·8	14·5 1·3
26	1 21·5	1 21·7	1 17·8	2·6 0·2	8·6 0·8	14·6 1·3
27	1 21·8	1 22·0	1 18·0	2·7 0·2	8·7 0·8	14·7 1·3
28	1 22·0	1 22·2	1 18·3	2·8 0·3	8·8 0·8	14·8 1·4
29	1 22·3	1 22·5	1 18·5	2·9 0·3	8·9 0·8	14·9 1·4
30	1 22·5	1 22·7	1 18·7	3·0 0·3	9·0 0·8	15·0 1·4
31	1 22·8	1 23·0	1 19·0	3·1 0·3	9·1 0·8	15·1 1·4
32	1 23·0	1 23·2	1 19·2	3·2 0·3	9·2 0·8	15·2 1·4
33	1 23·3	1 23·5	1 19·5	3·3 0·3	9·3 0·9	15·3 1·4
34	1 23·5	1 23·7	1 19·7	3·4 0·3	9·4 0·9	15·4 1·4
35	1 23·8	1 24·0	1 19·9	3·5 0·3	9·5 0·9	15·5 1·4
36	1 24·0	1 24·2	1 20·2	3·6 0·3	9·6 0·9	15·6 1·4
37	1 24·3	1 24·5	1 20·4	3·7 0·3	9·7 0·9	15·7 1·4
38	1 24·5	1 24·7	1 20·7	3·8 0·3	9·8 0·9	15·8 1·4
39	1 24·8	1 25·0	1 20·9	3·9 0·4	9·9 0·9	15·9 1·5
40	1 25·0	1 25·2	1 21·1	4·0 0·4	10·0 0·9	16·0 1·5
41	1 25·3	1 25·5	1 21·4	4·1 0·4	10·1 0·9	16·1 1·5
42	1 25·5	1 25·7	1 21·6	4·2 0·4	10·2 0·9	16·2 1·5
43	1 25·8	1 26·0	1 21·8	4·3 0·4	10·3 0·9	16·3 1·5
44	1 26·0	1 26·2	1 22·1	4·4 0·4	10·4 1·0	16·4 1·5
45	1 26·3	1 26·5	1 22·3	4·5 0·4	10·5 1·0	16·5 1·5
46	1 26·5	1 26·7	1 22·6	4·6 0·4	10·6 1·0	16·6 1·5
47	1 26·8	1 27·0	1 22·8	4·7 0·4	10·7 1·0	16·7 1·5
48	1 27·0	1 27·2	1 23·0	4·8 0·4	10·8 1·0	16·8 1·5
49	1 27·3	1 27·5	1 23·3	4·9 0·4	10·9 1·0	16·9 1·5
50	1 27·5	1 27·7	1 23·5	5·0 0·5	11·0 1·0	17·0 1·6
51	1 27·8	1 28·0	1 23·8	5·1 0·5	11·1 1·0	17·1 1·6
52	1 28·0	1 28·2	1 24·0	5·2 0·5	11·2 1·0	17·2 1·6
53	1 28·3	1 28·5	1 24·2	5·3 0·5	11·3 1·0	17·3 1·6
54	1 28·5	1 28·7	1 24·5	5·4 0·5	11·4 1·0	17·4 1·6
55	1 28·8	1 29·0	1 24·7	5·5 0·5	11·5 1·1	17·5 1·6
56	1 29·0	1 29·2	1 24·9	5·6 0·5	11·6 1·1	17·6 1·6
57	1 29·3	1 29·5	1 25·2	5·7 0·5	11·7 1·1	17·7 1·6
58	1 29·5	1 29·7	1 25·4	5·8 0·5	11·8 1·1	17·8 1·6
59	1 29·8	1 30·0	1 25·7	5·9 0·5	11·9 1·1	17·9 1·6
60	1 30·0	1 30·2	1 25·9	6·0 0·6	12·0 1·1	18·0 1·7

Figure 15.8. Yellow page for 5 minutes.

CONVERSION OF ARC TO TIME

0°–59°	h m	60°–119°	h m	120°–179°	h m	180°–239°	h m	240°–299°	h m	300°–359°	h m	′	0′.00 m s	0′.25 m s	0′.50 m s	0′.75 m s
0	0 00	60	4 00	120	8 00	180	12 00	240	16 00	300	20 00	0	0 00	0 01	0 02	0 03
1	0 04	61	4 04	121	8 04	181	12 04	241	16 04	301	20 04	1	0 04	0 05	0 06	0 07
2	0 08	62	4 08	122	8 08	182	12 08	242	16 08	302	20 08	2	0 08	0 09	0 10	0 11
3	0 12	63	4 12	123	8 12	183	12 12	243	16 12	303	20 12	3	0 12	0 13	0 14	0 15
4	0 16	64	4 16	124	8 16	184	12 16	244	16 16	304	20 16	4	0 16	0 17	0 18	0 19
5	0 20	65	4 20	125	8 20	185	12 20	245	16 20	305	20 20	5	0 20	0 21	0 22	0 23
6	0 24	66	4 24	126	8 24	186	12 24	246	16 24	306	20 24	6	0 24	0 25	0 26	0 27
7	0 28	67	4 28	127	8 28	187	12 28	247	16 28	307	20 28	7	0 28	0 29	0 30	0 31
8	0 32	68	4 32	128	8 32	188	12 32	248	16 32	308	20 32	8	0 32	0 33	0 34	0 35
9	0 36	69	4 36	129	8 36	189	12 36	249	16 36	309	20 36	9	0 36	0 37	0 38	0 39
10	0 40	70	4 40	130	8 40	190	12 40	250	16 40	310	20 40	10	0 40	0 41	0 42	0 43
11	0 44	71	4 44	131	8 44	191	12 44	251	16 44	311	20 44	11	0 44	0 45	0 46	0 47
12	0 48	72	4 48	132	8 48	192	12 48	252	16 48	312	20 48	12	0 48	0 49	0 50	0 51
13	0 52	73	4 52	133	8 52	193	12 52	253	16 52	313	20 52	13	0 52	0 53	0 54	0 55
14	0 56	74	4 56	134	8 56	194	12 56	254	16 56	314	20 56	14	0 56	0 57	0 58	0 59
15	1 00	75	5 00	135	9 00	195	13 00	255	17 00	315	21 00	15	1 00	1 01	1 02	1 03
16	1 04	76	5 04	136	9 04	196	13 04	256	17 04	316	21 04	16	1 04	1 05	1 06	1 07
17	1 08	77	5 08	137	9 08	197	13 08	257	17 08	317	21 08	17	1 08	1 09	1 10	1 11
18	1 12	78	5 12	138	9 12	198	13 12	258	17 12	318	21 12	18	1 12	1 13	1 14	1 15
19	1 16	79	5 16	139	9 16	199	13 16	259	17 16	319	21 16	19	1 16	1 17	1 18	1 19
20	1 20	80	5 20	140	9 20	200	13 20	260	17 20	320	21 20	20	1 20	1 21	1 22	1 23
21	1 24	81	5 24	141	9 24	201	13 24	261	17 24	321	21 24	21	1 24	1 25	1 26	1 27
22	1 28	82	5 28	142	9 28	202	13 28	262	17 28	322	21 28	22	1 28	1 29	1 30	1 31
23	1 32	83	5 32	143	9 32	203	13 32	263	17 32	323	21 32	23	1 32	1 33	1 34	1 35
24	1 36	84	5 36	144	9 36	204	13 36	264	17 36	324	21 36	24	1 36	1 37	1 38	1 39
25	1 40	85	5 40	145	9 40	205	13 40	265	17 40	325	21 40	25	1 40	1 41	1 42	1 43
26	1 44	86	5 44	146	9 44	206	13 44	266	17 44	326	21 44	26	1 44	1 45	1 46	1 47
27	1 48	87	5 48	147	9 48	207	13 48	267	17 48	327	21 48	27	1 48	1 49	1 50	1 51
28	1 52	88	5 52	148	9 52	208	13 52	268	17 52	328	21 52	28	1 52	1 53	1 54	1 55
29	1 56	89	5 56	149	9 56	209	13 56	269	17 56	329	21 56	29	1 56	1 57	1 58	1 59
30	2 00	90	6 00	150	10 00	210	14 00	270	18 00	330	22 00	30	2 00	2 01	2 02	2 03
31	2 04	91	6 04	151	10 04	211	14 04	271	18 04	331	22 04	31	2 04	2 05	2 06	2 07
32	2 08	92	6 08	152	10 08	212	14 08	272	18 08	332	22 08	32	2 08	2 09	2 10	2 11
33	2 12	93	6 12	153	10 12	213	14 12	273	18 12	333	22 12	33	2 12	2 13	2 14	2 15
34	2 16	94	6 16	154	10 16	214	14 16	274	18 16	334	22 16	34	2 16	2 17	2 18	2 19
35	2 20	95	6 20	155	10 20	215	14 20	275	18 20	335	22 20	35	2 20	2 21	2 22	2 23
36	2 24	96	6 24	156	10 24	216	14 24	276	18 24	336	22 24	36	2 24	2 25	2 26	2 27
37	2 28	97	6 28	157	10 28	217	14 28	277	18 28	337	22 28	37	2 28	2 29	2 30	2 31
38	2 32	98	6 32	158	10 32	218	14 32	278	18 32	338	22 32	38	2 32	2 33	2 34	2 35
39	2 36	99	6 36	159	10 36	219	14 36	279	18 36	339	22 36	39	2 36	2 37	2 38	2 39
40	2 40	100	6 40	160	10 40	220	14 40	280	18 40	340	22 40	40	2 40	2 41	2 42	2 43
41	2 44	101	6 44	161	10 44	221	14 44	281	18 44	341	22 44	41	2 44	2 45	2 46	2 47
42	2 48	102	6 48	162	10 48	222	14 48	282	18 48	342	22 48	42	2 48	2 49	2 50	2 51
43	2 52	103	6 52	163	10 52	223	14 52	283	18 52	343	22 52	43	2 52	2 53	2 54	2 55
44	2 56	104	6 56	164	10 56	224	14 56	284	18 56	344	22 56	44	2 56	2 57	2 58	2 59
45	3 00	105	7 00	165	11 00	225	15 00	285	19 00	345	23 00	45	3 00	3 01	3 02	3 03
46	3 04	106	7 04	166	11 04	226	15 04	286	19 04	346	23 04	46	3 04	3 05	3 06	3 07
47	3 08	107	7 08	167	11 08	227	15 08	287	19 08	347	23 08	47	3 08	3 09	3 10	3 11
48	3 12	108	7 12	168	11 12	228	15 12	288	19 12	348	23 12	48	3 12	3 13	3 14	3 15
49	3 16	109	7 16	169	11 16	229	15 16	289	19 16	349	23 16	49	3 16	3 17	3 18	3 19
50	3 20	110	7 20	170	11 20	230	15 20	290	19 20	350	23 20	50	3 20	3 21	3 22	3 23
51	3 24	111	7 24	171	11 24	231	15 24	291	19 24	351	23 24	51	3 24	3 25	3 26	3 27
52	3 28	112	7 28	172	11 28	232	15 28	292	19 28	352	23 28	52	3 28	3 29	3 30	3 31
53	3 32	113	7 32	173	11 32	233	15 32	293	19 32	353	23 32	53	3 32	3 33	3 34	3 35
54	3 36	114	7 36	174	11 36	234	15 36	294	19 36	354	23 36	54	3 36	3 37	3 38	3 39
55	3 40	115	7 40	175	11 40	235	15 40	295	19 40	355	23 40	55	3 40	3 41	3 42	3 43
56	3 44	116	7 44	176	11 44	236	15 44	296	19 44	356	23 44	56	3 44	3 45	3 46	3 47
57	3 48	117	7 48	177	11 48	237	15 48	297	19 48	357	23 48	57	3 48	3 49	3 50	3 51
58	3 52	118	7 52	178	11 52	238	15 52	298	19 52	358	23 52	58	3 52	3 53	3 54	3 55
59	3 56	119	7 56	179	11 56	239	15 56	299	19 56	359	23 56	59	3 56	3 57	3 58	3 59

The above table is for converting expressions in arc to their equivalent in time ; its main use in this Almanac is for the conversion of longitude for application to L.M.T. (*added if west, subtracted if east*) to give G.M.T. or vice versa, particularly in the case of sunrise, sunset, etc.

Figure 15.9. First yellow page of Almanac for conversion of angle to time.

Form F2. Reduction of Noon Sight for Latitude

Navigator _____

Zone date ___25 Feb___ , 19 _90_

D.R. lat. ___23 30___ N (or) S

D.R. long. ___61 20___ E (or)(W)(enter at 2.4)

1. To find GMT at DR position

1.1 Watch time at DR ___11 05___ (enter at 3.4)

1.2 Zone description ___4___

1.3 GMT watch time ___15 05___

1.4 GMT watch error ___00 05___ (+ if slow)

1.5 GMT ___15 05 05___ (enter at 4.2)

1.6 Greenwich date

2. To find LHA sun at DR

2.1 GHA sun _15_ hrs ___41 43.8___

2.2 corr. _5_ m _5_ s ___1 16.8___

2.3 GHA sun ___43 00.6___

2.4 DR long. ___61 20 W___

2.5 LHA sun ___−18 19.4___ (enter at 3.1)

3. Predict WT of local noon

3.1 LHA sun ___−18 19.4___ (subtract)

3.2 Deg. to noon ___18 19.4___

3.3 Time to noon ___1 13 18___ (enter at 4.1)

3.4 WT at DR ___11 05 00___ (add)

3.5 Pred. WT of noon ___12 18 18___

4. GMT & sun's dec. at noon

4.1 Interval to noon ___1 13 18___

4.2 GMT at DR ___15 05 05___ (add)

4.3 GMT of noon ___16 18 23___

4.4 Sun's dec. _16_ hrs. ___−9 01.2___ d 0.9(+)/−

4.5 d corr. _18_ m ___0.3___

4.6 Dec. at noon ___−9 00.9___ (enter at 6.3)

5. Reduction of sextant observation

5.1 Ht. of eye ___15___ ft.

	+	−	
5.2 Index corr.		1	(+ if off)
5.3 Ht. of eye corr.		3.8	(Table A2)
5.4 Sums		4.8	
5.5 Net	−4.8		
5.6 h_s	57 18.2		
5.7 Adjusted h_s	57 13.4		(add 5.5 to 5.6)
5.8 3rd correction to h_s	15.6		(Table A2, col. 1)
5.9 H_o	57 29.0		(enter at 6.1)

6. Derivation of noon latitude

Find zenith distance of sun by subtracting H_o from 90°. Mark it N if zenith is N of sun, mark it S if zenith is S of sun. If zenith distance and declination are both N or both S, add them. If one is N, and the other is S, subtract them. The result is the latitude, with the name of the greater.

89° 60.0′

6.1 H_o ___57 29.0___ (subtract)

6.2 Zenith distance ___32 31___ N (or)(S)

6.3 Dec. at noon ___9 01___ N (or)(S)

6.4 Latitude at noon ___23 30___ (N)(or) S

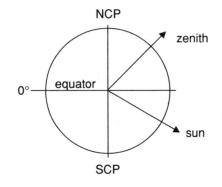

Figure 15.10.

subtracting longitude W, you find the LHA sun (−18°19.4′).

- **Part 3**—Convert the LHA sun to a time interval using the first yellow page in the *Almanac* (Figure 15.9). Adding this interval to the current watch time (WT) will give the predicted watch time of local noon.

- **Part 4**—Find the sun's declination at 1600 GMT from the daily page and add the correction for minutes, being careful to note whether the sun is moving north or south.

  Now make the sextant observation of the sun at the predicted time as illustrated in Figures 15.2-15.3. Suppose you obtained the value h_s = 57° 18.2′.

- **Part 5**—Reduce the sextant sighting, h_s, by adding the index correction and dip (height of eye) correction. With the adjusted sextant height find the altitude correction for the sun in column 1 of Table A2 in the Appendix. This correction includes atmospheric refraction and the radius of the sun, so there is no additional refraction correction. The radius correction is positive if you observed the lower limb of the sun and it is negative if you observed the upper limb.

- **Part 6**—Find the latitude by combining the observed zenith distance and declination of the sun according to the rule illustrated in Figures 15.1a and 15.1b, and verify your result by sketching the situation in the diagram at the bottom of the form.

LATITUDE AND LONGITUDE BY NOON CURVE

If you actually measure the time of the sun's greatest altitude you can find your longitude as well as latitude. Do this by constructing a curve showing the height of the sun every few minutes around noon. This is the "noon curve" method, and it gives an excellent determination of latitude because many observations are averaged into one. The determination of longitude is not as good, because the altitude changes slowly around noon, making the precise time of noon rather elusive. The longitude may not be precise enough for a reliable fix, but it can serve as a check on your DR position. Success in obtaining longitude depends on starting early and covering the rising and falling branches of the curve. If you learn to construct and analyze a noon curve, you could, in principle, navigate around the world using no other methods. All you would need

are the altitude corrections and an almanac of the sun.

Your first task in constructing a noon curve is to predict the time of noon, using the procedure outlined in Parts 1-3 of form F2. Then measure the sextant altitude of the sun, h_s, several dozen times during an interval of about two hours centered on the predicted time of local noon. As an example of what you are trying to determine, Figure 15.11 shows computed values for the altitude of the sun as seen from three latitudes around noon at the equinox. The curves are shallow, and in fact they are horizontal at noon, when the sun hangs momentarily at a constant altitude before beginning its descent toward sunset.

A measurement of altitude every 3 minutes is about right. If you can get someone to help you by noting the time on a watch and keeping records, so much the better. Otherwise, put on a wristwatch and fasten a small notebook on your left arm with a rubber band (if you are right-handed). This will allow you to record the measures and the times without putting down the sextant, which you will hold in your left hand while writing.

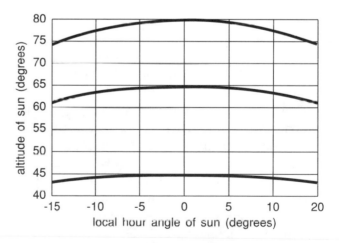

Figure 15.11. Altitude of the sun around noon at the time of the equinox as computed for three latitudes: 15° (upper), 30° (middle), 45° (lower). The altitudes are plotted as functions of LHA (degrees) for a span of one hour on each side of noon. The horizontal slope around noon means that a long series of observations is needed for determination of longitude from the time of noon. Real measures will have accidental errors and will give rougher curves, as in Figure 15.12.

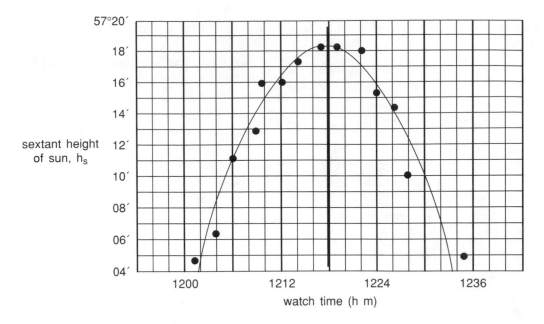

Figure 15.12. Noon curve of observed sextant altitudes, h$_S$, of the sun obtained for determining latitude and longitude. The data are raw sextant observations and uncorrected watch times. A vertical line bisecting the parabolic curve is drawn to determine time of local apparent noon.

After making each observation, write the time (WT, to the nearest second) and altitude (h$_s$ to the nearest 1′) neatly in columns. Do not pay attention to the sequence of altitudes as you collect these data, because your expectation may influence your readings. Simply write them down as they come and continue this process until the sun's altitude has decreased to the value it had when you started.

Then plot your uncorrected values of h$_s$ against watch time on square-ruled paper with a scale chosen so that the points fall in an area that is a few inches high and a few inches wide. Draw a smooth, symmetric parabola (∩) through the points and read off the maximum altitude and the time of maximum. Figure 15.12 is an example of a noon curve plotted against watch time.

After you have plotted all the sextant heights and have derived the noon height h$_s$ and the watch time of local apparent noon, you apply the sextant corrections and the watch error according to the entries in form F3. A sample is shown below.

POSTTEST

15.3. Plot the following noon curve and reduce it to find the latitude and longitude. What city were the observations made from?

Lower limb of sun; sun south of zenith

Height of eye = 20 feet

Index error = 5′ off the arc

Date February 25, 1990

GMT	h$_s$
16 40	52°34′
16 50	53 20
17 00	53 57
17 10	54 29
17 20	54 50
17 30	54 56
17 40	54 55
17 50	54 44
18 00	54 27
18 10	53 45
18 20	53 12
18 30	52 23

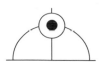

Form F3. Reduction of Noon Curve for Latitude and Longitude

Navigator _____

Zone date ___25 Feb___ , 19 _90_

D.R. lat. ___23 30___ (N)(or) S

D.R. long. ___61 20___ E (or)(W)

1. To find GMT of local noon

1.1 Zone watch time	12 18 20	(from curve)
1.2 Zone description	4	
1.3 GMT watch time	16 18 20	
1.4 GMT watch error	+ 05	(+ if slow)
1.5 GMT	16 18 25	
1.6 Greenwich date	25 Feb 90,	

2. Sun's dec. at noon

2.1 Dec. _16_ hrs.	−9 01.2	d 0.9 (+)/ −
2.2 d. corr. _18_ m _25_ s	0.3	
2.3 Dec. at noon	−9 00.9	(enter at 4.3)

3. Reduction of sextant observation

3.1 Ht. of eye _15_ ft.

	+	−	
3.2 Index corr.		1	(+ if off)
3.3 Ht. of eye corr.		3.8	(Table A2)
3.4 Sums		4.8	
3.5 Net	−4.8		
3.6 h_s	57 18.2		
3.7 Adjusted h_s	57 13.4		(add 3.5 to 3.6)
3.8 3rd corr. to h_s	+15.6		(Table A2)
3.9 H_0	57 29.0		(enter at 4.1)

4. Rule for derivation of noon latitude

Find zenith distance of sun by subtracting H_0 from 90°. Mark it N if zenith is N of sun, mark it S if zenith is S of sun. If zenith distance and declination are both N or both S, add them. If one is N, and the other is S, subtract them. The result is the latitude, with the name of the greater.

		89° 60.0′	
4.1 H_0		57 29.0	(subtract)
4.2 Zenith distance		32 31.0	N (or)(S)
4.3 Dec. at noon		9 00.9	N (or)(S)
4.4 Latitude at noon		23 30.1	(N)(or) S

5. Derivation of noon longitude

5.1 Sun GHA _16_ hrs.	56 43.9	
5.2 Corr. _18_ m _25_ s	4 36.3	
5.3 Sun GHA at noon	61 20.9	

= Long. W if less than 180°.

If greater than 180° subtract from 360°

359° 60′

GHA _____ (subtract)

Long. E =

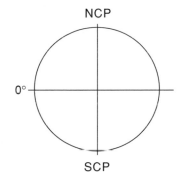

Figure 15.13.

CHAPTER SIXTEEN

Latitude and Longitude from Stars

Can you tie the Twins together
    or loosen the Hunter's cords?
Can you light the Evening Star
    or lead out the Bear and her cubs?
Do you know all the patterns of heaven
    and how they affect the earth?
         Book of Job, 38:31-33

INTRODUCTION

The stars can serve for the determination of latitude and longitude in much the same way that the sun does. However, they have certain disadvantages: they are a little more difficult to bring down to the horizon, and observations are usually restricted to twilight hours when the sky retains sufficient glow to reveal the horizon. The other side of the coin is that you can usually see many stars at the same time and can make many observations in a short interval, rather than having to wait for the sun to move. With techniques described in later chapters you can get a fix with the stars in much shorter time than is required for the sun.

HEIGHT OF THE CELESTIAL POLE FROM POLARIS OBSERVATION

For a person standing at the north pole of the earth, the north celestial pole (NCP) is directly overhead (altitude = 90°). From the equator it is seen on the horizon (altitude = 0°). Here is the rule:

Altitude of the celestial pole = latitude of the navigator

This applies to both the northern and southern hemispheres. The height of the south celestial pole (SCP) gives your southern latitude, but this is a difficult measure to take. There is no pole star in the south. Chapter 12 described how to estimate

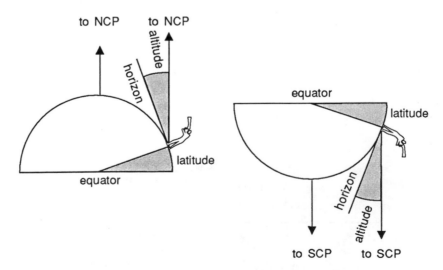

Figure 16.1. The altitude of the celestial pole and the latitude of the navigator are shown as angles. They are equal, as is depicted here for the northern hemisphere (left) and southern hemisphere (right). The south celestial pole is not marked by a star, and it is difficult to measure.

the location of the SCP, but you should not expect much precision when you try to determine your latitude this way. In the southern hemisphere you will need to use the sun or a star.

Finding the height of the celestial pole

Navigators in the northern hemisphere can observe the altitude of Polaris (the pole star) above the horizon, and this is the most direct way of determining latitude. Get out your sextant at twilight and determine h_s, the sextant height of Polaris. The value must be corrected for dip of the horizon and refraction before you can use it for determining latitude. Both corrections are found on the inside front cover of the *Nautical Almanac,* and their use is demonstrated in form F1, below.

Correcting the sextant altitude of Polaris

If Polaris were exactly at the NCP, your work would be almost done, but Chapter 12 described the slight displacement of Polaris from the NCP, and Figure 16.2 is a reminder. (In addition to the fact that Polaris is not precisely aligned with the earth's pole, the earth wobbles ever so slightly, like a spinning top.) To correct for the displacement of Polaris from the NCP, find LHA Aries and then go to the Polaris table in the *Nautical Almanac* and find the three corrections, a_0, a_1, and a_2, which must be added together.

Example—Suppose you measure the sextant height of Polaris as follows:

Time: May 23, 1990, at 2100 EST
h_s: 42°30′
Height of eye: 20 feet
DR location: long. 75°W, lat. 42°N
IC: 0′

Enter the date and DR location on the top line of form F1, and enter h_s in line 2.5. Then carry out the following steps:

- *Step 1*—Enter the watch time in line 1.1 and after applying the correction for its error, compute the GMT and enter the hours and minutes (ignore seconds) in line 1.5 and the GMT date in 1.6.

- *Step 2*—Open the front cover of the *Almanac* and scan down the Dip table to the height of eye entries that bracket 20 feet. You will see 19.1 ft. and 20.1 ft. Between them is the correction, −4.3′. Enter this in line 2.3 of the reduction form.

daily track of Polaris   range of altitude, 2°

northern horizon

Figure 16.2. The pole star traces a small circle around the NCP each day. When determining your latitude, you correct for this motion using the Polaris tables in the Almanac.

To find the refraction correction, scan down the Stars and Planets table to the apparent heights bracketing your value of apparent altitude, h_s = 42° 30′. You will see entries at 40°08′ and 42°44′. Between them is the correction, −1.1′. Enter this in line 2.8.

- *Step 3*—Enter the index correction for the sextant (we assume 0) and compute the observed height H_0 by combining the corrections and enter it in lines 2.9 and 4.1.

From the daily pages find GHA Aries for the hour and enter it in line 3.1, and enter the increments for minutes in line 3.2. Find GHA Aries and subtract the longitude (line 3.4) to find LHA Aries (line 3.5).

- *Step 4*—Turn to the Polaris tables in the *Almanac* for the correct year (Figure 16.3) and scan down the appropriate LHA column to the angle and read out a_0. Enter in line 4.3. Then scan down the same column to your latitude and read out a_1. Enter in line 4.4. Finally, continue down the column to the appropriate month and read a_2 and enter in line 4.5. Add the corrections, subtract 1° (line 4.2), and put the sum in line 4.6. This is your latitude.

POSTTEST

16.1 Reduce the following Polaris observation to find your latitude.
Time: May 28, 1990, at 0900 GMT
h_s : 30°30′
Height of eye: 16 feet
DR location: longitude 65°W, latitude 32°N
IC: 10′ on the arc

POLARIS (POLE STAR) TABLES, 1990
FOR DETERMINING LATITUDE FROM SEXTANT ALTITUDE AND FOR AZIMUTH

L.H.A. ARIES	0°–9°	10°–19°	20°–29°	30°–39°	40°–49°	50°–59°	60°–69°	70°–79°	80°–89°	90°–99°	100°–109°	110°–119°
	a_0	a_0	a_0	a_0	a_0	a_0	a_0	a_0	a_0	a_0	a_0	a_0
0	0 21·0	0 16·9	0 14·0	0 12·5	0 12·5	0 13·8	0 16·6	0 20·6	0 25·9	0 32·1	0 39·1	0 46·8
1	20·6	16·5	13·8	12·4	12·5	14·0	16·9	21·1	26·4	32·8	39·9	47·6
2	20·1	16·2	13·6	12·4	12·6	14·3	17·3	21·6	27·0	33·5	40·6	48·4
3	19·7	15·9	13·4	12·3	12·7	14·5	17·7	22·1	27·6	34·1	41·4	49·2
4	19·2	15·6	13·2	12·3	12·8	14·8	18·1	22·6	28·2	34·8	42·1	50·0
5	0 18·8	0 15·3	0 13·1	0 12·3	0 13·0	0 15·0	0 18·5	0 23·1	0 28·9	0 35·5	0 42·9	0 50·8
6	18·4	15·0	12·9	12·3	13·1	15·3	18·9	23·6	29·5	36·2	43·7	51·6
7	18·0	14·7	12·8	12·3	13·3	15·6	19·3	24·2	30·1	37·0	44·4	52·4
8	17·6	14·5	12·7	12·3	13·4	15·9	19·7	24·7	30·8	37·7	45·2	53·2
9	17·2	14·2	12·6	12·4	13·6	16·2	20·2	25·3	31·4	38·4	46·0	54·0
10	0 16·9	0 14·0	0 12·5	0 12·5	0 13·8	0 16·6	0 20·6	0 25·9	0 32·1	0 39·1	0 46·8	0 54·8
Lat.	a_1	a_1	a_1	a_1	a_1	a_1	a_1	a_1	a_1	a_1	a_1	a_1
0	0·5	0·6	0·6	0·6	0·6	0·6	0·5	0·4	0·4	0·3	0·3	0·2
10	·5	·6	·6	·6	·6	·6	·5	·5	·4	·4	·3	·3
20	·5	·6	·6	·6	·6	·6	·5	·5	·4	·4	·4	·3
30	·6	·6	·6	·6	·6	·6	·6	·5	·5	·5	·4	·4
40	0·6	0·6	0·6	0·6	0·6	0·6	0·6	0·6	0·5	0·5	0·5	0·5
45	·6	·6	·6	·6	·6	·6	·6	·6	·6	·6	·5	·5
50	·6	·6	·6	·6	·6	·6	·6	·6	·6	·6	·6	·6
55	·6	·6	·6	·6	·6	·6	·6	·6	·6	·7	·7	·7
60	·6	·6	·6	·6	·6	·6	·6	·7	·7	·7	·7	·8
62	0·7	0·6	0·6	0·6	0·6	0·6	0·7	0·7	0·7	0·8	0·8	0·8
64	·7	·6	·6	·6	·6	·6	·7	·7	·8	·8	·8	·9
66	·7	·6	·6	·6	·6	·6	·7	·7	·8	·8	·9	·9
68	0·7	0·6	0·6	0·6	0·6	0·6	0·7	0·8	0·8	0·9	1·0	1·0
Month	a_2	a_2	a_2	a_2	a_2	a_2	a_2	a_2	a_2	a_2	a_2	a_2
Jan.	0·7	0·7	0·7	0·7	0·7	0·7	0·7	0·7	0·7	0·7	0·7	0·7
Feb.	·6	·7	·7	·7	·8	·8	·8	·8	·8	·8	·8	·8
Mar.	·5	·5	·6	·6	·7	·8	·8	·8	·9	·9	·9	·9
Apr.	0·3	0·4	0·4	0·5	0·6	0·6	0·7	0·8	0·8	0·9	0·9	0·9
May	·2	·3	·3	·4	·4	·5	·6	·6	·7	·8	·8	·9
June	·2	·2	·2	·3	·3	·4	·4	·5	·6	·6	·7	·8
July	0·2	0·2	0·2	0·2	0·2	0·3	0·3	0·4	0·4	0·5	0·5	0·6
Aug.	·4	·3	·3	·3	·3	·3	·3	·3	·3	·3	·4	·4
Sept.	·5	·5	·4	·4	·3	·3	·3	·3	·3	·3	·3	·3
Oct.	0·7	0·7	0·6	0·6	0·5	0·4	0·4	0·3	0·3	0·3	0·2	0·2
Nov.	0·9	0·9	0·8	·7	·7	·6	·5	·5	·4	·3	·3	·2
Dec.	1·0	1·0	1·0	0·9	0·8	0·8	0·7	0·6	0·5	0·5	0·4	0·3
Lat.					AZIMUTH							
0	0·4	0·3	0·1	0·0	359·9	359·7	359·6	359·5	359·4	359·3	359·3	359·2
20	0·4	0·3	0·1	0·0	359·9	359·7	359·6	359·5	359·4	359·3	359·2	359·2
40	0·5	0·4	0·2	0·0	359·8	359·7	359·5	359·3	359·2	359·1	359·0	359·0
50	0·6	0·4	0·2	0·0	359·8	359·6	359·4	359·2	359·1	359·0	358·9	358·8
55	0·7	0·5	0·2	0·0	359·8	359·5	359·3	359·1	359·0	358·8	358·7	358·7
60	0·8	0·6	0·3	0·0	359·7	359·5	359·2	359·0	358·8	358·6	358·5	358·5
65	1·0	0·7	0·3	0·0	359·7	359·4	359·1	358·8	358·6	358·4	358·3	358·2

Latitude = Apparent altitude (corrected for refraction) − $1°$ + a_0 + a_1 + a_2

The table is entered with L.H.A. Aries to determine the column to be used; each column refers to a range of $10°$. a_0 is taken, with mental interpolation, from the upper table with the units of L.H.A. Aries in degrees as argument; a_1, a_2 are taken, without interpolation, from the second and third tables with arguments latitude and month respectively. a_0, a_1, a_2 are always positive. The final table gives the azimuth of *Polaris*.

Figure 16.3. Excerpt from the Polaris table for finding corrections to the altitude of Polaris in 1990.

Form F1. Latitude by Polaris

DR Lat. __42 N__ Long. __75W__ WT Date __23 May '90__

1. To find GMT

1.1 Zone watch time	21 00	
1.2 Zone description	+5	
1.3 GMT watch time	26 00	
1.4 GMT watch error	00 00	s+/f–
1.5 GMT	02 00	
1.6 GMT date	24 May	

2. Corrections to sextant observation

	+	–	
2.1 Ht. of eye __20__ ft.			
2.2 Index corr.		0	
2.3 Ht. of eye corr.		4.3	(Table A2)
2.4 Sums	0	4.3	
2.5 Net		–4.3	
2.6 h_s	42 30		
2.7 Adjusted h_s	42 25.7		(add 2.5 to 2.6)
2.8 Refraction corr.	–1.1		(*Almanac* Table A2, col. 2)
2.9 H_o	42 24.6		(enter at 4.1)

3. To find LHA Aries

3.1 GHA Aries __2__ hrs	93	
3.2 Corr. ___ m ___ s		
3.3 GHA Aries	93	
3.4 Long. (add if E)	75	
3.5 LHA Aries	18	

4. To find latitude

4.1 H_o	42 24.6
4.2 Subtract 1°	–1°
4.3 a_0	+ 14.5
4.4 a_1	+ 0.6
4.5 a_2	+ 0.3
4.6 Sum = Latitude	41 40.0N

Figure 16.4.

ZENITH PASSAGES OF STARS

If the pole star is hidden behind a cloud or a fog bank, any star that passes nearly through your zenith can be used for direct determination of latitude.

The rule is, the declination of a star that passes through your zenith equals your latitude:

Navigator's latitude = declination of zenith star

Identify the star and then find its declination in the *Almanac*.

Finding the zenith stars

This is the hard part, and it puts a limit on the precision of this method. You have to look overhead and turn your body because there is a tendency to put the zenith in front on you. Remember the warning of Figure 11.8: Visual determination of the zenith is quite tricky and requires practice. You can develop your own methods, such as sighting up the mast on a calm night. Using a sextant to verify the altitude of a star at the zenith is difficult, but it is worth trying.

Zenith passages are useful for navigators without instruments, but a far more accurate method—and one that is also simple mathematically—is to measure the altitude of a star when it is on the meridian. To do this, you must be able to predict the meridian passage. That is the topic of the next section.

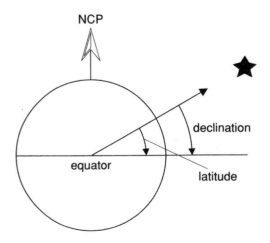

Figure 16.5. Rule for latitude by zenith stars. Declination of the zenith equals your latitude. (The size of the earth is highly exaggerated relative to the star's distance.)

PREDICTING A PARTICULAR STAR'S MERIDIAN PASSAGE

Latitude determination can be accomplished quite simply if you make a sextant sight when a star is on the local meridian (meridian passage). From an estimate of your longitude, you may predict the time of meridian passage for any star in the *Almanac*. The procedure is to find out when the geographic position of the star will have the same longitude (Greenwich hour angle) as your DR position.

We will use the symbol ☆ to indicate a star, so GP☆ and SHA☆ are the geographic position and the sidereal hour angle of the star. We start with the relationship from Figure 14.13:

Longitude (W) of GP ☆ = SHA☆ + GHA Aries

The meridian passage takes place when this longitude equals your DR longitude. That is, when

DR longitude (W) = SHA☆ + GHA Aries

How do you find a star that satisfies this equation? The DR longitude (W) is fixed by your location, but the SHA☆ depends on the star you select, and the GHA Aries depends on the Greenwich mean time. So you have two ways of satisfying the equation. Either select a favorite star and compute the GMT of its meridian passage, or select a convenient time (usually twilight or during a moonlit night) and find a star whose geographic position at that time will be near your longitude. The next paragraphs discuss both methods.

First method: Find the time of meridian passage for a particular star

If you have selected a star, you may find its SHA☆ in the Almanac and rewrite the key relation as

GHA Aries = DR longitude (W) – SHA☆

Suppose the date is July 15, 1990, and you are at longitude 71°05′W, and you have decided to observe Altair, whose SHA ☆ = 62°24.6′. (See Figure 16.6 for an extract of the Stars tables.)

You must find the GMT that gives this value for the GHA Aries. Proceed as in the following example.

STARS, 1990 JULY—DECEMBER

Mag.		Name and Number		S.H.A. °	JULY	AUG.	SEPT.	OCT.	NOV.	DEC.		Decl. °	JULY	AUG.	SEPT.	OCT.	NOV.	DEC.
3·4	γ	Cephei		5	15·3	14·7	14·4	14·5	14·9	15·5	N. 77		34·6	34·7	34·9	35·1	35·3	35·3
2·6		Markab	57	13	55·3	55·1	55·0	55·0	55·1	55·2	N. 15		09·3	09·4	09·5	09·6	09·6	09·6
2·6		Scheat		14	09·9	09·7	09·6	09·7	09·8	09·9	N. 28		01·9	02·0	02·1	02·2	02·3	02·3
1·3		Fomalhaut	56	15	42·5	42·4	42·3	42·3	42·4	42·5	S. 29		40·1	40·1	40·1	40·2	40·3	40·3
2·2	β	Gruis		19	27·8	27·5	27·5	27·5	27·7	27·8	S. 46		55·8	55·8	55·9	56·0	56·1	56·1
2·9	α	Tucanæ		25	31·2	30·9	30·9	31·0	31·2	31·5	S. 60		18·2	18·2	18·3	18·5	18·5	18·5
2·2		Al Na'ir	55	28	04·7	04·5	04·4	04·5	04·7	04·9	S. 47		00·2	00·2	00·3	00·4	00·5	00·5
3·0	δ	Capricorni		33	21·7	21·5	21·5	21·6	21·7	21·8	S. 16		10·1	10·1	10·1	10·1	10·1	10·1
2·5		Enif	54	34	03·7	03·6	03·6	03·6	03·8	03·8	N. 9		49·9	50·0	50·1	50·1	50·1	50·1
3·1	β	Aquarii		37	13·6	13·5	13·4	13·5	13·6	13·7	S. 5		36·7	36·6	36·6	36·6	36·6	36·7
2·6		Alderamin		40	24·1	24·0	24·1	24·3	24·7	25·0	N. 62		32·6	32·8	33·0	33·1	33·2	33·1
2·6	ε	Cygni		48	32·1	32·0	32·1	32·2	32·4	32·5	N. 33		56·0	56·2	56·3	56·4	56·4	56·3
1·3		Deneb	53	49	42·8	42·8	42·9	43·0	43·2	43·4	N. 45		14·7	14·9	15·0	15·1	15·1	15·1
3·2	η	Indi		50	45·6	45·5	45·5	45·7	45·9	46·0	S. 47		19·4	19·5	19·5	19·6	19·6	19·6
2·1		Peacock	52	53	45·4	45·3	45·4	45·6	45·9	46·0	S. 56		45·9	46·0	46·1	46·1	46·1	46·1
2·3	γ	Cygni		54	31·1	31·1	31·2	31·4	31·5	31·7	N. 40		13·5	13·7	13·8	13·9	13·9	13·8
0·9		Altair	51	62	24·6	24·6	24·7	24·8	24·9	25·0	N. 8		50·6	50·7	50·7	50·7	50·7	50·7
2·8	γ	Aquilæ		63	32·3	32·3	32·4	32·5	32·6	32·7	N. 10		35·4	35·5	35·5	35·6	35·5	35·5
3·0	δ	Cygni		63	49·2	49·3	49·4	49·6	49·8	49·9	N. 45		06·4	06·6	06·7	06·7	06·7	06·6
3·2		Albireo		67	24·4	24·4	24·5	24·6	24·8	24·8	N. 27		56·4	56·5	56·6	56·6	56·6	56·5
3·0	π	Sagittarii		72	41·4	41·3	41·4	41·5	41·7	41·7	S. 21		02·4	02·4	02·4	02·4	02·4	02·4
3·0	ζ	Aquilæ		73	44·8	44·8	44·9	45·1	45·2	45·2	N. 13		50·9	51·0	51·1	51·1	51·1	51·0
2·7	ζ	Sagittarii		74	29·2	29·2	29·3	29·4	29·5	29·5	S. 29		53·7	53·7	53·7	53·8	53·7	53·7
2·1		Nunki	50	76	19·2	19·2	19·3	19·4	19·5	19·5	S. 26		18·6	18·6	18·6	18·6	18·6	18·6
0·1		Vega	49	80	50·2	50·2	50·4	50·6	50·7	50·8	N. 38		46·5	46·6	46·7	46·7	46·6	46·5
2·9	λ	Sagittarii		83	08·6	08·6	08·7	08·8	08·9	08·9	S. 25		25·7	25·7	25·7	25·7	25·7	25·7
2·0		Kaus Australis	48	84	06·2	06·2	06·3	06·4	06·5	06·5	S. 34		23·5	23·5	23·5	23·5	23·5	23·5
2·8	δ	Sagittarii		84	53·5	53·5	53·6	53·8	53·9	53·9	S. 29		50·1	50·1	50·1	50·1	50·1	50·0
3·1	γ	Sagittarii		88	41·4	41·4	41·5	41·6	41·7	41·7	S. 30		25·6	25·6	25·6	25·6	25·6	25·6
2·4		Eltanin	47	90	53·6	53·8	54·0	54·2	54·4	54·5	N. 51		29·4	29·6	29·6	29·6	29·5	29·4
2·9	β	Ophiuchi		94	14·4	14·5	14·6	14·7	14·8	14·8	N. 4		34·2	34·3	34·3	34·3	34·2	34·2
2·5	κ	Scorpii		94	31·8	31·9	32·0	32·2	32·3	32·2	S. 39		01·7	01·7	01·8	01·7	01·7	01·6
2·0	θ	Scorpii		95	49·7	49·8	49·9	50·1	50·2	50·2	S. 42		59·7	59·8	59·8	59·8	59·7	59·6
2·1		Rasalhague	46	96	22·1	22·1	22·2	22·4	22·5	22·4	N. 12		34·0	34·0	34·1	34·1	34·0	33·9
1·7		Shaula	45	96	44·9	44·9	45·1	45·2	45·3	45·2	S. 37		06·0	06·0	06·1	06·0	06·0	05·9
3·0	α	Aræ		97	12·6	12·7	12·8	13·0	13·1	13·1	S. 49		52·4	52·4	52·4	52·4	52·3	52·3
3·0	β	Draconis		97	26·1	26·3	26·6	26·8	27·0	27·0	N. 52		18·5	18·7	18·7	18·7	18·6	18·4
2·8	υ	Scorpii		97	27·6	27·6	27·7	27·9	28·0	27·9	S. 37		17·5	17·5	17·5	17·5	17·5	17·4
2·8	β	Aræ		98	51·5	51·6	51·8	52·0	52·1	52·1	S. 55		31·5	31·6	31·6	31·6	31·5	31·4
Var.‡	α	Herculis		101	26·3	26·3	26·5	26·6	26·7	26·6	N. 14		24·0	24·1	24·1	24·1	24·0	23·9
2·6		Sabik	44	102	32·0	32·0	32·1	32·2	32·3	32·2	S. 15		42·9	42·9	42·9	42·9	42·9	42·9
3·1	ζ	Aræ		105	31·7	31·8	32·0	32·2	32·3	32·2	S. 55		58·9	58·9	58·9	58·8	58·7	58·6
2·4	ε	Scorpii		107	36·2	36·3	36·4	36·5	36·6	36·5	S. 34		16·8	16·8	16·8	16·8	16·7	16·7
1·9		Atria	43	108	04·0	04·3	04·6	05·0	05·1	05·0	S. 69		01·0	01·0	01·1	01·0	00·9	00·7
3·0	ζ	Herculis		109	45·6	45·7	45·8	46·0	46·1	46·0	N. 31		37·2	37·3	37·3	37·3	37·2	37·0
2·7	ζ	Ophiuchi		110	50·0	50·0	50·1	50·3	50·3	50·2	S. 10		33·0	33·0	33·0	33·0	33·0	33·0
2·9	τ	Scorpii		111	10·1	10·2	10·3	10·4	10·4	10·4	S. 28		12·0	12·0	12·0	12·0	11·9	11·9
2·8	β	Herculis		112	32·4	32·4	32·6	32·7	32·8	32·7	N. 21		30·6	30·7	30·7	30·6	30·5	30·4
1·2		Antares	42	112	47·1	47·2	47·3	47·4	47·4	47·3	S. 26		24·9	24·9	24·9	24·8	24·8	24·8
2·9	η	Draconis		114	01·5	01·7	02·1	02·4	02·6	02·6	N. 61		32·2	32·3	32·3	32·2	32·1	31·9
3·0	δ	Ophiuchi		116	31·8	31·9	32·0	32·1	32·1	32·0	S. 3		40·3	40·3	40·3	40·3	40·3	40·4
2·8	β	Scorpii		118	46·3	46·3	46·5	46·5	46·6	46·5	S. 19		47·0	46·9	46·9	46·9	46·9	46·9
2·5		Dschubba		120	03·0	03·0	03·2	03·2	03·3	03·1	S. 22		35·9	35·9	35·9	35·8	35·8	35·8
3·0	π	Scorpii		120	25·4	25·5	25·6	25·7	25·7	25·6	S. 26		05·4	05·4	05·4	05·4	05·3	05·3
3·0	β	Trianguli Aust.		121	24·7	25·0	25·2	25·5	25·5	25·3	S. 63		24·5	24·5	24·5	24·4	24·3	24·2
2·8	α	Serpentis		124	02·6	02·7	02·8	02·9	02·9	02·8	N. 6		27·3	27·3	27·3	27·3	27·2	27·1
3·0	γ	Lupi		126	21·9	22·0	22·2	22·3	22·3	22·1	S. 41		08·4	08·4	08·4	08·3	08·2	08·2
2·3		Alphecca	41	126	25·3	25·4	25·5	25·6	25·7	25·6	N. 26		44·8	44·9	44·8	44·8	44·7	44·5

‡ 3·0—3·7

Figure 16.6. Portion of Star tables for latter half of 1990.

1990 JULY 15, 16, 17 (SUN., MON., TUES.)

UT (GMT) d h	ARIES G.H.A.	VENUS −3.9 G.H.A.	VENUS Dec.	MARS +0.2 G.H.A.	MARS Dec.	JUPITER −1.8 G.H.A.	JUPITER Dec.	SATURN +0.1 G.H.A.	SATURN Dec.	STARS Name	S.H.A.	Dec.
15 00	292 35.3	209 16.7	N22 19.0	262 24.8	N10 05.7	178 19.0	N21 48.0	358 50.0	S21 34.3	Acamar	315 31.4	S40 20.2
01	307 37.8	224 15.9	19.3	277 25.7	06.3	193 20.8	47.9	13 52.6	34.3	Achernar	335 39.3	S57 16.6
02	322 40.2	239 15.2	19.5	292 26.5	06.9	208 22.7	47.8	28 55.3	34.3	Acrux	173 29.1	S63 03.2
03	337 42.7	254 14.4 · ·	19.7	307 27.4 · ·	07.5	223 24.6 · ·	47.7	43 58.0 · ·	34.4	Adhara	255 26.4	S28 57.4
04	352 45.1	269 13.6	20.0	322 28.3	08.0	238 26.4	47.6	59 00.6	34.4	Aldebaran	291 09.4	N16 29.6
05	7 47.6	284 12.9	20.2	337 29.1	08.6	253 28.3	47.5	74 03.3	34.4			
06	22 50.1	299 12.1	N22 20.5	352 30.0	N10 09.2	268 30.2	N21 47.5	89 05.9	S21 34.4	Alioth	166 35.6	N56 00.9
07	37 52.5	314 11.3	20.7	7 30.9	09.8	283 32.0	47.4	104 08.6	34.5	Alkaid	153 12.2	N49 21.8
08	52 55.0	329 10.5	21.0	22 31.7	10.4	298 33.9	47.3	119 11.3	34.5	Al Na'ir	28 04.7	S47 00.2
S 09	67 57.5	344 09.8 · ·	21.2	37 32.6 · ·	10.9	313 35.8 · ·	47.2	134 13.9 · ·	34.5	Alnilam	276 04.1	S 1 12.3
U 10	82 59.9	359 09.0	21.4	52 33.5	11.5	328 37.6	47.1	149 16.6	34.6	Alphard	218 13.3	S 8 37.0
N 11	98 02.4	14 08.2	21.7	67 34.3	12.1	343 39.5	47.0	164 19.2	34.6			
D 12	113 04.9	29 07.5	N22 21.9	82 35.2	N10 12.7	358 41.4	N21 46.9	179 21.9	S21 34.6	Alphecca	126 25.3	N26 44.8
A 13	128 07.3	44 06.7	22.1	97 36.1	13.2	13 43.2	46.8	194 24.6	34.7	Alpheratz	358 01.2	N29 02.3
Y 14	143 09.8	59 05.9	22.4	112 36.9	13.8	28 45.1	46.7	209 27.2	34.7	Altair	62 24.6	N 8 50.6
15	158 12.3	74 05.2 · ·	22.6	127 37.8 · ·	14.4	43 47.0 · ·	46.7	224 29.9 · ·	34.7	Ankaa	353 32.3	S42 21.1
16	173 14.7	89 04.4	22.8	142 38.7	15.0	58 48.9	46.6	239 32.5	34.8	Antares	112 47.1	S26 24.9
17	188 17.2	104 03.6	23.1	157 39.5	15.5	73 50.7	46.5	254 35.2	34.8			
18	203 19.6	119 02.8	N22 23.3	172 40.4	N10 16.1	88 52.6	N21 46.4	269 37.9	S21 34.8	Arcturus	146 11.3	N19 13.9
19	218 22.1	134 02.1	23.5	187 41.3	16.7	103 54.5	46.3	284 40.5	34.9	Atria	108 04.0	S69 01.0
20	233 24.6	149 01.3	23.7	202 42.1	17.2	118 56.3	46.2	299 43.2	34.9	Avior	234 25.8	S59 28.8
21	248 27.0	164 00.5 · ·	24.0	217 43.0 · ·	17.8	133 58.2 · ·	46.1	314 45.8 · ·	34.9	Bellatrix	278 50.7	N 6 20.6
22	263 29.5	178 59.8	24.2	232 43.9	18.4	149 00.1	46.0	329 48.5	35.0	Betelgeuse	271 20.2	N 7 24.5
23	278 32.0	193 59.0	24.4	247 44.7	19.0	164 01.9	46.0	344 51.2	35.0			
16 00	293 34.4	208 58.2	N22 24.6	262 45.6	N10 19.5	179 03.8	N21 45.9	359 53.8	S21 35.0	Canopus	264 04.3	S52 41.2
01	308 36.9	223 57.4	24.8	277 46.5	20.1	194 05.7	45.8	14 56.5	35.1	Capella	281 00.3	N45 59.4
02	323 39.4	238 56.7	25.1	292 47.3	20.7	209 07.5	45.7	29 59.1	35.1	Deneb	49 42.8	N45 14.7
03	338 41.8	253 55.9 · ·	25.3	307 48.2 · ·	21.3	224 09.4 · ·	45.6	45 01.8 · ·	35.1	Denebola	182 51.2	N14 37.5
04	353 44.3	268 55.1	25.5	322 49.1	21.8	239 11.3	45.5	60 04.5	35.2	Diphda	349 13.0	S18 02.0
05	8 46.8	283 54.3	25.7	337 50.0	22.4	254 13.1	45.4	75 07.1	35.2			
06	23 49.2	298 53.6	N22 25.9	352 50.8	N10 23.0	269 15.0	N21 45.3	90 09.8	S21 35.2	Dubhe	194 12.8	N61 48.3
07	38 51.7	313 52.8	26.2	7 51.7	23.5	284 16.9	45.2	105 12.4	35.3	Elnath	278 34.7	N28 36.1
08	53 54.1	328 52.0	26.4	22 52.6	24.1	299 18.7	45.2	120 15.1	35.3	Eltanin	90 53.6	N51 29.4
M 09	68 56.6	343 51.2 · ·	26.6	37 53.4 · ·	24.7	314 20.6 · ·	45.1	135 17.8 · ·	35.3	Enif	34 03.7	N 9 49.9
O 10	83 59.1	358 50.5	26.8	52 54.3	25.3	329 22.5	45.0	150 20.4	35.4	Fomalhaut	15 42.5	S29 40.1
N 11	99 01.5	13 49.7	27.0	67 55.2	25.8	344 24.3	44.9	165 23.1	35.4			
D 12	114 04.0	28 48.9	N22 27.2	82 56.0	N10 26.4	359 26.2	N21 44.8	180 25.7	S21 35.4	Gacrux	172 20.5	S57 04.0
A 13	129 06.5	43 48.1	27.4	97 56.9	27.0	14 28.1	44.7	195 28.4	35.5	Gienah	176 10.1	S17 29.5
Y 14	144 08.9	58 47.4	27.6	112 57.8	27.5	29 29.9	44.6	210 31.1	35.5	Hadar	149 12.5	S60 20.0
15	159 11.4	73 46.6 · ·	27.8	127 58.7 · ·	28.1	44 31.8 · ·	44.5	225 33.7 · ·	35.5	Hamal	328 20.3	N23 25.1
16	174 13.9	88 45.8	28.0	142 59.5	28.7	59 33.7	44.4	240 36.4	35.6	Kaus Aust.	84 06.2	S34 23.5
17	189 16.3	103 45.0	28.2	158 00.4	29.2	74 35.5	44.3	255 39.0	35.6			
18	204 18.8	118 44.3	N22 28.4	173 01.3	N10 29.8	89 37.4	N21 44.3	270 41.7	S21 35.6	Kochab	137 18.5	N74 11.8
19	219 21.2	133 43.5	28.6	188 02.1	30.4	104 39.3	44.2	285 44.4	35.7	Markab	13 55.3	N15 09.3
20	234 23.7	148 42.7	28.8	203 03.0	31.0	119 41.1	44.1	300 47.0	35.7	Menkar	314 33.2	N 4 03.3
21	249 26.2	163 41.9 · ·	29.0	218 03.9 · ·	31.5	134 43.0 · ·	44.0	315 49.7 · ·	35.7	Menkent	148 .27.9	S36 19.7
22	264 28.6	178 41.2	29.2	233 04.7	32.1	149 44.9	43.9	330 52.3	35.8	Miaplacidus	221 44.5	S69 40.8
23	279 31.1	193 40.4	29.4	248 05.6	32.7	164 46.8	43.8	345 55.0	35.8			
17 00	294 33.6	208 39.6	N22 29.6	263 06.5	N10 33.2	179 48.6	N21 43.7	0 57.7	S21 35.8	Mirfak	309 05.4	N49 49.6
01	309 36.0	223 38.8	29.8	278 07.4	33.8	194 50.5	43.6	16 00.3	35.9	Nunki	76 19.2	S26 18.6
02	324 38.5	238 38.0	30.0	293 08.2	34.4	209 52.4	43.5	31 03.0	35.9	Peacock	53 45.4	S56 45.9
03	339 41.0	253 37.3 · ·	30.2	308 09.1 · ·	34.9	224 54.2 · ·	43.5	46 05.6 · ·	35.9	Pollux	243 49.0	N28 03.1
04	354 43.4	268 36.5	30.4	323 10.0	35.5	239 56.1	43.4	61 08.3	36.0	Procyon	245 18.0	N 5 15.1
05	9 45.9	283 35.7	30.6	338 10.9	36.1	254 58.0	43.3	76 11.0	36.0			
06	24 48.4	298 34.9	N22 30.8	353 11.7	N10 36.6	269 59.8	N21 43.2	91 13.6	S21 36.0	Rasalhague	96 22.1	N12 34.0
07	39 50.8	313 34.1	31.0	8 12.6	37.2	285 01.7	43.1	106 16.3	36.1	Regulus	208 02.0	N12 00.9
T 08	54 53.3	328 33.4	31.2	23 13.5	37.8	300 03.6	43.0	121 18.9	36.1	Rigel	281 28.8	S 8 12.5
U 09	69 55.7	343 32.6 · ·	31.3	38 14.3 · ·	38.3	315 05.4 · ·	42.9	136 21.6 · ·	36.1	Rigil Kent.	140 15.2	S60 48.2
E 10	84 58.2	358 31.8	31.5	53 15.2	38.9	330 07.3	42.8	151 24.3	36.2	Sabik	102 32.0	S15 42.9
S 11	100 00.7	13 31.0	31.7	68 16.1	39.5	345 09.2	42.7	166 26.9	36.2			
D 12	115 03.1	28 30.2	N22 31.9	83 17.0	N10 40.0	0 11.0	N21 42.6	181 29.6	S21 36.2	Schedar	350 00.3	N56 29.0
A 13	130 05.6	43 29.4	32.1	98 17.8	40.6	15 12.9	42.6	196 32.2	36.3	Shaula	96 44.9	S37 06.0
Y 14	145 08.1	58 28.7	32.3	113 18.7	41.1	30 14.8	42.5	211 34.9	36.3	Sirius	258 49.2	S16 42.0
15	160 10.5	73 27.9 · ·	32.4	128 19.6 · ·	41.7	45 16.6 · ·	42.4	226 37.6 · ·	36.3	Spica	158 49.4	S11 06.9
16	175 13.0	88 27.1	32.6	143 20.5	42.3	60 18.5	42.3	241 40.2	36.4	Suhail	223 05.6	S43 23.7
17	190 15.5	103 26.3	32.8	158 21.3	42.8	75 20.4	42.2	256 42.9	36.4			
18	205 17.9	118 25.5	N22 33.0	173 22.2	N10 43.4	90 22.2	N21 42.1	271 45.5	S21 36.4	Vega	80 50.2	N38 46.5
19	220 20.4	133 24.8	33.1	188 23.1	44.0	105 24.1	42.0	286 48.2	36.5	Zuben'ubi	137 24.4	S16 00.3
20	235 22.9	148 24.0	33.3	203 24.0	44.5	120 26.0	41.9	301 50.9	36.5			
21	250 25.3	163 23.2 · ·	33.5	218 24.8 · ·	45.1	135 27.9 · ·	41.8	316 53.5 · ·	36.5		S.H.A.	Mer. Pass.
22	265 27.8	178 22.4	33.7	233 25.7	45.7	150 29.7	41.7	331 56.2	36.6	Venus	275 23.8	10 05
23	280 30.2	193 21.6	33.8	248 26.6	46.2	165 31.6	41.7	346 58.8	36.6	Mars	329 11.2	6 29
Mer. Pass.	4 25.0	v −0.8	d 0.2	v 0.9	d 0.6	v 1.9	d 0.1	v 2.7	d 0.0	Jupiter	245 29.4	12 02
										Saturn	66 19.4	0 00

Figure 16.7. Extract from daily pages for July 15, 1990.

1990 JULY 15, 16, 17 (SUN., MON., TUES.)

SUN / MOON

UT (GMT)	SUN G.H.A.	Dec.	MOON G.H.A.	v	Dec.	d	H.P.
15 00	178 32.1	N21 36.1	279 31.2	11.4	N10 55.9	14.6	58.7
01	193 32.0	35.7	294 01.6	11.3	11 10.5	14.4	58.7
02	208 31.9	35.3	308 31.9	11.2	11 24.9	14.4	58.7
03	223 31.9	.. 34.9	323 02.1	11.1	11 39.3	14.4	58.7
04	238 31.8	34.5	337 32.2	11.1	11 53.7	14.3	58.7
05	253 31.7	34.2	352 02.3	11.0	12 08.0	14.3	58.8
06	268 31.7	N21 33.8	6 32.3	10.9	N12 22.3	14.2	58.8
07	283 31.6	33.4	21 02.2	10.8	12 36.5	14.1	58.8
08	298 31.5	33.0	35 32.0	10.7	12 50.6	14.1	58.8
S 09	313 31.5	.. 32.6	50 01.7	10.6	13 04.7	14.0	58.9
U 10	328 31.4	32.2	64 31.3	10.6	13 18.7	14.0	58.9
N 11	343 31.3	31.8	79 00.9	10.4	13 32.7	13.9	58.9
D 12	358 31.3	N21 31.4	93 30.3	10.4	N13 46.6	13.9	58.9
A 13	13 31.2	31.0	107 59.7	10.3	14 00.5	13.8	58.9
Y 14	28 31.2	30.6	122 29.0	10.2	14 14.3	13.7	59.0
15	43 31.1	.. 30.2	136 58.2	10.1	14 28.0	13.6	59.0
16	58 31.0	29.8	151 27.3	10.0	14 41.6	13.6	59.0
17	73 31.0	29.4	165 56.3	9.9	14 55.2	13.5	59.0
18	88 30.9	N21 29.0	180 25.2	9.8	N15 08.7	13.5	59.0
19	103 30.8	28.6	194 54.0	9.7	15 22.2	13.3	59.1
20	118 30.8	28.2	209 22.7	9.7	15 35.5	13.3	59.1
21	133 30.7	.. 27.8	223 51.4	9.5	15 48.8	13.2	59.1
22	148 30.6	27.4	238 19.9	9.4	16 02.0	13.1	59.1
23	163 30.6	27.0	252 48.3	9.3	16 15.1	13.1	59.1
16 00	178 30.5	N21 26.6	267 16.6	9.3	N16 28.2	12.9	59.2
01	193 30.5	26.2	281 44.9	9.1	16 41.1	12.9	59.2
02	208 30.4	25.8	296 13.0	9.0	16 54.0	12.8	59.2
03	223 30.3	.. 25.4	310 41.0	8.9	17 06.8	12.7	59.2
04	238 30.3	25.0	325 08.9	8.8	17 19.5	12.6	59.2
05	253 30.2	24.6	339 36.7	8.7	17 32.1	12.5	59.3
06	268 30.2	N21 24.2	354 04.4	8.7	N17 44.6	12.4	59.3
07	283 30.1	23.8	8 32.1	8.5	17 57.0	12.4	59.3
08	298 30.0	23.4	22 59.6	8.4	18 09.4	12.2	59.3
M 09	313 30.0	.. 23.0	37 27.0	8.2	18 21.6	12.1	59.3
O 10	328 29.9	22.6	51 54.2	8.2	18 33.7	12.1	59.4
N 11	343 29.9	22.2	66 21.4	8.1	18 45.8	11.9	59.4
D 12	358 29.8	N21 21.8	80 48.5	8.0	N18 57.7	11.8	59.4
A 13	13 29.7	21.3	95 15.5	7.8	19 09.5	11.7	59.4
Y 14	28 29.7	20.9	109 42.3	7.8	19 21.2	11.6	59.4
15	43 29.6	.. 20.5	124 09.1	7.6	19 32.8	11.5	59.5
16	58 29.6	20.1	138 35.7	7.6	19 44.3	11.4	59.5
17	73 29.5	19.7	153 02.3	7.4	19 55.7	11.3	59.5
18	88 29.4	N21 19.3	167 28.7	7.3	N20 07.0	11.2	59.5
19	103 29.4	18.9	181 55.0	7.2	20 18.2	11.0	59.5
20	118 29.3	18.5	196 21.2	7.1	20 29.2	10.9	59.5
21	133 29.3	.. 18.0	210 47.3	7.0	20 40.1	10.8	59.6
22	148 29.2	17.6	225 13.3	6.9	20 50.9	10.7	59.6
23	163 29.2	17.2	239 39.2	6.7	21 01.6	10.6	59.6
17 00	178 29.1	N21 16.8	254 04.9	6.7	N21 12.2	10.4	59.6
01	193 29.0	16.4	268 30.6	6.6	21 22.6	10.3	59.6
02	208 29.0	16.0	282 56.2	6.4	21 32.9	10.2	59.6
03	223 28.9	.. 15.5	297 21.6	6.3	21 43.1	10.0	59.7
04	238 28.9	15.1	311 46.9	6.3	21 53.1	9.9	59.7
05	253 28.8	14.7	326 12.2	6.1	22 03.0	9.8	59.7
06	268 28.8	N21 14.3	340 37.3	6.0	N22 12.8	9.6	59.7
07	283 28.7	13.9	355 02.3	5.9	22 22.4	9.5	59.7
T 08	298 28.7	13.4	9 27.2	5.8	22 31.9	9.4	59.7
U 09	313 28.6	.. 13.0	23 52.0	5.7	22 41.3	9.2	59.8
E 10	328 28.5	12.6	38 16.7	5.6	22 50.5	9.0	59.8
S 11	343 28.5	12.2	52 41.3	5.4	22 59.5	9.0	59.8
D 12	358 28.4	N21 11.7	67 05.7	5.4	N23 08.5	8.7	59.8
A 13	13 28.4	11.3	81 30.1	5.3	23 17.2	8.7	59.8
Y 14	28 28.3	10.9	95 54.4	5.2	23 25.9	8.4	59.8
15	43 28.3	.. 10.5	110 18.6	5.0	23 34.3	8.4	59.8
16	58 28.2	10.0	124 42.6	5.0	23 42.7	8.1	59.9
17	73 28.2	09.6	139 06.6	4.9	23 50.8	8.1	59.9
18	88 28.1	N21 09.2	153 30.5	4.7	N23 58.9	7.8	59.9
19	103 28.1	08.8	167 54.2	4.7	24 06.7	7.7	59.9
20	118 28.0	08.3	182 17.9	4.6	24 14.4	7.5	59.9
21	133 28.0	.. 07.9	196 41.5	4.5	24 21.9	7.4	59.9
22	148 27.9	07.5	211 05.0	4.4	24 29.3	7.2	59.9
23	163 27.9	07.0	225 28.4	4.3	24 36.5	7.1	59.9
	S.D. 15.8	d 0.4	S.D. 16.1		16.2		16.3

Twilight / Sunrise / Moonrise

Lat.	Twilight Naut.	Civil	Sunrise	Moonrise 15	16	17	18
N 72	□	□	□	20 09	□	□	□
N 70	□	□	□	20 44	□	□	□
68	□	□	□	21 09	20 27	□	□
66	////	////	01 38	21 28	21 08	□	□
64	////	////	02 17	21 44	21 36	21 24	□
62	////	00 54	02 44	21 57	21 58	22 03	22 20
60	////	01 47	03 05	22 09	22 16	22 30	23 00
N 58	////	02 17	03 22	22 19	22 31	22 51	23 28
56	00 50	02 40	03 36	22 27	22 44	23 09	23 50
54	01 38	02 58	03 48	22 35	22 55	23 24	24 08
52	02 06	03 13	03 59	22 42	23 05	23 37	24 23
50	02 28	03 26	04 08	22 48	23 14	23 48	24 37
45	03 06	03 52	04 28	23 02	23 33	24 12	00 12
N 40	03 33	04 14	04 44	23 13	23 48	24 32	00 32
35	03 53	04 29	04 58	23 23	24 02	00 02	00 48
30	04 10	04 43	05 09	23 32	24 13	00 13	01 02
20	04 37	05 05	05 29	23 46	24 33	00 33	01 26
N 10	04 57	05 24	05 46	24 00	00 00	00 50	01 47
0	05 14	05 40	06 02	24 12	00 12	01 07	02 06
S 10	05 30	05 56	06 18	24 24	00 24	01 23	02 26
20	05 44	06 11	06 35	24 38	00 38	01 41	02 47
30	05 59	06 28	06 54	24 53	00 53	02 02	03 12
35	06 06	06 38	07 05	25 02	01 02	02 14	03 27
40	06 15	06 48	07 18	00 00	01 13	02 28	03 43
45	06 23	07 00	07 33	00 08	01 25	02 45	04 04
S 50	06 33	07 14	07 51	00 17	01 40	03 05	04 30
52	06 38	07 20	08 00	00 21	01 47	03 15	04 42
54	06 43	07 28	08 09	00 26	01 55	03 27	04 56
56	06 48	07 35	08 20	00 31	02 04	03 39	05 13
58	06 53	07 44	08 33	00 37	02 14	03 54	05 33
S 60	07 00	07 54	08 47	00 44	02 25	04 12	05 59

Sunset / Twilight / Moonset

Lat.	Sunset	Twilight Civil	Naut.	Moonset 15	16	17	18
N 72	□	□	□	15 22	□	□	□
N 70	□	□	□	14 49	□	□	□
68	□	□	□	14 26	16 59	□	□
66	22 30	////	////	14 08	16 19	□	□
64	21 52	////	////	13 53	15 52	18 06	□
62	21 06	23 11	////	13 41	15 31	17 28	19 21
60	21 06	22 22	////	13 31	15 15	17 01	18 41
N 58	20 49	21 53	////	13 22	15 00	16 41	18 14
56	20 35	21 31	23 16	13 15	14 48	16 23	17 52
54	20 23	21 13	22 31	13 08	14 38	16 09	17 34
52	20 03	20 58	22 04	13 02	14 29	15 56	17 19
50	20 03	20 45	21 43	12 56	14 20	15 45	17 06
45	19 43	20 19	21 06	12 44	14 03	15 22	16 39
N 40	19 27	19 59	20 39	12 34	13 48	15 04	16 18
35	19 14	19 43	20 18	12 26	13 36	14 48	16 00
30	19 02	19 29	20 02	12 19	13 26	14 35	15 45
20	18 43	19 07	19 35	12 06	13 08	14 12	15 19
N 10	18 25	18 48	19 15	11 55	12 52	13 53	14 57
0	18 07	18 32	18 58	11 45	12 37	13 35	14 36
S 10	17 54	18 16	18 42	11 35	12 23	13 17	14 16
20	17 37	18 01	18 28	11 24	12 08	12 57	13 53
30	17 18	17 44	18 13	11 12	11 50	12 35	13 28
35	17 07	17 35	18 06	11 04	11 40	12 22	13 13
40	16 54	17 24	17 58	10 56	11 28	12 07	12 55
45	16 40	17 12	17 49	10 47	11 14	11 49	12 34
S 50	16 21	16 58	17 39	10 36	10 58	11 27	12 08
52	16 13	16 52	17 35	10 31	10 50	11 17	11 55
54	16 03	16 45	17 30	10 25	10 42	11 05	11 40
56	15 52	16 37	17 25	10 19	10 32	10 52	11 23
58	15 40	16 28	17 19	10 12	10 21	10 36	11 03
S 60	15 25	16 19	17 13	10 04	10 09	10 18	10 37

SUN and MOON

Day	SUN Eqn. of Time 00h	12h	Mer. Pass.	MOON Mer. Pass. Upper	Lower	Age	Phase
15	05 52	05 55	12 06	05 33	17 58	23	
16	05 58	06 01	12 06	06 25	18 52	24	◗
17	06 03	06 06	12 06	07 21	19 50	25	

Figure 16.7. (cont.)

Example—

- **Step 1**—Find the GHA Aries that will put the star on the meridian. To do this, you carry out the subtraction given by the relation above:

Longitude	71° 05′ = 70° 65′	(converted to
–SHA☆	–62° 24.6	make arithmetic
GHA Aries	8° 40.4′	easier)

- **Step 2**—In the *Almanac* (Figure 16.7) find the values of GMT for which the GHA Aries brackets this desired value. Scanning the left-hand columns you find the following:

GMT	Aries
15d 05h	7° 47.6′
15d 06h	22° 50.1′

- **Step 3**—Compute by how much the desired value exceeds the smaller tabulated value:

GHA Aries	8° 40.4′ = 7°100.4′	(desired value,
Daily pages	7° 47.6	computed from
Difference	0° 52.8′	star in Step 1)

- **Step 4**—Thus, the angle you need differs from the smaller tabulated angle by 0° 52.8′. Turn to the Increments and Corrections table at the back of the *Almanac* and scan the Aries column until you find the time increment for this angle. (Be careful not to confuse minutes and seconds in reading this table.)

GMT Increment	3m 31s	(From Increments and Corrections table)

- **Step 5**—Add this increment to the whole hour of GMT, finding:

  GMT of meridian passage = July 15d 05h 03m 31s

- **Step 6**—If desired, find zone time by subtracting the zone description, ZD = 5h:

  Zone time of meridian passage = July 15d 00h 03m 31s ZT.

POSTTEST
16.2 Find the time of meridian passage for Deneb on July 15, 1990, at longitude 80°15′W.

Second method: Finding a star near the meridian at twilight

Suppose you wish to find a star that is near the meridian at civil twilight on the evening of July 15, 1990, at latitude 35°N and longitude 71°05′W. Proceed as follows:

- **Step 1**—From the daily pages (Figure 16.5) find the time (LMT) of civil twilight.

- **Step 2**—Find the corresponding GMT.

- **Step 3**—Then find the GHA Aries at that time.

- **Step 4**—From your longitude, find the required SHA☆ from

  SHA☆ = DR Longitude (W) – GHA Aries

Then scan the Stars table for a star with that SHA. Each step of the work is shown below. Step 2, the longitude correction to find the GMT of twilight was described in Chapter 14.

Example for July 15, 1990; lat. 35°N; long. 71°05′W

- **Step 1**—Find the time (LMT) of civil twilight from *Almanac* (Figure 16.6).

Twilight 1943 =	19 42 60 LMT	(converted to make the arithmetic easier)

- **Step 2**—Correction to your longitude.

Time corr. for 3°55′E	–00 15 40	(From Conversion of Arc to Time)
	19 27 20 ZT	
Zone description	+05	
Twilight July 16	00 27 20 GMT	(next day in Greenwich)

- **Step 3**—Find the GHA Aries at that time.

GHA Aries 16d 00h	293° 34.4′
Increment for 27m 20s	6° 51.1′
GHA Aries	300° 25.5′

- **Step 4**—From your longitude, find the required SHA☆

Longitude 71° 05 =	431° 05′	(360° added to
GHA Aries	–300° 25.5′	simplify sub-
SHA☆ needed	130° 39.5′	traction)

Now look in the Stars table to find a star with this SHA. According to the data in Figure 16.5, the closest star is β (beta) Librae, whose SHA = 130° 52.2′ in July 1990. This is 13′ greater than the desired SHA, 130°39.5′. Thus, the star will be 13′ west of the meridian at the time of twilight, July 16, 00 27 20 GMT (Figure 16.8 shows the sky at that time). The meridian passage of β Librae must have taken place a little earlier, and you can find the ex-

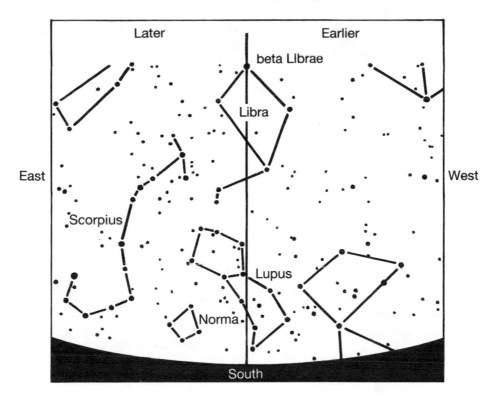

Figure 16.8. View looking south from long. 71°05′W, lat. 35°N at 1927 ZT on July 15, 1990. This is the time of civil twilight and the star beta Librae is on the meridian (vertical line). Stars are moving to the west (rightward), so those lying to the west were on the meridian earlier.

act time by converting the difference to a time interval. If the star had been 1° west, the meridian passage would have been 4 minutes earlier. But it is only $^{13}/_{60}$ of a degree, or $4 \times {}^{13}/_{60}$ minutes = 52 seconds early. So the meridian passage of β Librae took place at

July 16 00 26 80 GMT
Corr.   –52
July 16 00 26 28 GMT

The 52-second correction can be ignored because the altitude of the star will not change measurably in that time. Ordinarily, you will not be so lucky. If the closest star is more than 1° from the desired SHA, you will have to adjust the time of observation to catch the star on the meridian. If the star's SHA is greater than the desired value (so it is farther west), make your observation earlier, 4 minutes for each 1°. If it is smaller, make the observation later. (The amount of correction is the same as for a longitude correction, so use the Conversion of Arc to Time found in Table T6 in the Appendix or in the yellow pages of your *Almanac*.)

As another example, suppose you wished to observe the star Kochab (SHA = 137°) instead of β Librae. Kochab is 6° farther west. This means you must catch it 24 minutes earlier, or at 1903 GMT. At that time, Kochab will be on the meridian—but the sky may be too bright. (The time of twilight is not terribly precise, so you can make adjustments of several minutes without having the sky brightness change too much.)

Determining your latitude from such an observation is discussed in the next section.

POSTTEST
16.3 Find a convenient star for morning twilight at the same location on July 15, 1990.

LATITUDE FROM STAR ON THE MERIDIAN

Find the sextant height h_s and correct it for dip and refraction just as you did for Polaris. The result is H_o (observed height, or altitude). The remainder of the calculation is easier if you use zenith distance, derived from

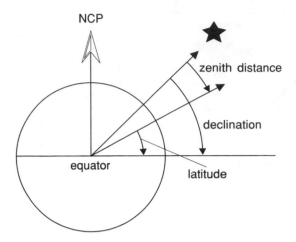

Figure 16.9. When a star is on your meridian, its distance from the zenith gives your distance from its geographic point. In this case the star is north of the navigator's zenith, so the relationship is latitude = declination – zenith distance. Southern latitudes and declinations are treated as negative numbers.

$$\text{Zenith distance} = 90° - H_o$$

There are two cases to be distinguished, and the best practice is to draw diagrams like Figures 16.9 and 16.10. In writing these rules, southern latitudes and declinations are considered as negative angles. All zenith distances are positive angles.

Star is north of the navigator's zenith
The situation is shown in Figure 16.8:

$$\text{Latitude} = \text{declination} - \text{zenith distance}$$

Examples—

1. A star at declination 40N is observed to the north at a zenith distance of 50°.

$$\text{Latitude} = 40 - 50 = -10° = 10S$$

2. A star at declination 10S is observed to the north at a zenith distance of 10°.

$$\text{Latitude} = -10° - 10° = -20° = 20S$$

Star is south of the navigator's zenith
The situation is shown in Figure 16.9:

$$\text{Latitude} = \text{declination} + \text{zenith distance}$$

Examples—

1. A star at declination 40S is observed to the south at a zenith distance of 50°.

$$\text{Latitude} = -40 + 50 = 10° = 10N$$

2. A star at declination 30S is observed to the south at a zenith distance of 10°.

$$\text{Latitude} = -30° + 10° = -20° = 20S$$

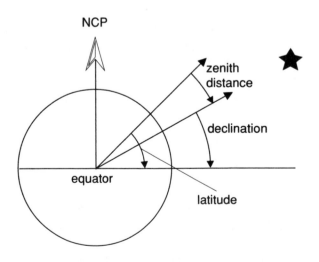

Figure 16.10. When a star is on your meridian, its distance from the zenith gives your distance from its geographic point. In this case the star is south of the navigator's zenith, so the relationship is latitude = declination + zenith distance.

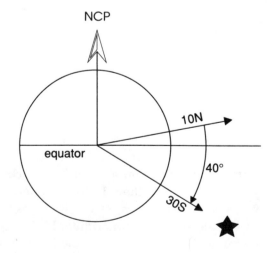

Figure 16.11. Sample meridian profile for helping compute the latitude from known declination and measured zenith distance of a star on the meridian. By inspection we see that, in this case, latitude = declination + zenith distance = 10N. Remember to treat southern latitudes and declinations as negative angles.

To help you see the relationships whenever you have to carry out this calculation, construct a simplified diagram (Figure 16.11) showing the profile of your meridian. Draw the equator and indicate the declination and the zenith distance of the star.

POSTTEST

16.4 The following table shows the results of other sample calculations of latitude for various assumed star observations. They are not all correct. Draw a diagram for each, carry out the arithmetic, and see if you can spot the errors.

Declination	Zenith distance	Direction	Latitude
10N	20°	North	10S
10N	30°	South	20N
30S	40°	North	70S
20S	25°	South	45N

CHAPTER SEVENTEEN

Celestial Orienteering

[Floyd] Bennett came up for a last talk and we decided to stake all on getting away—to give the *Josephine Ford* full power and full speed—and get off or crash at the end of the runway in the jagged ice. A few handclasps from our comrades and we set our faces toward our goal and the midnight sun, which at that moment lay almost due north.

Richard Evelyn Byrd, Skyward

INTRODUCTION

There are many ways to orient yourself by the sky. Some of them were probably used by navigators before the days of compasses, clocks, and almanacs. In one category are methods that determine the four cardinal directions: north, east, south, and west. They are simple to use. In another category are the methods that yield directions between the cardinal points. They depend on the positions of selected stars, and were used by Polynesians to navigate the Pacific Ocean.

Under a clear sky, the vessel's course can be set by the stars or the sun, and these methods can provide a check on the compass deviation. They require identifying the stars, so the next section introduces aids to star finding. A later section introduces the navigator's triangle, which is the key to the reduction of sextant sights to be discussed in Chapter 19.

PRETEST

17.1 The sun always rises due east as seen from the equator. T _____ F _____

17.2 In the course of the year, the rising points of the stars swing north and south around the horizon. T _____ F _____

STAR FINDERS

The surest road to success in identifying the planets and the stars is to (1) learn the major constellations, (2) concentrate on the navigation stars, and (3) keep track of the planets from month to month. (You probably won't have much trouble with the sun and moon!) All the necessary stars are bright and easily seen with the naked eye, but it takes some time to learn one's way around the sky. Several types of help are available.

Star atlases

These come in two varieties. First there are atlases of the sky, which represent the entire celestial sphere on a series of flat maps, or on a globe. These atlases make no reference to your location, so if you are trying to identify stars, you usually must start with a bit of sleuthing to find a reference point, such as a familiar constellation. These devices have the advantage of summarizing the entire sky and can be used anywhere in the world. The *Nautical Almanac* has an atlas presented in three portions: the equatorial region and the two polar regions.

The second type of star atlas shows the constellations in the evening for each month of the year from a particular latitude. They are usually designed for the midlatitudes, but with a little imagination and craning of the neck they can be used near the equator. And with a bit of practice, you can learn to use them for other times of the night, by shifting to another date. (Each two hours later at night requires looking at a chart for one month earlier in the book. That is, the stars on a chart for 11:00 P.M. on June 1 will be found in the same positions at 9:00 P.M. on July 1. This does not work for the planets, which were deservedly called "wanderers" by the ancients.)

Star finders

Adjustable star maps, called star finders, are available that have date and time scales on the outside so that when the star base is rotated to make the date and the time of day coincide, the visible stars will be shown inside an elliptical horizon. Such a star finder can be used to predict the times of sunset and sunrise and to find which constellations will be visible in the twilight on a particular date. To use it as a star clock when you know the calendar date, look at the stars visible in the sky and then rotate the star base until they appear in their proper positions. Then the time of day can be read against the date. Star finders are good for many years, so they make a sort of perpetual calendar/clock. But, because the height of the celestial pole (the pivot around which the stars rotate) depends on your latitude, each horizon is computed for a particular latitude, which must match your own to within 5° or 10°. Some come with adjustable horizons for different latitudes.

Bowditch Section 2210 gives a detailed description of the Rude Star Finder, which was patented by Captain G. T. Rude of the U.S. Coast and Geodetic Survey and was later sold to the U.S. Navy Hydrographic Office. It was distributed by the Hydrographic Office for a number of years as model No. 2102-D, and it is now available commercially. It consists of a star base, which is an opaque disc showing the southern hemisphere on one side and the northern hemisphere on the other. In the center is a small pin that acts as a pivot for transparent templates that show the horizon and the meridian of the navigator. The templates are designed for every 10° of latitude and can be used in either hemisphere. With the almanac and the time, the navigator sets the template in the proper orientation and then sees the navigation stars against scales of altitude and azimuth. This can be used for identifying individual stars, but it does not show the fainter stars or the constellations.

Activities with star finder

1. Use it for finding the stars that will be visible in the twilight.

2. Use it to calculate the azimuth and altitude of a bright star, and then verify your calculation by looking at the sky.

3. Measure the height and approximate azimuth of a star and try to identify it with the star finder.

4. Locate the sun among the constellations through the year.

5. Predict the times of sunrise and sunset on a particular date and compare them with newspaper or almanac values.

FINDING NORTH FROM POLARIS

Polaris is probably the easiest star to identify in the northern hemisphere, and it is directly under the pivoting rivet of most starfinders. (See Figures 12.7 and 12.8 for charts of the sky near Polaris.) It is always within a degree or so of true north; for most purposes, you can neglect this small discrepancy and assume Polaris shows true north. With a little work you can do better if you need higher accuracy. Here's how.

If Polaris were exactly at the north celestial pole, its azimuth would be 0°, due north. But because it is about a degree away, it makes a little circle about the pole, and its azimuth shifts east and west during the course of a day. If you want to find the north with high accuracy using Polaris, you must find its azimuth. Suppose it were 2° west. Then if you sight directly under Polaris, you will be looking at an azimuth of 358°. Shifting 2° east from Polaris will take you to the true north.

The first step in finding an accurate azimuth with Polaris is to compute the LHA Aries for your longitude at the time of your observation.

Example—Suppose you want to find the azimuth of Polaris from longitude 75W and latitude 40N at 0800 EST on July 15, 1990. Set up a small table as follows to find LHA Aries.

EST	0800	July 15, 1990
ZD	0500	(Zone description is 5 hours at longitude 75°W.)
GMT	1300	
GHA Aries	128°	(From daily pages in Figure 16.5. Nearest 1° is close enough.)
Longitude	75W	(Subtract for west longitude, add for east.)
Aries	53°	(The first point of Aries is 53° west of your meridian.)

Now turn to the Polaris Tables in the *Nautical Almanac.* Figure 16.3 is an excerpt. Scan across the top line, LHA Aries, until you come to the column headed 50°-59°, which includes the value you seek. Then scan down to the bottom of the page, Azimuth, and look for the row with your latitude (40°). You

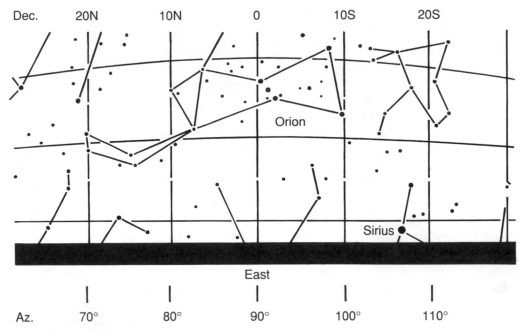

Figure 17.1. Eastern sky just before dawn as seen from the equator in mid-July. Sirius is rising with an azimuth of 107°. From the equatorial region, Sirius always rises with the same azimuth, and this was one of the keys to the Polynesian navigation technique of steering by the stars.

will find an azimuth of 359.7°, and this puts Polaris 0.3° west of the true north direction.

POSTTEST

17.3 Find the azimuth of Polaris at 2200 GMT Feb. 25, 1990, at latitude 40N and longitude 100W (see Figure 15.7 for the daily page).

POLYNESIAN STEERING BY THE RISINGS AND SETTINGS OF STARS

Long before the days of Nathaniel Bowditch and before the clock had been invented in Europe, the natives of Polynesia (in the South Pacific) had been navigating by the stars. Their techniques have been passed down to a few contemporaries, and we know they were simple and powerful, being derived from the appearance of the stars from season to season and year to year. There are three very simple facts that were the keys of the Polynesian methods. This section describes them in modern terms.

Yearly pattern seen from the equator

Imagine yourself at the equator under a clear evening sky. The date is June 20. The sun has set in the west-northwest and Sirius is following suit in the west-southwest. A careful measurement of the azimuth of Sirius with respect to Polaris shows it to be 253°. A few weeks later, in the morning twilight, you catch Sirius rising in the east-southeast. You determine its azimuth that morning to be 107°. Figure 17.1 shows the predawn sky in the east that day.

If you could keep track of the risings and settings of Sirius through the year from your spot on the equator, you would find something like the pattern shown in Table 17.1. Half of the events would be hidden by the sun.

Table 17.1. Risings and settings of Sirius as seen from the equator

Date	Rise		Set	
	LMT	Azimuth	LMT	Azimuth
Mar. 21	12 46*	107	00 46	253
Jun. 12	06 44*	107	18 44	253
Sep. 23	00 38	107	12 38*	253
Dec. 22	18 36	107	06 36*	253

*Hidden in sunlight

The pattern of Table 17.1 repeats every year. Let us see what it reveals:

Times of rising and setting—The times of risings and settings depend on the date; they are about four minutes earlier each day or two hours earlier each month. This accumulates to 24 hours per year. The advance in the rising and setting times is caused by the fact that your clock is running on sun time, and this is a little slower than star time because the sun moves among the stars. During the course of the year, the sun moves once around the zodiac. (The times of risings of various stars were used by the ancients as an annual calendar.)

POSTTEST

17.4 Suppose that the earth's annual motion around the sun were reversed but the daily spin were kept the same. Would the stars set later or earlier each night? Why?

17.5 Suppose that the annual motion and the daily spin were both reversed. Now what would happen to the stars? Would they rise earlier or later each night? Why?

Azimuths of rising and setting—Table 17.1 also shows that the azimuths of the rising and setting points are the same all year. This is the second key to the Polynesian methods of navigation. If you measure the direction in which a star rises one night, you can count on its rising in that same direction on successive nights. (Many modern-day skippers use this fact on overnight cruises.)

The directions of rising and setting for a handful of bright stars are shown in Table 17.2. These stars are all near the celestial equator, so they are useful in marking the east and west directions.

Table 17.2 Rising and setting of some bright stars as seen from the celestial equator

No.	Star Name	SHA	Dec.	Azimuth Rise	Set
10	Aldebaran	291	16N	74	286
–	δ Orionis	277	0	90	270
18	Sirius	259	16S	106	254
20	Procyon	245	5N	85	275
26	Regulus	208	12N	78	282
33	Spica	158	11S	101	259
–	β Aquarii	37	5S	95	265
51	Altair	62	–	82	278

To see how to compute the entries of such a table, imagine looking eastward from the equator. The due east direction is marked by the celestial equator; stars that are at declination 10°N will be 10° to the *left* of due east, and stars at declination 10°S will be 10° to the *right*. The corresponding azimuths will be 80° and 100° (Figures 17.2 a, b). The relationships are:

Azimuth of rising point as seen from the equator
= 90 − declination

Azimuth of setting point as seen from equator
= 270 + declination

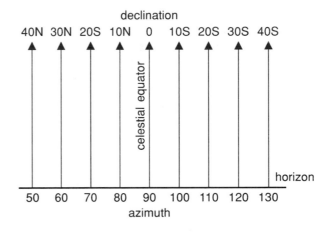

Figure 17.2a. Eastern horizon, showing the relationship between declination and azimuth of rising points as seen from the equator.

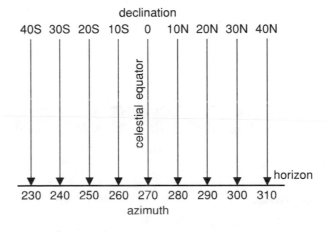

Figure 17.2b. Western horizon, showing the relationship between declination and azimuth of setting points as seen from the equator.

POSTTEST

17.6 If a star has a declination of 30°S what will be the azimuths of its rising and setting points, as seen from the equator?

17.7 Using the information in Table 17.2, what do you infer for the declination of Altair?

Yearly pattern seen from other latitudes

Figure 17.3 shows the predawn sky in mid-July as seen from a latitude of 20S. Compared to Figure 17.1, the azimuth of Sirius has increased slightly (shifted to the right) as the navigator moved away from the equator. A similar shift takes place if the navigator moves north from the equator.

Table 17.3 shows the rising and setting points of Sirius as seen from various latitudes. This table shows the third key to the Polynesian method.

Azimuths from different latitudes—The azimuths of Sirius change very little with latitude as long as the navigator stays within 20° of the equator. This means that, in going from one island to another, the Polynesians could assume that each star held the same direction throughout the voyage.

Table 17.3. Azimuths of risings and settings of Sirius as seen from various latitudes

Latitude N or S	Rise	Set
0	107	253
20	108	252
40	112	248
60	125	235

These properties of the rising and setting points meant that the Polynesian navigators merely had to memorize a short list of stars, and they could count on the stars holding true throughout the year and throughout all of Polynesia.

One word of caution: Typically, you will not be able to see a star when it is within 5° to 10° of the horizon. If you are at the equator, this has little effect on your estimate of the actual rising point, because the stars rise straight up from the horizon. But this is not the case at other latitudes. With a little practice you will be able to judge the actual rising and setting points by extending the visible path down to the horizon at its proper angle.

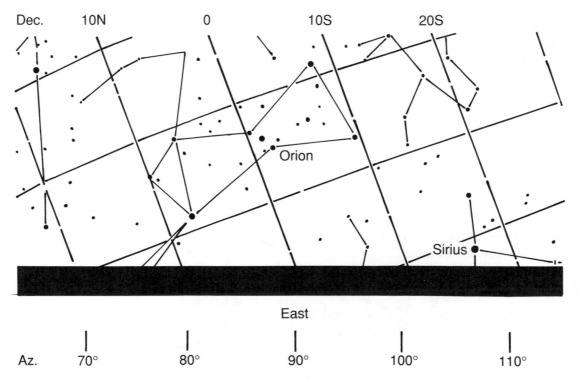

Figure 17.3. Predawn sky in the east as seen from a latitude of 20S. The scale at the bottom shows the azimuth along the eastern horizon. The azimuth of Sirius as seen from this latitude is about 108°. Comparison with Figure 17.1 (showing the sky as seen from the equator) shows this is about 1° greater than the azimuth as seen from the equator. The change is caused by the tilt of the celestial equator.

DIRECTIONS OF THE RISING AND SETTING SUN

At the times of the equinoxes, the sun rises (and sets) due east (and west). This is true for any latitude—except at the poles, where east and west are not defined. At other times of year, it wanders northward and southward from the cardinal points. It still can be used for determining directions, but this will require a calculation or looking in a few tables.

Seen from the equator

Figure 17.4 illustrates the seasonal motion of the sunrise point as seen from the equator. The sun changes its declination in a pattern that repeats each year. At any moment, the azimuths of rising and setting of the sun are computed from the declination by means of the same relationship that was used for the stars. The declination must be found from the *Almanac* for the date.

At other latitudes

For a navigator who is not at the earth's equator, the calculation of the sunrise and sunset points is more complicated. The situation at three latitudes is shown in Figure 17.5 for sunrise when the sun is at a declination of 10S.

When the sun is not on the celestial equator, the sunrise point is not due east. The amount of displacement is smallest for a navigator on the earth's

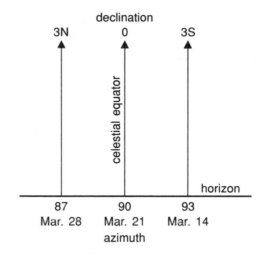

Figure 17.4. Diagram showing the sun in the eastern sky as seen from the equator at sunrise on three dates around the spring equinox. At the equinox, the sun rises due east. Before the equinox it rose slightly south of east. After the equinox, it has moved north, bringing summer to the northern hemisphere. Seen from the equator, the azimuth of the rising sun is 90° – declination, where southern declination is negative. At other latitudes, this simple relation does not hold (see text).

equator. It increases as the navigator moves away from the equator. Odd as it may seem, the sun moves in the same direction (south in this case) regardless of the direction the navigator moves from the equator.

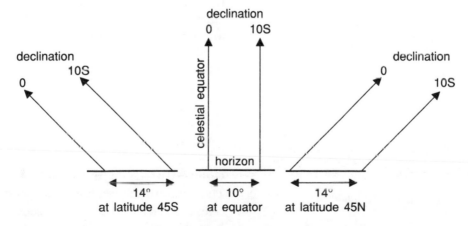

Figure 17.5. The direction of the sunrise point depends on the latitude as well as on the sun's declination. When the sun is off the celestial equator (here shown at a declination of 10S), the displacement of its rising point increases as the navigator moves away from the earth's equator. The length of the arrow indicates the sun's distance from the east point at sunrise. The arrow from the east point to the rising point is slightly longer when seen from latitude 45N. The sun is slightly more displaced toward the southeast when it is seen from northern or southern latitudes.

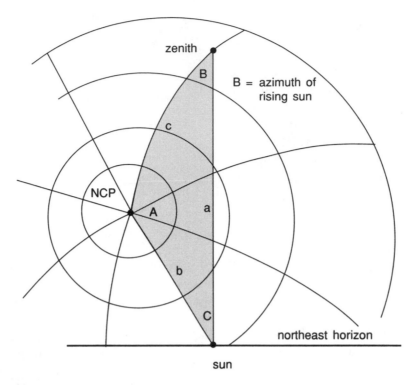

Figure 17.6. The position of the rising sun (C) relative to the north celestial pole (A) and the zenith (B) as seen from a latitude of 50N. These three points are the vertices of the navigator's triangle, which is to be solved for the azimuth of the rising sun. The three sides (a, b, c) are known (see text and Figure 17.7).

THE NAVIGATOR'S TRIANGLE

Introduction

In order to calculate the azimuth of the sun at latitudes other than the equator, we must exploit some spherical trigonometry. The triangle to be solved is illustrated in Figures 17.6 and 17.7. This is an example of the navigator's triangle.

Corners of navigator's triangle

- A = the north celestial pole

- B = the navigator's zenith

- C = the sun (or any other celestial body)

Sides of navigator's triangle

- a = zenith distance of sun (equal to 90° – altitude)

- b = 90° – declination of sun (also called codeclination)

- c = 90° – latitude of navigator (also called colatitude)

If we take an inventory of what we know about this triangle at sunrise, we find we know the three sides if we have a DR location. The sun is on the horizon, so it is 90° from the zenith. That gives us one side of the triangle: a = 90°. The other two sides are almost as easy to find. The distance from the zenith to the celestial pole is the navigator's colatitude: c = 90° – latitude. (Remember to treat southern latitudes and declinations as negative angles.) The third side of the triangle is the distance from the sun to the celestial pole. This is the sun's codeclination: b = 90° – declination.

Computing the azimuth of the rising sun

The azimuth of the sun is the angle between the celestial pole and the sun, as seen from the zenith. It is the angle at B. From spherical trigonometry, we have the law of cosines,

$$\cos B = \sin (90 - B) = (\cos b - \cos a \cos c) / (\sin a \sin c)$$

When the sun is on the horizon, a = 90°, and the equation simplifies to:

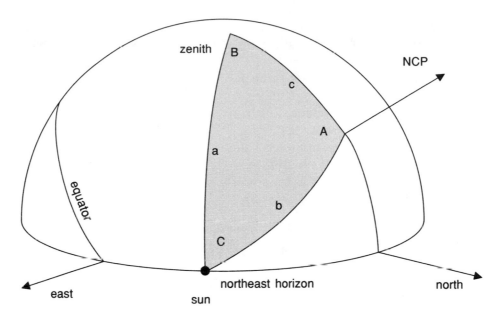

Figure 17.7. Navigator's triangle seen from outside the celestial sphere. As in Figure 17.6, the rising sun is 90° from the zenith and its distance from the north celestial pole is 90° – declination. The angle between the pole and the zenith is 90° – latitude. We seek the azimuth, B, which is an angle between the directions to the pole and to the sun as seen from the zenith.

$$\cos B = \sin (90 - B) = \cos b / \sin c$$

For a navigator on the equator, sin c = 1 and we find B = b.

We give these equations for completeness (and illustrate their use in a later section), but you will probably not need to use them, as several tables are available to do the work. The first are the tables of amplitudes.

The amplitudes of the sun

The amplitude of the sun is its angular distance on the horizon measured from the east or west point (Figure 17.8), and it is given by:

> Sunrise: Amplitude = B – 90
> Sunset: Amplitude = B – 270

Amplitudes in the east (sunrise) are prefixed with E, and those in the west with W. When the declination of the sun is north, the amplitude is suffixed with N; when south it is suffixed with S, as shown in Figure 17.8.

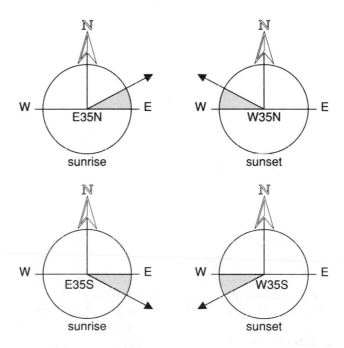

Figure 17.8. View looking down on the horizon circle. The amplitude of the sun (gray angle) is the angle of the rising or setting sun measured from the east or west cardinal point. It is prefixed E for sunrise and W for sunset; it is suffixed N for northern declinations and S for southern.

Example—If the sun rises 10° north of due east, its amplitude is E10°N. If it sets 20° south of due west its amplitude is W20°S.

The azimuth, Zn, is measured from north through east, and it can be found from the amplitude by sketching the triangle and noting the relationship between the cardinal point and the direction to the sun.

The amplitude is a convenient quantity, because a single table gives the azimuth of the sun from any latitude and at any time of year, as long as the sun's declination is known. *Bowditch* Table 27 (see Appendix) gives the amplitudes of the sun for its full range of declinations and for navigators within 77° of the equator. To use this table, find the declination of the sun on the date of interest. Scan down the column of the table to your latitude. Read out the amplitude and then label it, for example W23°N, and convert to azimuth according to the following rules, which are based on Figure 17.8.

Rules for finding azimuth, Zn, from amplitude and declination

1. Declination is south of the equator—amplitude will be toward the south.

    Sunrise: Zn = 90 + E Amplitude S
    Sunset: Zn = 270 – W Amplitude S

2. Declination is north of the equator—amplitude will be toward the north.

    Sunrise: Zn = 90 – E Amplitude N
    Sunset: Zn = 270 + W Amplitude N

Example—Suppose you wish to find the azimuths of sunrise and sunset on a day when the declination of the sun is 20N as observed from a latitude of 15N. According to Table 27 (see p. 302), the amplitude of the sun is 20.7N. It will be north of the east-west line, so its azimuth is Zn = 90 – E20.7N = 69.3 at sunrise and Zn = 270 + W20.7N = 290.7 at sunset.

Note on using old almanacs: For the purpose of steering or compass compensation, an accuracy of 0.5° is sufficient, so you may assume that the declination of the sun is the same on the same date in successive years. This means that you can use an old almanac to find the sun's declination as long as you use the right day of the year.

POSTTEST

17.8 Find the sun's declination from the *Almanac* and, using the table of Solar Amplitudes (Appendix), find the azimuths of sunrise and sunset on the following dates and at the listed latitudes.

Sunrise				
Date	Feb. 22	May 13	Aug. 8	Nov. 15
Sun's dec.				
Lat.		Amplitudes		
0				
15				
30				
44				

Sunset				
Date	Feb. 22	May 13	Aug. 8	Nov. 15
Sun's dec.				
Lat.		Amplitudes		
0				
15				
30				
44				

SOLVING THE NAVIGATOR'S TRIANGLE

Many of your navigation problems will involve setting up a navigator's triangle, deciding which parts of the triangle you know, and then setting out to compute the remaining parts. This section takes an example from the history of aviation and shows you two ways to approach the solution: by trigonometry and the law of cosines described above, or by the use of specially prepared tables published for this purpose. When you are at sea (in the literal and/or figurative sense) you will almost always prefer to use the tables, as they are quicker and more reliable than slugging through a series of equations or punching keys on a calculator. This section shows both ways so that you can make your own choice.

Azimuths of the sun during Byrd's polar flight

The quotation from Richard Byrd at the start of this chapter is an unusual example of orienteering by the sun. When Byrd and Bennett took off for the North Pole on May 9, 1926, 0222 GMT, the sun was in the north-northeast. (Byrd's comment that it was almost due north is a bit of poetic license.) By the time they reached the pole, the sun was, of course, in the south. Figure 17.9 is their record of the flight, showing the swing of the sun. The fliers arrived at the pole at 0902 GMT that day.

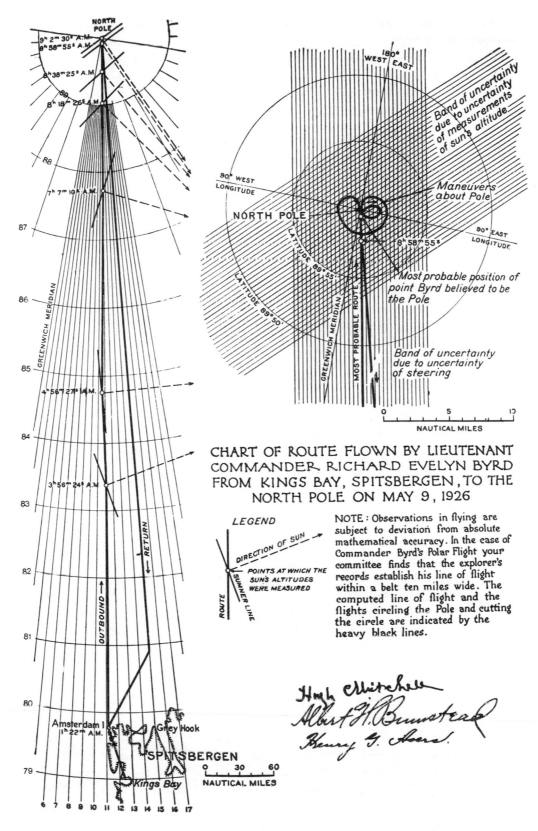

CHART OF ROUTE FLOWN BY LIEUTENANT COMMANDER RICHARD EVELYN BYRD FROM KINGS BAY, SPITSBERGEN, TO THE NORTH POLE ON MAY 9, 1926

LEGEND

NOTE: Observations in flying are subject to deviation from absolute mathematical accuracy. In the case of Commander Byrd's Polar Flight your committee finds that the explorer's records establish his line of flight within a belt ten miles wide. The computed line of flight and the flights circling the Pole and cutting the circle are indicated by the heavy black lines.

Figure 17.9. Chart of the Byrd-Bennett flight over the North Pole in 1926 (from Skyward, by Richard E. Byrd). All times on this chart are GMT, and the arrows indicate the observed directions of the sun. They compare well with the directions given in Table 17.4, based on modern calculations.

Solar azimuths calculated for various points on the track are given for comparison in Table 17.4, and this section shows how they were computed.

Table 17.4. Computed azimuths of the sun for the first leg of Byrd's polar flight on May 9, 1926

GMT	Lat.	Long.	Azimuth
01 22	79 40N	11E	31°
03 56	83 25N	11E	69°
04 56	84 45N	11E	84°
07 07	87 40N	11E	118°

Methods of solution

When the sun is not on the horizon, the solution of the navigator's triangle is slightly altered because you do not know side a in Figures 17.6 and 17.7. All you know about it is that a < 90° or else the sun would not be above the horizon. You know c, which is the zenith distance of the NCP, and you can find b, the colatitude of the sun, from the *Almanac*. But in order to solve the triangle you must know at least three quantities, so you must find one more angle before you can solve for the azimuth. That quantity is the local hour angle (LHA) of the sun, which is computed from the GMT and the navigator's longitude (Figure 17.10).

Proceed as follows to find the local hour angle of the sun.

- **Step 1**—Knowing the date and time, you can find the GHA of the sun (the longitude of its geographic point) as described in Chapter 14, and illustrated in Figure 14.13. Knowing your own longitude, you can find the LHA (sun) from the relation:

LHA (sun) = GHA (sun) − longitude (W)

Having done this, you know two sides (b and c) and the included angle A, and your task is to find the angle B, the azimuth. (In this triangle, A = LHA (sun) and B = azimuth, Zn.)

You must choose one of the following methods for solving the triangle. In method A, you call on the law of cosines for spherical triangles and do it the hard way—useful in case you don't have the proper tables for the easier methods. In method B, you avoid trigonometry by using some tables that are the favorites of many navigators: *H.O. 249*.

Method A: Solution with trigonometry—The calculation of B proceeds as follows, and if you are not familiar with the use of a hand-held calculator, turn to Chapter 23 for some hints.

- **Step 2A**—From the law of cosines we find side a using

$$\cos a = \cos b \cos c + \sin b \sin c \cos A$$

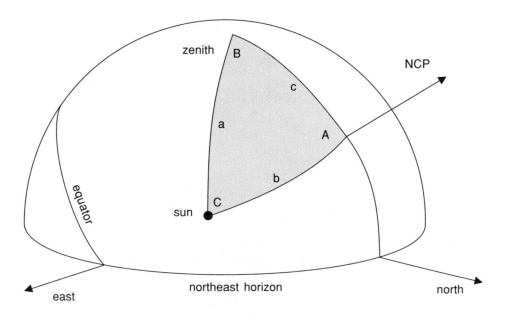

Figure 17.10. Navigator's triangle for sun above the horizon. Use a diagram like this for finding the azimuth of the sun (Zn) from its local hour angle (LHA) and codeclination (b), and the navigator's colatitude (c). The azimuth is angle B and the LHA (sun) is angle A.

which may be written

$$\cos a = \sin \text{(sun's declination)} \sin \text{(latitude)}$$
$$+ \cos \text{(sun's declination)} \cos \text{(latitude)} \cos \text{(LHA)}$$

- **Step 3A**—Evaluate cos a and find sin a from

$$\sin a = \sqrt{(1 - \cos^2 a)}$$

- **Step 4A**—Find B from the law of sines, sin a/sin A = sin b/sin B, written as

$$\sin B = \sin b \, \sin \text{(LHA)} / \sin a$$

or

$$\sin B = \cos \text{(sun's declination)} \sin \text{(LHA)} / \sin a$$

Then

$$Zn = B$$

Example—Let us recalculate the second point in Table 17.4 for Byrd and Bennett's flight, and carry out the calculation for a moment that is, to the day, 64 years later, using a modern almanac. We would expect the sun to be nearly where the explorers saw it.

Date: May 9, 1990/ 0356 GMT
Long. 11 00E, Lat. 83 20N

- **Step 1A**—GHA(sun) 239°53.6, dec. 17 16.5N
  (from the *Almanac*, Fig. 17.11)
  Long. (E)   11°
  LHA (sun) 250°53.6 (greater than 180°, so the sun is in the east)

- **Step 2A**—cos a = sin (17°16.5′) sin (83°20′) + cos (17°16.5′) cos (83°20′) cos (250°53.6′) = 0.2590

- **Step 3A**—sin a = $\sqrt{(1 - [0.259 \times 0.259])}$ = 0.9659; a = 75°00; Hc = 90° – a = 15°00 (the sun's altitude)

- **Step 4A**—sin B = cos (17°16.5′) sin (250°53.6′) / sin a = 0.9341
  B = 69°05′ (This is the azimuth shown in Table 17.4.)

Method B: Solution with H.O. 249—Figure 17.12 is a diagram of a page of *H.O. Pub. No. 249* in which the solutions to the navigator's triangle are tabulated. The actual page is shown in Figure 17.13. (A detailed explanation is published in the introduction to the tables.)

- **Step 2B**—Find the page marked with your latitude to the nearest degree (83°) and the declination of the sun. Because the latitude and declination are north, you take the page labelled *SAME* NAME. If one were north and one were south, you would use the page labelled *CONTRARY* NAME.

- **Step 3B**—Scan across the column headings to the nearest declination (17°) and then scan down the right-hand column to the LHA of the sun (251°). The headings are 252 and 250. Ignore Hc and write down both values of Z and then interpolate to the desired LHA:

	Z
252°:	70°
250°:	68
251°:	69 (interpolated)

- **Step 4B**—Look up at the top of the page and find the rule for converting from the tabulated Z to the azimuth, Zn, for navigators in the northern hemisphere:

N. Lat. $\begin{cases} \text{LHA greater than } 180° \ldots Zn = Z \\ \text{LHA less than } 180° \ldots Zn = 360 - Z \end{cases}$

The first case applies here, so we do nothing to Z, and we have Zn = 69°, which is the value we found with the other method.

At the bottom of the page you will find the rule for the southern hemisphere.

POSTTEST
17.9 Find the azimuth of the sun by both methods for:
Date: May 9, 1990/ 0445 GMT
Long. 13 00W, Lat. 83 20N

TWO COMMENTS ON ORIENTEERING

Using a pelorus

Once you have computed the sun's azimuth, you need a practical device to help you use that information. Such a device is the pelorus, which is described in Chapter 3. If, for example, you set the index of the pelorus to the true azimuth given by your calculations you will be able to read the true azimuths of objects sighted with the vanes. Then you can use those objects for compass checking or compensation.

1990 MAY 7, 8, 9 (MON., TUES., WED.)

UT (GMT)	ARIES G.H.A.	VENUS −4.1 G.H.A.	VENUS Dec.	MARS +0.7 G.H.A.	MARS Dec.	JUPITER −2.0 G.H.A.	JUPITER Dec.	SATURN +0.5 G.H.A.	SATURN Dec.	STARS Name	S.H.A.	Dec.
d h	° ′	° ′	° ′	° ′	° ′	° ′	° ′	° ′	° ′		° ′	° ′
7 00	224 34.7	221 04.1	S 0 05.2	240 32.3	S 8 34.3	125 52.9	N23 19.9	287 18.9	S20 54.7	Acamar	315 31.8	S40 20.5
01	239 37.2	236 03.9	04.2	255 33.0	33.6	140 54.9	19.9	302 21.3	54.7	Achernar	335 39.9	S57 17.0
02	254 39.6	251 03.8	03.1	270 33.7	32.9	155 56.8	19.9	317 23.8	54.7	Acrux	173 28.6	S63 03.1
03	269 42.1	266 03.6	·· 02.1	285 34.4	·· 32.2	170 58.8	·· 19.9	332 26.3	·· 54.7	Adhara	255 26.4	S28 57.6
04	284 44.6	281 03.4	01.1	300 35.1	31.5	186 00.8	19.8	347 28.8	54.7	Aldebaran	291 09.6	N16 29.5
05	299 47.0	296 03.3	S 0 00.1	315 35.8	30.8	201 02.8	19.8	2 31.2	54.7			
06	314 49.5	311 03.1	N 0 00.9	330 36.6	S 8 30.1	216 04.8	N23 19.8	17 33.7	S20 54.7	Alioth	166 35.1	N56 00.7
07	329 52.0	326 02.9	01.9	345 37.3	29.5	231 06.7	19.8	32 36.2	54.7	Alkaid	153 11.9	N49 21.6
08	344 54.4	341 02.8	02.9	0 38.0	28.8	246 08.7	19.7	47 38.7	54.7	Al Na'ir	28 05.4	S47 00.3
M 09	359 56.9	356 02.6	·· 03.9	15 38.7	·· 28.1	261 10.7	·· 19.7	62 41.1	·· 54.7	Alnilam	276 04.2	S 1 12.4
O 10	14 59.3	11 02.5	05.0	30 39.4	27.4	276 12.7	19.7	77 43.6	54.7	Alphard	218 13.1	S 8 37.1
N 11	30 01.8	26 02.3	06.0	45 40.1	26.7	291 14.7	19.7	92 46.1	54.7			
D 12	45 04.3	41 02.1	N 0 07.0	60 40.8	S 8 26.0	306 16.6	N23 19.7	107 48.6	S20 54.7	Alphecca	126 25.3	N26 44.6
A 13	60 06.7	56 02.0	08.0	75 41.6	25.3	321 18.6	19.6	122 51.0	54.7	Alpheratz	358 01.8	N29 02.1
Y 14	75 09.2	71 01.8	09.0	90 42.3	24.6	336 20.6	19.6	137 53.5	54.7	Altair	62 25.0	N 8 50.4
15	90 11.7	86 01.6	·· 10.0	105 43.0	·· 24.0	351 22.6	·· 19.6	152 56.0	·· 54.7	Ankaa	353 32.9	S42 21.3
16	105 14.1	101 01.5	11.1	120 43.7	23.3	6 24.6	19.6	167 58.5	54.8	Antares	112 47.2	S26 24.8
17	120 16.6	116 01.3	12.1	135 44.4	22.6	21 26.5	19.5	183 00.9	54.8			
18	135 19.1	131 01.1	N 0 13.1	150 45.1	S 8 21.9	36 28.5	N23 19.5	198 03.4	S20 54.8	Arcturus	146 11.2	N19 13.8
19	150 21.5	146 01.0	14.1	165 45.8	21.2	51 30.5	19.5	213 05.9	54.8	Atria	108 04.3	S69 00.7
20	165 24.0	161 00.8	15.1	180 46.6	20.5	66 32.5	19.5	228 08.4	54.8	Avior	234 25.4	S59 29.0
21	180 26.5	176 00.6	·· 16.1	195 47.3	·· 19.8	81 34.5	·· 19.4	243 10.8	·· 54.8	Bellatrix	278 50.9	N 6 20.5
22	195 28.9	191 00.5	17.2	210 48.0	19.1	96 36.4	19.4	258 13.3	54.8	Betelgeuse	271 20.3	N 7 24.4
23	210 31.4	206 00.3	18.2	225 48.7	18.4	111 38.4	19.4	273 15.8	54.8			
8 00	225 33.8	221 00.2	N 0 19.2	240 49.4	S 8 17.8	126 40.4	N23 19.4	288 18.3	S20 54.8	Canopus	264 04.2	S52 41.6
01	240 36.3	236 00.0	20.2	255 50.1	17.1	141 42.4	19.3	303 20.7	54.8	Capella	281 00.6	N45 59.5
02	255 38.8	250 59.8	21.2	270 50.9	16.4	156 44.3	19.3	318 23.2	54.8	Deneb	49 43.3	N45 14.4
03	270 41.2	265 59.7	·· 22.2	285 51.6	·· 15.7	171 46.3	·· 19.3	333 25.7	·· 54.8	Denebola	182 51.1	N14 37.5
04	285 43.7	280 59.5	23.3	300 52.3	15.0	186 48.3	19.3	348 28.2	54.8	Diphda	349 13.5	S18 02.3
05	300 46.2	295 59.3	24.3	315 53.0	14.3	201 50.3	19.2	3 30.6	54.8			
06	315 48.6	310 59.2	N 0 25.3	330 53.7	S 8 13.6	216 52.2	N23 19.2	18 33.1	S20 54.8	Dubhe	194 12.2	N61 48.4
07	330 51.1	325 59.0	26.3	345 54.4	12.9	231 54.2	19.2	33 35.6	54.8	Elnath	278 34.9	N28 36.1
T 08	345 53.6	340 58.8	27.3	0 55.2	12.2	246 56.2	19.2	48 38.1	54.8	Eltanin	90 53.8	N51 29.1
U 09	0 56.0	355 58.7	·· 28.3	15 55.9	·· 11.6	261 58.2	·· 19.1	63 40.6	·· 54.8	Enif	34 04.2	N 9 49.7
E 10	15 58.5	10 58.5	29.4	30 56.6	10.9	277 00.1	19.1	78 43.0	54.8	Fomalhaut	15 43.1	S29 40.3
S 11	31 01.0	25 58.3	30.4	45 57.3	10.2	292 02.1	19.1	93 45.5	54.8			
D 12	46 03.4	40 58.2	N 0 31.4	60 58.0	S 8 09.5	307 04.1	N23 19.1	108 48.0	S20 54.9	Gacrux	172 20.1	S57 03.9
A 13	61 05.9	55 58.0	32.4	75 58.7	08.8	322 06.1	19.0	123 50.5	54.9	Gienah	176 10.0	S17 29.5
Y 14	76 08.3	70 57.8	33.4	90 59.5	08.1	337 08.0	19.0	138 52.9	54.9	Hadar	149 12.2	S60 19.9
15	91 10.8	85 57.7	·· 34.5	106 00.2	·· 07.4	352 10.0	·· 19.0	153 55.4	·· 54.9	Hamal	328 20.8	N23 25.0
16	106 13.3	100 57.5	35.5	121 00.9	06.7	7 12.0	19.0	168 57.9	54.9	Kaus Aust.	84 06.5	S34 23.4
17	121 15.7	115 57.3	36.5	136 01.6	06.0	22 14.0	19.0	184 00.4	54.9			
18	136 18.2	130 57.2	N 0 37.5	151 02.3	S 8 05.3	37 15.9	N23 18.9	199 02.9	S20 54.9	Kochab	137 17.7	N74 11.6
19	151 20.7	145 57.0	38.5	166 03.1	04.6	52 17.9	18.9	214 05.3	54.9	Markab	13 55.8	N15 09.1
20	166 23.1	160 56.8	39.6	181 03.8	04.0	67 19.9	18.9	229 07.8	54.9	Menkar	314 33.5	N 4 03.2
21	181 25.6	175 56.7	·· 40.6	196 04.5	·· 03.3	82 21.9	·· 18.9	244 10.3	·· 54.9	Menkent	148 27.8	S36 19.6
22	196 28.1	190 56.5	41.6	211 05.2	02.6	97 23.8	18.8	259 12.8	54.9	Miaplacidus	221 43.7	S69 41.0
23	211 30.5	205 56.3	42.6	226 05.9	01.9	112 25.8	18.8	274 15.3	54.9			
9 00	226 33.0	220 56.1	N 0 43.6	241 06.6	S 8 01.2	127 27.8	N23 18.8	289 17.7	S20 54.9	Mirfak	309 05.9	N49 49.7
01	241 35.4	235 56.0	44.7	256 07.4	8 00.5	142 29.8	18.8	304 20.2	54.9	Nunki	76 19.6	S26 18.6
02	256 37.9	250 55.8	45.7	271 08.1	7 59.8	157 31.7	18.7	319 22.7	54.9	Peacock	53 46.2	S56 45.8
03	271 40.4	265 55.6	·· 46.7	286 08.8	·· 59.1	172 33.7	·· 18.7	334 25.2	·· 54.9	Pollux	243 49.0	N28 03.1
04	286 42.8	280 55.5	47.7	301 09.5	58.4	187 35.7	18.7	349 27.7	54.9	Procyon	245 18.0	N 5 15.0
05	301 45.3	295 55.3	48.8	316 10.2	57.7	202 37.6	18.7	4 30.2	54.9			
06	316 47.8	310 55.1	N 0 49.8	331 11.0	S 7 57.0	217 39.6	N23 18.6	19 32.6	S20 55.0	Rasalhague	96 22.3	N12 33.8
W 07	331 50.2	325 55.0	50.8	346 11.7	56.4	232 41.6	18.6	34 35.1	55.0	Regulus	208 01.8	N12 00.8
E 08	346 52.7	340 54.8	51.8	1 12.4	55.7	247 43.6	18.6	49 37.6	55.0	Rigel	281 29.0	S 8 12.7
D 09	1 55.2	355 54.6	·· 52.8	16 13.1	·· 55.0	262 45.5	·· 18.6	64 40.1	·· 55.0	Rigil Kent.	140 15.0	S60 47.9
N 10	16 57.6	10 54.5	53.9	31 13.8	54.3	277 47.5	18.5	79 42.6	55.0	Sabik	102 32.2	S15 43.0
E 11	32 00.1	25 54.3	54.9	46 14.6	53.6	292 49.5	18.5	94 45.0	55.0			
S 12	47 02.6	40 54.1	N 0 55.9	61 15.3	S 7 52.9	307 51.5	N23 18.5	109 47.5	S20 55.0	Schedar	350 01.1	N56 28.9
D 13	62 05.0	55 53.9	56.9	76 16.0	52.2	322 53.4	18.5	124 50.0	55.0	Shaula	96 45.1	S37 05.9
A 14	77 07.5	70 53.8	58.0	91 16.7	51.5	337 55.4	18.4	139 52.5	55.0	Sirius	258 49.2	S16 42.2
Y 15	92 09.9	85 53.6	0 59.0	106 17.4	·· 50.8	352 57.4	·· 18.4	154 55.0	·· 55.0	Spica	158 49.3	S11 06.9
16	107 12.4	100 53.4	1 00.0	121 18.2	50.1	7 59.3	18.4	169 57.5	55.0	Suhail	223 05.4	S43 23.9
17	122 14.9	115 53.3	01.0	136 18.9	49.4	23 01.3	18.3	184 59.9	55.0			
18	137 17.3	130 53.1	N 1 02.1	151 19.6	S 7 48.7	38 03.3	N23 18.3	200 02.4	S20 55.0	Vega	80 50.4	N38 46.1
19	152 19.8	145 52.9	03.1	166 20.3	48.0	53 05.2	18.3	215 04.9	55.0	Zuben'ubi	137 24.3	S16 00.3
20	167 22.3	160 52.7	04.1	181 21.0	47.3	68 07.2	18.3	230 07.4	55.0		S.H.A.	Mer. Pass.
21	182 24.7	175 52.6	·· 05.1	196 21.8	·· 46.7	83 09.2	·· 18.2	245 09.9	·· 55.0		° ′	h m
22	197 27.2	190 52.4	06.2	211 22.5	46.0	98 11.2	18.2	260 12.4	55.1	Venus	355 26.3	9 16
23	212 29.7	205 52.2	07.2	226 23.2	45.3	113 13.1	18.2	275 14.9	55.1	Mars	15 15.6	7 56
Mer. Pass.	h m 8 56.3	v −0.2 d 1.0		v 0.7 d 0.7		v 2.0 d 0.0		v 2.5 d 0.0		Jupiter Saturn	261 06.5 62 44.4	15 31 4 46

Figure 17.11. Excerpt of daily pages for May 9, 1990.

1990 MAY 7, 8, 9 (MON., TUES., WED.)

UT (GMT)	SUN G.H.A.	SUN Dec.	MOON G.H.A.	MOON v	MOON Dec.	MOON d	MOON H.P.	Lat.	Twilight Naut.	Twilight Civil	Sunrise	Moonrise 7	Moonrise 8	Moonrise 9	Moonrise 10
	° ′	° ′	° ′	′	° ′	′	′	°	h m	h m	h m	h m	h m	h m	h m
7 00	180 51.6	N16 40.9	32 11.4	15.9	S10 11.0	12.7	54.4	N 72	////	////	00 32	19 52	▬	▬	▬
01	195 51.6	41.6	46 46.3	15.9	10 23.7	12.6	54.4	N 70	////	////	01 48	19 21	21 57	▬	▬
02	210 51.7	42.3	61 21.2	15.8	10 36.3	12.6	54.3	68	////	01 06	02 25	18 58	21 01	▬	▬
03	225 51.7 ..	43.0	75 56.0	15.8	10 48.9	12.6	54.3	66	////	01 52	02 51	18 40	20 28	22 36	▬
04	240 51.8	43.7	90 30.8	15.8	11 01.5	12.6	54.3	64	////	02 21	03 11	18 26	20 04	21 49	23 52
05	255 51.8	44.4	105 05.6	15.8	11 14.1	12.4	54.3	62	00 59	02 43	03 27	18 14	19 45	21 19	22 55
06	270 51.9	N16 45.1	119 40.4	15.7	S11 26.5	12.5	54.3	60	01 40	03 00	03 40	18 04	19 29	20 56	22 22
07	285 51.9	45.8	134 15.1	15.7	11 39.0	12.4	54.3	N 58	02 07	03 15	03 52	17 55	19 16	20 38	21 57
08	300 51.9	46.5	148 49.8	15.7	11 51.4	12.3	54.3	56	02 28	03 27	04 02	17 48	19 05	20 23	21 38
M 09	315 52.0 ..	47.2	163 24.5	15.6	12 03.7	12.3	54.3	54	02 44	03 38	04 10	17 41	18 55	20 10	21 22
O 10	330 52.0	47.9	177 59.1	15.6	12 16.0	12.2	54.3	52	02 58	03 47	04 18	17 35	18 47	19 59	21 08
N 11	345 52.1	48.6	192 33.7	15.5	12 28.2	12.2	54.2	50	03 25	03 54	04 25	17 29	18 39	19 48	20 56
D 12	0 52.1	N16 49.3	207 08.2	15.6	S12 40.4	12.1	54.2	45	03 46	04 07	04 40	17 18	18 23	19 27	20 31
A 13	15 52.2	50.0	221 42.8	15.4	12 52.5	12.1	54.2	N 40	04 02	04 22	04 52	17 08	18 09	19 10	20 11
Y 14	30 52.2	50.6	236 17.2	15.5	13 04.6	12.0	54.2	35	04 15	04 35	05 03	17 00	17 58	18 56	19 54
15	45 52.2 ..	51.3	250 51.7	15.4	13 16.6	12.0	54.2	30	04 15	04 46	05 12	16 52	17 48	18 44	19 40
16	60 52.3	52.0	265 26.1	15.4	13 28.6	11.9	54.2	20	04 36	05 04	05 27	16 40	17 31	18 23	19 16
17	75 52.3	52.7	280 00.5	15.3	13 40.5	11.9	54.2	N 10	04 53	05 10	05 41	16 29	17 16	18 05	18 55
18	90 52.4	N16 53.4	294 34.8	15.3	S13 52.4	11.8	54.2	0	05 06	05 31	05 53	16 19	17 02	17 48	18 35
19	105 52.4	54.1	309 09.1	15.2	14 04.2	11.7	54.2	S 10	05 18	05 43	06 05	16 09	16 49	17 31	18 16
20	120 52.4	54.8	323 43.3	15.2	14 15.9	11.7	54.2	20	05 29	05 55	06 18	15 59	16 34	17 13	17 56
21	135 52.5 ..	55.5	338 17.5	15.2	14 27.6	11.6	54.2	30	05 39	06 08	06 33	15 47	16 18	16 53	17 32
22	150 52.5	56.1	352 51.7	15.1	14 39.2	11.6	54.1	35	05 45	06 15	06 42	15 40	16 08	16 41	17 18
23	165 52.6	56.8	7 25.8	15.0	14 50.8	11.5	54.1	40	05 50	06 23	06 51	15 32	15 57	16 27	17 02
								45	05 56	06 31	07 03	15 23	15 45	16 11	16 43
8 00	180 52.6	N16 57.5	21 59.8	15.1	S15 02.3	11.4	54.1	S 50	06 03	06 41	07 16	15 12	15 29	15 51	16 19
01	195 52.6	58.2	36 33.9	14.9	15 13.7	11.4	54.1	52	06 05	06 46	07 23	15 07	15 22	15 42	16 08
02	210 52.7	58.9	51 07.8	15.0	15 25.1	11.3	54.1	54	06 08	06 51	07 30	15 01	15 14	15 31	15 55
03	225 52.7	16 59.6	65 41.8	14.9	15 36.4	11.3	54.1	56	06 11	06 56	07 38	14 55	15 06	15 20	15 40
04	240 52.8	17 00.2	80 15.7	14.8	15 47.7	11.1	54.1	58	06 15	07 03	07 47	14 49	14 56	15 06	15 22
05	255 52.8	00.9	94 49.5	14.8	15 58.8	11.2	54.1	S 60	06 18	07 09	07 57	14 41	14 44	14 50	15 01

UT (GMT)	SUN G.H.A.	SUN Dec.	MOON G.H.A.	MOON v	MOON Dec.	MOON d	MOON H.P.	Lat.	Sunset	Twilight Civil	Twilight Naut.	Moonset 7	Moonset 8	Moonset 9	Moonset 10
06	270 52.8	N17 01.6	109 23.3	14.7	S16 10.0	11.0	54.1								
07	285 52.9	02.3	123 57.0	14.7	16 21.0	11.0	54.1	°	h m	h m	h m	h m	h m	h m	h m
T 08	300 52.9	03.0	138 30.7	14.7	16 32.0	10.9	54.1	N 72	▢	▢	▢	01 33	00 45	▬	▬
U 09	315 52.9 ..	03.6	153 04.4	14.6	16 42.9	10.9	54.1	N 70	22 11	////	////	01 50	01 18	00 12	▬
E 10	330 53.0	04.3	167 38.0	14.5	16 53.8	10.7	54.1	68	21 32	////	////	02 03	01 42	01 10	▬
S 11	345 53.0	05.0	182 11.5	14.5	17 04.5	10.7	54.1	66	21 05	22 56	////	02 14	02 01	01 44	01 11
D 12	0 53.0	N17 05.7	196 45.0	14.5	S17 15.2	10.7	54.1	64	20 44	22 05	////	02 23	02 17	02 09	01 59
A 13	15 53.1	06.4	211 18.5	14.4	17 25.9	10.5	54.0	62	20 28	21 35	////	02 31	02 30	02 29	02 29
Y 14	30 53.1	07.0	225 51.9	14.3	17 36.4	10.5	54.0	60	20 14	21 13	23 02	02 38	02 41	02 45	02 52
15	45 53.2 ..	07.7	240 25.2	14.3	17 46.9	10.4	54.0	N 58	20 03	20 55	22 17	02 44	02 50	02 58	03 11
16	60 53.2	08.4	254 58.5	14.2	17 57.3	10.4	54.0	56	19 53	20 40	21 49	02 50	02 50	03 10	03 27
17	75 53.2	09.1	269 31.7	14.2	18 07.7	10.3	54.0	54	19 44	20 27	21 28	02 55	03 06	03 21	03 40
18	90 53.3	N17 09.7	284 04.9	14.1	S18 18.0	10.1	54.0	52	19 36	20 16	21 11	02 59	03 13	03 30	03 52
19	105 53.3	10.4	298 38.0	14.1	18 28.1	10.2	54.0	50	19 29	20 07	20 57	03 03	03 19	03 38	04 03
20	120 53.3	11.1	313 11.1	14.0	18 38.3	10.0	54.0	45	19 14	19 47	20 29	03 12	03 32	03 56	04 25
21	135 53.4 ..	11.8	327 44.1	14.0	18 48.3	10.0	54.0	N 40	19 01	19 31	20 08	03 19	03 43	04 11	04 43
22	150 53.4	12.4	342 17.1	13.9	18 58.3	9.8	54.0	35	18 51	19 18	19 52	03 26	03 53	04 23	04 58
23	165 53.4	13.1	356 50.0	13.9	19 08.1	9.8	54.0	30	18 42	19 07	19 38	03 31	04 01	04 34	05 11
9 00	180 53.5	N17 13.8	11 22.9	13.7	S19 17.9	9.7	54.0	20	18 26	18 49	19 17	03 41	04 15	04 52	05 33
01	195 53.5	14.5	25 55.6	13.8	19 27.6	9.7	54.0	N 10	18 12	18 35	19 00	03 49	04 28	05 09	05 52
02	210 53.5	15.1	40 28.4	13.7	19 37.3	9.5	54.0	0	18 00	18 22	18 47	03 57	04 40	05 24	06 10
03	225 53.6 ..	15.8	55 01.1	13.6	19 46.8	9.5	54.0	S 10	17 48	18 09	18 35	04 06	04 52	05 39	06 29
04	240 53.6	16.5	69 33.7	13.6	19 56.3	9.4	54.0	20	17 34	17 57	18 24	04 14	05 04	05 56	06 48
05	255 53.6	17.1	84 06.3	13.5	20 05.7	9.3	54.0	30	17 19	17 45	18 13	04 24	05 19	06 15	07 11
06	270 53.7	N17 17.8	98 38.8	13.5	S20 15.0	9.2	54.0	35	17 11	17 37	18 08	04 30	05 28	06 26	07 24
W 07	285 53.7	18.5	113 11.3	13.4	20 24.2	9.1	54.0	40	17 01	17 30	18 02	04 37	05 37	06 39	07 40
E 08	300 53.7	19.1	127 43.7	13.3	20 33.3	9.0	54.0	45	16 50	17 21	17 56	04 44	05 49	06 54	07 58
D 09	315 53.8 ..	19.8	142 16.0	13.3	20 42.3	9.0	54.0	S 50	16 36	17 11	17 50	04 53	06 03	07 12	08 21
N 10	330 53.8	20.5	156 48.3	13.2	20 51.3	8.8	54.0	52	16 30	17 06	17 47	04 58	06 09	07 21	08 32
E 11	345 53.8	21.1	171 20.5	13.2	21 00.1	8.8	54.0	54	16 22	17 01	17 44	05 03	06 17	07 31	08 45
S 12	0 53.8	N17 21.8	185 52.7	13.1	S21 08.9	8.7	54.0	56	16 15	16 56	17 41	05 08	06 25	07 42	08 59
D 13	15 53.9	22.5	200 24.8	13.1	21 17.6	8.6	54.0	58	16 06	16 50	17 37	05 14	06 34	07 55	09 16
A 14	30 53.9	23.1	214 56.9	13.0	21 26.2	8.5	54.0	S 60	15 55	16 43	17 34	05 20	06 45	08 11	09 37
Y 15	45 53.9 ..	23.8	229 28.9	12.9	21 34.7	8.4	54.0								
16	60 54.0	24.5	244 00.8	12.9	21 43.1	8.3	54.0								
17	75 54.0	25.1	258 32.7	12.8	21 51.4	8.2	54.0								
18	90 54.0	N17 25.8	273 04.5	12.8	S21 59.6	8.1	54.0								
19	105 54.0	26.5	287 36.3	12.7	22 07.7	8.0	54.0								
20	120 54.1	27.1	302 08.0	12.6	22 15.7	7.9	54.0								
21	135 54.1 ..	27.8	316 39.6	12.6	22 23.6	7.9	54.0								
22	150 54.1	28.4	331 11.2	12.5	22 31.5	7.7	54.0								
23	165 54.2	29.1	345 42.7	12.5	22 39.2	7.6	54.0								

	SUN Eqn. of Time 00h	SUN Eqn. of Time 12h	SUN Mer. Pass.	MOON Mer. Pass. Upper	MOON Mer. Pass. Lower	Age	Phase
Day	m s	m s	h m	h m	h m		
7	03 26	03 28	11 57	22 29	10 08	12	
8	03 30	03 32	11 56	23 13	10 51	13	
9	03 34	03 35	11 56	23 59	11 36	14	◯

SUN S.D. 15.9	d 0.7	MOON S.D. 14.8	14.7	14.7

Figure 17.11. (cont.)

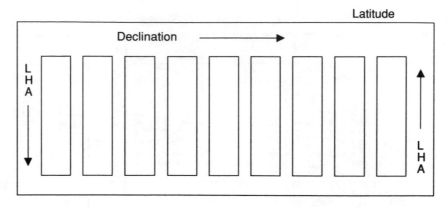

Figure 17.12. Layout of a page in H.O. Pub No. 249 *(see text).*

Steer not by the inconstant moon

Take Juliette's plea, ". . . not by th' inconstant moon," to heart and avoid using the moon for orienteering. During a single month, its rising point can swing north or south 10°, even if you stay at the same latitude. During the year, it will swing by 60° in a highly inconstant manner. Of course, it is predictable with an almanac, but it may not be worth the effort.

10°, 350° L.H.A. **LATITUDE SAME NAME AS DECLINATION**

N. Lat. { L.H.A. greater than 180°......Zn=Z
L.H.A. less than 180°............Zn=360°−Z

	23°			24°			25°			26°		
Dec.	Hc	d	Z	Hc	d	Z	Hc	d	Z	Hc	d	Z
°	° ′	′	°	° ′	′	°	° ′	′	°	° ′	′	°
0	65 01.7	+55.4	155.7	64 06.9	+55.7	156.6	63 11.6	+56.1	157.4	62 16.1	+56.4	158.1
1	65 57.1	55.0	154.8	65 02.6	55.4	155.7	64 07.7	55.9	156.6	63 12.5	56.2	157.3
2	66 52.1	54.6	153.8	65 58.0	55.1	154.8	65 03.6	55.5	155.7	64 08.7	55.9	156.6
3	67 46.7	54.1	152.7	66 53.1	54.7	153.8	65 59.1	55.1	154.8	65 04.6	55.5	155.7
4	68 40.8	53.7	151.5	67 47.8	54.2	152.7	66 54.2	54.8	153.8	66 00.1	55.3	154.8
5	69 34.5	+53.0	150.3	68 42.0	+53.7	151.6	67 49.0	+54.3	152.7	66 55.4	+54.8	153.8
6	70 27.5	52.3	148.9	69 35.7	53.1	150.3	68 43.3	53.8	151.6	67 50.2	54.4	152.8
7	71 19.8	51.6	147.4	70 28.8	52.5	148.9	69 37.1	53.2	150.3	68 44.6	53.9	151.6
8	72 11.4	50.7	145.8	71 21.3	51.7	147.5	70 30.3	52.6	149.0	69 38.5	53.3	150.4
9	73 02.1	49.7	144.0	72 13.0	50.8	145.8	71 22.9	51.8	147.5	70 31.8	52.7	149.0
10	73 51.8	+48.4	142.0	73 03.8	+49.8	144.1	72 14.7	+50.9	145.9	71 24.5	+51.9	147.6
11	74 40.2	47.1	139.9	73 53.6	48.6	142.1	73 05.6	49.9	144.1	72 16.4	51.1	146.0
12	75 27.3	45.4	137.4	74 42.2	47.2	139.9	73 55.5	48.8	142.2	73 07.5	50.1	144.2
13	76 12.7	43.5·	134.8	75 29.4	45.6	137.5	74 44.3	47.3	140.0	73 57.6	48.9	142.2
14	76 56.2	41.2·	131.8	76 15.0	43.7·	134.9	75 31.6	45.8	137.6	74 46.5	47.5	140.1
15	77 37.4	+38.6·	128.5	76 58.7	+41.4·	131.9	76 17.4	+43.9·	135.0	75 34.0	+45.9	137.7
16	78 16.0	35.4·	124.8	77 40.1	38.8·	128.6	77 01.3	41.6·	132.0	76 19.9	44.1·	135.1
17	78 51.4	31.8·	120.8	78 18.9	35.6·	124.9	77 42.9	39.0·	128.7	77 04.0	41.8·	132.1
18	79 23.2	27.6·	116.3	78 54.5	32.1·	120.9	78 21.9	35.9·	125.0	77 45.8	39.2·	128.8
19	79 50.8	22.8·	111.3	79 26.6	27.8·	116.3	78 57.8	32.2·	120.9	78 25.0	36.1·	125.1
20	80 13.6	+17.4·	106.0	79 54.4	+23.0·	111.4	79 30.0	+28.1·	116.4	79 01.1	+32.5·	121.1
21	80 31.0	11.5·	100.3	80 17.4	17.6·	106.0	79 58.1	23.2·	111.5	79 33.6	28.3·	116.5
22	80 42.5	+5.3·	94.2	80 35.0	11.6·	100.3	80 21.3	17.7·	106.1	80 01.9	23.4·	111.5
23	80 47.8	-1.2·	88.0	80 46.6	+5.4·	94.2	80 39.0	11.9·	100.3	80 25.3	18.0·	106.1
24	80 46.6	7.6·	81.8	80 52.0	-1.1·	88.0	80 50.9	+5.4·	94.2	80 43.3	12.0·	100.3
25	80 39.0	-13.7·	75.6	80 50.9	-7.6·	81.7	80 56.3	-1.0·	87.9	80 55.3	+5.6·	94.1
26	80 25.3	19.4·	69.7	80 43.3	13.8·	75.5	80 55.3	7.6·	81.5	81 00.9	-1.1·	87.8
27	80 05.9	24.6·	64.1	80 29.5	19.5·	69.5	80 47.7	13.8·	75.3	80 59.8	7.5·	81.4
28	79 41.3	29.2·	58.9	80 10.0	24.7·	63.9	80 33.9	19.6·	69.3	80 52.3	13.9·	75.1
29	79 12.1	33.2·	54.2	79 45.3	29.3·	58.6	80 14.3	24.8·	63.6	80 38.4	19.7·	69.0
30	78 38.9	-36.7·	49.8	79 16.0	-33.4·	53.8	79 49.5	-29.5·	58.3	80 18.7	-25.0·	63.3
31	78 02.2	39.6·	45.9	78 42.6	36.8·	49.5	79 20.0	33.5·	53.5	79 53.7	29.6·	58.0
32	77 22.6	42.1·	42.4	78 05.8	39.7·	45.6	78 46.5	37.0·	49.2	79 24.1	33.6·	53.2
33	76 40.5	44.2·	39.2	77 26.1	42.3·	42.0	78 09.5	39.9·	45.2	78 50.5	37.1·	48.8
34	75 56.3	46.1	36.3	76 43.8	44.3	38.8	77 29.6	42.4·	41.7	78 13.4	40.1·	44.9
35	75 10.2	-47.6	33.8	75 59.5	-46.2	36.0	76 47.2	-44.5	38.5	77 33.3	-42.6·	41.3
36	74 22.6	48.9	31.4	75 13.3	47.7	33.4	76 02.7	46.3	35.6	76 50.7	44.6	38.1
37	73 33.7	50.0	29.3	74 25.6	49.1	31.1	75 16.4	47.8	33.1	76 06.1	46.5	35.3
38	72 43.7	51.0	27.4	73 36.5	50.1	29.0	74 28.6	49.2	30.7	75 19.6	48.0	32.7
39	71 52.7	51.9	25.7	72 46.4	51.1	27.1	73 39.4	50.2	28.7	74 31.6	49.2	30.4
40	71 00.8	-52.6	24.1	71 55.3	-52.0	25.4	72 49.2	-51.3	26.8	73 42.4	-50.4	28.3
41	70 08.2	53.3	22.7	71 03.3	52.7	23.8	71 57.9	52.0	25.0	72 52.0	51.4	26.4
42	69 14.9	53.8	21.4	70 10.6	53.3	22.4	71 05.9	52.8	23.5	72 00.6	52.1	24.7
43	68 21.1	54.3	20.1	69 17.3	53.9	21.0	70 13.1	53.4	22.0	71 08.5	52.9	23.1
44	67 26.8	54.8	19.0	68 23.4	54.4	19.8	69 19.7	54.0	20.7	70 15.6	53.5	21.7
45	66 32.0	-55.1	18.0	67 29.0	-54.8	18.7	68 25.7	-54.5	19.5	69 22.1	-54.1	20.4
46	65 36.9	55.5	17.0	66 34.2	55.2	17.7	67 31.2	54.9	18.4	68 28.0	54.5	19.2
47	64 41.4	55.8	16.1	65 39.0	55.6	16.7	66 36.3	55.2	17.4	67 33.5	55.0	18.1
48	63 45.6	56.1	15.2	64 43.4	55.8	15.8	65 41.1	55.6	16.4	66 38.5	55.3	17.0
49	62 49.5	56.3	14.4	63 47.6	56.2	14.9	64 45.5	56.0	15.5	65 43.2	55.7	16.1
50	61 53.2	-56.6	13.7	62 51.4	-56.3	14.2	63 49.5	-56.1	14.7	64 47.5	-55.9	15.2
51	60 56.6	56.7	13.0	61 55.1	56.6	13.4	62 53.4	56.5	13.9	63 51.6	56.3	14.4
52	59 59.9	56.9	12.3	60 58.5	56.8	12.7	61 56.9	56.6	13.1	62 55.3	56.5	13.6
53	59 03.0	57.2	11.7	60 01.7	57.0	12.1	61 00.3	56.9	12.5	61 58.8	56.7	12.9
54	58 05.8	57.2	11.1	59 04.7	57.2	11.5	60 03.4	57.0	11.8	61 02.1	56.9	12.2
55	57 08.6	-57.4	10.6	58 07.5	-57.3	10.9	59 06.4	-57.2	11.2	60 05.2	-57.0	11.5
56	56 11.2	57.6	10.0	57 10.2	57.4	10.3	58 09.2	57.3	10.6	59 08.2	57.3	10.9
57	55 13.6	57.6	9.5	56 12.8	57.6	9.8	57 11.9	57.5	10.1	58 10.9	57.3	10.3
58	54 16.0	57.8	9.1	55 15.2	57.7	9.3	56 14.4	57.6	9.5	57 13.6	57.6	9.8
59	53 18.2	57.8	8.6	54 17.5	57.8	8.8	55 16.8	57.7	9.0	56 16.0	57.6	9.3
60	52 20.4	-58.0	8.2	53 19.7	-57.9	8.4	54 19.1	-57.8	8.6	55 18.4	-57.8	8.8
61	51 22.4	58.0	7.8	52 21.8	57.9	7.9	53 21.3	58.0	8.1	54 20.6	57.8	8.3
62	50 24.4	58.2	7.3	51 23.9	58.1	7.5	52 23.3	58.0	7.7	53 22.8	58.0	7.9
63	49 26.2	58.2	7.0	50 25.8	58.2	7.1	51 25.3	58.1	7.3	52 24.8	58.0	7.4
64	48 28.0	58.2	6.6	49 27.6	58.2	6.7	50 27.2	58.2	6.9	51 26.8	58.1	7.0
65	47 29.8	58.3	6.2	48 29.4	58.3	6.4	49 29.0	-58.2	6.5	50 28.7	-58.3	6.6
66	46 31.5	58.4	5.9	47 31.1	58.3	6.0	48 30.8	58.3	6.1	49 30.4	58.2	6.2
67	45 33.1	58.5	5.6	46 32.8	58.4	5.7	47 32.5	58.4	5.8	48 32.2	58.4	5.9
68	44 34.6	58.5	5.2	45 34.4	58.5	5.3	46 34.1	58.4	5.4	47 33.8	58.4	5.5
69	43 36.1	58.5	4.9	44 35.9	58.5	5.0	45 35.7	58.5	5.1	46 35.4	58.4	5.2
70	42 37.6	-58.6	4.6	43 37.4	-58.6	4.7	44 37.2	-58.6	4.8	45 37.0	-58.5	4.9
71	41 39.0	58.6	4.3	42 38.8	58.6	4.4	43 38.6	58.5	4.5	44 38.5	58.6	4.6
72	40 40.4	58.7	4.1	41 40.2	58.6	4.1	42 40.1	58.7	4.2	43 39.9	58.6	4.3
73	39 41.7	58.7	3.8	40 41.6	58.7	3.8	41 41.4	58.6	3.9	42 41.3	58.7	4.0
74	38 43.0	58.8	3.5	39 42.9	58.8	3.6	40 42.8	58.8	3.6	41 42.6	58.7	3.7
75	37 44.2	-58.7	3.3	38 44.1	-58.7	3.3	39 44.0	-58.7	3.4	40 43.9	-58.7	3.4
76	36 45.5	58.8	3.0	37 45.4	58.8	3.0	38 45.3	58.8	3.1	39 45.2	58.8	3.1
77	35 46.7	58.9	2.8	36 46.6	58.8	2.8	37 46.5	58.8	2.8	38 46.4	58.8	2.9
78	34 47.8	58.9	2.5	35 47.8	58.9	2.6	36 47.7	58.9	2.6	37 47.6	58.8	2.6
79	33 48.9	58.8	2.3	34 48.9	58.9	2.3	35 48.8	58.8	2.3	36 48.8	58.9	2.4
80	32 50.1	-59.0	2.1	33 50.0	-58.9	2.1	34 50.0	-58.9	2.1	35 49.9	-58.9	2.1
81	31 51.1	58.9	1.8	32 51.1	58.9	1.9	33 51.1	58.9	1.9	34 51.0	58.9	1.9
82	30 52.2	59.0	1.6	31 52.2	59.0	1.6	32 52.2	59.0	1.6	33 52.1	58.9	1.7
83	29 53.2	58.9	1.4	30 53.2	59.0	1.4	31 53.2	59.0	1.4	32 53.2	59.0	1.4
84	28 54.3	59.0	1.2	29 54.2	59.0	1.2	30 54.2	59.0	1.2	31 54.2	59.0	1.2
85	27 55.3	-59.1	1.0	28 55.2	-59.0	1.0	29 55.2	-59.0	1.0	30 55.2	-59.0	1.0
86	26 56.2	59.0	0.8	27 56.2	59.0	0.8	28 56.2	59.0	0.8	29 56.2	59.0	0.8
87	25 57.2	59.1	0.6	26 57.2	59.1	0.6	27 57.2	59.1	0.6	28 57.2	59.1	0.6
88	24 58.1	59.0	0.4	25 58.1	59.0	0.4	26 58.1	59.0	0.4	27 58.1	59.0	0.4
89	23 59.1	59.1	0.2	24 59.1	59.1	0.2	25 59.1	59.1	0.2	26 59.1	59.1	0.2
90	23 00.0	-59.1	0.0	24 00.0	-59.1	0.0	25 00.0	-59.1	0.0	26 00.0	-59.1	0.0
	23°			24°			25°			26°		

27°			28°			29°			30°			
Hc	d	Z	Hc	d	Z	Hc	d	Z	Hc	d	Z	Dec.
° ′	′	°	° ′	′	°	° ′	′	°	° ′	′	°	°
61 20.3	+56.7	158.8	60 24.3	+56.9	159.4	59 28.0	+57.2	160.0	58 31.5	+57.4	160.6	0
62 17.0	56.5	158.1	61 21.2	56.8	158.8	60 25.2	57.0	159.4	59 28.9	57.2	160.0	1
63 13.5	56.2	157.3	62 18.0	56.5	158.1	61 22.2	56.8	158.8	60 26.1	57.1	159.4	2
64 09.7	56.0	156.6	63 14.5	56.3	157.3	62 19.0	56.6	158.1	61 23.2	56.8	158.8	3
65 05.7	55.6	155.7	64 10.8	56.0	156.6	63 15.6	56.3	157.4	62 20.0	56.7	158.1	4
66 01.3	+55.3	154.8	65 06.8	+55.7	155.7	64 11.9	+56.1	156.6	63 16.7	+56.4	157.4	5
66 56.6	54.9	153.8	66 02.5	55.4	154.8	65 08.0	55.8	155.8	64 13.1	56.2	156.6	6
67 51.5	54.5	152.8	66 57.9	55.0	153.9	66 03.8	55.5	154.9	65 09.3	55.9	155.8	7
68 46.0	54.0	151.7	67 52.9	54.6	152.8	66 59.3	55.1	153.9	66 05.2	55.5	154.9	8
69 40.0	53.4	150.4	68 47.5	54.1	151.7	67 54.4	54.6	152.9	67 00.7	55.2	153.9	9
70 33.4	+52.8	149.1	69 41.6	+53.5	150.5	68 49.0	+54.2	151.8	67 55.9	+54.8	152.9	10
71 26.2	52.1	147.6	70 35.1	52.9	149.1	69 43.2	53.7	150.5	68 50.7	54.3	151.8	11
72 18.3	51.2	146.0	71 28.0	52.2	147.7	70 36.9	53.0	149.2	69 45.0	53.7	150.6	12
73 09.5	50.2	144.3	72 20.2	51.3	146.1	71 29.9	52.3	147.8	70 38.7	53.2	149.3	13
73 59.7	49.0	142.3	73 11.5	50.4	144.4	72 22.2	51.5	146.2	71 31.9	52.4	147.9	14
74 48.7	+47.7	140.2	74 01.9	+49.2	142.4	73 13.7	+50.5	144.5	72 24.3	+51.6	146.3	15
75 36.4	46.2	137.8	74 51.1	47.9	140.3	74 04.2	49.4	142.5	73 15.9	50.7	144.6	16
76 22.6	44.2·	135.2	75 39.0	46.3	137.9	74 53.6	48.0	140.4	74 06.6	49.5	142.7	17
77 06.8	42.1·	132.2	76 25.3	44.5·	135.3	75 41.6	46.6	138.1	74 56.1	48.3	140.5	18
77 48.9	39.4·	128.9	77 09.8	42.2·	132.4	76 28.2	44.6·	135.4	75 44.4	46.7	138.2	19
78 28.3	+36.4·	125.3	77 52.0	+39.7·	129.1	77 12.8	+42.5·	132.5	76 31.1	+44.9·	135.6	20
79 04.7	32.7·	121.2	78 31.7	36.6·	125.4	77 55.3	39.9·	129.2	77 16.0	42.7·	132.7	21
79 37.4	28.5·	116.6	79 08.3	33.0·	121.3	78 35.2	36.9·	125.5	77 58.7	40.2·	129.4	22
80 05.9	23.6·	111.6	79 41.3	28.7·	116.8	79 12.1	33.2·	121.4	78 38.9	37.1·	125.7	23
80 29.5	18.2·	106.2	80 10.0	23.9·	111.7	79 45.3	29.0·	116.9	79 16.0	33.5·	121.6	24
80 47.7	+12.1·	100.3	80 33.9	+18.4·	106.3	80 14.3	+24.1·	111.8	79 49.5	+29.2·	117.0	25
80 59.8	+5.7·	94.1	80 52.3	12.3·	100.3	80 38.4	18.6·	106.3	80 18.7	24.4·	112.0	26
81 05.5	-0.9·	87.7	81 04.6	+5.8·	94.1	80 57.0	12.5·	100.4	80 43.1	18.8·	106.4	27
81 04.6	7.6·	81.3	81 10.4	-0.9·	87.6	81 09.5	+5.9·	94.1	81 01.9	12.6·	100.4	28
80 57.0	13.9·	74.9	81 09.5	7.6·	81.1	81 15.4	-0.9·	87.6	81 14.5	+6.1·	94.1	29
80 43.1	-19.8·	68.8	81 01.9	-14.0·	74.7	81 14.5	-7.6·	81.0	81 20.6	-0.9·	87.5	30
80 23.3	25.1·	63.1	80 47.9	19.9·	68.6	81 06.9	14.0·	74.5	81 19.7	7.6·	80.9	31
79 58.2	29.8·	57.7	80 28.0	25.3·	62.8	80 52.9	20.1·	68.3	81 12.1	14.1·	74.3	32
79 28.4	33.8·	52.9	80 02.7	29.9·	57.4	80 32.8	25.4·	62.5	80 58.0	20.2·	68.0	33
78 54.6	37.3·	48.5	79 32.8	34.0·	52.5	80 07.4	30.1·	57.1	80 37.8	25.6·	62.2	34
78 17.3	-40.3·	44.5	78 58.8	-37.5·	48.1	79 37.3	-34.2·	52.1	80 12.2	-30.3·	56.7	35
77 37.0	42.7·	40.9	78 21.3	40.4·	44.1	79 03.1	37.7·	47.7	79 41.9	34.4·	51.8	36
76 54.3	44.8	37.7	77 40.9	42.9·	40.5	78 25.4	40.6·	43.7	79 07.5	37.9·	47.3	37
76 09.5	46.6	34.9	76 58.0	45.0	37.4	77 44.8	43.1·	40.1	78 29.6	40.8·	43.3	38
75 22.9	48.1	32.3	76 13.0	46.8	34.5	77 01.7	45.2	37.0	77 48.8	43.3·	39.7	39
74 34.8	-49.4	30.0	75 26.2	-48.2	31.9	76 16.5	-46.9	34.1	77 05.5	-45.3	36.5	40
73 45.4	50.5	27.9	74 38.0	49.6	29.6	75 29.6	48.4	31.5	76 20.2	47.1	33.7	41
72 54.9	51.5	26.1	73 48.4	50.6	27.6	74 41.2	49.7	29.3	75 33.1	48.6	31.1	42
72 03.4	52.3	24.3	72 57.8	51.6	25.7	73 51.5	50.8	27.2	74 44.5	49.9	28.9	43
71 11.1	53.0	22.8	72 06.2	52.4	24.0	73 00.7	51.7	25.3	73 54.6	50.9	26.8	44
70 18.1	-53.6	21.4	71 13.8	-53.1	22.4	72 09.0	-52.5	23.6	73 03.7	-51.8	24.9	45
69 24.5	54.1	20.1	70 20.7	53.7	21.0	71 16.5	53.1	22.1	72 11.9	52.6	23.2	46
68 30.4	54.6	18.9	69 27.0	54.2	19.7	70 23.4	53.8	20.7	71 19.3	53.3	21.7	47
67 35.8	55.0	17.8	68 32.8	54.7	18.5	69 29.6	54.4	19.4	70 26.0	53.9	20.3	48
66 40.8	55.5	16.7	67 38.1	55.1	17.4	68 35.2	54.7	18.2	69 32.1	54.4	19.0	49
65 45.3	-55.7	15.8	66 43.0	-55.5	16.4	67 40.5	-55.2	17.1	68 37.7	-54.9	17.8	50
64 49.6	56.0	14.9	65 47.5	55.8	15.5	66 45.3	55.6	16.1	67 42.8	55.3	16.7	51
63 53.6	56.3	14.1	64 51.7	56.1	14.6	65 49.7	55.9	15.1	66 47.5	55.6	15.7	52
62 57.3	56.5	13.3	63 55.6	56.3	13.8	64 53.8	56.1	14.3	65 51.9	55.9	14.8	53
62 00.8	56.8	12.6	62 59.3	56.6	13.0	63 57.7	56.4	13.4	64 56.0	56.3	13.9	54
61 04.0	-56.9	11.9	62 02.7	-56.8	12.3	63 01.3	-56.7	12.7	63 59.7	-56.4	13.1	55
60 07.1	57.2	11.2	61 05.9	57.0	11.6	62 04.6	56.8	12.0	63 03.3	56.7	12.4	56
59 09.9	57.2	10.6	60 08.9	57.2	11.0	61 07.8	57.1	11.3	62 06.6	57.0	11.7	57
58 12.7	57.5	10.1	59 11.7	57.3	10.4	60 10.7	57.2	10.7	61 09.6	57.1	11.0	58
57 15.2	57.5	9.5	58 14.4	57.5	9.8	59 13.5	57.4	10.1	60 12.5	57.2	10.4	59
56 17.7	-57.7	9.0	57 16.9	-57.6	9.2	58 16.1	-57.5	9.5	59 15.3	-57.4	9.8	60
55 20.0	57.8	8.5	56 19.3	57.7	8.7	57 18.6	57.6	9.0	58 17.9	57.6	9.2	61
54 22.2	57.9	8.0	55 21.6	57.8	8.2	56 21.0	57.8	8.5	57 20.2	57.7	8.7	62
53 24.3	58.0	7.6	54 23.8	58.0	7.8	55 23.2	57.9	8.0	56 22.6	57.8	8.2	63
52 26.3	58.1	7.2	53 25.8	58.0	7.3	54 25.3	57.9	7.5	55 24.8	57.9	7.7	64
51 28.2	-58.1	6.8	52 27.8	-58.1	6.9	53 27.4	-58.1	7.1	54 26.9	-58.0	7.3	65
50 30.1	58.2	6.4	51 29.7	58.2	6.5	52 29.3	58.1	6.7	53 28.9	58.1	6.8	66
49 31.9	58.4	6.0	50 31.5	58.3	6.1	51 31.2	58.3	6.3	52 30.8	58.2	6.4	67
48 33.5	58.3	5.6	49 33.2	58.3	5.8	50 32.9	58.3	5.9	51 32.6	58.2	6.0	68
47 35.2	58.5	5.3	48 34.9	58.4	5.4	49 34.6	58.3	5.5	50 34.4	58.4	5.6	69
46 36.7	-58.4	5.0	47 36.5	-58.4	5.1	48 36.3	-58.4	5.2	49 36.0	-58.4	5.3	70
45 38.3	58.6	4.6	46 38.1	58.6	4.7	47 37.9	58.5	4.8	48 37.6	58.4	4.9	71
44 39.7	58.6	4.3	45 39.5	58.5	4.4	46 39.4	58.6	4.5	47 39.2	58.5	4.6	72
43 41.1	58.6	4.0	44 41.0	58.6	4.1	45 40.8	58.6	4.2	46 40.7	58.6	4.2	73
42 42.5	58.7	3.7	43 42.4	58.7	3.8	44 42.2	58.6	3.9	45 42.1	58.6	3.9	74
41 43.8	-58.7	3.5	42 43.7	-58.7	3.5	43 43.6	-58.7	3.6	44 43.5	-58.7	3.6	75
40 45.1	58.7	3.2	41 45.0	58.7	3.2	42 44.9	58.7	3.3	43 44.8	58.7	3.3	76
39 46.4	58.8	2.9	40 46.3	58.8	3.0	41 46.2	58.8	3.0	42 46.1	58.7	3.1	77
38 47.6	58.9	2.7	39 47.5	58.8	2.7	40 47.4	58.8	2.7	41 47.4	58.8	2.8	78
37 48.7	58.8	2.4	38 48.7	58.9	2.4	39 48.6	58.8	2.5	40 48.6	58.8	2.5	79
36 49.9	-58.9	2.2	37 49.8	-58.8	2.2	38 49.8	-58.9	2.2	39 49.8	-58.9	2.3	80
35 51.0	58.9	1.9	36 51.0	58.9	1.9	37 50.9	58.9	2.0	38 50.9	58.9	2.0	81
34 52.1	58.9	1.7	35 52.1	59.0	1.7	36 52.0	58.9	1.7	37 52.0	58.9	1.8	82
33 53.2	59.0	1.5	34 53.1	58.9	1.5	35 53.1	58.9	1.5	36 53.1	58.9	1.5	83
32 54.2	59.0	1.2	33 54.2	59.0	1.3	34 54.2	59.0	1.3	35 54.2	59.0	1.3	84
31 55.2	-59.0	1.0	32 55.2	-59.0	1.0	33 55.2	-59.0	1.0	34 55.2	-59.0	1.1	85
30 56.2	59.0	0.8	31 56.2	59.0	0.8	32 56.2	59.0	0.8	33 56.2	59.0	0.8	86
29 57.2	59.1	0.6	30 57.2	59.1	0.6	31 57.2	59.1	0.6	32 57.2	59.1	0.6	87
28 58.1	59.0	0.4	29 58.1	59.0	0.4	30 58.1	59.0	0.4	31 58.1	59.0	0.4	88
27 59.1	59.1	0.2	28 59.1	59.1	0.2	29 59.1	59.1	0.2	30 59.1	59.1	0.2	89
27 00.0	-59.1	0.0	28 00.0	-59.1	0.0	29 00.0	-59.1	0.0	30 00.0	-59.1	0.0	90
27°			28°			29°			30°			

10°, 350° L.H.A. **LATITUDE SAME NAME AS DECLINATION**

Figure 17.13. Page from H.O. Pub. No. 249.

CHAPTER EIGHTEEN

Great-Circle Sailing

I sailed with a free wind day after day, marking the position of my ship on the chart with considerable precision; but this was done by intuition, I think, more than slavish calculations. For one whole month my vessel held her course true; I had not, the while, so much as a light in the binnacle. The Southern Cross I saw every night abeam. The sun every morning came up astern; every evening it went down ahead. I wished for no other compass to guide me, for these were true. If I doubted my reckoning after a long time at sea I verified it by reading the clock aloft made by the Great Architect, and it was right.

Joshua Slocum, Sailing Alone Around the World

INTRODUCTION

On a voyage of 1000 miles or more, the great-circle route can cut many miles from your trip—although weather and currents may dictate another route. In any case, the great-circle route is a useful reference, and you may want to know how to lay it out.

Using gnomonic charts (Chapter 3) is the easy way, but these charts are not always available. Direct calculation with spherical trigonometry is an alternative, and most hand-held navigational calculators can be used to calculate the great-circle route between any pair of points on the globe.

The aims of this chapter are (1) to show how the great-circle route can be viewed as one side of the navigator's triangle discussed in Chapter 17; and (2) to illustrate a painless solution to the problem using *H. O. Pub. No. 229.*

The exercises in this chapter will familiarize you with *H. O. Pub. No. 229* and will prepare you for its use in later chapters.

FINDING GREAT-CIRCLE ROUTES WITH *H. O. PUB. NO. 229*

Suppose you want to sail from the Hawaiian Islands to San Francisco. These points are marked H and S on the diagram in Figure 18.1.

You want answers to the following questions: (1) What is the great circle distance? (2) What is the true heading at the start of the trip? (The true heading will change as you move along the great-circle route. We will cope with that later.)

When it is properly set up, this problem is identical to the problem of the navigator's triangle discussed in Chapter 17. Figures 18.2a and b show the relationship between the labellings of the two triangles. The correspondence is set up by imagining that a star stands directly over your destination, and the star's zenith distance and azimuth is equivalent to the distance and course heading. The known quantities are shown in italic, and we need the angle marked "heading," which is the same as the azimuth of the star, and the side marked "dis-

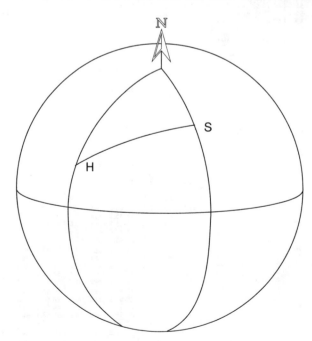

Figure 18.1. You want to sail from Hawaii (H) to San Francisco (S) and your task is to compute the great-circle distance and the initial heading of the track.

tance to be travelled," which is the same as the zenith distance of the star.

Knowing two sides and the included angle, we could apply the law of cosines, discussed in Chapter 17. But our goal is to use *H.O. Pub. No. 229,* which contains the solutions to the triangle. In conjunction with form F4 (Appendix), these tables are useful for sight reduction (as will be discussed in later

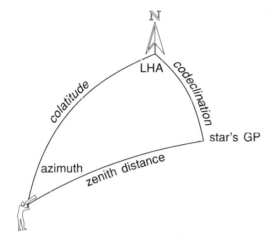

Figure 18.2a. The navigator's triangle viewed looking down on the celestial sphere as in Figure 17.10. Quantities in italic are known and the navigator wishes to compute the zenith distance and azimuth to the star. Compare with Figure 18.2b in which the navigator wishes to compute the distance to be travelled and the heading.

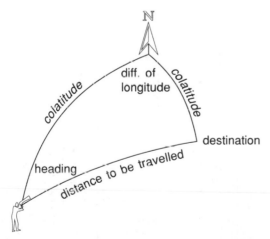

Figure 18.2b. This diagram represents the surface of the earth. The great-circle route has taken the place of the zenith distance to the star, and the course heading has become the azimuth. With this matching, the great-circle route may be found in the same way the star location was found in Chapter 17 with H.O. Pub. No. 249. Known quantities are shown in italic.

chapters) and they can be put to work in solving great-circle problems.

The page layout of *H.O. Pub. No. 229* is shown in Figure 18.3.

A portion of form F4 is shown below, and we have introduced the data for the great-circle sailing from Hawaii (entered as the navigator's DR position) and San Francisco (entered as the "star" to be sighted). We use coordinates rounded to the nearest degree to simplify the work, and this is usually appropriate for great-circle calculations.

Example—

DR Position (Hawaii): longitude 157°W, latitude 21°N. Target (San Francisco): GHA 122°W, declination 38°N.

The work proceeds as follows:

- *Step 1*—Enter the longitude and latitude of the starting point as the DR position of the navigator.

- *Step 2*—Enter the destination as the star name and enter its longitude and latitude as GHA (line 3.4) and declination (line 2.3) of the star.

- *Step 3*—Compute the LHA of the destination by subtracting from its longitude the longitude of the starting point. Enter in lines 3.6 and 5.3.

- *Step 4*—Enter the DR latitude of the navigator as assumed latitude in line 5.4.

- *Step 5*—Scan *H.O. Pub. No. 229* for the page with the appropriate LHA. (See excerpt in Figure 18.4a.) Find the column with the correct latitude of the navigator (*same* name or *contrary* name to declination) and scan down that column to the appropriate declination

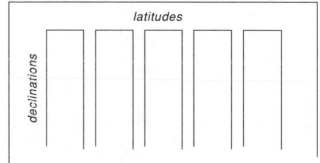

Figure 18.3. Page layout for H.O. Pub. No. 229. Each page is for one value of LHA (difference of longitude) and each horizontal row corresponds to a value of declination.

35°, 325° L.H.A. **LATITUDE SAME NAME AS DECLINATION** N. Lat. {L.H.A. greater than 180°......Zn=Z; L.H.A. less than 180°............Zn=360°−Z}

Dec.	15°			16°			17°			18°		
	Hc	d	Z	Hc	d	Z	Hc	d	Z	Hc	d	Z
°	° ′	′	°	° ′	′	°	° ′	′	°	° ′	′	°
0	52 18.1	+24.8	110.3	51 56.7	+26.3	111.5	51 34.1	+27.8	112.7	51 10.5	+29.0	113.8
1	52 42.9	23.7	108.8	52 23.0	25.2	110.0	52 01.9	26.6	111.2	51 39.5	28.1	112.4
2	53 06.6	22.5	107.3	52 48.2	24.0	108.5	52 28.5	25.5	109.8	52 07.6	27.0	111.0
3	53 29.1	21.3	105.7	53 12.2	22.8	107.0	52 54.0	24.4	108.3	52 34.6	25.9	109.5
4	53 50.4	20.0	104.1	53 35.0	21.7	105.5	53 18.4	23.2	106.7	53 00.5	24.7	108.0
5	54 10.4	+18.7	102.5	53 56.7	+20.3	103.9	53 41.6	+22.0	105.2	53 25.2	+23.6	106.5
6	54 29.1	17.3	100.9	54 17.0	19.1	102.3	54 03.6	20.7	103.6	53 48.8	22.3	105.0
7	54 46.4	16.0	99.2	54 36.1	17.7	100.6	54 24.3	19.4	102.0	54 11.1	21.1	103.4
8	55 02.4	14.7	97.6	54 53.8	16.4	99.0	54 43.7	18.1	100.4	54 32.2	19.8	101.8
9	55 17.1	13.1	95.9	55 10.2	14.9	97.3	55 01.8	16.7	98.7	54 52.0	18.4	100.1
10	55 30.2	+11.7	94.2	55 25.1	+13.5	95.6	55 18.5	+15.3	97.0	55 10.4	+17.1	98.5
11	55 41.9	10.3	92.4	55 38.6	12.1	93.9	55 33.8	13.9	95.3	55 27.5	15.6	96.8
12	55 52.2	8.7	90.7	55 50.7	10.6	92.1	55 47.7	12.4	93.6	55 43.1	14.3	95.1
13	56 00.9	7.2	88.9	56 01.3	9.0	90.4	56 00.1	10.9	91.9	55 57.4	12.7	93.3
14	56 08.1	5.6	87.1	56 10.3	7.5	88.6	56 11.0	9.4	90.1	56 10.1	11.2	91.6
15	56 13.7	+4.1	85.3	56 17.8	+6.0	86.8	56 20.4	+7.8	88.3	56 21.3	+9.8	89.8
16	56 17.8	2.6	83.5	56 23.8	4.4	85.0	56 28.2	6.3	86.5	56 31.1	8.1	88.0
17	56 20.4	+0.9	81.7	56 28.2	2.9	83.2	56 34.5	4.7	84.7	56 39.2	6.6	86.2
18	56 21.3	−0.6	79.9	56 31.1	+1.2	81.4	56 39.2	3.2	82.9	56 45.8	5.1	84.4
19	56 20.7	2.1	78.1	56 32.3	−0.3	79.6	56 42.4	+1.5	81.1	56 50.9	3.4	82.6
20	56 18.6	−3.8	76.3	56 32.0	−1.9	77.8	56 43.9	0.0	79.3	56 54.3	+1.8	80.8
21	56 14.8	5.3	74.5	56 30.1	3.5	76.0	56 43.9	−1.7	77.5	56 56.1	+0.2	79.0
22	56 09.5	6.8	72.7	56 26.6	5.1	74.2	56 42.2	3.2	75.6	56 56.3	−1.3	77.1
23	56 02.7	8.4	71.0	56 21.5	6.6	72.4	56 39.0	4.8	73.8	56 55.0	3.0	75.3
24	55 54.3	9.9	69.2	56 14.9	8.2	70.6	56 34.2	6.4	72.0	56 52.0	4.6	73.5
25	55 44.4	−11.4	67.4	56 06.7	−9.6	68.8	56 27.8	−8.0	70.2	56 47.4	−6.2	71.6
26	55 33.0	12.8	65.7	55 57.1	11.2	67.0	56 19.8	9.5	68.4	56 41.2	7.8	69.8
27	55 20.2	14.3	64.0	55 45.9	12.7	65.3	56 10.3	11.0	66.6	56 33.4	9.3	68.0
28	55 05.9	15.7	62.3	55 33.2	14.1	63.6	55 59.3	12.5	64.9	56 24.1	10.8	66.2
29	54 50.2	17.1	60.6	55 19.1	15.5	61.8	55 46.8	14.0	63.1	56 13.3	12.3	64.5
30	54 33.1	−18.4	58.9	55 03.6	−17.0	60.1	55 32.8	−15.4	61.4	56 01.0	−13.9	62.7
31	54 14.7	19.7	57.3	54 46.6	18.3	58.5	55 17.4	16.8	59.7	55 47.1	15.2	61.0
32	53 55.0	21.0	55.7	54 28.3	19.6	56.8	55 00.6	18.1	58.0	55 31.9	16.7	59.3
33	53 34.0	22.2	54.1	54 08.7	20.8	55.2	54 42.5	19.5	56.4	55 15.2	18.1	57.6
34	53 11.8	23.4	52.5	53 47.9	22.2	53.6	54 23.0	20.8	54.7	54 57.1	19.4	55.9
35	52 48.4	−24.6	51.0	53 25.7	−23.3	52.1	54 02.2	−22.1	53.1	54 37.7	−20.7	54.3
36	52 23.8	25.7	49.5	53 02.4	24.5	50.5	53 40.1	23.3	51.6	54 17.0	22.0	52.6
37	51 58.1	26.8	48.0	52 37.9	25.7	49.0	53 16.8	24.4	50.0	53 55.0	23.3	51.1
38	51 31.3	27.8	46.6	52 12.2	26.7	47.5	52 52.4	25.6	48.5	53 31.7	24.4	49.5
39	51 03.5	28.8	45.2	51 45.5	27.8	46.1	52 26.8	26.7	47.0	53 07.3	25.6	48.0
40	50 34.7	−29.8	43.8	51 17.7	−28.8	44.6	52 00.1	−27.8	45.5	52 41.7	−26.7	46.5
41	50 04.9	30.7	42.4	50 48.9	29.8	43.2	51 32.3	28.8	44.1	52 15.0	27.7	45.0
42	49 34.2	31.7	41.1	50 19.1	30.7	41.9	51 03.5	29.8	42.7	51 47.3	28.8	43.6
43	49 02.5	32.5	39.8	49 48.4	31.7	40.5	50 33.7	30.7	41.3	51 18.5	29.8	42.1
44	48 30.0	33.3	38.5	49 16.7	32.5	39.2	50 03.0	31.7	40.0	50 48.7	30.8	40.8
45	47 56.7	−34.1	37.3	48 44.2	−33.3	37.9	49 31.3	−32.5	38.7	50 17.9	−31.6	39.4
46	47 22.6	34.9	36.0	48 10.9	34.1	36.7	48 58.8	33.4	37.4	49 46.3	32.6	38.1
47	46 47.7	35.6	34.8	47 36.8	34.9	35.5	48 25.4	34.1	36.1	49 13.7	33.4	36.8
48	46 12.1	36.3	33.7	47 01.9	35.7	34.3	47 51.3	35.0	34.9	48 40.3	34.2	35.5
49	45 35.8	37.0	32.5	46 26.2	36.3	33.1	47 16.3	35.7	33.7	48 06.1	35.0	34.3
50	44 58.8	−37.6	31.4	45 49.9	−37.0	31.9	46 40.6	−36.3	32.5	47 31.1	−35.8	33.1
51	44 21.2	38.2	30.3	45 12.9	37.7	30.8	46 04.3	37.1	31.4	46 55.3	36.4	31.9
52	43 43.0	38.8	29.2	44 35.2	38.3	29.7	45 27.2	37.7	30.2	46 18.9	37.2	30.7
53	43 04.2	39.4	28.2	43 56.9	38.9	28.6	44 49.5	38.4	29.1	45 41.7	37.7	29.6
54	42 24.8	40.0	27.2	43 18.0	39.4	27.6	44 11.1	38.9	28.0	45 04.0	38.5	28.5
55	41 44.8	−40.4	26.2	42 38.6	−40.0	26.6	43 32.2	−39.5	27.0	44 25.5	−39.0	27.4
56	41 04.4	40.9	25.2	41 58.6	40.5	25.6	42 52.7	40.1	26.0	43 46.5	39.6	26.4
57	40 23.5	41.4	24.2	41 18.1	41.0	24.6	42 12.6	40.6	24.9	43 06.9	40.1	25.3
58	39 42.1	41.9	23.3	40 37.1	41.4	23.6	41 32.0	41.0	24.0	42 26.8	40.7	24.3
59	39 00.2	42.3	22.3	39 55.7	42.0	22.7	40 51.0	41.6	23.0	41 46.1	41.1	23.3
60	38 17.9	−42.7	21.4	39 13.7	−42.3	21.7	40 09.4	−42.0	22.0	41 05.0	−41.7	22.4
61	37 35.2	43.1	20.5	38 31.4	42.8	20.8	39 27.4	42.4	21.1	40 23.3	42.1	21.4
62	36 52.1	43.4	19.7	37 48.6	43.2	19.9	38 45.0	42.9	20.2	39 41.2	42.5	20.5
63	36 08.7	43.9	18.8	37 05.4	43.5	19.1	38 02.1	43.3	19.3	38 58.7	43.0	19.6
64	35 24.8	44.1	18.0	36 21.9	43.9	18.2	37 18.8	43.6	18.4	38 15.7	43.3	18.7
65	34 40.7	−44.5	17.1	35 38.0	−44.3	17.4	36 35.2	−44.0	17.6	37 32.4	−43.8	17.8
66	33 56.2	44.8	16.3	34 53.7	44.6	16.5	35 51.2	44.3	16.7	36 48.6	44.1	16.9
67	33 11.4	45.2	15.5	34 09.1	44.9	15.7	35 06.9	44.7	15.9	36 04.5	44.4	16.1
68	32 26.2	45.4	14.7	33 24.2	45.2	14.9	34 22.2	45.0	15.1	35 20.1	44.8	15.3
69	31 40.8	45.6	14.0	32 39.0	45.4	14.1	33 37.2	45.3	14.3	34 35.3	45.1	14.5
70	30 55.2	−46.0	13.2	31 53.6	−45.8	13.4	32 51.9	−45.6	13.5	33 50.2	−45.4	13.7
71	30 09.2	46.2	12.5	31 07.8	46.0	12.6	32 06.3	45.8	12.7	33 04.8	45.6	12.9
72	29 23.0	46.4	11.7	30 21.8	46.3	11.9	31 20.5	46.1	12.0	32 19.2	46.0	12.1
73	28 36.6	46.7	11.0	29 35.5	46.5	11.1	30 34.4	46.4	11.2	31 33.2	46.2	11.3
74	27 49.9	46.8	10.3	28 49.0	46.8	10.4	29 48.0	46.6	10.5	30 47.0	46.5	10.6
75	27 03.1	−47.1	9.6	28 02.2	−46.9	9.7	29 01.4	−46.9	9.8	30 00.5	−46.7	9.9
76	26 16.0	47.3	8.9	27 15.3	47.2	9.0	28 14.5	47.0	9.1	29 13.8	47.0	9.1
77	25 28.7	47.4	8.2	26 28.1	47.4	8.3	27 27.5	47.3	8.4	28 26.8	47.1	8.4
78	24 41.3	47.7	7.5	25 40.7	47.5	7.6	26 40.2	47.5	7.7	27 39.7	47.4	7.7
79	23 53.6	47.8	6.9	24 53.2	47.8	6.9	25 52.7	47.6	7.0	26 52.3	47.6	7.0
80	23 05.8	−48.0	6.2	24 05.4	−47.9	6.3	25 05.1	−47.8	6.3	26 04.7	−47.7	6.4
81	22 17.8	48.1	5.6	23 17.5	48.0	5.6	24 17.3	48.1	5.6	25 17.0	48.0	5.7
82	21 29.7	48.3	4.9	22 29.5	48.2	5.0	23 29.2	48.1	5.0	24 29.0	48.1	5.0
83	20 41.4	48.4	4.3	21 41.3	48.4	4.3	22 41.1	48.3	4.3	23 40.9	48.3	4.4
84	19 53.0	48.5	3.7	20 52.9	48.5	3.7	21 52.8	48.5	3.7	22 52.6	48.4	3.7
85	19 04.5	−48.7	3.0	20 04.4	−48.7	3.1	21 04.3	−48.6	3.1	22 04.2	−48.6	3.1
86	18 15.8	48.8	2.4	19 15.7	48.7	2.4	20 15.7	48.8	2.4	21 15.6	48.7	2.5
87	17 27.0	48.9	1.8	18 27.0	48.9	1.8	19 26.9	48.8	1.8	20 26.9	48.8	1.8
88	16 38.1	49.0	1.2	17 38.1	49.0	1.2	18 38.1	49.0	1.2	19 38.1	49.0	1.2
89	15 49.1	49.1	0.6	16 49.1	49.1	0.6	17 49.1	49.1	0.6	18 49.1	49.1	0.6
90	15 00.0	−49.2	0.0	16 00.0	−49.2	0.0	17 00.0	−49.2	0.0	18 00.0	−49.2	0.0
	15°			16°			17°			18°		

19°			20°			21°			22°			Dec.
Hc	d	Z	Hc	d	Z	Hc	d	Z	Hc	d	Z	
° ′	′	°	° ′	′	°	° ′	′	°	° ′	′	°	°
50 45.7	+30.4	114.9	50 19.9	+31.7	116.0	49 53.1	+32.9	117.1	49 25.2	+34.2	118.1	0
51 16.1	29.4	113.6	50 51.6	30.7	114.7	50 26.0	32.0	115.8	49 59.4	33.3	116.9	1
51 45.5	28.4	112.2	51 22.3	29.8	113.3	50 58.0	31.1	114.5	50 32.7	32.3	115.6	2
52 13.9	27.4	110.7	51 52.1	28.8	111.9	51 29.1	30.2	113.1	51 05.0	31.5	114.2	3
52 41.3	26.2	109.3	52 20.9	27.7	110.5	51 59.3	29.1	111.7	51 36.5	30.5	112.9	4
53 07.5	+25.1	107.8	52 48.6	+26.6	109.0	52 28.4	+28.1	110.3	52 07.0	+29.5	111.5	5
53 32.6	24.0	106.3	53 15.2	25.4	107.6	52 56.5	26.9	108.8	52 36.5	28.4	110.1	6
53 56.6	22.7	104.7	53 40.6	24.3	106.0	53 23.4	25.9	107.3	53 04.9	27.4	108.6	7
54 19.3	21.4	103.1	54 04.9	23.1	104.5	53 49.3	24.6	105.8	53 32.3	26.2	107.1	8
54 40.7	20.1	101.5	54 28.0	21.8	102.9	54 13.9	23.5	104.3	53 58.5	25.0	105.6	9
55 00.8	+18.8	99.9	54 49.8	+20.5	101.3	54 37.4	+22.1	102.7	54 23.5	+23.8	104.0	10
55 19.6	17.5	98.2	55 10.3	19.2	99.6	54 59.5	20.9	101.1	54 47.3	22.6	102.4	11
55 37.1	16.0	96.5	55 29.5	17.8	98.0	55 20.4	19.5	99.4	55 09.9	21.2	100.8	12
55 53.1	14.5	94.8	55 47.3	16.3	96.3	55 39.9	18.2	97.7	55 31.1	19.9	99.2	13
56 07.6	13.1	93.1	56 03.6	15.0	94.6	55 58.1	16.7	96.0	55 51.0	18.5	97.5	14
56 20.7	+11.6	91.3	56 18.6	+13.4	92.8	56 14.8	+15.3	94.3	56 09.5	+17.1	95.8	15
56 32.3	10.1	89.6	56 32.0	11.9	91.1	56 30.1	13.8	92.6	56 26.6	15.6	94.1	16
56 42.4	8.5	87.8	56 43.9	10.4	89.3	56 43.9	12.2	90.8	56 42.2	14.1	92.3	17
56 50.9	6.9	86.0	56 54.3	8.8	87.5	56 56.1	10.7	89.0	56 56.3	12.6	90.6	18
56 57.8	5.3	84.1	57 03.1	7.3	85.7	57 06.8	9.2	87.2	57 08.9	11.1	88.8	19
57 03.1	+3.7	82.3	57 10.4	+5.6	83.8	57 16.0	+7.5	85.4	57 20.0	+9.5	86.9	20
57 06.8	2.1	80.5	57 16.0	4.0	82.0	57 23.5	6.0	83.6	57 29.5	7.8	85.1	21
57 08.9	+0.5	78.6	57 20.0	2.4	80.2	57 29.5	4.2	81.7	57 37.3	6.2	83.3	22
57 09.4	−1.1	76.8	57 22.4	+0.7	78.3	57 33.7	2.7	79.8	57 43.5	4.6	81.4	23
57 08.3	2.8	74.9	57 23.1	−0.9	76.5	57 36.4	+1.0	78.0	57 48.1	2.9	79.5	24
57 05.5	−4.3	73.1	57 22.2	−2.5	74.6	57 37.4	−0.6	76.1	57 51.0	+1.3	77.7	25
57 01.2	6.0	71.3	57 19.7	4.1	72.7	57 36.8	2.3	74.2	57 52.3	−0.4	75.8	26
56 55.2	7.5	69.4	57 15.6	5.8	70.9	57 34.5	4.0	72.4	57 51.9	2.1	73.9	27
56 47.7	9.2	67.6	57 09.8	7.4	69.1	57 30.5	5.6	70.5	57 49.8	3.8	72.0	28
56 38.5	10.6	65.8	57 02.4	8.9	67.2	57 24.9	7.1	68.7	57 46.0	5.3	70.1	29
56 27.9	−12.2	64.0	56 53.5	−10.6	65.4	57 17.8	−8.8	66.8	57 40.7	−7.1	68.3	30
56 15.7	13.7	62.3	56 42.9	12.0	63.6	57 09.0	10.4	65.0	57 33.6	8.6	66.4	31
56 02.0	15.2	60.5	56 30.9	13.6	61.8	56 58.6	11.9	63.2	57 25.0	10.3	64.6	32
55 46.8	16.6	58.8	56 17.3	15.0	60.1	56 46.7	13.5	61.4	57 14.7	11.8	62.8	33
55 30.2	17.9	57.1	56 02.3	16.5	58.3	56 33.2	15.0	59.6	57 02.9	13.3	61.0	34
55 12.3	−19.4	55.4	55 45.8	−17.9	56.6	56 18.2	−16.4	57.9	56 49.6	−14.9	59.2	35
54 52.9	20.7	53.8	55 27.9	19.3	54.9	56 01.8	17.8	56.1	56 34.7	16.3	57.4	36
54 32.2	21.9	52.1	55 08.6	20.6	53.3	55 44.0	19.3	54.4	56 18.4	17.8	55.7	37
54 10.3	23.2	50.5	54 48.0	21.9	51.6	55 24.7	20.5	52.8	56 00.6	19.2	53.9	38
53 47.1	24.4	49.0	54 26.1	23.2	50.0	55 04.2	21.9	51.1	55 41.4	20.6	52.3	39
53 22.7	−25.6	47.4	54 02.9	−24.4	48.5	54 42.3	−23.2	49.5	55 20.8	−21.9	50.6	40
52 57.1	26.7	45.9	53 38.5	25.6	46.9	54 19.1	24.4	47.9	54 58.9	23.2	49.0	41
52 30.4	27.7	44.5	53 12.9	26.7	45.4	53 54.7	25.6	46.4	54 35.7	24.4	47.4	42
52 02.7	28.9	43.0	52 46.2	27.8	43.9	53 29.1	26.7	44.8	54 11.3	25.6	45.8	43
51 33.8	29.8	41.6	52 18.4	28.8	42.4	53 02.4	27.8	43.3	53 45.7	26.8	44.3	44
51 04.0	−30.8	40.2	51 49.6	−29.9	41.0	52 34.6	−28.9	41.9	53 18.9	−27.9	42.8	45
50 33.2	31.7	38.8	51 19.7	30.8	39.6	52 05.7	30.0	40.4	52 51.0	28.9	41.3	46
50 01.5	32.6	37.5	50 48.9	31.8	38.3	51 35.7	30.8	39.0	52 22.1	30.0	39.8	47
49 28.9	33.4	36.2	50 17.1	32.7	36.9	51 04.9	31.9	37.7	51 52.1	31.0	38.4	48
48 55.5	34.3	34.9	49 44.4	33.5	35.6	50 33.0	32.7	36.3	51 21.1	31.9	37.1	49
48 21.2	−35.1	33.7	49 10.9	−34.3	34.3	50 00.3	−33.6	35.0	50 49.2	−32.8	35.7	50
47 46.1	35.8	32.5	48 36.6	35.2	33.1	49 26.7	34.5	33.7	50 16.4	33.7	34.4	51
47 10.3	36.5	31.3	48 01.4	35.9	31.9	48 52.2	35.2	32.5	49 42.7	34.6	33.1	52
46 33.8	37.2	30.1	47 25.5	36.6	30.7	48 17.0	36.0	31.2	49 08.1	35.3	31.8	53
45 56.6	37.9	29.0	46 48.9	37.3	29.5	47 41.0	36.7	30.1	48 32.8	36.1	30.6	54
45 18.7	−38.5	27.9	46 11.6	−38.0	28.4	47 04.3	−37.5	28.9	47 56.7	−36.9	29.4	55
44 40.2	39.1	26.8	45 33.6	38.6	27.3	46 26.8	38.1	27.7	47 19.8	37.5	28.2	56
44 01.1	39.7	25.7	44 55.0	39.2	26.2	45 48.7	38.7	26.6	46 42.3	38.2	27.1	57
43 21.4	40.3	24.7	44 15.8	39.8	25.1	45 10.0	39.3	25.5	46 04.1	38.9	26.0	58
42 41.1	40.7	23.7	43 36.0	40.3	24.1	44 30.7	39.9	24.5	45 25.2	39.4	24.9	59
42 00.4	−41.3	22.7	42 55.7	−40.9	23.1	43 50.8	−40.5	23.4	44 45.8	−40.1	23.8	60
41 19.1	41.7	21.7	42 14.8	41.4	22.1	43 10.3	41.0	22.4	44 05.7	40.6	22.8	61
40 37.4	42.2	20.8	41 33.4	41.9	21.1	42 29.3	41.5	21.4	43 25.1	41.1	21.8	62
39 55.2	42.7	19.8	40 51.5	42.3	20.1	41 47.8	42.0	20.4	42 44.0	41.6	20.8	63
39 12.5	43.0	18.9	40 09.2	42.7	19.2	41 05.8	42.4	19.5	42 02.4	42.2	19.8	64
38 29.5	−43.5	18.0	39 26.5	−43.2	18.3	40 23.4	−42.9	18.6	41 20.2	−42.6	18.8	65
37 46.0	43.8	17.2	38 43.3	43.6	17.4	39 40.5	43.3	17.6	40 37.6	43.0	17.9	66
37 02.2	44.2	16.3	37 59.7	43.9	16.5	38 57.2	43.7	16.7	39 54.6	43.4	17.0	67
36 18.0	44.6	15.5	37 15.8	44.4	15.7	38 13.5	44.1	15.9	39 11.2	43.9	16.1	68
35 33.4	44.9	14.6	36 31.4	44.6	14.8	37 29.4	44.4	15.0	38 27.3	44.2	15.2	69
34 48.5	−45.2	13.8	35 46.8	−45.1	14.0	36 45.0	−44.9	14.2	37 43.1	−44.6	14.4	70
34 03.3	45.5	13.0	35 01.7	45.3	13.2	36 00.1	45.1	13.3	36 58.5	44.9	13.5	71
33 17.8	45.8	12.2	34 16.4	45.6	12.4	35 15.0	45.4	12.5	36 13.6	45.3	12.7	72
32 32.0	46.1	11.5	33 30.8	45.9	11.6	34 29.6	45.8	11.7	35 28.3	45.6	11.9	73
31 45.9	46.3	10.7	32 44.9	46.2	10.8	33 43.8	46.1	11.0	34 42.7	45.9	11.1	74
30 59.6	−46.6	10.0	31 58.7	−46.5	10.1	32 57.7	−46.3	10.2	33 56.8	−46.2	10.3	75
30 13.0	46.8	9.2	31 12.2	46.7	9.3	32 11.4	46.6	9.4	33 10.6	46.5	9.5	76
29 26.2	47.1	8.5	30 25.5	47.0	8.6	31 24.8	46.8	8.7	32 24.1	46.7	8.8	77
28 39.1	47.3	7.8	29 38.5	47.1	7.9	30 38.0	47.1	8.0	31 37.4	47.0	8.1	78
27 51.8	47.5	7.1	28 51.4	47.4	7.2	29 50.9	47.3	7.2	30 50.4	47.2	7.3	79
27 04.3	−47.6	6.4	28 04.0	−47.6	6.5	29 03.6	−47.6	6.5	30 03.2	−47.5	6.6	80
26 16.7	47.9	5.7	27 16.4	47.9	5.8	28 16.0	47.7	5.8	29 15.7	47.6	5.9	81
25 28.8	48.1	5.1	26 28.5	47.9	5.1	27 28.3	47.9	5.2	28 28.1	47.9	5.2	82
24 40.7	48.2	4.4	25 40.6	48.2	4.4	26 40.4	48.2	4.5	27 40.2	48.1	4.5	83
23 52.5	48.4	3.8	24 52.4	48.4	3.8	25 52.2	48.3	3.8	26 52.1	48.3	3.9	84
23 04.1	−48.5	3.1	24 04.0	−48.5	3.1	25 03.9	−48.4	3.2	26 03.8	−48.4	3.2	85
22 15.6	48.7	2.5	23 15.5	48.6	2.5	24 15.5	48.7	2.5	25 15.4	48.6	2.5	86
21 26.9	48.8	1.8	22 26.9	48.9	1.9	23 26.8	48.8	1.9	24 26.8	48.8	1.9	87
20 38.1	49.0	1.2	21 38.0	48.9	1.2	22 38.0	48.9	1.2	23 38.0	48.9	1.3	88
19 49.1	49.1	0.6	20 49.1	49.1	0.6	21 49.1	49.1	0.6	22 49.1	49.1	0.6	89
19 00.0	−49.2	0.0	20 00.0	−49.2	0.0	21 00.0	−49.2	0.0	22 00.0	−49.2	0.0	90
19°			20°			21°			22°			

35°, 325° L.H.A. **LATITUDE SAME NAME AS DECLINATION**

Figure 18.4a. Excerpt from H.O. Pub. No. 229 *for solving great-circle example.*

61°, 299° L.H.A. **LATITUDE SAME NAME AS DECLINATION**

N. Lat. {L.H.A. greater than 180°......Zn=Z; L.H.A. less than 180°............Zn=360°−Z}

Dec.	15°			16°			17°			18°			19°			20°			21°			22°			Dec.
	Hc	d	Z	Hc	d	Z	Hc	d	Z	Hc	d	Z	Hc	d	Z	Hc	d	Z	Hc	d	Z	Hc	d	Z	
°	° ′	′	°	° ′	′	°	° ′	′	°	° ′	′	°	° ′	′	°	° ′	′	°	° ′	′	°	° ′	′	°	°
0	27 55.4	+17.3	98.2	27 46.6	+18.5	98.7	27 37.3	+19.5	99.2	27 27.4	+20.7	99.7	27 17.0	+21.8	100.2	27 06.1	+22.8	100.7	26 54.7	+23.9	101.2	26 42.7	+25.0	101.7	0
1	28 12.7	16.8	97.1	28 05.1	17.9	97.6	27 56.8	19.1	98.1	27 48.1	20.1	98.7	27 38.8	21.2	99.2	27 28.9	22.4	99.7	27 18.6	23.4	100.2	27 07.7	24.5	100.7	1
2	28 29.5	16.3	96.0	28 23.0	17.4	96.5	28 15.9	18.5	97.1	28 08.2	19.7	97.6	28 00.0	20.8	98.1	27 51.3	21.9	98.6	27 42.0	23.0	99.2	27 32.2	24.0	99.7	2
3	28 45.8	15.7	94.9	28 40.4	16.9	95.4	28 34.4	18.1	96.0	28 27.9	19.2	96.5	28 20.8	20.3	97.1	28 13.2	21.3	97.6	28 05.0	22.4	98.1	27 56.2	23.6	98.6	3
4	29 01.5	15.3	93.8	28 57.3	16.4	94.3	28 52.5	17.5	94.9	28 47.1	18.6	95.4	28 41.1	19.8	96.0	28 34.5	20.9	96.5	28 27.4	22.0	97.1	28 19.8	23.1	97.6	4
5	29 16.8	+14.6	92.7	29 13.7	+15.8	93.2	29 10.0	+16.9	93.8	29 05.7	+18.1	94.4	29 00.9	+19.2	94.9	28 55.4	+20.4	95.5	28 49.4	+21.5	96.0	28 42.9	+22.6	96.6	5
6	29 31.4	14.1	91.6	29 29.5	15.2	92.1	29 26.9	16.5	92.7	29 23.8	17.6	93.3	29 20.1	18.7	93.8	29 15.8	19.9	94.4	29 10.9	21.0	94.9	29 05.5	22.1	95.5	6
7	29 45.5	13.5	90.5	29 44.7	14.7	91.0	29 43.4	15.8	91.6	29 41.4	17.0	92.2	29 38.8	18.2	92.7	29 35.7	19.3	93.3	29 31.9	20.5	93.9	29 27.6	21.6	94.4	7
8	29 59.0	13.0	89.3	29 59.4	14.2	89.9	29 59.2	15.3	90.5	29 58.4	16.5	91.1	29 57.0	17.6	91.6	29 55.0	18.8	92.2	29 52.4	19.9	92.8	29 49.2	21.0	93.4	8
9	30 12.0	12.3	88.2	30 13.6	13.5	88.8	30 14.5	14.8	89.4	30 14.9	15.9	89.9	30 14.6	17.1	90.5	30 13.8	18.2	91.1	30 12.3	19.4	91.7	30 10.2	20.6	92.3	9
10	30 24.3	+11.8	87.1	30 27.1	+13.0	87.7	30 29.3	+14.1	88.2	30 30.8	+15.3	88.8	30 31.7	+16.5	89.4	30 32.0	+17.7	90.0	30 31.7	+18.8	90.6	30 30.8	+19.9	91.2	10
11	30 36.1	11.2	85.9	30 40.1	12.3	86.5	30 43.4	13.6	87.1	30 46.1	14.8	87.7	30 48.2	15.9	88.3	30 49.7	17.1	88.9	30 50.5	18.3	89.5	30 50.7	19.5	90.1	11
12	30 47.3	10.6	84.8	30 52.4	11.8	85.4	30 57.0	12.9	86.0	31 00.9	14.1	86.6	31 04.1	15.4	87.2	31 06.8	16.5	87.8	31 08.8	17.7	88.4	31 10.2	18.8	89.0	12
13	30 57.9	9.9	83.6	31 04.2	11.2	84.2	31 09.9	12.4	84.8	31 15.0	13.6	85.4	31 19.5	14.7	86.0	31 23.3	15.9	86.7	31 26.5	17.1	87.3	31 29.0	18.3	87.9	13
14	31 07.8	9.4	82.5	31 15.4	10.5	83.1	31 22.3	11.7	83.7	31 28.6	12.9	84.3	31 34.2	14.1	84.9	31 39.2	15.3	85.5	31 43.6	16.5	86.1	31 47.3	17.7	86.8	14
15	31 17.2	+8.7	81.3	31 25.9	+10.0	81.9	31 34.0	+11.2	82.5	31 41.5	+12.3	83.2	31 48.3	+13.6	83.8	31 54.5	+14.7	84.4	32 00.1	+15.9	85.0	32 05.0	+17.1	85.6	15
16	31 25.9	8.1	80.2	31 35.9	9.3	80.8	31 45.2	10.5	81.4	31 53.8	11.7	82.0	32 01.9	12.9	82.6	32 09.2	14.1	83.2	32 16.0	15.3	83.9	32 22.1	16.4	84.5	16
17	31 34.0	7.5	79.0	31 45.2	8.6	79.6	31 55.7	9.8	80.2	32 05.5	11.1	80.8	32 14.8	12.2	81.5	32 23.3	13.5	82.1	32 31.3	14.6	82.7	32 38.5	15.9	83.4	17
18	31 41.5	6.8	77.8	31 53.8	8.1	78.5	32 05.5	9.3	79.1	32 16.6	10.4	79.7	32 27.0	11.6	80.3	32 36.8	12.8	80.9	32 45.9	14.0	81.6	32 54.4	15.2	82.2	18
19	31 48.3	6.2	76.7	32 01.9	7.3	77.3	32 14.8	8.5	77.9	32 27.0	9.8	78.5	32 38.6	11.0	79.1	32 49.6	12.2	79.8	32 59.9	13.4	80.4	33 09.6	14.6	81.1	19
20	31 54.5	+5.6	75.5	32 09.2	+6.8	76.1	32 23.3	+8.0	76.7	32 36.8	+9.1	77.3	32 49.6	+10.3	78.0	33 01.8	+11.5	78.6	33 13.3	+12.7	79.2	33 24.2	+13.9	79.9	20
21	32 00.1	4.9	74.3	32 16.0	6.1	74.9	32 31.3	7.2	75.6	32 45.9	8.3	76.2	32 59.9	9.7	76.8	33 13.3	10.9	77.4	33 26.0	12.1	78.1	33 38.1	13.3	78.7	21
22	32 05.0	4.2	73.2	32 22.1	5.4	73.8	32 38.5	6.6	74.4	32 54.4	7.8	75.0	33 09.6	9.0	75.6	33 24.2	10.2	76.3	33 38.1	11.4	76.9	33 51.4	12.5	77.6	22
23	32 09.2	3.6	72.0	32 27.5	4.7	72.6	32 45.1	6.0	73.2	33 02.2	7.1	73.8	33 18.6	8.3	74.4	33 34.4	9.5	75.1	33 49.5	10.7	75.7	34 03.9	12.0	76.4	23
24	32 12.8	2.9	70.8	32 32.2	4.1	71.4	32 51.1	5.3	72.0	33 09.3	6.5	72.6	33 26.9	7.6	73.3	33 43.9	8.8	73.9	34 00.2	10.0	74.5	34 15.9	11.2	75.2	24
25	32 15.7	+2.3	69.6	32 36.3	+3.5	70.2	32 56.4	+4.6	70.8	33 15.8	+5.7	71.4	33 34.5	+7.0	72.1	33 52.7	+8.1	72.7	34 10.2	+9.4	73.3	34 27.1	+10.5	74.0	25
26	32 18.0	1.6	68.4	32 39.8	2.7	69.0	33 01.0	3.9	69.6	33 21.5	5.1	70.2	33 41.5	6.3	70.9	34 00.8	7.5	71.5	34 19.6	8.6	72.2	34 37.6	9.8	72.8	26
27	32 19.6	1.0	67.3	32 42.5	2.1	67.8	33 04.9	3.2	68.4	33 26.6	4.4	69.1	33 47.8	5.5	69.7	34 08.3	6.7	70.3	34 28.2	7.9	71.0	34 47.4	9.2	71.6	27
28	32 20.6	+0.3	66.1	32 44.6	1.4	66.7	33 08.1	2.6	67.3	33 31.0	3.7	67.9	33 53.3	4.9	68.5	34 15.0	6.1	69.1	34 36.1	7.2	69.8	34 56.6	8.4	70.4	28
29	32 20.9	−0.4	64.9	32 46.0	0.8	65.5	33 10.7	1.9	66.1	33 34.7	3.1	66.7	33 58.2	4.2	67.3	34 21.1	5.3	67.9	34 43.3	6.5	68.5	35 05.0	7.7	69.2	29
30	32 20.5	−1.1	63.7	32 46.8	+0.1	64.3	33 12.6	+1.1	64.9	33 37.8	+2.3	65.5	34 02.4	+3.4	66.1	34 26.4	+4.6	66.7	34 49.8	+5.8	67.3	35 12.7	+6.9	68.0	30
31	32 19.4	1.7	62.5	32 46.9	−0.6	63.1	33 13.7	+0.5	63.7	33 40.1	1.6	64.3	34 05.8	2.8	64.9	34 31.0	3.9	65.5	34 55.6	5.1	66.1	35 19.6	6.2	66.8	31
32	32 17.7	2.3	61.3	32 46.3	1.3	61.9	33 14.2	−0.1	62.5	33 41.7	0.9	63.1	34 08.6	2.1	63.7	34 34.9	3.2	64.3	35 00.7	4.3	64.9	35 25.8	5.5	65.5	32
33	32 15.4	3.1	60.2	32 45.0	2.0	60.7	33 14.1	0.9	61.3	33 42.6	+0.3	61.9	34 10.7	1.3	62.5	34 38.1	2.5	63.1	35 05.0	3.6	63.7	35 31.3	4.8	64.3	33
34	32 12.3	3.6	59.0	32 43.0	2.6	59.5	33 13.2	1.6	60.1	33 42.9	−0.5	60.7	34 12.0	+0.6	61.2	34 40.6	1.7	61.8	35 08.6	2.9	62.5	35 36.1	4.0	63.1	34
35	32 08.7	−4.4	57.8	32 40.4	−3.3	58.3	33 11.6	−2.2	58.9	33 42.4	−1.2	59.5	34 12.6	−0.1	60.0	34 42.3	+1.0	60.6	35 11.5	+2.1	61.2	35 40.1	+3.2	61.9	35
36	32 04.3	5.0	56.6	32 37.1	4.0	57.1	33 09.4	2.9	57.7	33 41.2	1.8	58.3	34 12.5	0.7	58.8	34 43.3	+0.3	59.4	35 13.6	1.4	60.0	35 43.3	2.5	60.6	36
37	31 59.3	5.6	55.4	32 33.1	4.6	56.0	33 06.5	3.6	56.5	33 39.4	2.6	57.1	34 11.8	1.6	57.6	34 43.6	−0.4	58.2	35 15.0	+0.6	58.8	35 45.8	1.7	59.4	37
38	31 53.7	6.3	54.3	32 28.5	5.3	54.8	33 02.9	4.3	55.3	33 36.8	3.2	55.9	34 10.2	2.2	56.4	34 43.2	1.2	57.0	35 15.6	−0.1	57.6	35 47.5	1.0	58.2	38
39	31 47.4	6.9	53.1	32 23.2	5.9	53.6	32 58.6	4.9	54.1	33 33.6	4.0	54.7	34 08.0	2.9	55.2	34 42.0	1.9	55.8	35 15.5	0.8	56.3	35 48.5	+0.3	56.9	39
40	31 40.5	−7.6	51.9	32 17.3	−6.6	52.4	32 53.7	−5.7	52.9	33 29.6	−4.6	53.5	34 05.1	3.6	54.0	34 40.1	−2.6	54.6	35 14.7	−1.6	55.1	35 48.8	−0.6	55.7	40
41	31 32.9	8.2	50.8	32 10.7	7.3	51.2	32 48.0	6.3	51.7	33 25.0	5.4	52.3	34 01.5	4.4	52.8	34 37.5	3.3	53.3	35 13.1	2.3	53.9	35 48.2	1.2	54.5	41
42	31 24.7	8.8	49.6	32 03.4	7.9	50.1	32 41.7	6.9	50.6	33 19.6	6.0	51.1	33 57.1	5.0	51.6	34 34.2	4.1	52.1	35 10.8	3.0	52.7	35 47.0	2.1	53.2	42
43	31 15.9	9.4	48.4	31 55.5	8.5	48.9	32 34.8	7.6	49.4	33 13.6	6.6	49.9	33 52.1	5.7	50.4	34 30.1	4.7	50.9	35 07.8	3.8	51.5	35 44.9	2.8	52.0	43
44	31 06.5	10.1	47.3	31 47.0	9.2	47.7	32 27.2	8.3	48.2	33 07.0	7.4	48.7	33 46.4	6.5	49.2	34 25.4	5.5	49.7	35 04.0	4.5	50.2	35 42.1	3.5	50.8	44
45	30 56.4	−10.7	46.1	31 37.8	−9.8	46.6	32 18.9	−8.9	47.0	32 59.6	−8.0	47.5	33 39.9	−7.1	48.0	34 19.9	−6.2	48.5	34 59.5	−5.3	49.0	35 38.6	−4.3	49.6	45
46	30 45.7	11.2	45.0	31 28.0	10.4	45.4	32 10.0	9.6	45.9	32 51.6	8.7	46.3	33 32.8	7.8	46.8	34 13.7	6.9	47.3	34 54.2	6.0	47.8	35 34.3	5.0	48.3	46
47	30 34.5	11.9	43.9	31 17.6	11.0	44.3	32 00.4	10.2	44.7	32 42.9	9.4	45.1	33 25.0	8.4	45.6	34 06.8	7.6	46.1	34 48.2	6.6	46.6	35 29.3	5.8	47.1	47
48	30 22.6	12.4	42.7	31 06.6	11.7	43.1	31 50.2	10.8	43.5	32 33.5	10.0	44.0	33 16.6	9.2	44.4	33 59.2	8.3	44.9	34 41.6	7.4	45.4	35 23.5	6.5	45.9	48
49	30 10.2	13.1	41.6	30 54.9	12.2	42.0	31 39.4	11.5	42.4	32 23.5	10.6	42.8	33 07.4	9.8	43.2	33 50.9	8.9	43.7	34 34.2	8.2	44.2	35 17.0	7.2	44.7	49
50	29 57.1	−13.6	40.5	30 42.7	−12.9	40.8	31 27.9	−12.0	41.2	32 12.9	−11.3	41.6	32 57.6	−10.5	42.1	33 42.0	−9.7	42.5	34 26.0	−8.8	43.0	35 09.8	−8.0	43.4	50
51	29 43.5	14.1	39.3	30 29.8	13.4	39.7	31 15.9	12.7	40.1	32 01.6	11.9	40.5	32 47.1	11.1	40.9	33 32.3	10.3	41.3	34 17.2	9.5	41.8	35 01.8	8.7	42.2	51
52	29 29.4	14.8	38.2	30 16.4	14.0	38.6	31 03.2	13.3	38.9	31 49.7	12.5	39.3	32 36.0	11.8	39.7	33 22.0	11.0	40.1	34 07.7	10.2	40.6	34 53.1	9.4	41.0	52
53	29 14.6	15.3	37.1	30 02.4	14.6	37.4	30 49.9	13.9	37.8	31 37.2	13.2	38.2	32 24.2	12.4	38.6	33 11.0	11.7	39.0	33 57.5	10.9	39.4	34 43.7	10.1	39.8	53
54	28 59.3	15.8	36.0	29 47.8	15.2	36.3	30 36.0	14.4	36.7	31 24.0	13.7	37.0	32 11.8	13.0	37.4	32 59.3	12.3	37.8	33 46.6	11.5	38.2	34 33.6	10.8	38.6	54
55	28 43.5	−16.3	34.9	29 32.6	−15.7	35.2	30 21.6	−15.1	35.5	31 10.3	−14.4	35.9	31 58.8	−13.7	36.3	32 47.0	−12.9	36.6	33 35.1	−12.3	37.0	34 22.8	−11.5	37.4	55
56	28 27.2	16.9	33.8	29 16.9	16.2	34.1	30 06.5	15.6	34.4	30 55.9	14.9	34.8	31 45.1	14.3	35.1	32 34.1	13.6	35.5	33 22.8	12.9	35.9	34 11.3	12.1	36.2	56
57	28 10.3	17.4	32.7	29 00.7	16.8	33.0	29 50.9	16.1	33.3	30 41.0	15.6	33.6	31 30.8	14.8	34.0	32 20.5	14.2	34.3	33 09.9	13.5	34.7	33 59.2	12.9	35.1	57
58	27 52.9	17.9	31.6	28 43.9	17.3	31.9	29 34.8	16.7	32.2	30 25.4	16.0	32.5	31 16.0	15.5	32.8	32 06.3	14.9	33.2	32 56.4	14.2	33.5	33 46.3	13.5	33.9	58
59	27 35.0	18.4	30.5	28 26.6	17.8	30.8	29 18.1	17.3	31.1	30 09.4	16.7	31.4	31 00.5	16.1	31.7	31 51.4	15.4	32.0	32 42.2	14.8	32.4	33 32.8	14.2	32.7	59
60	27 16.6	−18.9	29.5	28 08.8	−18.4	29.7	29 00.8	−17.8	30.0	29 52.7	17.2	30.3	30 44.4	−16.6	30.6	31 36.0	−16.1	30.9	32 27.4	−15.4	31.2	33 18.6	−14.8	31.6	60
61	26 57.7	19.3	28.4	27 50.4	18.8	28.7	28 43.0	18.3	28.9	29 35.5	17.8	29.2	30 27.8	17.2	29.5	31 19.9	16.6	29.8	32 12.0	16.1	30.1	33 03.8	15.5	30.4	61
62	26 38.4	19.9	27.3	27 31.6	19.3	27.6	28 24.7	18.8	27.8	29 17.7	18.3	28.1	30 10.6	17.8	28.4	31 03.3	17.2	28.6	31 55.9	16.7	28.9	32 48.3	16.1	29.2	62
63	26 18.5	20.3	26.3	27 12.3	19.8	26.5	28 05.9	19.3	26.8	28 59.4	18.8	27.0	29 52.8	18.3	27.3	30 46.1	17.8	27.5	31 39.2	17.2	27.8	32 32.2	16.7	28.1	63
64	25 58.2	20.7	25.2	26 52.5	20.3	25.5	27 46.6	19.8	25.7	28 40.6	19.3	25.9	29 34.5	18.8	26.2	30 28.3	18.3	26.4	31 22.0	17.9	26.7	32 15.5	17.3	27.0	64
65	25 37.5	−21.2	24.2	26 32.2	−20.8	24.4	27 26.8	−20.3	24.6	28 21.3	−19.9	24.8	29 15.7	−19.4	25.1	30 10.0	−18.9	25.3	31 04.1	−18.4	25.6	31 58.2	−17.9	25.8	65
66	25 16.3	21.6	23.2	26 11.4	21.2	23.4	27 06.5	20.8	23.6	28 01.4	20.3	23.8	28 56.3	19.9	24.0	29 51.1	19.5	24.2	30 45.7	18.9	24.5	31 40.3	18.5	24.7	66
67	24 54.7	22.0	22.1	25 50.2	21.6	22.3	26 45.7	21.2	22.5	27 41.1	20.8	22.7	28 36.4	20.4	22.9	29 31.6	19.9	23.1	30 26.8	19.6	23.4	31 21.8	19.1	23.6	67
68	24 32.7	22.5	21.1	25 28.6	22.1	21.3	26 24.5	21.7	21.5	27 20.3	21.3	21.6	28 16.0	20.9	21.8	29 11.7	20.5	22.0	30 07.2	20.0	22.3	31 02.7	19.6	22.5	68
69	24 10.2	22.8	20.1	25 06.5	22.5	20.3	26 02.8	22.1	20.4	26 59.0	21.8	20.6	27 55.1	21.4	20.8	28 51.2	21.0	21.0	29 47.2	20.6	21.2	30 43.1	20.2	21.4	69
70	23 47.4	−23.3	19.1	24 44.0	−22.9	19.2	25 40.7	−22.6	19.4	26 37.2	−22.2	19.5	27 33.7	−21.8	19.7	28 30.2	−21.5	19.9	29 26.6	−21.1	20.1	30 22.9	−20.7	20.3	70
71	23 24.1	23.6	18.1	24 21.1	23.3	18.2	25 18.1	23.0	18.4	26 15.0	22.6	18.5	27 11.9	22.3	18.7	28 08.7	22.0	18.8	29 05.5	21.7	19.0	30 02.2	21.3	19.2	71
72	23 00.5	24.0	17.1	23 57.8	23.7	17.2	24 55.1	23.4	17.3	25 52.4	23.1	17.5	26 49.6	22.8	17.6	27 46.7	22.4	17.8	28 43.8	22.1	18.0	29 40.9	21.8	18.1	72
73	22 36.5	24.4	16.1	23 34.1	24.1	16.2	24 31.7	23.8	16.3	25 29.3	23.5	16.5	26 26.8	23.2	16.6	27 24.3	22.9	16.7	28 21.7	22.6	16.9	29 19.1	22.3	17.1	73
74	22 12.1	24.7	15.1	23 10.0	24.4	15.2	24 07.9	24.2	15.3	25 05.8	24.0	15.4	26 03.6	23.7	15.6	27 01.4	23.4	15.7	27 59.1	23.1	15.8	28 56.8	22.8	16.0	74
75	21 47.4	−25.1	14.1	22 45.6	−24.9	14.2	23 43.7	−24.6	14.3	24 41.8	−24.3	14.4	25 39.9	−24.0	14.5	26 38.0	−23.8	14.7	27 36.0	−23.5	14.8	28 34.0	−23.3	14.9	75
76	21 22.3	25.4	13.1	22 20.7	25.1	13.2	23 19.1	24.9	13.3	24 17.5	24.7	13.4	25 15.9	24.5	13.5	26 14.2	24.3	13.6	27 12.5	24.0	13.8	28 10.7	23.7	13.9	76
77	20 56.9	25.7	12.2	21 55.6	25.6	12.2	22 54.2	25.3	12.3	23 52.8	25.1	12.4	24 51.4	24.9	12.5	25 49.9	24.6	12.6	26 48.5	24.5	12.7	27 47.0	24.2	12.8	77
78	20 31.2	26.1	11.2	21 30.0	25.8	11.3	22 28.9	25.7	11.3	23 27.7	25.5	11.4	24 26.5	25.3	11.5	25 25.3	25.1	11.6	26 24.0	24.9	11.7	27 22.8	24.7	11.8	78
79	20 05.1	26.4	10.2	21 04.2	26.2	10.3	22 03.2	26.0	10.4	23 02.2	25.9	10.4	24 01.2	25.7	10.5	25 00.2	25.5	10.6	25 59.1	25.3	10.7	26 58.1	25.1	10.8	79
80	19 38.7	−26.6	9.3	20 38.0	−26.6	9.3	21 37.2	−26.4	9.4	22 36.3	−26.2	9.5	23 35.5	−26.0	9.5	24 34.7	−25.9	9.6	25 33.8	−25.7	9.7	26 33.0	−25.6	9.8	80
81	19 12.1	27.0	8.3	20 11.4	26.8	8.4	21 10.8	26.7	8.4	22 10.1	26.5	8.5	23 09.5	26.4	8.6	24 08.8	26.2	8.6	25 08.1	26.1	8.7	26 07.4	25.9	8.8	81
82	18 45.1	27.2	7.4	19 44.6	27.1	7.4	20 44.1	27.0	7.5	21 43.6	26.9	7.5	22 43.1	26.8	7.6	23 42.6	26.7	7.6	24 42.0	26.5	7.7	25 41.5	26.4	7.8	82
83	18 17.9	27.5	6.4	19 17.5	27.4	6.5	20 17.1	27.3	6.5	21 16.7	27.2	6.6	22 16.3	27.1	6.6	23 15.9	27.0	6.7	24 15.5	26.9	6.7	25 15.1	26.8	6.8	83
84	17 50.4	27.8	5.5	18 50.1	27.7	5.5	19 49.8	27.6	5.6	20 49.5	27.5	5.6	21 49.2	27.4	5.7	22 48.9	27.3	5.7	23 48.6	27.2	5.7	24 48.3	27.1	5.8	84
85	17 22.6	−28.1	4.6	18 22.4	−28.0	4.6	19 22.2	−27.9	4.6	20 22.0	−27.8	4.7	21 21.8	−27.8	4.7	22 21.6	−27.7	4.7	23 21.4	−27.6	4.8	24 21.2	−27.5	4.8	85
86	16 54.5	28.2	3.7	17 54.4	28.2	3.7	18 54.3	28.2	3.7	19 54.2	28.1	3.7	20 54.0	28.0	3.7	21 53.9	28.0	3.8	22 53.8	28.0	3.8	23 53.7	27.9	3.8	86
87	16 26.3	28.6	2.7	17 26.2	28.5	2.8	18 26.1	28.4	2.8	19 26.1	28.5	2.8	20 26.0	28.4	2.8	21 25.9	28.3	2.8	22 25.8	28.3	2.8	23 25.8	28.3	2.9	87
88	15 57.7	28.7	1.8	16 57.7	28.7	1.8	17 57.7	28.7	1.8	18 57.6	28.6	1.8	19 57.6	28.7	1.9	20 57.6	28.7	1.9	21 57.5	28.6	1.9	22 57.5	28.6	1.9	88
89	15 29.0	29.0	0.9	16 29.0	29.0	0.9	17 29.0	29.0	0.9	18 29.0	29.0	0.9	19 28.9	28.9	0.9	20 28.9	28.9	0.9	21 28.9	28.9	0.9	22 28.9	28.9	0.9	89
90	15 00.0	−29.2	0.0	16 00.0	−29.2	0.0	17 00.0	−29.2	0.0	18 00.0	−29.2	0.0	19 00.0	−29.2	0.0	20 00.0	−29.2	0.0	21 00.0	−29.2	0.0	22 00.0	−29.2	0.0	90
	15°			16°			17°			18°			19°			20°			21°			22°			

61°, 299° L.H.A. **LATITUDE SAME NAME AS DECLINATION**

Figure 18.4b. Extract from H.O. Pub. No. 229 *for posttest problem.*

Form F4. Reduction with *H.O. Pub. No. 229*

Navigator	Hawaii
Zone date	
DR lat.	21 _____ N (or) S
DR long.	157 _____ E (or) W

Planet/star name <u>San Francisco</u>
Sun/moon limb: Upper/Lower

1. (Not applicable)

2. To find declination

2.1 Dec. _____ N (or) S d ____ ±
2.2 d corr. _____ (skip for star)
2.3 Declination 38° _____ N (or) S

3. To find LHA

3.1 GHA ___ hrs. _____ v ____
3.2 corr. ___ m ___ s _____
3.3 v corr. _____ (skip for star)
3.4 GHA 122° _____
3.5 Assumed long. 157° _____ (add if E)
3.6 LHA −35° 00′ (enter at 5.3)

4. (Not applicable)

5. Solution by *H.O. Pub. No. 229*

5.1 Dec. difference __00′__
5.2 Dec. same _x_ name or contrary ___ name to lat.
5.3 LHA __−35° = 325° 00′__
5.4 Assumed lat. 21°00′ (nearest whole degree)
5.5 Tabulated H __55°24.7__ d 20.5 Z __52.8__ (to 5.11)
5.6 d corr. __0_____ (from dec. diff.)
5.7 H_c __55°24.7__ (enter at 5.9)
5.8 H_o _____
5.9 H_c _____
5.10 $H_o − H_c$ _____ (plus is toward Zn)
5.11 Zn 52.8 _____ (see rule below)

Rule for azimuth, Zn:
Northern Hemisphere: LHA < 180°: Zn = 360° − Z
LHA > 180°: Zn = Z
Southern Hemisphere: LHA < 180°: Zn = 180° + Z
LHA > 180°: Zn = 180° − Z

Figure 18.5.

of the star. Read out the values: $H_c = 55°24.7$ and $Z = 52.8$. Ignore the value of d. (This value is the difference of H_c for a 1° difference of declination, as you can easily verify. It is used for interpolating to minutes of declination, but we have rounded to the nearest degree, so it is not needed.) H_c is the great-circle distance to the destination, measured in degrees. (H_c is also the computed altitude of a star whose GP is at the location of the destination, that is, directly over San Francisco.) To convert to NM, multiply by 60. The result is 55° or $55 \times 60 = 3300$ NM.

- **Step 6**—To convert from Z to Zn, the azimuth of the destination, follow the rule at the bottom of the form, or make a sketch and derive the relationship by inspection. Result: LHA > 180°, so Zn = Z, and the initial course is about 053T.

POSTTEST

18.1 Compute the initial heading and distance from lat. 32°20′N, long. 66°45′W (near Bermuda) to Penzance, England (lat. 50°05′N, long. 5°35′W). See Figure 18. 4b for an excerpt from *H.O. Pub. No. 229.*

WAY POINTS ON THE GREAT-CIRCLE COURSE

The previous section showed how to compute the heading to be followed at the start of a great-circle course, but sailing a great circle requires gradually altering the ship's heading. The navigator needs to follow a series of way points and intermediate headings in order to approach the final destination along a great circle. (Remember, the rhumb line course that follows a constant heading is not a great circle.)

Figure 18.6 illustrates a way point. The locations of the way points can be calculated in advance. This can most easily be done on a gnomonic chart and then transferred to a Mercator, or it can be done on a hand-held calculator.

But rather than calculate the way points in advance, a more practical approach is to start off on the initial course—doing as well as you can to follow the prescribed heading—and then determine your position after a day or two. Do this by actual measurement if you can, or by dead reckoning if necessary. Call this new position the first way point. From this way point, solve for the new heading and distance to your destination. Change the helm to fit the new course. Repeat this procedure every day or every few days, depending on your progress. This method takes account of the fact that you can never follow a predicted great-circle course as precisely as you might wish, given the difficulty of predicting winds and currents.

Bon voyage!

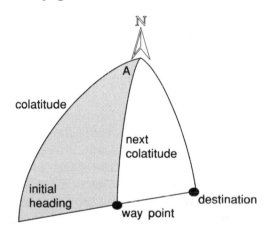

Figure 18.6. Location of a way point is found by solving the navigator's triangle with known initial azimuth and colatitude to find angle A (the LHA or difference of longitude) and next colatitude.

CHAPTER NINETEEN

Circles on the Globe

This was glorious sailing. A steady breeze; the light trade-wind clouds over our heads; the incomparable temperature of the Pacific [lat. 19° S.],—neither hot nor cold; a clear sun every day, and clear moon and stars each night; and new constellations rising in the south, and the familiar ones sinking in the north, as we went on our course,—"stemming nightly toward the pole." Already we had sunk the north star and the Great Bear in the northern horizon, and all hands looked out sharp to the southward for the Magellan Clouds, which each succeeding night, we expected to make. "The next time we see the north star," said one, "we shall be standing to the northward, the other side of the Horn." This was true enough, and no doubt it would be a welcome sight; for sailors say that in coming home from round Cape Horn or the Cape of Good Hope, the north star is the first land you make.

Richard Henry Dana, Jr., Two Years Before the Mast

INTRODUCTION

The sun and stars are so far away from earth that our planet would be a tiny dot if you went to one and looked back. This has an interesting consequence of great value to the navigator. When you observe a celestial object, its true direction is the same from all points on the globe of the earth. (This is not so for our moon. The direction of the moon depends on where you stand when you look at it. This leads to plenty of headaches when you come to reduce moon sights.) On the sky, the direction of any object is defined by its celestial coordinates (SHA and declination). On the other hand, the apparent direction with respect to your horizon depends on your location and on Greenwich mean time. This is the key to modern celestial navigation. If you know the time, and you know which star you are looking at, you can infer something about your location on the surface of the globe.

At any moment, every celestial object is directly overhead somewhere on earth. This is called its geographic point. The *Almanac* and the time will tell you where that point is. If you could accurately measure the azimuth and altitude of a celestial body, you could determine your distance and direction from its geographic point, and this would tell you where you are. But the measurement of azimuth is very difficult, and it has rarely been attempted by navigators at sea. You will have to content yourself with altitude measures, which will give your distance, but not direction, from the geographic point. This means that you will not completely determine your location from a single object. You will determine a circle of position (CoP) centered on the geographic point. Like the lines of position, discussed in earlier chapters, a CoP is a set of points which contains your location. You can be anywhere on the CoP. With several intersecting CoPs, you can find a unique point. This is the topic of this chapter.

RADAR FIX

A circle is a set of points on a plane that are the same distance from a specified point, called the center. In addition to giving distance, radar also permits determining the direction to the object by keeping track of the orientation of the antenna when the echo is received (Figure 19.1). The delay time of the echo, t, can be calculated from the distance D and the speed of light c as $t = 2D/c$. If t and c are known, D can be found. That is the principle of radar.

Celestial CoPs are derived from angles, rather than distances. The center of each celestial CoP is the geographic point (GP) of the celestial object, and the intersection of several CoPs determines a fix. Constructing the CoP on a globe is easy, but it is not very accurate unless the globe is large—this means it will be awkward to handle.

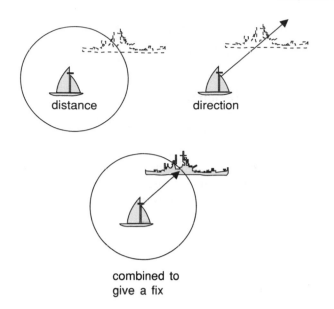

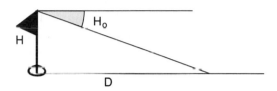

Figure 19.2. The first step in determining your distance from a flagpole of known height is to measure its vertical angle, H_0.

Figure 19.3. Making a scale drawing of the pole and constructing a back-sight line that makes an angle H_0 with the horizontal gives your location. Measurement then gives D. Alternatively, you can use trigonometry, as in the text.

Figure 19.1. Radar determines distance (and a circle of position) by the delay of the echo. It also determines the direction (and a line of position) by the orientation of the antenna. The combination of these two data will fix the position of the object relative to the radar equipment.

This chapter introduces CoPs on a globe and then applies them to sun sights in the tropics, where they occasionally can be made to fit on a chart. The next chapter discusses the more common case, when they can't.

ESTIMATING YOUR DISTANCE FROM A FLAGPOLE

Figure 19.2 shows a flagpole on a flat portion of the earth's surface. Suppose you know its height, H, and you want to find your distance by measuring it from the ground with a sextant. This will determine a CoP with its center at the base of the pole.

Suppose you find that the angular height from your position is H_0. To find your distance, you could make a scale drawing (Figure 19.3) of the pole and then draw a horizontal line from its top. At an angle H_0 from the horizontal line we draw a slanting line that will intersect the ground at your location. You can then measure the distance D from the drawing and compute its true value from the known scale of the drawing.

Alternatively, you can use the tangent function defined so that $H/D = \tan(H_0)$. Finding the numeri-

cal value in a trigonometric table, you can compute the desired distance from $D = H/\tan(H_0)$.

POSTTEST

19.1 You measure the angular height of a 60-foot flagpole and find it to be 30° above your head, which is 5 feet from the ground. How far are you from the base of the flagpole?

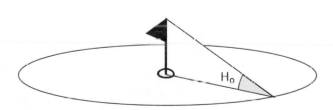

Figure 19.4. Circle of position around the flagpole. At any point on the circle, we would find the same angular height, H_0, for the flagpole. In doing a celestial circle of position, the tip of the flagpole is replaced by a celestial object, and a measurement of its altitude gives the navigator's distance from the point directly beneath the object.

NAVIGATING ON THE EDGE OF A CIRCULAR FLATLAND

Celestial CoPs look similar to the circle around this flagpole, but their construction differs from this example in two important ways. First, the celestial objects are extremely far away. Second, the surface of the earth is curved. Different navigators have different horizons and zeniths. If we observe that the direction of an object relative to our horizon has changed, that can only mean that the orientation of our horizon has changed. Either the earth has rotated and carried us with it, or we have moved along its surface. The *Nautical Almanac* keeps track of the earth's rotation, and we can determine a CoP on the earth if we can determine the zenith distance and geographical position of any celestial object.

To get the radius of the CoP from the zenith distance, let us take a simplified world, or *Flatland,* in the shape of a disc (Figure 19.5).

First, we must determine the radius of the circle, r. In our case, r = 3,440 nautical miles. The arc D in Figure 19.6 can be found from the ratio $D / (2\pi r) = \alpha / 360°$, or $D = (\alpha / 180°)\pi r$.

If we insert the radius of the earth into this expression we find:

$$D = 60 \, \alpha° \text{ (in NM)}$$

So if the zenith distance is 1° we have

$$\alpha = 1° \rightarrow D = 60 \text{ NM}$$

and if it is 1 arc-minute

$$\alpha = 1' \rightarrow D = 1 \text{ NM}$$

This is the rule we proclaimed in an earlier chapter; now we see where it came from. (It is no accident that it works out so nicely. This was the way the nautical mile was defined!)

POSTTEST

19.2 What distances in nautical miles correspond to the following zenith angles:

α	D (NM)
3°	_____
5°	_____
30'	_____
15'	_____

19.3 As an astronaut, you measure the zenith distance of the sun from a spot on the moon. You find it to be 10°, and then you quickly travel to the spot where the sun is directly overhead. You find the distance to be 158 NM. What do you infer for the radius of the moon?

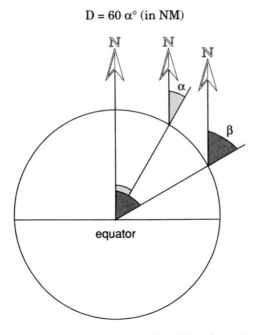

Figure 19.5. Our Flatland is a disc-shaped earth oriented toward Polaris and the NCP. As we move from the North Pole, the zenith distance α (alpha) increases. In this case β > α.

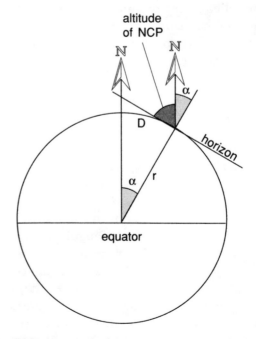

Figure 19.6. The navigator's distance from the GP of Polaris is D, and it can be computed from the zenith distance (alpha) and the known radius of the earth. The altitude is given by $H_0 = 90 - \alpha$.

CIRCLES OF POSITION ON A GLOBE

Now we must apply this to the globe. What do circles of position look like, and how do we plot them on a globe? The easiest way to start is to go back to our old friend, Polaris, because the GP of Polaris is always at the North Pole of the earth.

Latitudes: circles of position for Polaris

The latitude lines on a globe are ready-made circles of position (Figure 19.7). Their centers are at the North Pole, and their angular radius is the zenith distance of Polaris as seen from that latitude. The equator is a great circle and corresponds to Polaris on the horizon.

POSTTEST
19.4 If the CoP of the sun is a circle of longitude, what is the declination of the sun that day?

GP of a celestial object

Suppose you observe the sun and the moon at 1543 GMT on February 28, 1990. You find the center of the sun at an altitude of 54° and the center of the moon at an altitude of 30°. Using a globe, you can find your location.

First you need to find the GP of the sun and moon (see Figure 19.8). To find their exact coordinates you look in the *Almanac* for that date (Figure 19.9).

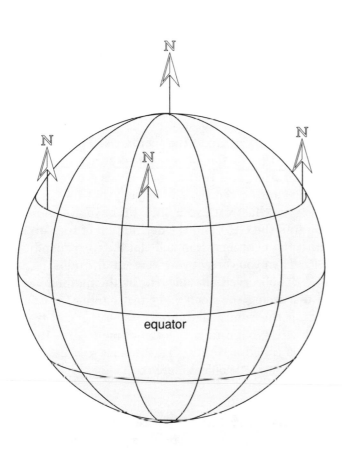

Figure 19.7. The earth as it might be seen from the moon, with latitude and longitude circles added. The latitude circles are circles of position for Polaris at the NCP. All points on a particular latitude circle see Polaris at an altitude equal to the latitude.

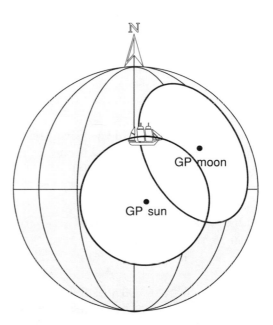

Figure 19.8. Earth as seen from the direction of the sun on February 28, 1990, at 1543 GMT. The geographic points (GP) of the sun and moon are indicated by the heavy dots, and two circles of position shown. All points on one CoP have the sun at the observed distance from the zenith (36°). A measurement of the sun's azimuth at that time would tell you where on the CoP you were, but this is not practical, although a rough estimate puts it in the south. So you must resort to using more than one CoP and finding their intersection. The larger circle represents the CoP for the moon, and the fix is at the ship. The other intersection can be rejected because the sun would have been to the north. See text for the calculations.

UT (GMT)	SUN		MOON				
d h	G.H.A. ° ′	Dec. ° ′	G.H.A. ° ′	v ′	Dec. ° ′	d ′	H.P. ′
28 00	176 49.8	S 8 08.8	146 03.6	10.2	N 9 45.8	15.8	59.9
01	191 49.9	07.8	160 32.8	10.2	10 01.6	15.8	59.9
02	206 50.0	06.9	175 02.0	10.1	10 17.4	15.6	59.9
03	221 50.1	.. 05.9	189 31.1	10.0	10 33.0	15.7	60.0
04	236 50.2	05.0	204 00.1	10.0	10 48.7	15.5	60.0
05	251 50.4	04.0	218 29.1	9.9	11 04.2	15.5	60.0
06	266 50.5	S 8 03.1	232 58.0	9.8	N11 19.7	15.5	60.0
W 07	281 50.6	02.1	247 26.8	9.8	11 35.2	15.4	60.0
E 08	296 50.7	01.2	261 55.6	9.8	11 50.6	15.3	60.0
D 09	311 50.8	8 00.3	276 24.4	9.7	12 05.9	15.2	60.0
N 10	326 50.9	7 59.3	290 53.1	9.6	12 21.1	15.2	60.0
E 11	341 51.0	58.4	305 21.7	9.5	12 36.3	15.1	60.0
S 12	356 51.2	S 7 57.4	319 50.2	9.5	N12 51.4	15.0	60.0
D 13	11 51.3	56.5	334 18.7	9.4	13 06.4	14.9	60.0
A 14	26 51.4	55.5	348 47.1	9.4	13 21.3	14.9	59.9
Y 15	41 51.5	.. 54.6	3 15.5	9.3	13 36.2	14.8	59.9
16	56 51.6	53.6	17 43.8	9.2	13 51.0	14.7	59.9
17	71 51.7	52.7	32 12.0	9.1	14 05.7	14.6	59.9
18	86 51.8	S 7 51.7	46 40.1	9.1	N14 20.3	14.5	59.9
19	101 52.0	50.8	61 08.2	9.0	14 34.8	14.5	59.9
20	116 52.1	49.8	75 36.2	9.0	14 49.3	14.4	59.9
21	131 52.2	.. 48.9	90 04.2	8.9	15 03.7	14.2	59.9
22	146 52.3	48.0	104 32.1	8.8	15 17.9	14.2	59.9
23	161 52.4	47.0	118 59.9	8.7	15 32.1	14.1	59.9

Figure 19.9. Excerpt from Nautical Almanac *for finding GHA sun on February 28, 1990, at 1543 GMT.*

Example—The calculation of the GP of the sun and moon are shown in the following table:

Date: February 28, 1990, 1543 GMT

	Sun	*Moon*
H_0	54°	30°
Zenith distance	36°	60°
GHA at 15 h	41°51.5	3°15′
Increment 43 m	10°45′	10°15′ (yellow pages)
GHA	52°36.5	13°30′
Dec.	7°55′S	13°46′N

Results:

Long.	52°36.5W	13°30′W
Lat.	7°55′S	13°46′N

With the help of an atlas, the GP of the sun is located in the valley of the Xingu river (a tributary of the Amazon) in Brazil, and the GP of the moon was in West Africa.

On Figure 19.8, a CoP has been drawn with a radius of 36° about the GP of the sun. All points on this circle will see the sun 36° from the zenith. The larger circle represents the CoP for the moon and it is drawn with a radius of 60°.

Activity—With a string, a ruler, and a globe, verify the great-circle distance (in degrees) from the GP of the sun in the valley of the Xingu to the Panama Canal.

POSTTEST

19.5 On February 28, 1990, at 1800 GMT, you observe the centers of the sun and the moon from the northern hemisphere at altitudes of 40° and 66°, respectively. On a globe of the earth, draw the GPs of the sun and moon and plot the CoPs. What are your latitude and longitude?

RUNNING FIX BY SUN SIGHTS IN THE TROPICS

When the celestial object is nearly overhead, the CoP is very small. You are close to its GP, and in such a situation you can draw the CoP on the chart. This is a common occurrence for the sun around noon in the tropics, and you can determine the location of your vessel by combining several altitude measurements of the sun.

Suppose you are at the spot marked by a ship in Figure 19.10. You observe the sun four times around noon and find that it comes within a few degrees of the zenith. This means that its GP will fit on the chart with your ship. From your *Almanac* you find the GHA and the declination of the sun at the times of observation and plot the corresponding GPs. Then you correct your sextant altitudes, h_s, to find the observed altitude, H_0, by the method used in discussing the noon sight in Chapter 15. Computing the zenith distances, 90° − H_0, you trace each circle, obtaining something like Figure 19.10. This is called a running fix, because you have observed the same object more than once.

POSTTEST

19.6 On February 28, 1990, you were off the east coast of Brazil and you made the following four observations of the altitude of the sun's lower limb. Your watch was set to GMT and there was no error. Find H_0 and zenith distance for each observation. Then find the GHA sun at each time and plot the circles of position. You noted that the sun was south of the zenith at noon. What were your longitude and latitude?

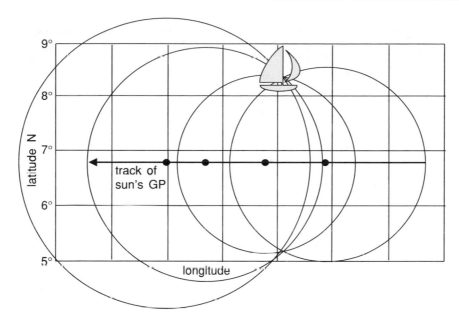

Figure 19.10. Schematic chart of the equatorial region showing the GPs of the sun at four times near noon. The navigator on the ship will measure four zenith distances. The location of the GPs are found in the Almanac, and when the CoPs are constructed, they all intersect at two points symmetrically placed north and south of the GP. One of these is the fix. The navigator resolves the ambiguity by noting that the sun was south of the zenith at noon, placing the navigator at the northern intersection.

Date: February 28, 1990; index error: 4′ off the arc

Time (GMT)	Observed h_s	Computed H_0	Zenith distance	Almanac GHA sun	Dec. sun
h m s	° ′				
14 02 00	87 43	——	——	——	——
14 05 00	88 25	——	——	——	——
14 09 00	89 08	——	——	——	——
14 12 00	88 53	——	——	——	——

CIRCLES OF POSITION FOR STARS

Stars near the zenith give small circles of position. You are near their geographic point, so the circles of position can be plotted directly on your chart. But you cannot usually find running fixes from the stars this way because your star sights are usually confined to a short interval during twilight. Thus, you cannot ordinarily obtain more than one CoP from a given star—the star will not have moved far enough during twilight.

But you can use the intersection of CoPs from different stars, as was illustrated for the sun and moon in Figure 19.8. Another example is shown in Figure 19.11, and the data are listed in Table 19.1

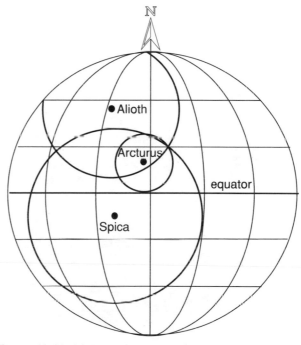

Figure 19.11. Globe of the earth with three geographical positions (GPs) drawn from the observations in Table 19.1. After measuring the height of each star, the navigator locates its GP and draws a CoP with a radius equal to the observed zenith distance. Their common intersection gives the navigator's position.

Table 19.1 Data for observations of three stars

Time: 15 July, 1990, 0100 GMT
GHA Aries: 307°38′

Star	Observation H_o	Observation Zenith distance	Almanac SHA	Almanac Dec.	Computed long.	Computed lat.
Arcturus	69°53′	20°	146°	19°N	94W	19°N
Alioth	52°14′	38°	166°	56°N	114W	56°N
Spica	38°59′	51°	159°	11° S	107W	11°S

POSTTEST

19.7 Set up another table like Table 19.1 and plot on a globe the GPs and CoPs given by the following observations to find your latitude and longitude. First you must find GHA Aries from the *Almanac*.

Time: 15 July, 1990, 0200 GMT
GHA Aries:

Star	Observation H_o	Observation Zenith distance	Almanac SHA	Almanac Dec.	Computed long.	Computed lat.
Arcturus	49°13′	____	____	____	____	____
Alioth	34°51′	____	____	____	____	____
Spica	24°15′	____	____	____	____	____

CHAPTER TWENTY

Sight Reduction for Lines of Position and Fixes

> ... Sextant observations of the sun, moon, or stars will give an accurate fix only if there is no blunder in working out the sights. I reckon to make some blunders in, I should guess, about one observation in ten or twenty, usually something quite silly, like using the wrong date in the almanac, or copying down the wrong figure from a 6-figure logarithm. Fortunately, I nearly always realize when a mistake has been made somewhere; I seem to develop an uncanny instinct for smelling out an error.
>
> *Sir Francis Chichester,* Gypsy Moth Circles the World

INTRODUCTION

Suppose you are too far from the geographical position (GP) of the celestial object to plot it on a single navigation chart with your own location. This is the common situation and it requires that you plot only a short segment of the circle—the line of position, LOP. (The LOP is nearly straight, so you may assume that it is exactly straight.)

An ingenious method suggested by Commander Marcq St.-Hilaire in 1875 requires navigators to start from an assumed position (AP), compute the altitude that would be observed if this were the true location, H_c, and compare it with the observed altitude, H_o. By evaluating $H_o - H_c$ and using the computed value of the azimuth you can construct a single LOP. The intersection of two or more LOPs provides a fix.

When it is done with tables, the work is nothing but arithmetic. The sequence of steps is rather long, so we provide forms for the navigator to fill out. Follow the steps, do the arithmetic correctly, and you won't get lost. If it seems a little "cookbook-ish," that is the way we intend it to be. When you are navigating at sea, you want to be able to do things without having to derive the mathematics each time. The theory can be amusing on a bright sunny morning, but on a stormy day when your stomach isn't feeling up to par, the cookbook procedures stand a higher chance of success.

LINES OF POSITION

The flagpole revisited

Imagine the following or, better yet, do it. Find a flagpole on level ground and mark it with a piece of sticky tape at your eye's height (Figure 20.1). Then stand back and measure with your sextant the angular height from the tape to the top of the pole, H_o. Pace off the distance (D) to the pole. Suppose you find D equals 75 feet. You know that if you walk around and remeasure the angular height and find the same value for H_o, you must be 75 feet from the base of the pole. If you find a smaller value you must be more than 75 feet from the pole. That is, if the difference $H_o' - H_o$ is *negative*, you must have moved *away* from the pole.

From the difference $H_o' - H_o$ you can infer the radius of your new circle of position relative to the old. That is the principle of the St.-Hilaire method.

Let's see how it works on the circular world of Flatland that was explored in Chapter 19 and is illustrated in Figures 20.2a and 20.2b. When you are at latitude H and you observe Polaris, it will have an altitude of H. Now suppose you are not quite sure what your latitude is, but you assume it to be H_c. This is your assumed position (AP), and the computed value of Polaris's altitude would be H_c. Now suppose you make a measure and find that

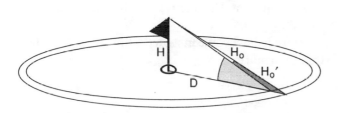

Figure 20.1. Measuring the angular height, H_o, of a flagpole from different distances. As you move away from the pole, H_o' decreases.

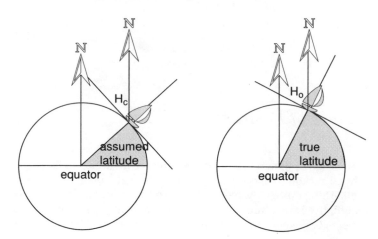

Figure 20.2a. Left side: *On a circular Flatland, you assume that you are at a latitude such that the altitude of the NCP would be* H_c. Right side: *But with your sextant you find that the altitude of the NCP is* H_o *rather than* H_c. *(See Figure 20.2b.)*

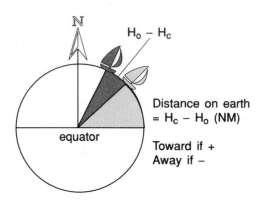

Figure 20.2b. Your latitude is different from what you thought, by *an amount* $H_o - H_c$. *The distance in NM equals* $H_o - H_c$ *in minutes of arc. If the difference is positive, your true position is closer to the pole than your assumed position. This is the essence of the Marcq St.-Hilaire method described in this chapter.*

it is actually H_o. Then you know you are at a distance $H_o - H_c$ along the north-south line from your assumed position.

That's all there is to it. Differences of altitude imply differences of distance from the GP of the celestial body. The distance in NM equals $H_o - H_c$ in minutes of arc. To see how this works when you are on a sphere, we now look at two very special situations, where the geometry is particularly simple.

First example: Navigation near the North Pole—You are flying in the region of the North Pole on May 9,

1990, and you measure the altitude of the sun at 0900 GMT. You find after correcting for dip and refraction that the center of the sun was at H_o 17°23′.

Here is how you construct a line of position from this information.

> Date: May 9, 1990
> GMT: 0900
> Watch error: 0 sec.
> H_o: 17°23′, center of sun, corrected for dip and refraction.

- **Step 1**—You pull out your *Almanac* and find on the daily pages (Figure 17.11): GHA sun = 315°54′, Declination sun = 17°19′N at 0900 GMT.

- **Step 2**—You assume, for the purpose of calculation, that you are exactly at the pole. Therefore: AP latitude = 90°; longitude is undefined at the poles.

  If this assumed position were correct, you would have found the altitude H_c of the sun to be equal to 17°19′. But you measured H_O at 17°23′, so the sun was higher than calculated. What does this imply?

- **Step 3**—Figure 20.3 summarizes the situation in a view looking down on the North Pole of the earth. The eastward longitude of the sun is 360° − GHA = 44° 06′E. If the value you measured were exactly equal to the value computed for the pole, $H_O = H_c$, you would know you were on a line that runs through the pole and perpendicular to the sun's azimuth. All points on that line would have the same value, $H_O = H_c$.

- **Step 4**—From the difference $H_O - H_c = 4′$ (which is *positive*) you conclude that you are 4 NM *toward* the GP of the sun from your assumed position at the North Pole. So you displace the line of position by a

distance 4 NM toward the sun and draw the new LOP (heavy line). You are somewhere on that line. That's how the method works.

Notice you didn't even have to solve the navigator's triangle. When you are near the pole, the problem is simplified, because you can take the pole as your assumed position and let the coordinate system do the work. There is one other situation where you can simplify the work by a good choice of assumed position, namely, when you and the sun are both on the equator. Then the zenith distance is just the difference of longitudes. This case is illustrated in the following example.

Second Example: On the equator at the equinox—On March 20, 1990, at 2100 GMT the sun was on the celestial equator and GHA sun was 133°09′. You were sailing in the Pacific Ocean near the equator south of Mexico at a DR longitude of 105°20′W. During the afternoon you measured the sun's altitude to be 62°40′ due west.

- **Step 1**—Figure 20.4 is a Mercator chart showing the equator and your assumed position on the equator at 105°W. You chose that spot because (1) the chart had a longitude mark reasonably close to your DR position, and (2) putting your AP directly east of the sun means that your LOP must go north and south.

- **Step 2**—Compute H_c, the altitude of the sun seen from the AP, and compare it with the observed altitude.

Observed altitude $H_O = 62°22′$.

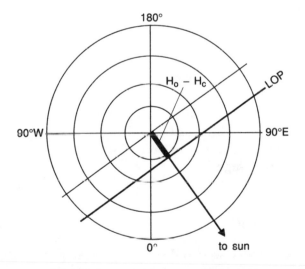

Figure 20.3. View looking down on the North Pole of the earth. The meridian of Greenwich (0°) and other longitude lines are indicated, as well as circles of latitude at 10-NM intervals. If you assume you are at the pole, the azimuth of the sun should be given by its GHA at that time. Its altitude will be given by its declination. You observed an altitude that was 4′ greater, so you must be 4 NM closer to the sun than the North Pole is. This puts you on the line marked LOP. It is perpendicular to the azimuth of the sun.

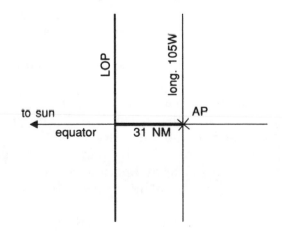

Figure 20.4. Solution for LOP when the sun is on the celestial equator and the navigator chooses an AP that is also on the equator. (See text.)

To find computed altitude:

Sun long.   133°09′W

AP long.   105°00′W

Zenith distance   28°09′   (= diff. of long. because both are on the equator)

Computed altitude from AP = H_c = 89°60′ − zenith distance = 61°51′.

Intercept, H_0 − H_c = 31′ (= 31 NM *toward* the sun)

POSTTEST

20.1 Follow the first example and use the daily pages in Figure 17.11 to calculate the GHA and the altitude of the center of the sun for 1100 GMT, May 9, 1990, as seen from the North Pole. Suppose you observe its altitude H_0 to be 17°30′. Draw a line of position taking the pole as your assumed position.

20.2 Following the second example, plot a line of position and determine your longitude from these data: On March 19, 1990, at 2100 GMT, you observe the sun at a corrected altitude H_0 of 45°10′ due east. Your DR position is 0°10′N, long. 177°30′W. (Use the *Almanac* in Figure 20.8a, b).

THE METHOD OF MARCQ ST.-HILAIRE

The fundamental idea of the St.-Hilaire method of sight reduction is to start from an assumed position AP, which can be selected for convenience of table entry. The observation will then tell you how far and in what direction you are from the AP. Your first step is to compute the sextant height h_s and azimuth Zn from the AP and then find the difference between computed and observed altitudes, H_0 − H_c. This difference is called the intercept, and it is used in constructing the line of position (LOP) from the AP.

To construct the LOP, you prepare a Mercator plotting sheet centered on your AP. Then you plot the AP (not the DR) and construct a line in the direction of the computed azimuth (see Figure 20.10). On this line, mark off a distance in nautical miles equal to the intercept H_0 − H_c in minutes. The distance is toward or away from the celestial object depending on the sign of the intercept. Here are the rules.

Rules for plotting intercept

If H_0 − H_c is *positive,* mark off a distance in nautical miles *toward* the sun equal to H_0 − H_c measured in minutes of arc.

If H_0 − H_c is *negative,* mark off a distance in nautical miles *away from* the sun equal to H_0 − H_c measured in minutes of arc.

Then construct a perpendicular to this line through the mark and label it the LOP.

Scenario of sight reduction examples

All the sight reductions we shall describe are based on the St.-Hilaire method, but they differ slightly in the data to be obtained from the *Almanac,* so we provide separate forms for each. We shall treat four cases in these two groups: afternoon LOP and morning position fix:

Afternoon LOP—The *sun sight* is the most common type of sighting and it includes correction for the radius of the sun's disc.

Morning position fix—Prediction of morning star sight is done ahead of time to assist in finding the stars.

Reduction of morning star sight is the simplest type because the celestial coordinates of the stars do not move appreciably in a year.

The morning sight of Venus reduction is similar to the sun sight, except there is no correction for the radius of the disc.

The moon sight reduction process is a bit more elaborate than for the other objects because the moon is relatively close to the earth. The moon can be seen during the day, and can give a good fix with the sun. It can also be seen on misty nights when the stars might not be visible, so it is often worth the effort (but beware of the distortion of the horizon by reflected moonlight if you sight it at night).

The morning sights will be combined into a fix.

THE CHOICE OF TABLES

The previous section discussed special cases of the navigator's triangle, where the solutions were fairly simple. However, in general, you will not be able to use such simplifications. You will have to solve the triangle, and this is where the DMA tables come in. The rest of this chapter leads you through the use of forms to be used with two sets of tables, *H.O. Pub. No. 229* and *H.O. Pub. No. 249*. These are not the only tables available, but they are probably the simplest to use.

You don't need *both* tables, so before sailing off you may want to decide which set to take with you.

They each have advantages. In order to clarify the differences and similarities, the following samples use both tables with the same sets of observations.

USING DMA *H. O. PUB. NO. 249*

This publication consists of three volumes (Figures 20.5 through 20.7). Reduction of the stars is very simple with *H. O. Pub. No. 249,* Volume 1, because the individual sidereal hour angle (SHA) for each navigation star is included in the calculation of the table. This makes the tables very popular, but they are limited to 41 navigation stars.

Volumes II and III are for the sun, moon, and planets. They make no special reference to the actual bodies; they simply solve the navigator's triangle. The tables are restricted to declinations within 29° of the equator because that is the belt in which these objects can be found. (There is, of course, no such restriction in latitude of the navigator.) This restriction (and the fact that the tables are rounded to the nearest minute of arc) means that only two volumes are needed.

The examples that follow refer to the DR position: long. 70°20'W; lat. 20°25'N. Figures 20.8a and 20.8b give excerpts from the daily pages of the *Almanac* for the relevant dates.

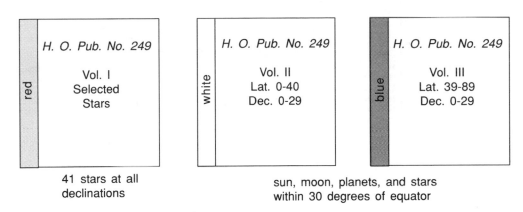

Figure 20.5. Organization of H.O. Pub. No. 249 *in three volumes. Volume I contains selected navigation stars and is based on their known SHAs and declinations. The other volumes apply to any objects of known declination and LHA. Because they are intended primarily for sun, moon, and planet sights, they are restricted to declinations in a 60° belt around the equator.*

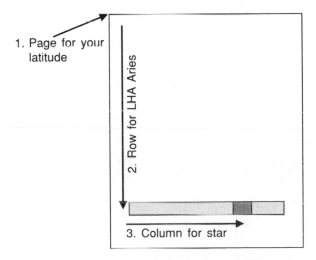

Figure 20.6. Entering Volume I of H.O. Pub. No. 249 *by navigator's latitude, then LHA Aries and name of star.*

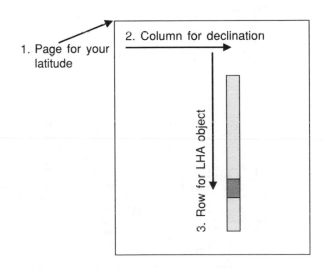

Figure 20.7. Entering Volumes II and III of H.O. Pub. No. 249 *by navigator's latitude, then declination and LHA of object.*

1990 MARCH 17, 18, 19 (SAT., SUN., MON.)

UT (GMT) d h	ARIES G.H.A.	VENUS −4.5 G.H.A.	VENUS Dec.	MARS +1.1 G.H.A.	MARS Dec.	JUPITER −2.3 G.H.A.	JUPITER Dec.	SATURN +0.6 G.H.A.	SATURN Dec.	STARS Name	S.H.A.	Dec.
17 00	174 18.6	222 16.3	S14 42.3	227 47.4	S20 13.0	82 42.3	N23 29.1	239 02.8	S21 11.6	Acamar	315 31.7	S40 20.7
01	189 21.1	237 16.5	42.0	242 48.0	12.6	97 44.6	29.1	254 05.1	11.6	Achernar	335 39.9	S57 17.3
02	204 23.5	252 16.7	41.7	257 48.5	12.2	112 46.9	29.1	269 07.4	11.5	Acrux	173 28.5	S63 02.8
03	219 26.0	267 16.9	·· 41.4	272 49.0	·· 11.8	127 49.2	·· 29.1	284 09.6	·· 11.5	Adhara	255 26.1	S28 57.7
04	234 28.5	282 17.1	41.1	287 49.6	11.4	142 51.4	29.1	299 11.9	11.5	Aldebaran	291 09.5	N16 29.5
05	249 30.9	297 17.3	40.8	302 50.1	11.0	157 53.7	29.1	314 14.2	11.5			
06	264 33.4	312 17.5	S14 40.5	317 50.6	S20 10.6	172 56.0	N23 29.1	329 16.4	S21 11.4	Alioth	166 35.1	N56 00.5
07	279 35.9	327 17.7	40.2	332 51.2	10.2	187 58.3	29.1	344 18.7	11.4	Alkaid	153 12.0	N49 21.4
S 08	294 38.3	342 17.9	39.9	347 51.7	09.7	203 00.6	29.1	359 21.0	11.4	Al Na'ir	28 05.8	S47 00.5
A 09	309 40.8	357 18.1	·· 39.7	2 52.3	·· 09.3	218 02.9	·· 29.1	14 23.2	·· 11.3	Alnilam	276 04.1	S 1 12.5
T 10	324 43.3	12 18.3	39.4	17 52.8	08.9	233 05.2	29.1	29 25.5	11.3	Alphard	218 13.0	S 8 37.1
U 11	339 45.7	27 18.5	39.1	32 53.3	08.5	248 07.4	29.1	44 27.8	11.3			
R 12	354 48.2	42 18.7	S14 38.8	47 53.9	S20 08.1	263 09.7	N23 29.1	59 30.1	S21 11.3	Alphecca	126 25.5	N26 44.5
D 13	9 50.7	57 18.9	38.5	62 54.4	07.7	278 12.0	29.1	74 32.3	11.2	Alpheratz	358 02.0	N29 02.2
A 14	24 53.1	72 19.1	38.2	77 54.9	07.3	293 14.3	29.1	89 34.6	11.2	Altair	62 25.4	N 8 50.3
Y 15	39 55.6	87 19.2	·· 37.9	92 55.5	·· 06.9	308 16.6	·· 29.1	104 36.9	·· 11.2	Ankaa	353 33.1	S42 21.6
16	54 58.0	102 19.4	37.6	107 56.0	06.5	323 18.9	29.1	119 39.1	11.1	Antares	112 47.6	S26 24.8
17	70 00.5	117 19.6	37.3	122 56.5	06.1	338 21.1	29.1	134 41.4	11.1			
18	85 03.0	132 19.8	S14 37.0	137 57.1	S20 05.6	353 23.4	N23 29.1	149 43.7	S21 11.1	Arcturus	146 11.3	N19 13.7
19	100 05.4	147 20.0	36.7	152 57.6	05.2	8 25.7	29.1	164 45.9	11.1	Atria	108 05.1	S69 00.5
20	115 07.9	162 20.2	36.4	167 58.2	04.8	23 28.0	29.1	179 48.2	11.0	Avior	234 24.9	S59 28.9
21	130 10.4	177 20.4	·· 36.1	182 58.7	·· 04.4	38 30.3	·· 29.1	194 50.5	·· 11.0	Bellatrix	278 50.8	N 6 20.5
22	145 12.8	192 20.6	35.8	197 59.2	04.0	53 32.6	29.1	209 52.8	11.0	Betelgeuse	271 20.2	N 7 24.4
23	160 15.3	207 20.7	35.5	212 59.8	03.6	68 34.8	29.1	224 55.0	10.9			
18 00	175 17.8	222 20.9	S14 35.2	228 00.3	S20 03.2	83 37.1	N23 29.1	239 57.3	S21 10.9	Canopus	264 03.8	S52 41.6
01	190 20.2	237 21.1	34.9	243 00.9	02.8	98 39.4	29.1	254 59.6	10.9	Capella	281 00.3	N45 59.6
02	205 22.7	252 21.3	34.6	258 01.4	02.3	113 41.7	29.1	270 01.8	10.9	Deneb	49 43.8	N45 14.4
03	220 25.2	267 21.5	·· 34.3	273 01.9	·· 01.9	128 44.0	·· 29.1	285 04.1	·· 10.8	Denebola	182 51.0	N14 37.4
04	235 27.6	282 21.7	33.9	288 02.5	01.5	143 46.2	29.1	300 06.4	10.8	Diphda	349 13.6	S18 02.5
05	250 30.1	297 21.8	33.6	303 03.0	01.1	158 48.5	29.1	315 08.7	10.8			
06	265 32.5	312 22.0	S14 33.3	318 03.6	S20 00.7	173 50.8	N23 29.1	330 10.9	S21 10.7	Dubhe	194 12.0	N61 48.2
07	280 35.0	327 22.2	33.0	333 04.1	20 00.3	188 53.1	29.1	345 13.2	10.7	Elnath	278 34.7	N28 36.1
08	295 37.5	342 22.4	32.7	348 04.6	19 59.8	203 55.4	29.1	0 15.5	10.7	Eltanin	90 54.3	N51 28.9
S 09	310 39.9	357 22.5	·· 32.4	3 05.2	·· 59.4	218 57.6	·· 29.1	15 17.8	·· 10.7	Enif	34 04.5	N 9 49.6
U 10	325 42.4	12 22.7	32.1	18 05.7	59.0	233 59.9	29.1	30 20.0	10.6	Fomalhaut	15 43.4	S29 40.5
N 11	340 44.9	27 22.9	31.8	33 06.3	58.6	249 02.2	29.1	45 22.3	10.6			
D 12	355 47.3	42 23.1	S14 31.5	48 06.8	S19 58.2	264 04.5	N23 29.1	60 24.6	S21 10.6	Gacrux	172 20.1	S57 03.6
A 13	10 49.8	57 23.2	31.1	63 07.3	57.8	279 06.7	29.1	75 26.8	10.6	Gienah	176 10.0	S17 29.5
Y 14	25 52.3	72 23.4	30.8	78 07.9	57.3	294 09.0	29.1	90 29.1	10.5	Hadar	149 12.5	S60 19.6
15	40 54.7	87 23.6	·· 30.5	93 08.4	·· 56.9	309 11.3	·· 29.2	105 31.4	·· 10.5	Hamal	328 20.8	N23 25.1
16	55 57.2	102 23.7	30.2	108 09.0	56.5	324 13.6	29.2	120 33.7	10.5	Kaus Aust.	84 07.0	S34 23.4
17	70 59.7	117 23.9	29.9	123 09.5	56.1	339 15.8	29.2	135 35.9	10.4			
18	86 02.1	132 24.1	S14 29.6	138 10.0	S19 55.7	354 18.1	N23 29.2	150 38.2	S21 10.4	Kochab	137 18.0	N74 11.3
19	101 04.6	147 24.2	29.2	153 10.6	55.2	9 20.4	29.2	165 40.5	10.4	Markab	13 56.1	N15 09.1
20	116 07.0	162 24.4	28.9	168 11.1	54.8	24 22.7	29.2	180 42.8	10.4	Menkar	314 33.5	N 4 03.1
21	131 09.5	177 24.6	·· 28.6	183 11.7	·· 54.4	39 24.9	·· 29.2	195 45.0	·· 10.3	Menkent	148 28.0	S36 19.5
22	146 12.0	192 24.7	28.3	198 12.2	54.0	54 27.2	29.2	210 47.3	10.3	Miaplacidus	221 43.0	S69 40.8
23	161 14.4	207 24.9	27.9	213 12.7	53.6	69 29.5	29.2	225 49.6	10.3			
19 00	176 16.9	222 25.1	S14 27.6	228 13.3	S19 53.1	84 31.8	N23 29.2	240 51.9	S21 10.2	Mirfak	309 05.8	N49 49.9
01	191 19.4	237 25.2	27.3	243 13.8	52.7	99 34.0	29.2	255 54.1	10.2	Nunki	76 20.0	S26 18.7
02	206 21.8	252 25.4	27.0	258 14.4	52.3	114 36.3	29.2	270 56.4	10.2	Peacock	53 46.8	S56 45.9
03	221 24.3	267 25.5	·· 26.6	273 14.9	·· 51.9	129 38.6	·· 29.2	285 58.7	·· 10.2	Pollux	243 48.8	N28 03.1
04	236 26.8	282 25.7	26.3	288 15.5	51.5	144 40.8	29.2	301 01.0	10.1	Procyon	245 17.8	N 5 15.0
05	251 29.2	297 25.8	26.0	303 16.0	51.0	159 43.1	29.2	316 03.2	10.1			
06	266 31.7	312 26.0	S14 25.7	318 16.5	S19 50.6	174 45.4	N23 29.2	331 05.5	S21 10.1	Rasalhague	96 22.6	N12 33.7
07	281 34.1	327 26.2	25.3	333 17.1	50.2	189 47.6	29.2	346 07.8	10.0	Regulus	208 01.7	N12 00.8
08	296 36.6	342 26.3	25.0	348 17.6	49.8	204 49.9	29.2	1 10.1	10.0	Rigel	281 28.9	S 8 12.8
M 09	311 39.1	357 26.5	·· 24.7	3 18.2	·· 49.3	219 52.2	·· 29.2	16 12.3	·· 10.0	Rigil Kent.	140 15.3	S60 47.7
O 10	326 41.5	12 26.6	24.3	18 18.7	48.9	234 54.5	29.2	31 14.6	10.0	Sabik	102 32.5	S15 43.0
N 11	341 44.0	27 26.8	24.0	33 19.3	48.5	249 56.7	29.2	46 16.9	09.9			
D 12	356 46.5	42 26.9	S14 23.7	48 19.8	S19 48.1	264 59.0	N23 29.2	61 19.2	S21 09.9	Schedar	350 01.3	N56 29.1
A 13	11 48.9	57 27.1	23.3	63 20.3	47.6	280 01.3	29.2	76 21.5	09.9	Shaula	96 45.6	S37 05.9
Y 14	26 51.4	72 27.2	23.0	78 20.9	47.2	295 03.5	29.2	91 23.7	09.9	Sirius	258 49.0	S16 42.3
15	41 53.9	87 27.4	·· 22.7	93 21.4	·· 46.8	310 05.8	·· 29.2	106 26.0	·· 09.8	Spica	158 49.4	S11 06.9
16	56 56.3	102 27.5	22.3	108 22.0	46.3	325 08.1	29.2	121 28.3	09.8	Suhail	223 05.1	S43 23.8
17	71 58.8	117 27.6	22.0	123 22.5	45.9	340 10.3	29.2	136 30.6	09.8			
18	87 01.3	132 27.8	S14 21.6	138 23.1	S19 45.5	355 12.6	N23 29.2	151 32.8	S21 09.7	Vega	80 50.9	N38 46.0
19	102 03.7	147 27.9	21.3	153 23.6	45.1	10 14.9	29.2	166 35.1	09.7	Zuben'ubi	137 24.6	S16 00.3
20	117 06.2	162 28.1	21.0	168 24.2	44.6	25 17.1	29.2	181 37.4	09.7		S.H.A.	Mer. Pass.
21	132 08.6	177 28.2	·· 20.6	183 24.7	·· 44.2	40 19.4	·· 29.2	196 39.7	·· 09.7			h m
22	147 11.1	192 28.4	20.3	198 25.2	43.8	55 21.7	29.2	211 42.0	09.6	Venus	47 03.2	9 10
23	162 13.6	207 28.5	19.9	213 25.8	43.4	70 23.9	29.2	226 44.2	09.6	Mars	52 42.6	8 48
Mer. Pass. 12 16.8		v 0.2	d 0.3	v 0.5	d 0.4	v 2.3	d 0.0	v 2.3	d 0.0	Jupiter	268 19.4	18 23
										Saturn	64 39.5	7 59

Figure 20.8a. Excerpt from daily pages.

1990 MARCH 17, 18, 19 (SAT., SUN., MON.)

UT (GMT) d h	SUN G.H.A.	SUN Dec.	MOON G.H.A.	MOON v	MOON Dec.	MOON d	MOON H.P.
17 00	177 51.6	S 1 32.3	300 16.7	11.7	S24 31.8	6.4	54.1
01	192 51.8	31.3	314 47.4	11.7	24 38.2	6.2	54.2
02	207 52.0	30.3	329 18.1	11.6	24 44.4	6.1	54.2
03	222 52.1	.. 29.3	343 48.7	11.6	24 50.5	6.0	54.2
04	237 52.3	28.3	358 19.3	11.5	24 56.5	5.9	54.2
05	252 52.5	27.3	12 49.8	11.4	25 02.4	5.8	54.2
06	267 52.7	S 1 26.3	27 20.2	11.4	S25 08.2	5.7	54.2
07	282 52.9	25.3	41 50.6	11.4	25 13.9	5.5	54.2
S 08	297 53.0	24.4	56 21.0	11.2	25 19.4	5.5	54.2
A 09	312 53.2	.. 23.4	70 51.2	11.3	25 24.9	5.3	54.2
T 10	327 53.4	22.4	85 21.5	11.1	25 30.2	5.2	54.2
U 11	342 53.6	21.4	99 51.6	11.2	25 35.4	5.1	54.2
R 12	357 53.8	S 1 20.4	114 21.8	11.0	S25 40.5	4.9	54.2
D 13	12 53.9	19.4	128 51.8	11.1	25 45.4	4.9	54.2
A 14	27 54.1	18.4	143 21.9	10.9	25 50.3	4.7	54.2
Y 15	42 54.3	.. 17.4	157 51.8	10.9	25 55.0	4.6	54.2
16	57 54.5	16.5	172 21.7	10.9	25 59.6	4.5	54.3
17	72 54.7	15.5	186 51.6	10.8	26 04.1	4.4	54.3
18	87 54.8	S 1 14.5	201 21.4	10.8	S26 08.5	4.2	54.3
19	102 55.0	13.5	215 51.2	10.7	26 12.7	4.1	54.3
20	117 55.2	12.5	230 20.9	10.7	26 16.8	4.0	54.3
21	132 55.4	.. 11.5	244 50.6	10.6	26 20.8	3.9	54.3
22	147 55.6	10.5	259 20.2	10.6	26 24.7	3.8	54.3
23	162 55.7	09.5	273 49.8	10.5	26 28.5	3.6	54.3
18 00	177 55.9	S 1 08.5	288 19.3	10.5	S26 32.1	3.5	54.3
01	192 56.1	07.6	302 48.8	10.4	26 35.6	3.4	54.3
02	207 56.3	06.6	317 18.2	10.4	26 39.0	3.2	54.4
03	222 56.5	.. 05.6	331 47.6	10.3	26 42.2	3.2	54.4
04	237 56.7	04.6	346 16.9	10.3	26 45.4	3.0	54.4
05	252 56.8	03.6	0 46.2	10.3	26 48.4	2.8	54.4
06	267 57.0	S 1 02.6	15 15.5	10.2	S26 51.2	2.8	54.4
07	282 57.2	01.6	29 44.7	10.2	26 54.0	2.6	54.4
08	297 57.4	1 00.6	44 13.9	10.1	26 56.6	2.5	54.4
S 09	312 57.6	0 59.6	58 43.0	10.1	26 59.1	2.3	54.4
U 10	327 57.7	58.7	73 12.1	10.1	27 01.4	2.2	54.5
N 11	342 57.9	57.7	87 41.2	10.0	27 03.6	2.1	54.5
D 12	357 58.1	S 0 56.7	102 10.2	10.0	S27 05.7	2.0	54.5
A 13	12 58.3	55.7	116 39.2	10.0	27 07.7	1.8	54.5
Y 14	27 58.5	54.7	131 08.2	9.9	27 09.5	1.7	54.5
15	42 58.7	.. 53.7	145 37.1	9.9	27 11.2	1.6	54.5
16	57 58.8	52.7	160 06.0	9.8	27 12.8	1.4	54.5
17	72 59.0	51.7	174 34.8	9.8	27 14.2	1.3	54.6
18	87 59.2	S 0 50.7	189 03.6	9.8	S27 15.5	1.2	54.6
19	102 59.4	49.8	203 32.4	9.8	27 16.7	1.0	54.6
20	117 59.6	48.8	218 01.2	9.7	27 17.7	0.9	54.6
21	132 59.8	.. 47.8	232 29.9	9.7	27 18.6	0.8	54.6
22	147 59.9	46.8	246 58.6	9.7	27 19.4	0.6	54.6
23	163 00.1	45.8	261 27.3	9.6	27 20.0	0.5	54.7
19 00	178 00.3	S 0 44.8	275 55.9	9.6	S27 20.5	0.4	54.7
01	193 00.5	43.8	290 24.5	9.6	27 20.9	0.2	54.7
02	208 00.7	42.8	304 53.1	9.6	27 21.1	0.1	54.7
03	223 00.9	.. 41.8	319 21.7	9.5	27 21.2	0.1	54.7
04	238 01.0	40.9	333 50.2	9.5	27 21.1	0.2	54.8
05	253 01.2	39.9	348 18.7	9.5	27 20.9	0.3	54.8
06	268 01.4	S 0 38.9	2 47.2	9.5	S27 20.6	0.5	54.8
07	283 01.6	37.9	17 15.7	9.5	27 20.1	0.6	54.8
08	290 01.8	36.9	31 44.2	9.4	27 19.5	0.7	54.8
M 09	313 02.0	.. 35.9	46 12.6	9.4	27 18.8	0.9	54.9
O 10	328 02.1	34.9	60 41.0	9.4	27 17.9	1.0	54.9
N 11	343 02.3	33.9	75 09.4	9.4	27 16.9	1.1	54.9
D 12	358 02.5	S 0 32.9	89 37.8	9.4	S27 15.8	1.3	54.9
A 13	13 02.7	31.9	104 06.2	9.4	27 14.5	1.5	54.9
Y 14	28 02.9	31.0	118 34.6	9.3	27 13.0	1.5	55.0
15	43 03.1	.. 30.0	133 02.9	9.3	27 11.5	1.7	55.0
16	58 03.3	29.0	147 31.3	9.3	27 09.8	1.9	55.0
17	73 03.4	28.0	161 59.6	9.3	27 07.9	2.0	55.0
18	88 03.6	S 0 27.0	176 27.9	9.3	S27 05.9	2.1	55.1
19	103 03.8	26.0	190 56.2	9.3	27 03.8	2.3	55.1
20	118 04.0	25.0	205 24.5	9.3	27 01.5	2.4	55.1
21	133 04.2	.. 24.0	219 52.8	9.3	26 59.1	2.5	55.1
22	148 04.4	23.0	234 21.1	9.3	26 56.6	2.7	55.1
23	163 04.6	22.0	248 49.4	9.3	26 53.9	2.8	55.2
	S.D. 16.1 d 1.0		S.D. 14.8	14.8	15.0		

Lat.	Twilight Naut.	Twilight Civil	Sunrise	Moonrise 17	18	19	20
N 72	03 36	05 03	06 10	■	■	■	■
N 70	03 53	05 09	06 10	■	■	■	■
68	04 06	05 14	06 10	■	■	■	■
66	04 16	05 18	06 09	■	■	■	■
64	04 25	05 22	06 09	02 54	■	■	■
62	04 32	05 25	06 09	02 05	03 43	04 57	05 21
60	04 38	05 27	06 09	01 34	02 57	04 01	04 39
N 58	04 43	05 30	06 09	01 11	02 27	03 29	04 11
56	04 48	05 31	06 08	00 53	02 04	03 04	03 48
54	04 52	05 33	06 08	00 37	01 46	02 45	03 30
52	04 55	05 35	06 08	00 24	01 30	02 28	03 15
50	04 58	05 36	06 08	00 12	01 17	02 14	03 01
45	05 04	05 38	06 08	24 49	00 49	01 45	02 34
N 40	05 09	05 40	06 07	24 27	00 27	01 23	02 12
35	05 12	05 42	06 07	24 09	00 09	01 04	01 54
30	05 15	05 43	06 07	23 54	24 48	00 48	01 39
20	05 19	05 44	06 06	23 28	24 21	00 21	01 12
N 10	05 20	05 45	06 06	23 05	23 58	24 49	00 49
0	05 20	05 44	06 05	22 45	23 36	24 28	00 28
S 10	05 19	05 43	06 04	22 24	23 14	24 07	00 07
20	05 15	05 41	06 03	22 01	22 51	23 44	24 40
30	05 10	05 38	06 02	21 36	22 24	23 18	24 16
35	05 06	05 36	06 01	21 21	22 08	23 02	24 02
40	05 02	05 33	06 00	21 03	21 50	22 44	23 45
45	04 55	05 30	05 59	20 42	21 27	22 22	23 25
S 50	04 47	05 26	05 58	20 16	20 59	21 54	23 00
52	04 43	05 24	05 57	20 03	20 45	21 40	22 48
54	04 39	05 21	05 57	19 48	20 29	21 25	22 34
56	04 34	05 19	05 56	19 31	20 10	21 06	22 18
58	04 28	05 16	05 55	19 10	19 46	20 43	21 59
S 60	04 22	05 12	05 54	18 44	19 15	20 13	21 35

Lat.	Sunset	Twilight Civil	Twilight Naut.	Moonset 17	18	19	20
N 72	18 08	19 16	20 44	■	■	■	■
N 70	18 09	19 10	20 27	■	■	■	■
68	18 09	19 04	20 13	■	■	■	■
66	18 09	19 00	20 03	■	■	■	■
64	18 09	18 56	19 54	05 12	■	■	■
62	18 09	18 53	19 46	06 01	06 07	06 40	08 05
60	18 09	18 50	19 40	06 32	06 53	07 36	08 47
N 58	18 09	18 48	19 35	06 56	07 23	08 09	09 16
56	18 09	18 46	19 30	07 15	07 46	08 33	09 38
54	18 09	18 44	19 26	07 31	08 05	08 53	09 56
52	18 09	18 43	19 23	07 44	08 20	09 09	10 11
50	18 09	18 41	19 19	07 56	08 34	09 23	10 24
45	18 09	18 39	19 13	08 22	09 02	09 52	10 51
N 40	18 10	18 37	19 08	08 42	09 24	10 14	11 12
35	18 10	18 35	19 04	08 58	09 42	10 33	11 30
30	18 10	18 34	19 01	09 13	09 58	10 49	11 45
20	18 10	18 32	18 58	09 37	10 25	11 16	12 11
N 10	18 11	18 32	18 56	09 59	10 48	11 39	12 33
0	18 11	18 32	18 56	10 19	11 09	12 01	12 54
S 10	18 12	18 33	18 57	10 39	11 31	12 23	13 14
20	18 13	18 35	19 00	11 00	11 54	12 46	13 36
30	18 14	18 38	19 06	11 25	12 20	13 13	14 01
35	18 14	18 40	19 09	11 40	12 36	13 28	14 16
40	18 15	18 42	19 13	11 57	12 54	13 47	14 33
45	18 16	18 45	19 20	12 18	13 17	14 09	14 54
S 50	18 17	18 50	19 28	12 43	13 45	14 37	15 19
52	18 18	18 51	19 31	12 56	13 59	14 51	15 32
54	18 18	18 54	19 35	13 11	14 15	15 07	15 46
56	18 19	18 56	19 41	13 27	14 34	15 26	16 02
58	18 20	18 59	19 46	13 48	14 57	15 49	16 22
S 60	18 21	19 02	19 53	14 14	15 28	16 19	16 47

Day	SUN Eqn. of Time 00ʰ	SUN Eqn. of Time 12ʰ	SUN Mer. Pass.	MOON Mer. Pass. Upper	MOON Mer. Pass. Lower	Age	Phase
17	08 34	08 25	12 08	04 07	16 32	20	
18	08 17	08 08	12 08	04 57	17 22	21	
19	07 59	07 50	12 08	05 48	18 15	22	◑

Figure 20.8b. Excerpt from daily pages.

Reducing a sun sight (Form F6)

On the afternoon of March 17, 1990, you obtained the following sun sight:

> Date: March 17, 1990
> Watch time: 16 41 50
> Watch error: 10 sec. slow
> h_S: 15°19′ (lower limb)
> Index error: 1′ off the arc
> Height of eye: 15′

Fill out Form F6—Figure 20.9 shows the sample work sheet. In the upper right, enter the date and DR (dead reckoning) position at the approximate time of the sight, leaving the coordinates of assumed position (AP lat. and AP long.) empty for the moment.

- **Part 1. Find GMT**—Enter the time of the sighting. If your watch is set to zone time, enter in 1.1 and add the zone description to find GMT according to your watch. Then apply the watch error: if slow, add the error; if fast, subtract it. Enter the resulting GMT in 1.5 and enter the corresponding date in 1.6. (In western longitudes in the evening, the GMT datum is often a day ahead.)

- **Part 2. Find declination**—From the sun column in the daily pages, find the declination at the nearest whole hour and enter in 2.1. Also copy the value of d (the change of Dec. in 1 hour) from the bottom of the Dec. column and circle N or S on the form according to whether the sun is moving north or south. The d correction must be interpolated for the number of minutes since the correction provided is for the whole hour (42 minutes = $\frac{2}{3}$ hour). This can be done in your head or by turning to the yellow pages for 42 minutes and looking for the value corresponding to 1′ in the v or d corrn. column. The correction is 0.7′, which is entered in 2.2 with the − sign, because it is to be subtracted from the numerical value of the declination. (The sun is moving north, so its southern declination is decreasing.) Add 2.2 to 2.1 and enter in 2.3, marking it N or S.

- **Part 3. Find LHA**—From the sun column in the daily pages, find the GHA sun at the nearest whole hour and enter in 3.1. The GHA sun increases 15° per hour and it must be interpolated for the number of minutes since the number provided is for the whole hour (42 minutes = $\frac{2}{3}$ hour). The increment for 42

minutes is found from the yellow pages in the column headed Sun/Planets. The whole minutes are at the top of the page and seconds are in successive rows down the page. For example, the value for 42 minutes 30 seconds is 10°37.5′. Add the interpolation increment and write the sum in 3.3. Adopt an AP long. with the same number of minutes and enter it in 3.4. Subtract it (if west) to find the LHA of the sun. The result must be a whole number of degrees for entering the tables later. Copy the value to 5.3.

- **Part 4. Reduction of sextant observation**—Enter the height of eye in 4.1 and find the corresponding dip correction in the inside front cover. In marine navigation, it is always negative and is to be entered in 4.3. Enter the index correction in 4.2 according to the rule ("If it's on it's off; if it's off it's on," which means that the IC is + if the error is *off* the arc, and it is − if the error is *on* the arc). Enter the net correction in 4.4 and write the observed sextant height h_S in 4.5, indicating whether you measured the upper or lower limb. Apply the correction and write the apparent altitude in 4.6. Find the third correction for the sun (which includes refraction and semidiameter for the appropriate limb) from the first column of Table A2 on the inside cover. Enter 4.6 + 4.7 into 4.8, for the observed height.

- **Part 5. Solution by H. O. Pub. No. 249**—In 5.1 enter the minutes of declination in excess of a whole degree, and in 5.2 place a check to indicate whether the declination and the latitude are on the same side or contrary side of the equator. Enter the tables with whole-degree LHA and AP lat. and read out the tabulated height, the d, and the Z value. This d value (−21′) is the change of tabulated altitude for a 1° change of declination, and the d correction in 5.6 accounts for the fact that the declination was not a whole degree. The appropriate value is found by linear interpolation using $-21 \times (11 / 60) = -4$. Enter 5.5 + 5.6 into 5.7 and copy the value into 5.9. Enter 5.8 − 5.9 into 5.10. This is the intercept, indicating the observed minus the computed altitude based on the AP. If the intercept is positive, you are closer to the sun than the AP is (toward); if it is negative, you are farther from the sun than the AP is (away). From Z compute the sun's azimuth Zn using the rules given lower on the form. You were in the northern hemisphere and LHA < 180°, so Zn = 360° − Z = 263°. This is the direction to the GP of the sun.

Form F6. Sun Sight by *H. O. Pub. No. 249* Vol. II or III

Limb: Upper / (Lower)

1. To find GMT

1.1 Zone watch time	16 41 50
1.2 Zone description	5
1.3 GMT watch time	21 41 50
1.4 GMT watch error	10 (s+) / f–
1.5 GMT	21 42 00
1.6 GMT date	Mar 17 1990

2. To find declination

2.1 Dec.	1°11.5 N (or)(S); d 1.0 (N)(or) S
2.2 d corr.	–0.7
2.3 Dec.	1°10.8 N (or)(S)

3. To find LHA

3.1 GHA 21 hrs.	132°55.4
3.2 Incr. 42 m ___ s	10°30.0
3.3 GHA	143°25.4
3.4 AP long.	70°25.4 (add if E)
3.5 LHA	73°00′ (enter at 5.3)

4. Reduction of sextant observation

4.1 Ht. of eye 15 ft.	+	–
4.2 Index corr.	1	
4.3 Ht. of eye corr.		3.8
4.4 Net	–2.8	
4.5 h_s	15°19.0	(U /(L) limb)
4.6 App. alt.	15°16.2	
4.7 3rd corr. to h_s	12.8	(first col. A2)
4.8 H_o	15°35	(enter at 5.8)

Navigator _____

Zone date	Mar 17 1990
DR lat.	20 25 (N)(or) S; AP Lat. 20
DR long.	70 29 E (or)(W) AP long. 70°25.4

5. Solution by *H. O. Pub. No. 249*

5.1 Dec. difference 10.8	
5.2 Dec. same ___ name or contrary ✓ name to lat.	
5.3 LHA	73° 00′
5.4 AP lat.	20° 00′ (nearest whole degree)
5.5 Tab. H 15°35 d –21 Z 97 (to 5.11)	
5.6 d corr.	–4′ (from Dec. diff.)
5.7 H_c	15°31 (enter at 5.9)
5.8 H_o	15°35
5.9 H_c	15°31
5.10 $H_o – H_c$	+04 (+ = toward; – = away)
5.11 Zn	263 (see rule below)

Rule for azimuth, Zn:

N. Hem: LHA < 180°: Zn = 360° – Z
           LHA > 180°: Zn = Z
S. Hem: LHA < 180°: Zn = 180° + Z
           LHA > 180°: Zn = 180° – Z

Figure 20.9. Form F6 for reduction of sun sight.

Plot the AP—Label it with the object and time (AP sun 1642). This has been done in Figure 20.10. Draw a line in the direction of Zn and label it "To sun." Measure along this line (toward the sun if intercept is +, away from the sun if intercept is –) a distance in NM equal to the intercept in minutes of arc.

Construct the line of position—It is a perpendicular to the line to the sun passing through the intercept. Label it "LOP sun 1642."

Predicting a star sight (Form F5)

Your next task is to prepare for a morning star sight by predicting the altitude and azimuth of a star that you know will be visible during morning twilight the next day. This preparation will help you find the star quickly and avoid losing time in case you oversleep. In preparing this prediction, you can ignore refinements such as index correction and dip. You will use the same DR position for this prediction.

You selected Arcturus, and you found that the nautical twilight starts at about 0517 LMT, so this is the time for which you make the prediction. The prediction is very simple with *H. O. Pub. No. 249*, Vol. I, and an excerpt is shown in Figure 20.11. See Figure 20.12, left column, for the details we now describe.

- *Part 1. To find GMT*—The procedure is the same as for the sun sight, except you may ignore the small watch error in computing GMT, as the prediction need not be more accurate than 1°.

- *Part 2. To find LHA Aries*—The coordinates of the navigation stars are built into *H. O. Pub. No. 249*, Vol. I, so you only need the LHA Aries. Find the value for the whole hour in the Aries column in the daily pages for this date, and find the increment for the extra minutes in the Aries column on the yellow pages for minutes. Enter the sum into 2.3 and adopt an AP long. with the same number of minutes, so the difference in 2.5 is a whole number of degrees.

- *Part 3. Reduction of sextant observation*—Skip this section, as you are making a prediction.

- *Part 4. Reduction*—Enter *H. O. Pub. No. 249*, Vol. I, with the AP lat. and the LHA Aries and read out the tabulated altitude, H_c. Read out the azimuth value Zn.

To make predictions for more stars at the same time and same DR location, you can scan the same row (LHA Aries) and find other stars listed. This is also a useful way to find stars that would make good objects for star sights. The stars marked with diamonds are about 120° apart in azimuth and would give a strong fix.

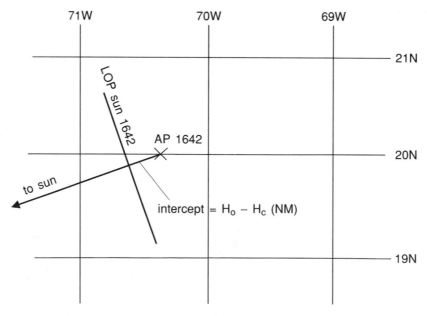

Figure 20.10. LOP from sun sight. From the AP (large X) draw a line toward the sun, along the indicated azimuth Zn. Measure a distance (in NM) equal to the intercept, toward the sun if the intercept is +, and away from the sun if the intercept is –. Through the intercept, construct the LOP (heavy line) perpendicular to the sun line.

LAT 20°N

LHA ♈	Hc	Zn	Hc	Zn	Hc	Zn	Hc	Zn	Hc	Zn	Hc	Zn	Hc	Zn
	♦Alkaid		ANTARES		♦SPICA		Gienah		♦REGULUS		POLLUX		Dubhe	
180	53 42	030	10 01	123	52 34	144	52 20	174	61 56	258	31 47	291	47 02	350
181	54 09	029	10 48	123	53 06	146	52 25	176	61 01	258	30 54	291	46 52	350
182	54 36	028	11 35	124	53 37	147	52 28	177	60 06	259	30 02	292	46 42	349
183	55 02	027	12 22	124	54 07	149	52 30	179	59 10	260	29 09	292	46 31	348
184	55 28	026	13 08	125	54 36	150	52 31	180	58 15	260	28 17	292	46 19	348
185	55 53	026	13 55	125	55 03	152	52 30	182	57 19	261	27 25	292	46 07	347
186	56 16	025	14 41	126	55 30	153	52 27	183	56 23	262	26 33	292	45 54	346
187	56 39	024	15 26	126	55 54	155	52 23	185	55 28	262	25 40	292	45 40	346
188	57 02	023	16 11	127	56 18	156	52 17	187	54 32	263	24 48	293	45 26	345
189	57 23	022	16 56	127	56 40	158	52 10	188	53 36	263	23 56	293	45 11	345
190	57 43	021	17 41	128	57 00	160	52 02	190	52 40	264	23 04	293	44 56	344
191	58 03	020	18 26	128	57 19	161	51 51	191	51 44	264	22 12	293	44 41	344
192	58 21	018	19 10	129	57 37	163	51 40	193	50 48	265	21 21	293	44 24	343
193	58 38	017	19 53	129	57 52	165	51 27	194	49 51	265	20 29	293	44 08	342
194	58 55	016	20 37	130	58 06	167	51 12	196	48 55	265	19 37	294	43 50	342
	Kochab		♦VEGA		Rasalhague		ANTARES		♦SPICA		♦REGULUS		Dubhe	
195	33 46	009	16 47	054	24 08	085	21 20	131	58 18	168	47 59	266	43 33	341
196	33 54	008	17 33	054	25 04	085	22 02	131	58 29	170	47 03	266	43 14	341
197	34 02	008	18 19	054	26 00	085	22 45	132	58 37	172	46 07	267	42 56	340
198	34 10	008	19 05	055	26 56	086	23 27	132	58 44	174	45 10	267	42 37	340
199	34 18	008	19 51	055	27 53	086	24 08	133	58 49	176	44 14	267	42 17	340
200	34 25	007	20 37	055	28 49	086	24 49	134	58 52	178	43 18	268	41 57	339
201	34 32	007	21 23	055	29 45	087	25 30	134	58 53	180	42 21	268	41 37	339
202	34 39	007	22 09	055	30 41	087	26 10	135	58 53	182	41 25	269	41 16	338
203	34 45	006	22 56	055	31 38	087	26 49	136	58 50	183	40 29	269	40 55	338
204	34 51	006	23 42	055	32 34	088	27 29	136	58 46	185	39 32	269	40 34	337
205	34 57	006	24 28	055	33 30	088	28 07	137	58 40	187	38 36	270	40 12	337
206	35 03	005	25 15	056	34 27	088	28 46	138	58 32	189	37 39	270	39 49	337
207	35 08	005	26 01	056	35 23	089	29 23	138	58 22	191	36 43	270	39 27	336
208	35 13	005	26 48	056	36 19	089	30 00	139	58 10	193	35 47	271	39 04	336
209	35 18	005	27 35	056	37 16	089	30 37	140	57 57	195	34 50	271	38 41	336
	Kochab		♦VEGA		Rasalhague		♦ANTARES		SPICA		♦REGULUS		Dubhe	
210	35 22	004	28 21	056	38 12	090	31 13	141	57 42	196	33 54	271	38 17	335
211	35 26	004	29 08	056	39 09	090	31 48	142	57 25	198	32 57	272	37 53	335
212	35 29	004	29 55	056	40 05	090	32 23	142	57 07	200	32 01	272	37 29	335
213	35 33	003	30 41	056	41 01	091	32 57	143	56 47	202	31 05	272	37 05	334
214	35 36	003	31 28	056	41 58	091	33 31	144	56 25	203	30 08	273	36 40	334
215	35 38	003	32 15	056	42 54	091	34 04	145	56 02	205	29 12	273	36 15	334
216	35 41	002	33 02	056	43 50	092	34 36	146	55 38	206	28 16	273	35 50	333
217	35 43	002	33 49	056	44 47	092	35 07	147	55 12	208	27 20	274	35 25	333
218	35 45	002	34 35	056	45 43	092	35 38	147	54 45	209	26 23	274	34 59	333
219	35 46	001	35 22	056	46 40	093	36 08	148	54 17	211	25 27	274	34 34	333
220	35 47	001	36 09	056	47 36	093	36 37	149	53 47	212	24 31	274	34 08	332
221	35 48	001	36 56	056	48 32	094	37 05	150	53 16	214	23 35	275	33 41	332
222	35 48	000	37 42	056	49 28	094	37 33	151	52 44	215	22 38	275	33 15	332
223	35 48	000	38 29	056	50 25	094	37 59	152	52 11	217	21 42	275	32 48	332
224	35 48	000	39 16	056	51 21	095	38 25	153	51 37	218	20 46	276	32 22	332
	VEGA		♦ALTAIR		Nunki		ANTARES		♦SPICA		Denebola		♦Alkaid	
225	40 02	056	19 18	087	16 39	127	38 50	154	51 02	219	44 08	271	57 14	338
226	40 49	056	20 15	088	17 24	127	39 14	155	50 26	220	43 12	272	56 52	337
227	41 35	055	21 11	088	18 08	128	39 37	156	49 49	222	42 16	272	56 30	336
228	42 21	055	22 07	088	18 53	129	40 00	157	49 11	223	41 19	272	56 06	335
229	43 08	055	23 04	089	19 37	129	40 21	158	48 33	224	40 23	272	55 42	334
230	43 54	055	24 00	089	20 20	130	40 41	160	47 53	225	39 27	273	55 17	333
231	44 40	055	24 57	089	21 03	130	41 00	161	47 13	226	38 30	273	54 51	332
232	45 26	055	25 53	090	21 46	131	41 18	162	46 32	227	37 34	273	54 25	332
233	46 12	054	26 49	090	22 29	131	41 35	163	45 51	228	36 38	274	53 58	331
234	46 58	054	27 46	090	23 11	132	41 51	164	45 09	229	35 41	274	53 30	330
235	47 43	054	28 42	091	23 53	133	42 06	165	44 26	230	34 45	274	53 01	329
236	48 29	054	29 38	091	24 34	133	42 20	166	43 42	231	33 49	275	52 32	328
237	49 14	053	30 35	091	25 15	134	42 33	168	42 58	232	32 53	275	52 02	328
238	49 59	053	31 31	092	25 55	135	42 44	169	42 14	233	31 57	275	51 32	327
239	50 44	053	32 28	092	26 35	135	42 55	170	41 29	233	31 00	275	51 01	327
	♦VEGA		ALTAIR		Nunki		♦ANTARES		SPICA		♦ARCTURUS		Alkaid	
240	51 28	052	33 24	093	27 15	136	43 04	171	40 43	234	65 20	273	50 30	326
241	52 13	052	34 20	093	27 54	137	43 12	172	39 57	235	64 24	273	49 58	325
242	52 57	051	35 17	093	28 32	137	43 19	174	39 11	236	63 27	273	49 25	325
243	53 41	051	36 13	094	29 10	138	43 25	175	38 24	237	62 31	273	48 53	324
244	54 25	050	37 09	094	29 48	139	43 29	176	37 37	237	61 35	274	48 19	324
245	55 08	050	38 05	094	30 24	140	43 32	177	36 49	238	60 39	274	47 46	323
246	55 51	049	39 01	095	31 01	140	43 35	179	36 01	239	59 42	274	47 12	323
247	56 34	049	39 58	095	31 37	141	43 35	180	35 13	239	58 46	274	46 38	322
248	57 16	048	40 54	096	32 12	142	43 35	181	34 24	240	57 50	275	46 03	322
249	57 58	048	41 50	096	32 46	143	43 33	182	33 35	241	56 54	275	45 28	321
250	58 39	047	42 46	097	33 20	144	43 31	183	32 45	241	55 58	275	44 53	321
251	59 20	046	43 42	097	33 53	144	43 27	185	31 56	242	55 01	275	44 17	321
252	60 00	045	44 38	097	34 26	145	43 21	186	31 06	243	54 05	275	43 41	320
253	60 40	045	45 34	098	34 58	146	43 15	187	30 15	243	53 09	276	43 05	320
254	61 19	044	46 29	098	35 29	147	43 07	188	29 25	244	52 13	276	42 28	320
	♦DENEB		ALTAIR		♦Nunki		ANTARES		SPICA		♦ARCTURUS		Alkaid	
255	38 18	048	47 25	099	35 59	148	42 59	190	28 34	244	51 17	276	41 52	319
256	39 00	047	48 21	099	36 29	149	42 49	191	27 43	245	50 21	276	41 15	319
257	39 41	047	49 16	100	36 57	150	42 38	192	26 52	246	49 25	277	40 38	319
258	40 22	047	50 12	100	37 25	151	42 25	193	26 01	246	48 29	277	40 01	318
259	41 03	047	51 07	101	37 52	152	42 12	194	25 09	247	47 33	277	39 23	318
260	41 44	047	52 03	102	38 19	153	41 57	195	24 17	247	46 37	277	38 45	318
261	42 25	046	52 58	102	38 44	154	41 42	197	23 25	248	45 41	277	38 08	318
262	43 06	046	53 53	103	39 09	155	41 25	198	22 33	248	44 45	278	37 30	318
263	43 46	046	54 48	103	39 32	156	41 07	199	21 41	249	43 49	278	36 52	317
264	44 27	045	55 43	104	39 55	157	40 49	200	20 48	249	42 54	278	36 13	317
265	45 07	045	56 37	105	40 17	158	40 29	201	19 55	250	41 58	278	35 35	317
266	45 47	045	57 32	106	40 37	159	40 08	202	19 02	250	41 02	279	34 57	317
267	46 26	044	58 26	106	40 57	160	39 46	203	18 09	250	40 06	279	34 18	317
268	47 05	044	59 20	107	41 16	161	39 24	204	17 16	251	39 10	279	33 40	317
269	47 45	044	60 14	108	41 33	162	39 00	205	16 23	251	38 15	279	33 01	317

LAT 20°N

LHA ♈	Hc	Zn	Hc	Zn	Hc	Zn	Hc	Zn	Hc	Zn	Hc	Zn	Hc	Zn
	♦DENEB		Enif		♦Nunki		ANTARES		♦ARCTURUS		Alkaid		Kochab	
270	48 23	043	35 15	092	41 50	163	38 35	206	37 19	279	32 22	317	30 10	347
271	49 02	043	36 11	092	42 05	165	38 10	207	36 24	280	31 43	316	29 57	346
272	49 40	042	37 08	093	42 20	166	37 43	208	35 28	280	31 04	316	29 44	346
273	50 18	042	38 04	093	42 33	167	37 16	209	34 32	280	30 25	316	29 30	346
274	50 55	041	39 00	093	42 45	168	36 48	210	33 37	280	29 46	316	29 17	346
275	51 32	041	39 57	094	42 56	169	36 19	211	32 42	281	29 07	316	29 03	346
276	52 09	040	40 53	094	43 06	171	35 50	212	31 46	281	28 28	316	28 49	346
277	52 45	040	41 49	095	43 14	172	35 19	213	30 51	281	27 49	316	28 35	345
278	53 21	039	42 45	095	43 22	173	34 48	214	29 55	281	27 10	316	28 20	345
279	53 56	038	43 41	096	43 28	174	34 16	215	29 00	281	26 31	316	28 06	345
280	54 31	038	44 37	096	43 33	175	33 44	216	28 05	282	25 52	316	27 51	345
281	55 05	037	45 34	096	43 37	177	33 11	217	27 10	282	25 13	316	27 37	345
282	55 39	036	46 30	097	43 40	178	32 37	217	26 15	282	24 34	316	27 22	345
283	56 12	035	47 25	097	43 41	179	32 02	218	25 20	282	23 55	316	27 07	345
284	56 44	035	48 21	098	43 41	180	31 27	219	24 24	283	23 16	316	26 52	344
	♦DENEB		Alpheratz		♦FOMALHAUT		Nunki		ANTARES		♦Rasalhague		Kochab	
285	57 16	034	20 34	065	14 21	130	43 40	182	30 51	220	68 12	253	26 37	344
286	57 47	033	21 25	066	15 04	130	43 38	183	30 15	221	67 18	254	26 22	344
287	58 17	032	22 17	066	15 47	131	43 35	184	29 38	221	66 23	255	26 06	344
288	58 46	031	23 08	066	16 30	131	43 30	185	29 01	222	65 29	256	25 51	344
289	59 15	030	24 00	066	17 12	132	43 24	187	28 23	223	64 34	257	25 35	344
290	59 43	029	24 51	066	17 54	132	43 17	188	27 44	223	63 39	258	25 20	344
291	60 10	028	25 43	067	18 36	133	43 09	189	27 05	224	62 44	258	25 04	344
292	60 35	027	26 35	067	19 17	133	42 59	190	26 26	225	61 48	259	24 48	344
293	61 00	026	27 27	067	19 58	134	42 49	191	25 46	225	60 53	260	24 32	344
294	61 24	024	28 18	067	20 38	134	42 37	193	25 05	226	59 57	260	24 16	344
295	61 47	023	29 10	067	21 18	135	42 24	194	24 24	227	59 02	261	24 00	343
296	62 08	022	30 02	067	21 58	136	42 10	195	23 43	227	58 06	262	23 44	343
297	62 29	020	30 54	067	22 37	136	41 55	196	23 01	228	57 10	262	23 28	343
298	62 48	019	31 46	068	23 16	137	41 39	197	22 19	229	56 14	263	23 12	343
299	63 06	018	32 39	068	23 54	138	41 21	198	21 37	229	55 18	263	22 56	343
	♦DENEB		Schedar		Alpheratz		♦FOMALHAUT		Nunki		♦Rasalhague		VEGA	
300	63 22	016	27 34	036	33 31	068	24 32	138	41 03	200	54 22	264	64 00	321
301	63 37	015	28 07	036	34 23	068	25 09	139	40 44	201	53 26	264	63 24	320
302	63 51	013	28 40	036	35 15	068	25 46	140	40 23	202	52 30	265	62 47	319
303	64 03	012	29 13	036	36 08	068	26 23	140	40 02	203	51 34	265	62 09	318
304	64 14	010	29 45	036	37 00	068	26 58	141	39 40	204	50 38	265	61 31	317
305	64 23	009	30 18	035	37 52	068	27 34	142	39 16	205	49 42	266	60 52	316
306	64 31	007	30 51	035	38 45	068	28 08	142	38 52	206	48 45	266	60 12	315
307	64 37	005	31 23	035	39 37	068	28 42	143	38 27	207	47 49	267	59 32	314
308	64 41	004	31 56	035	40 29	068	29 16	144	38 01	208	46 53	267	58 51	313
309	64 44	002	32 28	035	41 22	068	29 49	145	37 34	209	45 56	268	58 10	313
310	64 45	000	33 00	035	42 14	068	30 21	145	37 06	210	45 00	268	57 28	312
311	64 45	359	33 32	035	43 07	068	30 53	146	36 38	211	44 04	268	56 46	311
312	64 43	357	34 04	034	43 59	068	31 24	147	36 09	212	43 07	269	56 04	311
313	64 39	356	34 36	034	44 52	069	31 54	148	35 39	213	42 11	269	55 21	310
314	64 34	354	35 08	034	45 44	068	32 24	149	35 08	214	41 15	269	54 38	310
	♦Alpheratz		Diphda		♦FOMALHAUT		Nunki		Rasalhague		♦VEGA		DENEB	
315	46 36	068	23 22	121	32 53	150	34 36	214	40 18	270	53 54	309	64 27	352
316	47 29	068	24 10	122	33 21	150	34 04	215	39 22	270	53 10	309	64 19	351
317	48 21	068	24 58	122	33 48	151	33 31	216	38 25	270	52 26	308	64 09	349
318	49 14	068	25 46	123	34 15	152	32 57	217	37 29	271	51 42	308	63 58	348
319	50 06	068	26 33	123	34 41	153	32 23	218	36 33	271	50 57	308	63 45	346
320	50 59	068	27 20	124	35 06	154	31 48	219	35 36	271	50 12	307	63 30	345
321	51 51	068	28 06	125	35 30	155	31 12	219	34 40	272	49 27	307	63 15	343
322	52 43	068	28 53	125	35 53	156	30 36	220	33 44	272	48 42	307	62 58	342
323	53 35	068	29 39	126	36 16	157	30 00	221	32 47	272	47 57	306	62 39	340
324	54 28	068	30 24	127	36 37	158	29 22	222	31 51	273	47 11	306	62 20	339
325	55 20	068	31 09	127	36 58	159	28 45	222	30 55	273	46 26	306	61 59	338
326	56 12	067	31 54	128	37 18	160	28 06	223	29 58	273	45 40	306	61 37	336
327	57 04	067	32 38	129	37 37	161	27 27	224	29 02	274	44 54	305	61 13	335
328	57 56	067	33 22	129	37 54	162	26 48	225	28 06	274	44 08	305	60 49	334
329	58 48	067	34 05	130	38 11	163	26 08	225	27 10	274	43 22	305	60 24	333
	♦Mirfak		Hamal		Diphda		♦FOMALHAUT		ALTAIR		♦VEGA		DENEB	
330	20 56	043	33 03	074	34 48	131	38 27	164	56 45	255	42 35	305	59 58	332
331	21 34	043	33 57	075	35 30	132	38 42	165	55 51	256	41 49	305	59 30	331
332	22 13	043	34 52	075	36 12	132	38 56	166	54 56	256	41 03	305	59 02	330
333	22 51	043	35 46	075	36 54	133	39 09	167	54 01	257	40 16	304	58 33	329
334	23 30	043	36 41	075	37 34	134	39 21	168	53 06	258	39 29	304	58 03	328
335	24 09	043	37 35	075	38 15	135	39 32	170	52 11	258	38 43	304	57 33	327
336	24 47	043	38 30	075	38 54	136	39 41	171	51 16	259	37 56	304	57 02	326
337	25 26	043	39 24	076	39 33	137	39 50	172	50 20	259	37 10	304	56 30	325
338	26 05	043	40 19	076	40 12	138	39 57	173	49 25	260	36 23	304	55 57	324
339	26 43	043	41 14	076	40 49	139	40 04	174	48 29	261	35 36	304	55 24	323
340	27 22	043	42 08	076	41 26	140	40 09	175	47 33	261	34 49	304	54 50	323
341	28 01	043	43 03	076	42 02	141	40 13	176	46 38	262	34 03	304	54 15	322
342	28 39	043	43 58	076	42 38	142	40 17	177	45 42	262	33 16	304	53 40	321
343	29 18	043	44 53	076	43 12	143	40 19	179	44 46	262	32 29	304	53 05	321
344	29 57	043	45 47	077	43 46	144	40 19	180	43 50	263	31 42	304	52 29	320
	Schedar		Mirfak		♦ALDEBARAN		Diphda		♦FOMALHAUT		ALTAIR		♦DENEB	
345	49 04	021	30 35	043	11 11	076	44 19	145	40 19	181	42 54	263	51 52	319
346	49 24	020	31 14	043	12 05	077	44 51	146	40 18	182	41 58	264	51 16	319
347	49 43	019	31 52	043	13 00	077	45 23	147	40 15	183	41 02	264	50 38	318
348	50 01	019	32 31	043	13 55	077	45 53	148	40 12	184	40 06	265	50 01	318
349	50 19	018	33 09	043	14 50	078	46 22	149	40 07	185	39 10	265	49 23	317
350	50 36	017	33 47	043	15 45	078	46 51	150	40 01	186	38 14	265	48 44	317
351	50 53	017	34 26	043	16 40	078	47 18	152	39 54	188	37 17	266	48 06	317
352	51 08	016	35 04	042	17 36	078	47 44	153	39 46	189	36 21	266	47 27	316
353	51 23	015	35 42	042	18 31	079	48 09	154	39 37	190	35 25	267	46 48	316
354	51 38	014	36 20	042	19 26	079	48 33	156	39 27	191	34 29	267	46 08	315
355	51 51	013	36 57	042	20 22	079	48 56	157	39 16	192	33 32	267	45 28	315
356	52 04	013	37 35	042	21 17	079	49 17	158	39 03	193	32 36	268	44 48	315
357	52 15	012	38 12	042	22 12	080	49 38	160	38 50	194	31 40	268	44 08	314
358	52 26	011	38 50	041	23 08	080	49 57	161	38 36	195	30 43	269	43 28	314
359	52 37	010	39 27	041	24 04	080	50 15	162	38 20	196	29 47	269	42 47	314

Figure 20.11. Excerpt from H.O. Pub. No. 249.

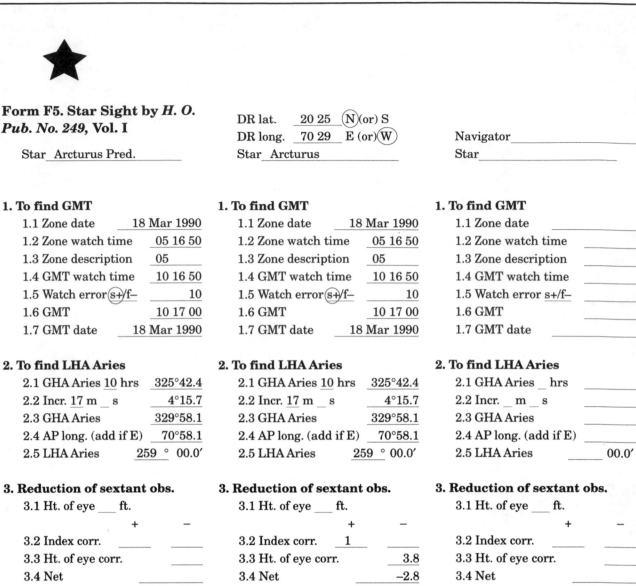

Form F5. Star Sight by *H. O. Pub. No. 249*, Vol. I

Star _Arcturus Pred._

DR lat.   20 25   (N)(or) S
DR long.   70 29   E (or)(W)

Star _Arcturus_

Navigator _____
Star _____

1. To find GMT

	Col 1	Col 2	Col 3
1.1 Zone date	18 Mar 1990	18 Mar 1990	
1.2 Zone watch time	05 16 50	05 16 50	
1.3 Zone description	05	05	
1.4 GMT watch time	10 16 50	10 16 50	
1.5 Watch error (s+)/f–	10	(s+)/f– 10	s+/f–
1.6 GMT	10 17 00	10 17 00	
1.7 GMT date	18 Mar 1990	18 Mar 1990	

2. To find LHA Aries

2.1 GHA Aries 10 hrs	325°42.4	325°42.4	___ hrs
2.2 Incr. 17 m __ s	4°15.7	4°15.7	__ m __ s
2.3 GHA Aries	329°58.1	329°58.1	
2.4 AP long. (add if E)	70°58.1	70°58.1	
2.5 LHA Aries	259 ° 00.0′	259 ° 00.0′	_____ 00.0′

3. Reduction of sextant obs.

	+	–	+	–	+	–
3.1 Ht. of eye ___ ft.						
3.2 Index corr.			1			
3.3 Ht. of eye corr.				3.8		
3.4 Net				–2.8		
3.5 h_s			47°18.7			
3.6 App. alt.			47°15.9			
3.7 3rd corr. to h_s				–.9		
3.8 H_o			47°15			

4. Reduction

	Col 1	Col 2	Col 3
4.1 AP lat.	20°	20°	20°
4.2 H_o		47°15	
4.3 H_c	47°33	47°33	47°33
4.4 $H_o - H_c$	t+ / a–	–18 t+ /(a–)	t+ / a–
4.5 Zn	277	277	277

Figure 20.12. Form F5 for reduction of star sight.

Reducing star sights (Form F5)

Now assume you have obtained the following sextant sight of Arcturus from the same DR position, and at the exact time for which you prepared the prediction (Figure 20.12, center column).

Date: March 18, 1990
Watch time: 05 16 50 ZT
Watch error: 10 sec. slow
h_S: 47°18.7′
Index error: 1′ off the arc
Height of eye: 15′

Fill out Form F5, center column

- ***Part 1. Find GMT***—Follow the same procedure as in filling out Form F6.

- ***Part 2. Find LHA Aries***—Same as for Form F6.

- ***Part 3. Reduction of sextant observation***—Enter your height of eye (15 feet) and index correction. (If it's on it's off; if it's off it's on.) Compute the net correction in 3.4 and write the h_S in 3.5. The sum, 3.4 + 3.5, goes into 3.6 as the apparent altitude. The refraction correction (third corr.) is found in the Stars and Planets column of Table A2 on the inside front cover according to apparent altitude. Enter in 3.7 and put the observed altitude in 3.8 and 4.2.

- ***Part 4. Reduction***—Enter *H. O. Pub. No. 249*, Vol. I, with the AP lat. and the LHA Aries and read out the computed altitude H_c and the azimuth Zn. There is no *d* correction because the exact declination of the star is built into the table. Compute the intercept $H_0 - H_c$ and note its sign.

Plot the AP—Draw a line in the direction of Zn and label it "To Arcturus" (see Figure 20.13). Measure along this line (toward the sun if intercept is +, away from the sun if intercept is −) a distance in NM equal to the intercept in minutes of arc.

Construct the line of position—It is a perpendicular to the line to the sun passing through the intercept. Label it "LOP Arcturus 0517."

Reducing a planet sight (Form F8)

Your diligent assistant obtained a sight of Venus at the same instant:

Date: March 18, 1990
Watch time: 05 16 50 ZT
Watch error: 10 sec. slow
h_S: 26°39.7
Index error: 1′ off the arc
Height of eye: 15′

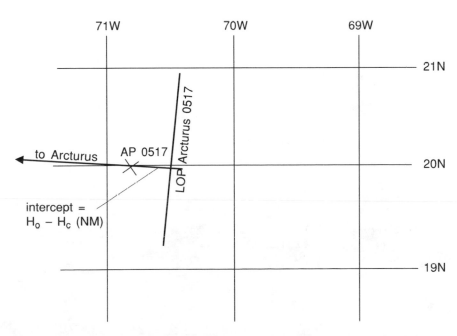

Fig. 20.13. LOP of Arcturus. From the AP (large X) a line is drawn toward the azimuth of Arcturus. The intercept is measured away from Arcturus and a perpendicular LOP is drawn and labeled.

Form F8. Planet or Star Sight by *H. O. Pub. No. 249*, Vol. II or III

Planet/Star Name ___Venus___

1. To find GMT

1.1 Zone watch time	05 16 50	
1.2 Zone description	05	
1.3 GMT watch time	10 16 50	
1.4 GMT watch error (s+)/ f–	10	
1.5 GMT	10 17 00	
1.6 GMT date	Mar 18 1990	

2. To find declination

2.1 Dec.   14°32.1 N (or)(S); d .3 (N)(or) S

2.2 d corr.   –.1 (skip for star)

2.3 Dec.   14°32.0 N (or)(S)

3. To find LHA

3.1 GHA _10_ hrs.	12°22.7 v .2	
3.2 Incr. _17_ m ___ s	4°15.0	
3.3 v corr.	0	(skip for star)
3.4 GHA	16°37.7	
3.5 AP long.	70°37.7	(add if E)
3.6 LHA	–54°00′	(enter at 5.3)

4. Reduction of sextant observation

4.1 Ht. of eye _15_ ft.	+	–	
4.2 Index corr.	1		
4.3 Ht. of eye corr.		3.8	
4.4 Net	–2.8		
4.5 h_s	26°39.7		
4.6 App. alt.	26°36.9		
4.7 3rd corr. to h_s	–1.9	(middle of A2)	
4.8 H_o	26°35.0	(enter at 5.8)	

Navigator _____

Zone date   Mar 18 1990

DR lat.   20 25 (N)(or) S; AP lat. _____

DR long.   70 29 E (or)(W;)AP long. _____

5. Solution by *H. O. Pub. No. 249*

5.1 Dec. difference _32_

5.2 Dec. same ___ name or contrary ✓ name to lat.

5.3 LHA   306°00′

5.4 AP lat.   20°00′ (nearest whole degree)

5.5 Tab. H _26°56.9_ d _–31.5_ Z _118_ (To 5.11)

5.6 d corr.   –16′ (from Dec. diff.)

5.7 H_c 26°40.9 (enter at 5.9)

5.8 H_o 26°35.0

5.9 H_c 26°40.9

5.10 $H_o - H_c$ –5.9 (+ = toward; – = away)

5.11 Zn   118 (see rule below)

Rule for azimuth, Zn:

N. Hem: LHA < 180°: Zn = 360° – Z

　　　　　LHA > 180°: Zn = Z

S. Hem: LHA < 180°: Zn = 180° + Z

　　　　　LHA > 180°: Zn = 180° – Z

Figure 20.14. Form F8 for sight reduction.

Fill out Form F8—The work is very similar to the reduction of the sun sight with Form F6 (see Figure 20.14) and goes as follows:

- **Part 1. Find GMT**—Follow the same procedure as for Form F6.

- **Part 2. Find Declination**—Same as for Form F6, except read from Venus column.

- **Part 3. Find LHA**—Same as for Form F6, except read from Venus column. The v correction is usually negligible for Venus.

- **Part 4. Reduction of sextant observation**—As before, compute the net correction in 4.4 and write the sextant height h_S in 4.5. The sum, 4.4 + 4.5, goes into 4.6 as the apparent altitude. The refraction correction (third corr.) is found in the Stars and Planets column of Table A2 on the inside front cover according to apparent altitude. Enter in 4.7 and put the observed altitude in 4.8 and 5.8. Note that there is an additional correction for the planets in the central part of Table A2. This is for geocentric parallax and depends on apparent altitude. It is usually negligible for the planets, and there is no place for it on the forms.

- **Part 5. Solution by H. O. Pub. No. 249**—Same as for Form F6.

Plot the AP—Draw a line in the direction of Zn and label it "To Venus" (Figure 20.15). Your AP for Venus is different from what you used for Arcturus, because Venus's LHA came out with a different number of minutes and you must enter *H. O. Pub. No. 249,* Vols. II and III, with a whole number LHA. Measure along this line (toward the sun if intercept is +, away from the sun if intercept is –) a distance in NM equal to the intercept in minutes of arc.

Construct the line of position—It is a perpendicular to the line to Venus passing through the intercept. Label it "LOP Venus 0517."

The plot has become more interesting (Figure 20.15) because the intersection indicates a fix. But it is not very strong because the angle of intersection is acute. Before labelling the fix there is a moon sight to add.

Reducing a moon sight (Form F7)

A third member of your party was able to obtain a simultaneous sight of the moon. The moon's phase

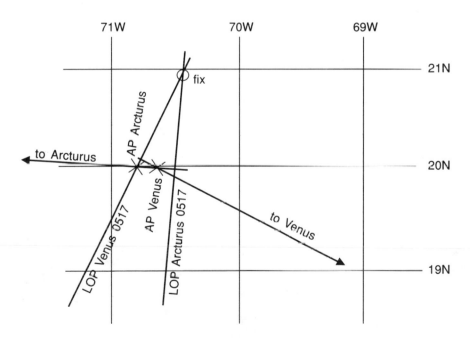

Figure 20.15. Plotting chart with the LOP Venus added. Note the AP used for Venus was not the same as the AP used for Arcturus, in order to enter the tables with a whole number LHA. The intersection of the two LOPs provides a weak fix, as the angle of intersection is very acute. A better fix would be obtained by adding an object in the south, as for the moon sight indicated in Figure 20.16.

Form F7. Moon Sight by *H. O. Pub No. 249*, Vol. II or III

Limb: (Upper)/ Lower

1. To find GMT

1.1 Zone watch time	05 16 50
1.2 Zone description	05
1.3 GMT watch time	10 16 50
1.4 GMT watch error (s+)/ f–	10
1.5 GMT	10 17 00
1.6 GMT date	Mar 18 1990

2. To find declination

2.1 Dec.	27°01.4 N (or)(S); d 2.2 N (or)(S)
2.2 d corr.	.6
2.3 Dec.	27°02.0 N (or)(S)

3. To find LHA

3.1 GHA 10 hrs.	73°12.1 v 10.1
3.2 Incr. 17 m s	4°03.4
3.3 v corr.	2.9
3.4 GHA	77°18.4
3.5 AP long.	70°18.4 (add if E)
3.6 LHA	7°00′ (enter at 5.3)

4. Reduction of sextant observation

4.1 Ht. of eye 15 ft. +	–
4.2 Index corr.	1
4.3 Ht. of eye corr.	3.8
4.4 Net	–2.8
4.5 h_s	41°41.8
4.6 App. alt.	41°39

Moon corrections, inside back cover *Almanac:*

4.7a Altitude corr.	+2.0
4.7b (HP 54.4) HP corr.	52.6
4.7c Upper limb? (= –30′)	–30′
4.8 H_o (enter at 5.8)	42°04

Navigator _____

Zone date   Mar 18 1990

DR lat.   20 25 (N)(or) S; AP lat.   20°

DR long.   70 29 E (or)(W); AP long.   70°18′

5. Solution by *H. O. Pub. No. 249*

5.1 Dec. difference 2.0	
5.2 Dec. same __ name or contrary ✓ name to lat.	
5.3 LHA	7° 00′
5.4 AP lat.	20° 00′ (nearest whole degree)
5.5 Tab. H 42°30.8 d –59.3 Z 171 (to 5.11)	
5.6 d corr.	–2.0′ (from Dec. diff.)
5.7 H_c	42°28.8 (enter at 5.9)
5.8 H_o	42°04
5.9 H_c	42°29
5.10 $H_o - H_c$	–25 (+ = toward; – = away)
5.11 Zn	189 (see rule below)

Rule for azimuth, Zn:

N. Hem: LHA < 180°: Zn = 360° – Z
               LHA > 180°: Zn = Z

S. Hem: LHA < 180°: Zn = 180° + Z
               LHA > 180°: Zn = 180° – Z

Figure 20.16. Form F7 for reduction of moon sight.

and orientation made the lower limb invisible, so the sight was made on the upper limb.

Date: March 18, 1990
Watch time: 05 16 50 ZT
Watch error: 10 sec. slow
h_s: 41°41.8′ (upper limb)
Index error: 1′ off the arc
Height of eye: 15′

Fill out Form F7—The sample is shown in Figure 20.16 and the details are as follows:

- *Part 1. Find GMT*—Same as for Form F6.

- *Part 2. Find declination*—For the moon, the v correction is usually significant. Find $d = 2.2$ and note the moon is moving south. You need to interpolate for 17 minutes, so turn to the yellow pages for 17 minutes and scan the v or d corrn. column until you find 2.2. Next to it is the interpolated value, 0.6. Add this to the value in 2.1 and enter the sum in 2.3. (This same procedure is used for planets when their d or v correction is significant.)

- *Part 3. Find LHA*—In the daily pages find the GHA moon and the v correction, 10.1. Add the increment for 17 minutes found in the yellow pages in the Moon column. Then find the v correction corresponding to 17 minutes in the yellow pages, just as you did for the d correction. Write the value, 2.9, in 3.3 and the sum of the three values in 3.4. Then subtract an assumed longitude to make LHA a whole degree. Write the assumed longitude in the AP long. place in the upper right corner of the form and enter LHA at 5.3.

- *Part 4. Reduction of sextant observation*—Parts 4.1 through 4.6 are the same as for star or planet. However, the refraction, semidiameter, and parallax corrections for the moon are inside the *back* cover of the *Almanac*. Before turning there, go to the daily page and find the HP (horizontal parallax, due to the size of the earth) and enter it in 4.7b. The value in this case is 54.4, and this is the maximum correction possible on this date. The actual correction will depend on the altitude of the moon from your location. The *Almanac* gives an explanation on the left-hand page.

  The moon corrections are combined into two tables, found at the top and the bottom of the page.

They are both taken from the column with the correct App. Alt. heading.

1) In your case, App. Alt. = 41°39′ so you go to the column headed 40°-44° and scan down to the lower half of the page until you come to the row labelled 54.3. This is the closest you can get to 54.4. The corresponding correction is 2.0 for the upper limb observation, so you write this in 4.7a.

2) Now go to the top of the table and find the group of entries corresponding to 41° and pick the one labelled 40′ in the left-hand column. The correction is 52.6 and you write this in 4.7b.

Finally, because you have an upper limb observation, write –30′ in 4.7c, and then combine all the corrections and write the result in 4.8. Copy this over to 5.8.

- *Part 5. Solution by H. O. Pub. No. 249*—From here on, the moon reduction is the same as for other objects. You have a d correction which accounts for the fact that the actual declination of the moon (S27°02.0′) is not a whole degree. The d value in the table (–59.3) must be interpolated for the additional 02.0′, leading to –59.3(2.0/60) = –2.0. This value is entered in 5.6. The final steps calculate the intercept and azimuth and plot the LOP.

Plot the AP on the chart

Construct the LOP for the moon—The LOP of the moon is shown in Figure 20.17, and the estimate of the fix is indicated by the triangle. In this case, the moon effectively determined the latitude because it was due south at the time of observation, while the star and the planet determined the longitude.

USING DMA *H. O. PUB. NO. 229* WITH FORM F4

Pub. No. 229 is a general-purpose table for solving the navigator's triangle. It covers an entire hemisphere in six volumes of 15° strips of latitude, and you may use it in either the northern or southern hemisphere. You enter *H. O. Pub. No. 229* by finding the page with the LHA of the object; then look for the column with your latitude and then find the row with the declination of the object, as illustrated in Figure 20.18.

Form F4 permits a variety of calculations concerning planets, stars, the sun, and the moon with

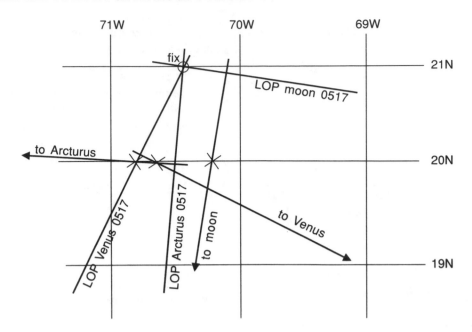

Figure 20.17. Plotting sheet after the addition of the LOP for the moon. The AP of the moon was between those used for Venus and Arcturus. The fix triangle is centered on the intersection with the moon's LOP because the intersection is nearly at right angles, so it is a strong one. The fix fell almost exactly on the DR position (lat. 20°25′N, long. 70°29′W).

H. O. Pub. No. 229. This distinguishes it from the other forms (and makes it a bit more difficult to use) because it is not tailored to specific calculations. The resulting plots look slightly different because the assumed positions will not be identical, although the fixes ought to be exactly the same.

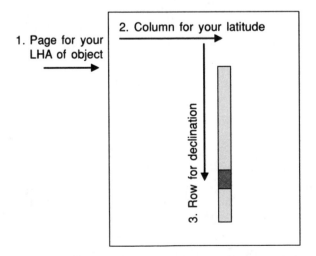

Figure 20.18. Diagram showing how to enter H.O. Pub. No. 229 in three steps: (1) Find page with LHA of object, (2) find column with your latitude, and (3) find row with declination of object.

Reduction of sun sight

We shall use the same data as before, to make it easier to compare the two tables. The sample sun sight is in Figure 20.9.

> Date: March 17, 1990
> Watch time: 16 41 50 ZT
> Watch error: 10 sec. slow
> h_s: 15°19′ (lower limb)
> Index error: 1′ off the arc
> Height of eye: 15′

- *Part 1. Find GMT*—Enter the time and compute GMT from the zone description and watch error.

- *Part 2. Find declination*—Find the declination and the GHA sun at the time of observation.

- *Part 3. Find LHA*—Find the increment for 3.2 from the yellow pages and put 3.1 + 2.3 into 3.4. Reduce to an angle less than 360°. Choose the AP longitude in 3.6 to have the same minutes as the GHA in 3.5, so the LHA in 3.7 is a whole degree. Enter the AP longitude in the upper right-hand corner of the page. At the same time, enter the AP latitude as the nearest whole degree to the DR latitude.

Form F4. Reduction with *H. O. Pub. No. 229*

Planet/star name   Sun

Sun/moon limb: upper / ⟨lower⟩

1. To find GMT

1.1 Zone watch time	16 41 50
1.2 Zone description	05
1.3 GMT watch time	21 41 50
1.4 GMT watch error ⟨s+⟩/ f–	10
1.5 GMT	21 42 00
1.6 GMT date	Mar 17 1990

2. To find declination

2.1 Dec.	1°11.5 N (or)⟨S;⟩d 1.0 ⟨N⟩(or) S	
2.2 d corr.	0.7	(skip for star)
2.3 Dec.	1°10.8 N (or)⟨S⟩	

3. To find LHA

3.1 GHA 21 hrs.	132°55.4 v ____	
3.2 Incr. 42 m ___ s	10°30.4	
3.3 v corr.	_____	(skip for star)
3.4 SHA☆	_____	(star only)
3.5 GHA	143°25.4	
3.6 AP long.	70°25.4	(add if E)
3.7 LHA	73°00′	(enter at 5.3)

4. Reduction of sextant observation

4.1 Ht. of eye 15 ft.	+	–
4.2 Index corr.	1	____
4.3 Ht. of eye corr.		3.8
4.4 Net	–2.8	
4.5 h_s	15°19.0	
4.6 App. alt.	15°16.2	

Sun, star, or planet

4.7 3rd corr. to h_s	12.8	(Table A2)

Moon corrections from inside back

4.7a Altitude corr.	_____
4.7b (HP ____) HP corr.	_____
4.7c (–30′ if upper limb)	_____
4.8 H_o (4.6 + 4.7)	15°29.0 (enter at 5.8)

Navigator   _____

Zone date   Mar 17 1990

DR lat.   20°25 ⟨N⟩(or) S; AP lat. 20°

DR long.   70 29 E (or)⟨W;⟩AP long. 70°25.4

5. Solution by *H. O. Pub. No. 229*

5.1 Dec. difference 10.8

5.2 Dec. same __ name or contrary ✓ name to lat.

5.3 LHA	73° 00′
5.4 AP lat.	20° 00′ (nearest whole degree)
5.5 Tab. H 15°35.0 d –21 Z 97 (to 5.11)	
5.6 d corr.	–4 (from Dec. diff.)
5.7 H_c	15°31.0 (enter at 5.9)
5.8 H_o	15°29.0
5.9 H_c	15°31.0
5.10 $H_o - H_c$	–2 (+ = toward; – = away)
5.11 Zn	263 (see rule below)

Rule for azimuth, Zn:

N. Hem: LHA < 180°: Zn = 360° – Z

               LHA > 180°: Zn = Z

S. Hem: LHA < 180°: Zn = 180° + Z

               LHA > 180°: Zn = 180° – Z

Figure 20.19. Form F4 for reduction of sun sight.

- *Part 4. Reduction of sextant observation*—Find the dip correction inside the front cover and combine it with the index error. Enter the net correction in 4.4 and enter h_S in 4.5. Add 4.4 to 4.5 and enter the sum as apparent altitude in 4.6. Find the third correction in the first two columns of Table A2 inside the front cover of the *Almanac,* being careful to use the entry for the proper month. Put 4.6 + 4.7 into 4.8 and copy to 5.8.

- *Part 5. Solution by* H. O. Pub. No. 229—Enter the minutes of declination (10.8′) in 5.1 as Dec. difference and note that the declination has the same name as the latitude. Enter *H. O. Pub. No. 229* with the LHA in 5.3, the latitude in 5.4, and the whole-degree declination from 2.1. Also copy down the value of d and Z in the same row.

   The d value is the change of H_c for $1°$ increase of declination. Interpolate to the value of the declination difference. In this case $9.2 \times (14/60) = 2.3$, to be added to 5.5. Enter the final computed altitude in 5.7 and repeat in 5.9. Enter H_0 in 5.8 and subtract H_c, to find the intercept in 5.10. Be sure to note the sign of the intercept.

   Compute the azimuth Zn from Z using the rule given on the form. In this case, you have LHA < $180°$: $Zn = 360° - Z = 263$. Ignore fractions of a degree of azimuth, as they are not important in plotting the LOP.

Reduction of star sight

The sighting of Arcturus gave the following data and Figure 20.20 shows the sample form:

   Date: March 18, 1990
   Watch time: 05 16 50 ZT
   Watch error: 10 sec. slow
   h_S: 47 °18.7′
   Index error: 1′ off the arc
   Height of eye: 15′

- *Part 1. Find GMT*—Enter the time and compute GMT from the zone description and watch error.

- *Part 2. Find declination*—Find the declination and the GHA Aries at the time of observation.

- *Part 3. Find LHA*—Enter SHA☆ (Arturus) in 3.4 from the daily page and enter sum of 3.1 + 3.2 + 3.4 into 3.5 for GHA☆. Reduce to an angle less than $360°$. Choose the AP longitude in 3.6 to have the same minutes as the GHA in 3.5, so the LHA in 3.7 is a whole degree. Enter the AP longitude in the upper right-hand corner of the page. At the same time, enter the AP latitude as the nearest whole degree to the DR latitude.

- *Part 4. Reduction of sextant observation*—Find the dip correction inside the front cover and combine it with the index error. Enter the net correction in 4.4 and enter h_S in 4.5. Add 4.4 to 4.5 and enter the sum as apparent altitude in 4.6. For a star, find the refraction correction in the center column of Table A2 and enter it in 4.7. Add this to 4.6 and put the result, H_0, into 4.8 and 5.8.

- *Part 5. Solution by* H. O. Pub. No. 229—Same as for the sun.

Reduction of Venus sight

The data are as follows and Figure 20.22 shows the sample form.

   Date: March 18, 1990
   Watch time: 05 16 50 ZT
   Watch error: 10 sec. slow
   h_S: 26°39.7
   Index error: 1′ off the arc
   Height of eye: 15′

- *Part 1. Find GMT*—Same as for the sun, except use GHA Venus from the daily pages.

- *Part 2. Find declination*—Now the d correction (for the change of declination since the whole hour) must be examined. It is $-0.3′$ per hour and is negligible.

- *Part 3. LHA*—Enter the GHA of Venus (not Aries) in 3.1. Find the increment for 17 minutes in the yellow pages, making sure to take if from the Sun/Planets column. Check the v correction (for incremental orbital motion relative to the sun) and enter if significant. Compute GHA Venus and subtract an AP longitude with the same minutes, so the LHA Venus is a whole number of degrees.

- *Part 4. Reduction of sextant observation*—From here on, the reduction is the same as for a star, as long as you are not trying to get accuracy better than $1′$. If you are, there is an additional correction for the parallax of Venus in the inside front cover. It is trivial for most marine navigation, but we mention it for completeness.

- *Part 5. Solution*—Same as for sun.

Form F4. Reduction with *H.O. Pub. No. 229*

Planet/star name ___Arcturus___
Sun/moon limb: upper/lower

1. To find GMT

1.1 Zone watch time	05 16 50
1.2 Zone description	05
1.3 GMT watch time	10 16 50
1.4 GMT watch error (s+)/ f–	10
1.5 GMT	10 17 00
1.6 GMT date	Mar 18 1990

2. To find declination

2.1 Dec.	19°14 (N)(or) S; d ___ N (or) S
2.2 d corr.	_____ (skip for star)
2.3 Dec.	_____ N (or) S

3. To find LHA

3.1 GHA 10 hrs.	325°42 v
3.2 Incr. _17_ m ___ s	4°16
3.3 v corr.	_____ (skip for star)
3.4 SHA☆	146°11 (star only)
3.5 GHA	116°09
3.6 AP long.	70°09 (add if E)
3.7 LHA	46°00′ (enter at 5.3)

4. Reduction of sextant observation

4.1 Ht. of eye _15_ ft. +	–
4.2 Index corr.	1 ___
4.3 Ht. of eye corr.	3.8
4.4 Net	–2.8
4.5 h_s	47°18.7
4.6 App. alt.	47°15.9 (4.4 + 4.5)

Sun, star, or planet

4.7 3rd corr. to h_s	–0.9 (Table A2)

Moon corrections from inside back

4.7a Altitude corr.	_____
4.7b (HP ___) HP corr.	____
4.7c (–30′ if upper limb)	_____
4.8 H_o (4.6 + 4.7)	47°15 (enter at 5.8)

Navigator _____
Zone date   Mar 18 1990
DR lat.   20°25 (N)(or) S; AP lat. __20°__
DR long.   70 29 E (or) (W;) AP long. 70°09

5. Solution by *H.O. Pub. No. 229*

5.1 Dec. difference 14′	
5.2 Dec. same ✓ name or contrary ___ name to lat.	
5.3 LHA	46°00′
5.4 AP lat.	20°00′ (nearest whole degree)
5.5 Tab. H 46°45.9 d +9.2 Z 83 (To 5.11)	
5.6 d corr.	2.3 (from Dec. diff.)
5.7 H_c	46°48.2 (enter at 5.9)
5.8 H_o	47°15 (from 4.8)
5.9 H_c	46°48
5.10 $H_o – H_c$	+27 (plus is toward Zn)
5.11 Zn	277° (see rule below)

Rule for azimuth, Zn:

N. Hem: LHA < 180°: Zn = 360° – Z
          LHA > 180°: Zn = Z

S. Hem: LHA < 180°: Zn = 180° + Z
          LHA > 180°: Zn = 180° – Z

Figure 20.20. Form F4 for reduction of star sight.

Reduction of moon sight

The moon is the trickiest, as you have already seen. The data are as follows and Figure 20.23 shows a sample form.

 Date: March 18, 1990
 Watch time: 16 41 50 ZT
 Watch error: 10 sec. slow
 h_s: 41°41.8′ (upper limb)
 Index error: 1′ off the arc
 Height of eye: 15′

- **Part 1. Find GMT**—Same as for other objects.

- **Part 2. Find declination**—For the moon, the v correction is usually significant. Find $d = 2.2$ and note the moon is moving south. You need to interpolate for 17 minutes, so turn to the yellow pages for 17 minutes and scan the v or d corrn. column until you find 2.2. Next to it is the interpolated value, 0.6. Add this to the value in 2.1 and enter the sum in 2.3. (This same procedure is used for planets when their d or v correction is significant.) Write the Dec. difference in 5.1 for later use.

- **Part 3. Find LHA**—In the daily pages find the GHA moon and the v correction, 10.1. Add the increment for 17 minutes found in the yellow pages in the Moon column. Then find the v correction corresponding to 17 minutes in the yellow pages, just as you did for the

d correction. Write the value, 2.9, in 3.3 and the sum of the three values in 3.5. Then subtract an assumed longitude to make LHA a whole degree. Write the assumed longitude in the AP long. place in the upper right corner of the form and enter LHA at 5.3.

- **Part 4. Reduction of sextant observation**—Steps 4.1 through 4.6 are the same as for star or planet. However, the refraction, semidiameter, and parallax corrections for the moon are inside the back cover of the *Almanac*. Before turning there, go to the daily page and find the HP (horizontal parallax, due to the size of the earth) and enter it in 4.7b. The value in this case is 54.4, and this is the maximum correction possible on this date. The actual correction will depend on the altitude of the moon from your location. The *Almanac* gives an explanation on the left-hand page.

 The moon corrections are combined into two tables, found at the top and the bottom of the page. They are both taken from the column with the correct App. Alt. heading.

1) In your case, App. Alt. = 41°39′ so you go to the column headed 40°-44° and scan down to the lower half of the page until you come to the row where HP = 54.3. This is the closest you can get to 54.4. The corresponding correction is 2.0 for the upper limb observation, so you write this in 4.7a.

Figure 20.21. Plotting the LOP for the sample sight of Arcturus at 0517, whose reduction is given in Figure 20.19. The Mercator plotting sheet has been constructed for the DR latitude of 20°.

Form F4. Reduction with *H.O. Pub. No. 229*

Planet/star name ___Venus___

Sun/moon limb: Upper/Lower

1. To find GMT

1.1 Zone watch time	05 16 50
1.2 Zone description	05
1.3 GMT watch time	10 16 50
1.4 GMT watch error (s+)/ f–	10
1.5 GMT	10 17 00
1.6 GMT date	Mar 18 1990

2. To find declination

2.1 Dec.	14°32.1 N (or)(S); d .3 (N)(or) S
2.2 d corr.	–.1 (skip for star)
2.3 Dec.	14°32.0 N (or)(S)

3. To find LHA

3.1 GHA _10_ hrs.	12°22.7 v .2
3.2 Incr. _17_ m ___ s	4°15.0
3.3 v corr.	_____ (skip for star)
3.4 SHA☆	_____ (star only)
3.5 GHA	16°37.7
3.6 AP long.	70°37.7 (add if E)
3.7 LHA	–54°00′ (enter at 5.3)

4. Reduction of sextant observation

4.1 Ht. of eye _15_ ft. + ___ –	
4.2 Index corr.	1 ___
4.3 Ht. of eye corr.	3.8
4.4 Net	–2.8
4.5 h_s	26°39.7
4.6 App. alt.	26°36.9 (4.4 + 4.5)

Sun, star, or planet

4.7 3rd corr. to h_s	–1.9 (Table A2)

Moon corrections from inside back

4.7a Altitude corr.	_____
4.7b (HP ____) HP corr.	____
4.7c (–30′ if upper limb)	_____
4.8 H_0 (4.6 + 4.7)	26°35 (enter at 5.8)

Navigator _____

Zone date ___Mar 18 1990___

DR lat. ___20°25 (N)(or) S; AP lat. _20°_

DR long. ___70 29__ E (or)(W;)AP long. _70°38_

5. Solution by *H.O. Pub. No. 229*

5.1 Dec. difference _32′_	
5.2 Dec. same __ name or contrary ✓ name to lat.	
5.3 LHA	306°00′
5.4 AP lat.	20°00′ (nearest whole degree)
5.5 Tab. H _26°56.9_ d _–31.5_ Z _118_ (to 5.11)	
5.6 d corr.	–16 (from Dec. diff.)
5.7 H_c	26°40.9 (5.5 + 5.6; enter at 5.9)
5.8 H_0	26°35 (from 4.8)
5.9 H_c	26°41
5.10 $H_0 – H_c$	–6′ (plus is toward Zn)
5.11 Zn	118° (see rule below)

Rule for azimuth, Zn:

N. Hem: LHA < 180°: Zn = 360° – Z

LHA > 180°: Zn = Z

S. Hem: LHA < 180°: Zn = 180° + Z

LHA > 180°: Zn = 180° – Z

Figure 20.22. Form F4 for reduction of Venus sight.

Form F4. Reduction with *H. O. Pub. No. 229*

Planet/star name   Moon

Sun/moon limb:⟨Upper⟩/ Lower

1. To find GMT

1.1 Zone watch time   05 16 50

1.2 Zone description   05

1.3 GMT watch time   10 16 50

1.4 GMT watch error ⟨s+⟩/ f–   10

1.5 GMT   10 17 00

1.6 GMT date   Mar 18 1990

2. To find declination

2.1 Dec.   27°01.4 N (or)⟨S;⟩d 2.2 N (or)⟨S⟩

2.2 d corr.   .6 (skip for star)

2.3 Dec.   27°02.0 N (or)⟨S⟩

3. To find LHA

3.1 GHA $\underline{10}$ hrs.   73°12.1 v $\underline{10.1}$

3.2 Incr. $\underline{17}$ m   s   4°03.4

3.3 v corr.   2.9 (skip for star)

3.4 SHA☆   (star only)

3.5 GHA   77°18.4

3.6 AP long.   70°18.4 (add if E)

3.7 LHA   7°00′ (enter at 5.3)

4. Reduction of sextant observation

4.1 Ht. of eye $\underline{15}$ ft. +   –

4.2 Index corr.   1

4.3 Ht. of eye corr.   3.8

4.4 Net   –2.8

4.5 h_s 41°41.8

4.6 App. alt.   41°39 (4.4 + 4.5)

Sun, star, or planet

4.7 3rd corr. to h_s (Table A2)

    Moon corrections from inside back

4.7a Altitude corr.   +2.0

4.7b (HP $\underline{54.4}$) HP corr. 52.6

4.7c (–30′ if upper limb)   –30

4.8 H_o (4.6 + 4.7)   42°04 (enter at 5.8)

Navigator

Zone date   Mar 18 1990

DR lat.   20°25 ⟨N⟩(or) S; AP lat.   20°

DR long.   70 29 E (or)⟨W;⟩AP long. 70°18

5. Solution by *H.O. Pub. No. 229*

5.1 Dec. difference $\underline{2′}$

5.2 Dec. same   name or contrary ✓ name to lat.

5.3 LHA   7°00′

5.4 AP lat.   20°00′ (nearest whole degree)

5.5 Tab. H $\underline{42°30.8}$ d $\underline{–59.3}$ Z $\underline{171}$ (to 5.11)

5.6 d corr.   –2.0 (from Dec. diff.)

5.7 H_c 42°28.6 (5.5 + 5.6; enter at 5.9)

5.8 H_o 42°04 (from 4.8)

5.9 H_c 42°29

5.10 $H_o – H_c$ –25′ (plus is toward Zn)

5.11 Zn   189° (see rule below)

Rule for azimuth, Zn:

N. Hem: LHA < 180°: Zn = 360° – Z

                LHA > 180°: Zn = Z

S. Hem: LHA < 180°: Zn = 180° + Z

                LHA > 180°: Zn = 180° – Z

Figure 20.23. Form F4 for reduction of moon sight.

2) Now go to the top of the table and find the group of entries corresponding to 41° and pick the one labelled 40′ in the left-hand column. The correction is 52.6 and you write this in 4.7b.

Finally, because you have an upper limb observation, write −30′ in 4.7c, and then combine all the corrections and write the result in 4.8. Copy this over to 5.8.

- **Part 5. Solution by H. O. Pub. No. 229**—From here on, the moon reduction is the same as for other objects. You have a *d* correction which accounts for the fact that the actual declination of the moon (27°02.2′) is not a whole degree. The *d* value in the table (−59.3) must be interpolated for the additional 02.2′, leading to −59.3 (2.2/60) = −2.2. This value is entered in 5.6, and the final steps calculate the intercept and azimuth and plot the LOP.

CORRECTING A FIX FOR PRECESSION
(*H. O. PUB. NO. 249, VOL. I ONLY*)

Note: You only make this correction if you are reducing star sights with *H. O. Pub. No. 249*, Vol. I.

If you obtain a fix using three star sights, and reduce the sights with *H. O. Pub. No. 249*, Vol. I, it is important to make sure you have used a table based on up-to-date star coordinates. To check whether this is the case, look at the front cover and read the Epoch. There you will find a date and if it is within a year or two of the current date, and you are satisfied with an accuracy of a mile or two, then you are in good shape. (*H. O. Pub. No. 249* is reissued every 5 years to keep it more or less up to date, so be sure to examine the cover when you purchase a copy.)

The star coordinates shift in a regular fashion due to the precession of the equinoxes ("wobbling of the earth" is an easier way to think of it). If your table is five years out of date, you may have a substantial error—about one mile per year, at most. Table 5 in the back of *H. O. Pub. No. 249*, Vol. I, will take care of this, and it is quite easy to use.

- **Step 1**—Do all the steps for star sights described above; plot the LOPs and the fix.

- **Step 2**—Find LHA Aries at the average time of the sights.

- **Step 3**—Look at Table 5 and find the portion for the current year, such as 1992. In that portion, find the column with your latitude and scan down to the row with the LHA Aries. Read out the two numbers. For example in 1992 at LHA Aries 90° and North latitude 50° you will find: 2′ 090°. These give the distance and the direction of the correction.

- **Step 4**—From your fix, draw a line with an azimuth of 90° and a length of 2 NM. This is the corrected location of the fix.

WHICH TABLES SHOULD YOU TAKE ON YOUR CRUISE—249 OR 229?

We can't answer that question for you, but here are some things to consider when you try to make up your mind.

1. Few navigators take *both* sets with them. It is probably a better practice to settle on one and get used to it.

2. The majority of your celestial sights will be of the sun, if you are a typical navigator, and this suggests using *H. O. Pub. No. 249*.

3. *H. O. Pub. No. 229* can be rather bulky if you are going to cover a wide range of latitude. But at each latitude it gives you the whole sky and it never gets out of date.

4. *H. O. Pub. No. 249* is popular because Vol. I is quick with the selected navigation stars, and Vols. II and III cover enough of the sky (within 30° of the equator) to satisfy your needs almost all the time. Although it can get out of date due to precession, the corrections to bring it up to date are very easy to apply.

5. If you take *H. O. Pub. No. 249*, you can go anywhere in the world—except the polar regions, where you will probably want *H. O. Pub. No. 229*.

All in all, *H. O. Pub. No. 249* is preferred by most sailors.

CHAPTER TWENTY-ONE

Running Fixes from Celestial Sights

When the sight had been worked out and the position line recorded on a plotting sheet, we resumed sailing and kept it up until just before noon. Then we stopped for the noon latitude sight, which usually took me twenty or thirty minutes, longer than was required for the morning or evening sights. By bringing forward the morning north-south position line, in accordance with the estimated distance and the course we had sailed, until it intersected the noon east-west position line, I got a fairly good idea of where we were at noon.

Robert Manry, Tinkerbelle

INTRODUCTION

The previous chapter discussed conventional celestial fixes that are obtained from either (1) two or more *simultaneous* lines of position, or (2) two lines of position at different times *from the same position*. The second case is illustrated in Figure 21.1. The basic assumption in both cases is that the boat has remained in the same place while you obtained the sights.

But what if the boat has moved during the interval between the sightings? There are many situations where you can see only one celestial object at a time. For example, if you have a series of hazy nights, the stars may be invisible although you can see the moon. During the day near the time of full moon or new moon you may see only the sun. (Or you may be one of many navigators who prefer to confine themselves to sights of the sun, as they are easier to make than star sights.)

How can you get a fix when the boat has moved, as you must do if there is only one object to observe?

We have already discussed a similar problem, in Chapter 6. There we supposed you were sailing along a coast and could identify only a single lighthouse. You were able to obtain your distance from the object by setting the boat on a straight course at a constant speed. You made two sightings of the same object at different times and took advantage of the assumed motion of the boat. You advanced the first LOP to the time of the second LOP and found the intersection. This was a form of *running fix,* and it is given that name because the boat is assumed to *run* a known distance between the sightings.

This chapter will focus on running fixes obtained with celestial objects. The principle is the same as for running fixes in coastal piloting. The trick is to use objects at different times of the day and then compensate by dead reckoning for the motion of the boat between the times of the sights. Chapter 19 gave an example of this when it showed how to combine a series of sun sights made around noon in the tropics.

SETTING UP A RUNNING FIX

First, suppose you in are a stationary boat. (Perhaps you have gone aground or are anchored near an unknown desert island!) In this case, you can take a morning sighting when the sun is in the east. This will give you an LOP that runs approximately north and south. Another sighting later in the day will produce an intersecting LOP, as indicated in Figure 21.1.

There is nothing new in this, because the sun at two times of day does, indeed, provide two independent LOPs.

From here it is a short step to obtain a running fix. Suppose you were to make a morning sight and then move to another island before making a noon sight. The situation is shown schematically in Figure 21.2. If you simply plot the two lines of position from the true assumed positions (APs) their inter-

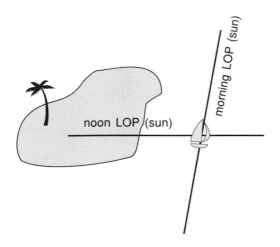

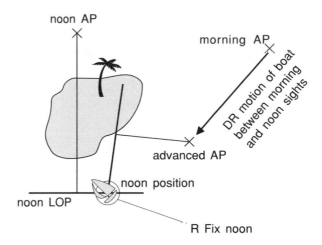

Figure 21.1. Two lines of position obtained from a boat at anchor by observing the sun at different times of day can fix your location near a desert island.

Figure 21.3. Observations made from two different locations may be combined into a running fix by carrying the first AP and LOP forward as though they had ridden on the boat during the interval. They intersect at the second observation point.

section will have little to do with your actual locations, because you did not make both observations from a single place.

What you can do is compensate for the motion of the boat between the sightings. Plot both APs in the usual way and then move the first AP and LOP forward by the amount and in the direction of your boat's motion during the interval between observations. In other words, you carry the first observation forward *as though it were riding on the boat.*

The result is a running fix (labelled "R fix noon" in Figure 21.3). (There is no reason, in principle, why you could not do it in reverse, carrying the

later observation back to the first. But you will probably want to advance it to the later point, to bring it up to date.)

SAMPLE RUNNING FIX FROM TWO OBSERVATIONS OF THE SUN

Here is an example of the process. Do the work using the excerpt from the *Nautical Almanac* in Figure 21.4 and check it against the solution given below.

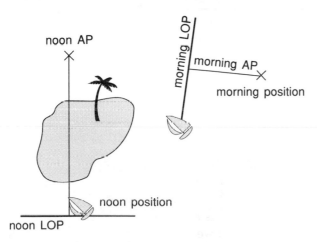

Figure 21.2. Lines of position for observations made from two different points, indicated by small boats. The LOPs will not intersect near either of the observation points.

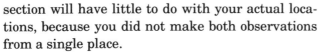

UT (GMT)		SUN			MOON				
		G.H.A.	Dec.		G.H.A.	v	Dec.	d	H.P.
d	h	° ′	° ′		° ′	′	° ′	′	′
17	00	180 04.4	N10 18.4		281 34.5	10.1	S25 30.9	5.2	55.1
	01	195 04.6	19.2		296 03.6	10.1	25 25.7	5.2	55.1
	02	210 04.7	20.1		310 32.7	10.1	25 20.5	5.4	55.2
	03	225 04.9	.. 21.0		325 01.8	10.2	25 15.1	5.6	55.2
	04	240 05.0	21.9		339 31.0	10.1	25 09.5	5.6	55.2
	05	255 05.1	22.8		354 00.1	10.2	25 03.9	5.8	55.2
	06	270 05.3	N10 23.7		8 29.3	10.2	S24 58.1	6.0	55.3
	07	285 05.4	24.5		22 58.5	10.2	24 52.1	6.0	55.3
T	08	300 05.6	25.4		37 27.7	10.3	24 46.1	6.2	55.3
U	09	315 05.7	.. 26.3		51 57.0	10.3	24 39.9	6.3	55.3
E	10	330 05.9	27.2		66 26.3	10.3	24 33.6	6.4	55.4
S	11	345 06.0	28.1		80 55.6	10.3	24 27.2	6.6	55.4
D	12	0 06.2	N10 28.9		95 24.9	10.3	S24 20.6	6.7	55.4
A	13	15 06.3	29.8		109 54.2	10.4	24 13.9	6.8	55.5
Y	14	30 06.4	30.7		124 23.6	10.4	24 07.1	6.9	55.5
	15	45 06.6	.. 31.6		138 53.0	10.5	24 00.2	7.1	55.5
	16	60 06.7	32.5		153 22.5	10.4	23 53.1	7.2	55.5
	17	75 06.9	33.3		167 51.9	10.5	23 45.9	7.3	55.6

Figure 21.4. Excerpt from Nautical Almanac *for reducing sample sun sights of April 17, 1990.*

Date: April 17, 1990
DR position: lat. 40°30′N, long: 50°05′W
Zone description: +3 hours
Watch error: 50 sec. slow
Height of eye: 10 feet
Index error: 3′ on the arc

First sun sight

Watch time: 07 03 10 ZT
h$_S$: 15°00 (lower limb of sun)

- **Step 1**—Carry out the reduction with Form F4 to find the intercept and azimuth of the line to the sun. We do not show the work of the reduction, so you should try it for yourself and check against the result shown below. You will need your own reduction tables for this work.

AP lat.: 40°00′N
AP long.: 50°06′W
Result: Intercept: +2; Zn: 89°

- **Step 2**—Plot the first AP on a universal plotting sheet (Figure 21.5). There is no need to plot the first LOP yet, as you will want to carry it forward to the time of the second sighting.

Second sun sight

Watch time: 12 13 10 ZT
h$_S$: 60°17′ (lower limb of sun)
Use same sextant and watch corrections.

- **Step 3**—Carry out the reduction and compare it with the following:

AP lat.: 40°00′N
AP long.: 50°36.6′W
Result: Intercept: −3; Zn: 176°

- **Step 4**—Plot this AP on the universal plotting sheet (Figure 21.5) and use the intercept and azimuth to construct the sun line and the LOP for the second sun sight.

- **Step 5**—According to your log, the boat sailed on a true course 200° at an average speed of 5 knots between the two observations. Use this information for carrying the first AP forward to the time of the second sighting. Calculate the DR motion of the boat between the two sightings:distance travelled: 25.8 NM, course 200T.

- **Step 6**—On the universal plotting sheet (Figure 21.6), draw a line from the first AP in the direction

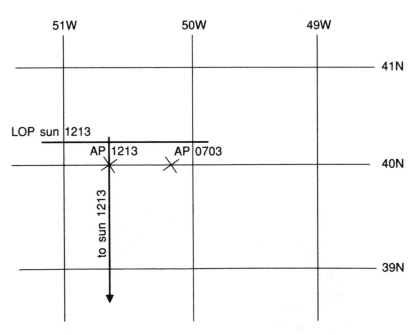

Figure 21.5. Plotting sheet showing first AP (0703 WT) as well as AP and LOP for second sight at 1213.

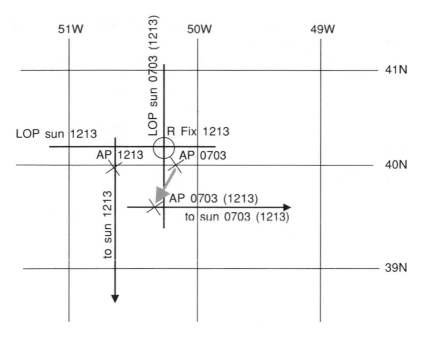

Figure 21.6. Plotting sheet after the first sun sight has been brought forward to the time of the second and its LOP has been constructed and labeled with the original and advanced times, indicating the advanced time with parentheses. The intersection of the two LOPs gives an R Fix corresponding to the advanced time, 1213 WT. The solution for the example given in the text is R Fix: lat. 40°03'N, long. 50°15'W.

200T and with a length of 25.8 NM. Mark the line with these data. The end of this line is the advanced AP for the morning sight. Label it with the original time and, in parentheses, the advanced time: "AP 0703 (1213)."

- **Step 7**—Construct the advanced LOP for the first sight using the intercept and azimuth you found. Label it with the original time and, in parentheses, the advanced time: "LOP sun 0703 (1213)."

- **Step 8**—Mark the intersection as "R Fix 1213." This is your location at the time of the second sight: lat. 40°03'N, long. 50°15'W.

VARIATIONS ON A THEME

Once you have mastered the practice of running fixes, you will be able to construct a wide variety of scenarios. You will, for example, be able to combine an LOP from a shore sighting with a later LOP from a celestial sighting, and you will be able to combine an LOP from a planet sighting in the evening with an LOP from the moon in morning. The principle is the same in all cases: Carry the AP and LOP of the first sighting forward to the time of the

second sighting using dead reckoning to account for the motion of your vessel.

And if there are *three* separate sightings, you can carry the first two forward to the third. The possibilities are endless.

When does a fix become a running fix?

Suppose you plan to get two or three twilight sightings of stars you have selected with the help of *H. O. Pub. No. 249*, Vol. I. You have made the predictions, and you know where to look for the stars, but after you finish the first sighting, you are interrupted—perhaps by a call for help with the rigging.

After 20 minutes you return to the navigation post and take up your sextant and make the sighting of the second star. How are you going to treat the lines of position? Is this a conventional fix or a running fix? Can you treat the LOPs as simultaneous when you come to plot them on the chart? And what if the delay had been 45 minutes?

There is no cut-and-dried answer to this question, but there is a guideline for making your own decision: How far did your boat move between the times of the first and last LOP? If the movement of the boat was less than a mile or two (the nominal accuracy of a single LOP) then you may ignore the motion and treat the LOPs as simultaneous. There is no need to treat the sightings as a running fix if the distance run during the interval between them is less than the typical errors of your fixes.

The validity of this rule depends on the geometry of the LOPs. If the LOPs are more or less perpendicular to each other, the rule is fairly safe.

Uncertainty of a running fix

An uncertainty is introduced by the estimate of the distance run between times of the two sightings. This error will be parallel to the course of the boat,

and there are situations in which the uncertainty can be greatly amplified by unfavorable geometry. Figure 21.7 shows a favorable case, in which the two LOPs are perpendicular to each other. The course of the boat is along a line of latitude, so the uncertainty in the estimated distance affects primarily the longitude, as indicated by the broad shape of the rectangular fix.

Figure 21.8 shows an unfavorable case, where the LOPs were nearly parallel to each other. This shows the importance of making sightings nearly perpendicular to each other to provide a strong fix.

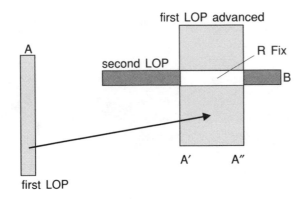

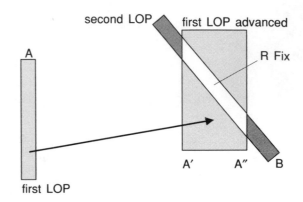

Figure 21.7. Illustrating how errors in carrying forward an LOP for a running fix depend on the geometry of the LOPs. Suppose A and B are LOPs obtained at different times. They each have an uncertainty (due to measurement errors) indicated schematically by the width of the gray line. If the first LOP is brought forward to the second along a course 070T, it will have a larger uncertainty due to the possible error in estimating the boat's speed. This is indicated by the increased width A'A". The white rectangle represents the region of the running fix, and the uncertainty is mostly in longitude because the boat was moving nearly eastward.

Figure 21.8. If B, the second LOP, had been nearly parallel to the first, the region of the R fix would have been much larger, as indicated by the white parallelogram.

CHAPTER TWENTY-TWO

Electronic Aids

The fine drizzle did not worry us at all, rather the reverse. It made the snow and ice smooth and flat to walk on, like the pavingstones of a market-place.

Andrée wrote a series of despatches, which we put into sheaths and attached to our carrier-pigeons.

The birds were then released, one by one. They circled round, disappeared for a few minutes into the white mist to the south of us, returned and flew round and round our camp. Six of them went back into their cages.

Some of them were attacked and driven off by large birds, whose name I did not know. They disappeared into the dense whiteness to the south and west.

Per Olof Sundman, Flight of the Eagle

INTRODUCTION

This chapter describes electronic equipment that has been developed to assist the small boat skipper. These consist of communication channels, piloting aids, emergency devices, and equipment for collecting information that will be a help in navigating.

We cannot give a description of state-of-the-art equipment, because these devices are developing rapidly and new ones are constantly being introduced. The aim of this chapter is merely to provide a selective introduction that will help you chart your way through a sea of possibilities. A mention in this chapter is not necessarily a recommendation, because our intent is merely to alert the reader to the variety of available equipment.

The best way to keep up to date is to read the pertinent magazines and request descriptive literature from manufacturers.

PILOTING

Chart corrections

One of the chores associated with sailing is the tedious job of making corrections to charts, as buoys move and lights are changed, etc. Typically, this has been done by scanning the weekly *Notice to Mariners* issued by the Defense Mapping Agency (DMA) and looking for the chart numbers of interest to you, copying out the corrections, and then transferring them to the charts. Those days can be put be-

hind if you have a telex machine or a computer with a modem.

The DMA has established the Navigation Information Network (NAVINFONET) for the electronic distribution of current navigational data. One service provided by NAVINFONET is the weekly *Notice to Mariners,* which can be obtained via Automated Notice to Mariners System (ANMS). With a computer or telex machine, the user may obtain a variety of information, including:

1. Chart corrections, by chart number, port, or weekly *Notice to Mariners*

2. Broadcast warnings, by region or by number

3. DMA *List of Lights* or corrections, by number or inclusive between numbers

4. Antishipping activity messages

5. Oil drill rig locations, by name or region

6. U.S. Coast Guard *Light Lists*

The first step is to obtain a user ID number, which is issued on request by:

Director
DMA Hydrographic/Topographic Center
ATTN: MCN/NAVINFONET
Washington, DC 20315-0030

An identification code and user manual will be sent by return mail. (A description of the system can also be found on the back of selected issues of the *Pilot Chart* for the North Atlantic.) Nearly any type of personal computer with a modem and communications software can be used to obtain data from the ANMS once your user ID has been obtained. A list of telephone lines for telex or 300-, 1200-, and 2400-baud modems is supplied, and the user must pay only for a telephone call to the 301 area. Once the contact has been established, a prompting menu will appear and the user can select the desired services. By saving the screen to disc, the data are stored for later editing and use. You do not need to be a computer wizard to use the system. As long as you know how to make telephone contact with your modem, you will be in business.

The DMA is working toward the day when the Electronic Chart Display and Information System (ECDIS) will be fully operational and navigators will have virtually instantaneous access to updated charts.

Radio direction finding

This is described in Chapter 7. In a pinch, you can make do with a hand-held radio, but a properly installed special-purpose device will have greater sensitivity and a more accurate directional readout.

Flux gate compass

This is a recent development in small-boat navigation and, although it may not entirely replace the old reliable magnetic card compass for some time to come, it can be a nice supplement. It detects the local magnetic field by generating its own field with a coil and an electric current and determining what is required to cancel out the ambient field. This means that it requires a small amount of electric power, but this may be provided by battery because the drain is low and the device can be turned off.

Like a conventional compass, the flux gate compass detects the local magnetic field, so it is affected by variation and deviation. There are three advantages to this type of compass:

1. There are no moving parts and no liquid chamber, so the compass is virtually maintenance-free, and it is not subject to the rocking motion of the boat. You can read it with a typical precision of about one degree.

2. You can mount the detector in a location on your boat that has been selected for having a small compass deviation.

3. The signal produced by the detector is electrical, so you can mount repeaters that display the reading virtually anywhere you want: at the helm, at the navigation station, and above your bunk. This is particularly useful if you are single-handing and want to keep up to date on the boat's heading.

Such compasses can also be linked to computers, auto-steering devices, and radar displays, and can automatically alert you to changes in the boat's heading.

Hand bearing compass

The value of this type of gadget in piloting is described in Chapter 5, and it cannot be overstated. No boat should be without one. Until recently, hand bearing compasses consisted of little magnetic compasses equipped with a simple sighting vane or mounted in binoculars. Hand-held flux gate compasses mounted in a monocular are now available from several sources, including KVH Industries (110 Enterprise Center, Middletown, RI 02840) and Autohelm America (New Whitfield St., Guilford, CT 06437). The KVH *Datascope* has a 5× monocular, a digital timer that can be keyed to observed sightings, and a range-finding scale. To use the range finder, you enter the known height of the object and then adjust a scale so the object is covered. The distance is then displayed.

Tide predictions

A number of small special-purpose calculators with the tidal cycles built in are advertised in sailing magazines. *Tidefinder* is available from Conex Electro-Systems (P.O. Box 1342, Bellingham, WA 98227); it has East and West Coast versions and claims to have 2000+ stored and programmed tide and current locations. *MacTides* is available from Nautasoft (Box 282, Rockland, DE 19732).

Electronic charts

Several private software companies offer digitally encoded charts that can be displayed on a Macintosh computer. Far Tide Technologies (18 Ray Ave., Burlington, MA 01803) offers *Navigate!* which is a stand-alone application intended for use on yachts between 30 and 60 feet in length. The program comes with one regional chart but further charts covering all U.S. waters, the Bahamas, and the Caribbean are available for $95 each.

Navico (Old Windsor Rd., Bloomfield, CT 06002) offers *NAVPlus,* which is described as "an electronic integration of charts, Loran and navigational functions." When installed in a Macintosh that has been linked to the electronic position devices, such as Loran and GPS, this program also provides automatic tracking of the boat's position on the computerized chart.

Software and digitized charts for IBM-compatible computers are available from DF Crane (341 W. Broadway, San Diego, CA 92101).

Electronic chart tables

For those who insist on using real paper charts, it is possible to purchase a digitizing tablet. When you mount a chart on it, the device can read the position of a special pen, and the output can be hooked to your Loran-C, GPS, or autopilot. Available from Maritime Pilot (500 North York Rd., Hatboro, PA 19040).

Radar

Radio pulses provide "eyes" to avoid land and ships in the fog and at night. A rotating antenna sweeps the horizon every few seconds and sends out a narrow beam of radio pulses. The pulses travel 300 meters per microsecond (10^{-6} sec), reflect from objects in their paths, and return to the antenna, which also acts as a receiver. The time delay between the emission of each pulse and the reception of the return echo is measured and displayed as a distance on the screen. (This is described in Chapter 19.) The pattern of echoes is also displayed on a screen with the radar antenna shown at the center of a concentric grid.

The effective range of the radar signals is similar to that of visible light on a clear day, because radio and visual waves behave similarly. The visual horizon in nautical miles is given by $1.15\sqrt{h}$, where h is the height above sea level in feet. Radar waves (3 cm) are refracted slightly more than visible light, and the expression for them is $1.22\sqrt{h}$. From the top of a 50-foot mast your radar horizon will be about 9 miles away, which is about one mile farther than the geometric horizon. You could see the tip of a 50-foot object at a distance twice as great, or about 18 miles. Small-boat radars are advertised to have ranges of from 16 to 48 NM.

Many boats carry passive radar reflectors high on the mast; this will produce an echo on radar sets and help make the boat "visible" at greater distances.

A feature available in some of the more elaborate radars is color coding to indicate the strength of the returned signal, so a tanker might be red and a buoy yellow. Another useful feature is target trailing, in which the speed and direction of the targets are indicated by trails on the screen. If a trail points directly at the center of the screen, you are probably on a collision course.

Another option is the manner in which the display is oriented. In the old days, before flux gate compasses, the screens were all "heading-up," so that the objects in front of the vessel appeared in the upper part of the screen. Now that flux gate compass directions can be electrically signalled to the radar, you have the additional options of "north-referenced" (in which the display is heading-up, but the bearings are true) and "north-up" (in which the display is oriented as in a conventional map, regardless of the vessel's heading).

NAVIGATION

Sight reduction equipment

For most of us, the main fun of celestial navigation is the planning (predicting, selecting, and finding the stars), taking a series of sights from the deck of a boat, and then plotting the fix. Between the sighting and the plotting comes the reduction procedure, which is less fun, even for the arithmeticians among us.

Calculator programs are available to do the arithmetic. After you have used one for a few days—completing your three-sight fixes in six minutes or less instead of 30 minutes or more—you will wonder how you got along without one. (You will also find yourself taking and reducing more sights, and that is good.) Some are expensive and some are not. You get what you pay for, so find the program/calculator you want and then ask the price and go to the bank if you need to. You will not regret the investment, once the pain of paying for it has passed.

Programs differ widely in their ease of use and their capacity for coping with error correction. The only way to find out what suits you is to try out a few and then send back the ones that are not satisfactory or not needed.

Here are some of the key features to look for when you start shopping:

- *Almanacs*—The great virtue of these devices is the time saved and errors eliminated when you don't have to page through the printed almanac looking for the data. We wouldn't consider buying a calculator/program that doesn't offer a complete stored almanac for the sun, moon, stars, and planets for at least the next ten years.

- *Clock*—A built-in clock is very handy, but probably not crucial. In some computers, you can adjust the rate of the clock and have it automatically store the time of the sight.

- *Plotting the fix*—A small printer to display the lines of position can be expensive and a drain on the batteries. Some of us prefer to do our own plotting, anyway.

- *Alphabetic prompting*—Programs that tell you what to do next are far easier to use than those that simply blink at you while you try to decide.

- *Auxiliary calculations*—In addition to sight reduction, there are other useful functions, such as solving for great-circle courses and solving drift and set problems, as well as quick distance-off calculations. These can be very handy.

- *Averaging of sights*—You will often want to take at least three, and possibly six, sights of each star to average out the motion of the boat. You can, of course, do this in your head from the list you have written, but it is safer and quicker to have a small preliminary program that will do the averaging for you before you start the main reduction.

- *Remembering input*—Programs differ in how much they will carry over from one sight reduction to the next. For example, if you have to re-enter the date for every sight, you will soon become irritated. These reduction programs do not use an assumed position—that was a trick we used to simplify table look-up, and that's no longer a consideration with a calculator. So you should be able to enter your dead reckoning position for a set of sights once and for all.

One final remark: Dedicated machines, which can serve no other purpose, become outdated quickly, and it seems to make more sense to buy a general-purpose calculator and then buy programs for it. You can add your own programs when you want.

Loran-C

This is currently the most popular and widespread system for locating yourself at sea, although it leaves most of the southern hemisphere without coverage (see Figure 22.1). It is relatively inexpensive, reliable, and easy to use—requiring little more than the flicking of a few buttons to produce a set of latitude and longitude coordinates.

Loran-C is called a "hyperbolic system" because it establishes lines of position (LOPs) that are hyperbolas. Your receiver locates itself by finding the intersections of two sets of hyperbolas. (Nonhyperbolic systems include radar, inertial guidance, and satellite ranging, as with global positioning satellites.) The LOPs are established by measuring the time of reception of low-frequency (LF: 100 kHz) radio pulses emitted by pairs of shore stations. The pulses spread out from the stations, as illustrated in Figure 22.2, and the receiver determines the difference of propagation time-delays from the two stations. In Figure 22.2, one LOP is indicated, corresponding to vessels that are equally distant from stations A and B. In this excample, the receiver has determined that the time delays are equal, so the LOP is midway between the stations.

In Figure 22.3, the vessel has moved down and to the right. Now the signals require 13 milliseconds (ms) to arrive from station A and only 7 ms to arrive from station B. The difference, 6 ms, determines a hyperbolic LOP which lies closer to B than A. The difference of distances from the two stations is given by the time difference (6×10^{-3} sec.) multiplied by the speed of light (300×10^{6} meters per second), giving 1,800 kilometers (1 km = 0.54 NM). This distance is the typical maximum range of Loran-C. Figure 22.4 is a schematic diagram of the lines of position from one pair of Loran-C stations.

There are two keys to the design of the Loran C system. They have to do with identifying the stations that are sending the pulse, and with the precise timing of pulses from pairs of stations:

1. All signals are sent at the same radio frequency (100 kHz), but the pulses from each station are sent at a group repetition rate that identifies the station, so the receiver knows how to interpret the information.

Numbers on the Loran-C chart, such as 9991, represent the pulse rate in tens of microseconds.

2. To ensure that the timing of received pulses will actually tell you the difference of distances from the stations, the pulses must be emitted at precisely the same instant. This is achieved in a clever way. A master station sends out its pulse, which starts on its way toward you. At the same time it travels toward a slave station that is a known distance away from the master. When it arrives at the slave, it triggers a pulse emission from the slave. (Because the distance between the slave and master is known, the time delay is also known.) This pulse and the original pulse arrive at your vessel and the time difference is measured and is then corrected for the slave's delay. This gives the the difference for the hyperbolic line of position. The process is illustrated in Figures 22.5 and 22.6.

Omega

This system operates at frequencies much lower than Loran-C, and its signals can be picked up at much longer range than Loran-C. Eight transmitting stations provide worldwide coverage, permitting fixes with an accuracy of 2 to 4 NM. To obtain a fix, the operator records numbers displayed on the panel and, with corrections obtained from a table, plots the data on an Omega plotting chart. The corrections depend on the season, time of day, and location. They are obtained from *H.O. Pub. No. 224* of the Defense Mapping Agency Hydrographic/Topographic Center, Washington, DC 20315-0030.

An Omega navigation receiver attached to a NAVSAT (see below) to provide continuous updating between satellite fixes is available, for example, from Tracor Instruments (6500 Tracor Lane, Austin, TX 78725)

NAVSAT

This satellite navigation system is operated by the U.S. Navy. It is rapidly becoming outdated, as it is slow and its fixes are far less frequent than is possible with GPS (below).

Global positioning satellites

By the end of 1992, a global network of two dozen Department of Defense satellites will be in orbit providing three- or four-station fixes on a 24-hour-a-day basis. Established for military purposes, the satellites will also be accessible (with slightly less precision) for civilian uses.

The system is as easy to use as Loran-C—merely turn it on and push a button or two and wait for the dial to display your coordinates—and it gives truly global coverage. The receiver detects timed radio signals from satellites whose orbits are about 12,000 NM in radius, have periods of 12 hours, and are tilted about 60° from the equator. It then determines your three-dimensional location by using distances and doppler shifts from the four satellites that are in the best positions above your horizon. Accuracy of a fix using nonmilitary equipment ought to be about 30 meters.

The GPS system is a remarkable achievement. Each satellite carries an atomic clock (actually four of them, including three backups) and a receiver and memory bank that can accept orbital parameters for itself and its companions. These data are radioed up from tracking stations on the ground. The transmitter of each satellite sends out a complex identifying signal that includes its own position and the approximate positions of other satellites. (These other positions are used by the vessel's GPS computer to decide which combination of satellites will give the strongest fix.) The satellite also sends out a carrier tone that is doppler-shifted by its orbital motion with respect to the vessel. As the satellite flies by, the distance and doppler shift vary in a way that depends on the precise location of the vessel and the vessel's clock error. The computer's task is to detect these patterns for four satellites and search for an assumed position and clock error of the vessel that makes the patterns consistent with the known orbits of the satellites. The result is a spatial fix, giving not only latitude and longitude, but height above sea level (which, if not close to zero, would indicate that something has gone wrong). Accurate time is also provided.

Many GPS receivers are already on the market and more are appearing each year. The prices are dropping rapidly, so don't buy a system until you are ready to use it.

At least two private groups are planning to launch their own satellite navigation systems (Geostar and Starfix). These may give nonmilitary customers a higher precision than planned for GPS. (See *Ocean Navigator,* May 1989, p. 53.)

At 14 minutes after every hour, station WWV broadcasts a brief status report on the GPS satellite system. (See Table 13.1.)

LORAN-C COVERAGE DIAGRAM

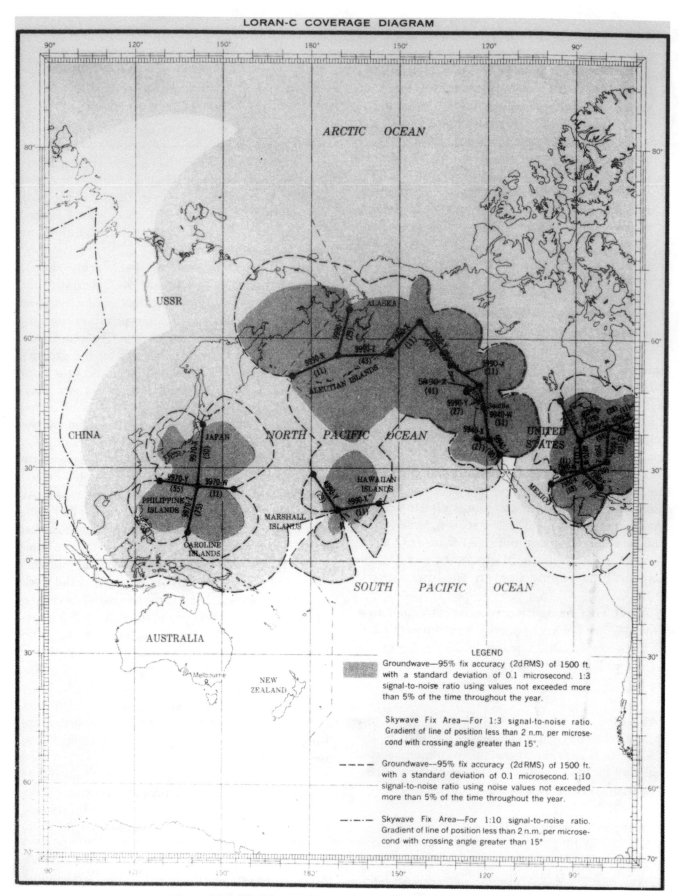

Figure 22.1. World map showing Loran-C coverage (Bowditch).

LORAN-C COVERAGE DIAGRAM

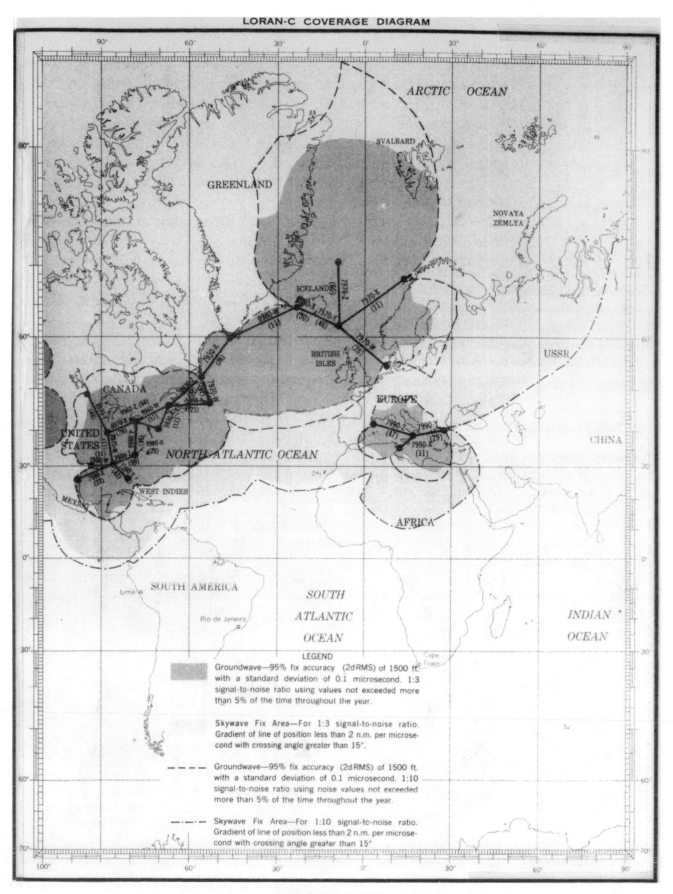

Figure 22.1. (cont.)

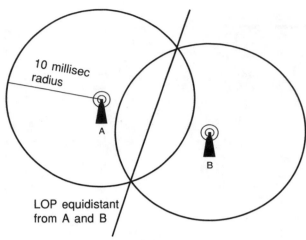

Figure 22.2. In Loran-C, two stations emit trains of pulses and their arrivals are timed at the vessel. In the case illustrated here, a vessel is equally distant from stations A and B, so it receives the pulses at the same time. The LOP is a hyperbola that lies midway between the stations. In this special case, the LOP is a straight line. A second LOP using pulses from at least one more station is required for a fix.

TWO-WAY COMMUNICATION

The radio spectrum

The behavior of radio waves in the earth's atmosphere depends on their frequency or wavelength and the state of the atmosphere. It is convenient to

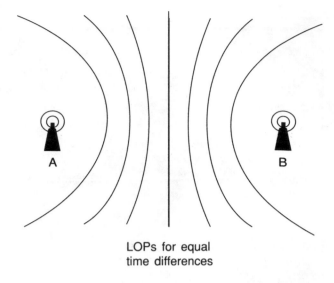

Figure 22.4. Network of hyperbolic lines of position from one pair of Loran-C stations.

measure wavelength in meters and frequency in megaherz (1 MHz = 10^6 cycles per second) or kiloherz (1 kHz = 10^3 cycles per second). These two parameters of radio waves are related by the expression:

Wave length (meters) × Frequency (MHz) = 300

So a 15-meter radio wave has a frequency of 20 MHz.

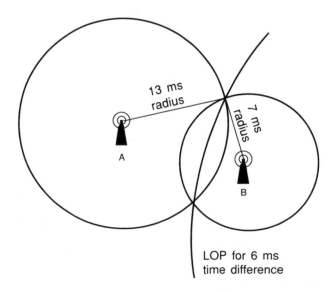

Figure 22.3. In this case, the Loran-C signals are received 6 milliseconds (ms) earlier from station B than station A. This puts the vessel on a hyperbolic LOP that is closer to B than A.

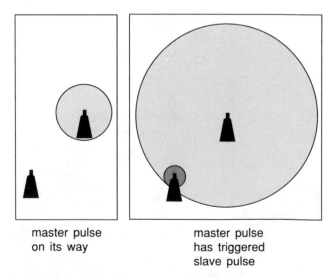

Figure 22.5. In Loran-C, a master station emits a pulse and this triggers the emission of a delayed pulse from the slave station. The delay is known precisely. See Figure 22.6.

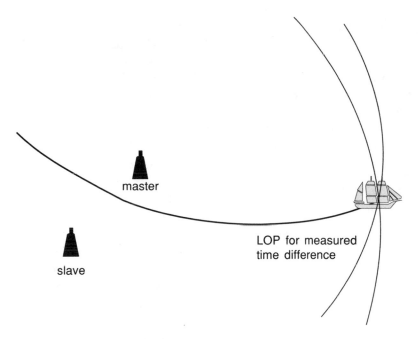

Figure 22.6. The master and slave pulses arrive at the vessel, where the Loran-C receiver recognizes them by their pulse repetition rate and corrects the arrival times for the known delay of the slave pulse. The corrected time difference gives a Loran line of position. By combining with data from another slave or another master-slave pair, the fix is obtained.

Table 22.1. Radio bands

Name of Band	Frequency (kHz)	Wavelength (meters)	Uses
VLF (very low)	10 to 30	30,000 to 10,000	Omega navigation
LF (low)	30 to 300	10,000 to 1,000	AM broadcast, RDF, Loran
MF (medium)	300 to 3,000 (MHz)	1,000 to 100	Coast Guard, radiotelephone
HF (high)	3 to 30	100 to 10	Shortwave, ham, CB
VHF (very high)	30 to 300	10 to 1	Ham, TV, aircraft, FM broadcast, maritime mobile
UHF (ultra high)	300 to 3,000	1m to 10 cm	TV, GPS
SHF (super high)	3,000 to 30,000	10 cm to 1 cm	Radar, microwave

Sensitivity to state of the atmosphere

For the most part the lower frequencies (VLF through HF) are not sensitive to meteorological conditions. However, VHF and UHF are affected by scatter from weather-related electrical irregularities in the troposphere. Also the very short SHF waves can be affected by rain, as exemplified by "weather radar" on the nightly news.

Electrification of the upper atmosphere in a broad layer called the ionosphere is critical to radio propagation at many frequencies. It produces a "mirror" that reflects upward-moving propagating waves back down toward the earth, as well as absorbing the waves of certain frequencies. Waves that have bounced down from the ionosphere are skywaves and waves that have come directly from the source are called groundwaves. The interplay and relative importance of these two types of waves vary radically with ionospheric conditions. Excellent discussions are found in *Bowditch* and the American Radio Relay League's *Handbook for the Amateur.*

Several key features of the behavior of radio waves are the following:

- The ionosphere traps the VLF waves near the earth, so they can propagate all the way around the earth, but antenna systems for VLF are very inefficient unless they are huge, so these frequencies are only used for specialized communication and navigation signals.

- LF is used for standard broadcast and direction finding, and the signals typically propagate hundreds of miles during the day and much farther at night.

- The MF and HF bands are used for long-range communication. Propagation varies drastically with the time of day and the amount of solar activity, so one of the challenges of shortwave work is finding the best conditions for communication between selected geographic locations.

- The VHF, UHF, and SHF waves are not reflected by the ionosphere, so there is usually no skywave at these frequencies, and propagation is typically along a line of sight and is cut off by the horizon, which is typical of FM and TV broadcasts. These frequencies are reliable over short distances and are much used for radiotelephones and digital communication by computers (packet radio).

Types of radio emission

When you scan a list of marine radio broadcasts you will often find a three-letter designation, such as A3J, which describes the nature of the emission.

Virtually all long-range communication is by amplitude modulation (AM), but this comes in a variety of modes. In the standard broadcast mode, the transmitter sends out a carrier wave of fixed frequency—that's the frequency you tune on your dial when you listen to the ball game on your AM radio. The carrier, by itself, is just a constant tone and it is totally dull. It carries no information by itself. In order to send music or voice, the radio transmitter modulates the carrier before sending it out (gives it a characteristic shape that conveys the useful information). In AM it is the amplitude of the radio wave that is modulated; in FM broadcast, it is the frequency of the wave that is modulated. (We won't discuss FM.)

The modulation is achieved by mixing the carrier with another wave that comes from the music. The beats of interference between the two waves produce two new frequencies by adding and sub-

tracting the two waves' frequencies. These are called the upper sideband (USB) and lower sideband (LSB) because they are quite close to the original carrier.

The result is that three signals are sent out: (1) the USB, (2) the carrier, and (3) the LSB. This is fine and dandy if the receiver is nearby. But it is a waste of energy to send out both sidebands and the carrier. All the music is carried in each of the sidebands, so it is unnecessary repetition to send all the signals. Better to pump all the energy into one of the sidebands and just send it. That is the essence of single sideband (SSB) broadcasting.

When your SSB receiver picks up the signal, you won't be able to make out the music or the voice until your receiver has provided a carrier signal and mixed it back in again, producing beats to reconstruct the original wave. A fuller discussion may be found in the latest edition of the American Radio Relay League's *Handbook for Amateurs*.

Each of these modes of broadcast has a special designation, but the system was changed recently, and many publications are still operating on the old system. We shall only describe the new.

1. First symbol: type of modulation of the main carrier
   N: unmodulated, carrier is sent out as a constant tone
   A: double sideband (DSB)
   H: single sideband (SSB), full carrier
   J: single sideband (SSB), suppressed carrier

2. Second symbol: nature of signal modulating the carrier
   0: no modulation
   1: digital pulses, for data transmission
   2: digital with modulating subcarrier
   3: single channel with analog signal, as voice or Morse code

3. Third symbol: type of information transmitted
   N: no information
   A: telegraphy for aural reception (Morse code)
   B: telegraphy for automatic reception (packet)
   C: facsimile
   D: telemetry, digital data
   E: telephony (voice and sound)
   F: television

Examples

1. Amplitude modulation (AM)
   A3E (A3 in old system): AM voice
   A1A: telegraphy

J3E (A3J in old system): SSB voice, suppressed carrier (This is a highly efficient mode of transmission and is frequently used for MF and HF communication.)

2. Frequency modulation (FM)
    F2D: data
    F2B: automatic telegraphy
    F3E: voice
    F3C: facsimile (FAX)

Communication bands and their uses

MF—The medium frequency band is used by the Coast Guard for coastal harbor communication in SSB at 2182 kHz (distress and calling) and 2670 kHz.

HF Coast Guard CALL system—If you plan long-range communication, as for a global trip, you may want a transceiver capable of HF-SSB operation. The U.S. Coast Guard monitors a set of frequencies for SSB communication as well as transmitting weather and emergency broadcasts in the HF band. This is the CALL (Contact and Long-range Liaison) system, and it is particularly useful where the MF and VHF transmission will not reach. Transmitting and receiving are done on different frequencies. Designated pairs of frequencies are as follows:

Transmit (kHz)	Receive (kHz)
4134.3	4428.7
6200.0	6506.4
8241.5	8765.4
12342.4	13113.2
16534.4	17307.3

HF High Seas Radiotelephone—In addition to the Coat Guard service, many coastal regions have high frequency (HF) single sideband (SSB) radio installations that offer links to a telephone service. In the United States, for example, AT&T runs three stations that can be used for two-way communication between ships and between ships and land telephones. These stations (KMI in Point Reyes, CA; WOM in Ft. Lauderdale, FL; WOO in Manahawkin, NJ) operate around the clock on several dozen channels in the 2 to 23 MHz frequency range. They use upper sideband (USB) in the duplex mode, so the coast station and the ship transmit in slightly different frequencies. By a proper choice of channel (frequency) it is usually possible to commu-

nicate over great distances with this system. Some channels also broadcast National Weather Service information several times a day.

For further information, call AT&T High Seas Radio Service at one of its coast stations (KMI: (414) 669-1055; WOM and WOO: (609) 597-2201). Also see *Marine Radio Telephone User's Handbook* (Radio Technical Commission for Marine Services, P.O. Box 19087, Washington, DC 20036).

Standard broadcast in the HF band—International programs of news, entertainment, and music are found in a series of HF bands, and these broadcasts are often beamed at particular geographic areas at times of day or night when propagation is expected to be best. An excellent source of frequencies and schedules is found in *World Radio TV Handbook* (see bibliography at end of chapter).

VHF-FM marine radio and radiotelephone—Certain VHF-FM frequencies in the range from 156.05 MHz to 162.425 MHz have been named as channels by the Coast Guard. Radios for these frequencies are found on nearly all vessels and are used for short-range communications, ship to ship or ship to harbor. The channels are numbered 1 to 80 and are obtained with special crystals in the VHF marine radio and are to be used for special aspects of marine communication. The uses of the principal channels are the following:

- Ch. 16 (156.8 MHz): Distress, safety, and calling; monitored by all Coast Guard stations and most marinas. After establishing contact on this channel, switch immediately to a working frequency.

- Ch. 22A (157.1 MHz): Coast Guard liaison, to be used after making contact on Ch. 16.

- Ch. 1, 5, 12, 14, 20, 63, 65, 66, 73, 74, 77: Port operations, for directing boat traffic in and near ports or waterways. Messages must be about the handling of the boat.

- Ch. 13, 67: Navigational or bridge-to-bridge channel, available to all ships. Messages must be about navigation. Also used as working channel at most locks and drawbridges.

- Ch. 6 (156.3 MHz): Intership safety messages and search-and-rescue operations.

- Ch. 9, 68, 69, 71, 72, 78: Noncommercial working channels for recreational boats. Messages must concern the needs of the boat. Use Ch. 72 for ship-to-ship only.

Citizens band (CB)—Forty channels in the HF band of the FM spectrum from 26.695 to 27.405 MHz have been assigned to CB. These may be used without an operator's license as long as the transceiver conforms to the FCC regulations. Ordinarily, however, the VHF marine bands (listed above) are more commonly used and monitored, so you should not count on using your CB unless you have made arrangements with someone else who has a CB radio.

Shortwave and amateur radio—The FCC has reserved certain frequencies for licensed amateur (ham) radio operation. Many special-purpose ham radios permit operation only in the small number of assigned bands, as distinguished from marine radios which usually permit general coverage. If you wish to receive international shortwave broadcasts (news, weather, etc.) as well as ham radio signals, you will need a general coverage radio.

The virtue of the ham operation is that it permits you to carry out personal communication not necessarily concerned with the vessel and its needs. It also puts you in touch with thousands of other amateurs around the world. Satellite and computer (packet) communication is also part of the ham radio world, as described below. One serious limitation of the ham bands is that you are not allowed to transact business, or even check up on the progress of your own business, on these frequencies. If you wish to do that, you will need to use marine SSB frequencies or a radiotelephone.

The five levels of ham license are Novice, Technician, General, Advanced, Extra. Tests for these licenses require some proficiency in Morse code and a basic understanding of the principle of radio, although the FCC has instituted a "Communicator" class that does not require Morse code. It is, however, limited to frequencies above 30 MHz (10 meters and shorter), so it will not permit HF operation and this limits its usefulness for marine operations.

The permitted frequency bands and the privileges of various levels of license are shown in Table 22.2. The more advanced the license, the broader the privileges.

Satellite communication by packet radio—In 1961 the first Orbiting Satellite Carrying Amateur Radio (OSCAR I) was launched into earth orbit. Since then, more than a dozen successors have been launched, and communication via satellite relay has become an important part of amateur radio—not to mention the commercial satellites that have been launched for telephone and TV communication. Most of the OSCAR ham-to-ham communication is by VHF and UHF *packet,* which is a computer-controlled, digital mode of transmission. It sends bursts, or packets, of data and this is preferred because it is fast. When the satellite flies over, there is no time for voice conversation or for a leisurely 10- to 15-wpm Morse code transmission. To send packet radio, you need a personal computer and a terminal node controller (TNC), in addition to your transceiver. The TNC sits between your computer and your transceiver and lets the two talk to each other. It can translate to and from Morse code, and it can decode radio teletype as well.

Here is how it works. From your computer, you initiate a message which is translated to a packet by your TNC and is sent out by your transceiver. The packet has the call sign of the station you are addressing, and it is picked up by the OSCAR satellite or, if you are very near the coast, it may be picked up by a land-based repeater. In either case, the packet is forwarded to the addressee, where it is automatically received, and if the error-check shows that the message is intact, it is acknowledged. Ideally, using packet radio will become as simple as mailing a letter. You address it, drop it in the box, and don't worry about the process by which it is delivered. Mariners have begun using this as a communication link to their home base.

See *Your Gateway to Packet Radio* (Horzepa, 1989) and *The Satellite Experimenter's Handbook* (Davidoff, 1984) both published by the ARRL (address at end of chapter).

Licenses required

A Federal Communications Commission (FCC) ship station license is required to operate an SSB or VHF marine radio. This no-test license is obtained with FCC Form 506 and it is not transferable. That is, each time a boat changes owners it must be re-licensed, and each time an owner changes boats the same is true. Application for a license is obtained from the FCC licensing bureau at P.O. Box 1040, Gettysburg, PA 17325. You will be issued a call sign that is to be used during all transmissions.

Table 22.2. Frequency allocations in the ham bands for various license levels. The communicator license is restricted to 30 MHz and above.

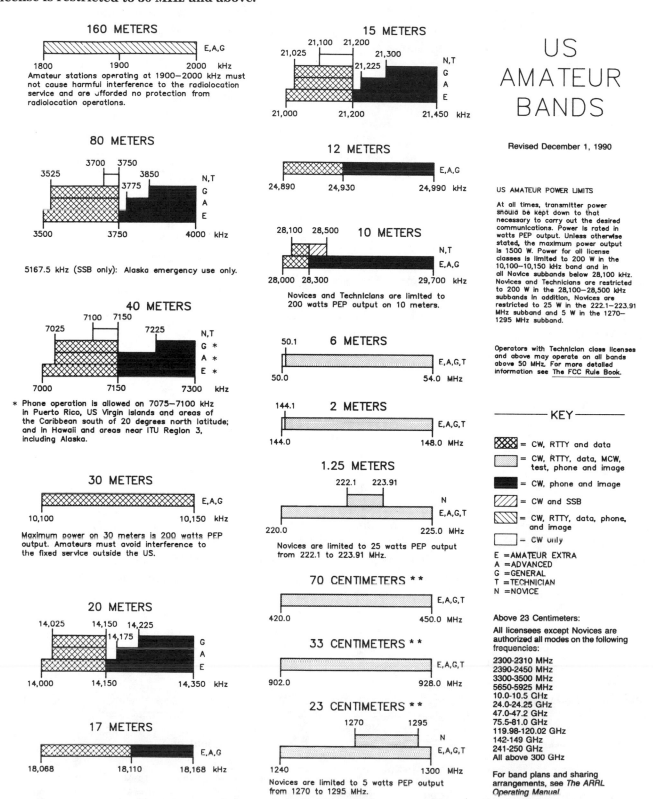

US AMATEUR BANDS

Revised December 1, 1990

US AMATEUR POWER LIMITS

At all times, transmitter power should be kept down to that necessary to carry out the desired communications. Power is rated in watts PEP output. Unless otherwise stated, the maximum power output is 1500 W. Power for all license classes is limited to 200 W in the 10,100–10,150 kHz band and in all Novice subbands below 28,100 kHz. Novices and Technicians are restricted to 200 W in the 28,100–28,500 kHz subbands. In addition, Novices are restricted to 25 W in the 222.1–223.91 MHz subband and 5 W in the 1270–1295 MHz subband.

Operators with Technician class licenses and above may operate on all bands above 50 MHz. For more detailed information see *The FCC Rule Book*.

KEY

- = CW, RTTY and data
- = CW, RTTY, data, MCW, test, phone and image
- = CW, phone and image
- = CW and SSB
- = CW, RTTY, data, phone, and image
- = CW only

E = AMATEUR EXTRA
A = ADVANCED
G = GENERAL
T = TECHNICIAN
N = NOVICE

Above 23 Centimeters:

All licensees except Novices are authorized all modes on the following frequencies:

2300-2310 MHz
2390-2450 MHz
3300-3500 MHz
5650-5925 MHz
10.0-10.5 GHz
24.0-24.25 GHz
47.0-47.2 GHz
75.5-81.0 GHz
119.98-120.02 GHz
142-149 GHz
241-250 GHz
All above 300 GHz

For band plans and sharing arrangements, see *The ARRL Operating Manual*

** Geographical and power restrictions apply to these bands. See *The FCC Rule Book* for information about your specific area.

If you plan to dock in a foreign port, you must also have a Restricted Radiotelephone Operator's Permit, obtained with FCC form 753.

Although these licenses do not require a test, you must stay out of the assigned amateur frequency bands. If you wish to operate in the amateur frequency bands, you will need an amateur (ham) license, for which there is a test. Details are given below.

How to get an amateur radio (ham) license—There is no age limit. (At least one four-year-old has done it, as well as people in their sixties and beyond.) More than two million people are licensed, and the fee is nominal, $5 or less.

Unless you decide to limit yourself to VHF frequencies and higher with a Communicator license, you will need to demonstrate an ability to copy Morse code at 5 words per minute (wpm). (There is no test of ability to transmit, because it is easier to send than to receive. According to a recent ruling, people with hearing impairment can be excused from the code requirement.)

You need to learn some of the basic terminology of radio and become acquainted with the Federal Communications Commission (FCC) rules concerning ham operation. There are plenty of instruction books and practice tapes available. Your first step should probably be to buy the American Radio Relay League (ARRL) *Handbook for the Radio Amateur.* (But don't try to read it like a novel. Pick the parts that apply to each step of your progress. The ARRL, by the way, is the largest amateur radio organization in the world, and it acts as the major liaison between the public and the FCC. It administers the FCC tests for ham radio licensing.)

The code is the most difficult part of the test for most of us, but it can be fun, and in six months you can be ready for your test. Here are some steps:

1. Get a complete copy of the Morse code, including abbreviations and the so-called Q signals. Start memorizing them.

2. Get a shortwave receiver capable of single sideband (SSB) reception.

3. Start listening to the ham bands (see list above).

4. Tune in to the practice code broadcasts from the ARRL station W1AW in Newington, CT (schedule below). Do this several times a week.

5. Get a tape recorder and record some of the broadcasts. Play the recordings to yourself when you are alone driving in a car or at home. You can also buy practice tapes from the ARRL.

Techniques for learning Morse code vary. At first you will probably want to write down the letters as you decode them. This is fine at low speeds, but you should soon shift to listening for words and writing down the entire word. Some people get in the habit of repeating the code to themselves and then speaking the translations. This will put a low ceiling on your code speed. The goal should be to make the process a reflex action, without losing time in a methodical letter-by-letter translation. Try to build up words and sentences in your head. You are learning a new language, and you should try to jump from the sound to the meaning as directly as possible. This can only be done with hours and hours of listening.

Table 22.3. W1AW practice code schedule*

All times EST/EDT
M, W, F: 9 AM and 7 PM
T, Th, S, Su: 4 PM and 10 PM
USB: 1818, 1890, 3580kHz, 7048kHz, and
14.07, 21.0675, 28.0675, 50.08 MHz

In addition to the code test, there will be a multiple-choice test on regulations and principles of radio. Get the special training materials for the novice and technician licenses and read through them. (You can get books that list all the questions in the pool from which your test will be chosen. If you can answer all of them, you are sure to pass.) If you need supplementary material to help you make sense of it, there are many things you can do. You can find a friend who is a ham operator, sign up for a course with a local radio ham club or a private tutor, or go to Heathkit and buy their self-help manual.

When you go to a test session run by the ARRL, you take the tests one license at a time, working your way up. The code test is the same for Novice

---

*Subject to change; check with ARRL. Each broadcast is about one hour and consists of code at 5, 7½, 10, 13, and 15 wpm. An easy way to remember the schedule is to number the days of the week starting with Sn = 0, M = 1, etc. The broadcasts on odd days are at the odd hours.

and Technician (5 wpm), so if you pass it and also pass the Novice written test, you may try the written test for Technician at the same session. Do it. Nothing is lost by failing, and you will be better prepared for the next time. Lots of people get their Technician licenses on the first try. The Technician license excludes a few useful bands, so you may want to go ahead to the General license, which is what you will probably want for marine cruising.

Ham or marine?

When it comes time to equip your vessel for short-wave communication, you must decide whether to get a marine or ham radio—or both. (As sold, radios are not able to serve both purposes.) The decision will depend on the purpose. If you need to transact business by radio, then ham is out. If you want global communication with a network of friendly people, then ham is in, and you will want to get a General license. The 1991 edition of *Ocean Voyager* (published by *Ocean Navigator* magazine as an annual supplement) has some informative articles that may help you make up your mind.

TIME SERVICE

Time signals throughout the world are listed in *H. O. Pub. No. 117, Radio Navigational Aids* and in Vol. 5 of the *Admiralty List of Radio Signals*. We mention only two of the many available signals. Their use is described in Chapter 10.

WWV, WWVH (2.5, 5, 10, 15, 20, 25 MHz)

The U.S. Department of Commerce, National Oceanic and Atmospheric Administration, Environmental Research Laboratory, Boulder, CO, maintains continuous broadcasts from Ft. Collins, CO, and Kuaui, HI. (The 25 MHz signal is not transmitted by WWVH). These signals are also useful for monitoring the quality of radio propagation. (See Chapter 13 for further details.)

CHU Canada (3.330, 7.337, 14.670 MHz)

The National Research Council of Canada broadcasts continuous signals from Montreal, giving Eastern Standard Time, alternating in French and English.

WEATHER PREDICTIONS

Private consultants

There are many private weather consultants who offer specialized forecasts for a fee. More than 100 are listed by the American Meteorological Society (45 Beacon Street, Boston, MA 02108), which will send the list on request.

Computer/telephone modem

Accu-weather Forecaster software for use with Apple Macintosh or IBM for downloading weather and forecast data by telephone and modem is available from Metacomet Software (Box 31337, Hartford, CT 06103). You telephone Accu-weather (which claims to be the nation's largest private weather service) and connect your computer modem to their computer using this communications software. You pay by the minute while the data are dumped into your computer; then you disconnect and use the software to print graphs and charts at your leisure.

Radio

Weather information is available by telex, voice, and computer. A good list of sources are the *Admiralty List of Radio Signals* and *H. O. Pub. No. 117, Radio Navigational Aids* The National Weather Service/National Oceanic and Atmospheric Administration (Silver Spring, MD 20910: 301-427-7730 or 301-427-7736) also publishes a list of *Selected Worldwide Marine Weather Broadcasts.* A brief article describing marine weather information sources is in *Cruising World,* December 1988. Government information is broadcast continuously and of course it is free, once you have the proper equipment to receive it.

NAVTEX—The U.S. Coast Guard broadcasts Notice to Mariners and marine weather forecasts from a network of coastal stations. These signals are digital and are sent on 518 kHz; they require special NAVTEX or SITOR receivers, about the size of Loran receivers, to decode the teletype signal.

MF (coastal harbor)—The U.S. Coast Guard broadcasts voice announcements several times a day on VHF-FM Ch. 22 and 2670 kHz in SSB. Schedules are listed in Read's *Almanac & Coast Pilot,* Chapter 12.

VHF—The National Weather Service broadcasts a continuous description of regional weather on three VHF channels. These can be picked up in U.S.

coastal waters with a standard VHF-FM receiver or with small special-purpose receivers, such as are sold by the Tandy Corporation. The frequencies of the weather channels are 162.55, 162.40, and 162.475 MHz.

WWV—Starting at the eighth minute after each hour, WWV broadcasts brief storm warnings in AM by voice, usually including the coordinates of barometric lows over North America or the North Atlantic (2.5, 5, 10, 15, 20, 25 MHz).

Facsimile (FAX)—The increasingly popular FAX machine, ordinarily connected to a telephone line, can now be connected to your single sideband (SSB) marine or ham radio. This means that you can get weather maps printed before your eyes on board your boat. You will have to pay for the service that sends you the map.

The National Weather Service (address above) transmits facsimile weather maps and extended forecasts.

EMERGENCY POSITION-INDICATING RADIOBEACON (EPIRB)

The EPIRB is a device that can be activated in dire emergency, either floating in the water if your boat has sunk, or attached to the boat in case you are incapacitated and require rescue. When it is turned on, the device sends a continuous homing signal (an audio signal consisting of a series of "whoops" on the carrier frequency) that can be picked up by polar orbiting search-and-rescue satellites (SARSAT in English and COSPAS in Russian) and by most commercial airplanes. When the signal is picked up and relayed, a search-and-rescue operation will be initiated from control centers in the northern hemisphere.

Currently, the signal is sent in the VHF band at 121.5 MHz and 243 MHz. This system was initially developed for detection by airborne receivers, and it is no longer adequate for satellite receivers, which require higher frequency stability. A new frequency (406 MHz in the UHF band) will soon be put in use to take care of this shortcoming and provide much better coverage than the current system.

As described by an article in *SAIL* magazine (October 1988), when a satellite passes over the EPIRB it measures the time of closest approach (by doppler shift) and this produces a line of position perpendicular to the satellite orbit. With the current system, a second satellite pass is required to provide a complete fix on the boat, but the new system will be able to make the fix on the first pass in 90 percent of the cases. When the new system has been put in place, the expected median notification time will be about two hours.

CHAPTER TWENTY-THREE

Special Topics

Life is a series of special cases.
Anonymous

INTRODUCTION

In this chapter, we collect four topics that might have been included in previous chapters. They were not discussed earlier because we felt that they would interrupt the flow of the narrative. The first, "Making a Mercator Chart," will enable you to make you own plotting sheets for solving problems involving lines of position and radio direction finding. The second, "Using an Artificial Horizon," will enable you to make sextant sights when the horizon is obscured. This can be useful on land, when you wish to practice determining your location with celestial sights. The third, "Sight Reduction with a Calculator," may be handy if you do not have any of the sight-reduction tables available. It is based on a description in the *Nautical Almanac,* and it gives the calculator keystrokes for solving the trigonometric equations for the navigator's triangle. The fourth, "Noon-Sight Reduction with an Analemma," is a graphical method of finding latitude and longitude from a noon sight without the help of the *Nautical Almanac.*

MAKING A MERCATOR CHART

Most of your plotting will be on Mercator maps—either on actual charts or on Universal Plotting Sheets. This type of map has so many uses that you should learn how to make your own from scratch, in case there is none at hand. Here is how to do it.

- *Step 1*—Draw a horizontal baseline at the bottom of the sheet of paper. This will represent a latitude line at the southern limit of the region to be charted.

- *Step 2*—Draw another horizontal line near the center of the paper, to represent the middle latitude line, Lm. This will usually be 1° (60 miles) from the bottom line. Mark it with the appropriate value, Lm. In our example Lm = 41°N.

- *Step 3*—At an equal distance northward, draw a the third latitude line, representing the northern limit of the region. Label the latitude lines (40°N, 41°N, 42°N). By now your sheet will look like Figure 23.1a.

- *Step 4*—Near the left side of the paper, erect a vertical line to be a meridian at the western end of the region. Note north is up and west is to the left, so the western longitudes increase to the left. Label this meridian. In our example (Figure 23.1b) it is 68°W.

- *Step 5*—Place the pin of a circular compass at A, where the horizontal baseline intersects the left-most meridian. Draw a quarter-circle from the meridian to the baseline.

- *Step 6*—Now you are ready to draw the middle meridian at 67°W. To locate it, place a circular protractor at A and draw a line at an angle of Lm = 41° from the horizontal baseline. This line will intersect the circle at B. With a triangle or protractor, erect a perpendicular to the baseline passing through B. Label this 67°W.

- *Step 7*—At an equal distance to the right, draw another meridian perpendicular to the baseline. (The quickest way is to mark off with dividers equal distances along the latitude lines and then draw a meridian through them.)

You now have a Mercator chart, with the same distance scale in all directions. (That, in fact, is the mathematical basis of the Mercator chart: the scales in both directions increase as 1/cos [latitude] and shapes of small regions are preserved.)

You will probably want to establish the scales in minutes of latitude and longitude. These will not be the same, because the meridians indicating each

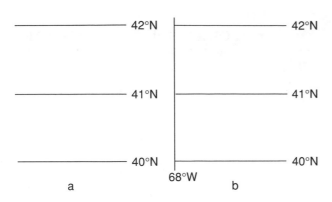

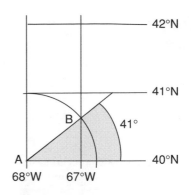

Figure 23.1. First four steps in constructing a Mercator chart. (a) Draw a baseline and two parallel lines of latitude at equal intervals (Steps 1-3). (b) Erect a perpendicular to the baseline at the western edge of the chart. Label all lines with desired latitudes and longitudes (Step 4).

Figure 23.2. Steps 5 and 6 in Mercator chart construction, showing the first meridian, the circle from A, and the line at an angle of 41° from the baseline to locate the next meridian which passes through B.

1° of longitude are closer together than the lines indicating each 1° of latitude. (This explains why the rectangles produced by latitude and longitude lines will look taller and narrower as you go to higher latitudes.)

- **Step 8**—To generate a scale, start with a compass or dividers and bisect one of the 1° intervals in latitude and in longitude, obtaining 30' intervals. Then bisect these, obtaining 15' intervals. Trisect these (perhaps with a ruler) and you will obtain 5' intervals which can be divided into 1' intervals by eye. The result is scales of minutes in latitude and longitude which you can use for deriving positions on the chart. You may use this scale with a pair of dividers to measure distances on the chart.

USING AN ARTIFICIAL HORIZON

The device commonly known as an artificial horizon is neither artificial nor is it, strictly speaking, a horizon. But it can be extremely useful for sun or moon sights when the horizon is invisible. Unfortunately, it is not practical to use an artificial horizon for star sights because the stars are not sufficiently bright.

While the device is not a horizon, it is horizontal. It consists of a container, such as a dish or a small watertight box partly filled with a liquid. As shown in Figure 23.3, you look through the sextant down onto the surface of the liquid, where you see the reflection of the celestial object. At the same

time you adjust the mirror to sight directly at the object and in this way you measure the angle between the object and its image. Because the surface of the liquid is horizontal (under the effect of gravity) this measured angle is exactly twice the altitude of the object. So you divide the measured angle by two and then apply the refraction correction, skipping the usual correction for the dip of the horizon. This gives H_o, the observed height.

You can use almost any liquid in the artificial horizon, but on a breezy day, there will be ripples on the surface if you use water. Try using cooking oil, liquid detergent, or motor oil, as they are thicker and will not be ruffled so easily by the breeze.

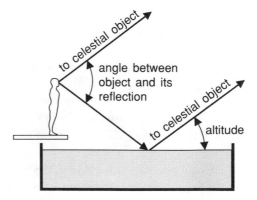

Figure 23.3. When using an artificial horizon with a sextant, you measure the angle between the object and its reflected image. This angle is twice the altitude of the object.

Finding both the object and its reflected image with a sextant is not very easy the first time, but keep trying and you will soon get the hang of it. You will quickly notice that the reflected image is much fainter (about ⅟₂₅ as bright) than the object itself, so you will have to adjust the filters for best visibility.

Start by setting the sextant arm at about twice the estimated altitude of the object, and then hunt around. When you sight the two images of the sun, rather than trying to align one edge against the opposite edge, it is easier if you put them right on top of each other. If you do it this way, you must not include the correction for the sun's radius, because you are measuring the actual center. So, take the refraction correction from the inside cover of the *Almanac,* Table A2 Stars/Planets, rather than the sun table.

Example for Sun—Suppose you estimate the sun to be about 30° above the (invisible) horizon. Set the sextant at 60° and sight down at the reflected image. Hunt around and adjust the arm until the two images are exactly superposed. Look at your watch, and then read the sextant.

Imagine that you find 50°34′. Divide by two, obtaining 25°17′ for the apparent altitude uncorrected for refraction. Look in A2 Stars/Planets for the apparent altitudes that bracket your measured value: 25°14′ and 26°22′. The tabulated correction is –2′, so you subtract 2′ from your apparent altitude, finding H_0 = 25°15′.

For a planet, the procedure is the same as for the sun.

When observing the moon with an artificial horizon, it is more practical to align one of the limbs (upper or lower) with its reflected image, as the correction tables all assume that you have made a limb observation. So you find the angle between the limb and its reflected image, divide by two to find the apparent altitude, then go to the altitude correction tables in the back inside cover of the *Almanac,* ignoring the dip correction.

SIGHT REDUCTION WITH A CALCULATOR

If you have an almanac but do not have access to sight-reduction tables, such as DMA *H. O. Pubs. No. 229* or *249,* you will need to solve the navigator's triangle by brute force—using the basic trigonometric formulae described in Chapter 17.

The purpose is to calculate the altitude and azimuth of the sighted object for comparison with your sextant altitude. The procedure is similar to what was described in Chapter 20, except you use the calculator instead of the tables for finding H_c and Z. The formulae are given in the *Almanac* section titled "Sight Reduction Procedures," and these are the formulae we shall use, so you can follow along in the *Almanac.* Form F9 (Figures 23.4a, b) will guide you in the calculation.

- *Step 1*—Find the GMT of the sextant observation from the watch time using any of the sight-reduction forms in the Appendix of this book. Enter in the Form F9.

- *Step 2*—Find interpolation factor x. See "Sight Reduction Procedures, Section 5, Interpolation of GHA and Dec." for an explanation. The interpolation factor is x = min/60 + sec/3600, and the keystrokes are represented by: min ÷ 60 + sec ÷ 3600 = [x → M]. The last step puts the value into memory for use later.

- *Steps 3 and 4*—Interpolate in the *Almanac* to find the Dec. and GHA of the object for the GMT of your observation. The keystrokes for the interpolation are shown on Form F9 in boldface. To prepare for the calculation, all of the angles must be converted from degrees and minutes (DD.MM) to degrees and decimals (DD.DDDD). To convert, divide the minutes of arc by 60 and add to the degrees. (For example: 60°34.2′ = 60 + 34.2/60 = 60.57.) In what follows, we assume that all angles are in the decimal form DD.DDDD. It is recommended that you carry four decimal figures and drop the last one when finished.

  Adopt an assumed position and enter in the form: (AP lat. and AP long.).

- *Step 5*—Find the sextant altitude, H_0, corrected for dip, refraction, and index error, using the tables in the inside cover of the *Almanac.* Enter in the form.

- *Step 6*—Calculate altitude and azimuth. The formulas are found in the *Almanac,* "Sight Reduction Procedures, Section 6. The calculated altitude and azimuth."

Figures 23.4a and 23.4b give examples of the calculation. (Note: Each figure corresponds to a different observation, so the LHA and Dec. are not the same.)

Form F9. Calculator Reduction of Sight

See *Almanac,* "Sight Reduction Procedures." Calculator entries in bold.

1. To find GMT

1.1 Zone watch time   _____

1.2 Zone description   _____

1.3 GMT watch time   _____

1.4 GMT watch error s+ / f–   _____

1.5 GMT h 15 min 47 sec 13

1.6 GMT Date D   Oct 6, 1990

2. Find interpolation factor, x

2.1 **min ÷ 60 + sec ÷ 3600 = [x → M]**; put x into memory.

2.2 x = __0.7869__ (All angles are assumed to be in form of decimal fraction DD.DDDD)

3. To find declination

3.1 Dec. (H + 1)   –5.1883

3.2 Dec. (H)   –5.1733

3.3 **Dec. (H + 1) – Dec (H) = × [M → x] +**

Dec. (H) =   –5.1851   (enter at 6.2)

4. To find GHA (Aries/sun/moon)

4.1 GHA (H + 1)   62.9667

4.2 GHA (H)   47.9633

4.3 **GHA (H + 1) – GHA (H) = × [M → x] +**

GHA (H) =   59.7701

4.4 GHA   _____

4.5 AP long.   _____ (add if E)

4.6 LHA   _____ (enter at 6.1)

5. Reduction of sextant observation

5.1 Ht. of eye ____ ft.   +   –

5.2 Index corr.   ____   ____

5.3 Ht. of eye corr.   ____

5.4 Net   _____

5.5 h_s _____ (upper/lower limb)

5.6 App. alt.   _____

5.7 3rd corr. to h_s _____ (first col. of A2)

5.8 H_o _____ (enter at 6.8)

6. Calculate altitude and azimuth

6.1 LHA   37.0000 (enter from 4.6)

6.2 Dec.   –15.0000 (enter from 3.3)

6.3 AP lat.   +32.0000

6.4 Find H_c: **Dec. sin × lat. sin + Dec. cos × LHA**

cos × lat. cos = 2ndF $\sin^{-1}$ **=**

       31.1346 H_c

6.5 H_o _____

6.6 $H_o – H_c$ _____ (+ = toward; – = away)

6.7 Find X: **Dec. sin × lat. cos – Dec. cos × LHA**

cos × lat.

sin = /   _____

H_c **cos =**   –0.7340   = X

6.8 Find Zn: **X 2ndF** $\cos^{-1}$ **=**

       137.2239 Z (see rule below)

Zn = 360 – z =   222.7761

Rule for azimuth, Zn:

N. Hem: LHA < 180°: Zn = 360° – Z

             LHA > 180°: Zn = Z

S. Hem: LHA < 180°: Zn = 180° + Z

             LHA > 180°: Zn = 180° – Z

Figure 23.4a. Example of interpolation to find Dec. and GHA of sun at time of observation.

Figure 23.4b. Example of calculation of sextant altitude, H_c, and azimuth, Zn, using pocket calculator.

REDUCING A NOON SIGHT WITH AN ANALEMMA (F10)

The sun's position at noon GMT each day is approximately on the meridian of Greenwich, England. If you were to stand somewhere on that meridian you would see the sun almost exactly north or south at noon, and during the year, the sun would swing back and forth across the celestial equator. That, of course, is why we must use an almanac for accurate navigation.

But, if you have lost your almanac, or if you are willing to accept an error of ten miles or so, you can replace the almanac with an analemma. This is a figure 8 pattern often found on terrestrial globes, usually floating in the Pacific Ocean off the coast of South America. The analemma (from the Greek for sundial) shows the yearly changes of the sun's declination and the equation of time. It shows the average behavior of the sun, and it applies to any year.

From the navigator's point of view, the analemma can be described another way. The analemma is a chart of the geographical position (GP) of the sun every day at noon, GMT. If you stood at that place, the sun would be directly overhead. The analemma is elongated north and south because the sun moves more than 46° in latitude; it is slightly spread out in the east-west direction because the equation of time puts the sun slightly east or west of the Greenwich meridian in the course of the year.

Here is how you may use it for sight reduction. Suppose you have plotted a noon curve (Figure 15.11) and have found that the highest observed altitude H_0 was 57°29′ and it occurred on February 25, 1990, at 16 18 25 GMT. The sun was observed south of the zenith at that time. (These data are the same as in Chapter 15, "Latitude and Longitude by Noon Curve.")

Refer to the sample Form F10 in Figure 23.5; we start at step 3, since the other work has already been done.

- **Part 3**—Calculate your longitude:

  Enter the date, February 25, and don't worry about the year. This analemma is an average that applies to any year.

  Enter the time of apparent noon, LAN: 16 18 25 GMT.

  Subtract 12 hours for the time at Greenwich noon. The difference is 4 18 25.

  Convert this to an angle using 1 hour = 15° and 1 minute = 15′, finding the difference in degrees = 64.60 degrees = 64°36′W.

  Find the analemma longitude by scanning around the figure-8 until you find the spot corresponding to February 25. Mark it with a sharp pencil. The longitude of the sun at noon GMT is –3°20′, which you find along the horizontal scale at the bottom. (The sun was actually a little east of the meridian at noon.)

  Find your longitude by summing these angles: 64°36 – 3°20 = 61°16′W.

  The reduction in Chapter 15 gave 61°21′W, which is about 4 NM farther west. The sight difference is due to the inaccuracy of the analemma and the difficulty in reading it to the nearest minute of arc. But it's very easy, and it's good enough for most purposes.

- **Part 4**—Calculate your latitude:

  Find the zenith distance of the sun at LAN by subtracting H_0 from 89°60′, finding LAN zenith distance = 89°60′ – 57°29′ = 32°31′.

  Find the sun's declination from the analemma: –8°40′.

  Find your latitude by summing these angles: 31°81′ – 8°40 = 23°41′N. Remember, though, the rule for finding your latitude depends on whether the sun is north or south of the zenith. Refer to Form F3 for the rule if you need it.

  The reduction in Chapter 15 gave 23°30′N, a difference of about 11 NM.

All in all, the method is quick and easy. And this means that it is safe. There are few places to go wrong.

Form F10. Noon Sight Reduction Using the Analemma

The easiest way to find your position on the surface of the earth by means of celestial navigation is by plotting a noon curve and using the analemma.

1. Measure the altitude of the sun at several times throughout the day. Measure more frequently when the sun is highest.

2. Graph and fit a smooth curve to this data.

3. Estimate the time at which the sun is highest in the sky. This is local apparent noon (LAN). Estimate the sun's maximum altitude in degrees and minutes of arc (1° = 60′).

LAN altitude: _____ . _____ ′ LAN time: _____ : _____

Zone time: _____

Date: _____

Convert zone time to Greenwich mean time (GMT) by adding in your zone description:

U.S. Time Zones	Standard Time Nov. to Apr.	Daylight Time May to Oct.
Eastern	+5	+4
Central	+6	+5
Mountain	+7	+6
Western	+8	+7

4. Calculate your longitude.

Time of LAN	_____ : _____ GMT
Subtract time at Greenwich noon	−12:00
± time difference at Greenwich noon	_____ : _____
Convert to degrees and minutes of arc	× 15°/hr
Difference in degrees	_____ ° _____ ′
Analemma longitude correction (+ = W)	_____ ° _____ ′
Longitude (+ = W)	_____ ° _____ ′

5. Calculate your latitude.

Zenith at 90°	89° 60′
Subtract LAN altitude	− _____ ° _____ ′
LAN zenith distance	_____ ° _____ ′
± declination from analemma (+ = N)	_____ ° _____ ′
Latitude (+ = N)	_____ ° _____ ′

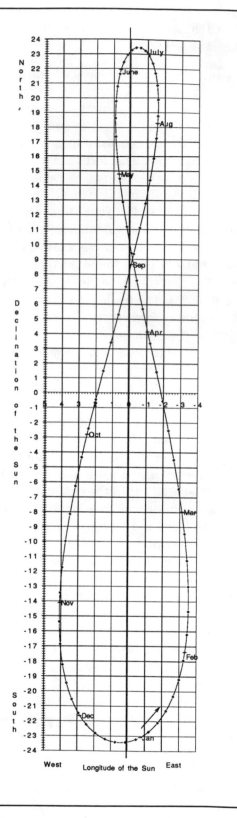

Figure 23.5. The analemma shows the annual pattern of the sun's latitude and longitude at noon GMT each day. As an example, on April 1 at 1200 GMT, the declination of the sun is 4°19′N and the longitude is 1°E. The diagram permits you to determine the geographic position of the sun at noon in your time zone; from this and a series of observations of the sun, you can determine latitude and approximate longitude. Use the form as a guide. Diagram courtesy Phil Sadler.

Descriptions of Almanacs

Two celestial almanacs are printed yearly by the U.S. Government Printing Office (Washington, D.C.): the *Nautical Almanac* and the *Air Almanac*. Several privately printed almanacs are also available, and they are somewhat less expensive than the government versions.

NAUTICAL ALMANAC

The *Nautical Almanac* (issued jointly by the U.S. Government and Her Majesty's Nautical Almanac Office, London) is intended for marine navigation and is found in most boating stores. It is available about two years before it becomes applicable, and it is the fundamental reference for all the celestial information needed for accurate reduction of celestial sights, including coordinates of the sun, moon, and bright planets as well as the coordinates of 173 bright stars. (These stars have been chosen for their distribution over the sky, and they will usually provide a good fix if the sky is not too cloudy. Fifty-seven of them—the navigation stars—are incorporated in special reduction tables: DMA *H. O. Pub. No. 249.*) The *Nautical Almanac* contains tables for making various corrections to sextant sights, such as correcting for the bending of light (refraction) in the earth's atmosphere. It also briefly describes methods for reducing sextant sights to obtain your location.

The following description is based on the 1990 edition, but it will change only slightly from year to year.

The *Nautical Almanac* Summary of Contents for 1990

Page	Contents
Inside front cover	Corrections to sextant sights to account for refraction, dip of the horizon, and the size of the sun.
4-5	Calendar for the year, giving phases of the moon.
6-7	Eclipse dates and tracks on the earth.
8-9	Visibility of planets described in general terms to facilitate finding them for navigation.
10-253	These are the main tables, giving declinations and Greenwich hour angles (GHA) as well as sunrise, sunset, twilight, moonrise and -set, and times of local meridian passage for moon and sun. Each pair of pages gives data for three days.
254-261	Explanation of the basis of the *Almanac* and the use of tables. This can be a very helpful section, and it should be looked at carefully so you will understand the contents of the *Almanac*. Don't worry if it doesn't all seem clear at first. The explanation also describes how you may use the *Almanac* for the following year, by making some corrections. The description reads like a nightmare but it can be understood with a little patience. It can be very useful if you are stuck in the middle of the ocean on New Year's Day with an old *Almanac* and can't find a bookstore or mailbox.
262-265	Lists of standard times (zone descriptions) in various parts of the earth. The information is given in two alphabetical tables: The first is for points east of Greenwich—from the Admiralty Islands (–10 hours) to Zimbabwe (–2 hours); the second is for points west—from Argentina (3 hours) to the Windward Islands (4 hours).

Page	Contents
266-267	Star identification charts for the equatorial and polar regions of the sky, indicating the navigation stars by name and number. Not very easy to use for constellation study, but a good reference.
268-273	Precise coordinates for navigation stars (for working to the nearest nautical mile), these include precession corrections month by month. You probably won't have much need for this table, unless you are trying to work to better than 1 NM.
274-276	Polaris tables for easily finding latitude from sextant altitude and for finding north.
277-283	Sight reduction procedures for direct computation by spherical triangle, using a pocket calculator with trigonometric functions. In Chapter 24, we describe this method in terms of calculator keystrokes, for those who are new to calculators. This method can be used if you do not have the usual sight reduction tables, DMA *H. O. Pub. No. 229* or *249*.
284-285	Description of reduction using concise reduction tables without an electronic calculator. (This is a relatively new section of the *Almanac*, and we find the method tricky and not much fun. We do not discuss it in this book.)
286-318	Concise reduction tables, to be used according to the description earlier.
Yellow pages	This portion contains information that is the same from year to year, such as conversion from arc to time and increments and corrections for converting from time to arc depending on the object (sun/planets, Aries, moon). There is also a list of selected navigation stars.
Inside back cover	Corrections to sextant sights of the moon. Because the moon is so close to the earth, it presents a few special problems and requires special tables. (Some people stay away from the moon until they have succeeded with all the other objects, but the moon is very handy.)

AIR ALMANAC

This is similar to the *Nautical Almanac* but is intended for airplane pilots, so it has additional information related to high-altitude observations. The main data are tabulated in much shorter intervals (10 minutes instead of 1 hour) to reduce the need for interpolation. This makes the book somewhat quicker to use, but it is much bulkier. (Many navigators reduce the bulk of the almanacs for sailing by tearing out the unneeded pages.)

The *Air Almanac* also has a number of sky diagrams to facilitate finding the navigation stars through the window of an airplane.

REED'S NAUTICAL ALMANAC AND COAST PILOT

This handy book is published annually by Thomas Reed Pub. Ltd., New Malden, Surrey, KT3 4QS, England. It is also distributed in the United States by Better Boating Association and is available in most boating stores.

Reed's contains a wealth of information for celestial navigation, piloting, and tide prediction. Its layout is different from the *Nautical Almanac* and it takes getting used to, but it's all here—along with helpful explanations. Published since 1973, this almanac has replaced a handful of government books on some sailors' navigation tables, at a fraction of the cost. We suggest you buy one and see whether it answers your needs. Chances are it will.

ELDRIDGE'S ALMANAC

This venerable little book has a history reaching back almost a century and a half. It was first published by Captain George Eldridge, of Chatham, MA, and has remained a family endeavor ever since. For piloting along the northeast coast from New York to Maine, this book and a set of charts will pretty well cover your needs. In effect, the publishers of this book have culled useful data from a variety of publications, focussing on the needs of a small boat, and the result is a compendium that you will learn to cherish if you sail in those waters.

Here is a list of its principal sections:

- Emergency first aid

- Rules and regulations

- Tide and current tables

- Current charts and diagrams

- Notes on tides and currents

- Lights and fog signals

- Courses and distances

- Flags and codes

- Astronomical data

- Radio navigational aids and data

- Weather

- Miscellaneous

Forms for Reducing Observations*

		Discussed in Chapter	Figure
F1.	Latitude by Polaris	16	16.4
F2.	Noon Sight for Latitude (from Predicted Time of Noon)	15	15.10
F3.	Noon Curve for Latitude and Longitude	15	15.13
F4.	Star Sights by *H.O. Pub. No. 229*	18, 20	20.19, 20.20, 20.22, 20.23
F5.	Star Sight (*H.O. Pub. No. 249,* Vol. I)	20	20.12
F6.	Sun Sight (*H.O. Pub. No. 249,* Vols. II, III)	20	20.9
F7.	Moon Sight (*H.O. Pub. No. 249,* Vols. II, III)	20	20.16
F8.	Planet or Star Sight (*H.O. Pub. No. 249,* Vols. II, III)	20	20.14
F9.	Calculator Reduction of Sight	23	23.4
F10.	Noon Sight Reduction with an Analemma	23	23.5
F11.	Universal Plotting Sheet	7	
F12.	Napier Diagram	5	

*May be photocopied for use at sea.

Form F1. Latitude by Polaris

DR Lat. _____ Long. _____ WT Date _____

1. To find GMT

1.1 Zone watch time _____

1.2 Zone description _____

1.3 GMT watch time _____

1.4 GMT watch error _____ s+/f–

1.5 GMT _____

1.6 GMT date _____

2. Corrections to sextant observation

2.1 Ht. of eye ____ ft. + _____ – _____

2.2 Index corr. ____ ____

2.3 Ht. of eye corr. ____ (Table A2)

2.4 Sums ____ ____

2.5 Net _____

2.6 h_s _____

2.7 Adjusted h_s _____ (add 2.5 to 2.6)

2.8 Refraction corr. – _____ (*Almanac* Table A2, col. 2)

2.9 H_o _____ (enter at 4.1)

3. To find LHA Aries

3.1 GHA Aries ____ hrs _____

3.2 Corr. ____ m ____ s _____

3.3 GHA Aries _____

3.4 Long. (add if E) _____

3.5 LHA Aries _____

4. To find latitude

4.1 H_o _____

4.2 Subtract 1° –1°

4.3 a_0 + _____

4.4 a_1 + _____

4.5 a_2 + _____

4.6 Sum = Latitude _____

Form F2. Reduction of Noon Sight for Latitude

Navigator _____

Zone date _____, 19 _____

D.R. lat. _____ N (or) S

D.R. long. _____ E (or) W (enter at 2.4)

1. To find GMT at DR position

1.1 Watch time at DR _____ (enter at 3.4)

1.2 Zone description _____

1.3 GMT watch time _____

1.4 GMT watch error _____ (+ if slow)

1.5 GMT _____ (enter at 4.2)

1.6 Greenwich date

2. To find LHA sun at DR

2.1 GHA sun _____ hrs _____

2.2 corr. ___ m ___ s _____

2.3 GHA sun _____

2.4 DR long. _____

2.5 LHA sun _____ (enter at 3.1)

3. Predict WT of local noon

3.1 LHA sun _____ (subtract)

3.2 Deg. to noon _____

3.3 Time to noon _____ (enter at 4.1)

3.4 WT at DR _____ (add)

3.5 Pred. WT of noon _____

4. GMT & sun's dec. at noon

4.1 Interval to noon _____

4.2 GMT at DR _____ (add)

4.3 GMT of noon _____

4.4 Sun's dec. _____ hrs. _____ d 0.9 + / −

4.5 d corr. ___ m _____

4.6 Dec. at noon _____ (enter at 6.3)

5. Reduction of sextant observation

5.1 Ht. of eye _____ ft.

	+	−	
5.2 Index corr.	____	____	(+ if off)
5.3 Ht. of eye corr.		____	(Table A2)
5.4 Sums	____	____	

5.5 Net _____

5.6 h_s _____

5.7 Adjusted h_s _____ (add 5.5 to 5.6)

5.8 3rd correction to h_s _____ (Table A2, col. 1)

5.9 H_o _____ (enter at 6.1)

6. Derivation of noon latitude

Find zenith distance of sun by subtracting H_o from 90°. Mark it N if zenith is N of sun, mark it S if zenith is S of sun. If zenith distance and declination are both N or both S, add them. If one is N, and the other is S, subtract them. The result is the latitude, with the name of the greater.

89° 60.0′

6.1 H_o _____ (subtract)

6.2 Zenith distance _____ N (or) S

6.3 Dec. at noon _____ N (or) S

6.4 Latitude at noon _____ N (or) S

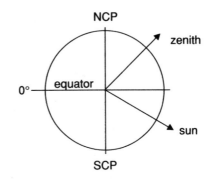

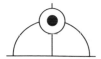

Form F3. Reduction of Noon Curve for Latitude and Longitude

    Navigator _____

    Zone date _____ , 19 _____

    D.R. lat. _____ N (or) S

    D.R. long. _____ E (or) W

1. To find GMT of local noon

    1.1 Zone watch time _____ (from curve)

    1.2 Zone description _____

    1.3 GMT watch time _____

    1.4 GMT watch error _____ (+ if slow)

    1.5 GMT _____

    1.6 Greenwich date _____

2. Sun's dec. at noon

    2.1 Dec. _____ hrs. _____ d _____ + / −

    2.2 d. corr. ___ m ___ s _____

    2.3 Dec. at noon _____ (enter at 4.3)

3. Reduction of sextant observation

    3.1 Ht. of eye _____ ft.

                       +   −

    3.2 Index corr. _____ _____ (+ if off)

    3.3 Ht. of eye corr. _____ (Table A2)

    3.4 Sums _____ _____

    3.5 Net _____

    3.6 h_s _____

    3.7 Adjusted h_s _____ (add 3.5 to 3.6)

    3.8 3rd corr. to h_s _____ (Table A2)

    3.9 H_o _____ (enter at 4.1)

4. Rule for derivation of noon latitude

Find zenith distance of sun by subtracting H_o from 90°. Mark it N if zenith is N of sun, mark it S if zenith is S of sun. If zenith distance and declination are both N or both S, add them. If one is N, and the other is S, subtract them. The result is the latitude, with the name of the greater.

                            89° 60.0′

    4.1 H_o _____ (subtract)

    4.2 Zenith distance _____ N (or) S

    4.3 Dec. at noon _____ N (or) S

    4.4 Latitude at noon _____ N (or) S

5. Derivation of noon longitude

    5.1 Sun GHA ___ hrs. _____

    5.2 Corr. ___ m ___ s _____

    5.3 Sun GHA at noon _____

          = Long. W if less than 180°.

If greater than 180° subtract from 360°

                       359° 60′

GHA _____ (subtract)

Long. E =

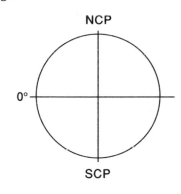

Form F4. Reduction with *H.O. Pub. No. 229*

Planet/star name ____
Sun/moon limb: upper/lower

1. To find GMT

1.1 Zone watch time   _____
1.2 Zone description   _____
1.3 GMT watch time   _____
1.4 GMT watch error s+ / f–   _____
1.5 GMT   _____
1.6 GMT date   _____

2. To find declination

2.1 Dec.   _____ N (or) S; d ___ N (or) S
2.2 d corr.   _____ (skip for star)
2.3 Dec.   _____ N (or) S

3. To find LHA

3.1 GHA ___ hrs.   _____ v ____
3.2 Incr. ___ m ___ s   _____
3.3 v corr.   _____ (skip for star)
3.4 SHA☆   _____ (star only)
3.5 GHA   _____
3.6 AP long.   _____ (add if E)
3.7 LHA   _____ (enter at 5.3)

4. Reduction of sextant observation

4.1 Ht. of eye ___ ft.   +   –
4.2 Index corr.   ____   ____
4.3 Ht. of eye corr.   ____
4.4 Net   _____
4.5 h_s _____
4.6 App. alt.   _____ (4.4 + 4.5)
    Sun, star, or planet
4.7 3rd corr. to h_s _____ (Table A2)
    Moon corrections from inside back
4.7a Altitude corr.   _____
4.7b (HP ____) HP corr.   _____
4.7c (–30′ if upper limb)   _____
4.8 H_o (4.6 + 4.7)   _____ (enter at 5.8)

Navigator   _____
Zone date   _____
DR lat.   _____ N (or) S; AP lat. _____
DR long.   _____ E (or) W; AP long. _____

5. Solution by *H.O. Pub. No. 229*

5.1 Dec. difference   _____
5.2 Dec. same _ name or contrary _ name to lat.
5.3 LHA   _____°00′
5.4 AP lat.   _____°00′ (nearest whole degree)
5.5 Tab. H   _____ d _____ Z _____ (to 5.11)
5.6 d corr.   _____ (from Dec. diff.)
5.7 H_c _____ (enter at 5.9)
5.8 H_o _____ (from 4.8)
5.9 H_c _____
5.10 $H_o - H_c$ _____ (plus is toward Zn)
5.11 Zn   _____ (see rule below)

Rule for azimuth, Zn:
N. Hem: LHA < 180°: Zn = 360° – Z
    LHA > 180°: Zn = Z
S. Hem: LHA < 180°: Zn = 180° + Z
    LHA > 180°: Zn = 180° – Z

Form F5. Star Sight by *H. O. Pub. No. 249*, Vol. I

Star_____

DR lat. _____ N (or) S
DR long. _____ E (or) W
Star_____

Navigator_____
Star_____

1. To find GMT
  1.1 Zone date ___ _____
  1.2 Zone watch time _____
  1.3 Zone description _____
  1.4 GMT watch time _____
  1.5 Watch error s+/f– _____
  1.6 GMT _____
  1.7 GMT date _____

2. To find LHA Aries
  2.1 GHA Aries __ hrs _____
  2.2 Incr. __ m __ s _____
  2.3 GHA Aries _____
  2.4 AP long. (add if E) _____
  2.5 LHA Aries ____° 00.0′

3. Reduction of sextant obs.
  3.1 Ht. of eye ___ ft.
                  +   –
  3.2 Index corr. _____ _____
  3.3 Ht. of eye corr. _____
  3.4 Net _____
  3.5 h_s _____
  3.6 App. alt. _____
  3.7 3rd corr. to h_s _____
  3.8 H_0 _____

4. Reduction
  4.1 AP lat. _____
  4.2 H_0 _____
  4.3 H_c _____
  4.4 $H_0 - H_c$ _____ t+ / a–
  4.5 Zn _____

1. To find GMT
  1.1 Zone date _____
  1.2 Zone watch time _____
  1.3 Zone description _____
  1.4 GMT watch time _____
  1.5 Watch error s+/f– _____
  1.6 GMT _____
  1.7 GMT date _____

2. To find LHA Aries
  2.1 GHA Aries __ hrs _____
  2.2 Incr. __ m __ s _____
  2.3 GHA Aries _____
  2.4 AP long. (add if E) _____
  2.5 LHA Aries ____° 00.0′

3. Reduction of sextant obs.
  3.1 Ht. of eye ___ ft.
                  +   –
  3.2 Index corr. _____ _____
  3.3 Ht. of eye corr. _____
  3.4 Net _____
  3.5 h_s _____
  3.6 App. alt. _____
  3.7 3rd corr. to h_s _____
  3.8 H_0 _____

4. Reduction
  4.1 AP lat. _____
  4.2 H_0 _____
  4.3 H_c _____
  4.4 $H_0 - H_c$ _____ t+ / a–
  4.5 Zn _____

1. To find GMT
  1.1 Zone date _____
  1.2 Zone watch time _____
  1.3 Zone description _____
  1.4 GMT watch time _____
  1.5 Watch error s+/f– _____
  1.6 GMT _____
  1.7 GMT date _____

2. To find LHA Aries
  2.1 GHA Aries __ hrs _____
  2.2 Incr. __ m __ s _____
  2.3 GHA Aries _____
  2.4 AP long. (add if E) _____
  2.5 LHA Aries ____ 00.0′

3. Reduction of sextant obs.
  3.1 Ht. of eye ___ ft.
                  +   –
  3.2 Index corr. _____ _____
  3.3 Ht. of eye corr. _____
  3.4 Net _____
  3.5 h_s _____
  3.6 App. alt. _____
  3.7 3rd corr. to h_s _____
  3.8 H_0 _____

4. Reduction
  4.1 AP lat. _____
  4.2 H_0 _____
  4.3 H_c _____
  4.4 $H_0 - H_c$ _____ t+ / a–
  4.5 Zn _____

Form F6. Sun Sight by *H. O. Pub. No. 249*
Vol. II or III

Limb: Upper / Lower

1. To find GMT

1.1 Zone watch time _____

1.2 Zone description _____

1.3 GMT watch time _____

1.4 GMT watch error _____ s+ / f–

1.5 GMT _____

1.6 GMT date _____

2. To find declination

2.1 Dec. _____ N (or) S; d ____ N (or) S

2.2 d corr. _____

2.3 Dec. _____ N (or) S

3. To find LHA

3.1 GHA ___ hrs. _____

3.2 Incr. ___ m ____ s _____

3.3 GHA _____

3.4 AP long. _____ (add if E)

3.5 LHA _____ (enter at 5.3)

4. Reduction of sextant observation

4.1 Ht. of eye ___ ft. + _____ –

4.2 Index corr. ____ ____

4.3 Ht. of eye corr. ____

4.4 Net _____

4.5 h_s _____ (U / L limb)

4.6 App. alt. _____

4.7 3rd corr. to h_s _____ (first col. A2)

4.8 H_0 _____ (enter at 5.8)

Navigator _____

Zone date _____

DR lat. _____ N (or) S; AP Lat. ___

DR long. _____ E (or) W; AP long. _____

5. Solution by *H. O. Pub. No. 249*

5.1 Dec. difference _____

5.2 Dec. same __ name or contrary __ name to lat.

5.3 LHA ____° 00′

5.4 AP lat. ____° 00′ (nearest whole degree)

5.5 Tab. H_____ d _____ Z _____ (to 5.11)

5.6 d corr. _____ (from Dec. diff.)

5.7 H_c _____ (enter at 5.9)

5.8 H_0 _____

5.9 H_c _____

5.10 $H_0 - H_c$ _____ (+ = toward; – = away)

5.11 Zn _____ (see rule below)

Rule for azimuth, Zn:

N. Hem: LHA < 180°: Zn = 360° – Z

LHA > 180°: Zn = Z

S. Hem: LHA < 180°: Zn = 180° + Z

LHA > 180°: Zn = 180° – Z

Form F7. Moon Sight by *H. O. Pub No. 249,* Vol. II or III

Limb: Upper / Lower

1. To find GMT

1.1 Zone watch time _____

1.2 Zone description _____

1.3 GMT watch time _____

1.4 GMT watch error s+ / f– _____

1.5 GMT _____

1.6 GMT date _____

2. To find declination

2.1 Dec. _____ N (or) S; d ____ N (or) S

2.2 d corr. _____

2.3 Dec. _____ N (or) S

3. To find LHA

3.1 GHA ___ hrs. _____ v _____

3.2 Incr. __ m __ s _____

3.3 v corr. _____

3.4 GHA _____

3.5 AP long. _____ (add if E)

3.6 LHA _____ 00′ (enter at 5.3)

4. Reduction of sextant observation

4.1 Ht. of eye ___ ft. + _____ –

4.2 Index corr. _____ _____

4.3 Ht. of eye corr. _____

4.4 Net _____

4.5 h_s _____

4.6 App. alt. _____

Moon corrections, inside back cover *Almanac:*

4.7a Altitude corr. _____

4.7b (HP _____) HP corr. _____

4.7c Upper limb? (= –30′) _____

4.8 H_o (enter at 5.8) _____

Navigator _____

Zone date _____ _____

DR lat. _____ N (or) S; AP lat. _____

DR long. _____ E (or) W; AP long. _____

5. Solution by *H. O. Pub. No. 249*

5.1 Dec. difference _____

5.2 Dec. same _ name or contrary _ name to lat.

5.3 LHA _____ ° 00′

5.4 AP lat. _____ ° 00′ (nearest whole degree)

5.5 Tab. H _____ d ____ Z ____ (to 5.11)

5.6 d corr. _____ (from Dec. diff.)

5.7 H_c _____ (enter at 5.9)

5.8 H_o _____

5.9 H_c _____

5.10 $H_o - H_c$ _____ (+ = toward; – = away)

5.11 Zn _____ (see rule below)

Rule for azimuth, Zn:

N. Hem: LHA < 180°: Zn = 360° – Z

LHA > 180°: Zn = Z

S. Hem: LHA < 180°: Zn = 180° + Z

LHA > 180°: Zn = 180° – Z

Form F8. Planet or Star Sight by *H. O. Pub. No. 249,* Vol. II or III

Planet/Star Name _____

1. To find GMT

1.1 Zone watch time _____

1.2 Zone description _____

1.3 GMT watch time _____

1.4 GMT watch error s+ / f– _____

1.5 GMT _____

1.6 GMT date _____

2. To find declination

2.1 Dec. _____ N (or) S; d ___ N (or) S

2.2 d corr. _____ (skip for star)

2.3 Dec. _____ N (or) S

3. To find LHA

3.1 GHA ___ hrs. _____ v ___

3.2 Incr. ___ m ___ s _____

3.3 v corr. _____ (skip for star)

3.4 GHA _____

3.5 AP long. _____ (add if E)

3.6 LHA _____ (enter at 5.3)

4. Reduction of sextant observation

4.1 Ht. of eye ___ ft.   +   –

4.2 Index corr. _____   _____

4.3 Ht. of eye corr. _____

4.4 Net _____

4.5 h_s _____

4.6 App. alt. _____

4.7 3rd corr. to h_s _____ (middle of A2)

4.8 H_o _____ (enter at 5.8)

Navigator _____

Zone date _____

DR lat. _____ N (or) S; AP lat. _____

DR long. _____ E (or) W; AP long. _____

5. Solution by *H. O. Pub. No. 249*

5.1 Dec. difference ___

5.2 Dec. same __ name or contrary __ name to lat.

5.3 LHA ____°00'

5.4 AP lat. ____°00' (nearest whole degree)

5.5 Tab. H _____ d ___ Z ___ (to 5.11)

5.6 d corr. _____ (from Dec. diff.)

5.7 H_c _____ (enter at 5.9)

5.8 H_o _____

5.9 H_c _____

5.10 $H_o – H_c$ _____ (+ = toward; – = away)

5.11 Zn _____ (see rule below)

Rule for azimuth, Zn:

N. Hem: LHA < 180°: Zn = 360° – Z

          LHA > 180°: Zn = Z

S. Hem: LHA < 180°: Zn = 180° + Z

          LHA > 180°: Zn = 180° – Z

Form F9. Calculator Reduction of Sight

See *Almanac,* "Sight Reduction Procedures."
Calculator entries in bold.

1. To find GMT

1.1 Zone watch time _____

1.2 Zone description _____

1.3 GMT watch time _____

1.4 GMT watch error s+ / f– _____

1.5 GMT h ___ min ___ sec _

1.6 GMT Date D _____

2. Find interpolation factor, x

2.1 **min ÷ 60 + sec ÷ 3600 = [x → M]**; put x into memory.

2.2 x – _____ (All angles are assumed to be in form of decimal fraction DD.DDDD)

3. To find declination

3.1 Dec. (H + 1) _____

3.2 Dec. (H) _____

3.3 **Dec. (H + 1) – Dec (H) = × [M → x] +**
Dec. (H) = _____ (enter at 6.2)

4. To find GHA (Aries/sun/moon)

4.1 GHA (H + 1) _____

4.2 GHA (H) _____

4.3 **GHA (H + 1) – GHA (H) = × [M → x] +**
GHA (H) = _____

4.4 GHA _____

4.5 AP long. _____ (add if E)

4.6 LHA _____ (enter at 6.1)

5. Reduction of sextant observation

5.1 Ht. of eye ___ ft.   +   –

5.2 Index corr. _____   _____

5.3 Ht. of eye corr. _____

5.4 Net _____

5.5 h_s _____ (upper/lower limb)

5.6 App. alt. _____

5.7 3rd corr. to h_s _____ (first col. of A2)

5.8 H_o _____ (enter at 6.8)

6. Calculate altitude and azimuth

6.1 LHA _____ (enter from 4.6)

6.2 Dec. _____ (enter from 3.3)

6.3 AP lat. _____

6.4 Find H_c: **Dec. sin × lat. sin + Dec. cos × LHA**
cos × lat. cos = 2ndF sin^{-1} =
_____ H_c

6.5 H_o _____

6.6 $H_o – H_c$ _____ (+ = toward; – = away)

6.7 Find X: **Dec. sin × lat. cos – Dec. cos × LHA**
cos × lat.
sin = / _____
H_c cos = _____ = X

6.8 Find Zn: **X 2ndF cos^{-1} =**
_____ Z (see rule below)

Zn = 360 – z = _____

Rule for azimuth, Zn:

N. Hem: LHA < 180°: Zn = 360° – Z
LHA > 180°: Zn = Z

S. Hem: LHA < 180°: Zn = 180° + Z
LHA > 180°: Zn = 180° – Z

Form F10. Noon Sight Reduction Using the Analemma

The easiest way to find your position on the surface of the earth by means of celestial navigation is by plotting a noon curve and using the analemma.

1. Measure the altitude of the sun at several times throughout the day. Measure more frequently when the sun is highest.

2. Graph and fit a smooth curve to this data.

3. Estimate the time at which the sun is highest in the sky. This is local apparent noon (LAN). Estimate the sun's maximum altitude in degrees and minutes of arc (1° = 60′).

LAN altitude: _____ . _____ ′ LAN time: _____ : _____

Zone time: _____

Date: _____

Convert zone time to Greenwich mean time (GMT) by adding in your zone description:

	Standard Time	Daylight Time
U.S. Time Zones	Nov. to Apr.	May to Oct.
Eastern	+5	+4
Central	+6	+5
Mountain	+7	+6
Western	+8	+7

4. Calculate your longitude.

Time of LAN	_____ : _____ GMT
Subtract time at Greenwich noon	−12:00
± time difference at Greenwich noon	_____ : _____
Convert to degrees and minutes of arc	× 15°/hr
Difference in degrees	_____ ° _____ ′
Analemma longitude correction (+ = W)	_____ ° _____ ′
Longitude (+ = W)	_____ ° _____ ′

5. Calculate your latitude.

Zenith at 90°	89° 60′
Subtract LAN altitude	− _____ ° _____ ′
LAN zenith distance	_____ ° _____ ′
± declination from analemma (+ = N)	_____ ° _____ ′
Latitude (+ = N)	_____ ° _____ ′

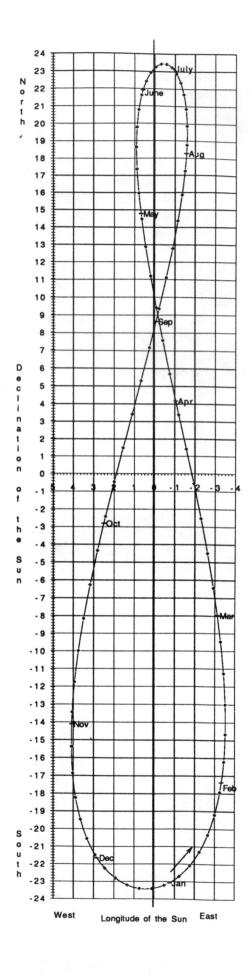

UNIVERSAL PLOTTING SHEET Navigator_____

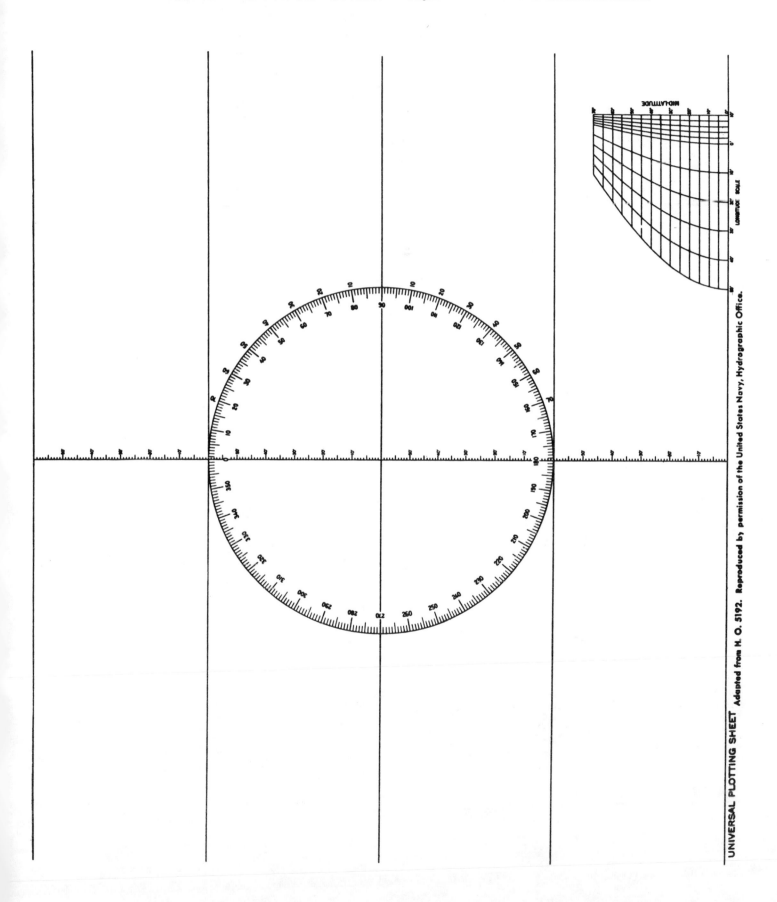

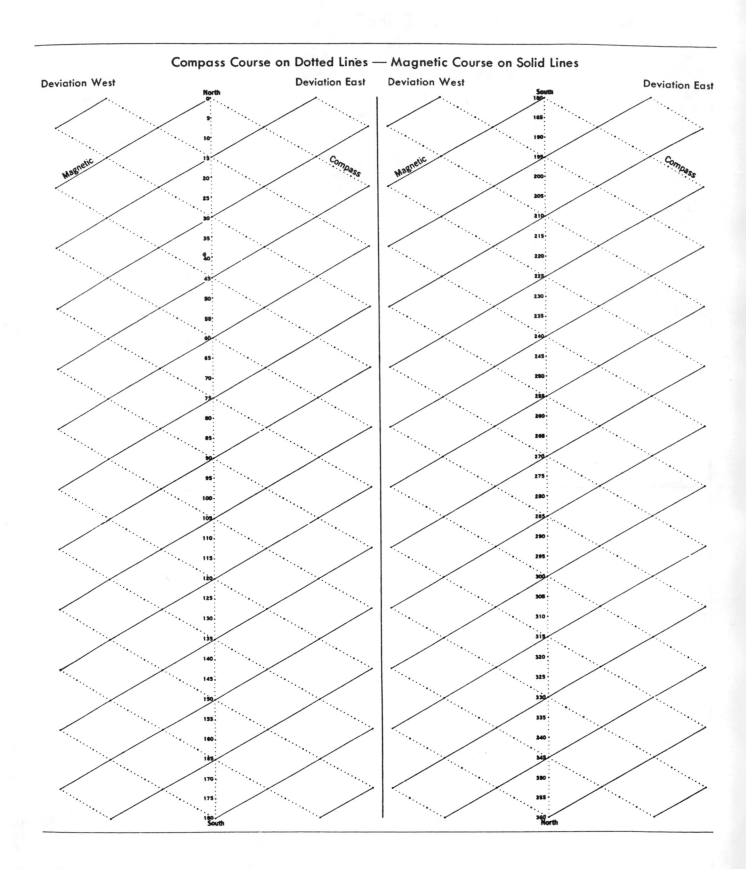

Compass Course on Dotted Lines — Magnetic Course on Solid Lines

Useful Tables

TABLE 19

Speed, Time, and Distance

Min-utes	Speed in knots																Min-utes
	0.5	1.0	1.5	2.0	2.5	3.0	3.5	4.0	4.5	5.0	5.5	6.0	6.5	7.0	7.5	8.0	
	Miles	Miles	Miles	Miles	Miles	Miles	Miles	Miles	Miles	Miles	Miles	Miles	Miles	Miles	Miles	Miles	
1	0.0	0.0	0.0	0.0	0.0	0.0	0.1	0.1	0.1	0.1	0.1	0.1	0.1	0.1	0.1	0.1	1
2	0.0	0.0	0.0	0.1	0.1	0.1	0.1	0.1	0.2	0.2	0.2	0.2	0.2	0.2	0.2	0.3	2
3	0.0	0.0	0.1	0.1	0.1	0.2	0.2	0.2	0.2	0.2	0.3	0.3	0.3	0.4	0.4	0.4	3
4	0.0	0.1	0.1	0.1	0.2	0.2	0.2	0.3	0.3	0.3	0.4	0.4	0.4	0.5	0.5	0.5	4
5	0.0	0.1	0.1	0.2	0.2	0.2	0.3	0.3	0.4	0.4	0.5	0.5	0.5	0.6	0.6	0.7	5
6	0.0	0.1	0.2	0.2	0.2	0.3	0.4	0.4	0.4	0.5	0.6	0.6	0.6	0.7	0.8	0.8	6
7	0.1	0.1	0.2	0.2	0.3	0.4	0.4	0.5	0.5	0.6	0.6	0.7	0.8	0.8	0.9	0.9	7
8	0.1	0.1	0.2	0.3	0.3	0.4	0.5	0.5	0.6	0.7	0.7	0.8	0.9	0.9	1.0	1.1	8
9	0.1	0.2	0.2	0.3	0.4	0.4	0.5	0.6	0.7	0.8	0.8	0.9	1.0	1.0	1.1	1.2	9
10	0.1	0.2	0.2	0.3	0.4	0.5	0.6	0.7	0.8	0.8	0.9	1.0	1.1	1.2	1.2	1.3	10
11	0.1	0.2	0.3	0.4	0.5	0.6	0.6	0.7	0.8	0.9	1.0	1.1	1.2	1.3	1.4	1.5	11
12	0.1	0.2	0.3	0.4	0.5	0.6	0.7	0.8	0.9	1.0	1.1	1.2	1.3	1.4	1.5	1.6	12
13	0.1	0.2	0.3	0.4	0.5	0.6	0.8	0.9	1.0	1.1	1.2	1.3	1.4	1.5	1.6	1.7	13
14	0.1	0.2	0.4	0.5	0.6	0.7	0.8	0.9	1.0	1.2	1.3	1.4	1.5	1.6	1.8	1.9	14
15	0.1	0.2	0.4	0.5	0.6	0.8	0.9	1.0	1.1	1.2	1.4	1.5	1.6	1.8	1.9	2.0	15
16	0.1	0.3	0.4	0.5	0.7	0.8	0.9	1.1	1.2	1.3	1.5	1.6	1.7	1.9	2.0	2.1	16
17	0.1	0.3	0.4	0.6	0.7	0.8	1.0	1.1	1.3	1.4	1.6	1.7	1.8	2.0	2.1	2.3	17
18	0.2	0.3	0.4	0.6	0.8	0.9	1.0	1.2	1.4	1.5	1.6	1.8	2.0	2.1	2.2	2.4	18
19	0.2	0.3	0.5	0.6	0.8	1.0	1.1	1.3	1.4	1.6	1.7	1.9	2.1	2.2	2.4	2.5	19
20	0.2	0.3	0.5	0.7	0.8	1.0	1.2	1.3	1.5	1.7	1.8	2.0	2.2	2.3	2.5	2.7	20
21	0.2	0.4	0.5	0.7	0.9	1.0	1.2	1.4	1.6	1.8	1.9	2.1	2.3	2.4	2.6	2.8	21
22	0.2	0.4	0.6	0.7	0.9	1.1	1.3	1.5	1.6	1.8	2.0	2.2	2.4	2.6	2.8	2.9	22
23	0.2	0.4	0.6	0.8	1.0	1.2	1.3	1.5	1.7	1.9	2.1	2.3	2.5	2.7	2.9	3.1	23
24	0.2	0.4	0.6	0.8	1.0	1.2	1.4	1.6	1.8	2.0	2.2	2.4	2.6	2.8	3.0	3.2	24
25	0.2	0.4	0.6	0.8	1.0	1.2	1.5	1.7	1.9	2.1	2.3	2.5	2.7	2.9	3.1	3.3	25
26	0.2	0.4	0.6	0.9	1.1	1.3	1.5	1.7	2.0	2.2	2.4	2.6	2.8	3.0	3.2	3.5	26
27	0.2	0.4	0.7	0.9	1.1	1.4	1.6	1.8	2.0	2.2	2.5	2.7	2.9	3.2	3.4	3.6	27
28	0.2	0.5	0.7	0.9	1.2	1.4	1.6	1.9	2.1	2.3	2.6	2.8	3.0	3.3	3.5	3.7	28
29	0.2	0.5	0.7	1.0	1.2	1.4	1.7	1.9	2.2	2.4	2.7	2.9	3.1	3.4	3.6	3.9	29
30	0.2	0.5	0.8	1.0	1.2	1.5	1.8	2.0	2.2	2.5	2.8	3.0	3.2	3.5	3.8	4.0	30
31	0.3	0.5	0.8	1.0	1.3	1.6	1.8	2.1	2.3	2.6	2.8	3.1	3.4	3.6	3.9	4.1	31
32	0.3	0.5	0.8	1.1	1.3	1.6	1.9	2.1	2.4	2.7	2.9	3.2	3.5	3.7	4.0	4.3	32
33	0.3	0.6	0.8	1.1	1.4	1.6	1.9	2.2	2.5	2.8	3.0	3.3	3.6	3.8	4.1	4.4	33
34	0.3	0.6	0.8	1.1	1.4	1.7	2.0	2.3	2.6	2.8	3.1	3.4	3.7	4.0	4.2	4.5	34
35	0.3	0.6	0.9	1.2	1.5	1.8	2.0	2.3	2.6	2.9	3.2	3.5	3.8	4.1	4.4	4.7	35
36	0.3	0.6	0.9	1.2	1.5	1.8	2.1	2.4	2.7	3.0	3.3	3.6	3.9	4.2	4.5	4.8	36
37	0.3	0.6	0.9	1.2	1.5	1.8	2.2	2.5	2.8	3.1	3.4	3.7	4.0	4.3	4.6	4.9	37
38	0.3	0.6	1.0	1.3	1.6	1.9	2.2	2.5	2.8	3.2	3.5	3.8	4.1	4.4	4.8	5.1	38
39	0.3	0.6	1.0	1.3	1.6	2.0	2.3	2.6	2.9	3.2	3.6	3.9	4.2	4.6	4.9	5.2	39
40	0.3	0.7	1.0	1.3	1.7	2.0	2.3	2.7	3.0	3.3	3.7	4.0	4.3	4.7	5.0	5.3	40
41	0.3	0.7	1.0	1.4	1.7	2.0	2.4	2.7	3.1	3.4	3.8	4.1	4.4	4.8	5.1	5.5	41
42	0.4	0.7	1.0	1.4	1.8	2.1	2.4	2.8	3.2	3.5	3.8	4.2	4.6	4.9	5.2	5.6	42
43	0.4	0.7	1.1	1.4	1.8	2.2	2.5	2.9	3.2	3.6	3.9	4.3	4.7	5.0	5.4	5.7	43
44	0.4	0.7	1.1	1.5	1.8	2.2	2.6	2.9	3.3	3.7	4.0	4.4	4.8	5.1	5.5	5.9	44
45	0.4	0.8	1.1	1.5	1.9	2.2	2.6	3.0	3.4	3.8	4.1	4.5	4.9	5.2	5.6	6.0	45
46	0.4	0.8	1.2	1.5	1.9	2.3	2.7	3.1	3.4	3.8	4.2	4.6	5.0	5.4	5.8	6.1	46
47	0.4	0.8	1.2	1.6	2.0	2.4	2.7	3.1	3.5	3.9	4.3	4.7	5.1	5.5	5.9	6.3	47
48	0.4	0.8	1.2	1.6	2.0	2.4	2.8	3.2	3.6	4.0	4.4	4.8	5.2	5.6	6.0	6.4	48
49	0.4	0.8	1.2	1.6	2.0	2.4	2.9	3.3	3.7	4.1	4.5	4.9	5.3	5.7	6.1	6.5	49
50	0.4	0.8	1.2	1.7	2.1	2.5	2.9	3.3	3.8	4.2	4.6	5.0	5.4	5.8	6.2	6.7	50
51	0.4	0.8	1.3	1.7	2.1	2.6	3.0	3.4	3.8	4.2	4.7	5.1	5.5	6.0	6.4	6.8	51
52	0.4	0.9	1.3	1.7	2.2	2.6	3.0	3.5	3.9	4.3	4.8	5.2	5.6	6.1	6.5	6.9	52
53	0.4	0.9	1.3	1.8	2.2	2.6	3.1	3.5	4.0	4.4	4.9	5.3	5.7	6.2	6.6	7.1	53
54	0.4	0.9	1.4	1.8	2.2	2.7	3.2	3.6	4.0	4.5	5.0	5.5	6.0	6.4	6.8	7.2	54
55	0.5	0.9	1.4	1.8	2.3	2.8	3.2	3.7	4.1	4.6	5.0	5.5	6.0	6.4	6.9	7.3	55
56	0.5	0.9	1.4	1.9	2.3	2.8	3.3	3.7	4.2	4.7	5.1	5.6	6.1	6.5	7.0	7.5	56
57	0.5	1.0	1.4	1.9	2.4	2.8	3.3	3.8	4.3	4.8	5.2	5.7	6.2	6.6	7.1	7.6	57
58	0.5	1.0	1.4	1.9	2.4	2.9	3.4	3.9	4.4	4.8	5.3	5.8	6.3	6.8	7.2	7.7	58
59	0.5	1.0	1.5	2.0	2.5	3.0	3.4	3.9	4.4	4.9	5.4	5.9	6.4	6.9	7.4	7.9	59
60	0.5	1.0	1.5	2.0	2.5	3.0	3.5	4.0	4.5	5.0	5.5	6.0	6.5	7.0	7.5	8.0	60

TABLE 19

Speed, Time, and Distance

Min-utes	Speed in knots																Min-utes
	8.5	9.0	9.5	10.0	10.5	11.0	11.5	12.0	12.5	13.0	13.5	14.0	14.5	15.0	15.5	16.0	
	Miles	Miles	Miles	Miles	Miles	Miles	Miles	Miles	Miles	Miles	Miles	Miles	Miles	Miles	Miles	Miles	
1	0.1	0.2	0.2	0.2	0.2	0.2	0.2	0.2	0.2	0.2	0.2	0.2	0.2	0.2	0.3	0.3	1
2	0.3	0.3	0.3	0.3	0.4	0.4	0.4	0.4	0.4	0.4	0.4	0.5	0.5	0.5	0.5	0.5	2
3	0.4	0.4	0.5	0.5	0.5	0.6	0.6	0.6	0.6	0.6	0.7	0.7	0.7	0.8	0.8	0.8	3
4	0.6	0.6	0.6	0.7	0.7	0.7	0.8	0.8	0.8	0.9	0.9	0.9	1.0	1.0	1.0	1.1	4
5	0.7	0.8	0.8	0.8	0.9	0.9	1.0	1.0	1.0	1.1	1.1	1.2	1.2	1.2	1.3	1.3	5
6	0.8	0.9	1.0	1.0	1.0	1.1	1.2	1.2	1.2	1.3	1.4	1.4	1.4	1.5	1.6	1.6	6
7	1.0	1.0	1.1	1.2	1.2	1.3	1.3	1.4	1.5	1.5	1.6	1.6	1.7	1.8	1.8	1.9	7
8	1.1	1.2	1.3	1.3	1.4	1.5	1.5	1.6	1.7	1.7	1.8	1.9	1.9	2.0	2.1	2.1	8
9	1.3	1.4	1.4	1.5	1.6	1.6	1.7	1.8	1.9	2.0	2.0	2.1	2.2	2.2	2.3	2.4	9
10	1.4	1.5	1.6	1.7	1.8	1.8	1.9	2.0	2.1	2.2	2.2	2.3	2.4	2.5	2.6	2.7	10
11	1.6	1.6	1.7	1.8	1.9	2.0	2.1	2.2	2.3	2.4	2.5	2.6	2.7	2.8	2.8	2.9	11
12	1.7	1.8	1.9	2.0	2.1	2.2	2.3	2.4	2.5	2.6	2.7	2.8	2.9	3.0	3.1	3.2	12
13	1.8	2.0	2.1	2.2	2.3	2.4	2.5	2.6	2.7	2.8	2.9	3.0	3.1	3.2	3.4	3.5	13
14	2.0	2.1	2.2	2.3	2.4	2.6	2.7	2.8	2.9	3.0	3.2	3.3	3.4	3.5	3.6	3.7	14
15	2.1	2.2	2.4	2.5	2.6	2.8	2.9	3.0	3.1	3.2	3.4	3.5	3.6	3.8	3.9	4.0	15
16	2.3	2.4	2.5	2.7	2.8	2.9	3.1	3.2	3.3	3.5	3.6	3.7	3.9	4.0	4.1	4.3	16
17	2.4	2.6	2.7	2.8	3.0	3.1	3.3	3.4	3.5	3.7	3.8	4.0	4.1	4.2	4.4	4.5	17
18	2.6	2.7	2.8	3.0	3.2	3.3	3.4	3.6	3.8	3.9	4.0	4.2	4.4	4.5	4.6	4.8	18
19	2.7	2.8	3.0	3.2	3.3	3.5	3.6	3.8	4.0	4.1	4.3	4.4	4.6	4.8	4.9	5.1	19
20	2.8	3.0	3.2	3.3	3.5	3.7	3.8	4.0	4.2	4.3	4.5	4.7	4.8	5.0	5.2	5.3	20
21	3.0	3.2	3.3	3.5	3.7	3.8	4.0	4.2	4.4	4.6	4.7	4.9	5.1	5.2	5.4	5.6	21
22	3.1	3.3	3.5	3.7	3.8	4.0	4.2	4.4	4.6	4.8	5.0	5.1	5.3	5.5	5.7	5.9	22
23	3.3	3.4	3.6	3.8	4.0	4.2	4.4	4.6	4.8	5.0	5.2	5.4	5.6	5.8	5.9	6.1	23
24	3.4	3.6	3.8	4.0	4.2	4.4	4.6	4.8	5.0	5.2	5.4	5.6	5.8	6.0	6.2	6.4	24
25	3.5	3.8	4.0	4.2	4.4	4.6	4.8	5.0	5.2	5.4	5.6	5.8	6.0	6.2	6.5	6.7	25
26	3.7	3.9	4.1	4.3	4.6	4.8	5.0	5.2	5.4	5.6	5.8	6.1	6.3	6.5	6.7	6.9	26
27	3.8	4.0	4.3	4.5	4.7	5.0	5.2	5.4	5.6	5.8	6.1	6.3	6.5	6.8	7.0	7.2	27
28	4.0	4.2	4.4	4.7	4.9	5.1	5.4	5.6	5.8	6.1	6.3	6.5	6.8	7.0	7.2	7.5	28
29	4.1	4.4	4.6	4.8	5.1	5.3	5.6	5.8	6.0	6.3	6.5	6.8	7.0	7.2	7.5	7.7	29
30	4.2	4.5	4.8	5.0	5.2	5.5	5.8	6.0	6.2	6.5	6.8	7.0	7.2	7.5	7.8	8.0	30
31	4.4	4.6	4.9	5.2	5.4	5.7	5.9	6.2	6.5	6.7	7.0	7.2	7.5	7.8	8.0	8.3	31
32	4.5	4.8	5.1	5.3	5.6	5.9	6.1	6.4	6.7	6.9	7.2	7.5	7.7	8.0	8.3	8.5	32
33	4.7	5.0	5.2	5.5	5.8	6.0	6.3	6.6	6.9	7.2	7.4	7.7	8.0	8.2	8.5	8.8	33
34	4.8	5.1	5.4	5.7	6.0	6.2	6.5	6.8	7.1	7.4	7.6	7.9	8.2	8.5	8.8	9.1	34
35	5.0	5.2	5.5	5.8	6.1	6.4	6.7	7.0	7.3	7.6	7.9	8.2	8.5	8.8	9.0	9.3	35
36	5.1	5.4	5.7	6.0	6.3	6.6	6.9	7.2	7.5	7.8	8.1	8.4	8.7	9.0	9.3	9.6	36
37	5.2	5.6	5.9	6.2	6.5	6.8	7.1	7.4	7.7	8.0	8.3	8.6	8.9	9.2	9.6	9.9	37
38	5.4	5.7	6.0	6.3	6.6	7.0	7.3	7.6	7.9	8.2	8.6	8.9	9.2	9.5	9.8	10.1	38
39	5.5	5.8	6.2	6.5	6.8	7.2	7.5	7.8	8.1	8.4	8.8	9.1	9.4	9.8	10.1	10.4	39
40	5.7	6.0	6.3	6.7	7.0	7.3	7.7	8.0	8.3	8.7	9.0	9.3	9.7	10.0	10.3	10.7	40
41	5.8	6.2	6.5	6.8	7.2	7.5	7.9	8.2	8.5	8.9	9.2	9.6	9.9	10.2	10.6	10.9	41
42	6.0	6.3	6.6	7.0	7.4	7.7	8.0	8.4	8.8	9.1	9.4	9.8	10.2	10.5	10.8	11.2	42
43	6.1	6.4	6.8	7.2	7.5	7.9	8.2	8.6	9.0	9.3	9.7	10.0	10.4	10.8	11.1	11.5	43
44	6.2	6.6	7.0	7.3	7.7	8.1	8.4	8.8	9.2	9.5	9.9	10.3	10.6	11.0	11.4	11.7	44
45	6.4	6.8	7.1	7.5	7.9	8.2	8.6	9.0	9.4	9.8	10.1	10.5	10.9	11.2	11.6	12.0	45
46	6.5	6.9	7.3	7.7	8.0	8.4	8.8	9.2	9.6	10.0	10.4	10.7	11.1	11.5	11.9	12.3	46
47	6.7	7.0	7.4	7.8	8.2	8.6	9.0	9.4	9.8	10.2	10.6	11.0	11.4	11.8	12.1	12.5	47
48	6.8	7.2	7.6	8.0	8.4	8.8	9.2	9.6	10.0	10.4	10.8	11.2	11.6	12.0	12.4	12.8	48
49	6.9	7.4	7.8	8.2	8.6	9.0	9.4	9.8	10.2	10.6	11.0	11.4	11.8	12.2	12.7	13.1	49
50	7.1	7.5	7.9	8.3	8.8	9.2	9.6	10.0	10.4	10.8	11.2	11.7	12.1	12.5	12.9	13.3	50
51	7.2	7.6	8.1	8.5	8.9	9.4	9.8	10.2	10.6	11.0	11.5	11.9	12.3	12.8	13.2	13.6	51
52	7.4	7.8	8.2	8.7	9.1	9.5	10.0	10.4	10.8	11.3	11.7	12.1	12.6	13.0	13.4	13.9	52
53	7.5	8.0	8.4	8.8	9.3	9.7	10.2	10.6	11.0	11.5	11.9	12.4	12.8	13.2	13.7	14.1	53
54	7.6	8.1	8.6	9.0	9.4	9.9	10.4	10.8	11.2	11.7	12.2	12.6	13.0	13.5	14.0	14.4	54
55	7.8	8.2	8.7	9.2	9.6	10.1	10.5	11.0	11.5	11.9	12.4	12.8	13.3	13.8	14.2	14.7	55
56	7.9	8.4	8.9	9.3	9.8	10.3	10.7	11.2	11.7	12.1	12.6	13.1	13.5	14.0	14.5	14.9	56
57	8.1	8.6	9.0	9.5	10.0	10.4	10.9	11.4	11.9	12.4	12.8	13.3	13.8	14.2	14.7	15.2	57
58	8.2	8.7	9.2	9.7	10.2	10.6	11.1	11.6	12.1	12.6	13.0	13.5	14.0	14.5	15.0	15.5	58
59	8.4	8.8	9.3	9.8	10.3	10.8	11.3	11.8	12.3	12.8	13.3	13.8	14.3	14.8	15.2	15.7	59
60	8.5	9.0	9.5	10.0	10.5	11.0	11.5	12.0	12.5	13.0	13.5	14.0	14.5	15.0	15.5	16.0	60

RUNNING FIX TABLE

DISTANCE OFF (at Second bearing) By TWO BEARINGS AND RUN BETWEEN THEM

EXAMPLE OF USING TABLE. At 0600 steering East (Magnetic) a vessel takes a bearing of a lighthouse 160°(M). Patent Log 56. Half an hour later the Patent Log reads 60 and the bearing is found to be 210°(M). Find the distance off at the Second bearing. Angle between Course Line and First bearing equals 70°. Angle between First and Second bearing equals 50°. Using Table, with above angles 70° at top and 50° at side, gives 1.2M. Distance run between bearings (P L 60 − 56) = 4 miles. Therefore 1.2 × 4 = 4.8 miles. Vessel's bearing and distance from the Lighthouse is therefore 210°, distance 4.8 miles. Speed must be estimated as accurately as possible if Patent Log is not available.

Angle between 1st and 2nd Bearings	Angle between Course Line (i.e. Ship's Head) and First Bearing															Angle between 1st and 2nd Bearings
	20°	25°	30°	35°	40°	45°	50°	55°	60°	65°	70°	75°	80°	85°	90°	
10°	2·0	2·4	2·9	3·3	3·7	4·1	4·4	4·7	5·0	5·2	5·4	5·5	5·7	5·7	5·8	
15°	1·3	1·6	1·9	2·2	2·5	2·7	3·0	3·2	3·3	3·5	3·7	3·8	4·0	4·0	4·0	
20°	1·0	1·2	1·5	1·7	1·9	2·1	2·2	2·4	2·5	2·6	2·8	2·8	2·9	2·9	2·9	160°
25°	0·8	1·0	1·2	1·4	1·6	1·7	1·8	1·9	2·0	2·1	2·2	2·3	2·3	2·4	2·4	155°
30°	0·7	0·9	1·0	1·1	1·3	1·4	1·5	1·6	1·7	1·8	1·9	1·9	2·0	2·0	2·0	150°
35°	0·6	0·8	0·9	1·0	1·1	1·3	1·4	1·5	1·5	1·6	1·7	1·7	1·7	1·7	1·7	145°
40°	0·5	0·7	0·8	0·9	1·0	1·1	1·2	1·3	1·4	1·4	1·5	1·5	1·6	1·6	1·6	140°
45°	0·5	0·6	0·7	0·8	0·9	1·0	1·1	1·2	1·2	1·3	1·3	1·4	1·4	1·4	1·4	135°
50°	0·4	0·6	0·7	0·8	0·8	0·9	1·0	1·1	1·1	1·2	1·2	1·3	1·3	1·3	1·3	130°
55°	0·4	0·5	0·6	0·7	0·8	0·9	0·9	1·0	1·1	1·1	1·1	1·2	1·2	1·2	1·2	125°
60°	0·4	0·5	0·6	0·7	0·7	0·8	0·9	0·9	1·0	1·1	1·1	1·1	1·1	1·2	1·2	120°
65°	0·4	0·5	0·5	0·6	0·7	0·8	0·9	0·9	0·9	1·0	1·0	1·1	1·1	1·1	1·1	115°
70°	0·4	0·5	0·5	0·6	0·7	0·7	0·8	0·8	0·9	0·9	1·0	1·0	1·1	1·1	1·1	110°
75°	0·3	0·4	0·5	0·6	0·7	0·7	0·8	0·8	0·9	0·9	1·0	1·0	1·0	1·0		105°
80°	0·3	0·4	0·5	0·6	0·7	0·7	0·8	0·8	0·9	0·9	0·9	1·0	1·0			100°
85°	0·3	0·4	0·5	0·6	0·6	0·7	0·8	0·8	0·9	0·9	0·9	1·0				95°
90°	0·3	0·4	0·5	0·6	0·6	0·7	0·8	0·8	0·9	0·9	0·9					90°
	160°	155°	150°	145°	140°	135°	130°	125°	120°	115°	110°	105°	100°	95°	90°	

Angle between Course Line (i.e. Ship's Head) and First Bearing

Note: When the angles exceed 90° use the right vertical column for the difference between bearings and the bottom horizontal row for the angle between Course Line and First Bearing. Interpolate for accuracy.

APPENDIX E

NAVIGATIONAL COORDINATES

Coordinate	Symbol	Measured from	Measured along	Direction	Measured to	Units	Precision	Maximum value	Labels
latitude	L, lat.	equator	meridian	N, S	parallel	°,′	0′.1	90°	N, S
colatitude	colat.	poles	meridian	S, N	parallel	°,′	0′.1	90°	—
longitude	λ, long.	prime meridian	parallel	E, W	local meridian	°,′	0′.1	180°	E, W
declination	d, dec.	celestial equator	hour circle	N, S	parallel of declination	°,′	0′.1	90°	N, S
polar distance	p	elevated pole	hour circle	S, N	parallel of declination	°,′	0′.1	180°	—
altitude	h	horizon	vertical circle	up	parallel of altitude	°,′	0′.1	90°*	—
zenith distance	z	zenith	vertical circle	down	parallel of altitude	°,′	0′.1	180°	—
azimuth	Zn	north	horizon	E	vertical circle	°	0°.1	360°	—
azimuth angle	Z	north, south	horizon	E, W	vertical circle	°	0°.1	180° or 90°	N, S...E, W
amplitude	A	east, west	horizon	N, S	body	°	0°.1	90°	E, W...N, S
Greenwich hour angle	GHA	Greenwich celestial meridian	parallel of declination	W	hour circle	°,′	0′.1	360°	—
local hour angle	LHA	local celestial meridian	parallel of declination	W	hour circle	°,′	0′.1	360°	—
meridian angle	t	local celestial meridian	parallel of declination	E, W	hour circle	°,′	0′.1	180°	E, W
sidereal hour angle	SHA	hour circle of vernal equinox	parallel of declination	W	hour circle	°,′	0′.1	360°	—
right ascension	RA	hour circle of vernal equinox	parallel of declination	E	hour circle	h, m, s	1s	24h	—
Greenwich mean time	GMT	lower branch Greenwich celestial meridian	parallel of declination	W	hour circle mean sun	h, m, s	1s	24h	—
local mean time	LMT	lower branch local celestial meridian	parallel of declination	W	hour circle mean sun	h, m, s	1s	24h	—
zone time	ZT	lower branch zone celestial meridian	parallel of declination	W	hour circle mean sun	h, m, s	1s	24h	—
Greenwich apparent time	GAT	lower branch Greenwich celestial meridian	parallel of declination	W	hour circle apparent sun	h, m, s	1s	24h	—
local apparent time	LAT	lower branch local celestial meridian	parallel of declination	W	hour circle apparent sun	h, m, s	1s	24h	—
Greenwich sidereal time	GST	Greenwich celestial meridian	parallel of declination	W	hour circle vernal equinox	h, m, s	1s	24h	—
local sidereal time	LST	local celestial meridian	parallel of declination	W	hour circle vernal equinox	h, m, s	1s	24h	—

*When measured from celestial horizon.

APPENDIX A

NAVIGATIONAL STARS AND THE PLANETS

Name	Pronunciation	Bayer name	Origin of name	Meaning of name	Dis-tance*
Acamar	ă′ká·măr	θ Eridani	Arabic	another form of Achernar	120
Achernar	ă′kĕr·năr	α Eridani	Arabic	end of the river (Eridanus)	72
Acrux	ă′krŭks	α Crucis	Modern	coined from Bayer name	220
Adhara	á·dä′rá	ε Canis Majoris	Arabic	the virgin(s)	350
Aldebaran	ăl dĕb′á·răn	α Tauri	Arabic	follower (of the Pleiades)	64
Alioth	ăl′ī·ôth	ε Ursa Majoris	Arabic	another form of Capella	49
Alkaid	ăl·kăd′	η Ursa Majoris	Arabic	leader of the daughters of the bier	190
Al Na′ir	ăl·nār′	α Gruis	Arabic	bright one (of the fish's tail)	90
Alnilam	ăl′nĭ·lăm	ε Orionis	Arabic	string of pearls	410
Alphard	ăl′fárd	α Hydrae	Arabic	solitary star of the serpent	200
Alphecca	ăl·fĕk′á	α Corona Borealis	Arabic	feeble one (in the crown)	76
Alpheratz	ăl·fē′răts	α Andromeda	Arabic	the horse's navel	120
Altair	ăl·tār′	α Aquilae	Arabic	flying eagle or vulture	16
Ankaa	ăn′ká	α Phoenicis	Arabic	coined name	93
Antares	ăn·tā′rēz	α Scorpii	Greek	rival of Mars (in color)	250
Arcturus	árk·tū′rús	α Bootis	Greek	the bear's guard	37
Atria	ăt′rĭ·á	α Trianguli Australis	Modern	coined from Bayer name	130
Avior	ā′vĭ·ôr	ε Carinae	Modern	coined name	350
Bellatrix	bĕ·lă′trĭks .	γ Orionis	Latin	female warrior	250
Betelgeuse	bĕt′ĕl·jūz	α Orionis	Arabic	the arm pit (of Orion)	300
Canopus	ká·nō′pŭs	α Carinae	Greek	city of ancient Egypt	230
Capella	ká·pĕl′á	α Aurigae	Latin	little she-goat	46
Deneb	dĕn′ĕb	α Cygni	Arabic	tail of the hen	600
Denebola	dĕ·nĕb′ŏ·lá	β Leonis	Arabic	tail of the lion	42
Diphda	dĭf′dá	β Ceti	Arabic	the second frog (Fomalhaut was once the first)	57
Dubhe	dŭb′ē	α Ursa Majoris	Arabic	the bear's back	100
Elnath	ĕl′năth	β Tauri	Arabic	one butting with horns	130
Eltanin	ĕl·tā′nĭn	γ Draconis	Arabic	head of the dragon	150
Enif	ĕn′ĭf	ε Pegasi	Arabic	nose of the horse	250
Fomalhaut	fō′mál·ôt	α Piscis Austrini	Arabic	mouth of the southern fish	23
Gacrux	gă′krŭks	γ Crucis	Modern	coined from Bayer name	72
Gienah	jē′ná	γ Corvi	Arabic	right wing of the raven	136
Hadar	hä′dár	β Centauri	Modern	leg of the centaur	200
Hamal	hăm′ál	α Arietis	Arabic	full-grown lamb	76
Kaus Australis	kôs ôs·trä′lĭs	ε Sagittarii	Ar., L.	southern part of the bow	163
Kochab	kō′kăb	β Ursa Minoris	Arabic	shortened form of "north star" (named when it was that, c. 1500 BC–AD 300)	100
Markab	már′kăb	α Pegasi	Arabic	saddle (of Pegasus)	100
Menkar	mĕn′kár	α Ceti	Arabic	nose (of the whale)	1,100
Menkent	mĕn′kĕnt	θ Centauri	Modern	shoulder of the centaur	55
Miaplacidus	mĭ′á·plăs′ĭ·dŭs	β Carinae	Ar., L.	quiet or still waters	86
Mirfak	mĭr′făk	α Persei	Arabic	elbow of the Pleiades	130
Nunki	nŭn′kē	σ Sagittarii	Bab.	constellation of the holy city (Eridu)	150
Peacock	pē′kŏk	α Pavonis	Modern	coined from English name of constellation	250
Polaris	pō·lā′rĭs	α Ursa Minoris	Latin	the pole (star)	450
Pollux	pŏl′ŭks	β Geminorum	Latin	Zeus' other twin son (Castor, α Geminorum, is first twin)	33
Procyon	prō′sĭ·ŏn	α Canis Minoris	Greek	before the dog (rising before the dog star, Sirius)	11
Rasalhague	rás′ál·hā′gwē	α Ophiuchi	Arabic	head of the serpent charmer	67
Regulus	rĕg′ù·lús	α Leonis	Latin	the prince	67
Rigel	rī′jĕl	β Orionis	Arabic	foot (left foot of Orion)	500
Rigil Kentaurus	rī′jĭl kĕn·tô′rŭs	α Centauri	Arabic	foot of the centaur	4.3
Sabik	sä′bĭk	η Ophiuchi	Arabic	second winner or conqueror	69
Schedar	shĕd′ár	α Cassiopeiae	Arabic	the breast (of Cassiopeia)	360
Shaula	shō′lá	λ Scorpii	Arabic	cocked-up part of the scorpion's tail	200
Sirius	sĭr′ĭ·ŭs	α Canis Majoris	Greek	the scorching one (popularly, the dog star)	8.6
Spica	spī′ká	α Virginis	Latin	the ear of corn	155
Suhail	sōō·hāl′	λ Velorum	Arabic	shortened form of Al Suhail, one Arabic name for Canopus	200
Vega	vē′gá	α Lyrae	Arabic	the falling eagle or vulture	27
Zubenelgenubi	zōō·bĕn′ĕl·jĕ·nū′bē	α Librae	Arabic	southern claw (of the scorpion)	66

PLANETS

Name	Pronunciation	Origin of name	Meaning of name
Mercury	mûr′kú·rĭ	Latin	god of commerce and gain
Venus	vē′nús	Latin	goddess of love
Earth	ûrth	Mid. Eng.	—
Mars	märz	Latin	god of war
Jupiter	jōō′pĭ·tēr	Latin	god of the heavens, identified with the Greek Zeus, chief of the Olympian gods
Saturn	săt′ĕrn	Latin	god of seed-sowing
Uranus	ū′rá·nŭs	Greek	the personification of heaven
Neptune	nĕp′tūn	Latin	god of the sea
Pluto	plōō′tō	Greek	god of the lower world (Hades)

Guide to pronunciations:
fāte, ădd, fĭnál, lást, á̇bound, ärm; bē, ĕnd, camĕl, readĕr; īce, bĭt, anĭmal; ōver, pŏetic, hŏt, lôrd, mōōn; tūbe, ûnite, tŭb, cìrcús, ûrn

*Distances in light-years.   One light-year equals approximately 63,300 AU, or 5,880,000,000,000 miles.   Authorities differ on distances of the stars; the values given are representative.

STAR CHARTS

NORTHERN STARS

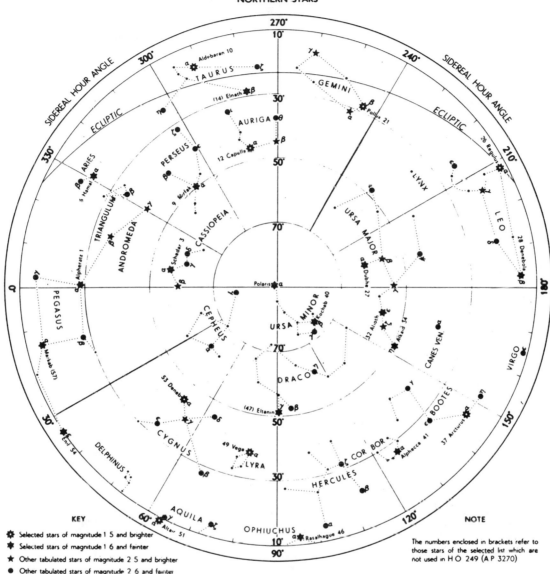

KEY

✦ Selected stars of magnitude 1·5 and brighter
✦ Selected stars of magnitude 1·6 and fainter
★ Other tabulated stars of magnitude 2·5 and brighter
● Other tabulated stars of magnitude 2·6 and fainter
· Untabulated stars

NOTE

The numbers enclosed in brackets refer to those stars of the selected list which are not used in H O 249 (A P 3270)

EQUATORIAL STARS (S.H.A. 0° to 180°)

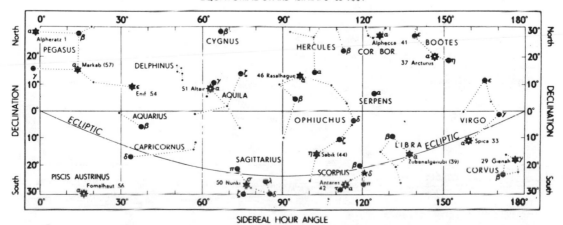

SIDEREAL HOUR ANGLE

STAR CHARTS

SOUTHERN STARS

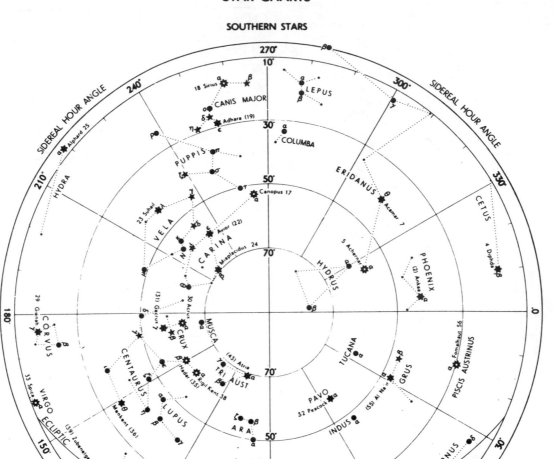

KEY

✹ Selected stars of magnitude 1·5 and brighter
✶ Selected stars of magnitude 1·6 and fainter
★ Other tabulated stars of magnitude 2·5 and brighter
● Other tabulated stars of magnitude 2·6 and fainter
· Untabulated stars

NOTE

The numbers enclosed in brackets refer to those stars of the selected list which are not used in H.O. 249 (A.P. 3270).

EQUATORIAL STARS (S.H.A. 180° to 360°)

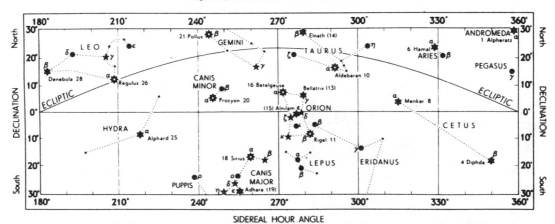

SIDEREAL HOUR ANGLE

ALTITUDE CORRECTION TABLES 0°–10°—SUN, STARS, PLANETS A3

App. Alt.	SUN OCT.–MAR. Lower Limb	Upper Limb	SUN APR.–SEPT. Lower Limb	Upper Limb	STARS PLANETS
° ′	′	′	′	′	′ ′
0 00	−18.2	−50.5	−18.4	−50.2	−34.5
03	17.5	49.8	17.8	49.6	33.8
06	16.9	49.2	17.1	48.9	33.2
09	16.3	48.6	16.5	48.3	32.6
12	15.7	48.0	15.9	47.7	32.0
15	15.1	47.4	15.3	47.1	31.4
0 18	−14.5	−46.8	−14.8	−46.6	−30.8
21	14.0	46.3	14.2	46.0	30.3
24	13.5	45.8	13.7	45.5	29.8
27	12.9	45.2	13.2	45.0	29.2
30	12.4	44.7	12.7	44.5	28.7
33	11.9	44.2	12.2	44.0	28.2
0 36	−11.5	−43.8	−11.7	−43.5	−27.8
39	11.0	43.3	11.2	43.0	27.3
42	10.5	42.8	10.8	42.6	26.8
45	10.1	42.4	10.3	42.1	26.4
48	9.6	41.9	9.9	41.7	25.9
51	9.2	41.5	9.5	41.3	25.5
0 54	−8.8	−41.1	−9.1	−40.9	−25.1
0 57	8.4	40.7	8.7	40.5	24.7
1 00	8.0	40.3	8.3	40.1	24.3
03	7.7	40.0	7.9	39.7	24.0
06	7.3	39.6	7.5	39.3	23.6
09	6.9	39.2	7.2	39.0	23.2
1 12	−6.6	−38.9	−6.8	−38.6	−22.9
15	6.2	38.5	6.5	38.3	22.5
18	5.9	38.2	6.2	38.0	22.2
21	5.6	37.9	5.8	37.6	21.9
24	5.3	37.6	5.5	37.3	21.6
27	4.9	37.2	5.2	37.0	21.2
1 30	−4.6	−36.9	−4.9	−36.7	−20.9
35	4.2	36.5	4.4	36.2	20.5
40	3.7	36.0	4.0	35.8	20.0
45	3.2	35.5	3.5	35.3	19.5
50	2.8	35.1	3.1	34.9	19.1
1 55	2.4	34.7	2.6	34.4	18.7
2 00	−2.0	−34.3	−2.2	−34.0	−18.3
05	1.6	33.9	1.8	33.6	17.9
10	1.2	33.5	1.5	33.3	17.5
15	0.9	33.2	1.1	32.9	17.2
20	0.5	32.8	0.8	32.6	16.8
25	−0.2	32.5	0.4	32.2	16.5
2 30	+0.2	−32.1	−0.1	−31.9	−16.1
35	0.5	31.8	+0.2	31.6	15.8
40	0.8	31.5	0.5	31.3	15.5
45	1.1	31.2	0.8	31.0	15.2
50	1.4	30.9	1.1	30.7	14.9
2 55	1.6	30.7	1.4	30.4	14.7
3 00	+1.9	−30.4	+1.7	−30.1	−14.4
05	2.2	30.1	1.9	29.9	14.1
10	2.4	29.9	2.1	29.7	13.9
15	2.6	29.7	2.4	29.4	13.7
20	2.9	29.4	2.6	29.2	13.4
25	3.1	29.2	2.9	28.9	13.2
3 30	+3.3	−29.0	+3.1	−28.7	−13.0

App. Alt.	SUN OCT.–MAR. Lower Limb	Upper Limb	SUN APR.–SEPT. Lower Limb	Upper Limb	STARS PLANETS
° ′	′	′	′	′	′
3 30	+3.3	−29.0	+3.1	−28.7	−13.0
35	3.6	28.7	3.3	28.5	12.7
40	3.8	28.5	3.5	28.3	12.5
45	4.0	28.3	3.7	28.1	12.3
50	4.2	28.1	3.9	27.9	12.1
3 55	4.4	27.9	4.1	27.7	11.9
4 00	+4.5	−27.8	+4.3	−27.5	−11.8
05	4.7	27.6	4.5	27.3	11.6
10	4.9	27.4	4.6	27.2	11.4
15	5.1	27.2	4.8	27.0	11.2
20	5.2	27.1	5.0	26.8	11.1
25	5.4	26.9	5.1	26.7	10.9
4 30	+5.6	−26.7	+5.3	−26.5	−10.7
35	5.7	26.6	5.5	26.3	10.6
40	5.9	26.4	5.6	26.2	10.4
45	6.0	26.3	5.8	26.0	10.3
50	6.2	26.1	5.9	25.9	10.1
4 55	6.3	26.0	6.0	25.8	10.0
5 00	+6.4	−25.9	+6.2	−25.6	−9.9
05	6.6	25.7	6.3	25.5	9.7
10	6.7	25.6	6.4	25.4	9.6
15	6.8	25.5	6.6	25.2	9.5
20	6.9	25.4	6.7	25.1	9.4
25	7.1	25.2	6.8	25.0	9.2
5 30	+7.2	−25.1	+6.9	−24.9	−9.1
35	7.3	25.0	7.0	24.8	9.0
40	7.4	24.9	7.2	24.6	8.9
45	7.5	24.8	7.3	24.5	8.8
50	7.6	24.7	7.4	24.4	8.7
5 55	7.7	24.6	7.5	24.3	8.6
6 00	+7.8	−24.5	+7.6	−24.2	−8.5
10	8.0	24.3	7.8	24.0	8.3
20	8.2	24.1	8.0	23.8	8.1
30	8.4	23.9	8.1	23.7	7.9
40	8.6	23.7	8.3	23.5	7.7
6 50	8.7	23.6	8.5	23.3	7.6
7 00	+8.9	−23.4	+8.6	−23.2	−7.4
10	9.1	23.2	8.8	23.0	7.2
20	9.2	23.1	9.0	22.8	7.1
30	9.3	23.0	9.1	22.7	7.0
40	9.5	22.8	9.2	22.6	6.8
7 50	9.6	22.7	9.4	22.4	6.7
8 00	+9.7	−22.6	+9.5	−22.3	−6.6
10	9.9	22.4	9.6	22.2	6.4
20	10.0	22.3	9.7	22.1	6.3
30	10.1	22.2	9.8	22.0	6.2
40	10.2	22.1	10.0	21.8	6.1
8 50	10.3	22.0	10.1	21.7	6.0
9 00	+10.4	−21.9	+10.2	−21.6	−5.9
10	10.5	21.8	10.3	21.5	5.8
20	10.6	21.7	10.4	21.4	5.7
30	10.7	21.6	10.5	21.3	5.6
40	10.8	21.5	10.6	21.2	5.5
9 50	10.9	21.4	10.6	21.2	5.4
10 00	+11.0	−21.3	+10.7	−21.1	−5.3

Additional corrections for temperature and pressure are given on the following page.

For bubble sextant observations ignore dip and use the star corrections for Sun, planets, and stars.

A2 ALTITUDE CORRECTION TABLES 10°-90°—SUN, STARS, PLANETS

OCT.—MAR. **SUN** APR.—SEPT.						**STARS AND PLANETS**				**DIP**				
App. Alt.	Lower Limb	Upper Limb	App. Alt.	Lower Limb	Upper Limb	App. Alt.	Corrⁿ	App. Alt.	Additional Corrⁿ	Ht. of Eye	Corrⁿ	Ht. of Eye	Ht. of Eye	Corrⁿ

OCT.—MAR. SUN App. Alt.	Lower Limb / Upper Limb	APR.—SEPT. SUN App. Alt.	Lower Limb / Upper Limb	STARS App. Alt.	Corrⁿ	PLANETS App. Alt.	Additional Corrⁿ	DIP Ht. Eye (m) Corrⁿ	Ht. Eye (ft)	Ht. Eye (m) Corrⁿ
9 34	+10·8 −21·5	9 39	+10·6 −21·2	9 56	−5·3	**1990 VENUS**		2·4 −2·8	8·0	1·0 − 1·8
9 45	+10·9 −21·4	9 51	+10·7 −21·1	10 08	−5·2	Jan. 1–Feb. 8		2·6 −2·9	8·6	1·5 − 2·2
9 56	+11·0 −21·3	10 03	+10·8 −21·0	10 20	−5·1			2·8 −3·0	9·2	2·0 − 2·5
10 08	+11·1 −21·2	10 15	+10·9 −20·9	10 33	−5·0			3·0 −3·1	9·8	2·5 − 2·8
10 21	+11·2 −21·1	10 27	+11·0 −20·8	10 46	−4·9	26 + 0·5		3·2 −3·2	10·5	3·0 − 3·0
10 34	+11·3 −21·0	10 40	+11·1 −20·7	11 00	−4·8	46 + 0·4		3·4 −3·2	11·2	See table
10 47	+11·4 −20·9	10 54	+11·2 −20·6	11 14	−4·7	60 + 0·3		3·6 −3·3	11·9	←
11 01	+11·5 −20·8	11 08	+11·3 −20·5	11 29	−4·6	73 + 0·2		3·8 −3·4	12·6	m
11 15	+11·6 −20·7	11 23	+11·4 −20·4	11 45	−4·5	84 + 0·1		4·0 −3·5	13·3	20 − 7·9
11 30	+11·7 −20·6	11 38	+11·5 −20·3	12 01	−4·4	Feb. 9–Feb. 23		4·3 −3·6	14·1	22 − 8·3
11 46	+11·8 −20·5	11 54	+11·6 −20·2	12 18	−4·3			4·5 −3·7	14·9	24 − 8·6
12 02	+11·9 −20·4	12 10	+11·7 −20·1	12 35	−4·2	29 + 0·4		4·7 −3·8	15·7	26 − 9·0
12 19	+12·0 −20·3	12 28	+11·8 −20·0	12 54	−4·1	51 + 0·3		5·0 −3·9	16·5	28 − 9·3
12 37	+12·1 −20·2	12 46	+11·9 −19·9	13 13	−4·0	68 + 0·2		5·2 −4·0	17·4	
12 55	+12·2 −20·1	13 05	+12·0 −19·8	13 33	−3·9	83 + 0·1		5·5 −4·1	18·3	30 − 9·6
13 14	+12·3 −20·0	13 24	+12·1 −19·7	13 54	−3·8	Feb. 24–Mar. 18		5·8 −4·2	19·1	32 −10·0
13 35	+12·4 −19·9	13 45	+12·2 −19·6	14 16	−3·7			6·1 −4·3	20·1	34 −10·3
13 56	+12·5 −19·8	14 07	+12·3 −19·5	14 40	−3·6	34 + 0·3		6·3 −4·4	21·0	36 −10·6
14 18	+12·6 −19·7	14 30	+12·4 −19·4	15 04	−3·5	60 + 0·2		6·6 −4·5	22·0	38 −10·8
14 42	+12·7 −19·6	14 54	+12·5 −19·3	15 30	−3·4	80 + 0·1		6·9 −4·6	22·9	
15 06	+12·8 −19·5	15 19	+12·6 −19·2	15 57	−3·3	Mar. 19–May 7		7·2 −4·7	23·9	40 −11·1
15 32	+12·9 −19·4	15 46	+12·7 −19·1	16 26	−3·2			7·5 −4·8	24·9	42 −11·4
15 59	+13·0 −19·3	16 14	+12·8 −19·0	16 56	−3·1	41 + 0·2		7·9 −4·9	26·0	44 −11·7
16 28	+13·1 −19·2	16 44	+12·9 −18·9	17 28	−3·0	76 + 0·1		8·2 −5·0	27·1	46 −11·9
16 59	+13·2 −19·1	17 15	+13·0 −18·8	18 02	−2·9	May 8–Dec. 31		8·5 −5·1	28·1	48 −12·2
17 32	+13·3 −19·0	17 48	+13·1 −18·7	18 38	−2·8			8·8 −5·2	29·2	ft.
18 06	+13·4 −18·9	18 24	+13·2 −18·6	19 17	−2·7	60 + 0·1		9·2 −5·3	30·4	2 − 1·4
18 42	+13·5 −18·8	19 01	+13·3 −18·5	19 58	−2·6			9·5 −5·4	31·5	4 − 1·9
19 21	+13·6 −18·7	19 42	+13·4 −18·4	20 42	−2·5			9·9 −5·5	32·7	6 − 2·4
20 03	+13·7 −18·6	20 25	+13·5 −18·3	21 28	−2·4			10·3 −5·6	33·9	8 − 2·7
20 48	+13·8 −18·5	21 11	+13·6 −18·2	22 19	−2·3	**MARS**		10·6 −5·7	35·1	10 − 3·1
21 35	+13·9 −18·4	22 00	+13·7 −18·1	23 13	−2·2	Jan. 1–Aug. 9		11·0 −5·8	36·3	See table
22 26	+14·0 −18·3	22 54	+13·8 −18·0	24 11	−2·1			11·4 −5·9	37·6	←
23 22	+14·1 −18·2	23 51	+13·9 −17·9	25 14	−2·0	60 + 0·1		11·8 −6·0	38·9	ft.
24 21	+14·2 −18·1	24 53	+14·0 −17·8	26 22	−1·9	Aug. 10–Oct. 21		12·2 −6·1	40·1	70 − 8·1
25 26	+14·3 −18·0	26 00	+14·1 −17·7	27 36	−1·8			12·6 −6·2	41·5	75 − 8·4
26 36	+14·4 −17·9	27 13	+14·2 −17·6	28 56	−1·7	41 + 0·2		13·0 −6·3	42·8	80 − 8·7
27 52	+14·5 −17·8	28 33	+14·3 −17·5	30 24	−1·6	76 + 0·1		13·4 −6·4	44·2	85 − 8·9
29 15	+14·6 −17·7	30 00	+14·4 −17·4	32 00	−1·5	Oct. 22–Dec. 17		13·8 −6·5	45·5	90 − 9·2
30 46	+14·7 −17·6	31 35	+14·5 −17·3	33 45	−1·4			14·2 −6·6	46·9	95 − 9·5
32 26	+14·8 −17·5	33 20	+14·6 −17·2	35 40	−1·3	34 + 0·3		14·7 −6·7	48·4	
34 17	+14·9 −17·4	35 17	+14·7 −17·1	37 48	−1·2	60 + 0·2		15·1 −6·8	49·8	
36 20	+15·0 −17·3	37 26	+14·8 −17·0	40 08	−1·1	80 + 0·1		15·5 −6·9	51·3	100 − 9·7
38 36	+15·1 −17·2	39 50	+14·9 −16·9	42 44	−1·0	Dec. 18–Dec. 31		16·0 −7·0	52·8	105 − 9·9
41 08	+15·2 −17·1	42 31	+15·0 −16·8	45 36	−0·9			16·5 −7·1	54·3	110 −10·2
43 59	+15·3 −17·0	45 31	+15·1 −16·7	48 47	−0·8	41 + 0·2		16·9 −7·2	55·8	115 −10·4
47 10	+15·4 −16·9	48 55	+15·2 −16·6	52 18	−0·7	76 + 0·1		17·4 −7·3	57·4	120 −10·6
50 46	+15·5 −16·8	52 44	+15·3 −16·5	56 11	−0·6			17·9 −7·4	58·9	125 −10·8
54 49	+15·6 −16·7	57 02	+15·4 −16·4	60 28	−0·5			18·4 −7·5	60·5	
59 23	+15·7 −16·6	61 51	+15·5 −16·3	65 08	−0·4			18·8 −7·6	62·1	130 −11·1
64 30	+15·8 −16·5	67 17	+15·6 −16·2	70 11	−0·3			19·3 −7·7	63·8	135 −11·3
70 12	+15·9 −16·4	73 16	+15·7 −16·1	75 34	−0·2			19·8 −7·8	65·4	140 −11·5
76 26	+16·0 −16·3	79 43	+15·8 −16·0	81 13	−0·1			20·4 −7·9	67·1	145 −11·7
83 05	+16·1 −16·2	86 32	+15·9 −15·9	87 03	−0·1			20·9 −8·0	68·8	150 −11·9
90 00		90 00		90 00	0·0			21·4 −8·1	70·5	155 −12·1

App. Alt. = Apparent altitude = Sextant altitude corrected for index error and dip.

TABLE 27
Amplitudes

Latitude	Declination 0°.0	0°.5	1°.0	1°.5	2°.0	2°.5	3°.0	3°.5	4°.0	4°.5	5°.0	5°.5	6°.0	Latitude
0	0.0	0.5	1.0	1.5	2.0	2.5	3.0	3.5	4.0	4.5	5.0	5.5	6.0	0
10	0.0	0.5	1.0	1.5	2.0	2.5	3.0	3.6	4.1	4.6	5.1	5.6	6.1	10
15	0.0	0.5	1.0	1.6	2.1	2.6	3.1	3.6	4.1	4.7	5.2	5.7	6.2	15
20	0.0	0.5	1.1	1.6	2.1	2.7	3.2	3.7	4.3	4.8	5.3	5.9	6.4	20
25	0.0	0.6	1.1	1.7	2.2	2.8	3.3	3.9	4.4	5.0	5.5	6.1	6.6	25
30	0.0	0.6	1.2	1.7	2.3	2.9	3.5	4.0	4.6	5.2	5.8	6.4	6.9	30
32	0.0	0.6	1.2	1.8	2.4	2.9	3.5	4.1	4.7	5.3	5.9	6.5	7.1	32
34	0.0	0.6	1.2	1.8	2.4	3.0	3.6	4.2	4.8	5.4	6.0	6.6	7.2	34
36	0.0	0.6	1.2	1.9	2.5	3.1	3.7	4.3	4.9	5.6	6.2	6.8	7.4	36
38	0.0	0.6	1.3	1.9	2.5	3.2	3.8	4.4	5.1	5.7	6.4	7.0	7.6	38
40	0.0	0.7	1.3	2.0	2.6	3.3	3.9	4.6	5.2	5.9	6.5	7.2	7.8	40
42	0.0	0.7	1.3	2.0	2.7	3.4	4.0	4.7	5.4	6.1	6.7	7.4	8.1	42
44	0.0	0.7	1.4	2.1	2.8	3.5	4.2	4.9	5.6	6.3	7.0	7.7	8.4	44
46	0.0	0.7	1.4	2.2	2.9	3.6	4.3	5.0	5.8	6.5	7.2	7.9	8.7	46
48	0.0	0.7	1.5	2.2	3.0	3.7	4.5	5.2	6.0	6.7	7.5	8.2	9.0	48
50	0.0	0.8	1.6	2.3	3.1	3.9	4.7	5.4	6.2	7.0	7.8	8.6	9.4	50
51	0.0	0.8	1.6	2.4	3.2	4.0	4.8	5.6	6.4	7.2	8.0	8.8	9.6	51
52	0.0	0.8	1.6	2.4	3.2	4.1	4.9	5.7	6.5	7.3	8.1	9.0	9.8	52
53	0.0	0.8	1.7	2.5	3.3	4.2	5.0	5.8	6.7	7.5	8.3	9.2	10.0	53
54	0.0	0.9	1.7	2.6	3.4	4.3	5.1	6.0	6.8	7.7	8.5	9.4	10.2	54
55	0.0	0.9	1.7	2.6	3.5	4.4	5.2	6.1	7.0	7.9	8.7	9.6	10.5	55
56	0.0	0.9	1.8	2.7	3.6	4.5	5.4	6.3	7.2	8.1	9.0	9.9	10.8	56
57	0.0	0.9	1.8	2.8	3.7	4.6	5.5	6.4	7.4	8.3	9.2	10.1	11.1	57
58	0.0	0.9	1.9	2.8	3.8	4.7	5.7	6.6	7.6	8.5	9.5	10.4	11.4	58
59	0.0	1.0	1.9	2.9	3.9	4.9	5.8	6.8	7.8	8.8	9.7	10.7	11.7	59
60	0.0	1.0	2.0	3.0	4.0	5.0	6.0	7.0	8.0	9.0	10.0	11.1	12.1	60
61	0.0	1.0	2.1	3.1	4.1	5.2	6.2	7.2	8.3	9.3	10.3	11.4	12.5	61
62	0.0	1.1	2.1	3.2	4.3	5.3	6.4	7.5	8.5	9.6	10.7	11.8	12.9	62
63	0.0	1.1	2.2	3.3	4.4	5.5	6.6	7.7	8.8	10.0	11.1	12.2	13.3	63
64	0.0	1.1	2.3	3.4	4.6	5.7	6.9	8.0	9.2	10.3	11.5	12.6	13.8	64
65.0	0.0	1.2	2.4	3.6	4.7	5.9	7.1	8.3	9.5	10.7	11.9	13.1	14.3	65.0
65.5	0.0	1.2	2.4	3.6	4.8	6.0	7.3	8.5	9.7	10.9	12.1	13.4	14.6	65.5
66.0	0.0	1.2	2.5	3.7	4.9	6.2	7.4	8.6	9.9	11.1	12.4	13.6	14.9	66.0
66.5	0.0	1.3	2.5	3.8	5.0	6.3	7.5	8.8	10.1	11.3	12.6	13.9	15.2	66.5
67.0	0.0	1.3	2.6	3.8	5.1	6.4	7.7	9.0	10.3	11.6	12.9	14.2	15.5	67.0
67.5	0.0	1.3	2.6	3.9	5.2	6.5	7.9	9.2	10.5	11.8	13.2	14.5	15.9	67.5
68.0	0.0	1.3	2.7	4.0	5.3	6.7	8.0	9.4	10.7	12.1	13.5	14.8	16.2	68.0
68.5	0.0	1.4	2.7	4.1	5.5	6.8	8.2	9.6	11.0	12.4	13.8	15.2	16.6	68.5
69.0	0.0	1.4	2.8	4.2	5.6	7.0	8.4	9.8	11.2	12.6	14.1	15.5	17.0	69.0
69.5	0.0	1.4	2.9	4.3	5.7	7.2	8.6	10.0	11.5	12.9	14.4	15.9	17.4	69.5
70.0	0.0	1.5	2.9	4.4	5.9	7.3	8.8	10.3	11.8	13.3	14.8	16.3	17.8	70.0
70.5	0.0	1.5	3.0	4.5	6.0	7.5	9.0	10.5	12.1	13.6	15.1	16.7	18.2	70.5
71.0	0.0	1.5	3.1	4.6	6.2	7.7	9.3	10.8	12.4	13.9	15.5	17.1	18.7	71.0
71.5	0.0	1.6	3.2	4.7	6.3	7.9	9.5	11.1	12.7	14.3	15.9	17.6	19.2	71.5
72.0	0.0	1.6	3.2	4.9	6.5	8.1	9.8	11.4	13.0	14.7	16.4	18.1	19.8	72.0
72.5	0.0	1.7	3.3	5.0	6.7	8.3	10.0	11.7	13.4	15.1	16.8	18.6	20.3	72.5
73.0	0.0	1.7	3.4	5.1	6.9	8.6	10.3	12.1	13.8	15.6	17.3	19.1	20.9	73.0
73.5	0.0	1.8	3.5	5.3	7.1	8.8	10.6	12.4	14.2	16.0	17.9	19.7	21.6	73.5
74.0	0.0	1.8	3.6	5.4	7.3	9.1	10.9	12.8	14.7	16.5	18.4	20.3	22.3	74.0
74.5	0.0	1.9	3.7	5.6	7.5	9.4	11.3	13.2	15.1	17.1	19.0	21.0	23.0	74.5
75.0	0.0	1.9	3.9	5.8	7.7	9.7	11.7	13.6	15.6	17.6	19.7	21.7	23.8	75.0
75.5	0.0	2.0	4.0	6.0	8.0	10.0	12.1	14.1	16.2	18.3	20.4	22.5	24.7	75.5
76.0	0.0	2.1	4.1	6.2	8.3	10.4	12.5	14.6	16.8	18.9	21.1	23.3	25.6	76.0
76.5	0.0	2.1	4.3	6.4	8.6	10.8	13.0	15.2	17.4	19.6	21.9	24.2	26.6	76.5
77.0	0.0	2.2	4.4	6.7	8.9	11.2	13.5	15.7	18.1	20.4	22.8	25.2	27.7	77.0

TABLE 27

Amplitudes

Latitude	Declination													Latitude
	6.0	6.5	7.0	7.5	8.0	8.5	9.0	9.5	10.0	10.5	11.0	11.5	12.0	
0	6.0	6.5	7.0	7.5	8.0	8.5	9.0	9.5	10.0	10.5	11.0	11.5	12.0	0
10	6.1	6.6	7.1	7.6	8.1	8.6	9.1	9.6	10.2	10.7	11.2	11.7	12.2	10
15	6.2	6.7	7.2	7.8	8.3	8.8	9.3	9.8	10.4	10.9	11.4	11.9	12.4	15
20	6.4	6.9	7.5	8.0	8.5	9.0	9.6	10.1	10.6	11.2	11.7	12.2	12.8	20
25	6.6	7.2	7.7	8.3	8.8	9.4	9.9	10.5	11.0	11.6	12.2	12.7	13.3	25
30	6.9	7.5	8.1	8.7	9.2	9.8	10.4	11.0	11.6	12.1	12.7	13.3	13.9	30
32	7.1	7.7	8.3	8.9	9.4	10.0	10.6	11.2	11.8	12.4	13.0	13.6	14.2	32
34	7.2	7.8	8.5	9.1	9.7	10.3	10.9	11.5	12.1	12.7	13.3	13.9	14.5	34
36	7.4	8.0	8.7	9.3	9.9	10.5	11.1	11.8	12.4	13.0	13.6	14.3	14.9	36
38	7.6	8.3	8.9	9.5	10.2	10.8	11.5	12.1	12.7	13.4	14.0	14.7	15.3	38
40	7.8	8.5	9.2	9.8	10.5	11.1	11.8	12.4	13.1	13.8	14.4	15.1	15.7	40
42	8.1	8.8	9.4	10.1	10.8	11.5	12.1	12.8	13.5	14.2	14.9	15.6	16.2	42
44	8.4	9.1	9.8	10.5	11.9	11.9	12.6	13.3	14.0	14.7	15.4	16.1	16.8	44
46	8.7	9.4	10.1	10.8	11.6	12.3	13.0	13.7	14.5	15.2	15.9	16.7	17.4	46
48	9.0	9.7	10.5	11.2	12.0	12.8	13.5	14.3	15.0	15.8	16.6	17.3	18.1	48
50	9.4	10.1	10.9	11.7	12.5	13.3	14.1	14.9	15.7	16.5	17.3	18.1	18.9	50
51	9.6	10.4	11.2	12.0	12.8	13.6	14.4	15.2	16.0	16.8	17.7	18.5	19.3	51
52	9.8	10.6	11.4	12.2	13.1	13.9	14.7	15.6	16.4	17.2	18.1	18.9	19.7	52
53	10.0	10.8	11.7	12.5	13.4	14.2	15.1	15.9	16.8	17.6	18.5	19.3	20.2	53
54	10.2	11.1	12.0	12.8	13.7	14.6	15.4	16.3	17.2	18.1	18.9	19.8	20.7	54
55	10.5	11.4	12.3	13.2	14.0	14.9	15.8	16.7	17.6	18.5	19.4	20.3	21.3	55
56	10.8	11.7	12.6	13.5	14.4	15.3	16.2	17.2	18.1	19.0	20.0	20.9	21.8	56
57	11.1	12.0	12.9	13.9	14.8	15.7	16.7	17.6	18.6	19.6	20.5	21.5	22.4	57
58	11.4	12.3	13.3	14.3	15.2	16.2	17.2	18.1	19.1	20.1	21.1	22.1	23.1	58
59	11.7	12.7	13.7	14.7	15.7	16.7	17.7	18.7	19.7	20.7	21.7	22.8	23.8	59
60	12.1	13.1	14.1	15.1	16.2	17.2	18.2	19.3	20.3	21.4	22.4	23.5	24.6	60
61	12.5	13.5	14.6	15.6	16.7	17.8	18.8	19.9	21.0	22.1	23.2	24.3	25.4	61
62	12.9	14.0	15.0	16.1	17.2	18.4	19.5	20.6	21.7	22.8	24.0	25.1	26.3	62
63	13.3	14.4	15.6	16.7	17.9	19.0	20.2	21.3	22.5	23.7	24.9	26.0	27.3	63
64	13.8	15.0	16.2	17.3	18.5	19.7	20.9	22.1	23.3	24.6	25.8	27.1	28.3	64
65.0	14.3	15.5	16.8	18.0	19.2	20.5	21.7	23.0	24.3	25.5	26.8	28.1	29.5	65.0
65.5	14.6	15.8	17.1	18.3	19.6	20.9	22.2	23.5	24.8	26.1	27.4	28.7	30.1	65.5
66.0	14.9	16.2	17.4	18.7	20.0	21.3	22.6	23.9	25.3	26.6	28.0	29.4	30.7	66.0
66.5	15.2	16.5	17.8	19.1	20.4	21.8	23.1	24.5	25.8	27.2	28.6	30.0	31.4	66.5
67.0	15.5	16.8	18.2	19.5	20.9	22.2	23.6	25.0	26.4	27.8	29.2	30.7	32.1	67.0
67.5	15.9	17.2	18.6	19.9	21.3	22.7	24.1	25.5	27.0	28.4	29.9	31.4	32.9	67.5
68.0	16.2	17.6	19.0	20.4	21.8	23.2	24.7	26.1	27.6	29.1	30.6	32.2	33.7	68.0
68.5	16.6	18.0	19.4	20.9	22.3	23.8	25.3	26.8	28.3	29.8	31.4	33.0	34.6	68.5
69.0	17.0	18.4	19.9	21.4	22.9	24.4	25.9	27.4	29.0	30.6	32.2	33.8	35.5	69.0
69.5	17.4	18.9	20.4	21.9	23.4	25.0	26.5	28.1	29.7	31.4	33.0	34.7	36.4	69.5
70.0	17.8	19.3	20.9	22.4	24.0	25.6	27.2	28.9	30.5	32.2	33.9	35.7	37.4	70.0
70.5	18.2	19.8	21.4	23.0	24.6	26.3	27.9	29.6	31.3	33.1	34.9	36.7	38.5	70.5
71.0	18.7	20.3	22.0	23.6	25.3	27.0	28.7	30.5	32.2	34.0	35.9	37.8	39.7	71.0
71.5	19.2	20.9	22.6	24.3	26.0	27.8	29.5	31.3	33.2	35.1	37.0	38.9	40.9	71.5
72.0	19.8	21.5	23.2	25.0	26.8	28.6	30.4	32.3	34.2	36.1	38.1	40.2	42.3	72.0
72.5	20.3	22.1	23.9	25.7	27.6	29.4	31.3	33.3	35.3	37.3	39.4	41.5	43.7	72.5
73.0	20.9	22.8	24.6	26.5	28.4	30.4	32.3	34.4	36.4	38.6	40.7	43.0	45.3	73.0
73.5	21.6	23.5	25.4	27.4	29.3	31.4	33.4	35.5	37.7	39.9	42.2	44.6	47.1	73.5
74.0	22.3	24.2	26.2	28.3	30.3	32.4	34.6	36.8	39.0	41.4	43.8	46.3	49.0	74.0
74.5	23.0	25.1	27.1	29.3	31.4	33.6	35.8	38.1	40.5	43.0	45.6	48.2	51.1	74.5
75.0	23.8	25.9	28.1	30.3	32.5	34.8	37.2	39.6	42.1	44.8	47.5	50.4	53.4	75.0
75.5	24.7	26.9	29.1	31.4	33.8	36.2	38.7	41.2	43.9	46.7	49.6	52.8	56.1	75.5
76.0	25.6	27.9	30.2	32.7	35.1	37.7	40.3	43.0	45.9	48.9	52.1	55.5	59.3	76.0
76.5	26.6	29.0	31.5	34.0	36.6	39.3	42.1	45.0	48.1	51.3	54.8	58.7	63.0	76.5
77.0	27.7	30.2	32.8	35.5	38.2	41.1	44.1	47.2	50.5	54.1	58.0	62.4	67.6	77.0

TABLE 27
Amplitudes

Latitude							Declination							Latitude
	12°0	12°5	13°0	13°5	14°0	14°5	15°0	15°5	16°0	16°5	17°0	17°5	18°0	
°	°	°	°	°	°	°	°	°	°	°	°	°	°	°
0	12.0	12.5	13.0	13.5	14.0	14.5	15.0	15.5	16.0	16.5	17.0	17.5	18.0	0
10	12.2	12.7	13.2	13.7	14.2	14.7	15.2	15.7	16.3	16.8	17.3	17.8	18.3	10
15	12.4	12.9	13.5	14.0	14.5	15.0	15.5	16.1	16.6	17.1	17.6	18.1	18.7	15
20	12.8	13.3	13.9	14.4	14.9	15.5	16.0	16.5	17.1	17.6	18.1	18.7	19.2	20
25	13.3	13.8	14.4	14.9	15.5	16.0	16.6	17.1	17.7	18.3	18.8	19.4	19.9	25
30	13.9	14.5	15.1	15.6	16.2	16.8	17.4	18.0	18.6	19.1	19.7	20.3	20.9	30
32	14.2	14.8	15.4	16.0	16.6	17.2	17.8	18.4	19.0	19.6	20.2	20.8	21.4	32
34	14.5	15.1	15.7	16.4	17.0	17.6	18.2	18.8	19.4	20.0	20.7	21.3	21.9	34
36	14.9	15.5	16.1	16.8	17.4	18.0	18.7	19.3	19.9	20.6	21.2	21.8	22.5	36
38	15.3	15.9	16.6	17.2	17.9	18.5	19.2	19.8	20.5	21.1	21.8	22.4	23.1	38
40	15.7	16.4	17.1	17.7	18.4	19.1	19.7	20.4	21.1	21.8	22.4	23.1	23.8	40
41	16.0	16.7	17.3	18.0	18.7	19.4	20.1	20.8	21.4	22.1	22.8	23.5	24.2	41
42	16.2	16.9	17.6	18.3	19.0	19.7	20.4	21.1	21.8	22.5	23.2	23.9	24.6	42
43	16.5	17.2	17.9	18.6	19.3	20.0	20.7	21.4	22.1	22.9	23.6	24.3	25.0	43
44	16.8	17.5	18.2	18.9	19.7	20.4	21.1	21.8	22.5	23.3	24.0	24.7	25.4	44
45	17.1	17.8	18.5	19.3	20.0	20.7	21.5	22.2	22.9	23.7	24.4	25.2	25.9	45
46	17.4	18.2	18.9	19.6	20.4	21.1	21.9	22.6	23.4	24.1	24.9	25.7	26.4	46
47	17.7	18.5	19.3	20.0	20.8	21.5	22.3	23.1	23.8	24.6	25.4	26.2	26.9	47
48	18.1	18.9	19.6	20.4	21.2	22.0	22.8	23.5	24.3	25.1	25.9	26.7	27.5	48
49	18.5	19.3	20.1	20.8	21.6	22.4	23.2	24.0	24.8	25.7	26.5	27.3	28.1	49
50	18.9	19.7	20.5	21.3	22.1	22.9	23.7	24.6	25.4	26.2	27.1	27.9	28.7	50
51	19.3	20.1	20.9	21.8	22.6	23.4	24.3	25.1	26.0	26.8	27.7	28.5	29.4	51
52	19.7	20.6	21.4	22.3	23.1	24.0	24.9	25.7	26.6	27.5	28.3	29.2	30.1	52
53	20.2	21.1	21.9	22.8	23.7	24.6	25.5	26.4	27.3	28.2	29.1	30.0	30.9	53
54	20.7	21.6	22.5	23.4	24.3	25.2	26.1	27.0	28.0	28.9	29.8	30.8	31.7	54
55	21.3	22.2	23.1	24.0	24.9	25.9	26.8	27.8	28.7	29.7	30.6	31.6	32.6	55
56	21.8	22.8	23.7	24.7	25.6	26.6	27.6	28.5	29.5	30.5	31.5	32.5	33.5	56
57	22.4	23.4	24.4	25.4	26.4	27.4	28.4	29.4	30.4	31.4	32.5	33.5	34.6	57
58	23.1	24.1	25.1	26.1	27.2	28.2	29.2	30.3	31.3	32.4	33.5	34.6	35.7	58
59	23.8	24.8	25.9	27.0	28.0	29.1	30.2	31.3	32.4	33.5	34.6	35.7	36.9	59
60	24.6	25.7	26.7	27.8	28.9	30.1	31.2	32.3	33.5	34.6	35.8	37.0	38.2	60
61	25.4	26.5	27.6	28.8	29.9	31.1	32.3	33.5	34.6	35.9	37.1	38.3	39.6	61
62	26.3	27.5	28.6	29.8	31.0	32.2	33.5	34.7	36.0	37.2	38.5	39.8	41.2	62
63	27.3	28.5	29.7	30.9	32.2	33.5	34.8	36.1	37.4	38.7	40.1	41.5	42.9	63
64	28.3	29.6	30.9	32.2	33.5	34.8	36.2	37.6	39.0	40.4	41.8	43.3	44.8	64
65.0	29.5	30.8	32.2	33.5	34.9	36.3	37.8	39.2	40.7	42.2	43.8	45.4	47.0	65.0
65.5	30.1	31.5	32.9	34.3	35.7	37.1	38.6	40.1	41.7	43.2	44.8	46.5	48.2	65.5
66.0	30.7	32.1	33.6	35.0	36.5	38.0	39.5	41.1	42.7	44.3	46.0	47.7	49.4	66.0
66.5	31.4	32.9	34.3	35.8	37.3	38.9	40.5	42.1	43.7	45.4	47.2	48.9	50.8	66.5
67.0	32.1	33.6	35.1	36.7	38.3	39.9	41.5	43.2	44.9	46.6	48.4	50.3	52.3	67.0
67.5	32.9	34.4	36.0	37.6	39.2	40.9	42.6	44.3	46.1	47.9	49.8	51.8	53.9	67.5
68.0	33.7	35.3	36.9	38.6	40.2	41.9	43.7	45.5	47.4	49.3	51.3	53.4	55.6	68.0
68.5	34.6	36.2	37.9	39.6	41.3	43.1	44.9	46.8	48.8	50.8	52.9	55.1	57.5	68.5
69.0	35.5	37.2	38.9	40.6	42.5	44.3	46.2	48.2	50.3	52.4	54.7	57.0	59.6	69.0
69.5	36.4	38.2	40.0	41.8	43.7	45.6	47.7	49.7	51.9	54.2	56.6	59.2	61.9	69.5
70.0	37.4	39.3	41.1	43.0	45.0	47.1	49.2	51.4	53.7	56.1	58.7	61.5	64.6	70.0
70.5	38.5	40.4	42.4	44.4	46.4	48.6	50.8	53.2	55.7	58.3	61.1	64.3	67.8	70.5
71.0	39.7	41.7	43.7	45.8	48.0	50.3	52.7	55.2	57.8	60.7	63.9	67.5	71.7	71.0
71.5	40.9	43.0	45.1	47.4	49.7	52.1	54.7	57.4	60.3	63.5	67.1	71.4	76.9	71.5
72.0	42.3	44.5	46.7	49.1	51.5	54.1	56.9	59.9	63.1	66.8	71.1	76.7	90.0	72.0
72.5	43.7	46.0	48.4	50.9	53.6	56.4	59.4	62.7	66.4	70.8	76.5	90.0		72.5
73.0	45.3	47.8	50.3	53.0	55.8	58.9	62.3	66.1	70.5	76.3	90.0			73.0
73.5	47.1	49.6	52.4	55.3	58.4	61.8	65.7	70.2	76.0	90.0				73.5
74.0	49.0	51.7	54.7	57.9	61.4	65.3	69.9	75.8	90.0					74.0
74.5	51.1	54.1	57.3	60.9	64.9	69.5	75.6	90.0						74.5

TABLE 27
Amplitudes

Latitude	Declination 18°0	18°5	19°0	19°5	20°0	20°5	21°0	21°5	22°0	22°5	23°0	23°5	24°0	Latitude
°	°	°	°	°	°	°	°	°	°	°	°	°	°	°
0	18.0	18.5	19.0	19.5	20.0	20.5	21.0	21.5	22.0	22.5	23.0	23.5	24.0	0
10	18.3	18.8	19.3	19.8	20.3	20.8	21.3	21.8	22.4	22.9	23.4	23.9	24.4	10
15	18.7	19.2	19.7	20.2	20.7	21.3	21.8	22.3	22.8	23.3	23.9	24.4	24.9	15
20	19.2	19.7	20.3	20.8	21.3	21.9	22.4	23.0	23.5	24.0	24.6	25.1	25.6	20
25	19.9	20.5	21.1	21.6	22.2	22.7	23.3	23.9	24.4	25.0	25.5	26.1	26.7	25
30	20.9	21.5	22.1	22.7	23.3	23.9	24.4	25.0	25.6	26.2	26.8	27.4	28.0	30
32	21.4	22.0	22.6	23.2	23.8	24.4	25.0	25.6	26.2	26.8	27.4	28.0	28.7	32
34	21.9	22.5	23.1	23.7	24.4	25.0	25.6	26.2	26.9	27.5	28.1	28.7	29.4	34
36	22.5	23.1	23.7	24.4	25.0	25.7	26.3	26.9	27.6	28.2	28.9	29.5	30.2	36
38	23.1	23.7	24.4	25.1	25.7	26.4	27.1	27.7	28.4	29.1	29.7	30.4	31.1	38
40	23.8	24.5	25.2	25.8	26.5	27.2	27.9	28.6	29.3	30.0	30.7	31.4	32.1	40
41	24.2	24.9	25.6	26.3	26.9	27.6	28.3	29.1	29.8	30.5	31.2	31.9	32.6	41
42	24.6	25.3	26.0	26.7	27.4	28.1	28.8	29.5	30.3	31.0	31.7	32.5	33.2	42
43	25.0	25.7	26.4	27.2	27.9	28.6	29.3	30.1	30.8	31.6	32.3	33.0	33.8	43
44	25.4	26.2	26.9	27.6	28.4	29.1	29.9	30.6	31.4	32.1	32.9	33.7	34.4	44
45	25.9	26.7	27.4	28.2	28.9	29.7	30.5	31.2	32.0	32.8	33.5	34.3	35.1	45
46	26.4	27.2	27.9	28.7	29.5	30.3	31.1	31.8	32.6	33.4	34.2	35.0	35.8	46
47	26.9	27.7	28.5	29.3	30.1	30.9	31.7	32.5	33.3	34.1	35.0	35.8	36.6	47
48	27.5	28.3	29.1	29.9	30.7	31.6	32.4	33.2	34.0	34.9	35.7	36.6	37.4	48
49	28.1	28.9	29.8	30.6	31.4	32.3	33.1	34.0	34.8	35.7	36.6	37.4	38.3	49
50	28.7	29.6	30.4	31.3	32.1	33.0	33.9	34.8	35.6	36.5	37.4	38.3	39.3	50
51	29.4	30.3	31.2	32.0	32.9	33.8	34.7	35.6	36.5	37.5	38.4	39.3	40.3	51
52	30.1	31.0	31.9	32.8	33.7	34.7	35.6	36.5	37.5	38.4	39.4	40.4	41.3	52
53	30.9	31.8	32.8	33.7	34.6	35.6	36.5	37.5	38.5	39.5	40.5	41.5	42.5	53
54	31.7	32.7	33.6	34.6	35.6	36.6	37.6	38.6	39.6	40.6	41.7	42.7	43.8	54
55	32.6	33.6	34.6	35.6	36.6	37.6	38.7	39.7	40.8	41.9	42.9	44.0	45.2	55
56	33.5	34.6	35.6	36.7	37.7	38.8	39.9	41.0	42.1	43.2	44.3	45.5	46.7	56
57	34.6	35.6	36.7	37.8	38.9	40.0	41.1	42.3	43.5	44.6	45.8	47.1	48.3	57
58	35.7	36.8	37.9	39.1	40.2	41.4	42.6	43.8	45.0	46.2	47.5	48.8	50.1	58
59	36.9	38.0	39.2	40.4	41.6	42.8	44.1	45.4	46.7	48.0	49.3	50.7	52.2	59
60.0	38.2	39.4	40.6	41.9	43.2	44.5	45.8	47.1	48.5	49.9	51.4	52.9	54.4	60.0
60.5	38.9	40.1	41.4	42.7	44.0	45.3	46.7	48.1	49.5	51.0	52.5	54.1	55.7	60.5
61.0	39.6	40.9	42.2	43.5	44.9	46.3	47.7	49.1	50.6	52.1	53.7	55.3	57.0	61.0
61.5	40.4	41.7	43.0	44.4	45.8	47.2	48.7	50.2	51.7	53.3	55.0	56.7	58.5	61.5
62.0	41.2	42.5	43.9	45.3	46.8	48.2	49.8	51.3	52.9	54.6	56.3	58.1	60.0	62.0
62.5	42.0	43.4	44.8	46.3	47.8	49.3	50.9	52.5	54.2	56.0	57.8	59.7	61.7	62.5
63.0	42.9	44.3	45.8	47.3	48.9	50.5	52.1	53.8	55.6	57.5	59.4	61.4	63.6	63.0
63.5	43.8	45.3	46.9	48.4	50.0	51.7	53.4	55.2	57.1	59.1	61.1	63.4	65.7	63.5
64.0	44.8	46.4	48.0	49.6	51.3	53.0	54.8	56.7	58.7	60.8	63.0	65.5	68.1	64.0
64.5	45.9	47.5	49.1	50.8	52.6	54.4	56.3	58.4	60.5	62.7	65.2	67.9	70.9	64.5
65.0	47.0	48.7	50.4	52.2	54.0	56.0	58.0	60.1	62.4	64.9	67.6	70.7	74.2	65.0
65.5	48.2	49.9	51.7	53.6	55.6	57.6	59.8	62.1	64.6	67.3	70.4	74.1	78.8	65.5
66.0	49.4	51.3	53.2	55.2	57.2	59.4	61.8	64.3	67.1	70.2	73.9	78.6	90.0	66.0
66.5	50.8	52.7	54.7	56.8	59.1	61.4	64.0	66.8	70.0	73.7	78.5	90.0		66.5
67.0	52.3	54.3	56.4	58.7	61.1	63.7	66.5	69.7	73.5	78.4	90.0			67.0
67.5	53.9	56.0	58.3	60.7	63.3	66.2	69.5	73.3	78.2	90.0				67.5
68.0	55.6	57.9	60.4	63.0	65.9	69.2	73.1	78.1	90.0					68.0
68.5	57.5	60.0	62.7	65.6	68.9	72.9	77.9	90.0						68.5
69.0	59.6	62.3	65.3	68.7	72.6	77.7	90.0							69.0
69.5	61.9	65.0	68.4	72.4	77.6	90.0								69.5
70.0	64.6	68.1	72.2	77.4	90.0									70.0
70.5	67.8	71.9	77.2	90.0										70.5
71.0	71.7	77.1	90.0											71.0
71.5	76.9	90.0												71.5
72.0	90.0													72.0

CONVERSION OF ARC TO TIME

0°–59°		60°–119°		120°–179°		180°–239°		240°–299°		300°–359°			0'.00	0'.25	0'.50	0'.75
°	h m	°	h m	°	h m	°	h m	°	h m	°	h m	'	m s	m s	m s	m s
0	0 00	60	4 00	120	8 00	180	12 00	240	16 00	300	20 00	0	0 00	0 01	0 02	0 03
1	0 04	61	4 04	121	8 04	181	12 04	241	16 04	301	20 04	1	0 04	0 05	0 06	0 07
2	0 08	62	4 08	122	8 08	182	12 08	242	16 08	302	20 08	2	0 08	0 09	0 10	0 11
3	0 12	63	4 12	123	8 12	183	12 12	243	16 12	303	20 12	3	0 12	0 13	0 14	0 15
4	0 16	64	4 16	124	8 16	184	12 16	244	16 16	304	20 16	4	0 16	0 17	0 18	0 19
5	0 20	65	4 20	125	8 20	185	12 20	245	16 20	305	20 20	5	0 20	0 21	0 22	0 23
6	0 24	66	4 24	126	8 24	186	12 24	246	16 24	306	20 24	6	0 24	0 25	0 26	0 27
7	0 28	67	4 28	127	8 28	187	12 28	247	16 28	307	20 28	7	0 28	0 29	0 30	0 31
8	0 32	68	4 32	128	8 32	188	12 32	248	16 32	308	20 32	8	0 32	0 33	0 34	0 35
9	0 36	69	4 36	129	8 36	189	12 36	249	16 36	309	20 36	9	0 36	0 37	0 38	0 39
10	0 40	70	4 40	130	8 40	190	12 40	250	16 40	310	20 40	10	0 40	0 41	0 42	0 43
11	0 44	71	4 44	131	8 44	191	12 44	251	16 44	311	20 44	11	0 44	0 45	0 46	0 47
12	0 48	72	4 48	132	8 48	192	12 48	252	16 48	312	20 48	12	0 48	0 49	0 50	0 51
13	0 52	73	4 52	133	8 52	193	12 52	253	16 52	313	20 52	13	0 52	0 53	0 54	0 55
14	0 56	74	4 56	134	8 56	194	12 56	254	16 56	314	20 56	14	0 56	0 57	0 58	0 59
15	1 00	75	5 00	135	9 00	195	13 00	255	17 00	315	21 00	15	1 00	1 01	1 02	1 03
16	1 04	76	5 04	136	9 04	196	13 04	256	17 04	316	21 04	16	1 04	1 05	1 06	1 07
17	1 08	77	5 08	137	9 08	197	13 08	257	17 08	317	21 08	17	1 08	1 09	1 10	1 11
18	1 12	78	5 12	138	9 12	198	13 12	258	17 12	318	21 12	18	1 12	1 13	1 14	1 15
19	1 16	79	5 16	139	9 16	199	13 16	259	17 16	319	21 16	19	1 16	1 17	1 18	1 19
20	1 20	80	5 20	140	9 20	200	13 20	260	17 20	320	21 20	20	1 20	1 21	1 22	1 23
21	1 24	81	5 24	141	9 24	201	13 24	261	17 24	321	21 24	21	1 24	1 25	1 26	1 27
22	1 28	82	5 28	142	9 28	202	13 28	262	17 28	322	21 28	22	1 28	1 29	1 30	1 31
23	1 32	83	5 32	143	9 32	203	13 32	263	17 32	323	21 32	23	1 32	1 33	1 34	1 35
24	1 36	84	5 36	144	9 36	204	13 36	264	17 36	324	21 36	24	1 36	1 37	1 38	1 39
25	1 40	85	5 40	145	9 40	205	13 40	265	17 40	325	21 40	25	1 40	1 41	1 42	1 43
26	1 44	86	5 44	146	9 44	206	13 44	266	17 44	326	21 44	26	1 44	1 45	1 46	1 47
27	1 48	87	5 48	147	9 48	207	13 48	267	17 48	327	21 48	27	1 48	1 49	1 50	1 51
28	1 52	88	5 52	148	9 52	208	13 52	268	17 52	328	21 52	28	1 52	1 53	1 54	1 55
29	1 56	89	5 56	149	9 56	209	13 56	269	17 56	329	21 56	29	1 56	1 57	1 58	1 59
30	2 00	90	6 00	150	10 00	210	14 00	270	18 00	330	22 00	30	2 00	2 01	2 02	2 03
31	2 04	91	6 04	151	10 04	211	14 04	271	18 04	331	22 04	31	2 04	2 05	2 06	2 07
32	2 08	92	6 08	152	10 08	212	14 08	272	18 08	332	22 08	32	2 08	2 09	2 10	2 11
33	2 12	93	6 12	153	10 12	213	14 12	273	18 12	333	22 12	33	2 12	2 13	2 14	2 15
34	2 16	94	6 16	154	10 16	214	14 16	274	18 16	334	22 16	34	2 16	2 17	2 18	2 19
35	2 20	95	6 20	155	10 20	215	14 20	275	18 20	335	22 20	35	2 20	2 21	2 22	2 23
36	2 24	96	6 24	156	10 24	216	14 24	276	18 24	336	22 24	36	2 24	2 25	2 26	2 27
37	2 28	97	6 28	157	10 28	217	14 28	277	18 28	337	22 28	37	2 28	2 29	2 30	2 31
38	2 32	98	6 32	158	10 32	218	14 32	278	18 32	338	22 32	38	2 32	2 33	2 34	2 35
39	2 36	99	6 36	159	10 36	219	14 36	279	18 36	339	22 36	39	2 36	2 37	2 38	2 39
40	2 40	100	6 40	160	10 40	220	14 40	280	18 40	340	22 40	40	2 40	2 41	2 42	2 43
41	2 44	101	6 44	161	10 44	221	14 44	281	18 44	341	22 44	41	2 44	2 45	2 46	2 47
42	2 48	102	6 48	162	10 48	222	14 48	282	18 48	342	22 48	42	2 48	2 49	2 50	2 51
43	2 52	103	6 52	163	10 52	223	14 52	283	18 52	343	22 52	43	2 52	2 53	2 54	2 55
44	2 56	104	6 56	164	10 56	224	14 56	284	18 56	344	22 56	44	2 56	2 57	2 58	2 59
45	3 00	105	7 00	165	11 00	225	15 00	285	19 00	345	23 00	45	3 00	3 01	3 02	3 03
46	3 04	106	7 04	166	11 04	226	15 04	286	19 04	346	23 04	46	3 04	3 05	3 06	3 07
47	3 08	107	7 08	167	11 08	227	15 08	287	19 08	347	23 08	47	3 08	3 09	3 10	3 11
48	3 12	108	7 12	168	11 12	228	15 12	288	19 12	348	23 12	48	3 12	3 13	3 14	3 15
49	3 16	109	7 16	169	11 16	229	15 16	289	19 16	349	23 16	49	3 16	3 17	3 18	3 19
50	3 20	110	7 20	170	11 20	230	15 20	290	19 20	350	23 20	50	3 20	3 21	3 22	3 23
51	3 24	111	7 24	171	11 24	231	15 24	291	19 24	351	23 24	51	3 24	3 25	3 26	3 27
52	3 28	112	7 28	172	11 28	232	15 28	292	19 28	352	23 28	52	3 28	3 29	3 30	3 31
53	3 32	113	7 32	173	11 32	233	15 32	293	19 32	353	23 32	53	3 32	3 33	3 34	3 35
54	3 36	114	7 36	174	11 36	234	15 36	294	19 36	354	23 36	54	3 36	3 37	3 38	3 39
55	3 40	115	7 40	175	11 40	235	15 40	295	19 40	355	23 40	55	3 40	3 41	3 42	3 43
56	3 44	116	7 44	176	11 44	236	15 44	296	19 44	356	23 44	56	3 44	3 45	3 46	3 47
57	3 48	117	7 48	177	11 48	237	15 48	297	19 48	357	23 48	57	3 48	3 49	3 50	3 51
58	3 52	118	7 52	178	11 52	238	15 52	298	19 52	358	23 52	58	3 52	3 53	3 54	3 55
59	3 56	119	7 56	179	11 56	239	15 56	299	19 56	359	23 56	59	3 56	3 57	3 58	3 59

The above table is for converting expressions in arc to their equivalent in time ; its main use in this Almanac is for the conversion of longitude for application to L.M.T. (*added if west, subtracted if east*) to give G.M.T. or vice versa, particularly in the case of sunrise, sunset, etc.

INDEX TO SELECTED STARS, 1990

Name	No.	Mag.	S.H.A.	Dec.
Acamar	7	3·1	316°	S. 40°
Achernar	5.	0·6	336	S. 57
Acrux	30	1·1	173	S. 63
Adhara	19	1·6	255	S. 29
Aldebaran	10	1·1	291	N. 16
Alioth	32	1·7	167	N. 56
Alkaid	34	1·9	153	N. 49
Al Na'ir	55	2·2	28	S. 47
Alnilam	15	1·8	276	S. 1
Alphard	25	2·2	218	S. 9
Alphecca	41	2·3	126	N. 27
Alpheratz	1	2·2	358	N. 29
Altair	51	0·9	62	N. 9
Ankaa	2	2·4	354	S. 42
Antares	42	1·2	113	S. 26
Arcturus	37	0·2	146	N. 19
Atria	43	1·9	108	S. 69
Avior	22	1·7	234	S. 59
Bellatrix	13	1·7	279	N. 6
Betelgeuse	16	Var.*	271	N. 7
Canopus	17	-0·9	264	S. 53
Capella	12	0·2	281	N. 46
Deneb	53	1·3	50	N. 45
Denebola	28	2·2	183	N. 15
Diphda	4	2·2	349	S. 18
Dubhe	27	2·0	194	N. 62
Elnath	14	1·8	279	N. 29
Eltanin	47	2·4	91	N. 51
Enif	54	2·5	34	N. 10
Fomalhaut	56	1·3	16	S. 30
Gacrux	31	1·6	172	S. 57
Gienah	29	2·8	176	S. 17
Hadar	35	0·9	149	S. 60
Hamal	6	2·2	328	N. 23
Kaus Australis	48	2·0	84	S. 34
Kochab	40	2·2	137	N. 74
Markab	57	2·6	14	N. 15
Menkar	8	2·8	315	N. 4
Menkent	36	2·3	148	S. 36
Miaplacidus	24	1·8	222	S. 70
Mirfak	9	1·9	309	N. 50
Nunki	50	2·1	76	S. 26
Peacock	52	2·1	54	S. 57
Pollux	21	1·2	244	N. 28
Procyon	20	0·5	245	N. 5
Rasalhague	46	2·1	96	N. 13
Regulus	26	1·3	208	N. 12
Rigel	11	0·3	281	S. 8
Rigil Kentaurus	38	0·1	140	S. 61
Sabik	44	2·6	103	S. 16
Schedar	3	2·5	350	N. 56
Shaula	45	1·7	97	S. 37
Sirius	18	-1·6	259	S. 17
Spica	33	1·2	159	S. 11
Suhail	23	2·2	223	S. 43
Vega	49	0·1	81	N. 39
Zubenelgenubi	39	2·9	137	S. 16

No.	Name	Mag.	S.H.A.	Dec.
1	Alpheratz	2·2	358°	N. 29°
2	Ankaa	2·4	354	S. 42
3	Schedar	2·5	350	N. 56
4	Diphda	2·2	349	S. 18
5	Achernar	0·6	336	S. 57
6	Hamal	2·2	328	N. 23
7	Acamar	3·1	316	S. 40
8	Menkar	2·8	315	N. 4
9	Mirfak	1·9	309	N. 50
10	Aldebaran	1·1	291	N. 16
11	Rigel	0·3	281	S. 8
12	Capella	0·2	281	N. 46
13	Bellatrix	1·7	279	N. 6
14	Elnath	1·8	279	N. 29
15	Alnilam	1·8	276	S. 1
16	Betelgeuse	Var.*	271	N. 7
17	Canopus	-0·9	264	S. 53
18	Sirius	-1·6	259	S. 17
19	Adhara	1·6	255	S. 29
20	Procyon	0·5	245	N. 5
21	Pollux	1·2	244	N. 28
22	Avior	1·7	234	S. 59
23	Suhail	2·2	223	S. 43
24	Miaplacidus	1·8	222	S. 70
25	Alphard	2·2	218	S. 9
26	Regulus	1·3	208	N. 12
27	Dubhe	2·0	194	N. 62
28	Denebola	2·2	183	N. 15
29	Gienah	2·8	176	S. 17
30	Acrux	1·1	173	S. 63
31	Gacrux	1·6	172	S. 57
32	Alioth	1·7	167	N. 56
33	Spica	1·2	159	S. 11
34	Alkaid	1·9	153	N. 49
35	Hadar	0·9	149	S. 60
36	Menkent	2·3	148	S. 36
37	Arcturus	0·2	146	N. 19
38	Rigil Kentaurus	0·1	140	S. 61
39	Zubenelgenubi	2·9	137	S. 16
40	Kochab	2·2	137	N. 74
41	Alphecca	2·3	126	N. 27
42	Antares	1·2	113	S. 26
43	Atria	1·9	108	S. 69
44	Sabik	2·6	103	S. 16
45	Shaula	1·7	97	S. 37
46	Rasalhague	2·1	96	N. 13
47	Eltanin	2·4	91	N. 51
48	Kaus Australis	2·0	84	S. 34
49	Vega	0·1	81	N. 39
50	Nunki	2·1	76	S. 26
51	Altair	0·9	62	N. 9
52	Peacock	2·1	54	S. 57
53	Deneb	1·3	50	N. 45
54	Enif	2·5	34	N. 10
55	Al Na'ir	2·2	28	S. 47
56	Fomalhaut	1·3	16	S. 30
57	Markab	2·6	14	N. 15

* 0·1—1·2

Table T11. Greek alphabet

A α a	Alpha		N ν	Nu
B β ϐ	Beta		Ξ ξ	Xi
Γ γ	Gamma		O ο	Omicron
Δ δ	Delta		Π π ϖ	Pi
E ε	Epsilon		P ρ	Rho
Z ζ	Zeta		Σ σ ς	Sigma
H η	Eta		T τ	Tau
Θ θ ϑ	Theta		Υ υ	Upsilon
I ι	Iota		Φ φ φ	Phi
K κ	Kappa		X χ	Chi
Λ λ	Lambda		Ψ ψ	Psi
M μ	Mu		Ω ω	Omega

Table T12. Conversion between English and metric systems

Value	US to Metric Multiply by	Find	Value	Metric to US Multiply by	Find
inches	25.4	millimeters	centimeters	0.394	inches
feet	0.3048	meters	meters	3.281	feet
yards	0.9114	meters	meters	1.094	yards
fathoms	1.829	meters	meters	0.5467	fathoms
statute miles	1.609	kilometers	kilometers	0.6214	statute miles
nautical miles	1.852	kilometers	kilometers	0.5400	nautical miles
pounds	0.4536	kilograms	kilograms	2.205	pounds
quarts	0.9464	liters	liters	1.057	quarts

Temperature

$C°$	$F°$	$C°$	$F°$	$C°$	$F°$	$C°$	$F°$	$C°$	$F°$
−20	−4	−7	19	6	43	19	66	32	90
−19	−2	−6	21	7	45	20	68	33	91
−18	0	−5	23	8	46	21	70	34	93
−17	1	−4	25	9	48	22	72	35	95
−16	3	−3	27	10	50	23	73	36	97
−15	5	−2	28	11	52	24	75	37	99
−14	7	−1	30	12	54	25	77	38	100
−13	9	0	32	13	55	26	79	39	102
−12	10	1	34	14	57	27	81	40	104
−11	12	2	36	15	59	28	82		
−10	14	3	37	16	61	29	84		
−9	16	4	39	17	63	30	86		
−8	18	5	41	18	64	31	88		

Nomogram Relating Time, Speed, and Distance Travelled

This nomogram is designed to help find the speed of a vessel in knots by measuring the distance it travels through the water in a measured time interval.

1. Measure a distance along the rail of the vessel in feet with a tape measure or ruler. Suppose it is 20 feet.

2. When the vessel is underway, use a stopwatch to determine how many seconds it takes for an object in the water to pass between the marks on the rail. Suppose it is 3 seconds.

3. Lay a straightedge across the paper so it intersects all three of the vertical lines. The three numerical scales then give values corresponding to the formula:

Distance (feet) = Speed (knots) × Time (seconds)

4. Adjust the straightedge so it strikes 20 on the distance scale and 3 on the time scale. Then read the speed on the center scale. In this case, you will find a speed of about 4 knots. Interpolate when necessary for higher accuracy.

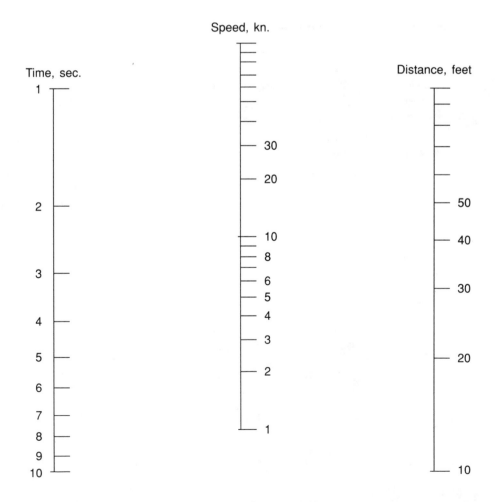

Index of Operations

PILOTING

TIME-RELATED TASKS

CELESTIAL

Sources

COMMERCIAL MAGAZINES

- *Sail* Magazine, P.O. Box 10210, Des Moines, IA 50336

- *Ocean Navigator,* P.O. Box 569, Portland, ME 04112-0569

- *Cruising World,* P.O. Box 3045, Harlan, IA 51537-3045

- *Popular Communications,* CQ Communications, Inc., 76 N. Broadway, Hicksville NY 11801-2953

- *QST,* American Radio Relay League, Newington, CT 06111

- *CQ Amateur Radio,* 76 N. Broadway, Hicksville, NY 11801

- *73 Amateur Radio,* WGE Center, Hancock, NH 03449

- *Sky and Telescope Magazine,* Sky Publishing Corp., 49 Bay State Road, Cambridge, MA 02238-1290

GOVERNMENT PUBLICATIONS ABOUT NAVIGATION

General

- *American Practical Navigator* (*Bowditch,* DMA *H. O. Pub. No. 9,* in 2 volumes)

Coastwise

- Chart catalogs

- *Radio Navigational Aids* (DMA *H. O. Pub. No. 117*)

- NOS *Coast Pilot*

- *Sailing Directions*

- *Tide Tables*

- *Tidal Current Tables*

- *Tidal Current Charts*

- *Tidal Current Diagrams*

- *Lists of Lights*

- *Notice to Mariners; Local Notice to Mariners*

Celestial

- *Nautical Almanac*

- *Air Almanac*

- DMA *H. O. Pub. No. 229, Sight Reduction Tables for Marine Navigation*

- DMA *H. O. Pub. No. 249, Sight Reduction Tables for Air Navigation*

- DMA *H. O. Pub. No. 260*

MISCELLANEOUS REFERENCE BOOKS

- *A Cruising Guide to the New England Coast,* Roger F. Duncan and John P. Ware, New York: G. P. Putnam.

- *Dutton's Navigation and Piloting,* by G. D. Dunlap and H. H. Shufeldt, Annapolis, MD: Naval Institute Press.

- *Chapman Piloting, Seamanship, and Small Boat Handling,* 59th ed., 1989, Elbert S. Maloney, New York: Motor Boating and Sailing Books.

- *Mariner's Guide to Single Sideband,* 4th ed., 1990, Frederick Graves, SEA Inc., 7030 220th S.W., Mountlake Terrace, WA 98043.

- *The ARRL Handbook for the Radio Amateur,* published annually by the American Radio Relay League, Newington, CT 06111.

- *World Radio TV Handbook,* published annually by Billboard Publications in Amsterdam, The Netherlands, with sales offices at 1515 Broadway, New York, NY 10036, and available in many electronics stores.

- *Passport to World Band Radio,* published yearly by International Broadcasting Services, Ltd., and intended primarily for shortwave listening.

- *Sailing, A Sailor's Dictionary,* Henry Beard and Roy McKie, New York: Workman Pub.

- *The Sextant Handbook,* Bruce Bauer, Camden, ME: International Marine Publishing Co., 1987.

- *Electronic Aids to Navigation,* L. Tetley and D. Calcutt, London: Edward Arnold Ltd., 1986.

SELECTED BOOKS ABOUT THE SEA AND SAILING

- *Moby Dick,* Herman Melville

- *Sailing Alone around the World,* Joshua Slocum

- *Riddle of the Sands,* Erskine Childers

- *South,* Sir Ernest Shackleton

- *Alone through the Roaring Forties,* Vito Dumas

- *Gypsy Moth Circles the World,* Sir Francis Chichester

- *Far Tortuga,* Peter Mathiessen

- *Tinkerbelle,* Robert Manry

- *A World of My Own,* Robin Knox-Johnston

A FEW AGENCIES AND ASSOCIATIONS

- Federal Communications Commission, 1919 M Street, N.W., Washington, DC 20554

- Defense Mapping Agency Hydrographic/Topographic Center, Washington, DC 20315-0030

- Superintendent of Documents, U.S. Government Printing Office, Washington, DC 20402

- Her Majesty's Stationery Office, 49 High Holborn, London WC 1, England

- Seven Seas Cruising Association, Box 38, Placida, FL 33946

- American Radio Relay League, Newington, CT 06111

Answers to Test Questions

CHAPTER 1

1.1 Small pea

1.2 Small pea

1.3 Slightly smaller

1.4 Slightly smaller

1.5 Most people think it looks larger on the horizon.

1.6 False

1.7 True

1.8 The ratio of distances will be the same as the ratio of diameters.

1.9 a) Moon's diameter = 240,000/100 = 2,400 miles; b) Sun's distance = 800,000 × 100 = 80,000,000 (eighty million) miles.

1.10 Ratio of distances = 2:1.

1.11 About 50:1 is typical.

1.12 0.7 NM

1.13 About 0.5 degrees

1.14 About 1 degree

1.15 D/S ratio for Venus = 4,750; Angular diameter = 0.012°; Distance = 4,750 × 8,000 = 38,000,000 miles.

1.16 D/S of airplane = 150; Distance = 34,500 feet = 5.7 NM.

CHAPTER 2

2.1 True

2.2 False. Only when you are at the North Pole.

2.3 False. It is measured along the horizon.

2.4 False. They are N, E, S, W.

2.5 N = 000, E = 090, S = 180, W = 270.

2.6 N = 90°, E = 0°, S = 90°, W = 0°.

2.7 40°, 70°, 20°, 75°.

2.8 90°

2.9 True

2.10 False. It increases from 0° to 90° toward each pole.

2.11 True

2.12 Quito, Ecuador, and Libreville, Gabon, are two.

2.13 Examples are New York and Bogotá, Colombia.

2.14 For example, at latitude 60°, longitude lines that are 10° apart are 300 NM apart.

2.16 105 NM

2.17 70 NM

2.18 Shorter

CHAPTER 3

3.1 A circular scale printed on a chart for measuring directions

3.2 1/1,000 NM or about 6 feet

3.3 It tells the vertical distance between points on adjacent contour lines.

3.4 Line of constant heading; because that is the course you follow if you steer in a constant true heading.

3.5 Mercator

3.6 A circle that divides the sphere in two; the intersection of a sphere with a plane through the center; the shortest and longest routes between two points on a sphere.

CHAPTER 4

4.1 045, 135, 225, 315

4.2 Increase

4.3 Both decrease

4.4 True

4.5

	Left	Right
Ship's true heading	030	120
True bearing of lighthouse	300	80
Relative bearing of lighthouse	270	320

CHAPTER 5

5.1 Variation is the difference between directions of true and magnetic north. It does not depend on the heading of the vessel.

5.2 Deviation is the difference between directions of magnetic north and compass north. It does depend on the heading of the vessel.

5.3 True

5.4 False. Usually compensation makes it point toward magnetic north.

5.5 The difference in direction between magnetic pole and north pole can be greatest when you are near one of the poles.

5.6 Cape Horn 15E, Chicago 0, Paris 2W, Tokyo 7W, Melbourne 10E.

5.7 Rock 1: 87M, Rock 2: 225M.

5.8 (The answers are shown it italic type.)

Identification	True	Var.	Magnetic	Dev.	Compass
Island 1	055T	*008W*	063M	*002W*	065psc
Island 2	090T	10E	*080M*	12W	*092W*
Island 3	*086T*	12W	*098M*	8E	090psc

5.9 It will return to the starting point, but the turn-around point will not be where the navigator thought it was.

5.10
Heading		N	E	S	W
Deviation	(a)	0	W	0	E
	(b)	E	0	W	0

5.11
Point	Magnetic (M)	Deviation	Compass (psc)
C	55	25E	030
D	72	27E	045
E	84	24E	060
F	90	15E	075

CHAPTER 6

6.1 Variation: 15°00′W in 1985; 15°33′W in 1996.

6.2 Course: 090T = 90° + 15°33′ − 5°00′ = 100°33′C.

6.3 (The answers are shown in italic type.)

Elapsed time (h)	Distance (NM)	Speed (kn)
1.25	6.0	*7.5*
0.4	15	6
2.5	*3.2*	8

6.4 8.45 feet

6.5 (The answers are shown in italic type.)

Elapsed time (sec.)	Distance (feet)	Speed (kn.)
2	20	*5.9*
3.5	35	6
4	*169*	25

6.6
Compass Heading to Steer
086 − 12 = 74
190 + 5 = 195
335 − 7 = 328

CHAPTER 7

7.1 (The answers are shown in italic type.)

	DR Pos.		Beacon	Diff. of	Tabulated	Observed	Corrected
	Lat.	Long.	Long.	Long.	Correction	Bearing	Bearing
	16N	60E	72E	*12*	*2*	040T	*042T*
	16S	60E	72E	*12*	*2*	040T	*038T*
	45N	120W	140W	*20*	*7*	220T	*213T*
	45S	120W	140W	*20*	*7*	310T	*317T*

7.2 Lat. = 42°21.6′N, long. = 72°25.4′W.

CHAPTER 8

8.1 A bearing is an angular measurement toward an object; a range line is a line passing through two visible objects.

8.2 There's no need to worry about compass corrections.

8.3 If an approaching object maintains a constant compass bearing from your vessel, you are on a collision course.

8.4 048T

8.5 183T, 003T

8.6 "A"

8.7 93 feet

8.8 "H"

8.9 "BR"

8.10 180°; 180°; 360°.

8.13 102 feet

CHAPTER 9

9.1 Two

9.2 The navigator doesn't have to look in two different directions at the same time.

9.3 The angle-measuring scale starts in the wrong place.

9.4 Superpose the two images of the horizon and read the angle.

9.5 Usually to 1 minute of arc. Gain precision by an average four or five measures.

9.6 48°53′

9.7 1°

9.8 50:1

9.9 200 feet

9.10 The angular diameter of the moon is about 32′ and D/S = 100:1.

9.11 The actual variation is about 0.5′, which is difficult to measure. The moon appears smaller when it is near the horizon than when it is high in the sky.

9.12 AOB

9.13 Twice as large; $\angle AOB = 65°$; $\angle ACB = 32.5°$; Ratio AOB/ACB = 2/1.

9.14 Stay the same

9.15 The angles measured by N1, N2, and N3 should be the same.

9.16 41°24.3′N, 71°20.0′W.

CHAPTER 10

10.1 The moon pulls the sea away from the earth on one side and it pulls the earth away from the sea on the other side.

10.2 The sun is 400 times farther away from the earth than the moon, and the tide-raising force drops with the cube of the distance.

10.3 Yes, in regions of the Pacific Ocean at certain times of the month.

10.4 There is a tide, but it is small and difficult to see.

10.5 It can take a long time for the water to flow across shallow regions near shore.

10.6 8:00 PM and 8:00 AM

10.8 a) A, F, C, H, D, B, G, E; b) (in days) A: 2, B: 21, C: 7, D: 16, E: 27, F: 4, G: 23, H: 9; c) Sunrise.

10.9 a) Midnight; b) 1:30 AM and PM; c) Midnight; d) 1:30 AM and PM.

10.10 Speed 6.3 knots toward 018T

10.11 Drift = 5.7 knots, set = 357.

10.12 Speed 6.6 knots toward 257 to make speed of 6.4 knots over the bottom

10.13 Course 345 at speed 6 knots will take you due north at 4.3 knots, and the trip will take 1.4 hours.

CHAPTER 11

11.1 14°25′W

11.2 26 NM; 4.5 hours.

11.3 284M

11.4 293 psc

11.5 Lat.: 41°18′33″N; Long.: 71°54′42″W.

11.6 264M, 272 psc.

11.7 0920 EDT

11.8 0950 EDT

11.9 3.55 NM, 2.96 knots.

11.10 The current is about 1 knot against you.

11.11 000T

11.12 215T, 6.0 NM.

11.13 About 67 feet

11.14 Race Rock is 1 NM off the port beam and has a relative bearing of 270R. You may use your heading (215T) to convert this to a true bearing, 125T. So you are in a direction 125 + 180 = 305T at a distance of 1 NM from the Race Rock light. This is not where your DR position would have put you.

11.15 Plot your DR position using the course (215T) and speed (4 kn) from the 1020 EDT position. Draw an arrow representing the current. Its direction (set) is 115T. Its length (0.6 NM) is the distance the tide travelled in 45 minutes, so the tide's speed (drift) is about 0.9 knot.

11.16 This is the second type of tide problem, and it is discussed in Chapter 10. You should head toward 238T, and your speed over the ground will be about 3.6 knots.

11.17 337T

11.18 It will take you about 56 minutes to get to R "44."

11.19 It will take an additional 13 minutes to get to Bartlett Reef.

11.20 354T, 008M, 357 psc.

11.21 Bartlett Reef: 280T; tank near Seaside Point: 347T.

11.22 072T, 4.3 NM.

11.23 About 1400 EDT

11.24 The current is about 1.2 kn from your stern.

11.25 1446.

11.26 We hope so.

CHAPTER 12

12.1 The time it takes for the sun to slide below the horizon is about 2 minutes.

12.2 No; it will be found slightly eastward.

12.3 It requires about 23h 56m on your watch.

12.4 False. It is *highest* at noon, but probably not overhead.

12.5 False. It only does this at the equator.

12.6 False. It rises once a year.

CHAPTER 13

13.1 False. But it usually is close.

13.2 False

13.3 False

13.4 False. But almost correct.

13.5 You would think local noon was an hour earlier than if you used true north.

13.6 14W: −1, 125E: −8, 125W: +8, 181E: −12.

13.7 When you are stationary, the sun moves west at 1,000 mph and there is no adjustment to your watch. If you move west at 1,000 mph, the sun is stationary and you retard your watch 1 hour every hour; so it doesn't move, except at the date line. If you move east at 1,000 mph, you enter a new time zone every hour, so you set your watch ahead 1 hour every hour. It moves twice as fast as normal. If you fly east at 2,000 mph, you enter a new time zone every half hour, so you set your watch ahead an hour every 30 minutes.

13.8 Set it back a day.

13.9 Four

13.10 East

13.11 It takes about ¼ second.

13.12 3m 05s fast

13.13 GMT = 05 54 50

13.14 LMT = 2000 – 4 min = 1956

13.15 WT = 22 01 20

13.16 You are 1° west of the central meridian of your zone. Meridian passage = 12 06 06 LMT, so LAN occurs at 12 10 06 ZT.

13.17 About 1,000 statute miles or 868 NM per hour.

13.18 Four seconds.

CHAPTER 14

14.1 False. Only around the equinoxes.

14.2 False. On the last day of northern spring.

14.3 The descent is slow at first and then faster.

14.4 True

14.5 True

14.6 True

14.7 At long. 0, sunrise is at 0319; it is 40 minutes earlier at long. 10E, so 0816.

14.8

	LMT	Corr.	ZT	ZD	GMT
Sunrise	0653	+08	0701	0500	1201
Sunset	1642	+08	1650	0500	2150

14.9

	Sun	
GHA	Longitude	LHA
156	156W	56W
217	143E	117W
117	117W	17W
100	100W	000

14.10 GHA sun = 20°55.2′, dec. = N17°22.5′.

CHAPTER 15

15.1

Zenith distance	Latitude
10	34N
50	40S
60	90S
30	20N

15.2 H₀ = 49°20′ –3.0′ –2.8′ – 16.9′ = 48°57.3′

15.3 Miami, FL

CHAPTER 16

16.1 Lat. = 30°05′N

16.2 GMT = July 15, 1990, at 0631

16.3 Any star with SHA near 3

16.4 The correct latitudes are: b) Lat. = 40N; d) lat. = 5N.

CHAPTER 17

17.1 False. It moves north and south.

17.2 False. They are stationary.

17.3 Azimuth = 0.2.

17.4 The stars would set later, because the motion of the sun would be reversed.

17.5 The stars would rise earlier. If both motions are reversed, the effect on setting times is null, so they would set earlier, as they normally do.

17.6 Rise: 120; set: 240.

17.7 Dec. of Altair = 8N.

17.8

Sunrise Azimuths

Date	Feb. 22	May 13	Aug. 8	Nov. 15
Sun's dec.	10S	18N	16N	18S
Lat.		Amplitudes		
0	100.0	72.0	74.0	108.0
15	100.4	71.3	73.4	108.7
30	101.6	69.1	71.4	110.9
44	104.0	64.6	67.5	115.4

Sunset Azimuths

Date	Feb. 22	May 13	Aug. 8	Nov. 15
Sun's dec.	10S	18N	16N	18S
Lat.		Amplitudes		
0	260.0	288.0	286.0	262.0
15	259.6	288.7	286.6	261.3
30	258.4	290.9	288.6	249.1
44	256.0	295.4	292.5	254.6

17.9 Azimuth = 57°34′

CHAPTER 18

18.1 Initial heading: 49T; distance = 42 × 60 = 2,520 NM.

CHAPTER 19

19.1 95.25 feet

19.2

α	D (NM)
3°	180
5°	300
30′	30
15′	15

19.3 Moon's radius = 905 NM.

19.4 The sun is on the equator. On that day, the sun's zenith distance at local noon will give your latitude.

19.5 Lat. = 35°N, long. = 60°W.

19.6 Lat. = 8°26′S, long. = 29°15′W.

19.7 Lat. = 25°N, long. = 65°W.

CHAPTER 20

20.1 The sun's dec. at 1100 GMT was 17°21′N, which is 9′ less than H_0. Therefore your LOP intercept is 9 NM toward the sun, along the direction long. = 15E.

20.2 On March 19, 1990, at 2100 GMT, the GHA sun was 133°04.2′. You observed a zenith distance of 44°50′ eastward, so your longitude is the sum, 177°54′.

Index